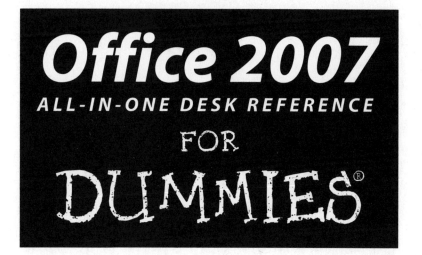

Office 2007
ALL-IN-ONE DESK REFERENCE
FOR
DUMMIES®

Office® 2007 All-in-One Desk Reference For Dummies®

Cheat Sheet

AutoRecovering from a Computer or Power Failure

It happens. Sometimes you're slaving away in an Office program and your computer fails or the power gets cut off. When you restart your computer and open the program again, you see the Document Recovery task pane with a list of files that were open when the failure occurred:

- *AutoSaved* files are files that Office saves as part of its AutoRecovery procedure.
- *Original* files are files that you save by clicking the Save button.

The Document Recovery task pane tells you when each file was saved. By studying the time listings, you can tell which version of a file — the AutoRecovery file or the file you saved — is most up to date.

Open the drop-down list for a file and choose one of these options:

- **Open:** Opens the file so that you can examine it. If you want to keep it, click the Save button.
- **Save As:** Opens the Save As dialog box so that you can save the file under a different name. Choose this command to keep a copy of the recovered file on hand in case you need it.
- **Delete:** Deletes the AutoRecovery file. (This command is available with AutoRecovery files, not files that you save on your own.)
- **Show Repairs:** Shows repairs made to the file as part of the AutoRecovery procedure.

For Dummies: Bestselling Book Series for Beginners

Office® 2007
All-in-One Desk Reference
For Dummies®

Indispensable Office Commands

Almost anywhere you go in an Office 2007 program, you can take advantage of these tricks and techniques:

- **Undoing mistakes:** Don't despair if you give a command and then realize that you shouldn't have done that. You can undo your mistake by clicking the Undo button (or pressing Ctrl+Z). The Undo command reverses your last action, whatever it happened to be. Keep clicking Undo to reverse several actions. You can also open the Undo drop-down list and undo many commands.

- **Repeating an action:** Click the Repeat button (or press F4 or Ctrl+Y) to repeat your latest action, whatever it was, and spare yourself from having to do it a second time. You can move to another place in your file before giving the command.

- **Opening files quickly:** Click the Office button and you see a list of the last several files you opened. If the one you want to open is on the list, click its name.

- **Zooming in and out:** Your eyes weren't meant to stare at a computer screen all day. To prevent eyestrain, use the Zoom controls:

  • *Zoom dialog box:* Click the Zoom button (or the % listing), and in the Zoom dialog box, select an option button or enter a Percent measurement.

  • *Zoom slider:* Drag the zoom slider to enlarge or shrink slides. Click the Zoom In or Zoom Out button to zoom in or out by ten percent increments.

  • *Mouse wheel:* If your mouse has a wheel, you can hold down the Ctrl key and spin the mouse wheel to zoom in or out.

- **Adding buttons to the Quick Access toolbar:** Right-click your favorite button and choose Add to Quick Access Toolbar to place your button on the *Quick Access toolbar,* the row of buttons that appears in the upper-left corner of the window. This way, you can find and click your button wherever your work takes you. To remove a button from the toolbar, right-click it and choose Remove from Quick Access Toolbar.

- **Entering symbols:** To enter a symbol or foreign character that isn't on your keyboard, go to the Insert tab and click the Symbol button. Then make a choice in the Symbol dialog box.

- **Identifying yourself:** Throughout the Office programs, you can enter your name, initials, and sometimes your address automatically in notes, revision marks, comments, address dialog boxes, and other places. For example, to make sure that PowerPoint knows who you are and can enter your personal information automatically, click the Office button and choose PowerPoint Options on the drop-down list. Then, in the Personalize category of the PowerPoint Options dialog box, enter your name and initials.

For Dummies: Bestselling Book Series for Beginners

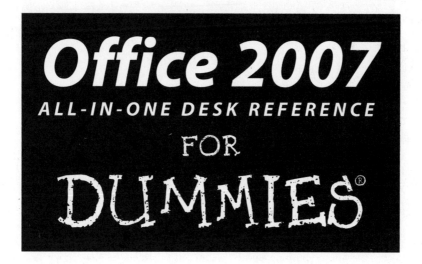

by Peter Weverka

Wiley Publishing, Inc.

Office 2007 All-in-One Desk Reference For Dummies®

Published by
Wiley Publishing, Inc.
111 River Street
Hoboken, NJ 07030-5774
www.wiley.com

For general information on our other products and services, please contact our Customer Care Department within the U.S. at 800-762-2974, outside the U.S. at 317-572-3993, or fax 317-572-4002.

For technical support, please visit www.wiley.com/techsupport.

Wiley also publishes its books in a variety of electronic formats. Some content that appears in print may not be available in electronic books.

Library of Congress Control Number: 2006925911

ISBN: 978-0-471-78279-7

Manufactured in the United States of America

10 9 8 7 6

1B/RV/QS/QY/IN

WILEY

About the Author

Peter Weverka is the bestselling author of several *For Dummies* books, including *PowerPoint 2007 All-in-One Desk Reference For Dummies* and *Microsoft Money For Dummies,* as well as 30 other computer books about various topics. Peter's humorous articles and stories — none related to computers, thankfully — have appeared in *Harper's, SPY, The Argonaut,* and other magazines for grown-ups.

Dedication

For Aiko Sofia and Henry Gabriel.

Author's Acknowledgments

Many hard-working people at Wiley Publishing in Indiana had a hand in this book, and I would like to thank all of them. I am especially grateful to Steve Hayes for giving me the opportunity to write this and other *For Dummies* books.

Many thanks as well go to Jean Rogers, this book's project editor, for her diligence and grace under pressure, and Jennifer Riggs and Mary Lagu for their copy editing skills. Technical editors Joyce Nielsen and Lee Musik made sure that all the explanations in this book are indeed accurate, and I would like to thank them for their excellent work and suggestions for improving this book. I would also like to give a special thanks to Joe Stockman for his work in Book VI about Access. I would also like to thank Rich Tennant for the witty cartoons you will find on the pages of this book and Richard Shrout for writing the index. Many other people at the Wiley office in Indianapolis gave their all to this book; their names are listed on the following page in the publisher's acknowledgements.

Finally, I owe my family — Sofia, Henry, and Addie — a debt for tolerating my vampire-like working hours and eerie demeanor at the breakfast table. How will I ever repay you?

Publisher's Acknowledgments

We're proud of this book; please send us your comments through our online registration form located at www.dummies.com/register/.

Some of the people who helped bring this book to market include the following:

Acquisitions, Editorial, and Media Development

Associate Project Editor: Jean Rogers

Acquisitions Editor: Steven Hayes

Copy Editors: Jennifer Riggs, Mary Lagu

Technical Editors: Joyce Nielsen, Lee Musick

Editorial Manager: Kevin Kirschner

Media Development Specialists: Angela Denny, Kate Jenkins, Steven Kudirka, Kit Malone

Media Development Coordinator: Laura Atkinson

Media Project Supervisor: Laura Moss

Media Development Manager: Laura VanWinkle

Media Development Associate Producer: Richard Graves

Editorial Assistant: Amanda Foxworth

Sr. Editorial Assistant: Cherie Case

Cartoons: Rich Tennant (www.the5thwave.com)

Composition Services

Project Coordinator: Erin Smith

Layout and Graphics: Claudia Bell, Joyce Haughey, Stephanie D. Jumper, Barbara Moore, Heather Ryan, Rashell Smith

Proofreaders: John Greenough, Sossity R. Smith, Melba Hopper, Brian H. Walls

Indexer: Richard Shrout

Anniversary Logo Design: Richard Pacifico

Publishing and Editorial for Technology Dummies

    Richard Swadley, Vice President and Executive Group Publisher

    Andy Cummings, Vice President and Publisher

    Mary Bednarek, Executive Acquisitions Director

    Mary C. Corder, Editorial Director

Publishing for Consumer Dummies

    Diane Graves Steele, Vice President and Publisher

    Joyce Pepple, Acquisitions Director

Composition Services

    Gerry Fahey, Vice President of Production Services

    Debbie Stailey, Director of Composition Services

Contents at a Glance

Table of Contents

Introduction

This book is for users of Office 2007 who want to get to the heart of the program without wasting time. Don't look in this book to find out how the different programs in the Office suite work. Look in this book to find out how *you* can get *your* work done better and faster with these programs.

I show you everything you need to make the most of the different Office programs. On the way, you have a laugh or two. No matter how much or how little skill you bring to the table, the guidance of this book will make you a better, more proficient, more confident user of the Office programs.

What's in This Book, Anyway?

Office 2007 is radically different from its predecessors — you can tell as soon as you open your first Office 2007 program. Office has been given a facelift. The menus and toolbars that used to appear along the top of the program windows are gone and have been replaced by command tabs and a Ribbon. Instead of opening menus, you click buttons or make gallery choices. Behind the scenes, the makers of Office have made many features — charts, diagrams, shapes, and others — available to all or most of the programs. The Office suite offers more commands and features than ever before. It gives you many, many opportunities to exercise your creativity and computer prowess.

This book is your guide to making the most of the Office programs. It's jam-packed with how-to's, advice, shortcuts, and tips. Here's a bare outline of the eight parts of this book:

✦ **Book I: Common Office Tools:** Looks into the many commands and features that are common to all or several of the Office programs. Master the material in Book I and you're well on your way to mastering all the programs. Book I explains handling text, the proofing tools, charts, diagrams, and tables. It explores speed techniques that can make you more productive in most of the Office programs, as well as how to draw and manipulate lines, shapes, clip-art, and other so-called objects.

✦ **Book II: Word 2007:** Explains the numerous features in Office's word processor, including how to create documents from letters to reports. Use the techniques described here to turn Word into a desktop-publishing program and quickly dispatch office tasks such as mass-mailings. You also discover how to get Word's help in writing indexes, bibliographies, and other items of interest to scholars.

- ✦ **Book III: Outlook 2007:** Shows you how to send and receive e-mail messages and files, as well as track tasks, maintain an address book, and keep a calendar with Outlook. If you're one of those people who receive numerous e-mail messages each day, you'll be delighted to discover all the ways to track and manage e-mail — and junk e-mail — in Outlook.

- ✦ **Book IV: PowerPoint 2007:** Demonstrates how to construct a meaningful presentation that makes the audience say, "Wow!" Included in Book IV are instructions for making a presentation livelier and more original, both when you create your presentation and when you deliver it.

- ✦ **Book V: Excel 2007:** Shows the many different ways to crunch the numbers with the bean counter in the Office suite. Along the way, you find out how to design worksheets that are easy to read and understand, use data-validation rules to cut down on entry mistakes, and analyze your data. You find out just how useful Excel can be for financial analyses, data tracking, and forecasting.

- ✦ **Book VI: Access 2007:** Describes how to create a relational database for storing information, as well as query the database for information and gather information into meaningful reports. Don't be frightened by the word "database." You'll be surprised to discover how useful Access can be in your work.

- ✦ **Book VII: Publisher 2007:** Shows how to create brochures, pamphlets, newsletters, and other publications with the "print shop in a can."

- ✦ **Book VIII: Office 2007 — One Step Beyond:** For people who want to take full advantage of Office, Book VIII delves into customizing the Office programs, recording and running macros, and collaborating with the SharePoint Services software. It looks into some auxiliary programs that come with Office, including OneNote, Picture Manager, and Clip Organizer. It also looks into alternative ways to distribute your work — in a blog or a Web page, for example.

What Makes This Book Different

You're holding in your hands a computer book designed to make mastering the Office programs as easy and comfortable as possible. Besides the fact that this book is easy to read, it's different from other books about Office. Read on to see why.

Easy-to-look-up information

This book is a *reference,* which means that readers have to be able to find instructions quickly. To that end, I have taken great pains to make sure that the material in this book is well organized and easy to find. The descriptive headings help you find information quickly. The bulleted and numbered lists make following instructions simpler. The tables make options easier to understand.

I want you to be able to look down the page and see in a heading or list the name of the topic that concerns you. I want you to be able to find instructions quickly. Compare the table of contents in this book to the book next to it on the bookstore shelf. The table of contents in this book is put together better and presents topics so that you can find them in a hurry.

A task-oriented approach

Most computer books describe what the software is, but this book explains how to complete tasks with the software. I assume that you came to this book because you want to know how to *do* something — print form letters, create a worksheet, or query a database. You came to the right place. This book describes how to get tasks done.

Meaningful screen shots

The screen shots in this book show only the part of the screen that illustrates what is being explained in the text. When instructions refer to one part of the screen, only that part of the screen is shown. I took great care to make sure that the screen shots in this book serve to help you understand the Office programs and how they work. Compare this book to the next one on the bookstore shelf. Do you see how clean the screen shots in this book are?

Foolish Assumptions

Please forgive me, but I made one or two foolish assumptions about you, the reader of this book. I assumed that:

✦ You own a copy of Office 2007, the latest edition of Office, and you have installed it on your computer.

✦ You use a Windows operating system, preferably either Windows XP or Windows Vista. All people who have the Windows operating system installed on their computers are invited to read this book, though.

✦ You are kind to foreign tourists and small animals.

Conventions Used in This Book

I want you to understand all the instructions in this book, and in that spirit, I've adopted a few conventions.

Where you see boldface letters or numbers in this book, it means to type the letters or numbers. For example, "Enter **25** in the Percentage text box" means to do exactly that: Enter the number 25.

To show you how to step through command sequences, I use the ⇨ symbol. For example, you can click the Office button and choose Print⇨Print Preview to see what the file you're working on will look like when you print it. The ⇨ symbol is just a shorthand method of saying "Choose Print and then choose Print Preview."

To give most commands, you can press combinations of keys. For example, pressing Ctrl+S saves the file you're working on. In other words, you can hold down the Ctrl key and press the S key to save a file. Where you see Ctrl+, Alt+, or Shift+ and a key name or key names, press the keys simultaneously.

 Yet another way to give a command is to click a button. When I tell you to click a button, you see a small illustration of the button in the margin of this book (unless the button is too large to fit in the margin). The button shown here is the Save button, the one you can click to save a file.

Icons Used in This Book

To help you get the most out of this book, I've placed icons here and there. Here's what the icons mean:

 Next to the Tip icon, you can find shortcuts and tricks of the trade to make your visit to Office Land more enjoyable.

 Where you see the Warning icon, tread softly and carefully. It means that you're about to do something that you may regret later.

 When I explain a juicy little fact that bears remembering, I mark it with a Remember icon. When you see this icon, prick up your ears. You'll discover something that you need to remember throughout your adventures with Word, Excel, PowerPoint, or the other Office program I'm demystifying.

When I am forced to describe high-tech stuff, a Technical Stuff icon appears in the margin. You don't have to read what's beside the Technical Stuff icons if you don't want to, although these technical descriptions often help you understand how a software feature works.

Good Luck, Reader!

If you have a comment about this book, a question, or a shortcut you would like to share with me, address an e-mail message to me at this address: weverka@sbcglobal.net. Be advised that I usually can't answer e-mail right away because I'm too darned busy. I do appreciate comments and questions, however, because they help me pass my dreary days in captivity.

Book I

Common Office Tools

The 5th Wave   By Rich Tennant

"No, that's not the icon for Excel, it's the icon for Excuse, the database of reasons why you haven't learned the other programs in Office."

Contents at a Glance

Chapter 1: Office Nuts and Bolts

Chapter 1 is where you get your feet wet with Office 2007. Walk right to the shore and sink your toes in the water. Don't worry; I won't push you from behind.

In this chapter, you meet the Office programs and discover speed techniques for opening programs and files. I show you around the new Office interface — the one that everybody's been talking about. I also show you how to save files, what the eXtensible Markup Language (XML) file format is all about, and how to clamp a password on a file.

A Survey of Office Programs

Office 2007, sometimes called the *Microsoft Office Suite,* is a collection of computer programs. Why is it called Office? I think because the people who invented it wanted to make software for completing tasks that need doing in a typical office. When you hear someone talk about "Office" or the "Office software," they're talking about several different programs:

✦ **Word:** A word processor for writing letters, reports, and so on. A Word file is a *document* (see Book II).

✦ **Outlook:** A personal information manager, scheduler, and e-mailer (see Book III).

+ **PowerPoint:** A means of creating computer presentations to give in front of audiences. A PowerPoint file is a *presentation,* or sometimes a *slide show* (see Book IV).

+ **Excel:** A number cruncher for performing numerical analyses. An Excel file is a *workbook* (see Book V).

+ **Access:** A database management program (see Book VI).

+ **Publisher:** A means of creating desktop-publishing files — pamphlets, notices, newsletters, and the like (see Book VII).

Office 2007 also comes with the *Clip Organizer,* for managing and inserting clip-art images in files, the *Picture Manger,* for inserting pictures and keeping track of the media files on your computer, and in some editions, *OneNote 2007,* a program for taking notes and brainstorming. These programs are explained in Book VIII.

If you're new to Office, don't be daunted by the prospect of having to study so many different computer programs. The programs have much in common. You find the same commands throughout Office. For example, the method of choosing fonts is the same in Word, Outlook, PowerPoint, Excel, and Publisher. Creating diagrams and charts works the same in Word, PowerPoint, and Excel. Book I describes tasks that are common to all or most of the Office programs. Master one Office program and you're well on your way to mastering the next.

Starting an Office Program

Unless you start an Office program, you can't create a document, construct a worksheet, or make a database. Many have tried to undertake these tasks with mud and paper-mâché without starting a program first, but all have failed. Here are the various and sundry ways to start an Office program:

+ **The old-fashioned way:** Click the Start button, choose All Programs⇨ Microsoft Office, and then choose the program's name on the submenu.

+ **The Start menu:** Click the program's name on the Start menu, as shown in Figure 1-1. The *Start menu* is the menu you see when you click the Start button. By placing a program's name on the Start menu, you can open the program simply by clicking the Start button and then clicking the program's name. To place an Office program on the Start menu:

   1. **Click the Start button and choose All Programs⇨Microsoft Office.**

   2. **Move the pointer over the program's name on the submenu, but don't click to select the program's name.**

3. **Right-click the program's name and choose Pin to Start Menu on the shortcut menu that appears.**

   To remove a program's name from the Start menu, right-click the name and choose Remove from This List.

Click a program name on the Start menu.   Double-click a shortcut icon.

Figure 1-1:
Three of several ways to start an Office program.

Click an icon on the Quick Launch toolbar.

✦ **Desktop shortcut icon:** Double-click the program's shortcut icon (see Figure 1-1). A *shortcut icon* is an icon you can click to do something in a hurry. By creating a shortcut icon on the Windows desktop, you can double-click the icon and immediately start an Office program. To place an Office shortcut icon on the desktop:

   1. **Click the Start button and choose All Programs⇨Microsoft Office.**

   2. **Move the pointer over the program's name on the submenu, but don't click the program's name.**

   3. **Right-click the program's name and choose Send To⇨Desktop (Create Shortcut) on the shortcut menu that appears.**

✦ **Quick Launch toolbar:** Click a shortcut icon on the Quick Launch toolbar, as shown in Figure 1-1. The Quick Launch toolbar appears on the Windows taskbar and is easy to find. Wherever your work takes you, you can see the Quick Launch toolbar and click its shortcut icons to start programs. Create a shortcut icon and follow these steps to place a copy of it on the Quick Launch toolbar:

1. **Click the shortcut icon to select it.**

2. **Hold down the Ctrl key.**

3. **Drag the shortcut icon onto the Quick Launch toolbar.**

To change an icon's position on the toolbar, drag it to the left or the right. To remove an icon, right-click it and choose Delete.

Yet another way to start an Office program is to make the program start automatically whenever you turn on your computer. If you're the president of the Office Fan Club and you have to run, for example, Outlook each time your computer starts, create an Outlook shortcut icon and copy it into this folder if your computer runs Windows XP:

```
C:\Documents and Settings\Username\Start Menu\Programs\
     Startup
```

Copy the shortcut icon into this folder if your computer runs Windows Vista:

```
C:\Users\Username\AppData\Roaming\Microsoft\Windows\
     Start Menu\Programs\Startup
```

Finding Your Way around the New Office Interface

If you're friendly with previous editions of Office, you probably got a shock when you opened this new edition for the first time. The new Office looks different. Gone is the main menu across the top of the screen and the many toolbars. The entire suite of programs has been given a facelift.

Why the change? The mighty muck-a-mucks of Microsoft decided that the number of features in Office had outgrown the old menu-and-toolbar structure. Users of Office had to take too many steps — they had to open too many menus and fiddle with too many toolbars — to find features and commands. Microsoft thought that features and commands were going unused because they were buried too deeply in the menu-and-toolbar structure.

To bring all the features and commands into the open, Microsoft designed a new interface for most of the Office programs. *Interface* — also called the *user interface* — is a computer term that describes how a software program presents itself to the people who use it (and you probably thought *interface* meant two people kissing). The new Office interface is daunting at first because it's hard to tell where to find commands. It's hard to know where to begin. However, I'm happy to report, having spent a lot of time with Office in the course of writing this book, that I like the new interface. Maybe I'm suffering from Stockholm Syndrome (a condition that makes kidnap victims fall in love with their kidnappers), but I've grown to like the interface.

These pages give you a quick tour of the new Office interface and explain what the various parts of the interface are. Click along with me as I describe the interface and you'll know what's what by the time you finish reading these pages.

The Office button

In the upper-left corner of the window is the *Office button,* as shown in Figure 1-2. Clicking this button opens a menu similar to the File menu in most computer programs. The Office menu offers commands for creating, opening, and saving files, as well as doing other file-management tasks.

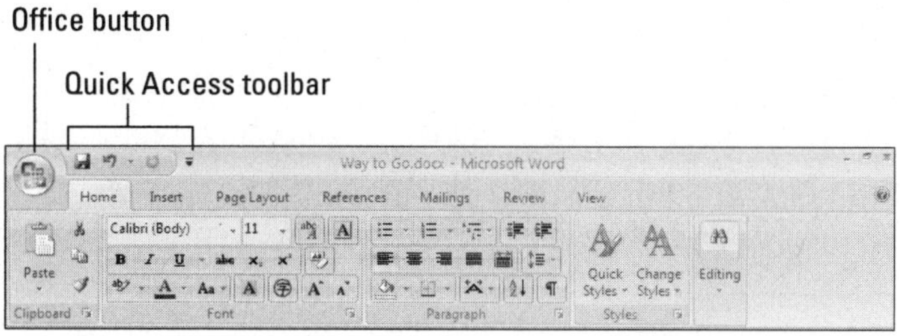

Office button

Quick Access toolbar

Figure 1-2:
The Office button and Quick Access toolbar are always available.

The Quick Access toolbar

No matter where you travel in an Office program, you see the *Quick Access toolbar* in the upper-left corner of the screen next to the Office button (see Figure 1-2). This toolbar offers three necessary buttons: the all-important Save button, the trusty Undo button, and the convenient Repeat button. You can place more buttons on the Quick Access toolbar as well as move the toolbar lower in the window. I explain how to customize the Quick Access toolbar in Book VIII, Chapter 1.

By the way, Microsoft says you can call the Quick Access toolbar the QAT, or "kwat," but I don't think you should do that. Others might think you have indigestion.

The Ribbon and its tabs

Across the top of the screen is the *Ribbon,* an assortment of different *tabs;* click a tab to undertake a task. For example, click the Home tab to format text; click the Insert tab to insert a table or chart. Figure 1-3 shows what you see in Word when you click the Home, Insert, and Page Layout tabs on the Ribbon. Each tab offers a different set of buttons and galleries.

The Ribbon

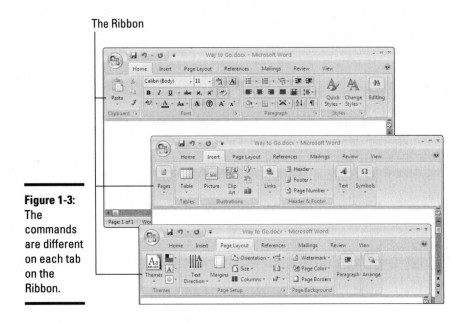

Figure 1-3: The commands are different on each tab on the Ribbon.

Practically speaking, your first step when you start a new task is to click a tab on the Ribbon. Knowing which tab to click takes awhile, but the names of tabs — Home, Insert, View, and so on — hint as to which commands you find when you visit a tab.

How many buttons appear on some of the tabs depends on the size of your monitor screen. On narrow 800 x 600 screens, Office sometimes can't find enough room to display all the buttons on a tab, so it presents you with a primary button to click in order to get to the other buttons. Throughout this book, I endeavor to tell you which button you click if your monitor has a narrow as well as a wide screen, but if the instructions in this book tell you to click a button and you don't see it, you have to click a primary button first. Look around for the primary button and then click it to get to the secondary button.

To make the Ribbon disappear and get more room to view slides, right-click the Ribbon and then choose Minimize the Ribbon on the shortcut menu. To see the Ribbon again, right-click a tab name or the Quick Access toolbar and then deselect Minimize the Ribbon on the shortcut menu. While the Ribbon is minimized, you can click a tab name to display a tab.

Context-sensitive tabs

Sorry for dropping the term *context-sensitive* on you. I usually steer clear of these horrid computer terms, but I can't help it this time because Microsoft calls some tabs context-sensitive, and by golly, I have to call them that, too.

To keep the Ribbon from getting too crowded with tabs, some tabs appear only in context — they appear on the Ribbon after you insert or click something. In Figure 1-4, for example, I inserted a table, and two additional tabs, the Design and the Layout tab, appear on the Ribbon under the heading Table Tools. These context-sensitive tabs offer commands for designing and laying out tables. When I click the (Table Tools) Design tab, as Figure 1-4 shows, I see commands for putting colors and borders on tables. The idea behind context-sensitive tabs is to direct you to the commands you need and exclude all other commands.

Select or insert an item. . .   . . .and you get context-sensitive tabs.

Figure 1-4:
After you insert or select an item, context-sensitive tabs appear on the Ribbon.

	Deer	Bear	Wombat
California	150,000	8,000	42,000
Nevada	45,000	2,000	23,000
Arizona	23,000	2,500	112,000

If you're looking for a tab on the Ribbon but can't find it, the tab is probably context-sensitive. You have to insert or select an item to make some tabs appear on the Ribbon. Context-sensitive tabs appear on the right side of the Ribbon under a heading with *Tools* in its name. In Figure 1-4, for example, the Design and Layout context-sensitive tabs pertain to handling tables, so they appear under the Table Tools heading.

Context-sensitive tab names can be confusing because sometimes they repeat the names of other tabs. When I refer to a context-sensitive tab name in this book, I sometimes include its Tools heading in parentheses if there is any confusion about which tab I'm referring to. In PowerPoint, for example, the Design tab that always appears on the Ribbon is the *Design tab,* but the context-sensitive Design tab is the *(Table Tools) Design tab*.

The anatomy of a tab

All tabs are different in terms of the commands they offer, but all are the same insofar as how they present commands. On every tab, you find groups and buttons. Some tabs also offer galleries. Groups, buttons, galleries — what's up with that?

Groups

Commands on each tab are organized into *groups*. For example, the Home tab in Excel is organized into several groups, including the Clipboard, Font, Alignment, Number, Cells, and Editing group, as shown in Figure 1-5. Group names appear below the buttons and galleries on tabs.

Group names

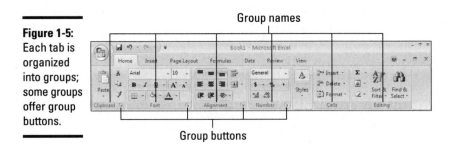

Figure 1-5: Each tab is organized into groups; some groups offer group buttons.

Group buttons

Groups serve two purposes:

✦ Groups tell you what the buttons and galleries above their names are used for. On the Home tab in Excel, for example, the buttons on the Font group are for formatting text. Read group names to help find the command you need.

✦ Many groups have *group buttons* that you can click to open a dialog box or task pane (officially, Microsoft calls these little buttons *dialog box launchers,* but let's act like grownups, shall we?). Group buttons are found to the right of group names. Moving the pointer over a group button opens a pop-up help box with a description and picture of the dialog box or task pane that appears when the button is clicked.

As with tabs on the Ribbon, group buttons are context-sensitive (there's that term again!). Whether you can click a group button to open a dialog box or task pane depends on the context in which you're working. Sometimes the buttons are grayed out because they don't pertain to the task you're currently doing.

Buttons

Go to any tab and you find buttons of all shapes and sizes. Square buttons and rectangular buttons. Big and small buttons. Buttons with labels and buttons without labels. Is there any rhyme or reason to these button shapes and sizes? No, there isn't.

What matters isn't a button's shape or size, but whether a down-pointing arrow appears on its face:

✦ **A button with an arrow:** Click a button *with* an arrow and you get a drop-down list. Sometimes the drop-down list presents still more buttons. Yet again, on these drop-down lists, clicking a button with an arrow gets you another drop-down list, but clicking a button without an arrow opens a dialog box or task pane.

✦ **A button without an arrow:** Click a button *without* an arrow and you open a dialog box or task pane.

✦ **A hybrid button with an arrow:** Some buttons serve a dual purpose as a button and a drop-down list. By clicking the symbol on the top half of the button, you complete an action; by clicking the arrow on the bottom half of the button, you open a drop-down list. On the Home tab, for example, clicking the top half of the Paste button pastes what is on the Clipboard into your file, but clicking the bottom half of the button opens a drop-down list with Paste options.

You can find out what clicking a button does by moving the pointer over it. You see a pop-up description of what the button is for.

Galleries

Built into some tabs are galleries like the one shown in Figure 1-6. The gallery in the figure pertains to charts: the Chart Styles gallery is for formatting charts. A *gallery* presents you with visual options for changing an item. Rather than visit numerous dialog boxes and task panes, you can select a gallery choice and give many commands at once. The item on your page or slide — the table, chart, or diagram, for example — changes in appearance when you move the pointer over different gallery choices.

Click the More button to open the gallery in a drop-down list.

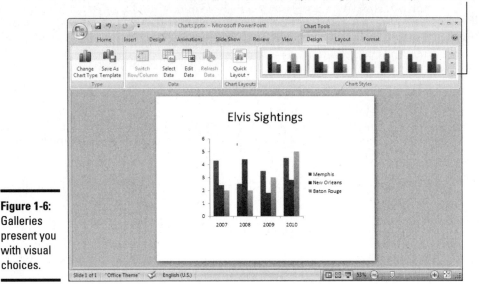

Figure 1-6:
Galleries
present you
with visual
choices.

To view and make choices on a gallery:

✦ Click a scroll arrow to see more gallery choices on the tab.

✦ Click the More button (see Figure 1-6) to open the gallery choices in a
   drop-down list and see many choices at once.

Galleries are unique because they present, in the form of visual choices, the
results of commands, not command names. All you have to do is glance at a
gallery option to see what selecting the option does to your chart, table,
shape, or whatever. By selecting gallery options, you can get very sophisticated layouts and formats without having to be a design expert or know
your way to all the layout and formatting commands. You can experiment
with formats and layouts in a matter of seconds merely by hovering the
pointer over gallery choices (see "Live previewing," the next section in this
chapter).

Live previewing

This new edition of Office comes with live previewing, a welcome and
inspired innovation. Thanks to *live previewing,* you can see the results of a
menu or gallery choice before actually making the choice.

Here's how live previewing works: Move the pointer over an option in a gallery or drop-down list and glance at the screen. You can see the results of selecting the option. For example, you see a different font or shape color. You can judge whether choosing the option is worthwhile without choosing the option first. Live previewing liberates you from repeatedly choosing commands, backtracking, and trying again until you get it right.

Follow these steps to experiment with live previewing:

1. **Enter some text.**

2. **Click and drag the pointer over the text to select it.**

   Drag means to hold down the mouse button while sliding the pointer over the text.

3. **Click the Home tab.**

4. **Open the Font drop-down list.**

5. **Slowly move your pointer over the options in the Font drop-down list.**

   When the pointer comes to different font names, the text on your slide changes fonts.

Mini Toolbars

A *Mini Toolbar* is a ghost-like menu that appears on-screen to help you do a task, as shown in Figure 1-7. Move the pointer over the Mini Toolbar, and it ceases being ghost-like, as Figure 1-7 demonstrates. Now you can choose an option from a drop-down list or click a button on the Mini Toolbar to complete a task.

Figure 1-7:
Move the pointer over the Mini Toolbar to make it come alive.

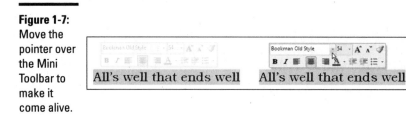

The Mini Toolbar, as shown in Figure 1-7, appears when you select text and then move the pointer over selected text. Don't be frightened of these ghost-like Mini Toolbars. Keep your eyes open for them. Mini Toolbars are very convenient, and they save you the trouble of going to a different tab to complete a task.

Right-clicking to open a shortcut menu

Similar to Mini Toolbars are the shortcut menus you get when you right-click. *Right-click* means to click the right — not the left — mouse button. Right-click just about anywhere and you get a shortcut menu of some kind. The shortcut menus differ, depending on what you right-click.

Right-clicking sometimes gets you to the command you need without having to select a different tab. I know I've been right-clicking more than usual in this new edition of Office to keep from switching from tab to tab on the Ribbon.

When you right-click text, the Mini Toolbar appears at the top or bottom of the shortcut menu. To see what I mean, compare this illustration to Figure 1-7.

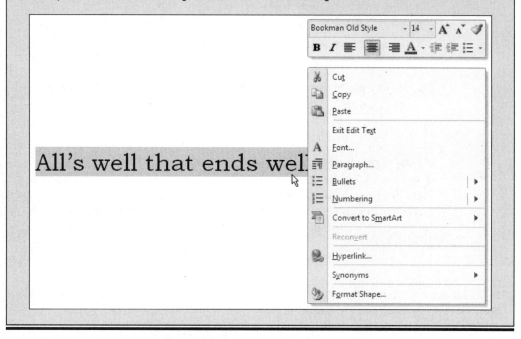

Office 2007 for keyboard lovers

People who like to give commands by pressing keyboard shortcuts may well ask, "Where are the keyboard shortcuts in the new edition of Office?" The answer is: They're still there. All keyboard shortcuts — press Ctrl+B for boldface text and Ctrl+U for underline text, for example — work the same way as they did in earlier editions of Office.

To find out the keyboard shortcuts for opening and choosing menu commands, press the Alt key. Letters — they're called *KeyTips* — appear on tab names. After you press the Alt key, follow these instructions to make use of KeyTips:

✦ **Go to a tab:** Press a KeyTip on a tab to visit a tab. As shown in Figure 1-8, letters, numbers, and combinations of letters and numbers appear on the commands.

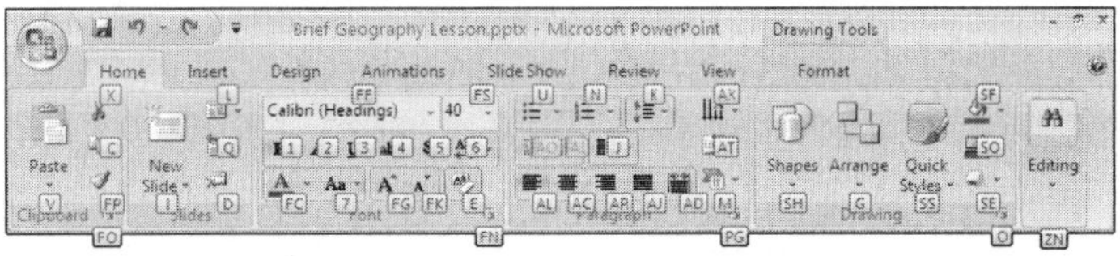

Figure 1-8:
Press the
Alt key to
see KeyTips.

✦ **Make KeyTips appear on menu items:** Press a KeyTip on a button or gallery to make KeyTips appear on menu items.

Saving Your Files

Soon after you create a new file, be sure to save it. And save your file from time to time while you work on it as well. Until you save your work, it rests in the computer's electronic memory (RAM), a precarious location. If a power outage occurs or your computer stalls, you lose all the work you did since the last time you saved your file. Make it a habit to save files every ten minutes or so or when you complete an important task.

To save a file:

✦ Click the Save button.

✦ Press Ctrl+S.

✦ Click the Office button and then choose Save on the drop-down list.

I wish that saving was always just a matter of clicking the Save button, but saving your work also entails declaring where you prefer to save files, saving files for use in earlier versions of the Office programs, and saving AutoRecovery files. Better read on.

Declaring where you like to save files

When you attempt to save a file for the first time in the Save As dialog box, Office shows you the contents of the My Documents folder (in Windows XP) or the Document folder (in Windows Vista) on the assumption that you keep most of your files in that folder. The My Documents folder is the center of the universe as far as Office is concerned, but perhaps you keep the majority of your files in a different folder. How would you like to see it first in the Save As and Open dialog boxes?

To direct Office to the folder you like best and make it appear first in the Save As and Open dialog boxes, follow these steps:

1. **In Word, Excel, or PowerPoint, click the Office button and then choose the Options button at the bottom of the drop-down list (in Word, for example, choose Word Options).**

   You see the Options dialog box.

2. **Select the Save category.**

   Figure 1-9 shows the topmost options in this category.

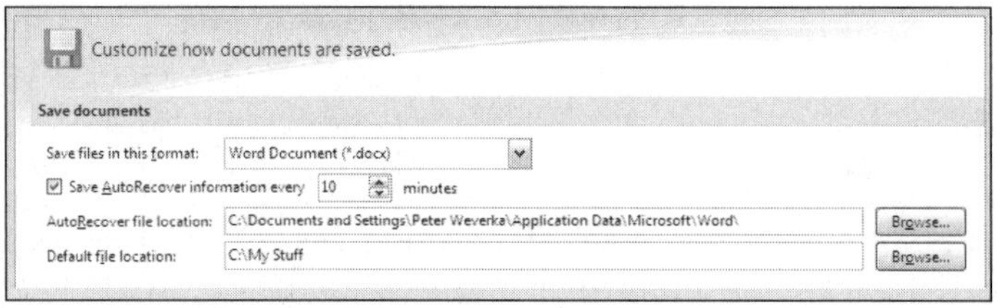

Figure 1-9: The Saving options in the Options dialog box.

Customize how documents are saved.

Save documents

Save files in this format: Word Document (*.docx)

☑ Save AutoRecover information every   10   minutes

AutoRecover file location: C:\Documents and Settings\Peter Weverka\Application Data\Microsoft\Word\   [Browse...]

Default file location: C:\My Stuff   [Browse...]

3. **In the Default File Location text box, enter the address of the folder where you prefer to keep your files.**

   For example, if you're fond of keeping files in the My Stuff folder on the C drive of your computer, enter **C:\My Stuff**, or click the Browse button and then select the My Stuff folder in the Modify Location dialog box.

4. **Click OK.**

Saving files for use in earlier versions of an Office program

Not everyone is a proud owner of Office 2007. Before you pass along a file to a co-worker who has an earlier version of Office, save your document so that your co-worker can open it. Files are stored in the XML format in Office 2007 (later in this chapter, "Understanding the New Office XML Format" explains XML). Unless you save your file for earlier versions of Office, people who don't have the latest version can't open them.

Saving a file for use in Office 97–2003

Follow these steps to save a file so that someone with Office 97, 2000, XP, or 2003 can open it:

1. **Click the Office button.**

2. **Choose Save As⇨*Program Name* 97–2003 Format.**

You see the Save As dialog box.

3. **Enter a new name for the file, if necessary.**

4. **Click the Save button.**

Files saved in the 97–2003 format have a different file extension. Instead of a four-letter file extension that ends in *x,* they have a three-letter extension without the *x.*

Before you save your file for an earlier version of the program you're working in, you can find out if anything will be lost when you save the file. Click the Office button and choose Prepare⇨Run Compatibility Checker. You see the Compatibility Checker dialog box. It tells you whether the earlier version of the program can't handle something in your file.

Saving files by default for earlier versions of Office

If you're way ahead of the pack and you always have to save files in a different format so that co-workers can open them, make the different format the default format for saving all your files. That way, you don't have to choose a new format whenever you pass off a file to a co-worker.

Follow these steps to change the default format for saving files:

1. **Click the Office button and choose Options on the drop-down list.**

The Options dialog box appears.

2. **Select the Save category (refer to Figure 1-9).**

3. **In the Save Files in This Format drop-down list, choose the 97–2003 format.**

4. **Click OK.**

Remember that you made 97–2003 the default format for saving files. Someday soon, your co-workers will catch up with you. They will acquire Office 2007. And when that happens, return to the Options dialog box and choose the most up-to-date format.

Converting Office 97–2003 files to 2007

When you open a file made in an earlier version of Office, the program switches to *compatibility mode*. Features that weren't part of earlier versions of the program are shut down. You can tell when a file is in compatibility mode because the words Compatibility Mode appear in the title bar next to the file's name.

Follow these steps to convert a 97–2003 file for use in an Office 2007 program:

1. **Click the Office button and choose Convert on the drop-down list.**

   A dialog box informs you what converting means. If you don't see the Convert option, your file has been converted already.

2. **Click OK.**

Island Tree.ppt [Compatibility Mode] - Microsoft PowerPoint

Microsoft Office PowerPoint

This action will convert the document to the newest format.
Converting allows you to use all the new features of PowerPoint and reduces the size of your file. This document will be replaced by the converted version.

☐ Do not ask me again about converting documents

Tell Me More...   OK   Cancel

Saving AutoRecovery information

To insure against data loss due to computer and power failures, Office saves files on its own every ten minutes. These files are saved in an AutoRecovery file. After your computer fails, you can try to recover some of the work you lost by getting it from the AutoRecovery file (see "When disaster strikes!").

Office saves AutoRecovery files every ten minutes, but if you want the program to save the files more or less frequently, you can change the AutoRecovery setting. Auto-recovering taxes a computer's memory. If your computer is sluggish, consider making AutoRecovery files at intervals longer than ten minutes; if your computer fails often and you're worried about losing data, make AutoRecovery files more frequently.

Follow these steps to tell Office how often to save data in an AutoRecovery file:

1. **Click the Office button and choose Options on the drop-down list.**

The Options dialog box appears.

2. **Select the Save category (refer to Figure 1-9).**

3. **Enter a Minutes setting in the Save AutoRecover Information Every box.**

4. **Click OK.**

When disaster strikes!

After your computer fails and you restart an Office program, you see the Document Recovery task pane with a list of files that were open when the failure occurred:

- ✔ *AutoSave* files are files that Office saves as part of its AutoRecovery procedure (see "Saving AutoRecovery information").

- ✔ *Original* files are files that you save by clicking the Save button.

The Document Recovery task pane tells you when each file was saved. By studying the time listings, you can tell which version of a file — the AutoRecovery file or the file you saved — is most up to date.

Open the drop-down list for a file and choose one of these options:

- ✔ **Open:** Opens the file so that you can examine it. If you want to keep it, click the Save button.

- ✔ **Save As:** Opens the Save As dialog box so that you can save the file under a different name. Choose this command to keep a copy of the recovered file on hand in case you need it.

- ✔ **Delete:** Deletes the AutoRecovery file (this command is available with AutoRecovery files, not files that you save on your own).

- ✔ **Show Repairs:** Shows repairs made to the file (for use with repaired Word documents).

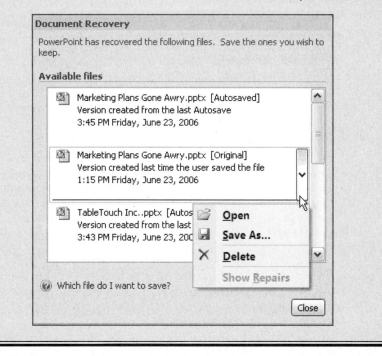

Opening and Closing Files

To get to work on a file, you have to open it first. And, of course, you close a file when you're finished working on it and want to carry on normal activities. The following pages explain all the intricate details of opening and closing files. In these pages, you find many tips for finding and opening the file you want to work on.

Opening a file

Between the two of them, Office and Windows offer many shortcuts for opening file. To open a file, take the standard route — click the Office button and then choose Open — or take advantage of the numerous ways to open files quickly.

The slow, conventional way to open a file

If you can't open a file by any other means, you have to resort to the Open dialog box:

1. **Click the Office button and choose Open on the drop-down list (or press Ctrl+O).**

   You see the Open dialog box, as shown in Figure 1-10.

2. **Locate and select the file you want to open.**

   Very shortly, I show you some tricks for locating a file in the Open dialog box.

3. **Click the Open button.**

   Your file opens. You can also double-click a filename to open a file.

The Open dialog box offers a bunch of different ways to locate a file:

+ **My Recent Documents button:** View the names of files you recently worked on in the dialog box.

+ **Look In drop-down list:** Look for folders or files on a different drive, network location, or disk. (You can also click the My Computer button.) Earlier in this chapter, "Declaring where you like to save files" explains how to make a folder of your choice appear first in the Look In drop-down list.

+ **Back button:** Revisit folders you saw before in the course of your search.

+ **Up One Level button:** Move up the folder hierarchy to show the contents of the folder one level above the one you're looking at.

Double-click a folder to see its contents.

Navigate to other folders.   Change views.

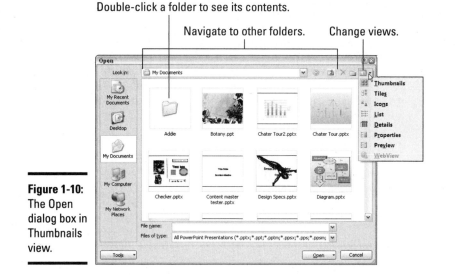

Figure 1-10:
The Open
dialog box in
Thumbnails
view.

✦ **Views drop-down list:** Display folder contents differently (see Figure 1-10). In the Thumbnails view and Preview view, you can see a pictorial representation of a file. Details view can be helpful when you have trouble finding a file. In Details view, you see how large files are and when they were edited last.

✦ **Folders:** Double-click a folder to see its contents in the Open dialog box.

If you know the first letter in the name of a file you want to open, type the letter in the File Name text box. Files whose names start with the letter you typed appear on the File Name drop-down list.

Deleting and renaming files in the Open dialog box

Deleting and renaming files is really the purlieu of the Windows operating system, but you can delete and rename documents one at a time inside the Open dialog box. Select the file that needs deleting or renaming and follow these instructions to delete or rename it:

✔ **Deleting a file:** Click the Delete button; click the Tools button and choose Delete on the drop-down list; or right-click and choose Delete. Then click Yes in the Confirm File Delete message box.

✔ **Renaming a file:** Click the Tools button and choose Rename on the drop-down list (or right-click and choose Rename). Then type a new name and press Enter.

Speed techniques for opening files

As shown in Figure 1-11, the fastest way to open a file is to click the Office button and then click the file's name on the Recent Documents list. This list shows the names of the last several files you opened. By moving the pointer over a name, you can see which folder a file is stored in. Click the pin next to a name to make the name remain on the list even if it isn't one of the last several files you opened (click the pin a second time to "unpin" a name).

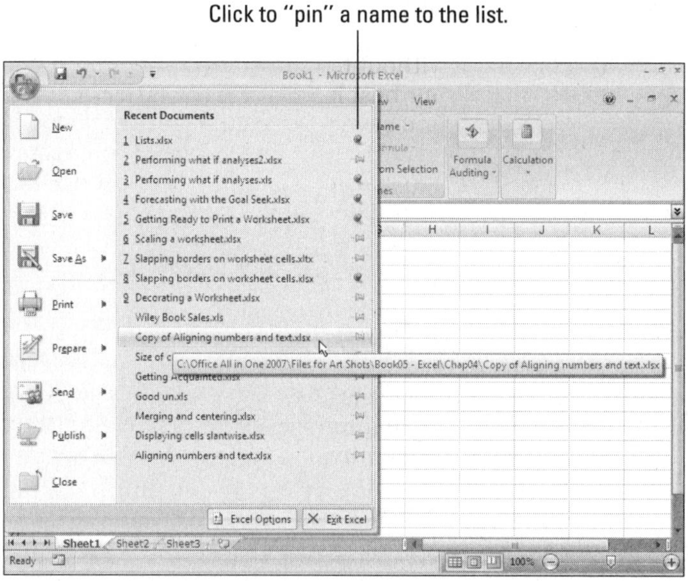

Click to "pin" a name to the list.

Figure 1-11:
Opening a
file on the
Recent
Documents
list.

To make more (or fewer) than nine filenames appear on the Recent Documents list, click the Office button and choose Options. In the Options dialog box, click the Advanced category. Then scroll to the Display section and enter a number in the Show This Number of Recent Documents text box.

Here are other speed techniques for opening files:

✦ **In Windows Explorer or My Computer:** Locate the file in one of these file-management programs and double-click its name. You can click the Start button and choose My Documents to open Windows Explorer to the My Documents folder.

✦ **Shortcut icon:** Create a shortcut icon to a file and place the icon on the Windows desktop. In Windows Explorer or the Open dialog box, right-click the file's name and choose Send To↔Desktop (Create Shortcut). To quickly open the file, double-click its shortcut icon on the desktop.

Closing a file

Closing a file is certainly easier than opening one. To close a file, save your file and use one of these techniques:

✦ Click the Office button and choose Close on the drop-down list. The program remains open although the file is closed.

✦ Click the Close button — the *X* in the upper-right corner of the window. (Alternatively, press Alt+F4.) Clicking the Close button closes the program as well as the file.

If you try to close a file without first saving it, a message box asks whether ditching your file is in your best interests, and you get a chance to click Yes in the message box and save your file. Sometimes closing a file without saving the changes you made to it is worthwhile. If you made a bunch of editorial mistakes and want to start over, you can close the file without saving the changes you made. Next time you open the file, you see the version that you had before you made all those mistakes.

Entering the Document Properties

Document properties are a means of describing a file. If you manage two dozen or more files, you owe it to yourself to record document properties. You can use them later to identify files.

 To record document-property descriptions, click the Office button and choose Prepare⇨Properties (in Access, choose Manage⇨Database Properties). You see the Properties pane, as shown in Figure 1-12. Enter information about your file in the text boxes. To record even more descriptions, click the Document Properties button and choose Advanced Properties on the drop-down list to display the Properties dialog box.

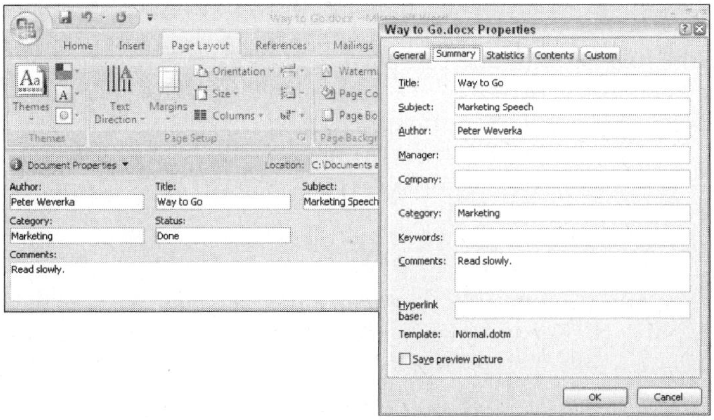

Figure 1-12: Enter document properties so you can identify files.

You can read a file's document properties without opening a file:

+ In Windows Explorer, My Computer, or the Open dialog box, right-click a file's name and choose Properties. You see the Properties dialog box, as shown on the right side of Figure 1-12.

+ In the Open dialog box, switch to Properties view (refer to Figure 1-10). You can do this in Windows XP but not Windows Vista.

Word, Excel, and PowerPoint offer a command for erasing document properties. Click the Office button and choose Prepare⇨Inspect Document. In the Document Inspector dialog box, click the Inspect button, and then click the Remove All button if you want to remove document properties.

Understanding the New Office XML Format

Not that you particularly need to know it if you don't share files with others, but Office 2007 files are formatted by using eXtensible Markup Language (XML), not the binary file format of previous versions. A *markup language* is a computer language, or set of codes, that determines how text, graphics, colors, and all else is displayed on a computer screen. You may have heard of Hypertext Markup Language (HTML). *HTML* is the markup language that Web browsers read to display Web pages on computer screens.

Microsoft adopted XML for Office 2007 (except Publisher) to make sharing information between the programs easier. Because files made in the Office 2007 programs are formatted in XML — because they're written in the same language — data from one Office program can be copied to another without the data having to be translated from one binary file format to another. What's more, files in the XML format are half the size of files written in the old binary formats. And because XML is an open format — all programmers can find the codes with which the XML is written — people outside Microsoft can write programs that produce XML data for use in Office programs. XML makes it easier for different programs to exchange information.

The new XML format matters to Office 2007 users who intend to give their files to people who don't have Office 2007. Because Office 2007 files are formatted in XML, not the binary file format with which Office 97, 2000, XP, and 2003 files are formatted, earlier versions of Office can't open files made in Office 2007. Before you give a file you create to someone who uses Office 97–2003, save it as an Office 97–2003 file. (See "Saving files for use in earlier versions of an Office program" earlier in this chapter.)

You can tell whether a Word, PowerPoint, Access, or Excel file is formatted for a 2007 program or an earlier version of the program by glancing at its file extension. PowerPoint, Excel, Access, and Word files have four-letter, not three-letter file extensions. Table 1-1 lists Office program file extensions. You can convert Office 97–2003 files for use in Office 2007. (See "Converting Office 97–2003 files to 2007" earlier in this chapter.)

Table 1-1	Office program file extensions		
Program	*2007*	*97–2003*	*Macro-enabled*
Access	`.accdb`	`.mlb`	
Excel	`.xlsx`	`.xls`	`.xlsm`
PowerPoint	`.pptx`	`.ppt`	`.pptm`
Publisher	`.pub`	`.pub`	
Word	`.docx`	`.doc`	`.docm`

Locking a File with a Password

Perhaps you want to submit your file to others for critical review but you don't want any Tom, Dick, or Harry to look at your file. In that case, lock your file with a password and only give out the password to people whose opinions you trust. These pages explain how to password-protect a file, open a file that is locked with a password, and remove the password from a file.

Password-protecting a file

Follow these steps to clamp a password on a file, such that others need a password to open and perhaps also edit it:

1. **Click the Office button and choose Save As.**

You see the Save As dialog box.

2. **Click the Tools button and choose General Options on the drop-down list.**

The General Options dialog box appears, as shown in Figure 1-13. (Your dialog box may look a little different, depending on which program you're in.)

3. **Enter a password in the Password to Open text box.**

Others need the password you enter to open the file. No ifs, ands, or buts. You have to enter this password.

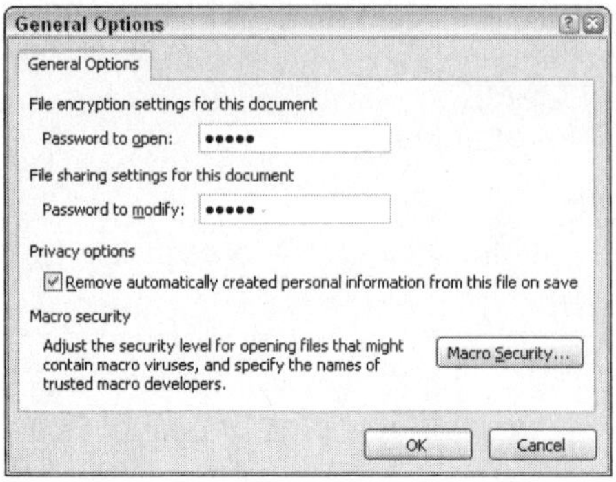

Figure 1-13:
Enter
passwords
for the file in
this dialog
box.

Passwords are case sensitive. In other words, you have to enter the correct combination of upper- and lowercase letters to successfully enter the password. If the password is *Valparaiso* (with an uppercase *V*), entering **valparaiso** (with a lowercase v) is deemed the wrong password and doesn't open the file.

4. **Enter a password in the Password to Modify text box if you want others to supply a password not only to open the file but also to edit it.**

   Unless they have this password, others can't edit this file or save it under a different name. The file opens as a read-only file. It can be viewed, but not altered.

5. **Click OK.**

   The Confirm Password dialog box appears.

6. **Enter the Open password you gave in Step 3, and if you entered a Modify password, enter it as well; then click OK.**

7. **Click the Save button in the Save As dialog box.**

   At last, the ordeal is over.

Opening a file that requires a password

When you try to open a file that has been given a password, you see the Password dialog box, as shown on the left side of Figure 1-14. And if a password is required as well to edit the file, the Password dialog box, as shown on the right side of Figure 1-14, appears shortly thereafter.

A person who doesn't have the Modify password can click the Read Only button to open the file. That person can view the file, but not edit it or save it under a different name.

Figure 1-14:
Open
sesame!

Removing a password from a file

Follow these steps to remove a password from a file:

1. **Open the file that needs its password removed.**

2. **Click the Office button and choose Save As.**

3. **In the Save As dialog box, click the Tools button and choose General Options on the drop-down list.**

You return to the General Options dialog box (refer to Figure 1-13).

4. **Delete the Open password and/or the Modify password and then click OK.**

5. **Click the Save button in the Save As dialog box.**

Chapter 2: Wrestling with the Text

In This Chapter

✔ Selecting, moving, copying, and deleting text

✔ Changing the appearance, size, and color of text

✔ Changing letters' case

✔ Inserting foreign characters and symbols

✔ Finding text — and replacing it if you want

✔ Hyperlinking to Web pages and other places in a file

To enter text, all you have to do is wiggle your fingers over the keyboard. Everybody knows that. But not everyone knows all the different ways to change the look and size of text in an Office 2007 file. This chapter explains how to do that as well as how to move, copy, and delete text. You find out how to quickly change letters' case, enter a symbol or foreign character, and find and replace text in a file. Finally, it shows you how to link your files to the Internet by fashioning a hyperlink.

Manipulating the Text

This short but important part of this chapter describes the many techniques for selecting, deleting, copying, and moving text. You find an inordinate number of tips on these pages because there are so many shortcuts for manipulating text. Master the many shortcuts and you cut down considerably on the time you spend editing text.

Selecting text

Before you can do anything to text — move it, boldface it, delete it, translate it — you have to select it. Here are speed techniques for selecting text:

To Select	Do This
A word	Double-click the word.
A few words	Drag over the words.
A paragraph	Triple-click inside the paragraph (in Word, PowerPoint, and Outlook messages).

To Select	Do This
A block of text	Click the start of the text you want to select, hold down the Shift key, and click the end of the text.
All text	Press Ctrl+A.

Word offers a special command for selecting text throughout a document. On the Home tab, click the Select button and choose Select Text with Similar Formatting (you may have to click the Editing button first). This command can come in handy when you need to make wholesale changes to text. For example, to change all italicized text to small caps, choose the Select Text with Similar Formatting command and then choose the Small Caps and Regular commands in the Font dialog box.

Moving and copying text

Office offers a number of different ways to move and copy text from place to place. Drum roll please . . . . Select the text you want to move or copy and then use one of these techniques to move or copy it:

✦ **Dragging and dropping:** Move the mouse over the text and then click and drag the text to a new location. If you want to copy rather than move the text, hold down the Ctrl key while you drag. *Drag* means to hold down the mouse button while you move the pointer on-screen.

✦ **Dragging and dropping with the right mouse button:** Drag the text while holding down the right, not the left, mouse button. After you release the right mouse button, a shortcut menu appears with Move Here and Copy Here options. Choose an option to move or copy the text.

✦ **Using the Clipboard:** Move or copy the text to the Clipboard by clicking the Cut or Copy button, pressing Ctrl+X or Ctrl+C, or right-clicking and choosing Cut or Copy on the shortcut menu. The text is moved or copied to an electronic holding tank called the *Clipboard.* Paste the text by clicking the Paste button, pressing Ctrl+V, or right-clicking and choosing Paste. You find the Paste, Cut, and Copy buttons on the Home tab.

Taking advantage of the Clipboard task pane

The Windows Clipboard is a piece of work. After you copy or cut text with the Cut or Copy command, the text is placed on the Clipboard. The Clipboard holds the last 24 items that you cut or copied. You can open the Clipboard task pane and view the last 24 items you cut or copied to the Clipboard, as shown in Figure 2-1.

To open the Clipboard task pane, go to the Home tab and click the Clipboard group button. Icons next to the items tell you where they came from. Open

---

A look at the Paste options

Text adopts the formatting of neighboring text when you move or copy it to a new location. Suppose, however, that you want the text you move or copy to keep its original formatting? In that case, click the Paste Options button. This button appears after you paste text. Click it to open a drop-down list with these options (among others, depending on the program you're working in):

✔ **Keep Source Formatting:** The text keeps its original formatting.

✔ **Match Destination Formatting:** The text adopts the formatting of surrounding text.

✔ **Keep Text Only:** The text is stripped of all formatting.

Some people think that the Paste Options button is a bother. If you're one of those people, click the Office button and choose Options on the drop-down list. You see the Options dialog box. Select the Advanced category and deselect the Show Paste Options Buttons check box.

---

an item's drop-down list and choose Paste to copy it. The Clipboard is available to all Office programs; it's especially useful for copying text and graphics from one Office program to another.

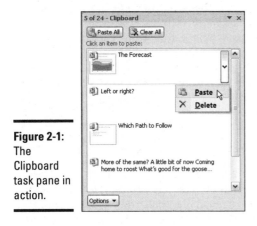

Figure 2-1:
The
Clipboard
task pane in
action.

The Options pop-up list at the bottom of the Clipboard task pane offers these options:

✦ **Show Office Clipboard Automatically:** Choose this option if you want the Clipboard task pane to open automatically when you cut or copy two items consecutively or you copy the same item twice.

✦ **Show Office Clipboard When Ctrl+C Pressed Twice:** Choose this option if you want to open the Clipboard task pane by pressing Ctrl+C and Ctrl+C again.

✦ **Collect Without Showing Office Clipboard:** Choose this option to be notified when an item has been cut or copied to the Clipboard by an icon in the system tray and/or a pop-up notice. To be notified, you must have selected either or both of the preceding two options on the Options menu.

✦ **Show Office Clipboard Icon on Taskbar:** Choose this option to be notified when an item has been cut or copied to the Clipboard by an icon in the *system tray,* the part of the Windows taskbar by the clock. (The icon appears after you cut or copy the first item to the Clipboard.) You can double-click the icon to open the Clipboard task pane. After an item is cut or copied to the Clipboard, a tiny page glides across the icon.

✦ **Show Status Near Taskbar When Copying:** Choose this item to be notified when an item has been cut or copied to the Clipboard by a pop-up notice in the lower-right corner of the screen. It tells you how many items have been collected on the Clipboard.

Deleting text

To delete a bunch of text at once, select the text you want to delete and press the Delete key. By the way, you can kill two birds with one stone by selecting text and then starting to type. The letters you type immediately take the place of and delete the text you selected.

You can always click the Undo button if you regret deleting text. You can find this button on the Quick Access toolbar.

Changing the Look of Text

What text looks like is determined by its font, the size of the letters, the color of the letters, and whether text effects or font styles, such as italics or boldface, are in the text. What text looks like really matters in Word, PowerPoint, and Publisher because files you create in those programs are meant to be read by all and sundry. Even in Excel, Access, and Outlook messages, however, font choices matter because the choices you make determine whether your work is easy to read and understand.

A *font* is a collection of letters, numbers, and symbols in a particular typeface, including all italic and boldface variations of the letters, numbers, and symbols. Fonts have beautiful names and some of them are many centuries old. Most computers come with these fonts: Arial, Tahoma, Times New Roman, and Verdana. By default, Office often applies the Calibri and Cambria fonts to text.

The Format Painter: A fast way to change the look of text

When you're in a hurry to change the look of text and reformat paragraphs, consider using the Format Painter. This nifty tool works something like a paintbrush. You drag it over text to copy formats from place to place. Follow these instructions to use the Format Painter:

1. **Click a place with text and paragraph formats that you want to copy elsewhere (or select the text).**

2. **On the Home tab (or the Format Text tab in an Outlook message), double-click the Format Painter button.**

   You can find this button in the Clipboard group. The pointer changes into a paintbrush. Unless

you double-click the Format Painter button, you can't copy format to more than one place.

3. **Drag the pointer across text to which you want to copy the formats.**

   You can go from place to place with the Format Painter.

4. **Click the Format Painter button a second time or press Esc when you're finished with the Format Painter.**

    At the opposite end of the spectrum from the Format Painter button is the Clear Formatting button on the Home tab. In Word and PowerPoint, you can select text and then click this button to strip text of all its formats, whatever they may be.

Font styles include boldface, italic, and underline. By convention, headings are boldface. Italics are used for emphasis and to mark foreign words in text. Office provides a number of text effects. *Text effects,* also known as *text attributes,* include strikethrough and superscript. Use text effects sparingly.

The following pages look at the different ways to change the font, font size, and color of text, as well as how to assign font styles and text effects to text.

Choosing fonts for text

If you aren't happy with the fonts you choose, select the text that needs a font change and change fonts with one of these techniques:

✦ **Mini Toolbar:** Move the pointer over the selected text. You see the Mini Toolbar. Move the pointer over this toolbar and choose a font in the Font drop-down list, as shown in Figure 2-2.

✦ **Shortcut menu:** Right-click the selected text and choose a new font on the Mini Toolbar attached to the shortcut menu.

✦ **Font drop-down list:** On the Home tab, open the Font drop-down list and choose a font. You can "live-preview" font choices on this menu.

✦ **Font dialog box:** On the Home tab, click the Font group button. You see the Font dialog box. Select a font and click OK.

Figure 2-2:
Changing
fonts by way
of the Mini
Toolbar.

 Another way to change fonts is to select a different theme font. In the Page Layout tab (in Word and Excel) or the Design tab (in PowerPoint), open the drop-down list on the Theme Fonts button and choose a font combination.

 Avoid using too many different fonts because a file with too many fonts looks like alphabet soup. The object is to choose a font that helps set the tone. An aggressive sales pitch calls for a strong, bold font; a technical presentation calls for a font that is clean and unobtrusive. Make sure that the fonts you select help communicate your message.

Installing and removing fonts on your computer

 If Windows is installed on your computer, so are many different fonts. The names of these fonts appear on the Font drop-down list, Font dialog box, and Mini Toolbar. Do you have enough fonts on your computer? Do you want to remove fonts to keep the Font drop-down list from being overcrowded?

Font files are kept in the `C:\Windows\Fonts` folder on your computer. Windows Explorer and My Computer (or Computer in Windows Vista) offer the File⇨Install New Font command for loading font files into this folder, but here are easier ways to handle fonts:

✔ **Installing new fonts:** Place the font file in the `C:\Windows\Fonts` folder.

✔ **Removing a font:** Move the font file out of the `C:\Windows\Fonts` folder. Store font files you don't want in another folder where you can resuscitate them if need be.

Besides opening the Fonts folder in Windows Explorer or My Computer, you can open it by double-clicking the Fonts icon in the Control Panel. The Fonts folder provides these amenities for handling fonts:

✔ **Examining fonts:** Double-click a font file to examine a font more closely. A window opens, and you see precisely what the font looks like. Do you know why "The quick brown fox jumps over the lazy dog"

appears in this window? Because that sentence includes every letter in the alphabet.

✔ **Finding similar fonts (Windows XP):** To list fonts that look similar to a certain font, click the Similarity button and choose the font's name on the List Fonts by Similarity To drop-down list. The list of fonts is arranged so that very similar fonts come first, fairly similar fonts come next, and dissimilar fonts come last in the list. Use this command to familiarize yourself with fonts or decide which fonts to remove when you have many that look nearly the same.

✔ **Shortening the font list (Windows XP):** To shrink the list of fonts and make font hunting a little easier, choose View⇨Hide Variations. Doing so removes boldface and italic versions of fonts from the list.

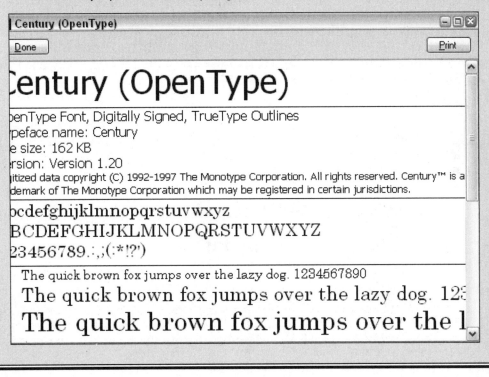

Changing the font size of text

Font size is measured in *points;* a point is $\frac{1}{72}$ of an inch. The golden rule of font sizes goes something like this: the larger the font size, the more important the text. This is why headings are larger than footnotes. Select your text and use one of these techniques to change the font size of the letters:

✦ **Mini Toolbar:** Move the pointer over the text and when you see the Mini Toolbar, move the pointer over the toolbar and choose a font size on the Font Size drop-down list (refer to Figure 2-2).

✦ **Shortcut menu:** Right-click the text and choose a new font size on the Mini Toolbar attached to the shortcut menu.

✦ **Font Size drop-down list:** On the Home tab, open the Font Size drop-down list and choose a font. You can "live-preview" font sizes this way.

✦ **Font dialog box:** On the Home tab, click the Font group button, and in the Font dialog box, choose a font size and click OK.

✦ **Grow Font and Shrink Font buttons:** Click these buttons (or press Ctrl+] or Ctrl+[) to increase or decrease the point size by the next interval on the Font Size drop-down list. You can find the Grow Font and Shrink Font buttons on the Home tab and the Mini Toolbar. Watch the Font Size list or your text and note how the text changes size. This is an excellent technique when you want to "eyeball it," and you don't care to fool with the Font Size list or Font dialog box.

Click the Grow Font and Shrink Font buttons when you're dealing with fonts of different sizes and you want to proportionally change the size of all the letters. Drag the pointer over the text to select it before clicking one of the buttons.

If the font size you want isn't on the Font Size drop-down list, enter the size. For example, to change the font size to 13.5 points, type **13.5** in the Font Size box and press Enter.

Applying font styles to text

There are four — count 'em four — font styles: regular, bold, italic, and underline:

✦ **Regular:** This style is just Office's way of denoting an absence of any font style.

✦ **Italic:** Italics are used for emphasis, when introducing a new term, and to mark foreign words such as *violà, gung hay fat choy,* and *Qué magnifico!* You can also italicize titles to make them a little more elegant.

✦ **Bold:** Boldface text calls attention to itself.

✦ **Underline:** Underline text to call attention to it but use underlining sparingly. Later in this chapter, "Underlining text" looks at all the ways to underline text.

Select text and use one of these techniques to apply a font style to it:

✦ **Home tab:** Click the Bold, Italic, or Underline button.

✦ **Keyboard:** Press Ctrl+B to boldface text, Ctrl+I to italicize it, or Ctrl+U to underline it.

✦ **Mini Toolbar:** The Mini Toolbar offers the Bold and Italic button.

✦ **Font dialog box:** Select a Font Style option in the Font dialog box. To open this dialog box, visit the Home tab and click the Font group button.

To remove a font style, click the Bold, Italic, or Underline buttons a second time. You can also select text and then click the Clear Formatting button on the Home tab (in Word and PowerPoint).

Applying text effects to text

Text effects have various uses, some utilitarian and some strictly for yucks. Be careful with text effects. Use them sparingly and to good purpose. To apply a text effect, start on the Home tab (or the Format Text tab in Outlook messages) and do one of the following:

✦ Click a text effect button.

✦ Click the Font group button and choose a text effect in the bottom half of the Font dialog box, as shown in Figure 2-3.

Here's a rundown of the different text effects (not all these effects are available in PowerPoint, Excel, and Outlook):

✦ **Strikethrough and Double Strikethrough:** By convention, *strikethrough* is used to show where passages are struck from a contract or other important document. Double strikethrough, for all I know, is used to show where passages are struck out forcefully. Use these text effects to demonstrate ideas that you reject.

✦ **Superscript:** A *superscripted* letter or number is one that is raised in the text. Superscript is used in mathematical and scientific formulas, in ordinal numbers (1st, 2nd, 3rd), and to mark footnotes. In the theory of relativity, the 2 is superscripted: $E = mc^2$.

✦ **Subscript:** A *subscripted* letter is lowered in the text. In this chemistry equation, the 2 is lowered to show that two atoms of hydrogen are needed along with one atom of oxygen to form a molecule of water: H_2O.

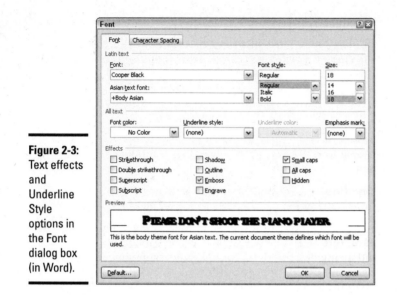

Figure 2-3:
Text effects
and
Underline
Style
options in
the Font
dialog box
(in Word).

✦ **Small Caps:** A *small cap* is a small capital letter. You can find many creative uses for small caps. An all small cap title looks elegant. Be sure to type lowercase letters in order to create small caps. Type an uppercase letter, and Office refuses to turn it into a small cap. Not all fonts can produce small capital letters.

✦ **All Caps:** The All Caps text effect merely capitalizes all letters. Use it in styles to make sure that you enter text in all capital letters.

✦ **Equalize Character Height (PowerPoint only):** This effect makes all characters the same height and stretches the characters in text. You can use it to add interesting effects in text box announcements.

The following text effects are available only in Word:

✦ **Shadow:** The Shadow effect makes letters cast a faint shadow on the page, as shown in Figure 2-4. To make the Shadow effect work, choose a heavy font (such as Copper Black or Franklin) so that the letters are wide enough to cast shadows.

Figure 2-4:
The Shadow
text effect.

✦ **Outline:** This effect presents letters in outline form. To use it success-fully, the letters must be heavy enough and tall enough to see as outlines.

✦ **Emboss:** This effect turns letters white. Embossed text looks as though it is raised from the paper. Be sure to choose a serif font, such as Times New Roman, with short, ornamental strokes to make the embossing stand out.

✦ **Engrave:** The Engrave effect also turns letters white. The letters are meant to look as though they have been chiseled into the paper. Be sure to choose a serif font with ornamental strokes to make the engraved let-ters stand out.

✦ **Character Shading:** This effect makes text look as though it has been selected. The effect is the same as what you get when you drag the pointer across letters to select them.

 ✦ **Enclose Characters:** This effect draws a circle, square, triangle, or dia-mond around a single character. After you click the Enclose Characters button, the Enclose Characters dialog box appears so you can tell Word how to enclose the character.

Underlining text

Word and PowerPoint offer 15 ways to underline text, with styles ranging from Words Only to Wavy Line, and you can select a color for the underline. If you decide to underline titles, do it consistently. To underline text, select the text that you want to underline, go to the Home tab and pick your poison:

✦ Click the Underline button. A single line runs under all the words you selected.

✦ Click the Font group button to open the Font dialog box (refer to Figure 2-3) and then choose an underline style from the drop-down list. You can also choose an underline color from the Underline Color drop-down list. The color you select applies to the underline, not to the words being underlined.

To remove an underline from text, select the text and then click the Underline button on the Home tab.

Changing the color of text

Before you change the color of text, peer at your computer screen and exam-ine the background theme or color you chose. Unless the color of the text is different from the theme or color, you can't read the text. Besides choosing a color that contributes to the overall tone, choose a color that is easy to read.

Select the text that needs touching up and use one of these techniques to change its color:

✦ On the Mini Toolbar, open the drop-down list on the Font Color button and choose a color, as shown in Figure 2-5.

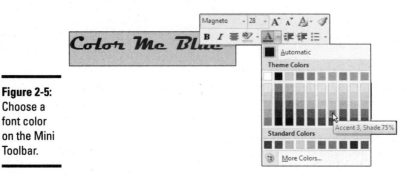

Figure 2-5:
Choose a
font color
on the Mini
Toolbar.

✦ Right-click, open the drop-down list on the Font Color button (you can see it on the Mini Toolbar attached to the shortcut menu), and choose a color.

✦ On the Home tab, open the drop-down list on the Font Color button and choose a color.

✦ On the Home tab, click the Font group button to open the Font dialog box, open the Font Color drop-down list, and choose a color.

The Font Color drop-down list offers theme colors and standard colors. You are well advised to choose a theme color. These colors are deemed *theme colors* because they jive with the theme you choose for your file.

Quick Ways to Handle Case, or Capitalization

Case refers to how letters are capitalized in words and sentences. Table 2-1 explains the different cases, and Figure 2-6 demonstrates why paying attention to case matters. In the figure, the PowerPoint slide titles are presented using different cases, and the titles are inconsistent with one another. In one slide, only the first letter in the title is capitalized (sentence case); in another slide, the first letter in each word is capitalized (capitalize each word); in another, none of the letters is capitalized (lowercase); and in another, all the letters are capitalized (uppercase). In your titles and headings, decide on a capitalization scheme and stick with it for consistency's sake.

Table 2-1	Cases for headings and titles	
Case	*Description*	*Example Title*
Sentence case	The first letter in the first word is capitalized; all other words are lowercase unless they are proper names.	Man bites dog in January
Lowercase	All letters are lowercase unless they are proper names.	man bites dog in January
Uppercase	All letters are uppercase no matter what.	MAN BITES DOG IN JANUARY
Capitalize each word	The first letter in each word is capitalized.	Man Bites Dog In January

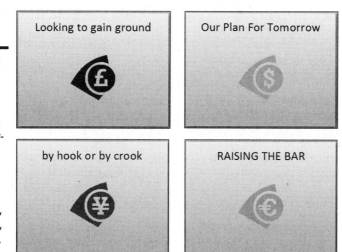

Figure 2-6: Capitalization schemes (clockwise from upper-left): sentence case, capitalize each word, uppercase, lowercase.

 To change case in Word and PowerPoint, all you have to do is select the text, click the Change Case button on the Home tab, and choose an option on the drop-down list:

+ **Sentence case**: Renders the letters in sentence case.

+ **lowercase:** Makes all the letters lowercase.

+ **UPPERCASE**: Renders all the letters as capital letters.

+ **Capitalize Each Word:** Capitalizes the first letter in each word. If you choose this option for a title or heading, go into the title and lowercase the first letter of articles *(the, a, an)*, coordinate conjunctions *(and, or, for, nor)*, and prepositions unless they're the first or last word in the title.

✦ **tOGGLE cASE:** Choose this option if you accidentally enter letters with the Caps Lock key pressed.

You can also change case by pressing Shift+F3. Pressing this key combination in Word and PowerPoint changes characters to uppercase, lowercase, each word capitalized, and back to uppercase again.

Entering Symbols and Foreign Characters

Don't panic if you need to enter an umlaut, grave accent, or cedilla because you can do it by way of the Symbol dialog box, as shown in Figure 2-7. You can enter just about any symbol and foreign character by way of this dialog box. Click where you want to enter a symbol or foreign character and follow these steps to enter it:

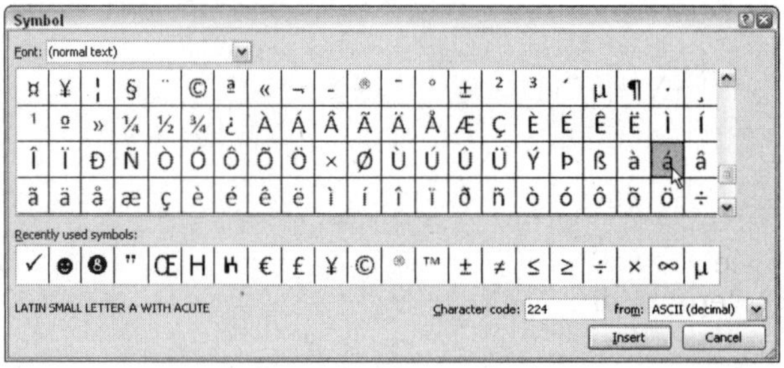

Figure 2-7:
To enter a symbol or foreign character, select it and click the Insert button.

1. **Click the Insert tab.**

2. **Click the Symbol button (you may have to click the Symbols button first, depending on the size of your screen).**

In Word, click More Symbols after you click the Symbol button. You see the Symbol dialog box (see Figure 2-7).

3. **If you're looking to insert a symbol, not a foreign character, choose Webdings or Wingdings 1, 2, or 3 in the Font drop-down list.**

Webdings and the Wingdings fonts offer all kinds of weird and whacky symbols.

4. **Select a symbol or foreign character.**

You may have to scroll to find the one you want.

5. **Click the Insert button to enter the symbol and then click Close to close the dialog box.**

TIP

The Symbol dialog box lists the last several symbols or foreign characters you entered under Recently Used Symbols. See whether the symbol you need is listed there. It spares you the trouble of rummaging in the Symbol dialog box. In Word, you see the last several symbols or foreign characters you entered on a drop-down list after you click the Symbol button.

Finding and Replacing Text

Use the Find command to locate a name or text passage. Use its twin, the powerful Replace command, to find and replace a name or text passage throughout a file. To give you an idea how useful the Replace command is, imagine that the company you work for just changed its name and the old company name is in many different places. By using the Replace command, you could replace the old company name with the new name throughout a long file in a matter of seconds.

Finding stray words and formats

To locate stray words, names, text passages, and formats, follow these steps:

1. **Press Ctrl+F.**

You see the Find and Replace (or Find) dialog box. Figure 2-8 shows the Find and Replace dialog box in Word. It offers many more Find options than are offered by Excel and PowerPoint, but the basics of looking for stray words and formats is the same in all programs.

You can also open the dialog box by going to the Home tab, clicking the Editing button (or the Find & Select button in Excel), and choosing Find on the drop-down list.

2. **Enter the word or phrase in the Find What text box.**

The words and phrases you looked for recently are on the Find What drop-down list. Open the Find What drop-down list and make a selection from that list if you want.

In Word, you can use wildcard characters in searches. See "Using wildcard operators to refine searches" later in this chapter.

3. **If necessary, click the More button (in Word) or the Options button (in Excel) and choose options for narrowing your search.**

What these options are is explained in "Narrowing your search," the next section in this chapter. If you want to search for text that has been formatted a certain way, see "Searching for formats in Word and Excel" later in this chapter.

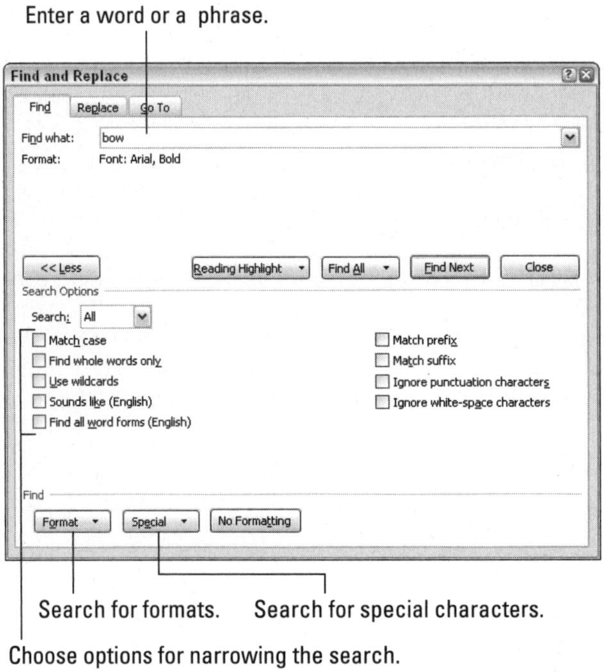

Enter a word or a phrase.

Figure 2-8: Conducting a Find operation in Word.

Search for formats.   Search for special characters.

Choose options for narrowing the search.

In Word, you can search for and highlight all instances of the thing you're looking for by clicking the Reading Highlight button and choosing Highlight All in the drop-down list.

4. **Click the Find Next button if you're looking for a simple word or phrase, or the Find All button to highlight all instances of a word or phrase in your file.**

   In PowerPoint, the Find All button is available only if you start your search in Slide Sorter view.

5. **To find the next instance of the thing you're looking for, click Find Next again.**

   In Word, you can close the Find and Replace dialog box and continue searching. Click either the Previous Find/Go To or Next Find/Go To button at the bottom of the scroll bar (or press Ctrl+Page Up or Ctrl+Page Down) to go to the previous or next instance of the thing you're looking for.

Narrowing your search

By clicking the More button (in Word) or the Options button (in Excel), you can take advantage of the following options to conduct a sophisticated search:

✦ **Match Case:** Searches for words with upper- and lowercase letters that exactly match those in the Find What box. With this box selected, a search for *bow* finds *bow,* but not *Bow* or *BOW.*

✦ **Find Whole Words Only:** Normally, a search for *bow* yields *elbow, bowler, bow-wow,* and all other words with the letters *b-o-w* (in that order). Click this option and you get only *bow.*

As shown in Figure 2-8, Word offers a number of other ways to narrow a search:

✦ **Use Wildcards:** Click here if you intend to use wildcards in searches. (See "Using wildcard operators to refine searches" later in this chapter.)

✦ **Sounds Like:** Looks for words that sound like the one in the Find What box. A search for *bow* with this option selected finds *beau,* for example. However, it doesn't find *bough.* This command isn't very reliable.

✦ **Find All Word Forms:** Takes into account verb conjugations and plurals. With this option clicked, you get *bows, bowing,* and *bowed* as well as *bow.*

✦ **Match Prefix:** A *prefix* is a syllable appearing before the root or stem of a word to alter its meaning. For example, *co, mid, non,* and *un* are prefixes in the words *coauthor, midtown, nonviolent,* and *unselfish.* Choose this option and enter a prefix in the Find What text box to locate words that begin with the prefix you enter.

✦ **Match Suffix:** A *suffix* is a syllable or two appearing at the end of a word to alter its meaning. For example, *age, ish,* and *ness* are suffixes in the words *spillage, smallish,* and *darkness.* Choose this option and enter a suffix in the Find What text box to find words that end with the same suffix.

✦ **Ignore Punctuation Characters:** Search in text for word phrases without regard for commas, periods, and other punctuation marks. For example, a search for *Yuma Arizona* finds *Yuma, Arizona* (with a comma) in the text.

✦ **Ignore White-Space Characters:** Search in text for word phrases without regard for white space caused by multiple blank spaces or tab entries.

Searching for formats in Word and Excel

In Word and Excel, you can search for formats or text that was formatted a certain way with these techniques:

✦ **In Word:** Click the Format button in the Find and Replace dialog box (refer to Figure 2-8), and on the drop-down list, choose a Format type — Font, Paragraph, Tabs, Language, Frame, Style, or Highlight. A Find dialog box opens so you can describe the format you're looking for. Select options in the dialog box to describe the format and click OK.

✦ **In Excel:** Click the Format button and choose a format in the Find Format dialog box. You can also open the drop-down list, select Choose Format from Cell on the drop-down list, and click a cell to describe the format you're looking for.

Be sure to click the No Formatting button (in Word) or open the Format drop-down list and choose Clear Find Format (in Excel) after you're finished looking for formats. Choosing these commands tells Word or Excel that you no longer want to look for formats or you want to search for a different set of formats.

Using wildcard operators to refine searches

A *wildcard operator* is a character that represents characters in a search expression. Wildcards aren't for everybody. Using them requires a certain amount of expertise, but after you know how to use them, wildcards can be very valuable in searches and macros. Table 2-2 explains the wildcard operators you can use in searches. Click the Use Wildcards check box if you want to search using wildcards.

Table 2-2	Wildcards for searches	
Operator	**What It Finds**	**Example**
?	Any single character	**b?t** finds *bat, bet, bit,* and *but.*
*	Zero or more characters	**t*o** finds *to, two,* and *tattoo.*
[*xyz*]	A specific character, *x, y,* or *z*	**t[aeiou]pper** finds *tapper, tipper,* and *topper.*
[*x-z*]	A range of characters, *x* through *z*	**[1-4]000** finds *1000, 2000, 3000,* and *4000,* but not *5000.*
[!*xy*]	Not the specific character or characters, *xy*	**p[!io]t** finds *pat* and *pet,* but not *pit* or *pot.*
<	Characters at the beginning of words	**<info** finds *information, infomaniac,* and *infomercial.*
>	Characters at the end of words	**ese>** finds *these, journalese,* and *legalese.*
@@	One or more instances of the previous character	**sho@@t** finds *shot* and *shoot.*
{*n*}	Exactly *n* instances of the previous character	**sho{2}t** finds *shoot* but not *shot.*

Operator	What It Finds	Example
{n,}	At least *n* instances of the previous character	**^p{3,}** finds three or more paragraph breaks in a row, but not a single paragraph break or two paragraph breaks in a row.
{n,m}	From *n* to *m* instances of the previous character	**10{2,4}** finds *100, 1000,* and *10000,* but not *10* or *100000.*

You can't conduct a whole-word-only search with a wildcard. For example, a search for **f*s** not only finds *fads* and *fits* but also all text strings that begin with *f* and end with *s,* such as *for the birds.* Wildcard searches can yield many, many results and are sometimes useless.

To search for an asterisk (*), question mark (?), or other character that serves as a wildcard search operator, place a backslash (\) before it in the Find What text box.

Searching for special characters in Word

Table 2-3 describes the *special characters* you can look for in Word documents. To look for the special characters listed in the table, enter the character directly in the Find What text box or click the Special button in the Find and Replace dialog box, and then choose a special character from the pop-up list. Be sure to enter lowercase letters. For example, you must enter **^n**, not **^N**, to look for a column break. *Note:* A caret (^) precedes special characters.

Table 2-3	Special characters for searches
To Find/Replace	*Enter*
Manual Formats That Users Insert	
Column break	^n
Field[1]	^d
Manual line break (⏎)	^l
Manual page break	^m
No-width nonbreak	^z
No-width optional break	^x
Paragraph break (¶)	^p
Section break[1]	^b
Section character	^%
Tab space (→)	^t
Punctuation Marks	
1/4 em space	^q

(continued)

Table 2-3 *(continued)*

To Find/Replace	Enter
Caret (^)	^^
Ellipsis	^i
Em dash (—)	^+
En dash (–)	^=
Full-width ellipses	^j
Nonbreaking hyphen	^~
Optional hyphen	^-
White space (one or more blank spaces)[1]	^w
Characters and Symbols	
Foreign character	You can type foreign characters in the Find What and Replace With text boxes
ANSI and ASCII characters and symbols	^*nnnn*, where *nnnn* is the four-digit code
Any character[1]	^?
Any digit[1]	^#
Any letter[1]	^$
Clipboard contents[2]	^c
Contents of the Find What box[2]	^&
Elements of Reports and Scholarly Papers	
Endnote mark[1]	^e
Footnote mark[1]	^f
Graphic[1]	^g

[1]*For use in find operations; can be entered only in the Find What text box*
[2]*For use in replace operations; can be entered only in the Replace With text box*

 Before searching for special characters in Word, click the Show/Hide¶ button in the Home tab. That way, you see special characters — also known as *hidden format symbols* — on-screen when Word finds them.

Creative people find many uses in the Find and Replace dialog box for special characters. The easiest way to find section breaks, column breaks, and manual line breaks in a document is to enter **^b**, **^n**, or **^l**, respectively, in the Find What text box and start searching. By combining special characters with text, you can make find-and-replace operations more productive. For example, to replace all double hyphens (- -) in a document with em dashes (—), enter – in the Find What text box and **^m** in the Replace With text box.

This kind of find-and-replace operation is especially useful for cleaning documents that were created in another program and then imported into Word.

Conducting a find-and-replace operation

Conducting a find-and-replace operation is the spitting image of conducting a find operation. Figure 2-9 shows (in PowerPoint) the Replace dialog box, the place where you declare what you want to find and what to replace it with. Do the options and buttons in the dialog box look familiar? They do if you read the previous handful of pages about searching because the Replace options are the same as the Find options.

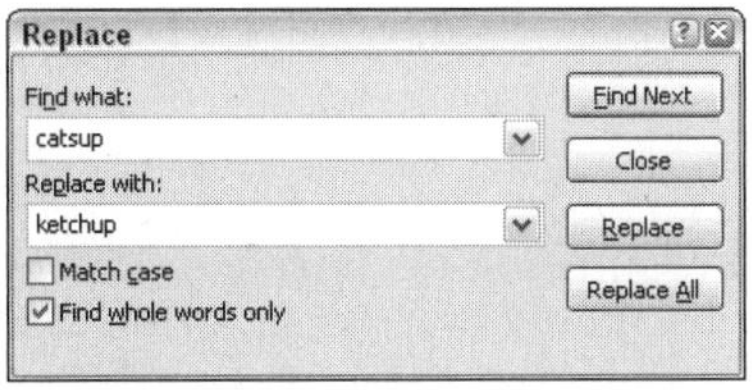

Figure 2-9: Using the powerful Replace command in PowerPoint.

The key to a successful find-and-replace operation is making sure you *find* exactly what you want to find and replace. One way to make sure that you find the right text is to start by running a Find operation. If the program finds precisely the text you want, you're in business. Click the Replace tab or Replace button in the Find dialog box and then enter the replacement text.

To locate and replace words, names, or text passages with the Find command, follow these steps:

1. **Press Ctrl+H or go to the Home tab and click the Editing button (or the Find & Select button in Excel), and choose Replace in the drop-down list.**

The Replace (or Find and Replace) dialog box appears (see Figure 2-9).

2. **Describe the text that needs replacing.**

Earlier in this chapter, "Finding stray words and formats" explains how to construct a search. Try to narrow your search so you find only the text you are looking for.

3. **Click the Find Next button.**

Did your program find what you're looking for? If it didn't, describe the search again.

4. **Enter the replacement text in the Replace With text box.**

You can select replacement text from the drop-down list.

5. Either replace everything simultaneously or do it one at a time.

Click one of these buttons:

- Click *Replace All* to make all replacements in an instant.
- Click *Find Next* and then either click Replace to make the replacement or Find Next to bypass it.

Click the Replace All button only if you are very, very confident that the thing your program found is the thing you want to replace.

Be sure to examine your file after you conduct a find-and-replace operation. You never know what the powerful Replace command will do. If the command makes a hash of your file, click the Undo button.

Creating Hyperlinks

A *hyperlink* is an electronic shortcut from one place to another. If you've spent any time on the Internet, you know what a hyperlink is. Clicking hyperlinks on the Internet takes you to different Web pages or different places on the same Web page. In the Office programs, you can use hyperlinks to connect readers to your favorite Web pages or to a different page, or slide, or file. You can fashion a link out of a word or phrase as well as any object — a clip-art image, text box or text frame, shape, or picture.

These pages explain how to insert a hyperlink to another place in your file as well as create links to Web pages. You also discover how to enter an e-mail hyperlink that makes it easy for others to e-mail you.

Linking a hyperlink to a Web page

It could well be that a Web page on the Internet has all the information your readers need. In that case, you can link to the Web page so that viewers can visit it in the course of viewing your file. To make this little trick work, however, Internet Explorer 4.0 or higher must be installed on your computer, and you must know the address of the Web page you will link to. When a viewer clicks the link, Internet Explorer opens and the Web page appears.

Follow these steps to hyperlink your file to a Web page on the Internet:

1. Select the text or object that will form the hyperlink.

For example, select a line of text or phrase if you want viewers to be able to click it to go to a Web page. Hyperlinked text is underlined on slides.

2. On the Insert tab, click the Hyperlink button (or press Ctrl+K).

Depending on the size of your screen, you may have to click the Links button before you can get to the Hyperlink button. You see the Insert Hyperlink dialog box, as shown in Figure 2-10. You can also open this dialog box by right-clicking an object or text and choosing Hyperlink on the shortcut menu.

Choose a Web page.   Click to go on the Internet to a Web page.

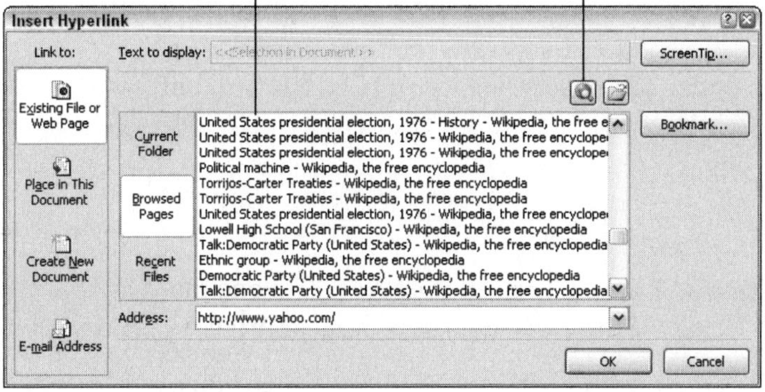

Figure 2-10: Enter the Web page target in the Address text box to create a hyperlink to a Web page.

3. Under Link To, select Existing File or Web Page.

4. Enter the address of the Web page to which you want to link in the Address text box, as shown in Figure 2-10.

From easiest to hardest, here are techniques for entering Web page addresses:

- *Click the Browse the Web button.* (Figure 2-10 shows where this button is.) Internet Explorer opens. Go to the Web page you want to link to and return to your program. The Web page's address appears in the Address text box.

- *Click Browsed Pages.* The dialog box lists Web pages you recently visited, as shown in Figure 2-10. Choose a Web page.

- *Type a Web page address in the Address text box.*

5. Click the ScreenTip button, enter a ScreenTip in the Set Hyperlink ScreenTip dialog box, and click OK.

Viewers can read the ScreenTip you enter when they move their pointers over the hyperlink.

6. Click OK in the Insert Hyperlink dialog box.

I would test the hyperlink if I were you to make sure it takes viewers to the right Web page. To test a hyperlink, Ctrl+click it or right-click it and choose Open Hyperlink on the shortcut menu.

Creating a hyperlink to another place in your file

Follow these steps to create a hyperlink to another place in your file:

1. **Select the text or object that will form the hyperlink.**

2. **On the Insert tab, click the Hyperlink button (or press Ctrl+K).**

You see the Insert Hyperlink dialog box. (Depending on the size of your screen, you may have to click the Links button before you see the Hyperlink button.) Another way to open this dialog box is to right-click and choose Hyperlink in the shortcut menu.

3. **Under Link To, select Place in This Document.**

What you see in the dialog box depends on which program you're working in:

- *Word:* You see bookmarks and headings to which you've assigned a heading style.

- *PowerPoint:* You see a list of slides in your presentation as well as links to the first, last, next, and previous slide, as shown in Figure 2-11.

- *Excel:* You see cell references and defined cell names.

Select Place in This Document.

Select a target.   Click to enter a ScreenTip.

Figure 2-11:
You can also create a hyperlink to a different place in a file.

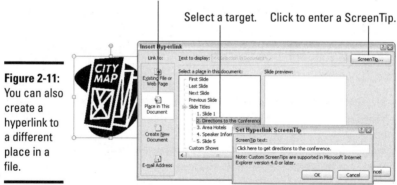

4. **Select the target of the hyperlink.**

5. **Click the ScreenTip button.**

You see the Set Hyperlink ScreenTip dialog box, as shown in Figure 2-11.

6. **Enter a ScreenTip and click OK.**

When viewers move their pointers over the link, they see the words you enter. Enter a description of where the hyperlink takes you.

7. **Click OK in the Insert Hyperlink dialog box.**

To test your hyperlink, move the pointer over it. You should see the ScreenTip description you wrote. Ctrl+click the link to see if it takes you to the right place.

Creating an e-mail hyperlink

An *e-mail hyperlink* is one that opens an e-mail program. These links are sometimes found on Web pages so that anyone visiting a Web page can conveniently send an e-mail message to the person who manages the Web page. When you click an e-mail hyperlink, your default e-mail program opens. And if the person who set up the link was thorough about it, the e-mail message is already addressed and given a subject line.

Include an e-mail hyperlink in a file if you're distributing the file to others and you would like them to be able to comment on your work and send the comments to you.

Follow these steps to put an e-mail hyperlink in a file:

1. **Select the words or object that will constitute the link.**

2. **On the Insert tab, click the Hyperlink button (or press Ctrl+K).**

The Insert Hyperlink dialog box appears.

3. **Under Link To, click E-Mail Address.**

Text boxes appear for entering an e-mail address and a subject message.

4. **Enter your e-mail address and a subject for the messages that others send you.**

Office inserts the word *mailto:* before your e-mail address as you enter it.

5. **Click OK.**

Test the link by Ctrl+clicking it. Your default e-mail program opens. The e-mail message is already addressed and given a subject.

Repairing and removing hyperlinks

From time to time, check the hyperlinks in your file to make sure they still work. Clicking a hyperlink and having nothing happen is disappointing. Hyperlinks get broken when Web pages and parts of files are deleted.

To repair or remove a hyperlink, right-click the link and choose Edit Hyperlink on the shortcut menu (or click in the link and then click the Hyperlink button on the Insert tab). You see the Edit Hyperlink dialog box. This dialog box looks and works just like the Insert Hyperlink dialog box.

✦ **Repairing a link:** Select a target in your file or a Web page and click OK.

✦ **Removing a link:** Click the Remove Link button. You can also remove a hyperlink by right-clicking the link and choosing Remove Hyperlink on the shortcut menu.

Chapter 3: Speed Techniques Worth Knowing About

In This Chapter

✔ **Undoing mistakes and repeating actions**

✔ **Zooming to get a better view of your work**

✔ **Working with two different files at the same time**

✔ **Instructing Office to correct typos automatically**

✔ **Entering hard-to-type text with the AutoCorrect command**

This brief chapter takes you on a whirlwind tour of shortcut commands that can save you time and effort no matter which Office 2007 program you're working in. This chapter is devoted to people who want to get it done quickly and get away from their computers. It explains the Undo and Repeat commands, zooming in and out, and opening more than one window on the same file. You also discover how to display windows in different ways, correct your typos automatically, and enter hard-to-type terminology with a simple flick of the wrist.

Undoing and Repeating Commands

If I were to choose two commands for the Hall of Fame, they would be the Undo command and the Repeat command. One allows you to reverse actions you regret doing, and the other repeats a previous action without you having to choose the same commands all over again. Undo and Repeat are explained forthwith.

Undoing a mistake

Fortunately for you, all is not lost if you make a big blunder because Office has a marvelous little tool called the Undo command. This command "remembers" your previous editorial and formatting changes. As long as you catch your error in time, you can undo your mistake.

Click the Undo button on the Quick Access toolbar to undo your most recent change. If you made your error and went on to do something else before you caught it, open the drop-down list on the Undo button. It lists your previous actions, as shown in Figure 3-1. Click the action you want to undo, or if it isn't on the list, scroll until you find the error and then click it.

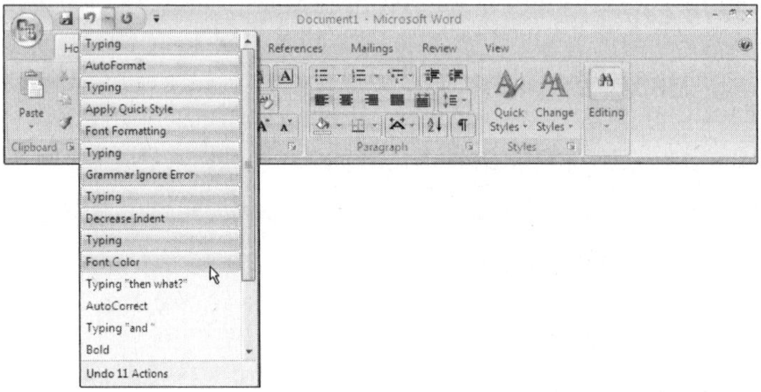

Figure 3-1:
Fixing a mistake with the Undo drop-down list.

Remember, however, that choosing an action far down the Undo list also reverses the actions before it on the list. For example, if you undo the 19th action on the list, you also undo the 18 more recent actions above it.

Repeating an action — and quicker this time

The Quick Access toolbar offers the Repeat button that you can click to repeat your last action. This button can be a mighty, mighty timesaver. For example, if you just changed fonts in one heading and you want to change another heading in the same way, select the heading and click the Repeat button (or press F4 or Ctrl+Y). Move the pointer over the Repeat button to see what clicking it does.

You can find many creative uses for the Repeat command if you use your imagination. For example, if you had to type **I will not talk in class** a hundred times as a punishment for talking in class, you could make excellent use of the Repeat command to fulfill your punishment. All you would have to do is write the sentence once and then click the Repeat button 99 times.

After you click the Undo button, the Repeat button changes names and becomes the Redo button. Click the Redo button to "redo" the command you "undid." In other words, if you regret clicking the Undo button, you can turn back the clock by clicking Redo.

Zooming In, Zooming Out

Eyes weren't meant to stare at the computer screen all day, which makes the Zoom controls all the more valuable. You can find these controls in the lower-right corner of the window and in the View tab, as shown in Figure 3-2. Use them freely and often to enlarge or shrink what is on the screen and preserve your eyes for important things, such as gazing at the sunset.

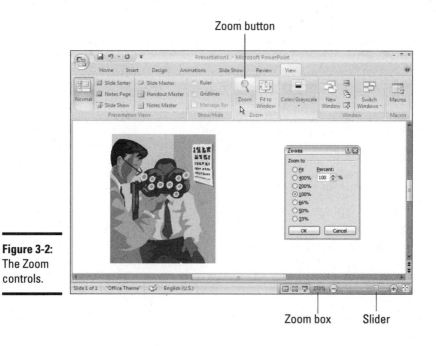

Zoom button

Zoom box   Slider

Figure 3-2:
The Zoom
controls.

Meet the Zoom controls:

✦ **Zoom slider:** Drag the *zoom slider* left to shrink or right to enlarge what is on your screen. Click the Zoom In (+) or Zoom Out (-) button to zoom in or out by 10-percent increments.

✦ **Zoom dialog box:** Click the *Zoom box* (the % listing) or the Zoom button (on the View tab) to display the Zoom dialog box, as shown in Figure 3-2. Then select an option button or enter a percent measurement in the dialog box and click OK.

✦ **Mouse wheel:** If your mouse has a wheel, you can hold down the Ctrl key and spin the wheel to quickly zoom in or out.

Each Office program offers its own special Zoom commands in the Zoom group on the View tab. In Word, for example, you can display one page or many pages; in Excel, you can click the Zoom to Selection button and enlarge a handful of cells. Make friends with the Zoom commands. They never let you down.

Viewing a File through More Than One Window

By way of the commands in the Window group on the View tab, you can be two places simultaneously, at least where Office is concerned. You can work on two files at once. You can place files side by side on the screen and do a number of other things to make your work a little easier.

Word, Excel, and PowerPoint all offer these buttons in the Window group:

✦ **New Window:** Opens another window on your file so you can be two places at once in the same file. To go back and forth between windows, click a taskbar button or click the Switch Windows button and choose a window name on the drop-down list. Click a window's Close button when you're finished looking at it.

✦ **Arrange All:** Arranges open windows side by side on-screen.

✦ **Switch Windows:** Opens a drop-down list with open windows so you can travel between windows.

You can also take advantage of these Window buttons in Word and Excel to compare files:

✦ **View Side by Side:** Displays files side by side so you can compare and contrast them.

✦ **Synchronous Scrolling:** Permits you to scroll two files at the same rate so you can proofread one against the other. To use this command, start by clicking the View Side by Side button. After you click the Synchronous Scrolling button, click the Reset Window Position button so both files are displayed at the same size on-screen.

✦ **Reset Window Position:** Gives files being shown side by side the same size on-screen to make comparing them easier.

Correcting Typos on the Fly

The unseen hand of Office 2007 corrects some typos and misspellings automatically. For example, try typing **accomodate** with one *m* — Office corrects the misspelling and inserts the second *m* for you. Try typing **perminent** with an *i* instead of an *a* — the invisible hand of Office corrects the misspelling, and you get *permanent*. While you're at it, type a colon and a close parenthesis **:)** — you get a smiley face ☺.

As good as the AutoCorrect feature is, you can make it even better. You can also add the typos and misspellings you often make to the list of words that are corrected automatically.

Opening the AutoCorrect dialog box

Office corrects common spelling errors and turns punctuation mark combinations into symbols as part of its AutoCorrect feature. To see which typos are corrected and which punctuation marks are turned into symbols, open the AutoCorrect dialog box by following these steps:

1. **Click the Office button and choose Options.**

   You see the Options dialog box.

2. **Click the Proofing category.**

3. **Click the AutoCorrect Options button.**

   The AutoCorrect dialog box opens.

4. **Click the AutoCorrect tab.**

   As shown in Figure 3-3, the AutoCorrect tab lists words that are corrected automatically. Scroll down the Replace list and have a look around. Go ahead. Make yourself at home.

Enter a typo and its replacement.

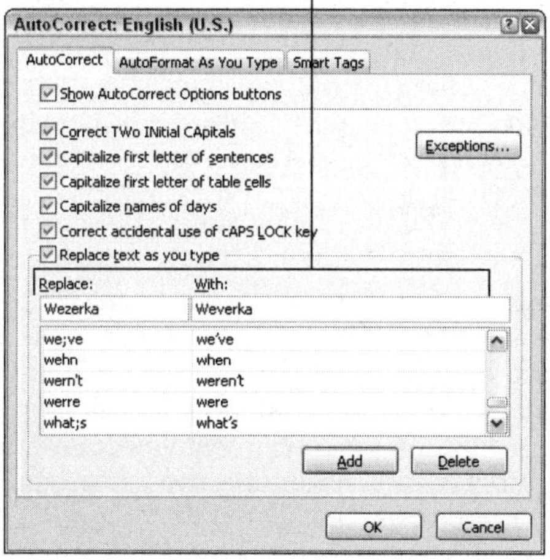

Figure 3-3:
As you type,
words in the
Replace
column are
replaced
auto-
matically
with words
in the With
column.

Telling Office which typos and misspellings to correct

No doubt you make the same typing errors and spelling errors time and time again. To keep from making these errors, you can tell Office to correct them for you automatically. You do that by entering the misspelling and its corrected spelling in the AutoCorrect dialog box (see Figure 3-3):

✦ Enter the misspelling in the Replace text box and its correct spelling in the With text box.

✦ Click the AutoCorrect button in the Spelling and Grammar dialog box when you spell check a file. This action automatically places the misspelling and its correction in the AutoCorrect dialog box so that the correction is made in the future.

You can also remove misspellings and typos from the list of words that are corrected automatically. To remove a word from the list of corrected words, select it in the AutoCorrect dialog box and click the Delete button.

Preventing capitalization errors with AutoCorrect

Near the top of the AutoCorrect dialog box (refer to Figure 3-3) are five check boxes whose job is to prevent capitalization errors. These options do their jobs very well, sometimes to a fault:

✦ **Correct TWo INitial Capitals:** Prevents two capital letters from appearing in a row at the start of a word with more than two letters. Only the first letter is capitalized. This option is for people who can't lift their little fingers from the Shift key fast enough after typing the first capital letter at the start of a word.

✦ **Capitalize first letter of sentences:** Makes sure that the first letter in a sentence is capitalized.

✦ **Capitalize first letter of table cells:** Makes sure that the first letter you enter in a table cell is a capital letter. A table cell holds one data item; it's the place in a table where a column and row intersect.

✦ **Capitalize names of days:** Makes sure that the names of the days of the week are capitalized.

✦ **Correct accidental usage of cAPS LOCK key:** Changes capital letters to lowercase letters if you press the Shift key to start a sentence while Caps Lock is on. The idea here is that if you press down the Shift key while Caps Lock is on, you don't know that Caps Lock is on because you don't need to hold down the Shift key to enter capital letters. AutoCorrect turns the first letter into a capital letter and the following letters into lowercase letters and then turns Caps Lock off.

Entering Text Quickly with the AutoCorrect Command

The preceding part of this chapter explains how you can use the AutoCorrect command to help correct typing errors, but with a little cunning you can also use it to quickly enter hard-to-type jargon, scientific names, and the like. To open the AutoCorrect dialog box, click the Office button, choose Options, click the Proofing category in the Options dialog box, and then click the AutoCorrect Options button. Select the AutoCorrect tab in the AutoCorrect dialog box, as shown in Figure 3-4.

Enter text to trigger AutoCorrect.

What's entered when you type the text.

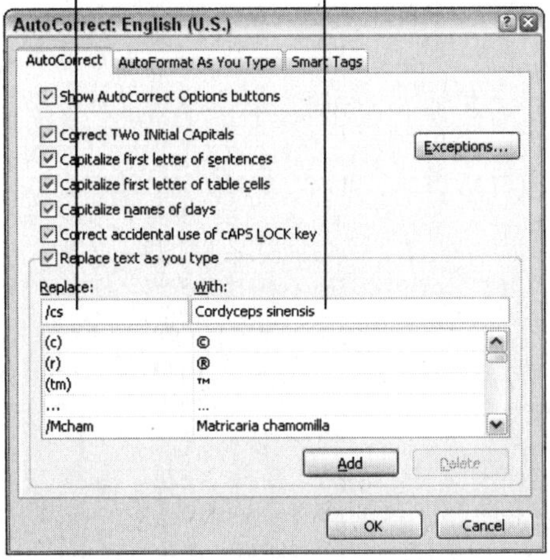

Figure 3-4:
With a little cunning, you can use AutoCorrect to enter hard-to-type text.

In the Replace column on the AutoCorrect tab are hundreds of common typing errors and codes that Office corrects automatically. The program corrects the errors by entering text in the With column whenever you mistakenly type the letters in the Replace column. However, you can also use this dialog box for a secondary purpose to quickly enter text.

To make AutoCorrect work as a means of entering text, you tell Office to enter the text whenever you type three or four specific characters. In Figure 3-4, for example, Office is instructed to insert the words *Cordyceps sinensis* (a mushroom genus) whenever I enter the characters **/cs** (and press the Spacebar). Follow these steps to use AutoCorrect to enter text:

1. **Open the AutoCorrect tab of the AutoCorrect dialog box (see Figure 3-4).**

2. **In the Replace text box, enter the three or four characters that will trigger the AutoCorrect mechanism and make it enter your text.**

Don't enter a word, or characters that you might really type someday, in the Replace box. If you do, the AutoCorrect mechanism might kick in when you least expect it. Enter three or four characters that never appear together. And start all AutoCorrect entries with a slash (/). You might forget which characters trigger the AutoText entry or decide to delete your AutoCorrect entry someday. By starting it with a slash, you can find it easily in the AutoCorrect dialog box at the top of the Replace list.

3. **In the With text box, enter the hard-to-type name or word(s) that will appear when you enter the Replace text.**

4. **Click the Add button.**

5. **Click OK.**

Test your AutoCorrect entry by typing the Replace text you entered in Step 2 (which, of course, includes the slash I recommended) and pressing the Spacebar. (AutoCorrect doesn't do its work until you press the Spacebar.)

To delete an AutoCorrect entry, open the AutoCorrect dialog box, select the entry, and click the Delete button.

Getting rid of the squiggly red lines

More than a few people think that the squiggly red lines that appear under misspelled words are annoying. To keep those lines from appearing, press F7 to open the Spelling and Grammar dialog box and then click the Options button. You see the Proofing category of the Options dialog box. Deselect the Check Spelling As You Type check box. (To reach this option in Publisher, choose Tools⇨Spelling⇨Spelling Options.)

Even with the red lines gone, you can do a quick spell check of a word that you suspect has been misspelled. To do so, select the word (double-click it) and press F7. The Spelling and Grammar dialog box appears if the word has indeed been misspelled. Select a word in the Suggestions box and then click the Change button.

You see the Spelling and Grammar (or Spelling) dialog box, as shown in Figure 4-2. Misspellings appear in the Not in Dictionary text box. As I explain shortly, your Office program offers all sorts of amenities for handling misspellings, but here are options for correcting known misspellings in the Spelling dialog box:

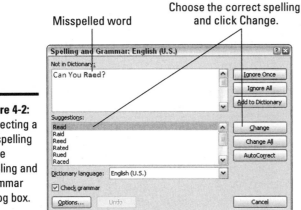

Misspelled word

Choose the correct spelling
and click Change.

Figure 4-2:
Correcting a
misspelling
in the
Spelling and
Grammar
dialog box.

✦ Select the correct spelling in the Suggestions box and then click the Change button.

✦ Click in the page or slide you're working on and correct the spelling there; then click the Resume button, located where the Ignore or Ignore Once button used to be. (You can't do this in Excel.)

✦ In Word, Excel, or Access, correct the spelling inside the Not in Dictionary text box and then click the Change button. (In PowerPoint, correct the spelling in the Change To box and then click the Change button.)

If the word in question isn't a misspelling, tell your program how to handle the word by clicking one of these buttons:

✦ **Ignore (or Ignore Once):** Ignores this instance of the misspelling but stops on it again if the same misspelling appears later.

✦ **Ignore All:** Ignores the misspelling throughout the file you're working on and in all other open Office files as well.

✦ **Change/Delete:** Enters the selected word in the Suggestions box in the file where the misspelling used to be. When the same word appears twice in a row, the Delete button appears where the Change button was. Click the Delete button to delete the second word in the pair.

✦ **Change All/Delete All:** Replaces all instances of the misspelled word with the word that you selected in the Suggestions box. Click the Change All button to correct a misspelling that occurs throughout a file. When two words appear in a row, this button is called Delete All. Click the Delete All button to delete the second word in the pair throughout your presentation.

✦ **Add (or Add to Dictionary):** Adds the misspelling to the Office spelling dictionary. By clicking the Add button, you tell Office that the misspelling is a legitimate word or name.

✦ **Suggest (in PowerPoint only):** Changes the list of words in the Suggestions box. Select a word in the Suggestions box and then click the Suggest button to see whether you can find a correct spelling.

✦ **AutoCorrect:** Adds the spelling correction to the list of words that are corrected automatically. If you find yourself making the same typing error over and over, place the error on the AutoCorrect list and never have to correct it again. (See Chapter 3 of this mini-book for details.)

Office programs share the same spelling dictionary. For example, words you add to the spelling dictionary in PowerPoint — by clicking the Add button in the Spelling and Grammar dialog box — are deemed correct spellings in Word documents, Excel spreadsheets, Publisher publications, Access databases, and Outlook e-mails.

Fine-tuning the spell checker

Especially if you deal in jargon and scientific terminology, you owe it to yourself to fine-tune the spell checker. No matter how arcane, it can make sure that your jargon gets used correctly. These pages explain the nuances of the spell checker.

Employing other dictionaries to help with spell-checking

To find spelling errors, Office compares each word on your page or slide to the words in its main dictionary and a second dictionary called `Custom.dic`. If a word you type isn't found in either dictionary, Office considers the word a misspelling. The main dictionary lists all known words in the English language; the `Custom.dic` dictionary lists words, proper names, and technical jargon that you deemed legitimate when you clicked the Add (or Add to Dictionary) button in the course of a spell-check and added a word to the `Custom.dic` dictionary.

From Office's standpoint, a dictionary is merely a list of words, one word per line, that has been saved in a `.dic` (dictionary) file. Besides the `Custom.dic` dictionary, you can employ other dictionaries to help with spell-checking. People who work in specialized professions, such as law or medicine, can also use legal dictionaries and medical dictionaries to spell check their work. You can create dictionaries of your own for slang words, colloquialisms, or special projects. Before you start spell-checking, you can tell Office which dictionaries to use. You can edit dictionaries as well. All this magic is done by way of the Custom Dictionaries dialog box, as shown in Figure 4-3.

Click to edit or delete the words in a dictionary.

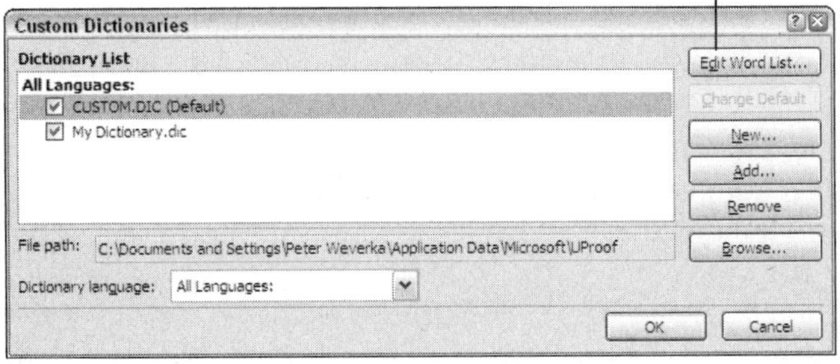

Figure 4-3:
Adding a
word to the
custom
dictionary.

Follow these steps to open the Custom Dictionaries dialog box:

1. Press F7.

You see the Spelling and Grammar (or Spelling) dialog box.

2. Click the Options button.

The Proofing category of the Options dialog box opens. (To reach this category in Publisher, choose Tools⇨Spelling⇨Spelling Options.)

3. Click the Custom Dictionaries button.

Starting in the Custom Dictionaries dialog box, you can create a new spelling dictionary, tell PowerPoint to use a third-party dictionary you acquired, edit words in a dictionary, and tell PowerPoint which diction-ary to use in a spell check. Better keep reading.

Creating a new spelling dictionary

People who work in law offices, research facilities, and medical facilities type hundreds of arcane terms each day, none of which are in the main diction-ary. One way to make sure that arcane terms are spelled correctly is to create or acquire a dictionary of legal, scientific, or medical terms and use it for spell-checking purposes. By Office's definition, a dictionary is simply a list of words saved in a dictionary (.dic) file.

Follow these steps to create a new spelling dictionary or tell Office that you want to use a secondary dictionary to check the spelling of words:

1. **Click the New button in the Custom Dictionaries dialog box (refer to Figure 4-3).**

   You see the Create Custom Dictionary dialog box.

2. **Enter a name for your new dictionary.**

3. **Click the Save button.**

   See "Entering and editing words in a dictionary" later in this chapter, to find out how to enter terms in your new spelling dictionary.

Using a third-party dictionary

Besides creating your own dictionary, you can acquire one and tell Office to use it by following these steps:

1. **Make note of where the dictionary file is located on your computer.**

   It doesn't have to be in the C:\Documents and Settings\ *Username*\Application Data\Microsoft\Proof (or UProof) folder along with the other dictionaries for Office to use it.

2. **Click the Add button in the Custom Dictionaries dialog box (refer to Figure 4-3).**

   The Add Custom Dictionary dialog box appears.

3. **Locate and select the dictionary on your computer.**

4. **Click Open.**

   The dictionary's name appears in the Custom Dictionaries dialog box. Ten dictionaries total can appear in the Dictionary List box.

Select a dictionary and click the Remove button to remove its name from the Dictionary List box. Removing a name in no way, shape, or form deletes the dictionary.

Entering and editing words in a dictionary

To edit the words in the Custom.dic dictionary or any other dictionary, select its name in the Custom Dictionaries dialog box (refer to Figure 4-3) and click the Edit Word List button. A dialog box opens with a list of the words in the dictionary, as shown in Figure 4-4. From there, you can delete words (by clicking the Delete button) and add words to the dictionary (by clicking the Add button).

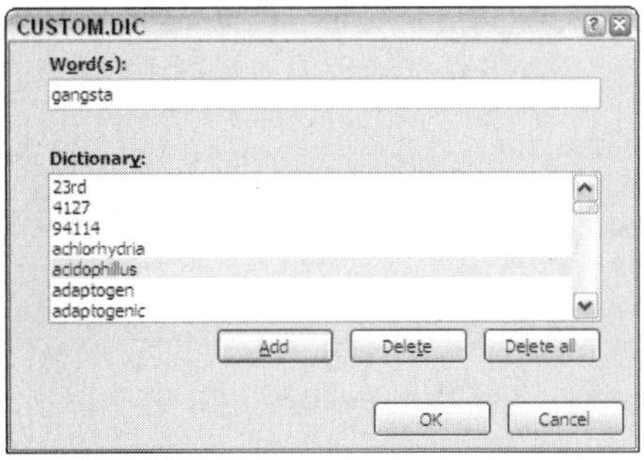

Figure 4-4:
Edit the
words in a
custom
dictionary in
this dialog
box.

Preventing text from being spell checked

Spell-checking address lists, lines of computer code, and foreign languages, such as Spanglish, for which Microsoft doesn't offer foreign language dictionaries is a thorough waste of time. Follow these steps in Word, PowerPoint, and Outlook to tell the spell checker to ignore text:

1. **Select the text.**

2. **On the Review tab, click the Set Language button (you may have to click the Proofing button first).**

You see the Language dialog box. (To open this dialog box in an Outlook message, open the drop-down list on the Spelling button and choose Set Language.)

3. **Select the Do Not Check Spelling or Grammar check box.**

4. **Click OK.**

Checking for Grammatical Errors in Word

Much of what constitutes good grammar is, like beauty, in the eye of the beholder. Still, you can do your best to repair grammatical errors in Word documents by getting the assistance of the grammar checker. The grammar checker identifies grammatical errors, explains what the errors are, and gives you the opportunity to correct the errors.

Figure 4-5 shows the grammar checker in action in the Spelling and Grammar dialog box. As long as the Check Grammar check box is selected, Word looks for grammatical errors along with spelling errors. To open the Spelling and Grammar dialog box, press F7 or go to the Review tab and then click the Spelling & Grammar button. (You may have to click the Proofing button first, depending on the size of your screen.)

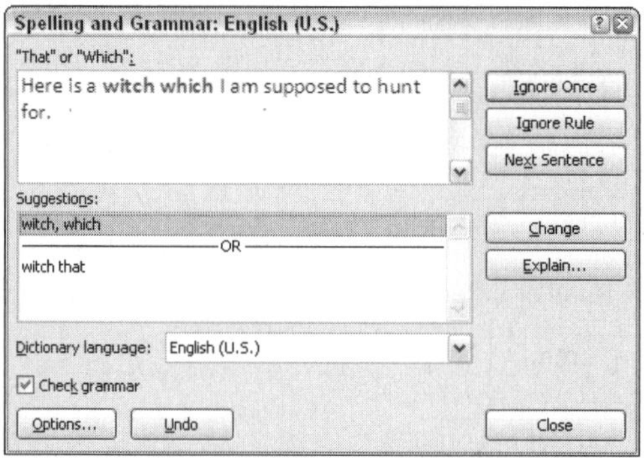

Figure 4-5:
Fix gram-
matical
errors with
the grammar
checker.

Sentences in which grammatical errors appear are underlined in green in your document. Meanwhile, the grammatical errors themselves appear in bright green in the box at the top of the Spelling and Grammar dialog box (along with spelling errors, which are red). When Word encounters an error, take one of these actions to correct it:

✦ Select a correction in the Suggestions box and click the Change button.

✦ Delete the grammatical error or rephrase the sentence in the top of the dialog box, enter a correction, and click the Next Sentence button.

✦ Click outside the Spelling and Grammar dialog box, correct the grammat-ical error in your document, and then click the Resume button. (You find it where the Ignore Once button used to be.)

Click one of the Ignore buttons or the Next Sentence button to let what Word thinks is a grammatical error stand.

If you want to fine-tune how Word runs its grammar checker, click the Options button in the Spelling and Grammar dialog box. You land in the Proofing category of the Word Options dialog box. Under When Correcting Spelling and Grammar in Word, choose whether to underline grammatical errors in your documents, whether to check for grammatical as well as spelling errors, and in the Writing Style drop-down list, how stringent you want the rules of grammar to be. Choose Grammar & Style, not Grammar Only, if you want Word to enforce style rules as well as the rules of grammar.

Researching a Topic inside an Office Program

Thanks to the Research task pane, your desk needn't be as crowded as before. The Research task pane offers dictionaries, foreign language dictionaries, a thesaurus, language translators, and encyclopedias, as well as Internet searching, all available from inside the Office programs. As shown in Figure 4-6, the Research task pane can save you a trip to the library. Table 4-1 describes the research services in the Research task pane. Use these services to get information as you compose a Word document, Excel worksheet, Outlook message, Publisher publication, or PowerPoint presentation.

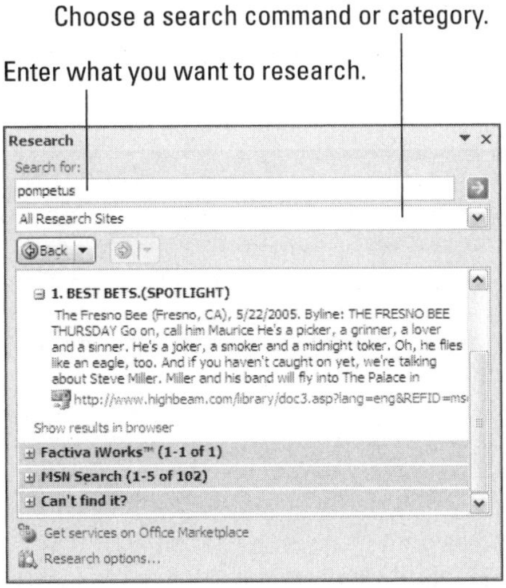

Choose a search command or category.

Enter what you want to research.

Figure 4-6:
The
Research
task pane is
like a mini-
reference
library.

Table 4-1	Research Services in the Research Task Pane
Research Service	*What It Provides*
All Reference Books	
Encarta dictionaries	Word definitions from the Microsoft Network's online dictionaries
Thesauruses	Synonyms from the Microsoft Network's online thesauruses
Translation service	Translations from one language to another
All Research Sites	
eLibrary*	Newspaper and magazine articles from the Highbeam Research Library (you must be a paid subscriber)
Encarta Encyclopedia	Encyclopedia articles from the Microsoft Network's online encyclopedias (you must be a paid subscriber to read most articles)
Factiva iWorks*	Business articles from Factiva (you must be a paid subscriber)
MSN Search*	Results from the Microsoft Network's search engine
All Business and Financial Sites	
MSN Money Stock Quotes*	Stock quotes from the Microsoft Network's Money Web site
Thomas Gale Company Profiles*	Thumbnail company profiles, including tickers, revenue, and Web site information

Requires an Internet connection.

Your computer must be connected to the Internet to run some of the services in the Research task plane. Bilingual dictionaries and thesauruses are installed as part of the Office software, but the research Web sites and the Encarta dictionaries and encyclopedia require an Internet connection.

In order to use some of the services offered by the Research task pane, you must pay a fee. These services are marked in search results with the Premium Content icon.

Using the Research task pane

No matter what you want to research in the Research task pane, start your search the same way. The task pane offers menus and buttons for steering a search in different directions. Follow these basic steps to use the Research task pane:

1. **Either click in a word or select the words that you want to research.**

   For example, if you want to translate a word, click it. Clicking a word or selecting words saves you the trouble of entering words in the Search For text box, but if no word in your file describes what you want to research, don't worry about it. You can enter the subject of your search later.

2. **On the Review tab, click the Research button (you may have to click the Proofing button first).**

   The Research task pane appears (refer to Figure 4-6). If you've researched since you started running your Office program, the options you chose for researching last time appear in the task pane. (In Publisher, choose Tools⇨Research to open the Research task pane; in Outlook, open the drop-down list on the Spelling button and choose Research.)

3. **Enter a research term in the Search For text box (if one isn't there already).**

   If you weren't able to click a word or select words in Step 1, enter research terms now.

4. **Open the Search For drop-down list and tell Office where to steer your search (refer to Table 4-1).**

   Choose a reference book, research Web site, or business and financial Web site. To research in a category, choose a category name — All Reference Books, All Research Sites, or All Business and Financial Sites. Later in this chapter, "Choosing your research options" explains how to decide which researching options appear on the drop-down list.

5. **Click the Start Searching button.**

   The results of your search appear in the Research task pane.

If your search yields nothing worthwhile or nothing at all, scroll to the bottom of the task pane and try the All Reference Books or All Reference Sites link. The first link searches all reference books — the dictionaries, thesauruses, and translation services. The second searches research sites — the Encarta Encyclopedia, Factiva iWorks and MSN Search.

You can retrace a search by clicking the Previous Search button or Next Search button in the Research task pane. These buttons work like the Back and Forward buttons in a Web browser.

Sometimes a hyperlink to a Web site appears in the search results. If you click one of these hyperlinks, your browser (if you're using Internet Explorer) opens with the Research task pane on the left, as shown in Figure 4-7. You can continue using the Research task pane in the browser window.

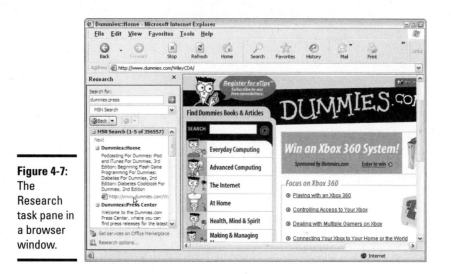

Figure 4-7:
The
Research
task pane in
a browser
window.

Choosing your research options

Which research options appear on the Search For drop-down list is up to you. Maybe you want to dispense with the for-a-fee services (eLibrary, Encarta Encyclopedia, and Factiva iWorks). Maybe you want to get stock quotes from a particular country. To decide which research options appear in the Research task pane, open the task pane and click the Research Options link (you can find this link at the bottom of the task pane). You see the Research Options dialog box. Select the research services you want and click OK.

Finding the Right Word with the Thesaurus

If you can't seem to find the right word or if the word is on the tip of your tongue but you can't quite remember it, you can always give the thesaurus a shot. To find synonyms for a word, start by right-clicking the word and choosing Synonyms on the shortcut menu, as shown in Figure 4-8 (you can't do this in Excel). With luck, the synonym you're looking for appears on the shortcut menu, and all you have to do is click to enter the synonym. Usually, however, finding a good synonym is a journey, not a Sunday stroll.

To search for a good synonym, click the word in question and open the thesaurus on the Research task pane with one of these techniques:

+ Press Shift+F7.

+ Right-click the word and choose Synonyms⇨Thesaurus. (In Publisher, right-click and choose Proofing Tools⇨Thesaurus.)

✦ Go to the Review tab and click the Thesaurus button (you may have to click the Proofing button first).

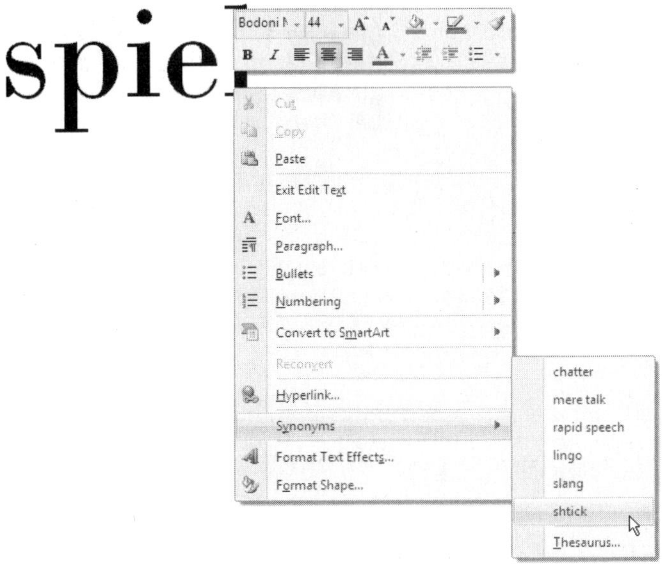

Figure 4-8:
Searching
for a
synonym.

The Research task pane opens. It offers a list of synonyms and sometimes includes an antonym or two at the bottom. Now you're getting somewhere:

✦ **Choosing a synonym:** Move the pointer over the synonym you want, open its drop-down list, and choose Insert.

✦ **Finding a synonym for a synonym:** If a synonym intrigues you, click it. The task pane displays a new list of synonyms.

✦ **Searching for antonyms:** If you can't think of the right word, type its antonym in the Search For box and then look for an "antonym of an antonym" in the Research task pane.

✦ **Revisit a word list:** Click the Back button as many times as necessary. If you go back too far, you can always click its companion Forward button.

If your search for a synonym comes up dry, scroll and click a link at the bottom of the Research task pane. Clicking All Reference Books gives you the opportunity to look up a word in the reference books you installed in the task pane; clicking All Research Sites gives you a chance to search the Internet (see "Researching a Topic inside an Office Program" earlier in this chapter, for details).

Proofing Text Written in a Foreign Language

In the interest of cosmopolitanism, Office gives you the opportunity to make foreign languages a part of Word documents, PowerPoint presentations, Publisher publications, and Outlook messages. To enter and edit text in a foreign language, you start by installing proofing tools for the language. With the tools installed, you tell Office where in your file a foreign language is used. After that, you can spell check text written in the language.

To spell check text written in anguages apart from English, you have to obtain the additional proofing tools from Microsoft. These can be obtained at the Microsoft Product Information Center at www.microsoft.com/products (enter **proofing tools** in the Search box). Proofing tools include a spell checker, grammar checker, thesaurus, hyphenator, AutoCorrect list, and translation dictionary, but not all these tools are available for every language.

In PowerPoint and Word, the status bar along the bottom of the window lists which language the cursor is in. Glance at the status bar if you aren't sure which language Office is whispering in your ear.

Telling Office which languages you will use

Follow these steps to inform Word, PowerPoint, Publisher, and Outlook that you will use a language or languages besides English in your files:

1. **Close all Office programs (if any are open).**

2. **Click the Start button and choose All Programs⇨Microsoft Office⇨ Microsoft Office Tools⇨Microsoft Office 2007 Language Settings.**

You see the Microsoft Office 2007 Language Settings dialog box. The Enabled Editing Languages box lists languages that Office is capable of proofing.

3. **Select a language in the Available Editing Languages box and click the Add button to make that language a part of your presentations, documents, and messages.**

If you see the words *limited support* next to a language's name in the Enabled Editing Languages box, you need to install language-proofing software. You can obtain this software at the Microsoft Product Information Center (www.microsoft.com/products).

4. **Click OK.**

Marking text as foreign language text

The next step is to tell Office where in your file you're using a foreign language. After you mark the text as foreign language text, Office can spell check it with the proper dictionaries. Follow these steps to mark text so that Office knows in which language it was written:

1. **Select the text that you wrote in a foreign language.**

2. **Click the Review tab.**

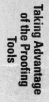

3. **Click the Set Language button (you may have to click the Proofing button first).**

You see the Language dialog box, as shown in Figure 4-9. (In Publisher, choose Tools⇨Language⇨Set Language; in Outlook, open the drop-down list on the Spelling button and choose Set Language.)

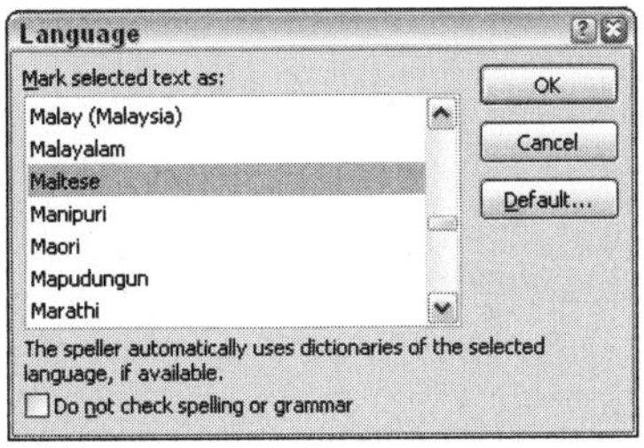

Figure 4-9:
Identifying foreign language words for spell-checking.

Language
Mark selected text as:
Malay (Malaysia)
Malayalam
Maltese
Manipuri
Maori
Mapudungun
Marathi
OK
Cancel
Default...
The speller automatically uses dictionaries of the selected language, if available.
☐ Do not check spelling or grammar

4. **Select a language and click OK.**

Translating Foreign Language Text

Office offers a little gizmo for translating words and phrases from one language to another. The translation gizmo is good only for translating single words and well-known phrases. To translate an entire file, you have to seek the help of a real, native speaker.

The fastest way to translate a word or phrase is to select it, right-click it, choose Translate, and then choose a language on the shortcut menu. With any luck, the translation is done. Usually, however, you have to follow these more intricate steps to translate text from one language to another:

1. **Select the word or phrase that needs translating.**

2. **On the Review tab, click the Translate button.**

The Research task pane opens, as shown in Figure 4-10. (In an Outlook message, open the drop-down list on the Spelling button and choose Translate; in Publisher and Excel, Alt+click to open the Research task pane and then choose Translation on the Search For drop-down list.) Earlier in this chapter, "Researching a Topic inside an Office Program" describes the Research task pane.

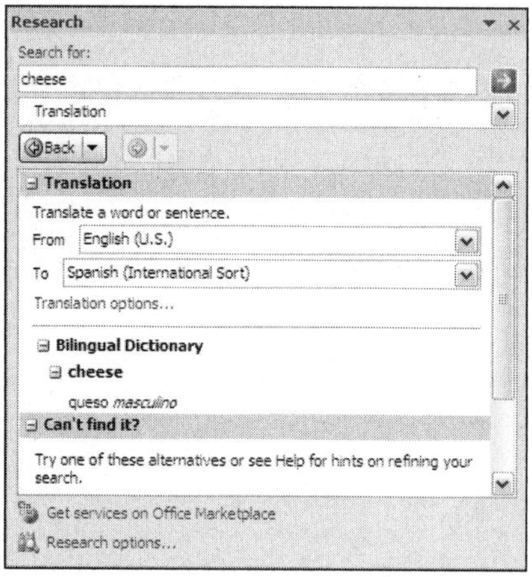

Figure 4-10:
Use the
Research
task pane to
translate a
word or
phrase.

3. Under Translation, choose a From option and a To option.

For example, to translate from English to Spanish, choose English in the From drop-down list and Spanish in the To drop-down list.

The translation — if Office can make it — appears in the task pane. You may have to scroll down to find it.

To copy a translation into your file, double-click or drag the pointer over the translation to select it. Then right-click and choose Copy to copy the word or phrase to the Clipboard. From there, you can paste it in your file.

Taking advantage of Word's Translation ScreenTips

If you're a jet-setter or other cosmopolitan type who often has to deal in foreign languages, you'll like the Word Translation ScreenTips. When you move the pointer over an English word, its translation appears in a pop-up box called a *ScreenTip*. Sometimes you get additional information about the word. For example, the ScreenTip tells you how the word is used in sayings and whether it is masculine or feminine.

To make Translation ScreenTips appear, go to the Review tab, click the Translation ScreenTip button (you may have to click the Proofing button first), and deselect Turn Off Translation ScreenTip. Then open the drop-down list again and choose the language for which you need translations.

Which languages appear on the list depends on which dictionaries are loaded on your computer and which languages you told Office you intended to use (see "Telling Office which languages you will use" earlier in this chapter).

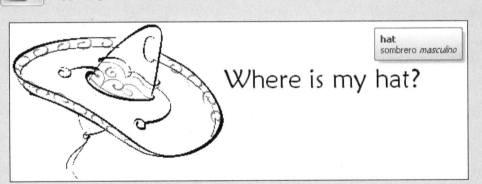

hat
sombrero *masculino*

Where is my hat?

Chapter 5: Creating a Table

In This Chapter

✔ Understanding table jargon

✔ Creating a table and entering the text and numbers

✔ Aligning table text in various ways

✔ Merging and splitting cells to make interesting layouts

✔ Changing the size of rows and columns

✔ Decorating a table with table styles, colors, and borders

✔ Doing calculations in a Word table

✔ Discovering an assortment of table tricks

The best way to present a bunch of data at once in Word or PowerPoint is to do it in a table. Viewers can compare and contrast the data. They can compare Elvis sightings in different cities or income from different businesses. They can contrast the number of socks lost in different washing machine brands. A table is a great way to plead your case or defend your position. On a PowerPoint slide, the audience can see right away that the numbers back you up. In a Word document, readers can refer to your table to get the information they need.

As everyone who has worked on tables knows, however, tables are a chore. Getting all the columns to fit, making columns and rows the right width and height, and editing the text in a table isn't easy. I explain in this chapter how to create tables, enter text in tables, change the number and size of columns and rows, lay out tables, format tables, and (in Word) do the math in tables. You'll also discover a few tricks — including using a picture for the background — that only magicians know. And to start you on the right foot, I begin by explaining table jargon.

Talking Table Jargon

As with much else in Computerland, tables have their own jargon. Figure 5-1 describes this jargon. Sorry, but you need to catch up on these terms to construct the perfect table:

✦ **Cell:** The box that is formed where a row and column intersect. Each cell holds one data item.

✦ **Header row:** The name of the labels along the top row that explain what is in the columns below.

✦ **Row labels:** The labels in the first column that describe what is in each row.

✦ **Borders:** The lines in the table that define where the rows and columns are.

✦ **Gridlines:** The gray lines that show where the columns and rows are. Unless you've drawn borders around all the cells in a table, you can't tell where rows and columns begin and end without gridlines. To display or hide the gridlines, click the View Gridlines button on the (Table Tools) Layout tab.

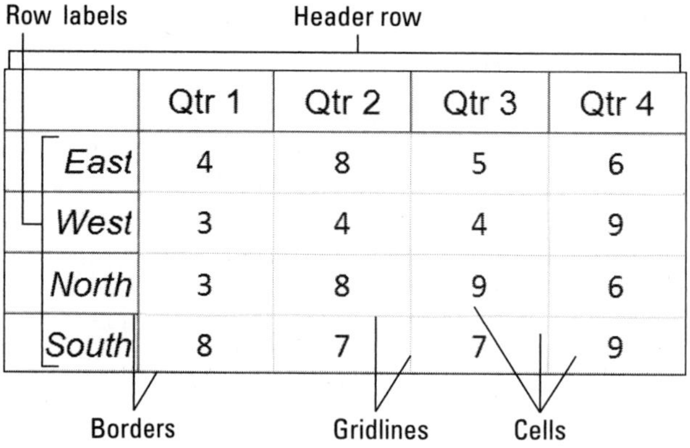

Row labels   Header row

	Qtr 1	Qtr 2	Qtr 3	Qtr 4
East	4	8	5	6
West	3	4	4	9
North	3	8	9	6
South	8	7	7	9

Borders   Gridlines   Cells

Figure 5-1:
The parts of a table.

Creating a Table

Word and PowerPoint offer several ways to create a table:

✦ **Drag from the Table menu (Word and PowerPoint).** On the Insert tab, click the Table button, point on the drop-down list to the number of columns and rows you want, click, and let go of the mouse button.

✦ **Use the Insert Table dialog box (Word and PowerPoint).** On the Insert tab, click the Table button and choose Insert Table on the drop-down list. The Insert Table dialog box appears. Enter the number of columns and rows you want and click OK. In PowerPoint, you can also open the Insert Table dialog box by clicking the Table icon in a content place-holder frame.

✦ **Draw a table (Word and PowerPoint).** On the Insert tab, click the Table button and then choose Draw Table on the drop-down list. The pointer changes into a pencil. Use the pencil to draw table borders, rows, and columns. If you make a mistake, click the Eraser button on the (Table Tools) Design tab and drag it over the parts of the table you regret drawing (you may have to click the Draw Borders button first). When you're finished drawing the table, press Esc.

✦ **Create a quick table (Word).** On the Insert tab, click the Table button and choose Quick Tables on the drop-down list. Then select a ready-made table on the shortcut menu. You have to replace the sample data in the quick table, however, with your own data.

✦ **Convert text to a table (Word).** Press Tab or enter a comma in the text where you want columns divided. For example, to turn an address list into a table, put each name and address on its own line and press Tab or enter a comma after the first name, the last name, the street address, the city, the state, and the ZIP Code. For this feature to work, each name and address — each line — must have the same number of tab spaces or commas in it. Select the text you'll convert to a table, click the Table button on the Insert tab, and choose Convert Text to Table. Under Separate Text At in the Convert Text to Table dialog box, choose Tabs or Commas to tell Word how the columns are separated. Then click OK.

After you create a table, you get two new tabs on the Ribbon. The (Table Tools) Design tab offers commands for changing the look of the table; the (Table Tools) Layout tab is for changing around the rows and columns.

Constructing your table from an Excel worksheet

Fans of Microsoft Excel will be glad to know that you can construct an Excel worksheet in a Word document or PowerPoint slide. Excel worksheets, which present data in columns and rows, are very much like tables and can serve as such in documents and slides.

To create an Excel worksheet, go to the Insert tab, click the Table button, and choose Excel Spreadsheet. An Excel worksheet appears on the slide and — *gadzooks!* — you see Excel menus and commands where Word or PowerPoint menus and commands used to be. The worksheet you just created is embedded in your file. Whenever you click the worksheet, Excel menus and commands instead of Word or PowerPoint menus and commands appear on-screen. Click outside the worksheet to return to Word or PowerPoint. Book VIII, Chapter 8 explains how embedded objects work.

Entering the Text and Numbers

After you've created the table, you can start entering text and numbers. All you have to do is click in a cell and start typing. Select your table and take advantage of these techniques to make the onerous task of entering table data a little easier:

✦ **Quickly changing a table's size:** In *Word,* drag the bottom or side of a table to change its size. You can also go to the Layout tab, click the AutoFit button, and choose AutoFit Window to make the table stretch from margin to margin. In PowerPoint, drag a selection handle on a corner or side of the table.

✦ **Moving a table:** In *Word,* switch to Print Layout view and drag the table selector (the square in the upper-left corner of the table). In PowerPoint, move the pointer over the table's perimeter and when you see the four-headed arrow, click and then drag.

✦ **Choosing your preferred font and font size:** Entering table data is easier when you're working in a font and font size you like. Select the table by going to the Layout tab, clicking the Select button, and choosing Select Table on the drop-down list. Then click the Home tab and choose a font and font size there.

✦ **Quickly inserting a new row:** Click in the last column of the last row in your table and press the Tab key to quickly insert a new row at the bottom of the table.

Here are some shortcuts for moving the cursor in a table:

Press	Moves the Cursor to
Tab	Next column in row
Shift+Tab	Previous column in row
↓	Row below
↑	Row above
Alt+Page Up	Top of column
Alt+Page Down	Bottom of column

Selecting Different Parts of a Table

It almost goes without saying, but before you can reformat, alter, or diddle with table cells, rows, or columns, you have to select them:

✦ **Selecting cells:** To select a cell, click in it. You can select several adjacent cells by dragging the pointer over them.

✦ **Selecting rows:** Drag across rows to select them; or go to the Layout tab, click inside the row you want to select, click the Select button, and choose Select Row on the drop-down list. To select more than one row at a time, select cells in the rows before choosing the Select Row command.

✦ **Selecting columns:** Drag across columns to select them, or start from the Layout tab, click in the column you want to select, click the Select button, and choose Select Column on the drop-down list. To select several columns, select cells in the columns before choosing the Select Column command.

✦ **Selecting a table:** Click the Layout tab, click the Select button, and choose Select Table on the drop-down list. In PowerPoint, you can also right-click a table and choose Select Table on the shortcut menu.

Aligning Text in Columns and Rows

Aligning text in columns and rows is a matter of choosing how you want the text to line up vertically and how you want it to line up horizontally. Select the cells, columns, or rows, with text that you want to align (or select your entire table) and then align the text:

✦ **In Word:** On the (Table Tools) Layout tab, click an Align button (you may have to click the Alignment button first, depending on the size of your screen). Word offers nine of them in the Alignment group.

✦ **In PowerPoint:** On the (Table Tools) Layout tab, click one Horizontal Align button (Align Left, Center, or Align Right), and one Vertical Align button (Align Top, Center Vertically, or Align Bottom). You may have to click the Alignment button first.

Merging and Splitting Cells

Merge and split cells to make your tables a little more elegant than run-of-the-mill tables. *Merge* cells to break down the barriers between cells and join them into one cell; *split* cells to divide a single cell into several cells (or several cells into several more cells). In the table shown in Figure 5-2, the cells in rows two, four, and six merged and a baseball player's name is in each merged cell. Where rows two, four, and six originally had nine cells, they now have only one.

Merge and split cells.

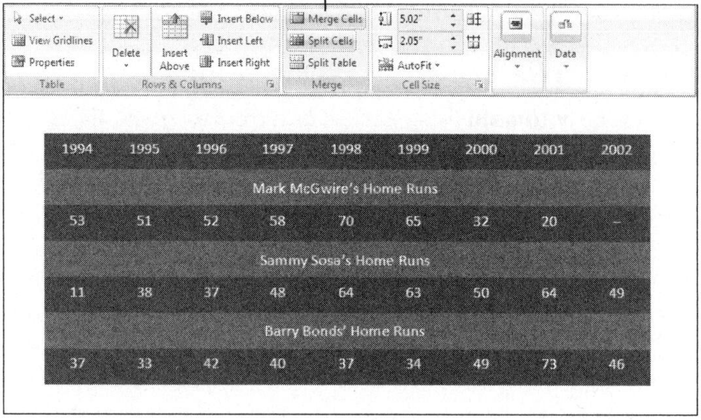

Select
View Gridlines
Properties
Table
Delete
Insert Above
Insert Below
Insert Left
Insert Right
Rows & Columns
Merge Cells
Split Cells
Split Table
Merge
5.02"
2.05"
AutoFit
Cell Size
Alignment
Data
1994 1995 1996 1997 1998 1999 2000 2001 2002
Mark McGwire's Home Runs
53 51 52 58 70 65 32 20 –
Sammy Sosa's Home Runs
11 38 37 48 64 63 50 64 49
Barry Bonds' Home Runs
37 33 42 40 37 34 49 73 46

Figure 5-2: Merge cells to create larger cells.

Select the cells you want to merge or split, go to the Layout tab, and follow these instructions to merge or split cells:

Merge Cells

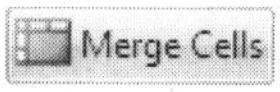

- ✦ **Merging cells:** Click the Merge Cells button. You can also right-click and choose Merge Cells.

Split Cells

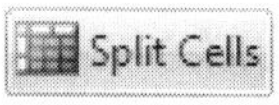

- ✦ **Splitting cells:** Click the Split Cells button. In the Split Cells dialog box, declare how many columns and rows you want to split the cell into and then click OK.

Another way to merge and split cells is to click the Draw Table or Eraser button on the (Table Tools) Design tab (you may have to click the Draw Borders button first). Click the Draw Table button and then draw lines through cells to split them. Click the Eraser button and drag over the boundary between cells to merge cells. Press Esc when you're finished drawing or erasing table cell boundaries.

Split Table

Need to split a table? In Word, place the pointer in what you want to be the first row of the new table and then click the Split Table button.

Laying Out Your Table

Very likely, you created too many or too few columns or rows for your table. Some columns are probably too wide and others too narrow. If that's the case, you have to change the table layout by deleting, inserting, and changing the size of columns and rows, not to mention changing the size of the table itself. In other words, you have to modify the table layout. (Later in this chapter, "Decorating your table with borders and colors" shows how to put borders around tables and embellish them in other ways.)

Changing the size of a table, columns, and rows

The fastest way to adjust the width of columns, the height of rows, and the size of a table itself is to "eyeball it" and drag the mouse:

- ✦ **Column or row:** Move the pointer onto a gridline or border, and when the pointer changes into a double-headed arrow, start dragging. Tug and pull, tug and pull until the column or row is the right size.

  You can also go to the (Table Tools) Layout tab and change the measurements in the Height and Width text boxes to change the width of a column or the height of a row. The measurements affect entire columns or rows, not individual cells.

- ✦ **A table:** Select your table and use one of these techniques to change its size in Word and PowerPoint:

  - *In Word:* Drag the lower-right corner of the table. You can also click the Cell Size group button on the Layout tab, and in the Table Properties dialog box, enter a preferred width measurement on the Table tab.

  - *In PowerPoint:* Drag a selection handle on a side or corner, as shown in Figure 5-3. You can also go to the Layout tab, click the Table Size button (if necessary), and enter inch measurements in the Height and Width text boxes, as shown in Figure 5-3. Click the Lock Aspect Ratio check box to keep the table's proportions when you change its height or width.

  Because resizing columns and rows can be problematic, you can also click these handy buttons in the Layout tab to adjust the width and height of rows and columns:

- ✦ **Distribute Rows:** Click this button to make all rows in the table the same height. Select the rows before clicking the button to make only the rows you select the same height.

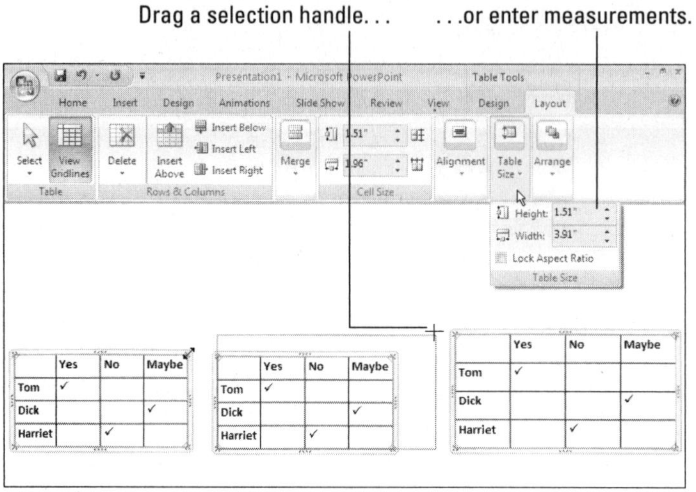

Drag a selection handle. . .   . . .or enter measurements.

Figure 5-3:
The two
ways to
change a
table's
size in
PowerPoint.

✦ **Distribute Columns:** Click this button to make all columns the same width. Select the columns before giving this command to make only the columns you select the same width.

✦ In Word, you can also click the AutoFit button on the Layout tab and take advantage of these commands on the drop-down list for handling columns and rows:

✦ **AutoFit Contents:** Makes each column wide enough to accommodate its widest entry.

✦ **AutoFit Window:** Stretches the table so that it fits across the page between the left and right margin.

✦ **Fixed Column Width:** Fixes the column widths at their current settings.

Sorting, or reordering a table (in Word)

On the subject of moving columns and rows, the fastest way to rearrange the rows in a Word table is to sort the table. *Sorting* means to rearrange all the rows in a table on the basis of data in one or more columns. For example, a table that shows candidates and the number of votes they received could be sorted in alphabetical order by the candidates' names or in numerical order by the number of votes they received. Both tables present the same information, but the information is sorted in different ways.

The difference between ascending and descending sorts is as follows:

- ✔ Ascending arranges text from A to Z, numbers from smallest to largest, and dates from earliest to latest.

- ✔ Descending arranges text from Z to A, numbers from largest to smallest, and dates from latest to earliest.

When you rearrange a table by sorting it, Word rearranges the formatting as well as the data. Do your sorting before you format the table.

Follow these steps to sort a table:

1. **On the (Table Tools) Layout tab, click the Sort button.**

   You see the Sort dialog box. Depending on the size of your screen, you may have to click the Data button before you see the Sort button.

2. **In the first Sort By drop-down list, choose the column you want to sort with.**

3. **If necessary, open the first Type drop-down list and choose Text, Number, or Date to describe what kind of data you're dealing with.**

4. **Select the Ascending or Descending option button to declare whether you want an ascending or descending sort.**

5. **If necessary, on the first Then By drop-down list, choose the tiebreaker column.**

   If two items in the Sort By columns are alike, Word looks to your Then By column choice to break the tie and place one row before another in the table.

6. **Click OK.**

When you sort a table, Word ignores the *header row* — the first row in the table — and doesn't move it. However, if you want to include the header row in the sort, click the No Header Row option button in the Sort dialog box.

Inserting and deleting columns and rows

The trick to inserting and deleting columns and rows is to correctly select part of the table first. You can insert more than one column or row at a time by first selecting more than one column or row. To insert two columns, select two columns and choose an Insert command; to insert three rows, select three rows and choose an Insert command. Earlier in this chapter, "Selecting Different Parts of a Table" explains how to make table selections.

Go to the (Table Tools) Layout tab and follow these instructions to insert and delete columns and rows:

✦ **Inserting columns:** Select a column or columns and click the Insert Left or Insert Right button. If you want to insert just one column, click in a column and then click the Insert Left or Insert Right button. You can also right-click, choose Insert, and choose an Insert command.

✦ **Inserting rows:** Select a row or rows and click the Insert Above or Insert Below button. If you want to insert just one row, click in a row and click the Insert Above or Insert Below button. You can also right-click, choose Insert, and choose an Insert command on the shortcut menu.

To insert a row at the end of a table, move the pointer into the last cell in the last row and press the Tab key.

✦ **Deleting columns:** Click in the column you want to delete, click the Delete button, and choose Delete Columns on the drop-down list. Select more than one column to delete more than one. (Pressing the Delete key deletes the data in the column, not the column itself.)

✦ **Deleting rows:** Click in the row you want to delete, click the Delete button, and choose Delete Rows. Select more than one row to delete more than one. (Pressing the Delete key deletes the data in the row, not the row itself.)

Moving columns and rows

Because there is no elegant way to move a column or row, you should move only one at a time. If you try to move several simultaneously, you open a can of worms that is best left unopened. To move a column or row:

1. **Select the column or row you want to move.**

Earlier in this chapter, "Selecting Different Parts of a Table" explains how to select columns and rows.

2. **Right-click in the selection and then choose Cut on the shortcut menu.**

The column or row is moved to the Clipboard.

The preceding section of this chapter explains how to insert columns and rows.

3. **Move the column or row:**

- *Column:* Click in the topmost cell in your new column. Then right-click and choose Paste Columns (in Word) or Paste (in PowerPoint).

- *Row:* Click in the first column of the row you inserted. Then right-click and choose Paste Rows (in Word) or Paste (in PowerPoint).

Formatting Your Table

After you have entered the text, placed the columns and rows, and made them the right size, the fun begins. Now you can dress up your table and make it look snazzy. You can change text fonts, choose colors for columns and rows, and even land a graphic in the background of your table. You can also play with the borders that divide the columns and rows and *shade* columns, rows, and cells by filling them with gray shades or a black background. Read on to find out how to do these tricks.

Designing a table with a table style

By far the fastest way to get a good-looking table is to select a table style in the Table Styles gallery and let Word or PowerPoint do the work for you, as shown in Figure 5-4. A *table style* is a ready-made assortment of colors and border choices. You can save yourself a lot of formatting trouble by selecting a table style. After you've selected a table style, you can modify it by selecting or deselecting check boxes in the Table Style Options group.

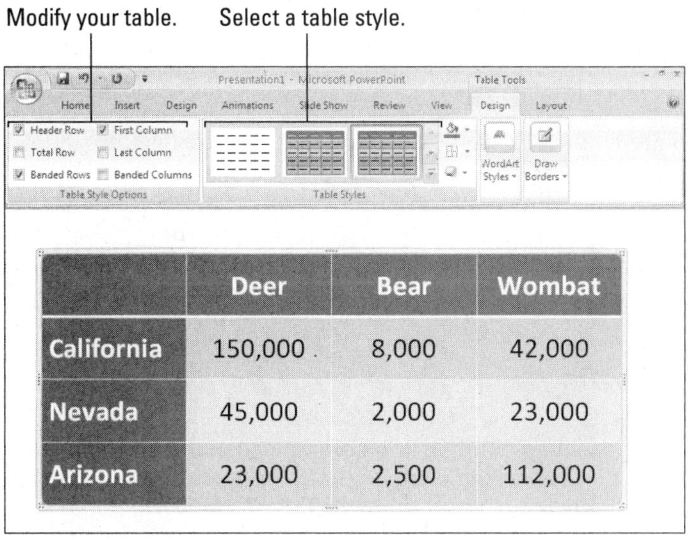

Modify your table.   Select a table style.

Figure 5-4:
You have
lots of
choices in
the Table
Styles
gallery.

	Deer	Bear	Wombat
California	150,000	8,000	42,000
Nevada	45,000	2,000	23,000
Arizona	23,000	2,500	112,000

Select your table and follow these steps to choose a table style:

1. **Click the (Table Tools) Design tab.**

2. **Open the Table Styles gallery and move the pointer over table style choices to live-preview the table.**

3. **Select a table style.**

    To remove a table style, choose Clear (in Word) or Clear Table (in PowerPoint) on the bottom of the Table Styles gallery.

For consistency's sake, choose a similar table style — or better yet the same table style — for all the tables in your document or presentation. This way, your work doesn't become a showcase for table styles.

Calling attention to different rows and columns

On the (Table Tools) Design tab, Word and PowerPoint offer Table Style Options check boxes for calling attention to different rows or columns (refer to Figure 5-4). For example, you can make the header row — the first row in the table — stand out by selecting the Header Row check box. If your table presents numerical data with total figures in the last row, you can call attention to the last row by choosing the Total Row check box. Select or deselect these check boxes to make your table easier to read and understand:

+ **Header Row and Total Row:** These check boxes make the first row and last row in a table stand out. Typically, the header row is a different color or contains boldface text because it is the row that identifies the data in the table. Click the Header Row check box to make the first row stand out; if you also want the last row to stand out, click the Total Row check box.

+ **Banded Columns and Banded Rows:** *Banded* means "striped" in Office lingo. For striped columns or striped rows — columns or rows that alternate in color — select the Banded Columns or Banded Rows check box.

+ **First Column and Last Column:** Often the first column stands out in a table because it identifies what type of data is in each row (refer to Figure 5-4). Select the First Column check box to make it a different color or boldface its text. Check the Last Column check box if you want the rightmost column to stand out.

Decorating your table with borders and colors

Rather than rely on a table style, you can play interior decorator on your own. You can slap color on the columns and rows of your table, draw borders around columns and rows, and choose a look for borders. Figure 5-5 shows the drop-down lists on the (Table Tools) Design tab that pertain to table decoration. Use these lists to shade table column and rows and draw table borders.

Line Style (Pen Style) list

Shading button   Borders button   Line Weight (Pen Weight) list

Figure 5-5:
Tools on the
(Table Tools)
Design tab
for decorat-
ing tables.

Designing borders for your table

Follow these steps to fashion a border for your table or a part of your table:

1. **Click the (Table Tools) Design tab.**

2. **Select the part of your table that needs a new border.**

To select the entire table, go to the Layout tab, click the Select button, and choose Select Table.

3. **Open the Line Style drop-down list (in Word) or the Pen Style drop-down list (in PowerPoint) and choose a line style for the border, as shown in Figure 5-5 (you may have to click the Draw Borders button first, depending on the size of your screen).**

Stay away from the dotted and dashed lines unless you have a good reason for choosing one. These lines can be distracting and keep others from focusing on the data presented in the table.

4. **Open the Line Width drop-down list (in Word) or the Pen Weight drop-down list (in PowerPoint) and choose a thickness for the border, as shown in Figure 5-5 (you may have to click the Draw Borders button first).**

5. **If you want your borders to be a color apart from black, click the Pen Color button and choose a color on the drop-down list (you may have to click the Draw Borders button first).**

6. **Open the drop-down list on the Borders button (refer to Figure 5-5) and choose where to place borders on the part of the table you selected in the previous step.**

This is the tricky part. The Borders commands have different effects, depending on which part of the table you selected. For example, if you selected two rows and you choose the Top Border command, the command applies only to the top of the uppermost row. If you're anywhere near typical, you have to repeat Steps 5 and 6 until you get it just right.

In Word, you can also change borders by clicking the Draw Borders group button and making selections in the Borders and Shading dialog box.

Selecting colors for columns, rows, or your table

Follow these steps to paint columns, rows, or your table a new color:

1. **Select the part of the table that needs a paint job.**

2. **On the (Table Tools) Design tab, open the drop-down list on the Shading button and choose a color (refer to Figure 5-5).**

Later in this chapter, "Using a picture as the table background" explains how to use a picture as the background in a table.

Using Math Formulas in Word Tables

No, you don't have to add the figures in columns and rows yourself; Word gladly does that for you. Word can perform other mathematical calculations as well. Follow these steps to perform mathematical calculations and tell Word how to format sums and products:

1. **Put the cursor in the cell that will hold the sum or product of the cells above, below, to the right, or to the left.**

2. **On the (Table Tools) Layout tab, click the Formula button.**

Depending on the size of your screen, you may have to click the Data button first. The Formula dialog box appears, as shown in Figure 5-6. In its wisdom, Word makes a very educated guess about what you want the formula to do and places a formula in the Formula box.

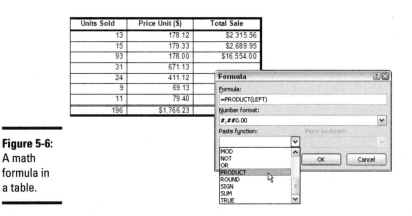

Figure 5-6:
A math
formula in
a table.

3. **If this isn't the formula you want, delete everything except the equal sign in the Formula box, open the Paste Function drop-down list, and choose another function for the formula.**

   For example, choose PRODUCT to multiply figures. You may have to type **left**, **right**, **above**, or **below** in the parentheses within the formula to tell Word where the figures that you want it to compute are.

4. **In the Number Format drop-down list, choose a format for your number.**

5. **Click OK.**

Word doesn't calculate blank cells in formulas. Enter **0** in blank cells if you want them to be included in calculations. You can copy functions from one cell to another to save yourself the trouble of opening the Formula dialog box.

Neat Table Tricks

The rest of this chapter details a handful of neat table tricks to make your tables stand out in a crowd. Why should all tables look alike? Read on to discover how to make text in the header row stand on its ear, put a picture behind a table, draw diagonal border lines, draw on top of a table, and wrap slide text around a table.

Changing the direction of header row text

In a top-heavy table in which the *header row cells* — the cells in the first row — contain text and the cells below contain numbers, consider changing the direction of the text in the header row to make the table easier to read. Changing text direction in the header row is also a good way to squeeze more columns onto a table. Consider how wide the table shown in Figure 5-7 would be if the words in the first row were displayed horizontally.

Figure 5-7:
Change the direction of text to squeeze more columns on a table.

	Yes	No	Maybe	Often	Never
Prof. Plum in the Library	✓				
Miss Scarlet in the Drawing Room		✓			
Col. Mustard in the Dining Room					✓

Follow these steps to change the direction of text on a table.

1. **Select the row that needs a change of text direction.**

   Usually, that's the first row in a table.

2. **Go to the (Table Tools) Layout tab.**

3. **Click the Text Direction button.**

   What happens next depends on whether you're operating in Word or PowerPoint:

   - *In Word:* Keep clicking the Text Direction button until text lands where you want it to land. (You may have to click the Alignment button before you can see the Text Direction button.)

   - *In PowerPoint:* Choose a Text Direction option on the drop-down list. (You may have to click the Alignment button to get to the Text Direction button, depending on the size of your screen.)

4. **Change the height of the row to make the vertical text fit.**

   As "Changing the size of a table, columns, and rows" explains earlier in this chapter, you can change the height of a row by going to the Layout tab and entering a measurement in the Height box. (You may have to click the Table Size button in order to see the Height box.)

Using a picture as the table background

As Figure 5-8 demonstrates, a picture used as the background in a table looks mighty nice. To make it work, however, you need a graphic that serves well as the background. For Figure 5-8, I got around this problem by recoloring my graphic (Book VIII, Chapter 3 explains how to recolor a graphic). You also need to think about font colors. Your audience must be able to read the table text, and that usually means choosing a white or light font color for text so that the text can be read over the graphic. For Figure 5-8, I selected a white font color.

Besides putting a graphic behind a table, PowerPoint gives you the opportunity to make the graphic appear in every table cell, as shown on the right side of Figure 5-8. Sorry, you can't do that feat in Word, but you can place a picture behind a table, as the following pages explain.

Placing a picture behind the table

Placing a graphic behind a table requires a fair bit of work, but the results are well worth the effort. First you have to insert the graphic and perhaps recolor it. Then you have to create the table. Lastly, you have to make the table fit squarely on top of the graphic and perhaps group the objects together.

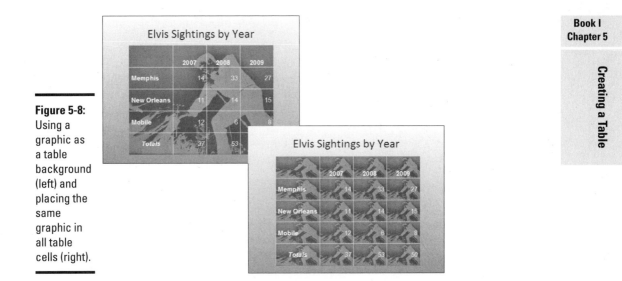

Figure 5-8:
Using a
graphic as
a table
background
(left) and
placing the
same
graphic in
all table
cells (right).

In Word and PowerPoint, follow these steps to place a graphic behind a table:

1. **Insert the graphic, resize it, and format the graphic.**

Book VIII, Chapter 3 explains how to insert and resize graphics. To insert a graphic, go to the Insert tab and click the Picture button. To resize it, drag a selection handle; make the graphic as big as you want your table to be. To recolor a graphic similar to the job done to the graphic in Figure 5-8, select the (Picture Tools) Format tab, click the Recolor button, and choose an option.

2. **Insert the table and make it roughly the same size as the graphic.**

These tasks are explained earlier in this chapter. To change the size of a table, drag a selection handle on its corner or side. Place the table nearby the graphic, but not right on top of it.

3. **Select the (Table Tools) Design tab, open the Table Styles gallery, and choose Clear (in Word) or Clear Table (in PowerPoint).**

With the table styles out of the way, you can see the graphic clearly through your table.

4. **Enter the data in the table, select a font and font color, select a border and border color, and align the text.**

These tasks (except for selecting fonts) are described throughout this chapter. The easiest way to choose a font and font color for a table is to select the table and then go to the Home tab and select a font and font size.

5. **Move the table squarely on top of the graphic and then make the table and graphic roughly the same size.**

Here are a few tricks that are worth knowing when you're handling a graphic and table:

✦ In Word, you have to turn off text wrapping in order to bring the graphic behind the table. To do that, select your graphic, go to the (Picture Tools) Format tab, click the Text Wrapping button, and choose Behind Text on the drop-down list.

✦ If the graphic is in front of the table, select the graphic, go to the (Picture Tools) Format tab, open the drop-down list on the Send to Back button, and choose Send to Back (in PowerPoint) or Send Behind Text (in Word).

✦ To make the graphic and table the same size, enter the same measurements for both. Select the table, go to the (Table Tools) Layout tab, and enter measurements for the table in the Height and Width boxes. Then select the graphic, go to the (Picture Tools) Format tab, and enter the same measurements in the Height and Width boxes. (You may have to click the Size button to see these boxes, depending on the size of your screen.)

Placing a background picture in each PowerPoint table cell

PowerPoint offers a special command for placing a picture in each table cell (refer to Figure 5-8). For this trick to work, you need a graphic of uniform color; otherwise, the text is too hard to read. (You might consult Book VIII, Chapter 3, which explains how to alter graphics with the Office Picture Manager.) Follow these steps to place a background picture in each PowerPoint table cell:

1. **Right-click your table and choose Select Table.**

2. **Click the (Table Tools) Design tab.**

3. **Open the drop-down list on the Shading button and choose Picture.**

The Insert Picture dialog box opens.

4. **Select a picture and click the Insert button.**

To remove the background pictures from a table, open the drop-down list on the Shading button and choose No Fill or choose Clear Table in the Table Styles gallery.

Drawing diagonal lines on tables

Draw diagonal lines across table cells to cancel out those cells or otherwise make cells look different. In Figure 5-9, diagonal lines are drawn on cells to show that information that would otherwise be in the cells is either not available or is not relevant.

	Mon.	Tues.	Wed.	Thurs.	Fri.	Sat.	Sun.
McKeef	8:00			3:00		8:00	2:15
Arnez	9:00	6:00	2:30	12:00	8:15		4:00
Danes	9:30		2:00	7:30		3:30	7:30
Minor		12:00	4:15	5:15	2:00		
Krupf	3:30	6:00		12:00	2:30	9:00	9:00
Gough	3:00			7:00	3:30	4:530	3:30
Gonzalez	12:00	7:15	8:30				10:15

Figure 5-9:
Diagonal
lines mark
off cells as
different.

Select the cells that need diagonal lines, go to the (Table Tools) Design tab, and use one of these techniques to draw diagonal lines across cells:

✦ **Draw Table button:** Click the Draw Table button (you may have to click the Draw Borders button first). The pointer changes into a pencil. Drag to draw the diagonal lines. Press Esc or click the Draw Table button a second time when you're finished drawing.

✦ **Borders button:** Open the drop-down list on the Borders button and choose Diagonal Down Border or Diagonal Up Border.

To remove diagonal lines, click the Eraser button and drag across the diagonals.

Drawing on a table

When you want the audience to focus on data in one part of a table, draw a circle around the data. By "draw" I mean make an Oval shape and place it over the data you want to highlight, as shown in Figure 5-10. Book I, Chapter 8 explains the drawing tools in detail. To spare you the trouble of turning to that chapter, here are shorthand instructions for drawing on a table:

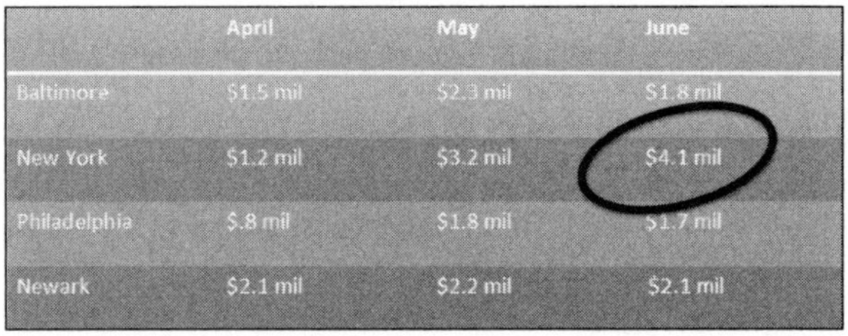

	April	May	June
Baltimore	$1.5 mil	$2.3 mil	$1.8 mil
New York	$1.2 mil	$3.2 mil	$4.1 mil
Philadelphia	$.8 mil	$1.8 mil	$1.7 mil
Newark	$2.1 mil	$2.2 mil	$2.1 mil

Figure 5-10:
You can
circle data to
highlight it.

1. **On the Insert tab, open the Shapes gallery and select the Oval shape.**

2. **On a corner of your page or slide, away from the table, drag to draw the oval.**

Shape Fill *3.* **On the (Drawing Tools) Format tab, open the drop-down list on the Shape Fill button and choose No Fill.**

Shape Outline *4.* **Open the drop-down list on the Shape Outline button and choose a very dark color.**

5. **Open the drop-down list on the Shape Outline button, choose Weight, and choose a thick line.**

6. **Drag the oval over the data on your table that you want to highlight.**

If the oval is obscured by the table, go to the (Drawing Tools) Format tab, and click the Bring to Front button (click the Arrange button, if necessary, to see this button). While you're at it, consider rotating the oval a little way to make it appear as though it was drawn by hand on the table.

In the course of a live PowerPoint presentation, you can draw on slides with the Pen to highlight data. See Book IV, Chapter 4.

Chapter 6: Creating a Chart

In This Chapter

✔ Looking at the different parts of a chart

✔ Creating a chart

✔ Examining the different types of charts

✔ Entering chart data in an Excel worksheet

✔ Positioning a chart in Excel, Word, and PowerPoint

✔ Changing the appearance of a chart

✔ Saving a customized chart as a template so that you can use it again

✔ Exploring some fancy-schmancy chart tricks

✔ Fixing common problems with charts

*N*othing is more persuasive than a chart. The bars, pie slices, lines, or columns show instantaneously that production is up or down, that cats are better than dogs or dogs better than cats, or that catsup tastes better than ketchup. Fans of charts and graphs will be glad to know that putting a chart in a Word document, Excel worksheet, or PowerPoint slide is fairly easy.

This explains how to create a chart. It looks at which charts are best for presenting different kinds of data, how to change a chart's appearance, and how to save charts in a template that you can use again. You discover some nice chart tricks, including how to make a picture the backdrop for a chart and how to annotate a chart. It also addresses common chart problems.

A Mercifully Brief Anatomy Lesson

Throughout this chapter, I show you many ways to tinker with charts, but before you can begin tinkering, you need to know what you're tinkering with. In other words, you have to know what the different parts of a chart are. Here is a brief chart anatomy lesson. Figure 6-1 points out where some of the terms described here are found on a real, live chart:

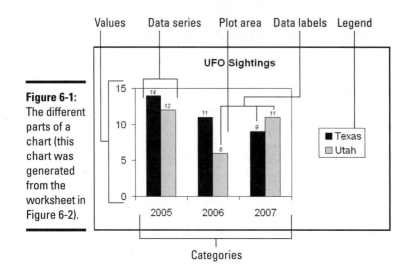

Figure 6-1: The different parts of a chart (this chart was generated from the worksheet in Figure 6-2).

✦ **Plot area:** The center of the chart, apart from the legend and data labels, where the data itself is presented.

✦ **Values:** The numerical values with which the chart is plotted. The values you enter determine the size of the *data markers* — the bars, columns, pie slices, and so on — that portray value. In the column chart in Figure 6-1, values determine the height of the columns.

✦ **Gridlines:** Lines on the chart that indicate value measurements. Gridlines are optional in charts (none are shown in Figure 6-1).

✦ **Worksheet:** Where you enter (or retrieve) the data used to plot the chart. The worksheet resembles a table. Figure 6-2 shows the worksheet I used to enter the data that produced the chart in Figure 6-1. Notice how the numbers at the top of the columns correspond to the numbers entered in the worksheet shown in Figure 6-2. A worksheet is called a *data table* when it appears along with a chart.

Categories

Data labels   Data Series

Figure 6-2: The information entered in this worksheet produced the chart shown in Figure 6-1.

	A	B	C
1		Texas	Utah
2	2005	14	12
3	2006	11	6
4	2007	9	11

✦ **Data series:** A group of related data points presented by category on a chart. The chart in Figure 6-1 has two data series — one for Texas and one for Utah.

✦ **Categories:** The actual items that you want to compare or display in your chart. In Figure 6-1, the categories are the three years in which UFO sightings occurred in the two states.

✦ **Legend:** A text box located to the side, top, or bottom of a chart that identifies the chart's data labels.

✦ **Horizontal and vertical axes:** For plotting purposes, one side of the plot area. In the chart in Figure 6-1, UFO sightings are plotted on the *horizontal axis;* categories are plotted on the *vertical axis.* Sometimes these axes are called the *category axis* (or *x axis*) and the *value axis* (or *y axis*).

Axes can be confusing, but these axes aren't as evil as they seem. All you really need to know about them is this: You can label the axes in different ways and you can rotate the chart so that the horizontal becomes the vertical axis and vice versa (click the Switch Row/Column button).

✦ **Data point:** A value plotted on a chart that is represented by a column, line, bar, pie slice, dot, or other shape. Each data point corresponds to a value entered in the worksheet. In Figure 6-1, for example, the data points for Texas UFO sightings are 14 in 2005, 11 in 2006, and 9 in 2007. Hence the Texas columns in the table rise to the 14, 11, and 9 level.

✦ **Data marker:** Shapes on a chart that represent data points. Data markers include columns, lines, pie slices, bubbles, and dots. In Figure 6-1, columns are the data markers.

✦ **Data label:** A label that shows the actual values used to construct the data markers. In the chart in Figure 6-1, there are six data labels, one on the top of each column. Displaying data labels in charts is optional.

The good news where the anatomy of a chart is concerned is that you can click anywhere on a chart and see a pop-up box that tells you what part of the chart you just clicked. I wish biology class were that easy!

The Basics: Creating a Chart

Throughout this chapter, I explain the whys, wherefores, and whatnots of creating a chart. Before going into detail, here are the basic steps that everyone needs to know to create a chart in Word, Excel, and PowerPoint:

1. **Click the Insert tab.**

2. **If you're working in Excel, select the data you'll use to generate the chart (in Word and PowerPoint, skip to Step 3).**

In Excel, you select the data on a worksheet before creating the chart, but in Word and PowerPoint, you enter the data for the chart in Excel in Step 4. Yes, you heard me right — in Word and PowerPoint. Excel opens after you begin creating your chart so you can enter data for the chart in an Excel worksheet.

3. Select the kind of chart you want.

How you select a chart type depends on which program you're working in:

- *Excel:* Either open the drop-down list in one of the buttons on the Chart group (Column, Line, Pie, Bar, Area, Scatter, or Other Charts) and then select a chart type, or click the Chart group button drop-down list to open the Insert Chart dialog box and select a chart there. As shown in Figure 6-3, the Insert Chart dialog box shows all the kinds of charts you can create.

Chart type   Chart variations

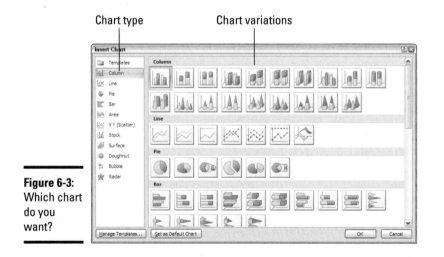

Figure 6-3: Which chart do you want?

- *Word and PowerPoint:* Click the Chart button. You see the Insert Chart dialog box, as shown in Figure 6-3. Select a chart and click OK. The Excel program opens on the right side of your computer screen.

The next portion of this chapter, "Choosing the Right Chart," describes all the charts types and advises you which to choose.

4. In Word and PowerPoint, replace the sample data in the Excel worksheet with the data you need for generating your chart.

Later in this chapter, "Providing the Raw Data for Your Chart" explains how to enter data in an Excel worksheet. After you finish entering the data, you can close Excel by clicking the Close button in the Excel window or by clicking the Office button and choosing Close.

5. **To modify your chart, start by selecting it.**

   Click a chart to select it. Selecting a chart makes the Chart Tools tabs appear in the upper-right corner of the window. Use these tabs — Design, Layout, and Format — to make your chart just-so.

   In Word, you must be in Print Layout view to see a chart.

6. **Select the (Chart Tools) Design tab when you want to change the chart's layout, alter the data with which the chart was generated, or select a different chart type.**

   Later in this chapter, "Changing a Chart's Appearance" explains how to change the design of a chart.

7. **Select the (Chart Tools) Layout tab when you want to change the chart's title, labels, or gridlines.**

   You can add or remove parts of a chart starting at the Layout tab. Later in this chapter, "Changing the layout of a chart" describes how to change around the text and gridlines on a chart.

8. **Select the (Chart Tools) Format tab when you want to change the appearance of your chart.**

   You can change colors and fills on your chart, as "Changing a chart element's color, font, or other particular" explains later in this chapter.

And if you decide to delete the chart you created? Click its perimeter to select it and then press the Delete key.

Choosing the Right Chart

If you're a fan of charts, the huge selection of charts can make you feel like a kid in a candy store, but if charts aren't your forte, the wealth of charts you can choose from can be daunting. You can choose among six dozen charts in 11 categories (refer to Figure 6-3). Which chart is best? The golden rule for choosing a chart type is to choose the one that presents information in the brightest possible light. The purpose of a chart is to compare information across different categories. Select a chart that draws out the comparison so that others can clearly make comparisons. Table 6-1 describes the 11 chart categories and explains in brief when to use each type of chart.

Table 6-1		Chart Types
Symbol	**Chart Type**	**Best Use/Description**
	Area	Examine how values in different categories fluctuate over time and see the cumulative change in values. (Same as a line chart except that the area between trend lines is colored in.)
	Bar	Compare values in different categories against one another, usually over time. Data is displayed in horizontal bars. (Same as a column chart except that the bars are horizontal.)
	Bubble	Examine data relationships by studying the size and location of the bubbles that represent the relationships. Bubble charts are often used in financial analyses and market research. (Similar to an XY scatter chart except that you can use three instead of two data series, and the data points appear as bubbles.)
	Column	Compare values in different categories against one another, usually over time. Data is displayed in vertical columns. (Same as a bar chart except that the bars are vertical.)
	Doughnut	See how values compare as percentages of a whole. (Similar to a pie chart except that you can use more than one data series and create concentric doughnut rings in the chart.)
	Line	Examine how values fluctuate over time. Data is displayed in a set of points connected by a line.
	Pie	See how values compare as percentages of a whole. Data from categories is displayed as a percentage of a whole. (Similar to a doughnut chart.)
	Radar	Examine data as it relates to one central point. Data is plotted on radial points from the central point. This kind of chart is used to make subjective performance analyses.
	XY (Scatter)	Compare different numeric data point sets in space to reveal patterns and trends in data. (Similar to a bubble chart except that the data appears as points instead of bubbles.)
	Stock	See how the value of an item fluctuates as well as its daily, weekly, or yearly high, low, and closing price. This chart is used to track stock prices, but it can also be used to track air temperature and other variable quantities.
	Surface	Examine color-coded data on a 3D surface to explore relationships between data values.

Providing the Raw Data for Your Chart

Every chart is constructed from *raw data* — the numbers and category names you select in an Excel worksheet (in Excel) or enter in an Excel worksheet (in Word and PowerPoint). Book V, Chapter 1 explains in detail how to enter data in an Excel worksheet, but here are the basics of entering data in case you're new to Excel:

✦ **Entering the data in a cell:** A cell is the box in a worksheet where a column and row intersect; each cell can contain one data item. To enter data in a cell, click the cell and start typing. When you're finished, press Enter, press Tab, or click a different cell. You can also click in the Formula bar (above the worksheet) and enter the data there.

✦ **Deleting the data in a cell:** To delete the data in a cell, including the sample data Excel provides for charts, click the cell and press Delete.

✦ **Displaying the numbers:** When a number is too large to fit in a cell, Excel displays pound signs (###) or it displays the number in scientific notation. Don't worry — the number is still recorded and is used to generate your chart. You can display large numbers by widening the columns in which the numbers are found. Move the pointer between column letters (A, B, and so on at the top of the worksheet), and when you see the double-headed arrow, click and start dragging to the right.

Positioning Your Chart in a Workbook, Page, or Slide

To change the position of a chart, click to select it, click its perimeter, and when you see the four-headed arrow, start dragging. Otherwise, follow these instructions to land your chart where you want it to be:

✦ **Excel:** To move your chart to a different worksheet or create a new worksheet to hold your chart, click the Move Chart button in the (Chart Tools) Design tab. You see the Move Chart dialog box.

   • To move your chart to a different worksheet, click the Object In option button, choose the worksheet in the drop-down list, and click OK.

   • To create a new worksheet for a chart, click the New Sheet option button, enter a name for the new worksheet, and click OK.

✦ **Word:** Starting in Print Layout view, select your chart, and in the Page Layout or (Chart Tools) Format tab, click the Position button (you may have to click the Arrange button first, depending on the size of your screen). You see a drop-down list with text-wrapping options. Choose the option that describes how you want surrounding text to behave when it crashes into your chart. Book II, Chapter 4 looks in detail at wrapping text around charts and other objects in Word.

✦ **PowerPoint:** Select the chart and drag it on the slide to the right position.

Changing a Chart's Appearance

Charts are awfully nice already, but perhaps you want to redesign one. Perhaps you're the interior decorator type, and you want to give charts your own personal touch. Excel, PowerPoint, and Word offer these Chart Tools tabs for redecorating charts:

✦ **Design tab:** For quickly changing a chart's appearance. Go to the Design tab if you're in a hurry. The ready-made gallery choices give you the opportunity to change a chart's layout and appearance in a matter of seconds. You can also choose a new chart type from the Design tab. See "Relying on a chart style to change appearances," later in this chapter.

✦ **Layout tab:** For rearranging, hiding, and displaying various parts of a chart, including the legend, labels, title, gridlines, and scale. Go to the Layout tab to tweak your chart and make different parts of it stand out or recede into the background. For example, you can display axis labels more prominently or make them disappear, enter a title for your chart, or display more or fewer gridlines. See "Changing the layout of a chart" and "Handling the gridlines," later in this chapter.

✦ **Format tab:** For changing the color, outline, font, and font size of various parts of a chart, including the labels, bars, and pie slices. You have to really know what you're doing and have a lot of time on your hands to change colors and fonts throughout a chart. See "Changing a chart element's color, font, or other particular," later in this chapter.

These pages explain how to change a chart's appearance, starting with the biggest change you can make — exchanging one type of chart for another.

Changing the chart type

The biggest way to overhaul a chart is to ditch it in favor of a different chart type. Luckily for you, Office 2007 makes this task simple. I wish that changing jobs was this easy. Follow these steps to change a pumpkin into a carriage or an existing chart into a different kind of chart:

1. **Click your chart to select it.**

2. **On the (Chart Tools) Design tab, click the Change Chart Type button, or right-click your chart and choose Change Chart Type on the short-cut menu.**

The Change Chart Type dialog box appears. Does it look familiar? This is the same dialog box you can use to create a chart in the first place.

3. **Select a new chart and click OK.**

Not all chart types can be converted successfully to other chart types. You may well have created a monster, in which case go back to Step 1 and start all over or click the Undo button.

Changing the size and shape of a chart

To make a chart taller or wider, follow these instructions:

✦ Click the perimeter of the chart to select it and then drag a handle on the side to make it wider, or a handle on the top or bottom to make it taller.

✦ Select the (Chart Tools) Format tab and enter measurements in the Height and Width boxes. You can find these boxes in the Size group (you may have to click the Size button to see them, depending on the size of your screen).

Relying on a chart style to change appearances

By far the easiest way to change the look of a chart is to choose an option in the Chart Styles gallery in the (Chart Tools) Design tab, as shown in Figure 6-4. You can choose among 50 options. These gallery options are quite sophisticated — you would have a hard time fashioning these charts on your own.

Select a Chart Style.

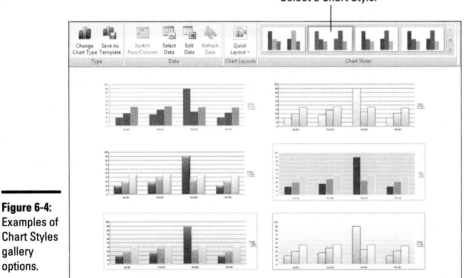

Figure 6-4:
Examples of
Chart Styles
gallery
options.

If your file includes more than one chart, make the charts consistent with one another. Give them a similar appearance so that your file doesn't turn into a chart fashion show. You can make charts consistent with one another by choosing similar options for charts in the Chart Styles gallery.

Changing the layout of a chart

Figure 6-5 identifies the chart elements that you can lay out in different ways. Some of these elements can be removed as well as placed on different parts of a chart. For example, you can display the legend on any side of a chart or not display it at all. Some of the elements can be labeled in different ways. To decide on the layout of a chart, select it and then visit the (Chart Tools) Layout tab.

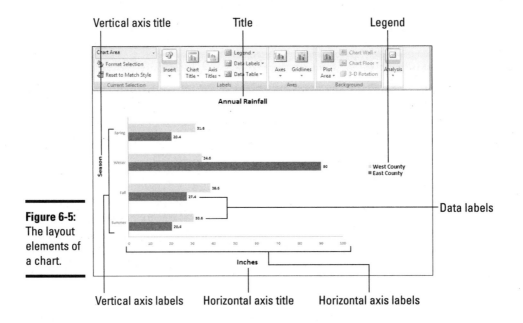

Figure 6-5:
The layout elements of a chart.

Vertical axis title   Title   Legend

Vertical axis labels   Horizontal axis title   Horizontal axis labels

Data labels

The following explains how to change the layout of a chart starting on the (Chart Tools) Layout tab. However, before hurrying to the Layout tab to change your chart's layout, you may consider taking a detour to the (Chart Tools) Design tab (refer to Figure 6-4). The Chart Layouts gallery on the Design tab offers ten ready-made layouts, one of which may meet your high expectations and spare you a trip to the Layout tab.

Deciding where chart elements appear and how they are labeled

The first four buttons on the Labels group of the Layout tab are for determining where elements appear on your chart and how or whether these elements are labeled. Open the drop-down list on these buttons and choose options to determine how and whether chart elements are labeled:

◆ **Chart Title:** The chart title appears above the chart and describes what the chart is about (see Figure 6-5). Place a centered title inside or above the chart. The Above Chart option shrinks the chart a bit to make room for the title. Click in the text box and enter the title after Office creates a chart title text box.

◆ **Axis Titles:** Axis titles list the series name and category name of the data being plotted in the chart (see Figure 6-5). You can select Rotated Title for the vertical axis to make the axis label read vertically instead of horizontally (see Figure 6-5).

◆ **Legend:** The legend is the box to the side, top, or bottom of the chart that describes what is being plotted (see Figure 6-5). Choose an option from the drop-down list to place the chart's legend above, below, or to the side of a chart.

◆ **Data Labels:** Data labels show the numeric values by which the data markers — the bars, columns, pie slices, or dots — in your chart are constructed (refer to Figure 6-5). For example, if a bar in your chart represents the number 400, the data label 400 appears in the bar. You can also label the series name or category name by choosing More Data Label Options on the drop-down list and making selections in the Format Data Labels dialog box.

◆ **Axes:** The axes labels are the series names and scale markers that appear in the chart. Choose Primary Horizontal Axis or Primary Vertical Axis and then select None to remove series names and scale markers from your chart. The other axes options are for deciding how to display axes labels (and are explained in the next section of this chapter).

Deciding how the chart's scale and axes labels are presented

The labels and scale on the horizontal and vertical axes of a chart tell viewers what is being plotted on the chart. By clicking the Axes button on the (Chart Tools) Layout tab (refer to Figure 6-5), you can fine-tune the axes labels and scale on your chart.

After you click the Axes button, you see options for changing around your chart's horizontal or vertical axis. What the horizontal and vertical axis options are depends on whether the axis you're dealing with presents text labels, expresses numerical values, or expresses date values.

Text axis options

Choose a text axis option on the drop-down list to remove the labels or present category name labels in reverse order from the way in which these labels are listed on the worksheet.

Numerical and date axis options

The axis options that pertain to numbers and dates are for declaring how to present the scale on your chart. You can present the numbers in thousands, millions, billions, or with a log scale. By opening the Format Axis dialog box, as shown in Figure 6-6, you can get quite specific about how the scale is presented on your chart. To open this dialog box, click the Axes button, choose the appropriate axis option on the drop-down list, and choose More Options on the submenu. Which options you see in this dialog box depends greatly on which chart type you're dealing with.

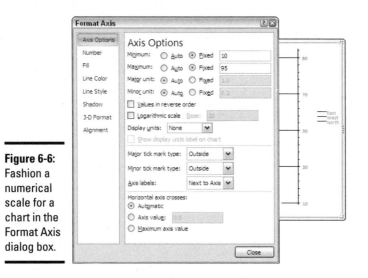

Figure 6-6:
Fashion a numerical scale for a chart in the Format Axis dialog box.

The Format Axis dialog box offers these opportunities for changing around the scale of a chart:

✦ **Changing the scale's range:** By default, the scale ranges from 0 to 10 percent more than the largest value being plotted, but you can change the scale's range by selecting a Fixed option button and entering a new value in the Minimum and Maximum text box.

✦ **Changing the number of unit measurement labels:** Label measurements (and gridlines) appear at intervals on a chart according to the number entered in the Major Unit text box. For example, an entry of 10 tells Office to mark each 10 units with a measurement label. Select the Fixed option button and change the number in the Major Unit text box to draw fewer or more unit labels (and gridlines) on your chart. If your chart displays minor tick marks, do the same in the Minor Unit text box.

✦ **Displaying numbers as thousandths, millionths, or billionths:** If your chart presents large numbers, consider listing these numbers in thousandths, millionths, or billionths by selecting an option in the Display Units drop-down list. You can also select the Logarithmic Scale check box to display numbers as logarithms.

✦ **Changing the tick-mark scale markers:** Choose Tick Mark options to tell Office where or whether to place *tick marks* — small unit markers — on the scale.

✦ **Changing the location of axis labels:** Choose an option in the Axis Labels drop-down list to tell Office where to place the unit labels on the scale.

✦ **Change the horizontal axis cross:** Select the Axis Value option button and then enter a measurement in the Axis Value text box if you want to change the baseline of your chart. Usually, the horizontal axis is set at 0, and markers rise from 0 on the chart; but by entering a different measurement, you can make markers rise or fall from the baseline. For example, if the Axis Value baseline is 5, markers less than 5 fall from a baseline in the middle of the chart and markers greater than 5 rise above it.

Handling the gridlines

Gridlines are lines that cross a chart and indicate value measurements. In most charts, you can include major gridlines to show where bars or columns meet or surpass a major unit of measurement. You can also include fainter, minor gridlines that mark less significant measurements. Figure 6-7 shows a chart with gridlines displayed in different ways.

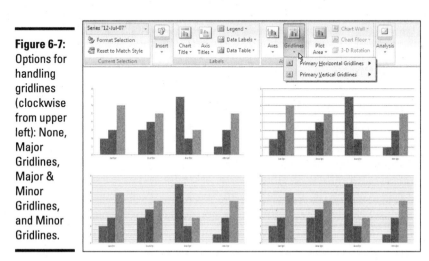

Figure 6-7: Options for handling gridlines (clockwise from upper left): None, Major Gridlines, Major & Minor Gridlines, and Minor Gridlines.

Select your chart and follow these instructions to hide or display gridlines, change the lines' width, or change the lines' color:

✦ **Hiding and choosing the frequency of gridlines:** On the Layout tab, click the Gridlines button, choose Primary Horizontal Gridlines or Primary Vertical Gridlines on the drop-down list, and choose an option on the submenu. You can hide gridlines (by choosing None), display major gridlines, display minor gridlines, or display major and minor gridlines (refer to Figure 6-7).

The frequency of gridlines on a chart is tied to the scale. If you want to control the frequency of the gridlines on your own without relying on a Gridlines option, change your chart's scale. The preceding section in this chapter explains how to handle scales.

✦ **Changing gridline width:** On the Format tab, open the Chart Elements drop-down list and choose Axis Major Gridlines or Axis Minor Gridlines (display gridlines on your chart if you don't see these options). Then click the Format Selection button, and in the Line Style category of the Format Gridlines dialog box, enter a measurement in the Width text box to make the gridlines wider or narrower.

✦ **Changing gridline color:** On the Format tab, open the Chart Elements drop-down list and select Axis Major Gridlines or Axis Minor Gridlines (display gridlines on your chart if you don't see these options). Then open the drop-down list on the Shape Outline button and choose a color. You can also click the Format Selection button, and in the Line category of the Format Gridlines dialog box, select the Solid Line option button and then click the Color Picker button and choose a color there.

Gridlines are essential for helping read charts, but be very, very careful about displaying minor gridlines on charts. These lines can make your chart unreadable. They can turn a perfectly good chart into a gaudy pinstripe suit.

Changing a chart element's color, font, or other particular

Generally speaking, the (Chart Tools) Format tab is the place to go if you want to change the color, line width, font, or font size of a chart element. As I explain shortly, you can do some interior decorating tasks on the Layout tab as well.

Follow these basic steps on the Format tab to change a color, line width, font, or font size in part of a chart:

1. **Select the (Chart Tools) Format tab.**

The tools on the (Chart Tools) Format tab are very similar to the tools found on the (Drawing Tools) Format tab. You can find all the tools you need here to change the color, outline, and size of a chart element. These tools are explained in detail in Book I, Chapter 8.

2. **Select the chart element that needs a facelift.**

To select a chart element, either click it or select its name on the Chart Elements drop-down list. You can find this list in the upper-left corner of the window, as shown in Figure 6-8.

Select part of the chart.   Click the Format Selection button.

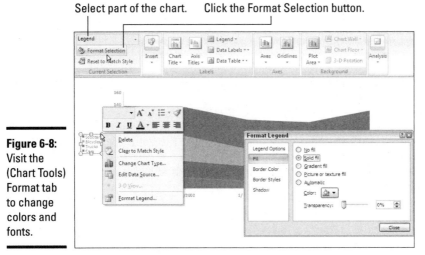

Figure 6-8:
Visit the (Chart Tools) Format tab to change colors and fonts.

3. **Format the chart element you selected.**

Use one of these techniques to format the chart element:

- *Open a Format dialog box.* Click the Format Selection button to open a Format dialog box, as shown in Figure 6-8. The dialog box offers commands for formatting the element you select.

- *Do the work on your own.* Format the chart element as you would any object. For example, to change fonts in the chart element you select, right-click and then choose a font in the Mini Toolbar, as shown in Figure 6-8. Or go to the Home tab to change font sizes. Or open the drop-down list on the Shape Fill button on the Format tab and select a new color.

The (Chart Tools) Layout tab also offers these convenient commands for changing the color of a chart element:

✦ **Plot area:** The *plot area* is the rectangle in which the chart's gridlines, bars, columns, pie slices, or lines appear. In some chart designs, the plot area is filled with color. To remove this color or choose a different color, click the Plot Area button and choose an option. Choose More Plot Area Options to open the Format Plot Area dialog box and select a new fill color.

✦ **3D chart wall and chart floor:** Three-dimensional charts have chart walls and a chart floor. The *chart wall* forms the backdrop of a 3D chart; the *chart floor* forms the bottom of the chart. Click the Chart Wall button and choose an option to remove the chart wall or change its color; click the Chart Floor button and choose an option to remove the chart floor or change its color.

Saving a Chart as a Template so You Can Use It Again

If you go to the significant trouble of redecorating a chart and you expect to do it again the same way in the future, save your chart as a template. This way, you can call on the template in the future to create the same chart and not have to decorate it again. Perhaps you've created charts with your company's colors or you've created a chart that you're especially proud of. Save it as a template to spare yourself the work of reconstructing it.

A chart template holds data series colors, gridline settings, plot area colors, font settings, and the like. It doesn't hold data. These pages explain how to save a chart as a template and how to create a chart with a template you created.

Saving a chart as a template

Follow these steps to make a template out of a chart:

1. **Save your file to make sure the chart settings are saved on your computer.**

2. **Select your chart.**

3. **Click the (Chart Tools) Design tab.**

4. **Click the Save As Template button.**

   You can find this button in the Type group. You see the Save Chart Template dialog box.

5. Enter a descriptive name for the template and click the Save button.

Include the type of chart you're dealing with in the name. This helps you understand which template you're selecting when the time comes to choose a chart template.

By default, chart templates are saved in this folder in Windows XP:

```
C:\Documents and Settings\Username\Application
     Data\Microsoft\Templates\Charts
```

In computers that run Windows Vista, chart templates are saved in this folder:

```
C:\Users\Username\AppData\Roaming\
     Microsoft\Templates\Charts
```

The templates have the .rctrx extension. If you want to delete or rename a template, open the Charts folder in Windows Explorer or My Computer and do your deleting and renaming there. You can open the Charts folder very quickly by clicking the Manage Templates button in the Insert Chart dialog box.

Creating a chart from a template

To create a chart from your own customized template, open the Create Chart dialog box and then click Templates in the dialog box. The dialog box shows a list of templates you created. Move the pointer over a template to read its name in a pop-up box. Select a template and click OK.

Chart Tricks for the Daring and Heroic

This chapter wouldn't be complete without a handful of chart tricks to impress your friends and intimidate your enemies. In the pages that follow, you discover how to make charts roll over and play dead. You also find out how to decorate a chart with a picture, annotate a chart, display worksheet data alongside a chart, and create an overlay chart.

Decorating a chart with a picture

As shown in Figure 6-9, a picture looks mighty nice on the plot area of a chart — especially a column chart. If you have a picture in your computer that would serve well to decorate a chart, you are hereby encouraged to start decorating. Follow these steps to place a picture in the plot area of a chart:

1. Select your chart.

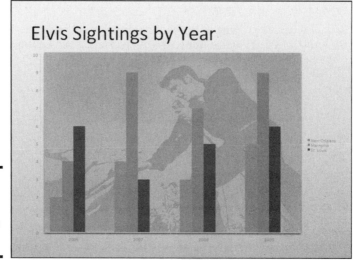

Elvis Sightings by Year

Figure 6-9:
Use a picture as the backdrop of a chart.

 Shape Fill ▾

2. On the (Chart Tools) Format tab, open the drop-down list on the Shape Fill button and choose Picture.

You see the Insert Picture dialog box.

3. Locate the picture you need and select it.

Try to select a light-colored picture that will serve as a background. Book VIII, Chapter 3 explains how you can recolor a picture to make it lighter.

4. Click the Insert button.

The picture lands in your chart.

5. On the (Chart Tools) Format tab, open the Chart Elements drop-down list and choose Plot Area.

In Word and Excel, the plot area obscures the picture. In the next step, you fix this problem.

Shape Fill ▾ **6. Still in the (Chart Tools) Format tab, open the drop-down list on the Shape Fill button and choose No Fill.**

You may need to change the color of the *data markers* — the columns, bars, lines, or pie slices — on your chart to make them stand out against the picture you chose. See "Changing a chart element's color, font, or other particular," earlier in this chapter.

Annotating a chart

To highlight part of a chart — an especially large pie slice, a tall column, or a bar showing miniscule sales figures — annotate it with a callout text box and place the text box beside the pie slice, column, or bar. Figure 6-10 shows an example of an annotated chart. The annotation tells you that one sector isn't performing especially well and somebody ought to get on the ball.

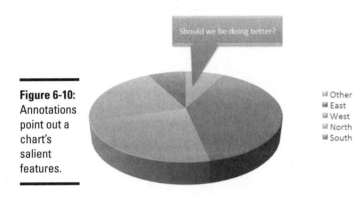

Figure 6-10: Annotations point out a chart's salient features.

To annotate a chart, select a callout shape, enter text in the callout shape, and connect the shape to part of your chart. Follow these steps to annotate a chart:

1. **Select your chart and go to the (Chart Tools) Layout tab.**

2. **Click the Shapes button, scroll to the Callouts section of the drop-down list, and choose a callout.**

   Depending on the size of your screen, you may have to click the Insert button to get to the Shapes button.

3. **Drag your slide to draw the callout shape.**

   Book I, Chapter 8 explains drawing shapes in gory detail.

4. **Type the annotation inside the callout shape.**

5. **Resize the callout shape as necessary to make it fit with the chart.**

6. **Drag the yellow diamond on the callout shape to attach the callout to the chart.**

   You probably have to do some interior decorating to make the callout color fit with the chart. Book I, Chapter 8 explains how to change an object's color.

Displaying the raw data alongside the chart

Showing the worksheet data used to produce a chart is sort of like showing the cops your I.D. It proves you're the real thing. It makes your chart more authentic. If yours is a simple pie chart or other chart that wasn't generated with a large amount of raw data, you can display the data alongside your chart in a data table. Anyone who sees the table knows you're not kidding or fudging the numbers.

Select your chart and use of one of these techniques to place a table with the raw data below your chart:

✦ In the (Chart Tools) Layout tab, click the Data Table button and choose an option on the drop-down list.

✦ In the (Chart Tools) Design tab, open the Chart Layouts gallery and select a layout that includes a data table.

To format a data table, go to the (Chart Tools) Format tab and select Data Table in the Chart Elements drop-down list. Then click the Format Selection button. You see the Format Data Table dialog box, where you can fill the table with color and choose colors for the lines in the table.

Creating an overlay chart

An *overlay chart* is a secondary chart that appears over another chart, the idea is to contrast two sets of data. Create an overlay chart by selecting one data series in a chart you already created and instructing Office to use the data in the series for the overlay chart. To create an overlay chart, the original chart must plot more than one data series. Figure 6-11 shows a bar chart overlaying a stacked area chart.

Figure 6-11:
An overlay chart — in this case, a bar chart overlaying a stacked area chart.

Yields at Blue, Muddy, and Mirror Lake

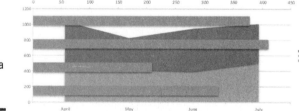

Follow these steps to create an overlay chart:

1. **In a chart you created, click to select the data series that you will use to create the secondary chart.**

    The easiest way to select a data series is to click the chart itself, but you can also go to the (Chart Tools) Format tab and choose a series in the Chart Elements drop-down list.

2. **Right-click the data series you selected and choose Change Series Chart Type.**

    You see the Change Chart Type dialog box.

3. **Choose a chart type for the overlay chart and click OK.**

    Be sure to click a chart type different from the one in the other chart.

Troubleshooting a Chart

Sometimes tinkering with a chart opens a Pandora's Box of problems. You find yourself having to correct little errors that appear in charts. Here are some shorthand instructions for fixing common chart problems:

✦ *The dates in the chart aren't formatted right:* Dates in a chart are inherited from the Excel worksheet from which the chart is generated. Therefore, to change date formats, you have to go back to the worksheet and change date formats there. Book V, Chapter 1 explains how to format dates and numbers in Excel.

✦ *The numbers in the chart aren't formatted right:* To change the number of decimal places, include comma separators in numbers, display currency symbols, or do all else that pertains to numbers, click the (Chart Tools) Format tab, open the Chart Elements drop-down list, and choose Horizontal (Value) Axis or Vertical (Value) Axis. Then click the Format Selection button. You see the Format Axis dialog box. Click the Number category and select options for displaying numbers.

✦ *"Category 1" or "Series 1" appears in the chart legend:* To direct you to the right place to enter data in Excel worksheets, phantom names such as "Category 1" and "Series 1" appear in worksheets. Sometimes these phantoms wind up in chart legends as well. To remove them, click the Select Data button on the Design tab. The Excel worksheet and the Select Data Source dialog box open. Select Category 1 or Series 1 in the dialog box, click the Remove button, and click OK.

✦ *In 3D charts, small markers are obscured by large markers in the foreground:*
For all the data markers to be shown in a 3D chart, the smaller ones
have to be in the foreground. To rearrange data markers, go to the
Design tab, click the Select Data button to open the Select Data Source
dialog box. Then select a series and click the Up or Down button to
rearrange the series in your chart. Series that are high on the list go to
the back of the chart; series that are low on the list go to the front.

✦ *The chart doesn't gather all data from the worksheet:* Click the trusty
Select Data Source button to open the Select Data Source dialog box.
In the dialog box, click the Chart Data Range button (it's located to the
right of the Chart Data Range text box). Then, on the Excel worksheet,
drag to select the data you want to generate your chart and press Enter.
Click OK in the Select Data Source dialog box.

✦ *The scale is too big for my chart:* Especially if the scale range on a chart is
small, the scale can be too big compared to the data markers. To change
the scale range, go to the (Chart Tools) Layout tab, click the Axes
button, choose the appropriate axis option on the drop-down list, and
choose More Options. Then in the Format Axis dialog box, select the
Fixed option button and enter a Maximum value to establish the top of
the scale for your chart. For more details, see "Deciding how the chart's
scale and axes labels are presented," earlier in this chapter.

Chapter 7: Making a SmartArt Diagram

In This Chapter

✔ Creating a diagram

✔ Repositioning and resizing diagrams

✔ Laying out and changing the look of diagram shapes

✔ Entering text on a diagram shape

✔ Changing the appearance of a diagram

✔ Creating a diagram from shapes

*A*long with charts and tables, diagrams are the best way to present your ideas. Diagrams clearly show, for example, employees' relationships with one another, product cycles, workflow processes, and spheres of influence. A diagram is an excellent marriage of images and words. Diagrams allow an audience to literally visualize a concept, idea, or relationship.

This chapter explains how to construct diagrams from SmartArt graphics and how to create a diagram. It shows how to customize diagrams by changing the size of diagrams and diagram shapes, adding and removing shapes, and changing shapes' colors. You also discover how to change the direction of a diagram and enter the text. Finally, this chapter demonstrates how to create a diagram from scratch with shapes and connectors.

The Basics: Creating SmartArt Diagrams

In Word, PowerPoint, and Excel, diagrams are made from *SmartArt graphics*. These diagram graphics are "interactive" in the sense that you can move, alter, and write text on them. In other words, you can use them to construct diagrams. Because SmartArt graphics are based on the eXtensible Markup Language (XML) format (Book I, Chapter 1 explains XML), you can alter them to your liking. You can make the diagram portray precisely what you want it to portray, although you usually have to wrestle with the diagram a bit.

The first step in creating a diagram is to select a layout in the dialog box, as shown in Figure 7-1. After you create the initial diagram, you customize it to create a diagram of your own. About 80 diagrams are in the dialog box. They fall into these seven types:

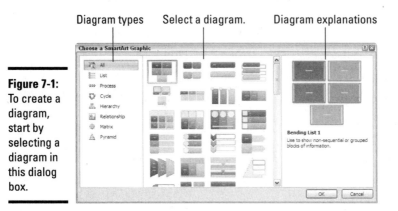

Figure 7-1: To create a diagram, start by selecting a diagram in this dialog box.

Diagram Type	Use
List	For describing blocks of related information as well as sequential steps in a task, process, or workflow
Process	For describing how a concept or physical process changes over time or is modified
Cycle	For illustrating a circular progression without a beginning or end, or a relationship in which the components are in balance
Hierarchy	For describing hierarchical relationships between people, departments, and other entities, as well as portraying branchlike relationships in which one decision or action leads to another
Relationship	For describing the relationship between different components (but not hierarchical relationships)
Matrix	For showing the relationship between quadrants
Pyramid	For showing proportional or hierarchical relationships

If you intend to construct a "flow chart type" diagram with many branches and levels, go to the Hierarchy category and select the Organization Chart or one of the hierarchy diagrams. As "Laying Out the Diagram Shapes" explains later in this chapter, only these choices permit you to make a diagram with many different branches and levels.

After you select a generic diagram in the Choose a SmartArt Graphic dialog box and click OK, the next step is to make the diagram your own by completing these tasks:

✦ **Change the diagram's size and position:** Change the size and position of a diagram to make it fit squarely on your slide. See "Changing the Size and Position of a Diagram," later in this chapter.

✦ **Add shapes to (or remove shapes from) the diagram:** Adding a shape involves declaring where to add the shape, promoting or demoting the shape with respect to other shapes, and declaring how the new shape connects to another shape. See "Laying Out the Diagram Shapes," later in this chapter.

✦ **Enter text:** Enter text on each shape, or component, of the diagram. See "Handling the Text on Diagram Shapes," later in this chapter.

If you so desire, you can also customize your diagram by taking on some or all of these tasks:

✦ **Changing its overall appearance:** Choose a different color scheme or 3D variation for your diagram. See "Choosing a Look for Your Diagram," later in this chapter.

✦ **Changing shapes:** Select a new shape for part of your diagram, change the size of a shape, or assign different colors to shapes to make shapes stand out. See "Changing the Appearance of Diagram Shapes," later in this chapter.

If you're comfortable creating a diagram of your own by drawing shapes and lines, no law says you have to begin in the Choose a SmartArt Graphic dialog box. Later in this chapter, "Creating a Diagram from Scratch" looks into creating a diagram by making use of text boxes, lines, and shapes.

Creating the Initial Diagram

The first step in fashioning a diagram is to choose a SmartArt graphic in the Choose a SmartArt Graphic dialog box. After that, you roll up your sleeves, change the diagram's size and shape, and enter the text. If you select the wrong diagram to start with, all is not lost. You can choose another diagram in its place, although how successful swapping one diagram for another is depends on how lucky you are and how far along you are in creating your diagram. These pages explain how to create an initial diagram and swap one diagram for another.

Creating a diagram

Follow these steps to create a diagram:

1. On the Insert tab, click the SmartArt button.

You see the Choose a SmartArt Graphic dialog box (refer to Figure 7-1). In PowerPoint, you can also open the dialog box by clicking the SmartArt icon in a content placeholder frame.

2. Select a diagram in the Choose a SmartArt Graphic dialog box.

Diagrams are divided into seven types, as I explain earlier in this chapter. The dialog box offers a description of each diagram. Either select a type on the left side of the dialog box or scroll the entire list to find the graphic that most resembles the diagram you want.

In the Hierarchy category, select the Organization Chart, Hierarchy, or Horizontal Hierarchy if you want to create a graph with many levels and branches. These three diagrams are much more complex than the others. See "Laying Out the Diagram Shapes," later in this chapter, for details.

3. Click OK.

The next section in this chapter explains how to swap one diagram for another, in case you chose wrongly in the Choose a SmartArt Graphic dialog box.

Starting from a sketch

You can spare yourself a lot of trouble by starting from a sketch when you create a diagram. Find a pencil with a good eraser, grab a blank piece of paper, and start drawing. Imagine what your ideal diagram looks like. Draw the arrows or lines connecting the different parts of the diagram. Write the text. Draw the diagram that best illustrates what you want to communicate.

Later, in the Choose a SmartArt Graphic dialog box (refer to Figure 7-1), you can select the diagram that most resembles the one you sketched. The dialog box offers about 80 types of diagrams. Unless you start from a sketch and have a solid idea of the diagram you want, you can get lost in the dialog box. Also, if you don't start from a sketch, adding shapes to the diagram and landing them in the right places can be a chore.

Swapping one diagram for another

If the diagram you chose initially doesn't do the job, you can swap it for a different diagram. How successful the swap is depends on how far along you are in creating your diagram and whether your diagram is simple or complex. Follow these steps to swap one diagram for another:

1. **Click your diagram to select it.**

2. **Click the (SmartArt Tools) Design tab.**

3. **Open the Layout gallery. (You may have to click the Change Layout button first.)**

You see a gallery with diagrams of the same type as the diagram you're working with.

4. **Select a new diagram or choose More Layouts to open the Choose a SmartArt Graphic dialog box and select a diagram there.**

You may have to click the trusty Undo button and start all over if the diagram you selected for the swap didn't do the job.

Changing the Size and Position of a Diagram

To make a diagram fit squarely on a page or slide, you have to change its size and position. Resizing and positioning diagrams and other objects is the subject of Book I, Chapter 8, but in case you don't care to travel that far to get instructions, here are shorthand instructions for resizing and positioning diagrams:

✦ **Resizing a diagram:** Select the diagram, move the pointer over a selection handle on the corner or side, and start dragging after the pointer changes into a two-headed arrow. You can also go to the (SmartArt Tools) Format tab and enter new measurements in the Width and Height boxes (you may have to click the Size button to see these text boxes, depending on the size of your screen).

✦ **Repositioning a diagram:** Select the diagram, move the pointer over its perimeter, and when you see the four-headed arrow, click and start dragging.

Notice when you resize a diagram that the shapes in the diagram change size proportionally. Most diagrams are designed so that shapes fill out the diagram. When you change the size of a diagram, remove a shape from a diagram, or add a shape, shapes change size within the diagram.

Laying Out the Diagram Shapes

At the heart of every diagram are the rectangles, circles, arrows, and what-nots that make the diagram what it is. These shapes illustrate the concept or idea you want to express to your audience. Your biggest challenge when creating a diagram is laying out the diagram shapes.

How you add shapes depends on what kind of diagram you're working with. Hierarchy diagrams present problems where adding shapes is concerned because these diagrams branch into many levels and can be very complex. For that reason, the techniques for adding shapes to hierarchy diagrams are different from the techniques for adding shapes to the other diagrams.

These pages explain how to select diagram shapes, add shapes, and remove shapes from diagrams. They offer instructions specific to working with hierarchy diagrams.

Selecting a diagram shape

Before you can remove a shape from a diagram or indicate where you want to add a new shape, you have to select a diagram shape. Selecting a shape isn't simply a matter of clicking if text has been written on the shape. Follow these instructions to select a diagram shape:

✦ **Selecting a shape with text:** Click the shape twice, as shown in Figure 7-2. First, click anywhere in the shape and then move the pointer to the perimeter of the shape; click after a four-headed arrow appears beside the pointer.

✦ **Selecting a shape without text:** Simply click anywhere in the shape.

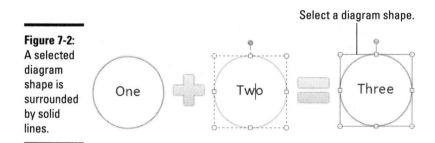

Select a diagram shape.

Figure 7-2: A selected diagram shape is surrounded by solid lines.

You can tell when a diagram shape is selected because a solid, not a dotted line, appears around the shape (see Figure 7-2). When you see dotted lines around a shape, you're expected to enter text.

Removing a shape from a diagram

Removing a shape from a diagram is as easy as falling off a turnip truck as long as you correctly select the shape before you remove it (the preceding section in this chapter explains how to select shapes). To remove a shape, select it and then press Delete. Other shapes grow larger when you remove a shape in keeping with the "fill out the diagram by any means necessary" philosophy.

Adding shapes to diagrams apart from hierarchy diagrams

Unlike hierarchy diagrams, list, process, cycle, relationship, and matrix diagrams don't have branches. They always travel in one direction only. This makes adding shapes to these diagrams fairly straightforward. To add a shape, you select a shape in the diagram and then add the new shape so that it appears before or after the shape you selected, as shown in Figure 7-3.

Choose Add Shape After or Add Shape Before.   Select a shape.   The new shape.

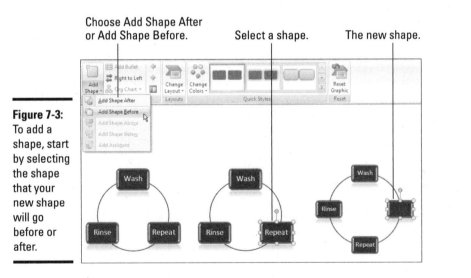

Figure 7-3:
To add a shape, start by selecting the shape that your new shape will go before or after.

Follow these steps to add a shape to a list, process, cycle, relationship, matrix, or pyramid diagram:

1. **In your diagram, select the shape that your new shape will appear before or after.**

Earlier in this chapter, "Selecting a diagram shape" explains how to select shapes.

2. Choose the Add Shape After or Add Shape Before command.

To get to these commands, use one of these techniques:

- On the (SmartArt Tools) Design tab, open the drop-down list on the Add Shape button and choose Add Shape After or Add Shape Before, as shown in Figure 7-3.

- Right-click the shape you selected, choose Add Shape on the short-cut menu, and then choose Add Shape After or Add Shape Before on the submenu.

The new shape appears in your diagram.

Although the Add Shape drop-down list offers an Add Shape Above and Add Shape Below command (see Figure 7-3), these commands don't apply to list, process, cycle, relationship, or matrix diagrams. Ignore them. They're strictly for hierarchy and pyramid diagrams.

Adding shapes to hierarchy diagrams

Hierarchy diagrams are more complex than other diagrams because they branch out such that shapes are found on different levels. This branching out makes adding shapes to hierarchy diagrams problematic.

In the first place, the Add Shape commands do different things on hierarchy diagrams, depending on whether the diagram is horizontally or vertically oriented. In hierarchy diagrams, you can promote and demote shapes. You can't do that in other diagrams. If you're working with an Organization Chart, you get a set of commands — the Layout commands — for making shapes *hang* rather than fall below other shapes.

These pages explain how to add shapes to vertically oriented diagrams, horizontally oriented diagrams, and Organization Charts. (One hierarchy diagram, Hierarchy List, is just two right-hanging diagram shapes, and it isn't truly a hierarchy diagram.)

Adding shapes to horizontally oriented diagrams

A *horizontally oriented diagram* (Horizontal Hierarchy and Horizontal Labeled Hierarchy) is a simple branching, horizontal diagram. In a horizontally oriented diagram, shapes can branch only from a shape in the level above; shapes can't branch sideways from one another, as they can in an Organization Chart diagram. Figure 7-4 shows a Horizontal Hiserarchy diagram along with the Add Shape drop-down list for adding shapes to diagrams.

As Figure 7-4 shows, the Add Shape commands are a little cockeyed when you apply them to a horizontally oriented diagram. The Add Shape Above command, for example, places a new shape to the left, not above, the shape you selected. For the purpose of adding shapes to horizontally oriented diagrams, the Add Shape commands are based on rank, not gravity. The Add

Shape Above command, for example, places a new shape a rank above, not directly above, another shape.

Follow these steps to add a shape to a horizontally oriented diagram:

1. **In your diagram, select the shape to which your new shape will be connected.**

Earlier in this chapter, "Selecting a diagram shape" demonstrates how to select a shape.

2. **Choose an Add Shape command.**

Figure 7-4 shows what Add Shape commands do. You can choose Add Shape commands with one of these techniques:

- On the (SmartArt Tools) Design tab, open the drop-down list on the Add Shape button and choose an Add Shape command (refer to Figure 7-4).

- Right-click the shape you selected, choose Add Shape on the short-cut menu, and then choose an Add Shape command.

In effect, you choose two commands when you choose Add Shape Above — you insert a shape above the shape you selected and you demote the shape you selected to the next level in the hierarchy. The Add Shape Above command demotes the shape you selected to the next lowest level to make room for the new shape. Rather than choose the Add Shape Above command, you might consider selecting a shape in the level above and then choosing the Add Shape Below command.

Choose an Add Shape command.   Select a shape.

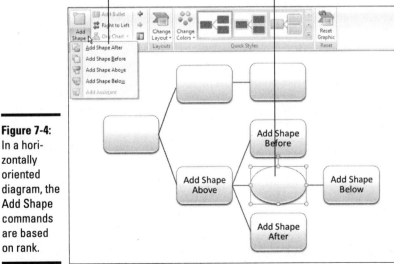

Figure 7-4:
In a hori-
zontally
oriented
diagram, the
Add Shape
commands
are based
on rank.

Adding shapes to vertically oriented diagrams

Follow these steps to add a shape to the vertically oriented Hierarchy, Labeled Hierarchy, or Table Hierarchy diagram:

1. **Select the shape to which your new shape will be connected.**

Earlier in this chapter, "Selecting a diagram shape" demonstrates how to select a shape.

2. **Choose an Add Shape command.**

You can choose Add Shape commands with either of these techniques:

- On the (SmartArt Tools) Design tab, open the drop-down list on the Add Shape button and choose an Add Shape command.

- Right-click the shape you selected, choose Add Shape on the short-cut menu, and then choose an Add Shape command.

The Add Shape Before command places the new shape to the left of the shape you selected; the Add Shape After command places the new shape to the right.

Be careful about choosing the Add Shape Above command because it inserts a new shape above the one you selected and demotes the selected shape. You add another layer to the hierarchy when you select the Add Shape Above command.

Handling shapes on Organization Charts

An Organization Chart offers many opportunities for connecting shapes. The shapes can branch out from one another in four directions as well as appear to the side in the "assistant" position. When you place one shape below another shape, you can make the new shape *hang* so that it is joined to a line, not joined directly to the shape above it. Figure 7-5 shows what hanging shapes look like. Compare the standard connection to the hanging connections — Left Hanging, Right Hanging, and Both. Hanging shapes connect to a line that drops, or hangs, from a shape above.

To add a shape to an Organization Chart diagram, decide where you want the shape to go, and if you want to place one shape below another, decide whether you want a hanging or standard relationship. These pages explain how to add shapes and create hanging relationships between one shape and the shapes below it.

Click the Layout button to establish a hanging relationship between shapes.

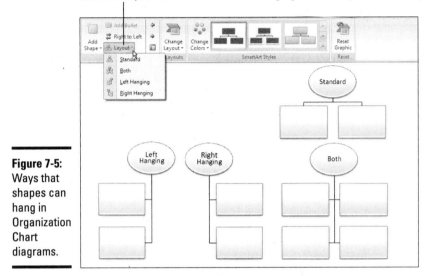

Figure 7-5:
Ways that
shapes can
hang in
Organization
Chart
diagrams.

Adding a shape

Follow these steps to add a shape to an Organization Chart diagram:

***1.* Select the shape to which you will add a new shape.**

Earlier in this chapter, "Selecting a diagram shape" explains how to
select shapes. As shown in Figure 7-6, shapes are surrounded by solid
lines, not dotted lines, when you select them properly.

***2.* Choose an Add Shape command.**

You can choose Add Shape commands in two ways:

* On the (SmartArt Tools) Design tab, open the drop-down list on the
Add Shape button and choose an Add Shape command (see Figure 7-6).

* Right-click the shape you selected, choose Add Shape on the shortcut menu, and then choose an Add Shape command on the submenu.

Figure 7-6 demonstrates what the Add Shape commands do. Notice that
Add Shape Before places a new shape to the left of the shape you selected;
Add Shape After places a new shape to the right.

Be careful about choosing the Add Shape Above command. This command effectively bumps the shape you selected to a lower level in order
to make room for the new shape. In effect, you demote one shape when
you place a new shape above it.

Choose an Add Shape command.　　　　　　Select a shape.

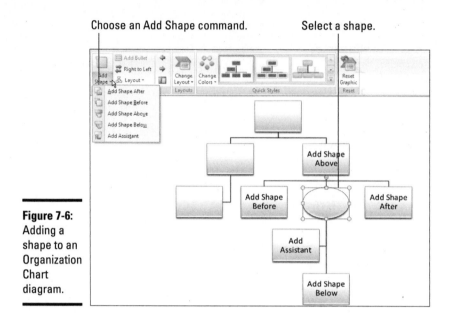

Figure 7-6:
Adding a
shape to an
Organization
Chart
diagram.

The Add Assistant command creates an intermediary shape between two levels, as shown in Figure 7-6. The command is called "Add Assistant" because assistants don't have a ranking in organization charts. Executive assistants, secretaries, and the like are attached to the bigwigs of the organization and don't have a real place in the hierarchy, although everyone knows they do most of the work.

Add Assistant shapes land on the left side of the line to which they're attached, but if you prefer the assistant shape to be on the right side of the line, you can drag it to the right.

Hanging a shape below another shape

Besides the standard relationship between shapes above and below one another, you can create a *hanging relationship*. Earlier in this chapter, Figure 7-5 shows the three kinds of hanging relationships — Both, Left Hanging, and Right Hanging. In a hanging relationship, the line hangs from a shape, and subordinate shapes are connected to the line.

You can create a hanging relationship between shapes before or after you create the subordinate shapes. Follow these steps to create a hanging relationship:

1. **Select the shape to which other shapes will hang or are hanging.**

2. **Select the (SmartArt Tools) Design tab.**

3. **Click the Layout button (refer to Figure 7-5).**

4. **Select an option on the drop-down list — Both, Left Hanging, or Right Hanging.**

   The Standard option on the drop-down list is for creating a standard relationship, not a hanging relationship.

Promoting and demoting shapes in hierarchy diagrams

Shapes in hierarchy diagrams are ranked by level. If a shape is on the wrong level, you can move it higher or lower in the diagram by clicking the Promote or Demote button on the (SmartArt Tools) Design tab. Promoting and demoting shapes can turn into a donnybrook if you aren't careful. If the shapes being promoted or demoted are attached to subordinate shapes, the subordinate shapes are promoted or demoted as well. This can have unforeseen and sometimes horrendous consequences.

Follow these steps to promote or demote a shape (and its subordinates) in a hierarchy diagram:

1. **Select the shape that needs a change of rank.**

   You can select more than one shape by Ctrl+clicking.

2. **Select the (SmartArt Tools) Design tab.**

3. **Click the Promote or Demote button.**

   Do you like what you see? If not, you may have to click the Undo button and start all over.

Handling the Text on Diagram Shapes

When you create a new diagram, "[Text]" (the word *Text* enclosed in brackets) appears on shapes. Your job is to replace this generic placeholder with something more meaningful and less bland. These pages explain how to enter text and bulleted lists on shapes. You also discover how to enter text on shapes you create. These shapes don't come with the generic [Text], which makes entering the text slightly problematic.

Entering text on a shape

You can click in the middle of a shape and start typing to enter text, or you can visit the Text pane, which provides another, simpler way to enter text. Follow these steps to open the Text pane and enter the text there:

1. **Select your diagram.**

2. **Select the (SmartArt Tools) Design tab.**

3. **Either click the Text Pane button or click the same button to the left of the diagram.**

> The Text pane opens to the left of the diagram, as shown on the bottom of Figure 7-7. The figure also shows the two places you can click to open the Text pane.

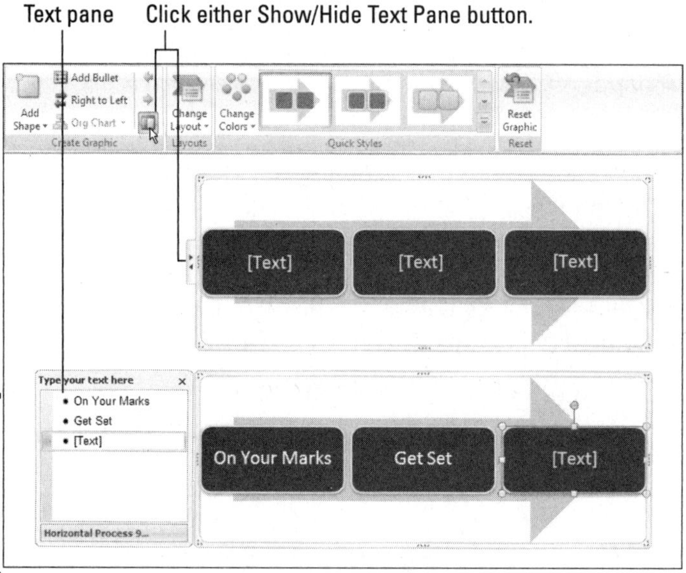

Text pane   Click either Show/Hide Text Pane button.

Figure 7-7:
The easiest way to enter text is on the Text pane.

4. **Enter the text in the Text pane.**

> As you enter text, the diagram shapes are selected so that you know which shape you're entering text on.

5. **Click the Close button (the *X*) in the Text pane to close the pane.**

> If you make a spelling error, click either Text Pane button to reopen the Text pane and correct it.

The text in diagrams shrinks as you enter more text so that all text is the same size. If you want to make the text larger or smaller in one shape, see "Changing fonts and font sizes on shapes," later in this chapter.

Entering text in a diagram shape you added

Diagram shapes you add on your own don't come with the generic [Text] placeholder. Select your newly minted shape and do one of the following to enter text on it:

 ✦ Click the Text Pane button to display the Text pane (see Figure 7-7). You see a blank place in the Text pane for entering text for your new shape. Enter the text in the Text pane.

✦ Click in the diagram shape and start typing. That's all there is to it.

Turning a bulleted list into a diagram

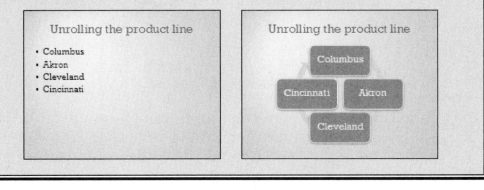

Suppose you're working along when suddenly it strikes you — a bulleted list in a text frame or text box would work much better as a diagram. For those occasions, you can click the Convert to SmartArt button. By clicking this button, you can turn the text in a text frame or text box into a diagram. If the text frame or box contains a bulleted list, each bulleted item becomes a diagram shape.

Follow these steps to turn a text frame or text box into a diagram:

1. **Select the text frame or text box.**

2. **Click the Home tab.**

3. **Click the Convert to SmartArt button.**

   You see a drop-down list with basic diagram choices.

4. **Either select a diagram on the list or choose More SmartArt Graphics to open the Choose a SmartArt Graphic dialog box and select a diagram there.**

Entering bulleted lists on diagram shapes

Some diagram shapes have built-in bulleted lists, but no matter — whether a shape is prepared to be bulleted or not, you can enter bullets in a diagram shape. Here are instructions for entering and removing bullets:

✦ **Entering a bulleted list:** Select the shape that needs bullets, and in the (SmartArt Tools) Design tab, click the Add Bullet button. When you click inside the shape, the first bullet appears. Either enter the bulleted items directly into the shape (pressing Enter as you type each entry), or click the Text Pane button to open the Text pane (refer to Figure 7-7) and enter bullets there.

✦ **Removing bulleted items:** Click before the first bulleted entry and keep pressing the Delete key until you have removed all the bulleted items. You can also start in the Text pane (refer to Figure 7-7) and press the Delete key there until you've removed the bulleted items, or drag to select several bulleted items and then press Delete.

Changing a Diagram's Direction

As long as your diagram is horizontally oriented, you can change its direction. As shown in Figure 7-8, you can flip it over such that the rightmost shape in your diagram becomes the leftmost shape, and what was the leftmost shape becomes the rightmost shape. If arrows are in your diagram, the arrows point the opposite direction after you flip the diagram. You can't flip vertically oriented diagrams this way. Sorry, but diagrams that run north to south, not west to east, can't be rolled over.

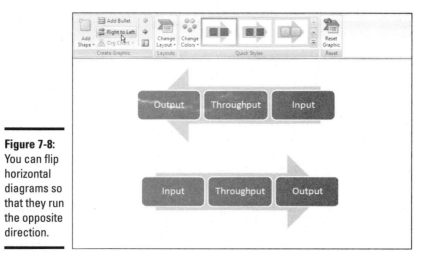

Figure 7-8:
You can flip horizontal diagrams so that they run the opposite direction.

Follow these steps to flip a horizontally oriented diagram like the one in Figure 7-8:

1. **Select the diagram.**

2. **Select the (SmartArt Tools) Design tab.**

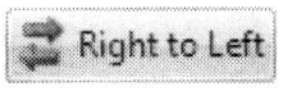

3. **Click the Right to Left button.**

If you don't like what you see, click the button again or click the Undo button.

Choosing a Look for Your Diagram

Decide how a diagram looks by starting on the (SmartArt Tools) Design tab. Starting there, you can choose a color scheme for your diagram and a 3D or other style. Between the Change Colors drop-down list and the SmartArt Styles gallery, you can find a combination of options that presents your diagram in the best light:

✦ **Change Colors drop-down list:** Offers color schemes for your diagram, as shown in Figure 7-9. Point at a few options to "live-preview" them.

✦ **SmartArt Styles gallery:** Offers Simple and 3D variations on the diagram.

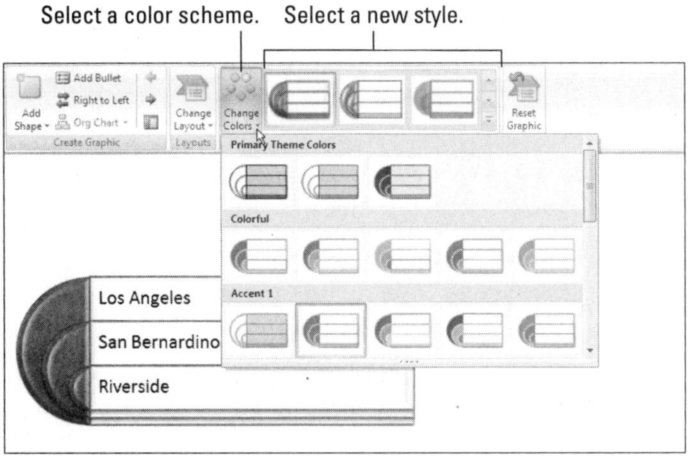

Select a color scheme.   Select a new style.

Figure 7-9:
Experiment
freely with
the Change
Colors and
SmartArt
Styles
gallery
options.

Los Angeles

San Bernardino

Riverside

If you experiment too freely and wish to backpedal, click the Reset Graphic button. Clicking this button reverses all the formatting changes you made to your diagram.

If your Word document, Excel worksheet, or PowerPoint presentation includes many diagrams, make sure your diagrams are consistent in appearance. Choose similar colors for diagrams. If you like 3D diagrams, make the majority of your diagrams 3D. Don't let the diagrams overwhelm the ideas they are meant to express. The point is to present ideas in diagrams, not turn your work into a SmartArt diagram showcase.

Changing the Appearance of Diagram Shapes

To call attention to one part of a diagram, you can change the appearance of a shape and make it stand out. Any part of a diagram that is different from the other parts naturally gets more attention. To change the appearance of a shape, consider changing its size or color, exchanging one shape for another, or changing the font and font size of the text. These topics are covered in the following pages.

Before you can do anything to a diagram shape, you have to properly select it. Earlier in this chapter, "Selecting a diagram shape" explains selecting shapes in detail.

Changing the size of a diagram shape

A shape that is larger than other shapes in a diagram gets the attention of the audience. Select your shape and use one of these techniques to enlarge or shrink it:

✦ In the (SmartArt Tools) Format tab, click the Larger or Smaller button as many times as necessary to make the shape the right size.

✦ Move the pointer over a corner selection handle, and when the pointer changes to a two-headed arrow, click and start dragging.

Notice that the text inside the shape remains the same size although the shape is larger. To change the size of the text in a shape, see "Changing fonts and font sizes on shapes," later in this chapter.

To return a diagram shape to its original size after you've fooled with it, right-click the shape and choose Reset Shape or click the Reshape button on the (SmartArt Tools) Design tab.

Exchanging one shape for another

Another way to call attention to an important part of a diagram is to change shapes, as shown in Figure 7-10. Rather than a conventional shape, use an oval, block arrow, or star. You can substitute a shape in the Shapes gallery for any diagram shape (Book I, Chapter 8 explores the Shapes gallery). To exchange one shape for another in a diagram, select the shape and use one of these techniques:

◆ In the (SmartArt Tools) Format tab, click the Change Shape button and select a shape in the Shapes gallery.

◆ Right-click the shape, choose Change Shape on the shortcut menu, and select a shape on the submenu.

Figure 7-10:
Introducing a different shape in a diagram calls attention to the shape.

Changing a shape's color, fill, or outline

Yet another way to call attention to a shape is to change its color, fill, or outline border. Select a shape and go to the (SmartArt Tools) Format tab, as shown in Figure 7-11, to change a shape's color, fill, or outline.

Figure 7-11:
Ways to make a diagram shape stand out.

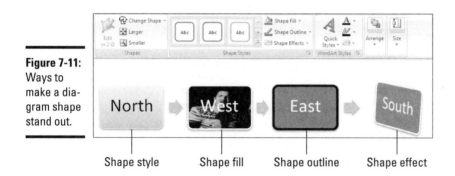

Shape style   Shape fill   Shape outline   Shape effect

◆ **Restyling a shape:** Select an option in the Shape Styles gallery to give a shape a makeover.

◆ **Filling a shape with a new color:** Click the Shape Fill button and make a choice from the drop-down list to choose a color, picture, two-color gradient, or texture for the shape.

◆ **Changing the outline:** Click the Shape Outline button and choose a color and weight for the shape's border on the drop-down list.

◆ **Applying a shape effect:** Click the Shape Effects button to select a shape effect for your shape.

Editing 3D diagrams in 2D

Three-dimensional diagrams are wonderful. You can impress your friends with a 3D diagram. All you have to do to turn a mundane two-dimensional diagram into a three-dimensional showpiece is go to the (SmartArt Tools) Design tab, open the SmartArt Styles gallery, and select a 3D option.

Unfortunately, editing a 3D diagram can be difficult. The shapes and text are all aslant. It's

hard to tell where to click or what to drag when you're editing a 3D diagram.

Fortunately, you can get around the problem of editing a 3D diagram by temporarily displaying it in two dimensions. On the (SmartArt Tools) Format tab, click the Edit in 2-D button to temporarily render a 3D graphic in two dimensions. Click the button a second time to get the third dimension back.

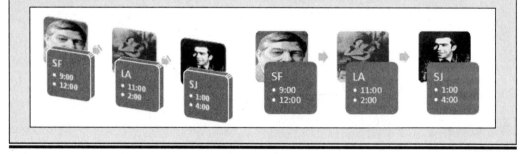

Changing fonts and font sizes on shapes

To make a diagram shape stand out, try changing the font and font size of the text on the diagram. Before you change fonts and font sizes, however, you should know that changing fonts in a shape effectively disconnects the shape from the other shapes in the diagram. Normally when you remove or add a shape in a diagram, the other shapes change size and text on the shapes changes size accordingly. But when you change the font size on one shape, the text on the shape no longer changes along with its brethren.

Follow these steps to choose a different font or font size for the text on a diagram shape:

1. **Select the text.**

2. **Click the Home tab.**

3. **Open the Font Size drop-down list and choose a font size.**

4. **Open the Font drop-down list and choose a font.**

Creating a Diagram from Scratch

If you have the skill and the wherewithal, you can create a diagram from scratch by piecing together shapes, arrows, and connectors on the Insert tab. The diagram in Figure 7-12, for example, was made not from SmartArt graphics but from shapes, arrows, and connectors. Book I, Chapter 8 explains how to draw shapes and lines between shapes. You can enter text on any shape merely by clicking inside it and wiggling your fingers over the keyboard.

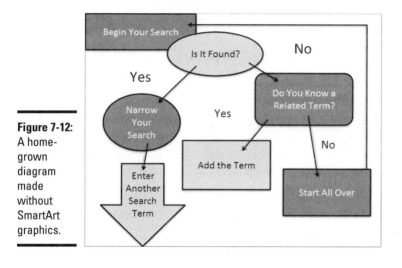

Figure 7-12:
A home-grown diagram made without SmartArt graphics.

Making a diagram from scratch has some advantages. You can draw the connectors any which way. Lines can cross the diagram chaotically. You can include text boxes as well as shapes (the diagram in Figure 7-12 has four text boxes). Don't hesitate to fashion your own diagrams when a presentation or document calls for it.

Chapter 8: Drawing and Manipulating Lines, Shapes, and Other Objects

---

In This Chapter

✔ **Drawing and manipulating lines, arrows, and connectors**

✔ **Creating and modifying shapes**

✔ **Creating WordArt images**

✔ **Selecting, resizing, moving, aligning, overlapping, rotating, and grouping objects**

✔ **Changing the color and border around an object**

*W*hether you know it or not, Office 2007 comes with drawing commands for drawing lines, arrows, shapes, block arrows, stars, banners, and callout shapes. And Office provides numerous ways to manipulate these objects after you draw them. The drawing commands are meant to bring out the artist in you. Use them to make diagrams, fashion your own ideagrams, and illustrate difficult concepts and ideas. Lines and shapes give you a wonderful opportunity to exercise your creativity. A picture is worth a thousand words, so they say, and the drawing commands give you a chance to say it without having to write a thousand words.

In this chapter, you discover all the many ways to manipulate lines, shapes, text boxes, WordArt images, clip-art images, and graphics. You discover how to lay out these objects on a page or slide, flip them, change their colors, resize them, move them, and otherwise torture them until they look just right. You discover how to draw lines and arrows, draw connections between shapes, and draw ovals, squares, and other shapes, as well as WordArt images. Use the techniques I describe in this chapter to bring something more to your Word documents, PowerPoint presentations, and Excel worksheets — originality. With the techniques I describe in this chapter, you can bring the visual element into your work. You can communicate with images as well as words.

The Basics: Drawing Lines, Arrows, and Shapes

Figure 8-1 demonstrates how you can use lines, arrows, and shapes (not to mention text boxes) to illustrate ideas and concepts. Sometimes saying it with lines and shapes is easier and more informative than saying it with words. Even in Excel worksheets, you can find opportunities to use lines, arrows, and shapes. For example, draw arrows and lines on worksheets to illustrate which cells are used to compute formulas.

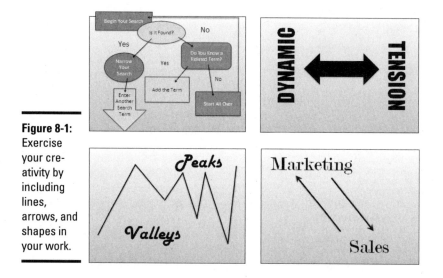

Figure 8-1:
Exercise your creativity by including lines, arrows, and shapes in your work.

Follow these basic steps to draw a line, arrow, or shape:

1. **Click the Insert tab.**

   In Word, you must be in Print Layout view to draw and see lines and shapes. PowerPoint also offers the Shapes button on the Home tab.

2. **Click the Shapes button to open the Insert Shapes gallery.**

   As shown in Figure 8-2, the Shapes gallery appears. The shapes are divided into several categories, including Lines, Basic Shapes, and Block Arrows, as well as a category at the top of the gallery where shapes you chose recently are shown.

3. **Select a line, arrow, or shape in the Insert Shapes gallery.**

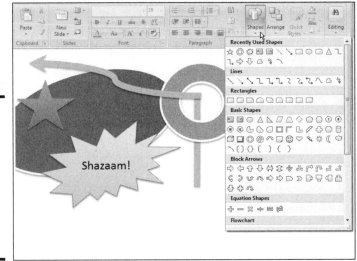

Figure 8-2:
To draw a
line, arrow,
or shape,
choose it in
the Insert
Shapes
gallery on
the Insert
tab.

4. **Drag on your page, slide, or worksheet.**

   As you drag, the line, arrow, or shape appears before your eyes.

5. **To alter your line, arrow, or shape — to change its size, color, or outline — select the (Drawing Tools) Format tab.**

   This tab offers many commands for manipulating lines and shapes (they are explained throughout this chapter). You must select a line or shape to make the (Drawing Tools) Format tab appear. Click a line or shape to select it.

   In the upper-left corner of the (Drawing Tools) Format tab is another Shapes gallery for creating new shapes to go along with the one you created. You can click the Edit Shape button (in the Insert Shapes group) on the Format tab to exchange one shape for another.

Handling Lines, Arrows, and Connectors

Figure 8-1 shows examples of how you can use lines and arrows to present ideas. As well as lines and arrows, the Insert Shapes gallery offers *connectors,* special lines that link shapes and can bend and stretch as you move shapes around. Use connectors along with lines and arrows to describe the relationships between the people or things in a diagram. These pages explain how to handle lines, arrows, and connectors.

Changing the length and position of a line or arrow

To change the length or angle of a line or arrow, start by clicking to select it. You can tell when a line has been selected because round selection handles appear at either end. Follow these instructions to move a line or adjust its length or angle:

✦ **Changing the angle of a line:** Drag a selection handle up, down, or sideways. A faint line shows where your line will be when you release the mouse button.

✦ **Changing the length:** Drag a selection handle away from or toward the opposite selection handle.

✦ **Changing the position:** Move the pointer over the line itself and click when you see the four-headed arrow. Then drag the line to a new location.

Changing the appearance of a line, arrow, or connector

What a line looks like is a matter of its color, its *weight* (how wide it is), its *dash status* (it can be filled out or dashed), and its *cap* (its ends can be rounded, square, or flat). To change the appearance of a line, start by selecting it, going to the (Drawing Tools) Format tab, and opening the drop-down list on the Shape Outline button (you can find it in the Shape Styles group). As shown in Figure 8-3, you see a drop-down list with commands for handling the appearance of lines, arrows, and connectors:

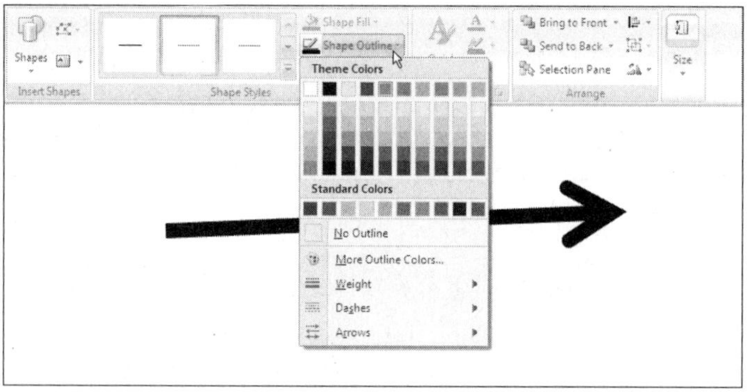

Figure 8-3: Open the drop-down list on the Shape Outline button to change the appearance of lines.

✦ **Color:** Choose a color on the drop-down list (see Figure 8-3).

✦ **Width:** Choose Weight on the drop-down list (see Figure 8-3) and then choose a line width on the submenu. You can also choose More Lines on the submenu to open the Format Shape (or Format AutoShape) dialog box and change the width there. Enter a setting in points to make the line narrower or wider.

✦ **Dotted or dashed lines:** Choose Dashes on the drop-down list (see Figure 8-3) and then choose an option on the submenu. Again, you can choose More Lines to open the Format Shape (or Format AutoShape) dialog box and choose from many dash types and compound lines.

✦ **Line caps (PowerPoint and Excel only):** Click the Shape Styles group button to open the Format Shape (or Format AutoShape) dialog box. In the Line Style category, select a cap type.

You can also change the appearance of a line by opening the Shape Styles gallery on the (Drawing Tools) Format tab and selecting a style.

Attaching and handling arrowheads on lines and connectors

Arrows, of course, have arrowheads, and arrowheads on lines and connectors can go on either side or both sides of a line. What's more, arrowheads come in different sizes and shapes. To handle arrowheads on lines and connectors, select your line or connector and go to the (Drawing Tools) Format tab. Then use one of these techniques to handle the arrowheads:

✦ Open the drop-down list on the Shape Outline button, choose Arrows (refer to Figure 8-3), and select an arrow on the submenu.

✦ Click the Shape Styles group button to open the Format Shape (or Format AutoShape) dialog box. In the Line Style category (or Colors and Lines tab), choose Arrow settings to describe where you want the arrowheads to be, what you want them to look like, and what size you want them to be.

Choosing a default line style for consistency's sake

One of the secrets to making an attractive drawing is to make the lines consistent with one another. Lines should be the same width and color. They should be the same style. Unless you observe this rule, your drawings will be infested with lines of varying width and different colors. They will look like a confetti parade in a windstorm.

You can get around the problem of making lines consistent with one another by creating a model line and making it the default line style. After

you declare a default style, all new lines you create are assigned the style. You don't have to spend as much time making the lines look alike.

Give a line the style, weight, and color that you want for all (or most) lines and then follow these steps to make that line the default style:

1. **Select and right-click the line.**

2. **Choose Set AutoShape Defaults (in Word) or Set As Default Line (in PowerPoint and Excel) on the shortcut menu.**

To attach an arrowhead or arrowheads to a line or connector you've already drawn, select the line and proceed as though you were attaching arrowheads to a line that already has an arrow.

Connecting shapes by using connectors

Under Lines, the Insert Shapes gallery offers six different connectors. Use *connectors* to link shapes and text boxes to form a diagram. Connectors differ from conventional lines in an important way: After you attach one to a shape, it stays with the shape when you move the shape. You don't have to worry about remaking all the connections after you move a shape. You can move shapes at will and let the connectors between shapes take care of themselves. Figure 8-4 shows three types of connectors in action. By the way, if you came here to explore how to make a diagram, be sure to check out Book I, Chapter 7 as well. It explains the Office SmartArt diagramming gizmos.

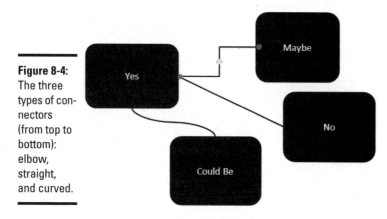

Figure 8-4: The three types of connectors (from top to bottom): elbow, straight, and curved.

To connect shapes in Word, the shapes must be on the drawing canvas. Book II, Chapter 4 describes the Word drawing canvas. (Click the Shapes button and choose New Drawing Canvas to create one.)

Making the connection

Before you draw the connections, draw the shapes and arrange them on the slide where you want them to be in your diagram. Then follow these steps to connect two shapes with a connector:

1. **Select the two shapes that you want to connect.**

To select the shapes, hold down the Ctrl key and click each one.

2. **On the Format tab, click the Shapes button to open the Shapes gallery.**

3. **Under Lines, select the connector that will best fit between the two shapes you want to link together.**

4. **Move the pointer over a side selection handle on one of the shapes you want to connect.**

   The selection handles turn red (except in Word, which doesn't register any changes).

5. **Click and drag the pointer over the other shape, and when you see red selection handles on that shape, release the mouse button.**

   As shown earlier in Figure 8-4, red, round selection handles appear on the shapes where they're connected. These red handles tell you that the two shapes are connected and will remain connected when you move them.

If your connector is attached to the wrong shape, don't despair. Select the connector, and on the Format tab, click the Edit Shape button and choose Reroute Connectors. Then move the pointer over the red handle on the side of the connector that needs to be attached elsewhere, click, drag the connector onto the other shape, and release the mouse button when you see the red selection handles on the other shape.

Adjusting a connector

Chances are your connector needs adjusting to make it fit correctly between the two shapes. Click to select your connector and follow these techniques for adjusting it:

✦ **Changing the shape of a connector:** Drag the yellow diamond on the connector. As you drag, the connector assumes different shapes.

✦ **Changing the connector type:** Right-click the connector, choose Connector Types, and choose Straight Connector, Elbow Connector, or Curved Connector on the submenu.

✦ **Handling arrows on connectors:** If the arrows on the connector aren't there, are pointing in the wrong direction, or shouldn't be there, change around the arrowheads using the same techniques you use with standard arrows. See "Attaching and handling arrowheads on lines and connectors," earlier in this chapter.

Make sure that the connector lines in your diagram are consistent with one another. Give them the same style and appearance, or else it will be hard to make sense of your diagram.

Handling Rectangles, Ovals, Stars, and Other Shapes

As I mention earlier in this chapter, shapes can come in very handy for illustrating concepts and ideas, as shown in Figure 8-5. You can combine shapes to make your own illustrations. Apart from the standard rectangle and oval, you can draw octagons and various other "-agons," arrows, stars, and banners. You are hereby encouraged to make shapes a part of your work, and you'll be glad to know that drawing shapes is not difficult. These pages explain how to draw a shape, exchange one shape for another, change a shape's symmetry, and enter words on a shape.

Figure 8-5:
An example
of using
shapes (and
connectors)
to convey
an idea.

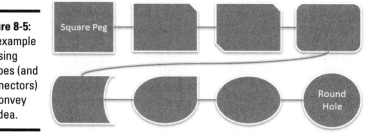

 In Word, you must be in Print Layout view to draw and handle shapes. If you intend to draw more than one shape in Word, create a drawing canvas to hold the shapes (click the Shapes button and choose New Drawing Canvas). Book II, Chapter 4 describes the drawing canvas in Word.

Drawing a shape

Follow these steps to draw a shape:

 1. **On the Insert tab, click the Shapes button to open the Shapes gallery.**

You can also find a Shapes button on the (Drawing Tools) Format tab.

2. **Select a shape in the gallery.**

If you've drawn the shape recently, you may be able to find it at the top of the gallery under Recently Used Shapes.

3. **Click on-screen and drag slantwise to draw the shape, as shown at the top of Figure 8-6.**

 Hold down the Shift key as you drag if you want the shape to retain its symmetry. For example, to draw a circle, select the Oval shape and hold down the Shift key as you draw.

Drag to draw a shape.

Figure 8-6:
Drag on-
screen to
draw a
shape (top);
drag a
diamond to
change a
shape's
symmetry
(bottom).

Drag a diamond to change a shape's symmetry.

Selection handles appear on the corners and sides of a shape when you select it. With the selection handles showing, you can change a shape's size and shape:

✦ Hold down the Shift key and drag a corner handle to change a shape's size and retain its symmetry.

✦ Drag a side, top, or bottom handle to stretch or scrunch the shape.

To exchange one shape for another, select the shape and follow these instructions:

✦ **In Word:** On the Format tab, click the Change Shape button (you can find it in the Shape Styles group), and select a new shape on the Change Shape drop-down list.

✦ **In PowerPoint and Excel:** On the Format tab, click the Edit Shape button in the Insert Shapes group, choose Change Shape on the drop-down list, and select a new shape on the Change Shape drop-down list.

Turning a text box into a text box shape

You can turn a conventional text box into a text box shape by following these instructions:

- **In Word:** Select the text box, go to the (Text Box Tools) Format tab, click the Change Shape button (you can find it in the Text Box Styles group), and select a shape in the Change Shape drop-down list.

- **In PowerPoint and Excel:** Select the text box by clicking its perimeter, select the (Drawing Tools) Format tab, click the Edit Shape button, choose Change Shape, and then select a shape in the Change Shape drop-down list.

Unless your text box shape has a dark outline, you won't be able to see the shape it's in. After the conversion, you usually have to enlarge the shape to accommodate the text.

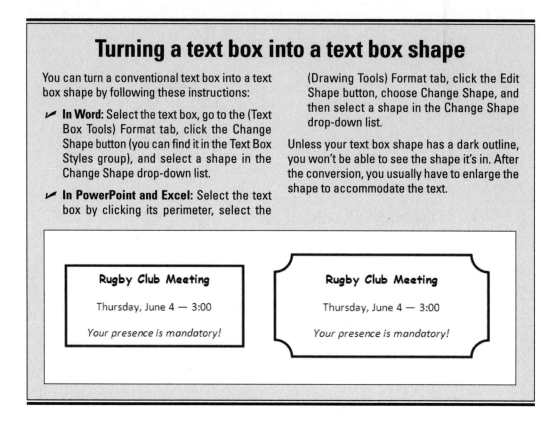

Changing a shape's symmetry

A yellow diamond — sometimes two or three — appears on some shapes. By dragging a diamond, you can change a shape's symmetry. Figure 8-6, for example, shows the same shape — the Sun shape — altered into different symmetries. Notice where the diamonds are. By dragging a diamond even a very short distance, you can do a lot to change a shape's symmetry.

Using a shape as a text box

Here's a neat trick: Rather than use the conventional rectangle as a text box, you can use a shape. Figure 8-7 shows examples of shapes being used as text boxes. By placing words on shapes, you can make the shapes serve to illustrate ideas and concepts.

Follow these instructions to handle text box shapes:

- **Entering the text:** Click in the shape and start typing. In Word, right-click and choose Add Text before you type.

✦ **Editing the text:** Click in the text and start editing. That's all there is to it. If you have trouble getting PowerPoint or Excel to understand that you want to edit text, select the shape, right-click it, and choose Edit Text on the shortcut menu.

✦ **Changing the font, color, and size of text:** Right-click in the text and choose Font. Then, in the Font dialog box, choose a font, font color, and a font size for the text.

✦ **Allowing the shape to enlarge for text:** In PowerPoint and Excel, you can allow the shape to enlarge and receive more text. Right-click the shape and choose Format Shape. Then, in the Text Box category of the Format Shape dialog box, select the Resize Shape to Fit Text option button.

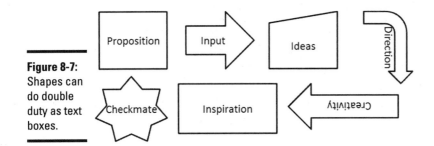

Figure 8-7: Shapes can do double duty as text boxes.

WordArt for Bending, Spindling, and Mutilating Text

A *WordArt image* consists of a word that has been stretched, crumpled, or squeezed into an odd shape. Actually, a WordArt image can include more than one word. Figure 8-8 shows the WordArt gallery, where WordArt images are made, and an example of a WordArt image. After you insert a WordArt image, you can fool with the buttons on the WordArt toolbar and torture the word or phrase even further.

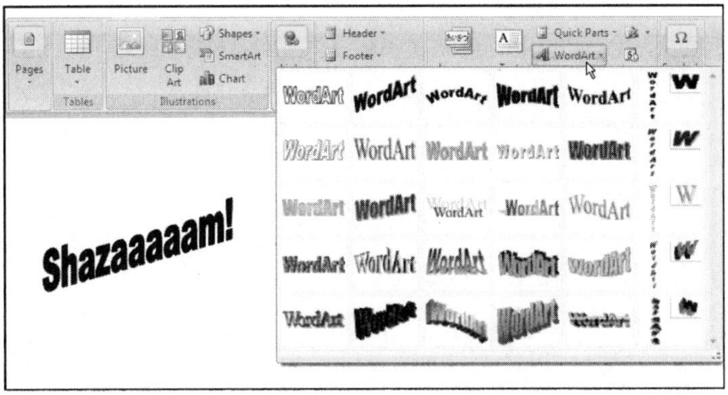

Figure 8-8: Creating a WordArt image.

Creating a WordArt image

Follow these steps to create a WordArt image:

1. **Click the Insert tab.**

2. **Click the WordArt button.**

   A drop-down list with WordArt styles appears (refer to Figure 8-8).

3. **Select a WordArt style.**

   Don't worry about selecting the right style — you can choose a different one later. In Word, you see the Edit WordArt Text dialog box.

4. **Enter the text for the image in the dialog box (in Word) or in the WordArt text box (in PowerPoint and Excel).**

   Congratulations. You just created a WordArt image.

Editing a WordArt image

Usually, you have to wrestle with a WordArt image before it comes out right. Select the image, go to the Format tab, and use these techniques to win the wrestling match:

+ **Editing the words:** In Word, click the Edit Text button and edit the words in the Edit WordArt Text dialog box. In PowerPoint and Excel, click in the WordArt text box and edit the text there.

+ **Choosing a new WordArt style:** Open the WordArt gallery and select a style. Depending on the size of your screen and which program you're working in, you may have to click the WordArt button or Quick Styles button first.

+ **Changing the image's shape:** In Word, you can click the Change WordArt Shape button and choose a shape on the drop-down list.

+ **Changing the letters' color:** Click the Shape Fill button (in Word) or the Text Fill button (in PowerPoint and Excel) and choose a color on the drop-down list.

+ **Changing the letters' outline:** Click the Shape Outline button (in Word) or open the drop-down list on the Text Outline button (in PowerPoint and Excel) and make choices to change the letters' outline.

Manipulating Lines, Shapes, Art, Text Boxes, and Other Objects

After you insert a shape, line, text box, clip-art image, graphic, diagram, WordArt image, chart, or embedded object in a file, it ceases being what it was before and becomes an *object*. Figure 8-9 shows eight objects on a slide.

I'm not sure whether these eight objects resent being objectified, but Office objectifies them. As far as manipulating these items in Office is concerned, these are just objects.

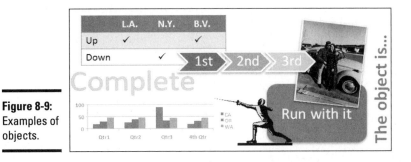

Figure 8-9:
Examples of
objects.

The techniques for manipulating objects are the same whether you're dealing with a line, shape, graphic, clip-art image, diagram, or text box. The good news from your end is that you have to master only one set of techniques for handling these objects. Whether you want to move, change the size of, or change the outline of a text box, clip-art image, graphic, or shape, the techniques are the same.

In the remainder of this chapter are instructions for doing these tasks with objects:

✦ **Selecting:** Before you can do anything to objects, you have to select them. See "Selecting objects so that you can manipulate them."

✦ **Making use of the rulers and grid:** Rulers (in Word, PowerPoint, and Excel) and the grid (in Word and PowerPoint) can be very helpful for aligning and placing objects. See "Hiding and displaying the rulers and grid."

✦ **Changing an object's size and shape:** You can enlarge, shrink, stretch, and scrunch objects to make them wider or taller. See "Changing an object's size and shape."

✦ **Moving and positioning:** You can land objects with precision in a Word document, PowerPoint slide, or Excel worksheet. See "Moving and positioning objects."

✦ **Aligning and distributing:** Another way to move and position objects is to realign or redistribute them across a page, slide, or worksheet. See "Tricks for aligning and distributing objects."

✦ **Overlapping:** When you're dealing with several objects, they're bound to overlap. And sometimes overlapping objects make for an interesting effect. On the right side of Figure 8-9, for example, several objects overlap and give the impression that they were "dropped there." See "When objects overlap: Choosing which appears above the other," to handle overlapping objects.

✦ **Rotating and flipping:** Viewers turn their heads when they see an object that has been flipped or rotated. You can rotate and flip shapes, lines, text boxes, graphics, clip-art images, and WordArt images. See "Rotating and flipping objects."

✦ **Grouping:** To make working with several different objects easier, you can *group* them so that they become a single object. After objects have been grouped, manipulating them — manipulating it, I should say — is easier. See "Grouping objects to make working with them easier."

✦ **Applying outlines and fills:** Putting outlines and color fills on objects makes them stand out. You can also fill some kinds of objects with a color or pattern. See "Changing an Object's Color, Outline Color, and Transparency."

If you sighed after you finished reading this long list, I don't blame you. But be of good cheer: Most of these commands are easy to pick up, and including lines, shapes, text boxes, WordArt images, clip art, and graphics in your work is a good way to impress your friends and intimidate your enemies.

Selecting objects so that you can manipulate them

Before you can move or change the border of a graphic, text box, or other object, you have to select it. To select an object, simply click it. Sometimes, to align or decorate several objects simultaneously, you have to select more than one object at the same time. To select more than one object:

✦ Ctrl+click them. In other words, hold down the Ctrl key as you click the objects.

✦ "Lasso" the objects (in Word and PowerPoint). Click on one side of the objects you want to select and drag the pointer across the other objects. In Word, the objects must be on the drawing canvas for you to select them this way.

After you select an object, its selection handles appear. Objects have eight selection handles, one at each corner and one at each side. To tell whether an object is selected, look for its selection handles.

Hiding and displaying the rulers and grid

Word, PowerPoint, and Excel offer two rulers, one along the top of the window and one along the left side. Use the rulers to help place and align objects. To display or hide these rulers, use one of these techniques:

✦ On the View tab, click the Ruler check box (you may have to click the Show/Hide button first, depending on the size of your screen). To see the rulers, you must be in Print Layout view in Word and Page Layout view in Excel.

✦ In PowerPoint, you can also hide or display rulers by right-clicking a slide (but not an object or frame) and choosing Ruler on the shortcut menu.

In Word and PowerPoint, the grid can come in very handy for aligning objects. On the View tab, click the Gridlines check box to see the grid (you may have to click the Show/Hide button first). The grid settings in PowerPoint are quite sophisticated (see Book IV, Chapter 4 for details).

Changing an object's size and shape

Usually when an object arrives on-screen, you have to wrestle with it. You have to change its size (and sometimes its shape as well). Figure 8-10 demonstrates how to resize an object. Select your object and use one of these methods to change its size and shape:

✦ **"Eyeball it":** Hold down the Shift key and drag a *corner* selection handle to make the object larger or smaller but maintain its proportions. Drag a selection handle on the *side* to stretch or crimp an object and change its shape as well as its size.

✦ **Enter height and width measurements:** On the Format tab, enter measurements in the Height and Width boxes (see Figure 8-10). Depending on the size of your screen, you may have to click the Size button before you can see these boxes.

✦ **Open the Size and Position (or Format) dialog box:** Click the Size group button on the Format tab to open the Size dialog box (in PowerPoint and Excel) or the Format dialog box (in Word). Then change the Height and Width settings in the dialog box (see Figure 8-10).

Enter measurements . . .

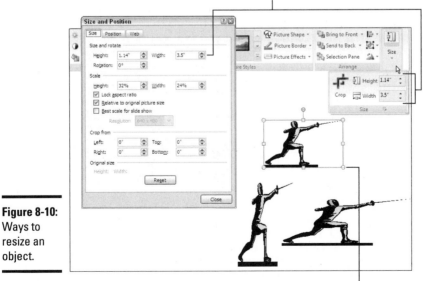

Figure 8-10:
Ways to resize an object.

. . . or drag a selection handle.

Whether you can change an object's shape as well as its size depends on whether the object's aspect ratio is *locked.* If you're wrestling with an object and it won't do your bidding — if it refuses to change shape or it changes shape, and you don't want it to do that — change its aspect ratio setting. Click the Size group button to open the Size (or Format) dialog box. Then select or deselect the Lock Aspect Ratio check box. When an object's aspect ratio is locked, it maintains its shape as you change its size, but when it's *unlocked,* you can change its shape.

You can change the size and shape of several objects at one time by selecting all the objects before giving a command to change sizes. Being able to change an object's size this way is convenient when you want to change the size of objects with respect to one another.

Moving and positioning objects

Moving objects is considerably easier than moving furniture. Select the object you want to reposition and use one of these techniques to land it in the right place:

✦ **Dragging:** Move the pointer over the object, click when you see the four-headed arrow, and drag the object to a new location. Hold down the Shift key as you drag to move an object either horizontally or vertically in a straight line.

✦ **Using a dialog box (in PowerPoint and Word):** On the Format tab, click the Size group button (depending on the size of your screen, you may have to click the Size button first). You see the Size dialog box (in PowerPoint) or the Format dialog box (in Word). In the Position tab (in PowerPoint) or the Size tab (in Word), enter Horizontal and Vertical measurements and then choose options on the From drop-down list to declare where you want to make the measurements from.

✦ **Nudging:** If you can't quite fit an object in the right place, try using a Nudge command. Nudge commands move objects up, down, left, or right. Press one of the arrow keys ($\uparrow$, $\downarrow$, $\leftarrow$, $\rightarrow$) to move the object a little bit. Hold down the Ctrl key as you press to move an object ever so slightly.

Use the dialog box method of positioning objects when you want objects to be in the exact same position on different pages or slides.

Tricks for aligning and distributing objects

When several objects appear in the same place, use the Align and Distribute commands to give the objects an orderly appearance. You can make your Word page, PowerPoint slide, or Excel worksheet look tidier by aligning the objects or by distributing them so that they are an equal distance from one another. Office offers special commands for doing these tasks — and the Align and Distribute commands are easy to execute.

Aligning objects

The Align commands come in handy when you want objects to line up with one another. Suppose you need to paste several photos in a row or column. Lining up the photos neatly gives your page or slide an orderly appearance. Figure 8-11 shows the two different ways to align objects. When you choose an Align command in Word and PowerPoint, you have the option of aligning objects with respect to one another, or to the page or page margin (in Word), or the slide itself (in PowerPoint). In Figure 8-11, the stars — there are four in a set — are left-aligned with respect, first, to a slide, and second, to one another.

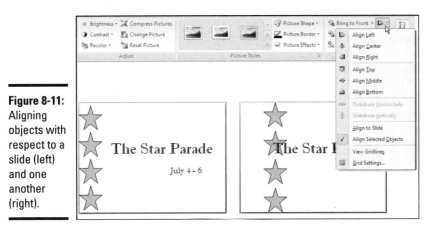

Figure 8-11:
Aligning
objects with
respect to a
slide (left)
and one
another
(right).

Follow these steps to line up objects on a slide:

1. **Move the objects where you roughly want them to be, and if you want to align objects with respect to one another, move one object to a point that the others will align to.**

   When Word, PowerPoint, or Excel aligns objects with respect to one another, it aligns them to the object in the leftmost, centermost, rightmost, topmost, middlemost, or bottommost position, depending on which Align command you choose.

2. **Select the objects you want to align.**

   Earlier in this chapter, "Selecting objects so that you can manipulate them" looks at selection techniques.

3. **Click the Format tab.**

   You can also click the Page Layout tab (in Word and Excel) or the Home tab (in PowerPoint).

4. **Click the Align button, and on the drop-down list, choose whether to align the objects with respect to one another or with respect to the page or page margin (in Word) or a slide (in PowerPoint).**

Depending on the size of your screen, you may have to click the Arrange button to get to the Align button. Figure 8-11 shows the Align drop-down list.

5. **Click the Align button again and choose an Align command — Left, Center, Right, Top, Middle, or Bottom (refer to Figure 8-11).**

6. **If necessary, drag the objects on the page.**

That's right — drag them. After you give an Align command, the objects are still selected, and you can drag to adjust their positions.

Distributing objects so that they are equidistant

The Distribute commands — Distribute Horizontally and Distribute Vertically — come in handy for laying out objects on a page or slide. These commands arrange objects so that the same amount of space appears between each one. Rather than go to the trouble of pushing and pulling objects until they are distributed evenly, you can simply select the objects and choose a Distribute command.

Figure 8-12 demonstrates how the Distribute commands work. First, you select the objects that need the same amount of space between them and then you give a Distribute command. In the figure, I chose the Distribute Horizontally command so that the same amount of horizontal (side-by-side) space appears between the objects. Distributing objects such as these on your own, perhaps by entering measurements in the Size or Format dialog box, is a waste of time when you can use the Distribute commands.

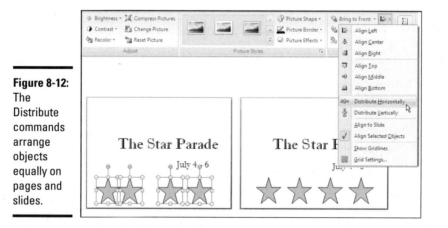

Figure 8-12: The Distribute commands arrange objects equally on pages and slides.

Follow these steps to distribute objects horizontally or vertically on a page or slide:

1. **Arrange the objects so that the outermost objects — the ones that will go on the top and bottom or left side and right side — are where you want them to be.**

In other words, if you want to distribute objects horizontally across a page, place the leftmost object and rightmost object where you want them to be. Office distributes the other objects equally between the leftmost and rightmost object.

2. **Select the objects by Ctrl+clicking or "lassoing" them.**

3. **Click the Format tab.**

You can also click the Page Layout tab (in Word and Excel) or the Home tab (in PowerPoint).

4. **Click the Align button and choose a Distribute option on the drop-down list.**

Figure 8-12 shows the Align drop-down list. To find the Align button, you may have to click the Arrange button first, depending on the size of your screen.

When objects overlap: Choosing which appears above the other

On a page or slide that is crowded with text boxes, shapes, graphics, and clip-art images, objects inevitably overlap, and you have to decide which object goes on top of the stack and which on the bottom. In a Word document, you have to decide as well whether text appears above or below objects. Objects that deliberately overlap can be interesting and attractive to look at. On the right side of Figure 8-13, for example, a clip-art image and text box appear in front of a shape. Makes for a nice effect, no?

Choose a Bring or Send command.

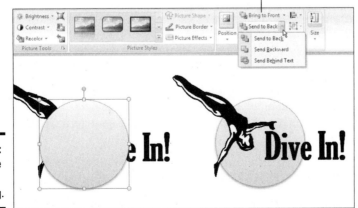

Figure 8-13:
An example
of objects
overlapping.

The Bring and Send commands

Word, PowerPoint, and Excel offer four commands for handling objects in a stack:

✦ **Bring to Front:** Places the object in front of all other objects in the stack

✦ **Bring Forward:** Moves the object higher in the stack

✦ **Send to Back:** Places the object behind all other objects

✦ **Send Backward:** Moves the object lower in the stack

Word offers these additional commands:

✦ **Bring in Front of Text:** Moves the object in front of text on the page

✦ **Send Behind Text:** Moves the object behind text on the page so that the text appears over the object

In Word, you can't choose a Bring or Send command unless you've chosen a text-wrapping option apart from In Line with Text for the object. Select your object, click the Format tab, click the Text Wrapping button, and choose an option on the drop-down list apart from In Line with Text. Book II, Chapter 4 looks at text wrapping in Word.

Giving a Bring or Send command

Select an object and use one of these techniques to give a Bring or Send command:

✦ **Format tab, or Page Layout tab (in Word and Excel), and Home tab (in PowerPoint):** Click the Bring to Front or Send to Back button, or open the drop-down list on one of these buttons and choose a command (refer to Figure 8-13). Depending on the size of your screen, you may have to click the Arrange button before you can get to a Bring or Send command.

✦ **Right-clicking:** Right-click and choose a Bring to Front or Send to Back command.

If an object on the bottom of the stack shows through after you place it on the bottom, the object on the top of the stack is transparent or semi-transparent. Transparent objects are like gauze curtains — they reveal what's behind them. If you want to make the object on the top of the stack less transparent, see "Making a color transparent," later in this chapter.

Rotating and flipping objects

Rotating and flipping objects — that is, changing their orientation — is a neat way to spruce up a page or slide, as Figure 8-14 demonstrates. You can rotate and flip these kinds of objects: lines, shapes, text boxes, clip-art images, graphics, and WordArt images. To flip or rotate an object, select it and do one of the following:

Drag the rotation handle . . .   . . . or choose a Rotate command.

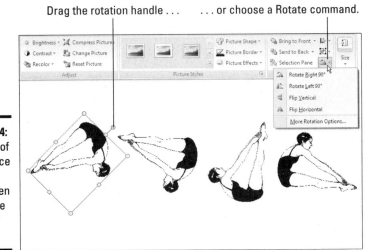

Figure 8-14:
Members of an audience turn their heads when objects are rotated or flipped.

+ **Choose a Rotate or Flip command:** On the Format tab, click the Rotate button and choose an option on the drop-down list (refer to Figure 8-14). The Rotate commands rotate objects by 90 degrees; the Flip commands flip objects over. The Rotate button is also found on the Page Layout tab (in Word and Excel) and the Home tab (in PowerPoint). You may have to click the Arrange button to see the Rotate button, depending on the size of your screen.

+ **Roll your own:** Drag the object's *rotation handle,* the green dot that appears after you select it. Hold down the Shift key as you drag to rotate the shape by 15-degree increments.

+ **Open the Size dialog box:** On the Rotate drop-down list, select More Rotation Options to open the Size dialog box. Enter a degree measurement in the Rotation text box.

To rotate several objects simultaneously, Ctrl+click to select each object and then give a rotation command.

Grouping objects to make working with them easier

Consider the clip-art image, shape, and text box in Figure 8-15. To move, resize, or reshape these objects, I would have to laboriously move them one at a time — that is, I would have to do that if it weren't for the Group command.

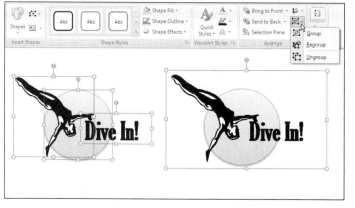

Figure 8-15: You can move, resize, and reshape grouped objects as though they were a single object.

The Group command assembles different objects into a single object to make moving, resizing, and reshaping objects easier. With the Group command, you select the objects that you want to "group" and then you wrap them into a single bundle so that they become easier to work with. Office remembers which objects were grouped so that you can ungroup objects after you've moved or resized them.

To group objects in Word, the objects must be on the same drawing canvas. Book II, Chapter 4 explains the drawing canvas.

Grouping objects

Select objects by Ctrl+clicking or "lassoing" them and then do either of the following to group the objects:

✦ On the Format tab (or the Page Layout tab in Word and Excel, and the Home tab in PowerPoint), click the Group button and choose Group on the drop-down list, as shown in Figure 8-15. Depending on the size of your screen, you may have to click the Arrange button to get to the Group button.

✦ Right-click one of the objects you selected, choose Group (or Grouping) and then choose Group.

After objects are grouped, they form a single object with the eight selection handles.

To add an object to a group, select the object and the grouped objects by Ctrl+clicking and then choosing the Group command.

Ungrouping and regrouping

To ungroup an object and break it into its components, perhaps to fiddle with one of the objects in the group, select the object, click the Group button, and choose Ungroup (refer to Figure 8-15).

Office remembers which objects were in a group after you ungroup it. To reassemble the objects in a group, click an object that was formerly in the group and then choose the Regroup command. You can find this command on the Group button (refer to Figure 8-15).

Changing an Object's Color, Outline Color, and Transparency

If an object's color or outline color doesn't suit you, you have the right to change colors. For that matter, you can opt for a "blank" object with no color or remove the color from around the perimeter of the object. As the saying goes, "It's a free country."

Office has its own lingo when it comes to an object's color. Remember these terms when you make like Picasso with your shapes, text boxes, graphics, and clip-art images:

✦ **Shape fill colors:** The color that fills in an object is called the *shape fill*. You can apply shape fills to shapes, text boxes, and WordArt images, but not clip-art or graphics. Besides colors, you can fill a shape with a picture, a gradient, or a texture. (See the next section in this chapter, "Filling an object with a color, picture, or texture.")

✦ **Shape outline colors:** The line that goes around the perimeter of the object is called the *shape outline*. You can choose a color, style, and line width for outlines. (See "Putting the outline around an object," later in this chapter.)

The easiest way to decorate a shape, text box, or WordArt image is to visit the Format tab and make a selection in the Shape Styles gallery. These ready-made gallery selections can spare you the work of dealing with fill colors, outlines, and shape effects. Just remember not to mix and match different Shape Style options; use them with consistency.

Filling an object with a color, picture, or texture

Shapes, text boxes, and WordArt images are empty when you first create them, but you can fill them with a color, picture, gradient, or texture by following these basic steps:

1. **Select the object that needs a facelift.**

2. **Click the Format tab.**

3. **Click the Shape Fill button.**

As shown in Figure 8-16, a drop-down list appears.

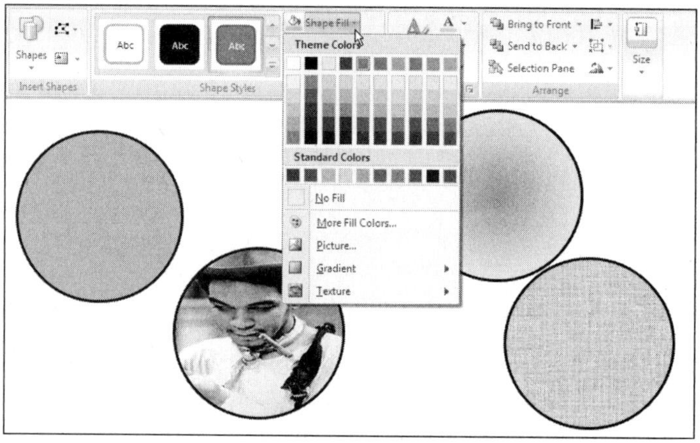

Figure 8-16:
Shape fills
(from left to
right): a
color,
picture,
gradient,
and texture.

4. **Choose a fill color, picture, gradient, or texture.**

Choose No Fill to remove the fill color, picture, gradient, or texture from an object.

Figure 8-16 shows the same object filled with a color, picture, gradient, and texture. Which do you prefer? Your choices are as follows:

✦ **Color:** Applies a single color to the object. *Theme colors* are colors that the makers of Office believe are compatible with the theme you choose for your presentation. If these colors don't suit you, choose a standard color or choose More Fill Colors to open the Colors dialog box, where you can choose from many different colors.

✦ **Picture:** Places a picture in the object. You see the Insert (or Select) Picture dialog box. Choose a picture and click the Insert button.

✦ **Gradient:** Applies two- or three-color shading to the object. You can choose between various shading styles.

✦ **Texture:** Offers 24 patterns meant to simulate various surfaces. The choices include Granite, Paper Bag, and Pink Tissue Paper. Be sure to use the scroll bar to see all the choices.

✦ **Pattern (Word only):** Applies a pattern to the object. Select a pattern on the Pattern tab of the Fill Effects dialog box.

Making a color transparent

A transparent color is like gauze because instead of being solid, it shows what's behind it. Transparent colors are especially useful in text boxes because the text shows through and can be read easily. Follow these steps to make the fill color in a text box, shape, or WordArt image transparent or semi-transparent:

1. **Right-click the object and choose Format Shape (or Format AutoShape).**

You see the Format dialog box.

2. **In the Fill category, drag the Transparency slider to choose how transparent a color you want.**

At 100%, the color is completely transparent and, in fact, not there; at 1%, the color is hardly transparent at all.

3. **Click the Close or OK button.**

You can also make a graphic transparent by recoloring it. See Book VIII, Chapter 3.

Putting the outline around an object

The *outline* is the line that runs around the perimeter of an object. Put an outline color around an object to give it more definition or make it stand out. Figure 8-17 shows examples of outlines. What a shape outline looks like has to do with the color, weight, and dash style you choose for it.

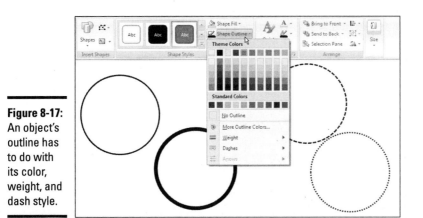

Figure 8-17: An object's outline has to do with its color, weight, and dash style.

Designating a fill and outline color for all your objects

Rather than go to the significant trouble of giving all or most of your objects the same look, you can make one object the model for all others to follow, and declare it the default style. After that, all new objects you insert appear in the same style, your objects have a uniform appearance, and you don't have to spend as much time formatting objects.

Select an object with a fill and an outline color that you want as your model, right-click the object, and choose Set As Default (or Set AutoShape Defaults) to make your object the default that all other objects start from.

Select your object and follow these steps to change its outline:

1. **Click the Format tab.**

2. **Click the Shape Outline button.**

A drop-down list appears (see Figure 8-17).

3. **Choose a color, weight, or dash.**

You may have to return to the Shape Outline drop-down list more than once to make the outline just so.

- *Color:* Choose a theme color deemed right for borders by the makers of your program or choose a standard color.

- *Weight:* Choose how thick or thin you want the border to be. You can choose More Lines on the submenu to open the Format dialog box. In the Line Style (or Line) category, you can choose compound lines and select point-size width for the outline.

- *Dashes:* Choose straight lines, dashed lines, or broken lines.

- *Pattern (Word only):* Select a line pattern in the Patterned Lines dialog box.

The (Picture Tools) Format tab — the one you see when you're dealing with pictures and clip art — offers the Picture Border drop-down list instead of the Shape Outline drop-down list, but the options on the lists are the same.

To remove an outline from an object, choose No Outline on the Shape Outline (or Picture Border) drop-down list.

Contents at a Glance

Chapter 1: Speed Techniques for Using Word

In This Chapter

✔ Getting acquainted with the Word screen

✔ Creating a Word document

✔ Changing your view of a document

✔ Selecting text so you can copy, move, or delete it

✔ Getting from place to place in long documents

✔ Pasting one Word document into another

✔ Creating data-entry forms

*T*his chapter explains shortcuts and commands that can help you become a speedy user of Word. Everything in this chapter was put here so that you can get off work earlier and take the slow, scenic route home. Starting here, you discover how to create and change your view of documents. You find out how to select text, get from place to place — and mark your place — in long documents. You also explore how to insert one document into another and create data-entry forms to make entering information a little easier.

Introducing the Word Screen

Seeing the Word screen for the first time is sort of like trying to find your way through Tokyo's busy Ikebukuro subway station. It's intimidating. But when you start using Word, you quickly discover what everything is. To help you get going, Figure 1-1 shows you the different parts of the screen. Here are shorthand descriptions of these screen parts:

✦ **Title bar:** At the top of the screen, the title bar tells you the name of the document you're working on.

✦ **Quick Access toolbar:** This toolbar offers the Save, Undo, and Repeat buttons. Wherever you go in Word, you see the Quick Access toolbar. Book I, Chapter 1 explains the toolbar in detail; Book VIII, Chapter 1 explains how to customize and move the Quick Access toolbar.

✦ **Minimize, Restore, Close buttons:** These three magic buttons make it very easy to shrink, enlarge, and close the window you're working in.

✦ **The Ribbon:** Select a tab on the Ribbon to undertake a new task. Book I, Chapter 1 explains the Ribbon in detail, as well as the new Office 2007 interface.

✦ **Scroll bars:** The scroll bars help you get from place to place in a document.

✦ **Status bar:** The status bar gives you basic information about where you are and what you're doing in a document. It tells you what page and what section you're in, the total number of pages and words in your document, and what language the text is written in. Book VIII, Chapter 1 explains how to customize the status bar.

✦ **View buttons:** Click one of these buttons — Print Layout, Full Screen Reading, Web Layout, Outline, or Draft — to change your view of a document.

✦ **Zoom controls:** Use these controls to zoom in and out on your work. See Book I, Chapter 3 for details.

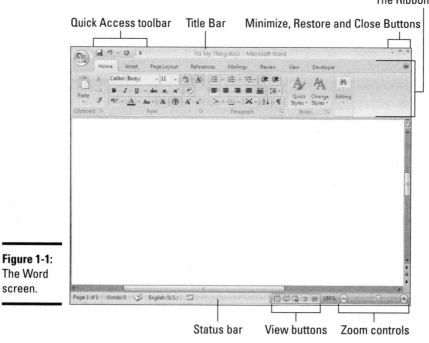

The Ribbon

Quick Access toolbar   Title Bar   Minimize, Restore and Close Buttons

Figure 1-1:
The Word
screen.

Status bar   View buttons   Zoom controls

Creating a New Document

Document is just a fancy word for a letter, report, announcement, or proclamation that you create with Word. When you first start Word, you see a new, blank document with the generic name *Document1*. You can start working right away on this document, or you can create a new document from a template. A *template* is a special kind of file that is used as the starting point for creating other files. Each template comes with many preformatted styles. If your aim is to create an academic report, flyer, newsletter, calendar, résumé, or other sophisticated document, see if you can spare yourself the formatting work by creating your document from a template.

No matter what kind of document you want, you can start creating it by clicking the Office button and choosing New on the drop-down list. You see the New Document dialog box, as shown in Figure 1-2. Create your document with one of these techniques:

Find a template.

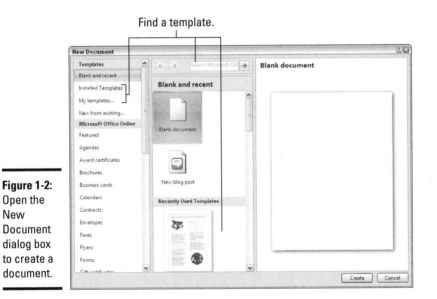

Figure 1-2:
Open the
New
Document
dialog box
to create a
document.

  ✦ **Blank document:** Double-click the Blank Document icon. (By pressing Ctrl+N, you can create a new, blank document without opening the New Document dialog box.)

✦ **Document from a template:** Take your pick of these techniques to create a document from a template:

- *Use a template on your computer:* Click Installed Templates (you can find this button under Templates). Templates that you loaded on your computer when you installed Office appear in the dialog box. Double-click a template to create a document.

- *Search for a template online at Microsoft:* Enter a search term in the Search box, make sure your computer is connected to the Internet, and click the Start Searching button. Templates appear in the dialog box. Double-click a template to download it and use it to create a document.

- *Use a template you created (or downloaded earlier from Microsoft or acquired from a third party):* Click the My Templates button. The New dialog box appears. Select a template and click OK.

- *Choose a recently used template:* Click an icon under Recently Used Templates.

✦ **Recycle another document:** If you can use another document as the starting point for creating a new document, click the New from Existing button. In the New from Existing Document dialog box, select the document and click the Create New button.

Book I, Chapter 1 explains how to save documents after you create them, as well as how to open the document you want to work on.

Constructing your default document

When you open a new, blank document by pressing Ctrl+N or double-clicking the Blank Document icon in the New Document dialog box (refer to Figure 1-2), does the document meet your specifications? When you start typing, does the text appear in your favorite font? Are the margins just-so?

You can get a head start in creating documents by telling Word what you want new documents

to look like. To do that, open the Font dialog box (click the Font group button on the Home tab) and then the Page Setup dialog box (click the Page Setup group button on the Page Layout tab), make your formatting choices, and click the Default button in these dialog boxes. Changes you make this way are saved to the Normal document template (Chapter 3 of this mini-book explains what templates are).

Getting a Better Look at Your Documents

A computer screen can be kind of confining. There you are, staring at the darn thing for hours at a stretch. Do you wish the view were better? The Word screen can't be made to look like the Riviera, but you can examine documents in different ways and work in two places at one time in the same document. Better read on.

Viewing documents in different ways

In word processing, you want to focus sometimes on the writing, sometimes on the layout, and sometimes on the organization of your work. To help you stay in focus, Word offers different ways of viewing a document. Figure 1-3 shows these views. To change views, click one of the five View buttons on the status bar or go to the View tab and click one of the five buttons in the Document Views group. These pages explain the five views and why to select one over the other. (Be sure to visit Book I, Chapter 3 as well; it describes how to view a document through more than one window and how to open a second window on a document.)

**Book II
Chapter 1**

**Speed Techniques
for Using Word**

Print Layout view

Switch to Print Layout view to see the big picture. In this view, you can see what your document will look like when you print it. You can see graphics, headers, footers, and even page borders in Print Layout view. You can also see clearly where page breaks occur — that is, where one page ends and the next begins. In Print Layout view, you can click the One Page, Two Pages, or Page Width button to display more or fewer pages on your screen.

Full Screen Reading view

Switch to Full Screen Reading view to focus on the text itself and proofread your documents. In this view, everything gets stripped away — the Ribbon, scroll bars, status bar, and all. All you see is the text and artwork in your documents. You can't enter or edit text (unless you open the View Options drop-down list and choose Allow Typing).

Click the View Options button to open a drop-down list with options for improving your view. For example, you can increase or decrease the size of text, show one or two document pages at a time, and display page margins. To get from page to page, click buttons along the top of the window. Click the Close button to leave this view.

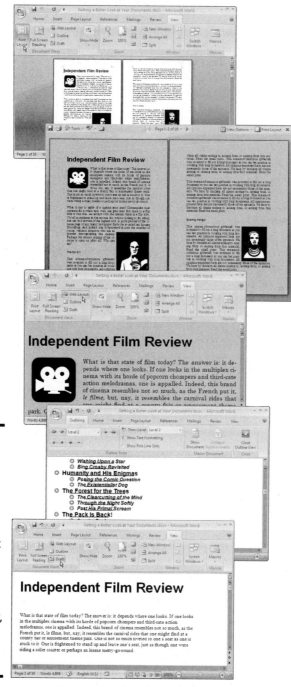

Figure 1-3:
Different
ways of
viewing
documents
(top to
bottom):
Print Layout
view, Full
Screen
Reading
view, Web
Layout view,
Outline
view, and
Draft view.

Web Layout view

Switch to Web Layout view to see what your document would look like as a Web page. Background colors appear (if you chose a theme or background color for your document). Text is wrapped to the window rather than around the artwork in the document. Book VIII, Chapter 2 explains how to save an Office file, a Word document included, as a Web page.

Outline view

Switch to Outline view to see how your work is organized. In this view, you can see only the headings in a document. You can get a sense of how your document unfolds and easily move sections of text backward and forward in a document. In other words, you can reorganize a document in Outline view. To switch to this view, click the Outline button on the status bar or the Outline button on the View tab. Chapter 6 of this mini-book explains outlines in torturous detail.

Book II
Chapter 1

Speed Techniques
for Using Word

Draft view

Switch to Draft view when you're writing a document and you want to focus on the words. Clip-art images, shapes, and other objects don't appear in this view, nor do page breaks (although you can clearly see section breaks). Draft view is best for writing first drafts.

Splitting the screen

Besides opening a second window on a document (a subject of Book I, Chapter 3), you can be two places at once in a Word document by splitting the screen. One reason you might do this: You're writing a long report and want the introduction to support the conclusion, and you also want the conclusion to fulfill all promises made by the introduction. That's difficult to do sometimes, but you can make it easier by splitting the screen so you can be two places at once as you write your introduction and conclusion.

Splitting a window divides it into north and south halves, as shown in Figure 1-4. In a split screen, two sets of scroll bars appear so that you can travel in one half of the screen without disturbing the other half. Word offers two ways to split the screen:

✦ Move the mouse pointer to the *split box* at the top of the scroll bar on the right. Move it just above the View Ruler button. When the pointer turns into double-arrows, click and drag the gray line down the screen. When you release the mouse button, you have a split screen.

✦ On the View tab, click the Split button. A gray line appears on-screen. Roll the mouse down until the gray line is where you want the split to be, and click. You get two screens split down the middle.

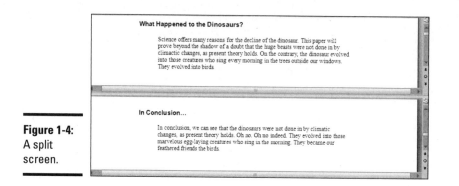

Figure 1-4:
A split
screen.

When you tire of this schizophrenic arrangement, click the Remove Split button on the View tab or drag the line to the top or bottom of the screen. You can also double-click the line that splits the screen in two.

In a split screen, you can choose a view for the different halves. For example, choose Outline view for one half and Draft view for the other to see the headings in a document while you write the introduction.

Selecting Text in Speedy Ways

Book I, Chapter 2 explains how to enter text and change its appearance and size. After you enter text, the need may arise for you to copy, move, or delete it, but you can't do those tasks until you select it first. Table 1-1 describes shortcuts for selecting text.

Viewing the hidden format symbols

Sometimes it pays to see the hidden format symbols when you're editing and laying out a document. The symbols show line breaks, tab spaces, paragraph breaks, and the space or spaces between words. To see the hidden format symbols, click the Show/Hide¶ button. Click the button again to hide the symbols.

Here's what the hidden symbols look like on-screen.

Symbol	How to Enter
Line break (↵)	Press Shift+Enter.
Optional hyphen (¬)	Press Ctrl+hyphen.
Paragraph (¶)	Press Enter.
Space (·)	Press the spacebar.
Tab (→)	Press Tab.

Table 1-1	Shortcuts for Selecting Text
To Select This	*Do This*
A word	Double-click the word.
A line	Click in the left margin next to the line.
Some lines	Drag the mouse pointer over the lines or drag it down the left margin.
A sentence	Ctrl+click the sentence.
A paragraph	Double-click in the left margin next to the paragraph.
A mess of text	Click at the start of the text, hold down the Shift key, and click at the end of the text.
A gob of text	Put the cursor where you want to start selecting, press F8, and press an arrow key, drag the mouse, or click at the end of the selection.
Text with the same formats	On the Home tab, click the Select button and choose Select Text with Similar Formatting (you may have to click the Editing button first).
A document	Hold down the Ctrl key and click in the left margin; triple-click in the left margin; press Ctrl+A; or go to the Home tab, click the Editing button (if necessary), and choose Select⇨Select All.

If you have a bunch of highlighted text on-screen and you want it to go away but it won't (because you pressed F8), press the Esc key.

After you press F8, all the keyboard shortcuts for moving the cursor also work for selecting text. For example, press F8 and then press Ctrl+Home to select everything from the cursor to the top of the document. Later in this chapter, "Keys for getting around quickly" describes keyboard shortcuts for getting from place to place.

Moving Around Quickly in Documents

Besides sliding the scroll bar, Word offers a handful of very speedy techniques for jumping around in documents: pressing shortcut keys, browsing in the Select Browse Object menu, using the Go To command, and navigating with the Document Map or thumbnails. Read on to discover how to get there faster, faster, faster.

Keys for getting around quickly

One of the fastest ways to go from place to place is to press the keys and key combinations listed in Table 1-2.

Table 1-2	Keys for Moving Around Documents
Key to Press	*Where It Takes You*
Page Up	Up the length of one screen
Page Down	Down the length of one screen
Ctrl+Page Up	To the previous page in the document
Ctrl+Page Down	To the next page in the document
Ctrl+Home	To the top of the document
Ctrl+End	To the bottom of the document

If pressing Ctrl+Page Up or Ctrl+Page Down doesn't get you to the top or bottom of a page, it's because you clicked the Select Browse Object button at the bottom of the vertical scroll bar, which makes Word go to the next bookmark, comment, heading, or whatever. Click the Select Browse Object button and choose Browse by Page to make these key combinations work again.

Here's a useful keystroke for getting from place to place: Shift+F5. Press it once to go to the location of your most recent edit. Press it two or three times to go back one or two edits before that. Pressing Shift+F5 is useful when you want to return to the place where you made an edit but can't quite remember where that place is.

Clicking thumbnail pages

In lengthy documents, such as the one shown in Figure 1-5, the best way to get from page to page is to display the Thumbnails pane and click a thumbnail image of a page. When you display thumbnail pages, a thumbnail image of each page in the document appears on the left side of the screen. Each thumbnail is numbered so that you always know which page you're viewing. To quickly move from page to page, use the scroll bar on the left side of the screen and click a page thumbnail. To display the thumbnails, go to the View tab and click the Thumbnails check box (you may have to click the Show/Hide button first).

"Browsing" around a document

A really fast way to move around quickly is to click the Select Browse Object button in the lower-right corner of the screen. When you click this button, Word presents 12 *Browse By* icons: Go To, Find, Edits, Heading, Graphic, Table, Field, Endnote, Footnote, Comment, Section, and Page. Select the icon that represents the element you want to go to, and Word takes you there immediately. For example, click the Browse by Heading icon to get to the next heading in your document (provided that you assigned heading styles to headings).

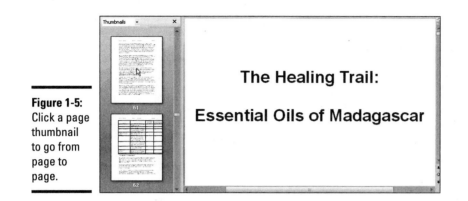

Figure 1-5:
Click a page
thumbnail
to go from
page to
page.

After you select a Browse By icon, the navigator buttons — the double-arrows
directly above and below the Select Browse Object button — turn blue.
Click a blue navigator button to get to the next example or the previous
example of the element you chose. For example, if you selected the Browse
by Heading icon, all you have to do is click the blue navigator buttons to get
from heading to heading, backward or forward in your document.

Going there fast with the Go To command

Another fast way to go from place to place in a document is to use the Go To
command. On the Home tab, open the drop-down list on the Find button and
choose Go To (you may have to click the Editing button first). You see the
Go To tab of the Find and Replace dialog box, as shown in Figure 1-6. You can
also open this dialog box by pressing Ctrl+G or F5.

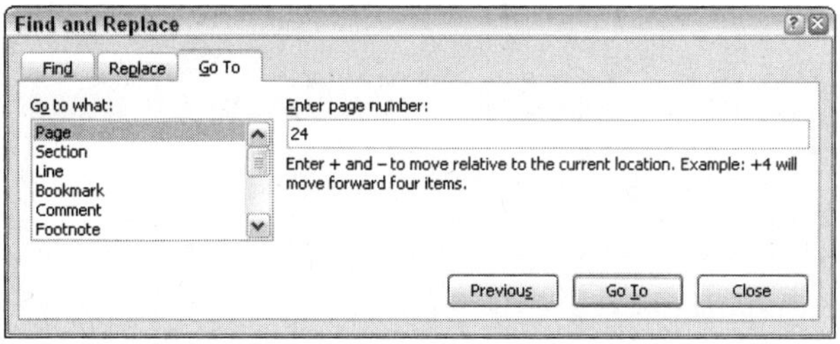

Figure 1-6:
Using the
Go To
command.

The Go to What menu in this dialog box lists everything that can conceivably be numbered in a Word document, and other things, too. Everything
that you can get to with the Select Browse Object button, as well as lines,
equations, and objects, can be reached by way of the Go To tab. Click a
menu item, enter a number, choose an item from the drop-down list, or click
the Previous, Next, or Go To buttons to go elsewhere.

Hopping from place to place in the document map

Yet another way to hop from place to place is by turning on the *document map.* To do so, go to the View tab and click the Document Map check box (you may have to click the Show/Hide button first). As shown in Figure 1-7, the headings in your document appear along the left side of the screen (provided you assigned heading styles to headings).

Select a heading to scroll to it.

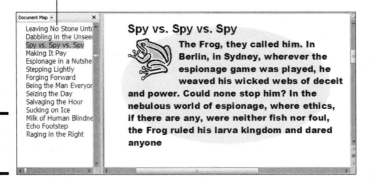

Figure 1-7:
The document map.

Select an item in the Document Map, and Word takes you there in the twinkling of an eye. The document map is like a table of contents whose headings you can click to get from place to place. Right-click the document map and choose a heading-level option on the shortcut menu to tell Word which headings to display in the map. You can also right-click a heading and choose Expand or Collapse on the shortcut menu to see or hide lower-level headings.

Bookmarks for hopping around

Rather than press Page Up or Page Down or click the scroll bar to thrash around in a long document, you can use *bookmarks.* All you do is put a bookmark in an important spot in your document that you'll return to many times. When you want to return to that spot, go to the Insert tab, click the Bookmark button (you may have to click the Links button first), double-click the bookmark in the Bookmark dialog box, and click the Close button. True to the craft, the mystery writer whose bookmarks are shown in Figure 1-8 wrote the end of the story first and used bookmarks to jump back and forth between the beginning and end to make all the clues fit together.

Follow these instructions to handle bookmarks:

+ **Adding a bookmark:** To place a bookmark in a document, click where you want the bookmark to go and click the Bookmark button on the Insert tab (you may have to click the Links button first, depending on the size of your screen). Then, in the Bookmark dialog box, type a descriptive name in the Bookmark Name box, and click the Add button. Bookmarks can't start with numbers or include blank spaces. You can also open the Bookmark dialog box by pressing Ctrl+Shift+F5.

+ **Deleting a bookmark:** To delete a bookmark, select it in the Bookmark dialog box and click the Delete button.

Word uses bookmarks for many purposes. For example, bookmarks indicate where cross-references are located in a document.

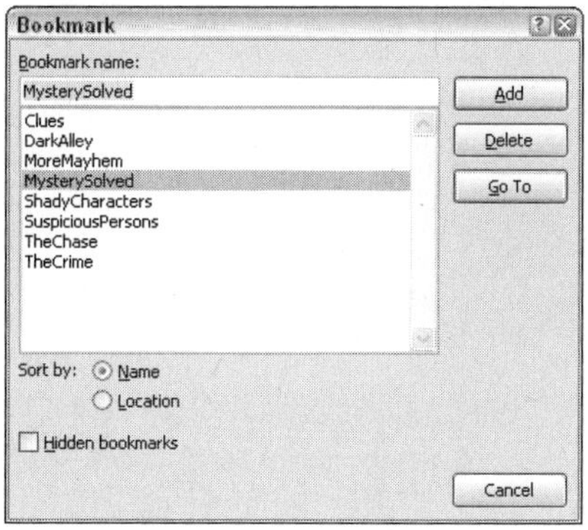

Figure 1-8:
The
Bookmark
dialog box.

Inserting a Whole File into a Document

One of the beautiful things about word processing is that you can recycle documents. Say that you wrote an essay on the Scissor-Tailed Flycatcher that would fit very nicely in a broader report on North American birds. You can insert the Scissor-Tailed Flycatcher document into your report document:

1. **Place the cursor where you want to insert the document.**

2. **On the Insert tab, open the drop-down list on the Object button and choose Text from File.**

You see the Insert File dialog box.

3. **Find and select the file you want to insert.**

4. **Click the Insert button.**

Entering Information Quickly in a Computerized Form

A *form* is a means of soliciting and recording information. You can use forms, like the one shown in Figure 1-9, to enter data faster and to reduce data-entry errors. Instead of entering all the information by hand, you or a data-entry clerk can choose entries from combo boxes, drop-down lists, and date pickers. You save time because you don't have to enter all the information by hand, and the information you enter is more likely to be accurate because you choose it from prescribed lists instead of entering it yourself.

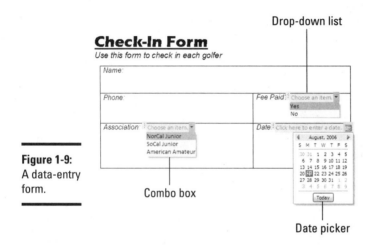

Figure 1-9:
A data-entry form.

To create a form like the one shown in Figure 1-9, start by creating a template for your form and putting *data-entry controls* — the combo boxes, drop-down lists, and date pickers — in the form. To fill out a form, you create a document from the form template and go to it. These pages explain how to create a form and use forms to record information.

Creating a computerized form

The first step in creating a data-entry form is to create a template for holding the form. After that, you design the form itself by labeling the data fields and creating the data-entry controls. Better keep reading.

Creating a template to hold the form

Follow these steps to create a new template:

1. **Click the Office button and choose New on the drop-down list.**

You see the New Document dialog box.

2. **Click the My Templates button.**

The New dialog box appears. It lists Word templates that are on your computer.

3. **Click the Template option button.**

You can find this button under Create New in the lower-right corner of the dialog box.

4. **Click OK.**

5. **Click the Save button to open the Save As dialog box.**

6. **Enter a descriptive name for your template and click the Save button.**

Chapter 3 of this mini-book explains templates in detail.

Creating the form and data-entry controls

Your next task is to create the form and data-entry controls for your template. Enter labels on the form where you will enter information. The form in Figure 1-9, for example, has five labels: Name, Phone, Fee Paid?, Association, and Date. After you've entered the labels, follow these steps to create the data-entry controls:

1. **Display the Developer tab, if necessary.**

If this tab isn't showing, click the Office button, choose Word Options, and on the Popular tab of the Word Options dialog box, click the Show Developer Tab in the Ribbon check box and click OK.

2. **Click where you want to place a control and then create the control.**

Here are instructions for creating three types of controls:

✦ *Drop-down list:* A *drop-down list* is a menu that "drops" when you open it to reveal different option choices (refer to Figure 1-9). Click the Dropdown List button and then the Properties button. You see the Content Control Properties dialog box, as shown in Figure 1-10. For each option you want to place on the drop-down list, click the Add button, and in the Add Choice dialog box, enter the option's name in the Display Name text box and click OK, as shown in Figure 1-10.

✦ *Combo box:* Like a drop-down list, a *combo box* "drops" to reveal choices. However, as well as choosing an option on the drop-down list, data-entry clerks can enter information in the box (refer to Figure 1-9). Click the Combo Box button and then the Properties button. In the Content Control Properties dialog box, enter option names the same way you enter them in a drop-down list, as shown in Figure 1-10.

✦ *Date picker:* A *date picker* is a mini-calendar from which data-entry clerks can enter a date (refer to Figure 1-9). Click the Date Picker button and then the Properties button. In the Content Control Properties dialog box, choose a display format for dates and click OK.

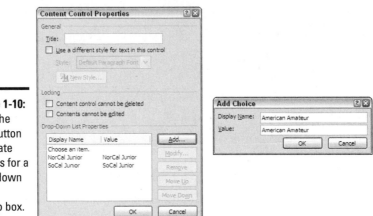

Figure 1-10:
Click the
Add button
to create
options for a
drop-down
list or
combo box.

3. **Click the Save button to save your template.**

Now you're ready to use your newly made form to enter data.

Entering data in the form

Now that you have the template, you or someone else can enter data cleanly in easy-to-read forms:

1. **Click the Office button and choose New on the drop-down list.**

You see the New Document dialog box.

2. **Click the My Templates button.**

The New dialog box opens and shows you Word templates on your computer.

3. **Double-click the name of the template you created for entering data in your form.**

The form appears.

4. **Enter information in the input fields.**

Press the up or down arrow, or press Tab and Shift+Tab to move from field to field. You can also click input fields to move the cursor there.

5. **When you're done, print the document or save it.**

Chapter 2: Laying Out Text and Pages

In This Chapter

- ✔ Entering a section break
- ✔ Starting a new line and page
- ✔ Changing the margins
- ✔ Indenting text
- ✔ Numbering pages and handling headers and footers
- ✔ Adjusting the space between lines and paragraphs
- ✔ Handling bulleted and numbered lists
- ✔ Hyphenating the text

This chapter explains how to format text and pages. A well-laid-out document says a lot about how much time and thought went into it. This chapter presents tips, tricks, and techniques for making pages look just right.

In this chapter, you learn what section breaks are and why they are so important to formatting. You discover how to establish the size of margins, indent text, number pages, construct headers and footers, determine how much space appears between lines of text, handle lists, and hyphenate text.

Paragraphs and Formatting

Back in English class, your teacher taught you that a paragraph is a part of a longer composition that presents one idea, or in the case of dialogue, presents the words of one speaker. Your teacher was right, too, but for word-processing purposes, a paragraph is a lot less than that. In word processing, a paragraph is simply what you put on-screen before you press the Enter key.

For instance, a heading is a paragraph. If you press Enter on a blank line to go to the next line, the blank line is considered a paragraph. If you type **Dear John** at the top of a letter and press Enter, "Dear John" is a paragraph.

It's important to know this because paragraphs have a lot to do with formatting. If you click the Paragraph group button on the Home tab and monkey around with the paragraph formatting in the Paragraph dialog box, your changes affect everything in the paragraph where the cursor is located. To make format changes to a whole paragraph, all you have to do is place the cursor there. You don't have to select the paragraph. And if you want to make format changes to several paragraphs in a row, all you have to do is select those paragraphs.

Inserting a Section Break for Formatting Purposes

When you want to have different page numbering schemes, headers and footers, margin sizes, and page orientations in a document, you have to create a *section break* to start a new section. Word creates a new section for you when you create newspaper-style columns or change the size of margins.

Follow these steps to create a new section:

1. **Click where you want to insert a section break.**

2. **On the Page Layout tab, click the Breaks button.**

You open a drop-down list.

3. **Under Section Breaks on the drop-down list, choose a section break.**

All four section break options create a new section, but they do so in different ways:

✦ **Next Page:** Inserts a page break as well as a section break so that the new section can start at the top of a new page (the next one). Select this option to start a new chapter, for example.

✦ **Continuous:** Inserts a section break in the middle of a page. Select this option if, for example, you want to introduce newspaper-style columns in the middle of a page.

✦ **Even Page:** Starts the new section on the next even page. This option is good for two-sided documents in which the headers on the left- and right-side pages are different.

✦ **Odd Page:** Starts the new section on the next odd page. You might choose this option if you have a book in which chapters start on odd pages. (By convention, that's where they start.)

To delete a section break, make sure that you're in Draft view, click the dotted line, and press the Delete key.

Editing a document with many sections can be confusing, and if you accidentally delete a section break, you can turn a perfectly good document into guacamole. In the same way that paragraph marks store formats for a paragraph, section breaks store formats for an entire section. If you accidentally delete a section break, you apply new formats because the section is folded into the section that formerly followed it and adopts that next section's formats. Because it's easy to accidentally delete a section break and create havoc, I recommend working in Draft view when your document has many section breaks. In Draft view, you can tell where a section ends because `Section Break` and a double dotted line appear on-screen. The only way to tell where a section ends in Print Layout view is to glance at the Sec listing on the status bar or click the Show/Hide¶ button on the Home tab. (If the Sec listing doesn't appear on the status bar, right-click the status bar and choose Section on the pop-up list.)

Seeing what the formats are

Sometimes seeing how text was formatted merely by looking is difficult. However, by pressing Shift+F1, you can see precisely how text and paragraphs were formatted in the Reveal Formatting task pane. It describes how the text, paragraph, and section where the pointer is located are formatted.

While the Reveal Formatting task pane is open, you can take advantage of these amenities:

✔ **Compare one part of a document to another:** Click the Compare to Another Section check box and then click another part of your document. The Reveal Formatting task pane describes how the two parts differ. Knowing how parts of a document differ can be invaluable when you're creating and modifying styles.

✔ **Find out which style was assigned:** Click the Distinguish Style Source check box. The task pane lists the style you assigned to the part of your document where the cursor is located.

✔ **See the formatting marks:** Click the Show All Formatting Marks check box. Clicking this box has the same results as clicking

the Show/Hide¶ button on the Home tab — you can tell where paragraphs end, where line breaks are, and where tab spaces were entered.

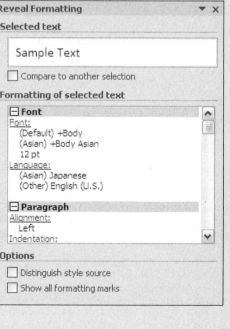

Breaking a Line

To break a line of text before it reaches the right margin without starting a new paragraph, press Shift+Enter. Figure 2-1 shows how you can press Shift+Enter to make lines break better. The paragraphs are identical, but I broke lines in the right-side paragraph to make the text easier to read. Line breaks are marked with the ↵ symbol. To erase line breaks, click the Show/Hide¶ button to see these symbols and then backspace over them.

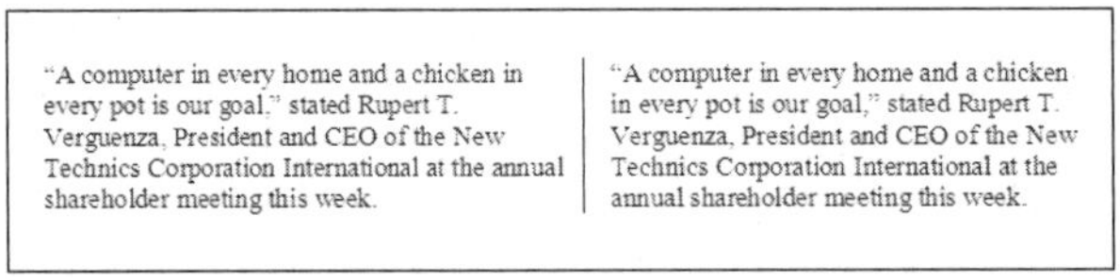

Figure 2-1:
Break lines
to make
reading
easier.

"A computer in every home and a chicken in every pot is our goal," stated Rupert T. Verguenza, President and CEO of the New Technics Corporation International at the annual shareholder meeting this week.

"A computer in every home and a chicken in every pot is our goal," stated Rupert T. Verguenza, President and CEO of the New Technics Corporation International at the annual shareholder meeting this week.

Starting a New Page

Word gives you another page so that you can keep going when you fill up one page. But what if you're impatient and want to start a new page right away? Whatever you do, *don't* press Enter again and again until you fill up the page. Instead, create a *hard page break* by doing either of the following:

✦ Press Ctrl+Enter.

✦ Click the Breaks button on the Page Layout tab and choose Page on the drop-down list.

In Draft view, you can click the Show/Hide¶ button on the Home tab and tell where you inserted a hard page break because you see the words `Page Break` and a dotted line on-screen. You can't tell where hard page breaks are in Print Layout view.

To delete a hard page break, switch to Draft view, click the Show/Hide¶ button on the Home tab, click the words `Page Break`, and press the Delete key.

Setting Up and Changing the Margins

Margins are the empty spaces along the left, right, top, and bottom edges of a page, as shown in Figure 2-2. Headers and footers fall, respectively, in the top and bottom margins. And you can put graphics, text boxes, and page numbers in the margins as well. Margins serve to frame the text and make it easier to read.

Outside margin   Inside margin   Outside margin

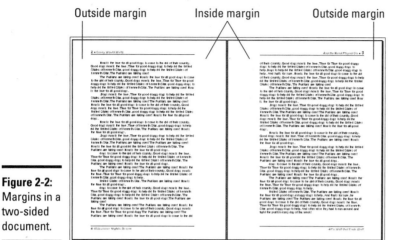

Figure 2-2:
Margins in a
two-sided
document.

When you start a new document, give a moment's thought to the margins. Changing the size of margins after you enter the text, clip art, graphics, and whatnot can be disastrous. Text is indented from the left and right margins. Pages break on the bottom margin. If you change margin settings, indents and page breaks change for good or ill throughout your document. By setting the margins carefully from the beginning, you can rest assured that text lands on the page where you want it to land.

Don't confuse margins with indents. Text is indented from the margin, not from the edge of the page. If you want to change how far text falls from the page edge, indent it. To change margin settings in the middle of a document, you have to create a new section.

To set up or change the margins, go to the Page Layout tab and click the Margins button. You see a drop-down list with margin settings. Either choose a setting or select Custom Margins to open the Margins tab of the Page Setup dialog box and choose among these commands for handling margins:

✦ **Changing the size of the margins:** Enter measurements in the Top, Bottom, Left, and Right boxes to tell Word how much blank space to put along the sides of the page.

✦ **Making room for the gutter:** The *gutter* is the part of the paper that the binding eats into when you bind a document. Enter a measurement in the Gutter box to increase the left or inside margin and make room for the binding. Notice on the pages of this book, for example, that the margin closest to the binding is wider than the outside margin. Choose Top on the Gutter Position menu if you intend to bind your document from the top, not the left, or inside, of the page. Some legal documents are bound this way.

✦ **Handling two-sided documents (inside and outside margins):** In a bound document in which text is printed on both sides of the pages, the terms left margin and right margin are meaningless. What matters instead is in the *inside margin,* the margin in the middle of the page spread next to the bindings, and the *outside margin,* the margin on the outside of the page spread that isn't affected by the bindings (refer to Figure 2-2). Choose Mirror Margins on the Multiple Pages drop-down list and adjust the margins accordingly if you intend to print on both sides of the paper.

✦ **Applying margin changes:** On the Apply To drop-down list, choose Whole Document to apply your margin settings to the entire document; This Section to apply them to a section; or This Point Forward to change margins in the rest of a document. When you choose This Point Forward, Word creates a new section.

If you're in a hurry to change margins, you can change them on the ruler. Display the ruler and drag the Left Margin, Right Margin, or Top Margin marker. You can find these markers by moving the pointer onto a ruler and looking for the two-headed arrow near a margin boundary. It appears, along with a pop-up label, when the pointer is over a margin marker.

To get a good look at where margins are as you're working in a document, click the Office button and choose Word Options. In the Word Options dialog box, select the Advanced category, and click the Show Text Boundaries check box (you'll find it under Show Document Content).

Indenting Paragraphs and First Lines

An *indent* is the distance between a margin and the text, not the edge of the page and the text. Word offers a handful of different ways to change the indentation of paragraphs. You can change the indentation of first lines as well as entire paragraphs. To start, select all or part of the paragraphs you want to re-indent (just click in a paragraph if you want to re-indent only on paragraph). Then click an Indent button, fiddle with the indentation marks on the ruler, or go to the Paragraph dialog box. All three techniques are described here.

Clicking an Indent button (for left-indents)

Click the Increase Indent or Decrease Indent button (or press Ctrl+M or Ctrl+Shift+M) on the Home tab to move a paragraph a half-inch farther away from or closer to the left margin. If you created tab stops, text is indented to the next or previous tab stop as well as to the next or previous half-inch. This is the fastest way to indent text, although you can't indent first lines or indent from the right margin this way.

"Eye-balling it" with the ruler

You can also change indentations by using the ruler to "eyeball it." This technique requires some dexterity with the mouse, but it allows you to see precisely where paragraphs and the first lines of paragraphs are indented. If necessary, display the ruler by going to the View tab and clicking the Ruler check box. Then click in or select the paragraph or paragraphs that need indenting and use these techniques to re-indent them:

✦ **Indenting an entire paragraph from the left margin:** Drag the *left-indent marker* on the ruler to the right. Figure 2-3 shows where this marker is on the ruler. Dragging the left-indent marker moves the first-line indent marker as well.

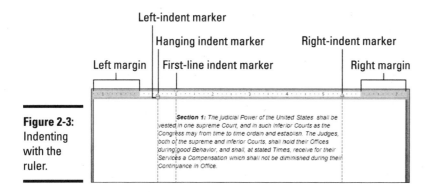

Figure 2-3:
Indenting
with the
ruler.

✦ **Indenting the first line of a paragraph:** Drag the *first-line indent marker* to the right (see Figure 2-3). This marker determines how far the first line of the paragraph is indented.

✦ **Making a hanging indent:** Drag the *hanging indent marker* to the right of the first-line indent marker (see Figure 2-3). A *hanging indent* is one in which the first line of a paragraph appears to "hang" into the margin because the second and subsequent lines are indented to the right of the first line.

✦ **Indenting an entire paragraph from the right margin:** Drag the *right-indent marker* to the left (see Figure 2-3).

Notice the shaded areas on the left and right sides of the ruler. These areas represent the page margins.

Going to the Paragraph dialog box

Yet another way to indent a paragraph or first line is to visit the Paragraph dialog box. Click in or select the paragraph or paragraphs in question and then click the Paragraph group button on the Home tab. You see the Indents and Spacing tab of the Paragraph dialog box. Change the indentation settings. If you want to indent the first line or create a hanging indent, choose First Line or Hanging on the Special drop-down list and enter a measurement in the By box.

Numbering the Pages

Word numbers the pages in a document automatically. How do you want page numbers to appear in your document? You can number them in sequence starting with the number 1, number pages starting with a different number, use different number formats, include chapter numbers in page numbers, and number the pages by section. You can make page numbers a part of headers and footers or use "prefabricated" numbers, as shown in Figure 2-4.

Figure 2-4: A "prefabricated" page number (left) and a page number in a header (right).

Prefabricated page numbers are elegant (see Figure 2-4). You would have a hard time creating them on your own. However, you can't change their number formats or adjust their position on the page. Include the page number in a header or footer if you want an unusual number formatting scheme for your page numbers.

To handle page numbers (as well as headers and footers), you must be in Print Layout view. Click the Print Layout view button or click the Print Layout button on the View tab.

Using "prefabricated" page numbers

[Page Number ▾]

To insert a prefabricated page number, click the Page Number button on the Insert tab, choose where on the page you want to put the page number (Top, Bottom, or Page Margins), and choose a prefabricated number on the submenu.

You can do one or two things to change a prefabricated page number. If necessary, switch to Print Layout view and double-click in the Header or Footer area of your page to work with the header or footer (you can also go to the Insert tab and click the Header or Footer button). Then follow these steps to alter a prefabricated page number:

1. **Move the pointer over the page number and double-click it.**

As shown in Figure 2-5, double-clicking the page number selects it and places it in a text frame.

2. **Change the look and format of the page number.**

With the page number selected, you can change the number's appearance and formatting:

- *Changing a number's appearance:* Choose a new font or font size on the Mini Toolbar (right-click the page number if you have trouble making the Mini Toolbar appear).

- *Changing number formats:* Click the Page Number button on the (Header & Footer Tools) Design tab and choose Format Page Numbers on the drop-down list. You see the Page Number Format dialog box, as shown in Figure 2-5. You can't change number formats for prefabricated page numbers in this dialog box, but you can include the chapter number in the page number, continue numbering from a previous section, and start numbering from a numeral other than 1. See "Changing page number formats" later in this chapter.

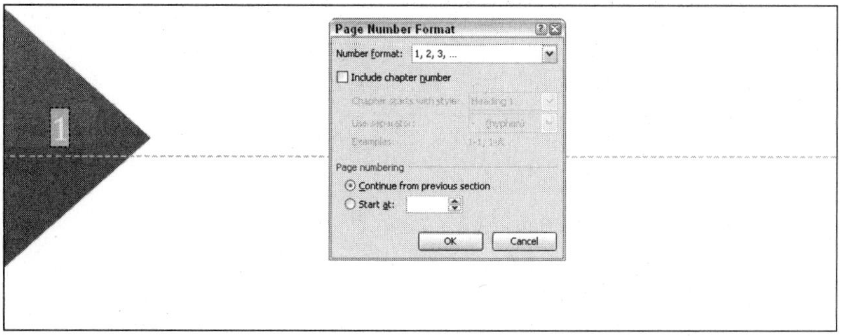

Figure 2-5:
Working with a "prefabricated" page number.

To remove a prefabricated page number, double-click the header or footer where it is located, click the Page Number button on the (Header & Footer Tools) Design tab, and choose Remove Page Numbers on the drop-down list.

Including a page number in a header or footer

To make the page number a part of a header or footer, double-click in the header or footer where you want the page number to appear. (Later in this chapter, "Putting Headers and Footers on Pages" explains headers and footers.) Then follow these steps to insert the page number:

`[#] Page Number ∨`

1. **On the (Header & Footer Tools) Design tab, click the Page Number button and choose a position (Top of Page, Bottom of Page, or Page Margins) on the drop-down list.**

   You see a submenu with page number choices.

2. **Scroll through the submenu and choose a page number format.**

   The "Page X of Y" options are for listing the total number of pages in a document as well as the page number. For example, page 2 of a 10-page document is numbered "Page 2 of 10." You can change the font and font size of page numbers and the word *page* by selecting them and giving a font or font-size command.

Changing page number formats

Change page number formats in the Page Number Format dialog box (refer to Figure 2-5). To display this dialog box, make sure you're in Print Layout view and double-click your header or footer. Then use one of the following methods:

✦ On the Insert tab, click the Page Number button and choose Format Page Numbers on the drop-down list.

✦ On the (Header & Footer Tools) Design tab, click the Page Number button and choose Format Page Numbers on the drop-down list.

In the Page Number Format dialog box, get to work to make your page numbers just-so:

✦ **Choosing a different number format:** Open the Number Format drop-down list and choose a page-numbering format. You can use numbers, letters, and Roman numerals.

✦ **Including chapter numbers in page numbers:** If your document generates chapter numbers automatically from headings assigned the same style (a subject not covered in this book), you can include the chapter number in the page number. Click the Include Chapter Number check box, choose a style, and choose a separator to go between the chapter number and page number.

✦ **Numbering each section separately:** Click the Start At option button (not the Continue from Previous Section button) to begin counting pages anew at each section in your document. Earlier in this chapter, "Inserting a Section Break for Formatting Purposes" explains sections.

✦ **Start numbering pages at a number other than 1:** Click the Start At option button and enter a number other than 1.

To keep some pages in a document from being numbered, create a section for those pages, and then remove page numbers from the section. To paginate your document, Word skips the section you created and resumes numbering pages in the following section.

Putting Headers and Footers on Pages

A *header* is a little description that appears along the top of a page so that the reader knows what's what. Usually, headers include the page number and a title, and often the author's name appears in the header as well. A *footer* is the same thing as a header except that it appears along the bottom of the page, as befits its name.

These pages explain everything a mere mortal needs to know about headers and footers. Meanwhile, here are the ground rules for managing them:

✦ **Switching to Print Layout view:** To enter, read, edit or delete headers and footers, you must be in Print Layout view. You can't see headers and footers in the other views.

✦ **Displaying the (Header & Footer Tools) Design tab:** As shown in Figure 2-6, you manage headers and footers by way of buttons on the (Header & Footer Tools) Design tab. To display this tab after you create a header or footer, switch to Print Layout view and double-click a header or footer.

✦ **Closing the (Header & Footer Tools) Design tab:** Click the Close Header and Footer button.

✦ **Placing different headers and footers in the same document:** To change headers or footers in the middle of a document, you have to create a new section. See "Inserting a Section Break for Formatting Purposes" earlier in this chapter.

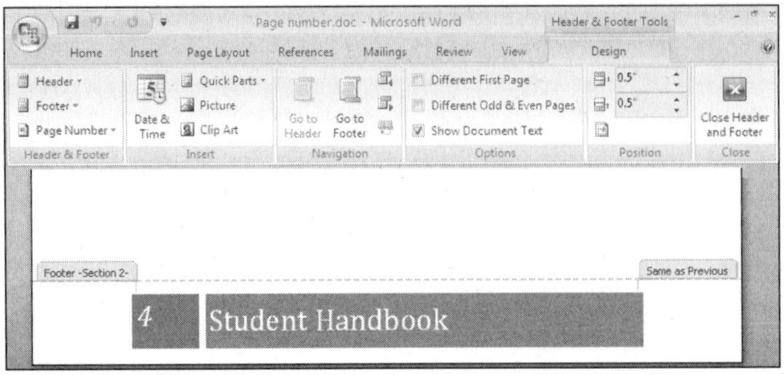

Figure 2-6:
Manage
headers and
footers on
the (Header
& Footer
Tools)
Design tab.

Creating, editing, and removing headers and footers

Follow these instructions to create, edit, and delete headers and footers:

✦ **Creating a header or footer:** On the Insert tab, click the Header or Footer button, and on the drop-down list, choose a header or footer. You can find several ready-made headers or footers on the drop-down list; the fancier ones are at the bottom. You can find preformatted page numbers, dates, and places to enter a document title and author's name on many headers and footers.

✦ **Choosing a different header or footer:** Don't like the header or footer you chose? If necessary, double-click your header or footer to display the (Header & Footer Tools) Design tab. Then click the Header or Footer button and choose a new header or footer on the drop-down list.

✦ **Editing a header or footer:** Click the Header or Footer button and choose Edit Header or Edit Footer on the drop-down list. The cursor moves into the header or footer so you can enter or format text.

✦ **Removing a header or footer:** Click the Header or Footer button and choose Remove Header or Remove Footer on the drop-down list.

To switch back and forth between the header and footer, click the Go to Header or Go to Footer button on the (Header & Footer Tools) Design tab.

As you work away on your header and footer, you can call on most of the text-formatting commands on the Home tab. You can change the text's font and font size, click an alignment button, and paste text from the Clipboard. Tabs are set up in most headers and footers to make it possible to center, left-align, and right-align text. To center a header or footer, for example, press the Tab key once to go to the Center tab mark, and start typing.

Fine-tuning a header or footer

Here is advice for making a perfect header or footer:

+ **Inserting a page number:** See "Including a page number in a header or footer" and "Changing page number formats" earlier in this chapter.

+ **Inserting the date and time:** Click the Date & Time button, choose a date format in the Date and Time dialog box, and click OK. Click the Update Automatically check box if you want the date to record when you print the document, not when you created your header or footer.

+ **Changing headers and footers from section to section:** Use the Link to Previous button to determine whether headers and footers are different from section to section (you must divide the document into sections to have different headers and footers). Unpressing (clicking to release) this button tells Word that you want your header or footer to be different from the header or footer in the previous section of the document; pressing this button (clicking it so it looks selected) tells Word that you want your header or footer to be the same as the header or footer in the previous section of your document. To make a different header or footer, deselect the Link to Previous button and enter a different header or footer.

When the header or footer is the same as that of the previous section, the Header or Footer box reads `Same as Previous` (refer to Figure 2-6); when the header or footer is different from that of the previous section, the words `Same as Previous` don't appear. You can click the Show Previous or Show Next button to examine the header or footer in the previous or next section.

+ **Different headers and footers for odd and even pages:** Click the Different Odd & Even Pages check box to create different headers and footers for odd and even pages. As "Setting Up and Changing the Margins" explains earlier in this chapter, documents in which text is printing on both sides of the page can have different headers and footers for the left and right side of the page spread. The Header or Footer box reads Odd or Even to tell you which side of the page spread you're dealing with when you enter your header or footer.

+ **Removing headers and footers from the first page:** Click the Different First Page check box to remove a header or footer from the first page of a document or section. Typically, the first page of letters and reports are not numbered.

Book II
Chapter 2

Laying Out Text
and Pages

Including a logo in a header or footer

As long as it's small enough, you can include a company logo in a header or footer. To do so, click the Picture button on the (Header & Footer Tools) Design tab, select the logo graphic in the Insert Picture dialog box, and click the Insert button. (Book VIII, Chapter 3 describes how to recolor and change the size of graphics; Book I, Chapter 8 explains how to manipulate graphics.)

If you often insert the same header and footer with a logo in headers and footers, you can place it in the Building Blocks gallery and be able to enter it in a hurry:

- **Placing a logo header or footer in the Building Blocks gallery:** Place a logo in the header or footer, being careful to locate it where you want it to go when you insert it in the future. Then select your header or footer by dragging over it or by clicking once in the margin to its left. On the (Header & Footer Tools) Design tab, click the Quick Parts button and choose Save Selection to Quick Part Gallery on the drop-down list. You see the Create New Building Block dialog box. Enter

a descriptive name for the header or footer with the logo, choose Footers or Headers on the Gallery drop-down list, and click OK.

- **Inserting a header or footer from the Building Blocks gallery:** On the Insert tab, click the Quick Parts button and choose Building Blocks Organizer. The Building Blocks Organizer dialog box appears. Select your logo (select it under the name you gave it) and click the Insert button.

Create New Building Block	? ☒
Name:	Footer - Company Logo
Gallery:	Footers ▾
Category:	General ▾
Description:	Footer with company logo, date, company name, and words "First Draft"
Save in:	Building Blocks.dotx ▾
Options:	Insert content only ▾
	OK Cancel

Adjusting the Space between Lines

To change the spacing between lines, select the lines whose spacing you want to change, or simply put the cursor in a paragraph if you're changing the line spacing throughout a paragraph (if you're just starting a document, you're ready to go). Then, on the Home tab, click the Line Spacing button and choose an option on the drop-down list.

To take advantage of more line-spacing options, click the Paragraph group button on the Home tab or choose Line Spacing Options on the Line Spacing button drop-down list. You see the Paragraph dialog box. Select an option on the Line Spacing drop-down list:

✦ **At Least:** Choose this one if you want Word to adjust for tall symbols or other unusual text. Word adjusts the lines but makes sure there is, at minimum, the number of points you enter in the At box between each line.

✦ **Exactly:** Choose this one and enter a number in the At box if you want a specific amount of space between lines.

✦ **Multiple:** Choose this one and put a number in the At box to get triple-spaced, quadruple-, quintuple-, or any other number of spaced lines.

 To quickly single-space text, click the text or select it if you want to change more than one paragraph, and press Ctrl+1. To quickly double-space text, select the text and press Ctrl+2. Press Ctrl+5 to put one and a half lines between lines of text.

Adjusting the Space between Paragraphs

Rather than press Enter to put a blank line between paragraphs, you can open the Paragraph dialog box and enter a point-size measurement in the Before or After text box. The Before and After measurements place a specific amount of space before and after paragraphs.

 Truth be told, the Before and After options are for use with styles (a subject of Chapter 3 in this mini-book). When you create a style, you can tell Word to always follow a paragraph in a certain style with a paragraph in another style. For example, a paragraph in the Chapter Title style might always be followed by a paragraph in the Chapter Intro style. In cases like these, when you know that paragraphs assigned to one type of style will always follow paragraphs assigned to another style, you can confidently put space before and after paragraphs. But if you use the Before and After styles indiscriminately, you can end up with large blank spaces between paragraphs.

Go to the Home tab and use one of these techniques to adjust the amount of space between paragraphs:

✦ Click the Line Spacing button and choose Add Space Before Paragraph or Add Space after Paragraph on the drop-down list. These commands place ten points of blank space before or after the paragraph that the cursor is in.

✦ Click the Paragraph group button to open the Paragraph dialog box, and enter point-size measurements in the Before and After boxes (or choose Auto in these boxes to enter one blank line between paragraphs in whatever your Line-Spacing choice is). The Don't Add Space between Paragraphs of the Same Style check box tells Word to ignore Before and After measurements if the previous or next paragraph is assigned the same style as the paragraph that the cursor is in.

Creating Numbered and Bulleted Lists

What is a word-processed document without a list or two? It's like an emperor with no clothes. Numbered lists are invaluable in manuals and books like this one that present a lot of step-by-step procedures. Use bulleted lists when you want to present alternatives to the reader. A *bullet* is a black, filled-in circle or other character. These pages explain numbered lists, bulleted lists, and multilevel lists.

Simple numbered and bulleted lists

The fastest, cleanest, and most honest way to create a numbered or bulleted list is to enter the text without any concern for numbers or bullets. Just press Enter at the end of each step or bulleted entry. When you're done, select the list and click the Numbering or Bullets button on the Home tab (or the Bullets button on the Mini Toolbar). You can also click the Numbering or Bullets button and start typing the list. Each time you press Enter, Word enters the next number or another bullet.

Meanwhile, here are some tricks for handling lists:

✦ **Ending a list:** Press the Enter key twice after typing the last entry in the list. You can also right-click the list, choose Bullets or Numbering, and choose None on the submenu.

✦ **Removing the number or bullets:** Select the list and click the Numbering or Bullets button.

✦ **Adjusting how far a list is indented:** Right-click anywhere in the list, choose Adjust List Indents, and enter a new measurement in the Text Indent box.

✦ **Resuming a numbered list:** Suppose that you want a numbered list to resume where a list you entered earlier ended. In other words, suppose that you left off writing a four-step list, put in a graphic or some paragraphs, and now you want to resume the list at Step 5. Click the Numbering button to start numbering again. The AutoCorrect Options button appears. Click it and choose Continue Numbering, or right-click and choose Continue Numbering on the shortcut menu.

✦ **Starting a new list:** Suppose that you want to start a brand-new list right away. Right-click the number Word entered and choose Restart at 1 on the shortcut menu.

Constructing lists of your own

If you're an individualist and you want numbered and bulleted lists to work your way, follow these instructions for choosing unusual bulleted characters and number formats:

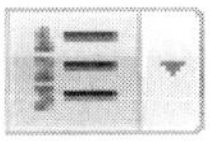

✦ **Choosing a different numbering scheme:** On the Home tab, open the drop-down list on the Numbering button and choose a numbering scheme on the drop-down list. You can also choose Define New Number Format. As shown in Figure 2-7, you see the Define New Number Format dialog box, where you can choose a number format, choose a font for numbers, and toy with number alignments.

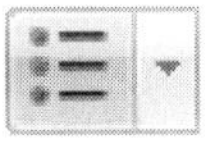

✦ **Choosing a different bullet character:** On the Home tab or Mini Toolbar, open the drop-down list on the Bullets button and choose a different bullet character on the drop-down list. You can also choose Define New Bullet to open the Define New Bullet dialog box, as shown in Figure 2-7, and click the Symbol button to choose a bullet character in the Symbol dialog box (Book I, Chapter 2 describes symbols). The dialog box also offers opportunities for indenting bullets and the text that follows them in new ways.

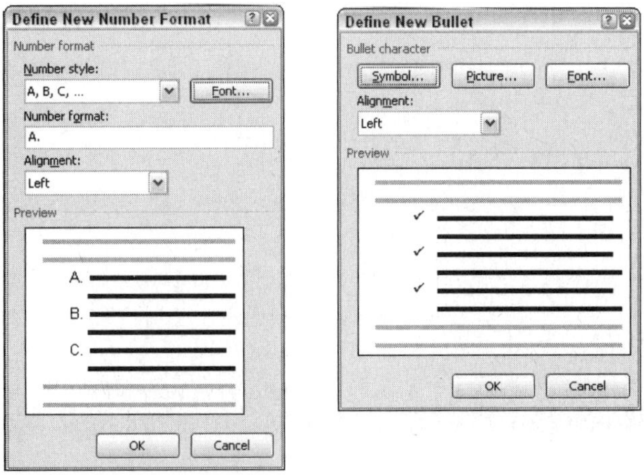

Figure 2-7:
Customizing a numbered or bulleted list.

Automatic lists and what to do about them

Word creates automatic lists for you whether you like it or not. To see what I mean, type the number 1, type a period, and press the spacebar. Word immediately creates a numbered list. In the same manner, Word creates a bulleted list when you type an asterisk (*) and press the spacebar.

Some people find this kind of behind-the-scenes skullduggery annoying. If you're one such person, do one of the following to keep Word from making lists automatically:

✔ Click the AutoCorrect Options button — it appears automatically — and choose Stop Automatically Creating Lists.

✔ Click the Office button, choose Word Options, select the Proofing category, and click the AutoCorrect Options button. On the AutoFormat As You Type tab in the AutoCorrect dialog box, deselect the Automatic Numbered Lists and Automatic Bulleted Lists check boxes.

Managing a multilevel list

A *multilevel list,* also called a *nested list,* is a list with subordinate entries, as shown in Figure 2-8. To create a multilevel list, you declare what kind of list you want, and then, when you enter items for the list, you indent the items that you want to be subordinate. Follow these steps to create a multi-level list:

Figure 2-8:
Examples of multilevel lists.

1. **On the Home tab, click the Multilevel List button and choose what kind of list you want.**

   If none of the lists suit you, you can choose Define New Multilevel List and create a new kind of list in the Define New Multilevel List dialog box.

2. **Enter the items for the list, pressing Enter as you complete each one.**

3. **Select a list item (or items) and click the Increase Indent button (or press Ctrl+M) to make the items subordinate in the list; click the Decrease Indent button (or press Ctrl+Shift+M) to raise their rank in the list.**

   Repeat Step 3 until the list is just-so.

Working with Tabs

Tabs are a throwback to the days of the typewriter, when it was necessary to make tab stops in order to align the next item. Except for making leaders and aligning text in headers and footers, everything you can do with tabs can also be done by creating a table — and it can be done far faster. All you have to do is align the text inside the table and then remove the table borders. Book I, Chapter 5 explains tables.

A *tab stop* is a point on the ruler around which or against which text is formatted (on the View tab, click the Ruler check box to display the ruler). When you press the Tab key, you advance the text cursor by one tab stop. Tab stops are set at half-inch intervals on the ruler, but you can change that if you want. You can also change the type of tab. By default, tabs are left-aligned, which means that when you enter letters after you press the Tab key, the letters move toward the right in the same way that they move toward the right when text is left-aligned. However, Word also offers right, center, decimal, and bar tabs. Figure 2-9 shows the differences between the tab settings. Notice the symbols on the ruler — they tell you what type of tab you're dealing with.

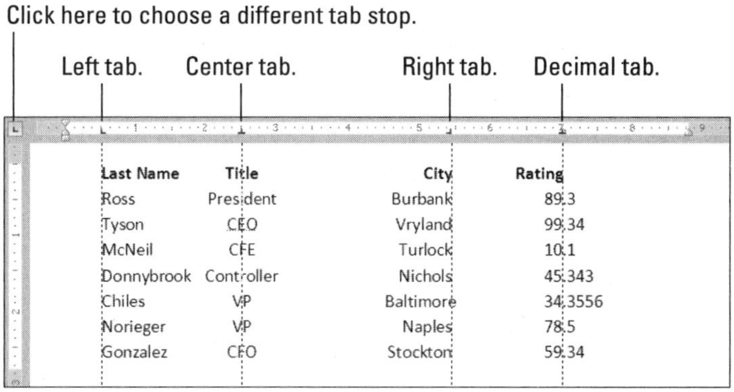

Click here to choose a different tab stop.

Left tab.   Center tab.   Right tab.   Decimal tab.

Last Name	Title	City	Rating
Ross	President	Burbank	89.3
Tyson	CEO	Vryland	99.34
McNeil	CFE	Turlock	10.1
Donnybrook	Controller	Nichols	45.343
Chiles	VP	Baltimore	34.3556
Norieger	VP	Naples	78.5
Gonzalez	CFO	Stockton	59.34

Figure 2-9:
Different
kinds of tab
stops.

To change tabs or change where tabs appear on the ruler, start by selecting the paragraphs for which you need different tabs. Then click in the Tab box on the left side of the ruler as many times as necessary to choose the kind of tab you want, and click the ruler where you want the tab to go. You can click as many times as you want and enter more than one kind of tab.

To move a tab, simply drag it to a new location on the ruler. Text that has been aligned with the tab moves as well. To remove a tab, drag it off the ruler. When you remove a tab, the text to which it was aligned is aligned to the next remaining tab stop on the ruler or to the next default tab stop if you didn't create any tab stops of your own.

¶ Sometimes it's hard to tell where tabs were put in the text. To find out, click the Show/Hide¶button on the Home tab to see the formatting characters, including the arrows that show where the Tab key was pressed.

All about tab leaders

In my opinion, the only reason to fool with tabs and tab stops is to create tab leaders like the ones shown in the following figure. A *leader* is a series of punctuation marks — periods in the illustration — that connect text across a page. Leaders are very elegant. For the figure, I used left-aligned tab stops for the characters' names and right-aligned tab stops for the players' names. I included leaders so that you can tell precisely who played whom.

Follow these steps to create tab leaders:

1. **Enter the text, and in each line, enter a tab space between the text on the left side and the text on the right side.**

2. **Select the text you entered.**

3. **On the Home tab, click the Paragraph group button, and in the Paragraph dialog box, click the Tabs button.**

   You see the Tabs dialog box.

4. **Enter a position for the first new tab in the Tab Stop Position box.**

5. **Under Leader in the dialog box, select the punctuation symbol you want.**

6. **Click OK, display the ruler, and drag tab markers to adjust the space between the text on the left and right.**

THE PLAYERS

Romeo...McGeorge Wright
Juliet.....................................Gabriela Hernandez
Mercutio ....Chris Suzuki
Lady Capulet...........................Mimi Hornstein

Hyphenating a Document

The first thing you should know about hyphenating the words in a document is that you may not need to do it. Text that hasn't been hyphenated is much easier to read, which is why the majority of text in this book, for example, isn't hyphenated. It has a *ragged right margin,* to borrow typesetter lingo. Hyphenate only when text is trapped in columns or in other narrow places, or when you want a very formal-looking document.

Do not insert a hyphen simply by pressing the hyphen key, because the hyphen stays there even if the word moves to the middle of a line and doesn't need to be broken in half. Instead, when a big gap appears in the right margin and a word is crying out to be hyphenated, put the cursor where the hyphen needs to go and press Ctrl+hyphen. This way, you tell Word to make the hyphen appear only if the word breaks at the end of a line. (To remove a manual hyphen, press the Show/Hide ¶button so that you can see it; then backspace over it.)

Automatically and manually hyphenating a document

To hyphenate a document, tell Word to do it automatically or pick and choose where the hyphens go by hyphenating your document manually:

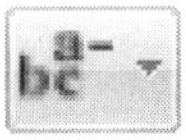

✦ **Automatic hyphenation:** On the Page Layout tab, click the Hyphenation button and choose Automatic on the drop-down list. Word hyphenates your document (or a portion of your document, if you selected it first).

You can tell Word how to hyphenate automatically by clicking the Hyphenation button and choosing Hyphenation Options. You see the Hyphenation dialog box, as shown in Figure 2-10. Deselect the Hyphenate Words in CAPS check box if you don't care to hyphenate words in upper-case. Words that fall in the hyphenation zone are hyphenated, so enlarging the large zone means a less ragged right margin but more ugly hyphens, and a small zone means fewer ugly hyphens but a more ragged right margin. You can limit how many hyphens appear consecutively by entering a number in the Limit Consecutive Hyphens To box.

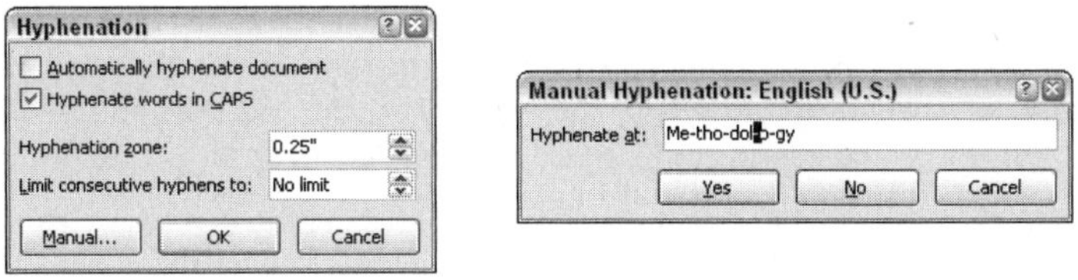

Book II Chapter 2

Laying Out Text and Pages

Figure 2-10: Telling Word how to hyphenate (left) and deciding where a hyphen goes (right).

✦ **Manual hyphenation:** On the Page Layout tab, click the Hyphenation button and choose Manual on the drop-down list. Word displays a box with some hyphenation choices in it, as shown in Figure 2-10. The cursor blinks on the spot where Word suggests putting a hyphen. Click Yes or No to accept or reject Word's suggestion. Keep accepting or rejecting Word's suggestions until the text is hyphenated.

Em and en dashes

Here is something about hyphens that editors and typesetters know, but the general public does not know: Hyphens and dashes are different. Most people insert a hyphen where they ought to use an em dash or an en dash:

✔ An *em dash* looks like a hyphen but is wider — it's as wide as the letter m. The previous sentence has an em dash in it. Did you notice?

✔ An *en dash* is the width of the letter *n*. Use en dashes to show inclusive numbers or time periods, like so: pp. 45–50; Aug.–Sept.

1998; Exodus 16:11–16:18. An en dash is a little bit longer than a hyphen.

To place em or en dashes in your documents and impress your local typesetter or editor, not to mention your readers, press Alt+Ctrl+– (the minus sign key on the Numeric keypad) to enter an em dash, or Ctrl+– (on the numeric keypad) to enter an en dash. You can also go to the Insert tab, click the Symbol button, choose More Symbols on the drop-down list, select the Special Characters tab in the Symbol dialog box, and choose Em Dash or En Dash.

Unhyphenating and other hyphenation tasks

More hyphenation esoterica:

✦ **Unhyphenating:** To "unhyphenate" a document you hyphenated automatically, click the Hyphenation button on the Page Layout tab and choose Hyphenation Options. In the Hyphenation dialog box (see Figure 2-10), deselect the Automatically Hyphenate Document check box and click OK.

✦ **Preventing text from being hyphenated:** Select the text and click the Paragraph group button on the Home tab. In the Paragraph dialog box, select the Line and Page Breaks tab, and click the Don't Hyphenate check box. (If you can't hyphenate a paragraph, it's probably because this box was checked unintentionally.)

✦ **Hyphenating a single paragraph or two:** To hyphenate a paragraph or two in the middle of a document — maybe because it's a long quote or some other thing that needs to stand out — select the paragraph and hyphenate it manually by clicking the Manual button in the Hyphenation dialog box.

Chapter 3: Word Styles

*W*elcome to what may be the most important chapter of this book — the most important in Book II, anyway. Styles can save a ridiculous amount of time that you would otherwise spend formatting and wrestling with text. And many Word features rely on styles. You can't create a table of contents or use the document map unless each heading in your document has been assigned a heading style. Nor can you take advantage of Outline view and the commands for moving text around in that view. You can't cross-reference headings or number the headings in a document.

If you want to be stylish, at least where Word is concerned, you have to know about styles.

All about Styles

A *style* is a collection of commands and formats that have been bundled under one name. With styles, you don't have to visit a bunch of dialog boxes to change the formatting of text or paragraphs. Instead, you simply choose a style from the Quick Styles gallery or the Styles window. You can be certain that all parts of the document that were assigned the same style look the same. In short, you can fool everybody into thinking your documents were created by a pro.

The template you used to create your document determines which styles are available. Each template comes with its own set of styles, and you can create your own styles, too. A simple document created with the Normal template — a document that you created by double-clicking the Blank Document icon or pressing Ctrl+N — has but a few styles, but a document that was created with an advanced template comes with many styles. (Later in this chapter, "Creating and Managing Templates" explains templates.)

To see which styles are available in your document, go to the Home tab and open the Styles gallery (you may have to click the Quick Styles button first) or click the Styles group button to display the Styles window. As shown in Figure 3-1, the Styles gallery and Styles window show which styles are available to you. Want to know which style has been assigned to text or a paragraph? Click the text or paragraph and glance at the Styles gallery or Styles window.

Figure 3-1:
The three ways to apply a style: Styles window (left), Apply Styles task pane (middle), and Styles gallery (right).

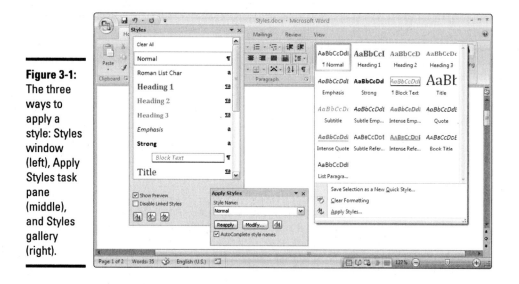

In the Styles gallery and Style window (if you click the Show Preview check box), each style name is formatted to give you an idea of what it does to text when you apply it in your document. Word offers four types of styles:

✦ **Paragraph styles:** Determine the formatting of entire paragraphs. A paragraph style can include these settings: font, paragraph, tab, border, language, and bullets and numbering. Paragraph styles are marked with the paragraph symbol (¶).

✦ **Character styles:** Apply to text, not to paragraphs. You select text before you apply a character style. Create a character style for text that is hard to lay out and for foreign language text. A character style can include these settings: font, border, and language. When you apply a character style to text, the character-style settings override the paragraph-style settings. If the paragraph style calls for a 14-point Arial text but the character style calls for 12-point Times Roman font, the character style wins. Character styles are marked with the letter *a*.

+ **Linked (paragraph and character):** Apply paragraph formats as well as the text formats throughout a paragraph. These styles are marked with the paragraph symbol (¶) as well as the letter *a*.

+ **Table styles:** Apply to tables (Book I, Chapter 5 describes creating and formatting tables). Table styles are marked with a grid icon.

+ **List styles:** Apply to lists. List styles are marked with the paragraph icon.

The beauty of styles is this: After you modify a style, all paragraphs or text to which the style has been assigned are instantly changed. You don't have to go back and reformat text and paragraphs throughout your document.

Applying a Style to Text and Paragraphs

Word offers several ways to apply a style, and you're invited to choose the one that works best for you. These pages explain how to choose a style set, apply a style, and tell Word how to present style names in various places for your enjoyment and pleasure.

Experimenting with style sets

A *style set* is a slight variation on the styles in the template you chose for your document. Style sets include Classic, Elegant, Fancy, and Modern. When you choose a style set, you impose a slightly different look on your document — you make it classier, more elegant, fancier, or more modern. All templates, even those you create yourself, offer style sets. Style sets are a convenient way to experiment with the overall look of a document.

To experiment with style sets, click the Change Styles button on the Home tab, choose Style Set on the drop-down list, and do one of the following:

+ **Choose a new style set:** Choose a style set on the submenu.

+ **Use the original styles in the template:** Choose Reset to Quick Styles from Template on the submenu.

Applying a style

The first step in applying a style is to select the paragraph you want to apply the style to, or to apply a style to several paragraphs, select all or part of them; if you're applying a character style, select the letters whose formatting you want to change. Then apply the style using one of these techniques:

✦ **Styles gallery:** On the Home tab, choose a style in the Styles gallery (refer to Figure 3-1). Depending on the size of your screen, you may have to click the Quick Styles button to open the gallery. The formatted letters above each style name give you an idea of what your style choice will do to paragraphs or text. You can't tell from looking which type of style — Paragraph, Character, or Linked — you're choosing from, but you can "live-preview" styles on the Quick Styles gallery.

If styles from your template don't appear in the Quick Styles gallery and you want them to appear there, click the Change Styles button, choose Style Set on the drop-down list, and choose Reset to Quick Styles from Template on the submenu.

✦ **Styles window:** On the Home tab, click the Styles group button to open the Styles window, and select a style (refer to Figure 3-1). By clicking the Show Preview check box, you can view formatted style names and get an idea of what the different styles are. You can drag the Styles window to different locations on your screen.

✦ **Apply Styles task pane:** Choose a style on the Apply Styles task pane (refer to Figure 3-1). To display this task pane, open the Styles gallery and choose Apply Styles (look for this option at the bottom of the gallery). You can drag the Apply Styles task pane to a corner of the screen.

To strip a paragraph or text of its style and give it the generic Normal style, select it, open the Styles gallery, and choose Clear Formatting. You can also click the Clear All command at the top of the Styles window. To "unapply" a style throughout a document, open its drop-down list in the Styles window and choose Remove All.

Shortcuts for applying styles

A handful of keyboard shortcuts can be very handy when applying paragraph styles:

✔ Normal: Ctrl+Shift+N

✔ Bulleted List: Ctrl+Shift+L

✔ Heading 1: Ctrl+Alt+1

✔ Heading 2: Ctrl+Alt+2

✔ Heading 3: Ctrl+Alt+3

✔ Next higher heading: Alt+Shift+→

✔ Next lower heading: Alt+Shift+←

You can assign keyboard shortcuts to styles. Book VIII, Chapter 1 explains how.

Choosing which style names appear on the Style menus

As I explain, you can apply a style by way of the Styles gallery, Styles window, and Apply Styles task pane. The latter two can become crowded with many style names, which makes choosing styles difficult. To make choosing styles easier, you can decide for yourself which style names appear on the Styles gallery, Styles window, and Apply Styles task pane.

In the Styles gallery, remove a style name by right-clicking it and choosing Remove from Quick Style Gallery. If you regret removing style names from the Styles gallery, click the Change Styles button and choose Style Set⇨Reset Document Quick Styles.

To decide for yourself which style names appear in the Styles window and Apply Styles task pane, click the Styles group button, and in the Styles window, click the Options link (you can find this link near the bottom of the window). You see the Style Pane Options dialog box, as shown in Figure 3-2. Choose options in the dialog box to tell Word which style names to present in the Styles window and Apply Styles task pane:

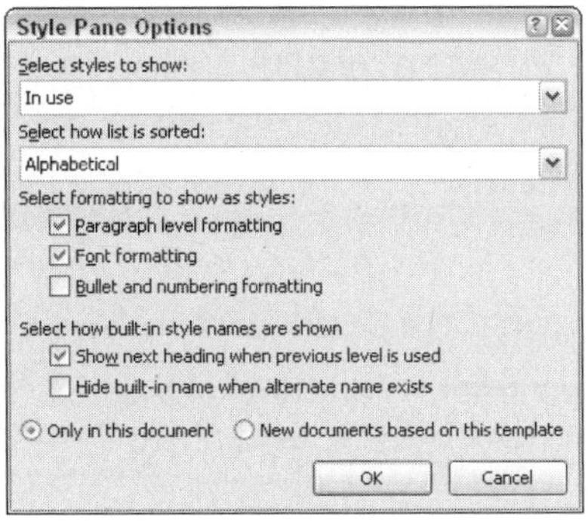

Figure 3-2: Deciding which names to put in the Styles window and Apply Styles task pane.

+ **Select Styles to Show:** Choose All Styles to show all style names. The other options place a subset of names in the window and task pane. Recommended style names are those Microsoft thinks you need most often.

+ **Select How List Is Sorted:** Choose an option to describe how to list styles. Except for Based On, these options, I think, are self-explanatory. The Based On option lists styles in alphabetical order according to which style each is based on. (Later in this chapter, "Creating a style from the ground up" explains how the based on style is used in constructing styles.)

✦ **Select Formatting to Show As Styles:** Choose options to declare which styles to list — those that pertain to paragraph level formatting, fonts, and bulleted and numbered lists.

✦ **Select How Built-In Style Names Are Shown:** Choose options to tell how to handle built-in styles, the styles that Word applies on its own when you create tables of contents and other self-generating lists.

✦ **Apply to this document or to the template as well:** Click the Only in This Document option button to apply your choices only to the document you're working on; click the New Documents Based on This Template option button to apply your choices to your document and all future documents you create with the template you're using.

Creating a New Style

You can create a new style in two ways: by creating it from a paragraph or building it from the ground up. To do a thorough job, build it from the ground up because styles you create this way can be made part of the template you're currently working in and can be copied to other templates (later in this chapter, "Creating and Managing Templates" explains templates).

Creating a style from a paragraph

Follow these steps to create a new style from a paragraph:

1. **Click in a paragraph whose formatting you would like to turn into a style.**

2. **Right-click and choose Styles➪Save Selection As a New Quick Style.**

You see the Create New Style from Formatting dialog box. You can also open this dialog box by choosing Save Selection As a New Quick Style in the Quick Styles gallery.

3. **Enter a name for your new style.**

4. **Click OK.**

A style you create this way becomes a part of the document you're working on — it isn't made part of the template from which you created your document.

Creating a style from the ground up

If you want to make a style available in documents you will create in the future, make it part of a template and build it from the ground up. In the Styles window, click the New Style button (you can find it in the lower-left corner of the window). You see the Create New Style from Formatting dialog box, as shown in Figure 3-3. Fill in the dialog box and click OK.

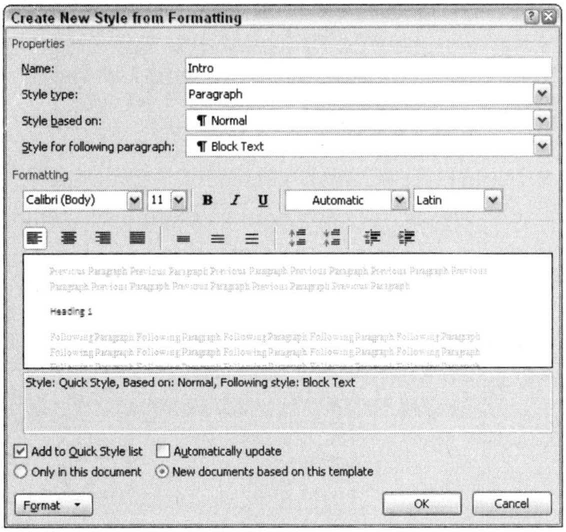

Figure 3-3:
Creating a
brand-
spanking-
new style.

Here's a rundown of the options in the Create New Style from Formatting dialog box:

+ **Name:** Enter a descriptive name for the style, one you will recognize in the Styles window and Quick Styles gallery.

+ **Style Type:** On the drop-down list, choose a style type ("All about Styles," earlier in this chapter, describes the five style types).

+ **Style Based On:** If your new style is similar to a style that is already part of the template with which you created your document, choose the style to get a head start on creating the new one. Be warned, however, that if you or someone else changes the Based On style, your new style will inherit those changes and be altered as well.

+ **Style for Following Paragraph:** Choose a style from the drop-down list if the style you're creating is always followed by an existing style. For example, a new style called Chapter Title might always be followed by a style called Chapter Intro Paragraph. If that were the case, you would choose Chapter Intro Paragraph from this drop-down list.

+ **Formatting:** Choose options from the menus or click buttons to fashion or refine your style (you can also click the Format button to do this).

+ **Add to Quick Style List:** Click this check box to make the style's name appear in the Styles gallery, Styles window, and Apply Styles task pane.

+ **Automatically Update:** Normally, when you make a formatting change to a paragraph, the style assigned to the paragraph does not change at all, but the style does change if you check this box. By checking this box, you tell Word to alter the style itself each time you alter a paragraph to which you've assigned the style. With this box checked, all paragraphs in the document that were assigned the style are altered each time you change a single paragraph that was assigned the style.

✦ **Only in This Document/New Documents Based on This Template:** To make your style a part of the template from which you created your document as well as the document itself, click the New Documents Based on This Template option button. This way, new documents you create that are based on the template you're using can also make use of the new style.

✦ **Format:** This is the important one. Click the button and make a formatting choice. Word takes you to dialog boxes so that you can create or refine the style.

Modifying a Style

What if you decide at the end of an 80-page document that all 35 introductory paragraphs to which you've assigned the Intro Para style look funny? If you click the Automatically Update check box in the New Style dialog box when you create the style, all you have to do is alter a paragraph to which you assigned the Intro Para style to alter all 35 introductory paragraphs. However, if you decide against updating styles automatically, you can still change the introductory paragraphs throughout your document.

Follow these steps to modify a style that isn't updated automatically:

1. **Click in any paragraph, table, or list to which you've assigned the style; if you want to modify a character style, select the characters to which you've assigned the style.**

2. **In the Styles window or Apply Styles task pane, make sure the name of the style you want to modify is selected.**

   If the right name isn't selected, select it now in the Styles window or Apply Styles task pane.

3. **In the Styles window, open the style's drop-down list and choose Modify; in the Apply Styles task pane, click the Modify button.**

   You see the Modify Style dialog box. Does the box look familiar? That's because it's virtually identical to Create New Style from Formatting dialog box you used to create the style in the first place (refer to Figure 3-3). The only difference is that you can't choose a style type in the Modify Style dialog box.

4. **Change the settings in the Modify Styles dialog box and click OK.**

   The preceding section in this chapter explains the settings.

While the Modify Style dialog box is open, you can check the Automatically Update check box if you want future modifications that you make to the style to be applied automatically. This way, when you change a paragraph or text to which the style has been applied, all other paragraphs and text in your document are changed accordingly.

Creating and Managing Templates

Every document you create is founded upon a *template*. When you double-click the Blank Template icon in the New Document dialog box or press Ctrl+N, you create a document founded on the Normal template. And if you create a document with a template from Microsoft Office Online or a template from the New dialog box, you create a complex document with many different styles.

Each template comes with its own styles. Suppose that you create a complex document and you want to be able to use its styles in other documents. To be able to do that, you can create a template from your document. For that matter, you can create a template from scratch by assembling styles from other templates and documents.

Attaching a different template to a document

It happens in the best of families. You create or are given a document only to discover that the wrong template is attached to it. For times like those, Word gives you the opportunity to switch templates. Follow these steps:

1. **On the Developer tab, click the Document Template button.**

   You see the Templates and Add-Ins dialog box. If the Developer tab isn't displayed, click the Office button, choose Word Options, select the Popular category in the Word Options dialog box, click the Show Developer Tab in the Ribbon check box, and click OK.

2. **Click the Attach button to open the Attach Template dialog box.**

3. **Find and select the template you want, and click the Open button.**

   You return to the Templates and Add-ins dialog box, where the name of the template you chose appears in the Document Template box.

4. **Click the Automatically Update Document Styles check box.**

   Doing so tells Word to apply the styles from the new template to your document.

5. **Click OK.**

Creating a new template

Here are the ways to create a new template:

+ **Creating a template from scratch:** Create a new document, click the Office button, and choose Save As⇨Word Template. You see the Save As dialog box. Click the Trusted Templates button, enter a name for your template, and click the Save button.

+ **Creating a template from a document:** Open your document and follow the preceding instructions for creating a template from scratch. Your new template will have all the styles found in the document.

+ **Assembling styles from other templates:** Create a new template by following the preceding instructions and then copy styles to your new template ("Copying styles from different documents and templates," later in this chapter, explains the details). To choose a template from which to copy styles, click the Close File button on the left side of the Organizer dialog box, click the Open File button, select the template in the Open dialog box, and click the Open button.

Where templates are stored depends on which version of Windows your computer runs under:

+ **Windows Vista:** `C:\Users\`*Username*`\AppData\Roaming\` `Microsoft\Templates` folder

+ **Windows XP:** `C:\Documents and Settings\`*Username*`\` `Application Data\Microsoft\Templates` folder

+ **Windows NT, 95, 98, 2000, and ME:** `C:\Windows\Profiles\` `Application Data\`*Username*`\Application Data\Microsoft\` `Templates` folder, or the `C:\Windows\Profiles\Application` `Data\Application Data\Microsoft\Templates` folder

To get into the Application Data folder where templates are stored, it may be necessary to display hidden folders on your computer. Click the Start button and choose Control Panel. Then double-click the Folder Options icon (you may have to click the Switch to Classic View link first), select the View tab in the Folder Options dialog box, and click the Show Hidden Files and Folders option button.

To create a document from a template you created yourself, open the New Document dialog box and double-click the My Templates icon. You see the name of the template you created on the My Templates tab of the New dialog box. Select your template and click OK.

Deleting and renaming styles in templates

Suppose that you need to delete styles or rename styles in a template.
Follow these steps:

1. In the Styles window, click the Manage Styles button.

You see the Manage Styles dialog box.

2. Click the Import/Export button to open the Organizer dialog box.

3. Click the Close File button on the right side of the dialog box.

4. Click the Open File button, and in the Open dialog box, select the template that needs modifying; then click the Open button.

The names of styles in the template appear in the right side of the dialog box.

5. Select the item you want to rename or delete.

Follow these steps to rename or delete the item:

- *Rename an item:* Click the Rename button, enter a new name in the Rename dialog box, and click OK.

- *Delete an item:* Click the Delete button and then click Yes in the dialog box.

**Book II
Chapter 3**

Word Styles

Copying styles from different documents and templates

Suppose that you like a style in one document and you want to copy it to another so that you can use it there. How you make the copy depends on whether you want to copy the style into a document or into a template. By copying it into a template, you make the style part of the template, and the style is available for all documents that are created with that template. However, if you need the style solely for a particular document, you may as well copy it into the document. Doing that is easy enough.

Copying a style from one document to another

Copy a style from one document to another when you need the style on a one-time basis. Follow these steps:

1. Select a paragraph that was assigned the style you want to copy.

Be sure to select the entire paragraph. If you want to copy a character style, select text to which you have assigned the character style.

2. **Choose Edit⇨Copy or press Ctrl+C to copy the paragraph to the Clipboard.**

3. **Switch to the document you want to copy the style to and choose Edit⇨Paste or press Ctrl+V.**

4. **Delete the text.**

   The style remains in the Styles window, Styles gallery, and Apply Styles task pane even though the text is deleted. You can call upon the style whenever you need it.

Copying styles between templates

Use the Organizer to copy styles into other templates. By making the style a part of a template, you can call upon the style in other documents. You can call upon it in each document you create or created with the template. Follow these steps to copy a style into a template:

1. **In the Styles window, click the Manage Styles button.**

   The Manage Styles dialog box appears.

2. **Click the Import/Export button.**

   You see the Organizer dialog box, as shown in Figure 3-4. Styles in the document that you opened appear in the In Document list box on the left side of the dialog box.

Select the styles you want to copy.

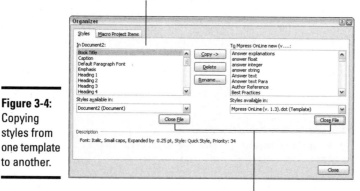

Figure 3-4: Copying styles from one template to another.

Click to close on template or open another.

3. **Click the Close File button on the right side of the dialog box.**

   The button changes names and becomes the Open File button.

4. **Click the Open File button, and in the Open dialog box, find and select the template to which you want to copy styles; then click the Open button.**

   Where the templates are stored depends on which version of Windows you are working in:

   - *Windows Vista:* `C:\Users\`*Username*`\AppData\Roaming\Microsoft\Templates` folder

   - *Windows XP:* `C:\Documents and Settings\`*Username*`\Application Data\Microsoft\Templates` folder

   - *Windows NT, 95, 98, 2000, and ME:* `C:\Windows\Profiles\Application Data\`*Username*`\Application Data\Microsoft\Templates` folder, or the `C:\Windows\Profiles\Application Data\Application Data\Microsoft\Templates` folder

   The names of styles in the template you chose appear on the right side of the Organizer dialog box.

5. **In the Organizer dialog box, Ctrl+click the names of styles on the left side of the dialog box that you want to copy to the template listed on the right side of the dialog box.**

   When you click the names, they become highlighted.

6. **Click the Copy button.**

   The names of styles that you copied appear on the right side of the Organizer dialog box.

7. **Click the Close button and click Yes when Word asks whether you want to save the new styles in the template.**

Chapter 4: Desktop Publishing with Word

In This Chapter

✔ Considering ways to desktop-publish in Word

✔ Fine-tuning tables

✔ Wrapping text around graphics and other objects

✔ Running text in newspaper-style columns

✔ Putting text boxes in documents

✔ Putting borders on pages

✔ Decorating pages with drop caps and watermarks

✔ Printing landscape documents

*O*nce upon a time, word processors were nothing more than glorified typewriters. They were good for typing and basic formatting, and not much else. But over the years, Microsoft Word has become a desktop publishing program in its own right. This chapter explains a few desktop publishing features that can make your documents stand out in the crowd — columns, text boxes, page borders, watermarks, and drop caps, to name a few.

Making Use of Charts, Diagrams, Shapes, Clip Art, and Photos

Figure 4-1 shows a newsletter that includes a chart, diagram, shape, clip-art image, and photo. You're invited to include these items in your Word documents, and you'll be glad to know that including them isn't very much trouble.

 ✦ **Charts:** A chart is an excellent way to present data for comparison purposes. The pie slices, bars, columns, or lines tell readers right away which business is more productive, for example, or who received the most votes. Book I, Chapter 6 explains how to create charts.

♦ **Diagrams:** A diagram allows readers to quickly grasp an idea, relationship, or concept. Instead of explaining an abstract idea, you can portray it in a diagram. Book I, Chapter 7 explains diagrams.

♦ **Shapes and lines:** Shapes and lines can also illustrate ideas and concepts. You can also use them for decorative purposes in Word documents. Book I, Chapter 8 explains how to draw lines, arrows, and shapes.

♦ **Clip-art images:** Clip-art images can make a document livelier. They add a little color to documents. Book VIII, Chapter 4 explains how to place clip-art images in documents.

♦ **Photos:** A well-placed photo or two can make a newsletter or brochure that much more attractive. Book VIII, Chapter 3 explains how to include photos in Word documents.

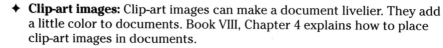

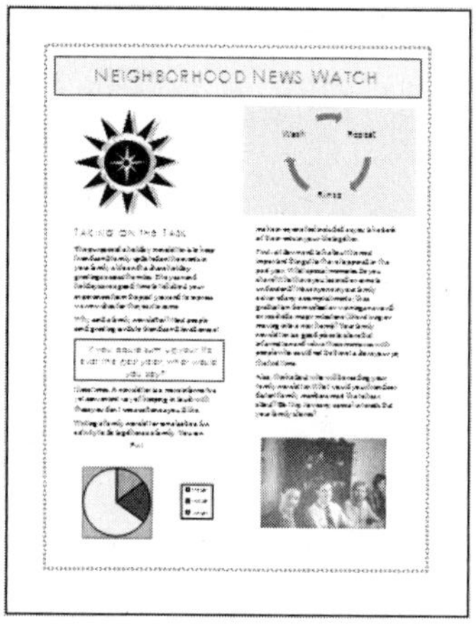

Figure 4-1: This newsletter includes a clip-art image, shape, chart, diagram, and photo.

Constructing the Perfect Table

Create a table to present raw data to your readers or plead your case with numbers and facts. Provided the row labels and column headings are descriptive, looking up information in a table is the easiest way to find it. And tables impose order on chaos. What used to be a knotty lump of non-descript data can be turned into an orderly statement of fact if the data is presented in a table. No report is complete without one or two of them.

Book I, Chapter 5 explains how to create a table, as well as how to include mathematical calculations in Word tables. These pages explain a few table techniques that pertain strictly to Word documents — repeating the heading rows, fitting a table on a single page, and turning a list into a table.

Repeating heading rows on subsequent pages

Making sure that the *heading row,* sometimes called the *header row,* appears on a new page if the table breaks across pages is absolutely essential. The heading row is the first row in the table, the one that usually describes what is in the columns below. Without a heading row, readers can't tell what the information in a table means. Follow these steps to make the heading row (or rows) repeat on the top of each new page that a table appears on:

1. **Place the cursor in the heading row or select the heading rows if you have more than one at the top of your table.**

2. **On the (Table Tools) Layout tab, click the Repeat Header Rows button (depending on the size of your screen, you may have to click the Data button first).**

   Heading rows appear only in Print Layout view, so don't worry if you can't see them in Draft view.

**Book II
Chapter 4**

**Desktop Publishing
with Word**

Turning a list into a table

In order to turn a list into a table, all components of the list — each name, address, city name, state, and zip code listing, for example — must be separated from the next component by a tab space or a comma. Word looks for tab spaces or commas when it turns a list into a table, and the program separates data into columns according to where the tab spaces or commas are located. You have to prepare your list carefully by entering tab spaces or commas in all the right places before you can turn your list into a table.

Follow these steps to turn a list into a table after you've done all the preliminary work:

1. **Select the list.**

2. **On the Insert tab, click the Table button and choose Convert Text to Table on the drop-down list.**

   You see the Convert Text to Table dialog box.

   Note the number in the Number of Columns box. It should list the number of components into which you separated your list. If the number doesn't match the number of components, you misplaced a tab entry or comma in your list. Click Cancel, return to your list, and examine it to make sure each line has been divided into the same number of components.

3. **Under Separate Text At, choose the Tabs or Commas option, depending on which you used to separate the components on the list.**

4. **Click OK.**

You can turn a table into a list by clicking the Convert to Text button on the (Table Tools) Layout tab (you may have to click the Data button first, depending on the size of your screen).

Fitting a table on the page

Ideally, a table should fit on a single page because studying table data that is spread across two or more pages can be difficult. Here are a couple of suggestions for fitting a table on a single page:

➤ **Present the table in landscape mode:** In Landscape mode, a page is turned on its ear so that it is wider than it is tall and you have room for more columns. To print in Landscape mode, however, you must create a new section for the pages in question. Later in this chapter, "Landscape Documents" explains how to switch from Portrait to Landscape mode.

➤ **Shrink the font size:** Sometimes shrinking the font size throughout a table shrinks the table just enough to fit it on a page. To shrink fonts throughout a table by 1 point, select the table and press Ctrl+[. Keep pressing this key combination until the table fits on one page. While you're at it,

click the AutoFit button on the Layout tab and choose AutoFit Contents on the drop-down list to make each column wide enough to accommodate its widest entry.

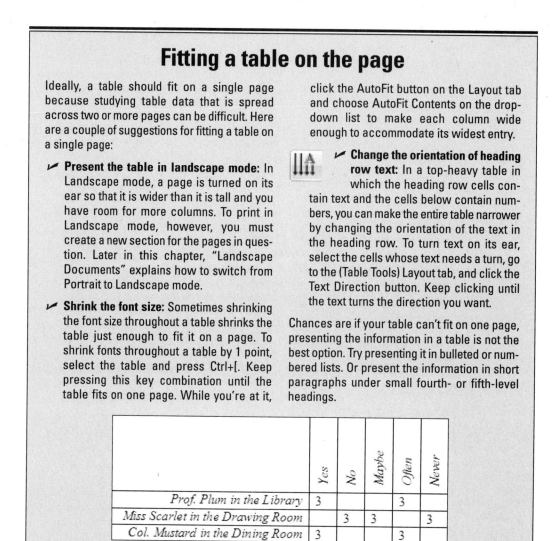

➤ **Change the orientation of heading row text:** In a top-heavy table in which the heading row cells contain text and the cells below contain numbers, you can make the entire table narrower by changing the orientation of the text in the heading row. To turn text on its ear, select the cells whose text needs a turn, go to the (Table Tools) Layout tab, and click the Text Direction button. Keep clicking until the text turns the direction you want.

Chances are if your table can't fit on one page, presenting the information in a table is not the best option. Try presenting it in bulleted or numbered lists. Or present the information in short paragraphs under small fourth- or fifth-level headings.

	Yes	No	Maybe	Often	Never
Prof. Plum in the Library	3			3	
Miss Scarlet in the Drawing Room		3	3		3
Col. Mustard in the Dining Room	3			3	

Positioning and Wrapping Objects Relative to the Page and Text

"Object" is just Office's generic term for a shape, line, text box, clip-art image, photo, diagram, WordArt image, or chart that you insert in a document. Book I, Chapter 8 explains how to manipulate an object — how to change its size, shape, and other qualities. When you place an object in a Word document, you have to consider more than its size and shape. You also have to consider where to position it on the page and how to wrap text around it. In Word lingo, *wrap* refers to what text does when it butts heads with a shape, text box, photo, diagram, or other object. You must be in Print Layout view to wrap and position objects on a page.

When you insert an object, it lands *inline with text.* That means it lands against the left margin and text doesn't wrap around its side. What's more important, to change the position of an object, you must select it and choose a text-wrapping option apart from Inline with Text.

Wrapping text around an object

Figure 4-2 shows the 15 different ways you can wrap text around an object. Select the object you want to wrap text around, go to the Format tab, and use one of these techniques to wrap text around the object:

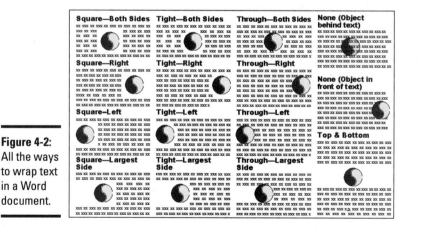

Figure 4-2: All the ways to wrap text in a Word document.

✦ Click the Text Wrapping button and choose an option on the drop-down list. (You may have to click the Arrange button first, depending on the size of your screen.)

✦ Click the Text Wrapping button, choose More Layout Options on the drop-down list, and on the Text Wrapping tab of the Advanced Layout dialog box, choose a wrapping style and side around which to wrap text. Figure 4-2 shows what the different combinations of Wrapping Style and Wrap Text options do.

Wrapped text looks best when it is justified and hyphenated. That way, text can get closer to the object that is being wrapped.

Click the Text Wrapping button and choose Edit Wrap Points to choose precisely how close or far text is from the object. After you choose the command, *wrap points* — small black squares — appear around the object. Click and drag the wrap points to push text away from or bring text closer to the object in question.

Positioning an object on a page

To position an object in a Word page, you can drag it to a new location. As Book I, Chapter 8 explains in torturous detail, dragging means to select the object, move the pointer over its perimeter, click when you see the four-headed arrow, and slide the object to a new location.

To make positioning objects on a page a little easier, Word also offers Position commands for moving objects. Select your object, go to the Format tab, and use one of these techniques to move your object precisely into place:

✦ Click the Position button and select a With Text Wrapping option on the drop-down list, as shown in Figure 4-3. (You may have to click the Arrange button first, depending on the size of your screen.) These options position an object squarely in a corner, side, or the middle of the page.

✦ Click the Position button, choose More Layout Options on the drop-down list, and choose options on the Picture Position tab of the Advanced Layout dialog box. Go to the Advanced Layout dialog box when you want to place objects in the very same position on different pages.

Select the object.   Choose a With Text Wrapping option.

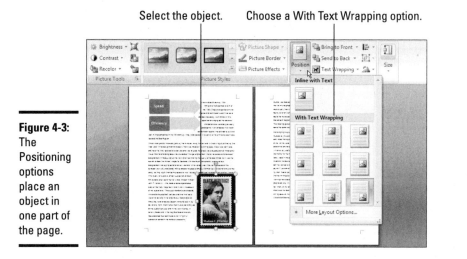

Figure 4-3:
The
Positioning
options
place an
object in
one part of
the page.

An object you position with an option on the Position drop-down list travels from page to page if you move the paragraph to which it's connected. This happens because when you insert an object, Word attaches it to the paragraph where the cursor is located when you make the insertion. If you move that paragraph to another page or the paragraph gets moved as you edit text, the object moves right along with the paragraph. You can locate the paragraph to which an object is connected by clicking the Show/Hide¶ button on the Home tab and then clicking the object; the anchor symbol appears beside the paragraph that the object is connected to.

Working with the Drawing Canvas

As Book I, Chapter 8 explains, shapes and lines are a great way to illustrate ideas. You can in effect doodle on the page and give readers another insight into what you want to explain. In Word, however, drawing lines and shapes is problematic unless you draw them on the drawing canvas. The *drawing canvas* works like a corral to hold lines and shapes. After you create a drawing canvas, you can draw inside it as though you were drawing on a little page, as shown in Figure 4-4. Then you can treat the drawing canvas as an object in its own right and move it — and the things inside it — to new locations. You can also, by way of the (Drawing Tools) Format tab, give the drawing canvas an outline shape and fill color. The drawing canvas makes working with objects on a page, especially lines and shapes, that much easier.

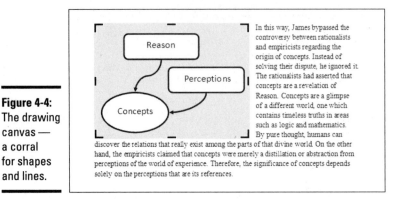

In this way, James bypassed the controversy between rationalists and empiricists regarding the origin of concepts. Instead of solving their dispute, he ignored it. The rationalists had asserted that concepts are a revelation of Reason. Concepts are a glimpse of a different world, one which contains timeless truths in areas such as logic and mathematics. By pure thought, humans can discover the relations that really exist among the parts of that divine world. On the other hand, the empiricists claimed that concepts were merely a distillation or abstraction from perceptions of the world of experience. Therefore, the significance of concepts depends solely on the perceptions that are its references.

Figure 4-4:
The drawing canvas — a corral for shapes and lines.

Follow these steps to create a drawing canvas for holding lines and shapes:

1. **Place the cursor roughly where you want the drawing canvas to be.**

2. **Click the Insert tab.**

3. **Click the Shapes button and choose New Drawing Canvas.**

You can find the New Drawing Canvas command at the bottom of the Shapes drop-down list. A drawing canvas appears on your screen.

The drawing canvas is an object in its own right. You can wrap text around it, give it an outline, and give it a color fill. You can drag it to a new location. To change its size, drag a handle on the side or corner.

Choosing a Theme for Your Document

When you installed Word on your computer, you also installed a dozen or more themes. A *theme* is a colorful, ready-made design for headings and text. Each theme imposes a slightly different look on a document. If you want to experiment with themes, more power to you; but be prepared to click the Undo button and backtrack as you rummage around for the right one. In my experience, themes are more suitable to Web pages than to Word documents that you intend to print. They apply too much color into documents.

Starting on the Page Layout tab, follow these instructions to experiment with themes:

✦ **Choosing a new theme:** Click the Themes button and choose a theme on the drop-down list.

✦ **Choosing a new set of colors for your theme:** Click the Theme Colors button, slide the pointer over the different color sets on the drop-down list, and see what effect they have on your document.

✦ **Changing the fonts:** Click the Theme Fonts button and choose a combination of fonts on the drop-down list for the headings and text in your document.

✦ **Changing theme effects:** Click the Theme Effects button and choose a theme effect on the drop-down list. A *theme effect* is a slight refinement to a theme.

Putting Newspaper-Style Columns in a Document

Columns look great in newsletters and similar documents. And you can pack a lot of words in columns. I should warn you, however, that the Columns command is only good for creating columns that appear on the same page. Running text to the next page with the Columns command can be problematic. If you're serious about running text in columns, I suggest either constructing the columns from text boxes or using Publisher, another Office program. Book VII explains Publisher.

Before you put text in newspaper-style columns, write it. Take care of the spelling, grammar, and everything else first because making text changes to words after they've been arranged in columns is difficult. Columns appear only in Print Layout view.

Sometimes it is easier to create columns by creating a table or by using text boxes, especially when the columns refer to one another. In a two-column résumé, for example, the left-hand column often lists job titles ("Facsimile Engineer") whose descriptions are found directly across the page in the right-hand column ("I Xeroxed stuff all day long"). Creating a two-column résumé with Word's Columns command would be futile because making the columns line up is nearly impossible. Each time you add something to the left-hand column, everything *snakes* — it gets bumped down in the left-hand column and the right-hand column as well.

To "columnize" text, select it, go to the Page Layout tab, and click the Columns button. Then either choose how many columns you want on the drop-down list, or choose More Columns to create columns of different widths. You see the Columns dialog box, as shown in Figure 4-5. Here are the options in the Columns dialog box:

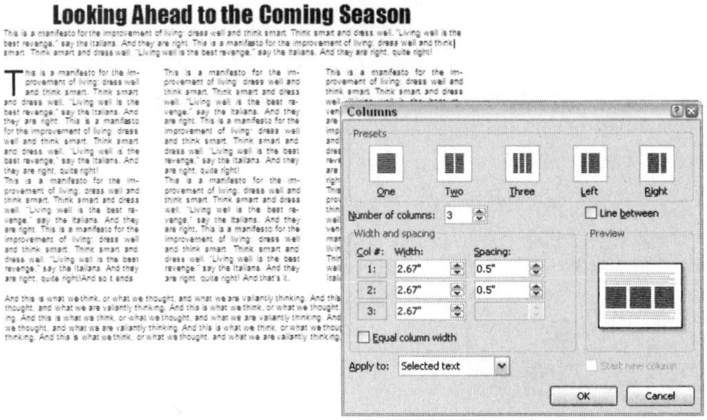

Figure 4-5:
Running text
in columns.

✦ **Preset columns:** Select a Presets box to choose a preset number of columns. Notice that, in some of the boxes, the columns aren't of equal width.

✦ **Number of columns:** If a preset column doesn't do the trick, enter the number of columns you want in the Number of Columns box.

✦ **Line between columns:** A line between columns is mighty elegant and is difficult to do on your own. Select the Line Between check box to run lines between columns.

✦ **Columns width:** If you deselect the Equal Column Width check box, you can make columns of unequal width. Change the width of each column by using the Width boxes.

✦ **Space between columns:** Enter a measurement in the Spacing boxes to determine how much space appears between columns.

✦ **Start New Column:** This box is for putting empty space in a column, perhaps to insert a text box or picture. Place the cursor where you want the empty space to begin, open the Columns dialog box, choose This Point Forward on the Apply To drop-down list, and click the Start New Column check box. Text below the cursor moves to the next column.

Word creates a new section if you selected text before you columnized it, and you see your columns in Print Layout view. Chapter 2 of this mini-book explains sections.

To "break" a column in the middle and move text to the next column, click where you want the column to break and press Ctrl+Shift+Enter or click the Breaks button on the Page Layout tab and choose Column on the drop-down list.

Working with Text Boxes

Put text in a text box when you want a notice or announcement to stand out on the page. Text boxes can be shaded, filled with color, and given borders, as the examples in Figure 4-6 demonstrate. You can also lay them over graphics to make for interesting effects. I removed the borders and the fill color from the text box on the right side of Figure 4-6, but rest assured, the text in this figure lies squarely in a text box.

Book II
Chapter 4

Desktop Publishing with Word

Figure 4-6: Examples of text boxes.

Announcing a
FROG JUMPING
CONTEST
~~Calaveras County~~
July 5-6

Announcing a
FROG JUMPING
CONTEST
~~Calaveras County~~
July 5-6

You can move a text box around at will on the page until it lands in the right place. You can even use text boxes as columns and make text jump from one text box to the next in a document — a nice feature, for example, when you want a newsletter article on page 1 to be continued on page 2. Instead of cutting and pasting text from page 1 to page 2, Word moves the text for you as the column on page 1 fills up. (Book I, Chapter 8 explains how to give borders, shading, and color to objects such as text boxes.)

Inserting a text box

To draw a text box, go to the Insert tab, click the Text Box button, and use one of these techniques:

- ✦ **Choose a ready-made text box**: Scroll in the drop-down list and choose a preformatted text box.

- ✦ **Draw a conventional text box:** Choose Draw Text Box on the drop-down list, and then click and drag to draw the text box. Lines show you how big it will be when you release the mouse button.

- ✦ **Draw a "vertical" text box:** In a vertical text box, text reads from top to bottom or bottom to top, not from left to right. To create a vertical text box, create a text box, enter the text, and then go to the (Text Box Tools) Format tab and click the Text Direction button as many times as necessary to make the text land where you want it to land.

After you've inserted the text box, you can type text in it and call on all the formatting commands on the (Text Box Tools) Format tab. These commands are explained in Book I, Chapter 8.

Book I, Chapter 8 also describes how to turn a shape such as a circle or triangle into a text box (create the shape, right-click it and choose Add Text, and start typing).

Making text flow from text box to text box

As I mention earlier, you can link text boxes so that the text in the first box is pushed into the next one when it fills up. To link text boxes, start by creating all the text boxes that you need. You cannot link one text box to another if the second text box already has text in it. Starting on the (Text Box Tools) Format tab, follow these directions to link text boxes:

✦ **Creating a forward link:** Click a text box and then click the Create Link button to create a forward link. When you click the button, the pointer changes into a very odd-looking pointer that is supposed to look like a pitcher. Move the odd-looking pointer to the next text box in the chain and click there to create a link.

✦ **Breaking a link:** To break a link, click the text box that is to be the last in the chain and then click the Break Link button.

Decorating a Page with a Border

Word offers a means of decorating title pages, certificates, menus, and similar documents with a page border. Besides lines, you can decorate the sides of a page with stars, pieces of cake, and other artwork. If you want to place a border around a page in the middle of the document, you must create a section break where the page is.

Before you create your border, place the cursor on the page where the border is to appear. Place the cursor on the first page of a document if you want to put a border around only the first page. If your document is divided into sections and you want to put borders around certain pages in a section, place the cursor in the section — either in the first page, if you want the borders to go around it, or in a subsequent page.

⬜ Page Borders   With the cursor in the right place, follow these steps to decorate your page or pages with a border:

1. **Go to the Page Layout tab and click the Page Borders button.**

You see the Borders and Shading dialog box, as shown in Figure 4-7.

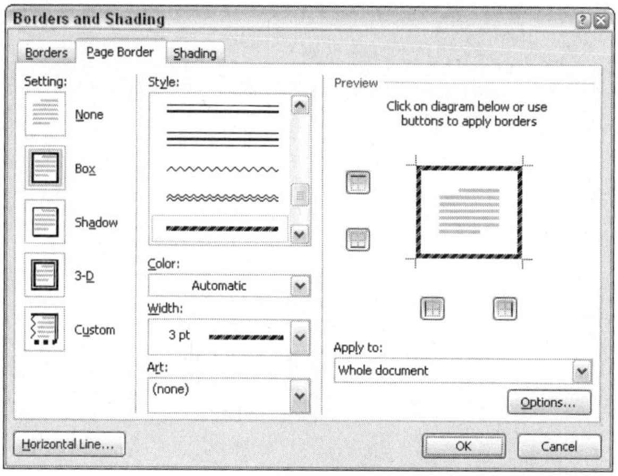

Figure 4-7:
Putting
borders on
pages.

2. **Under Setting, choose which kind of border you want.**

   The Custom setting is for putting borders on one, two, or three sides of the page, not four. Use the None setting to remove borders.

3. **Under Apply To, tell Word which page or pages in the document get borders.**

4. **Select options to construct the border you want and then click OK.**

The Page Border tab offers a bunch of tools for fashioning a border:

✦ **Line for borders:** Under Style, scroll down the list and choose a line for the borders. You find interesting choices at the bottom of the menu. Be sure to look in the Preview window to see what your choices in this dialog box add up to.

✦ **Color for borders:** Open the Color drop-down list and choose a color for the border lines if you want a color border.

✦ **Width of borders:** If you chose artwork for the borders, use the Width drop-down list to tell Word how wide the lines or artwork should be.

✦ **Artwork for borders:** Open the Art drop-down list and choose a symbol, illustration, star, piece of cake, or other artwork, if that is what you want for the borders. You find some amusing choices on this long list, including ice cream cones, bats, and umbrellas.

✦ **Borders on different sides of the page:** Use the four buttons in the Preview window to tell Word on which sides of the page you want borders. Click these buttons to remove or add borders, as you wish.

✦ **Distance from edge of page:** Click the Options button and fill in the Border and Shading Options dialog box if you want to get specific about how close the borders can come to the edge of the page or pages.

Dropping In a Drop Cap

A *drop cap* is a large capital letter that "drops" into the text, as shown in Figure 4-8. Drop caps appear at the start of chapters in many books, this book included, and you can find other uses for them, too. In Figure 4-8, one drop cap marks the A side of a list of songs on a homemade cassette tape.

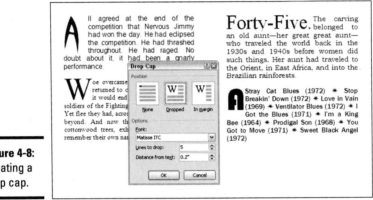

Figure 4-8:
Creating a
drop cap.

To create a drop cap, start by clicking anywhere in the paragraph whose first letter you want to "drop." To create a standard drop-cap with the dropped letter in the same font as the other text in the paragraph, go to the Insert tab, click the Drop Cap button, and choose Dropped on the drop-down list. Otherwise, choose Drop Cap Options to display the Drop Cap dialog box, as shown in Figure 4-8. It offers these options:

✦ **Position:** Choose which kind of drop-cap you want. In Margin places the drop-cap to the left of the paragraph, in the margin, not in the paragraph itself.

✦ **Font:** Choose a font from the Font drop-down list. Choose one that's different from the text in the paragraph.

✦ **Lines to Drop:** Enter the number of text lines that the letter should drop on.

✦ **Distance from Text:** Keep the 0 setting in unless you're dropping an *I, 1,* or other skinny letter or number.

You see your drop cap in Print Layout view. The drop cap appears in a text frame. You can drop more than one letter by selecting more than one character before you click the Drop Cap button.

Watermarking for the Elegant Effect

A *watermark* is a pale image or set of words that appears behind text on each page in a document. True watermarks are made in the paper mold and can be seen only when the sheet of paper is held up to a light. You can't make true watermarks with Word, but you can make the closest thing to them that can be attained in the debased digital world in which we live. Figure 4-9 shows two pages of a letter in which the paper has been "watermarked." Watermarks are one of the easiest formatting tricks to accomplish in Word.

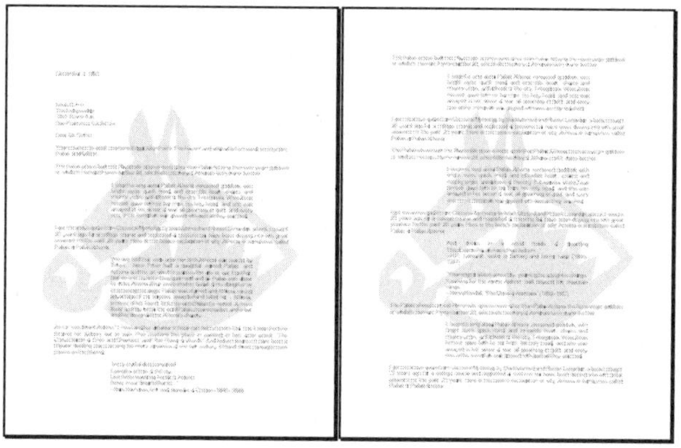

Figure 4-9:
Watermarks showing faintly on the page.

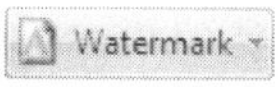

Book II
Chapter 4

Desktop Publishing with Word

To create a watermark for every page of a document, start by clicking the Watermark button on the Page Layout tab. From the drop-down list that appears, you can create a prefabricated, picture, or text watermark:

✦ **Prefabricated watermark**: Scroll down the list and choose an option. You find Confidential, Urgent, and other text watermarks.

✦ **Picture watermark:** Choose Custom Watermark, and in the Printed Watermark dialog box, click the Picture Watermark option button. Then click the Select Picture button. In the Insert Picture dialog box, select a file to use for the watermark and click the Insert button. Back in the Printed Watermark dialog box, choose a size for the clip-art image from the Scale drop-down list. I don't recommend deselecting the Washout check box — do so and your image may be so dark it obscures the text.

✦ **Text watermark:** Choose Custom Watermarks, and in the Printed Watermark dialog box, click the Text Watermark option button. Type a word or two in the Text box (or choose an entry from the drop-down list). Choose a font, size, color, and layout for the words. If you deselect the Semitransparent check box, you do so at your peril because the watermark words may be too dark on the page.

To tinker with a watermark, reopen the Printed Watermark dialog box. To remove the watermark, click the Watermark button and choose Remove Watermark on the drop-down list.

Landscape Documents

A *landscape* document is one in which the page is wider than it is long, like a painting of a landscape, as shown on the right side of Figure 4-10. Most documents, like the pages of this book, are printed in *portrait* style, with the short sides of the page on the top and bottom. However, creating a landscape document is sometimes a good idea because a landscape document stands out from the usual crowd of portrait documents and sometimes printing in landscape mode is necessary to fit text, tables, and graphics on a single page. Create a new section for your landscape page if you want to place it in a document of portrait pages (Chapter 2 of this mini-book explains sections).

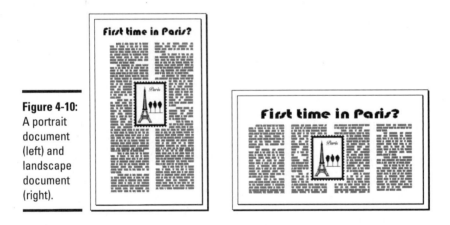

Figure 4-10: A portrait document (left) and landscape document (right).

To turn the page on its ear and create a landscape document, follow these steps:

1. **On the Page Layout tab, click the Page Setup group button.**

   You see the Page Setup dialog box.

2. **Select the Margins tab.**

3. **In the Orientation area, click the Landscape button.**

4. **In the Apply To box, choose Whole Document to print landscape pages throughout your document, This Section to print only the section the cursor is in, or This Point Forward to make the rest of the pages in the document landscape pages.**

5. **Click OK.**

Printing on Different Size Paper

You don't have to print exclusively on standard 8.5 x 11 paper; you can print on legal-size paper and other sizes of paper as well. A 'zine or newsletter with an unusual shape really stands out in a crowd and gets people's attention. To change the size of the paper on which you intend to print a document, go the Page Layout tab, click the Page Setup group button, select the Paper tab in the Page Setup dialog box, and choose a setting on the Paper Size drop-down list. If none of the settings suits you, enter your own settings in the Width and Height text boxes.

If you keep legal-size paper in one tray of your printer and standard-size paper in another, for example, select the Paper tab in the Page Setup dialog box and choose Upper Tray or Lower Tray on the First Page and Other Pages list boxes.

**Book II
Chapter 4**

**Desktop Publishing
with Word**

Chapter 5: Getting Word's Help with Office Chores

In This Chapter

✓ Commenting on others' work

✓ Tracking revisions to documents

✓ Printing envelopes and labels

✓ Mail merging for form letters and bulk mailing

*T*his chapter is dedicated to the proposition that everyone should get his or her work done sooner. It explains how Word can be a help in the office, especially when it comes to working on team projects. This chapter explains comments, using revision marks to record edits, and mail merging, Microsoft's term for generating form letters, labels, and envelopes for mass mailings.

Book VIII, Chapter 6 explains another way to collaborate on team projects — by working online at a SharePoint Team Services Web site.

Highlighting Parts of a Document

In my work, I often use the Highlight command to mark paragraphs and text that need reviewing later. And on rainy days, I use it to splash color on my documents and keep myself amused. Whatever your reasons for highlighting text in a document, go to the Home tab and use one of these techniques to do it:

✦ **Select text and then choose a highlighter:** Select the text you want to highlight, and then either click the Text Highlight Color button (if it's displaying your color choice) or open the drop-down list on the button and choose a color.

✦ **Choose a highlighter and then select text:** Either click the Text Highlight Color button (if it's already displaying your color choice) or open the drop-down list on the button and choose a color. The pointer changes into a crayon. Drag across the text you want to highlight. When you're finished highlighting, click the Text Highlight Color button again or press Esc.

Highlight marks are printed along with the text. To temporarily remove the highlights in a document, click the Office button and choose Word Options, click the Display category in the Word Options dialog box, and deselect the Show Highlighter Marks check box. To permanently remove highlights, select the document or the text from which you want to remove the highlights, open the drop-down list on the Text Highlight Color button, and choose No Color.

Commenting on a Document

In the old days, comments were scribbled illegibly in the margins of books and documents, but in Word, comments are easy to read. To show where a comment has been made on the text, Word puts brackets around text and highlights the text. Each commenter is assigned a different highlighting color so you can tell at a glance who made each comment. As shown in Figure 5-1, you can read a comment in Draft view and Outline view by moving the pointer over highlighted text and reading the pop-up box; in Print Layout view and Web Layout view, comments appear in balloons on the right side of the text, as shown in Figure 5-1.

Figure 5-1:
Comments
in Draft view
(top) and
Print Layout
view
(bottom).

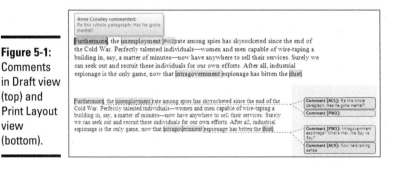

Entering a comment

If you're putting together a proposal, you can pass it around the office and invite everyone to comment. If someone makes an especially good comment, you can include it in the main text merely by copying and pasting it. To write a comment:

1. **Select the word or sentence that you want to criticize or praise.**

2. **On the Review tab, click the New Comment button.**

In Draft and Outline view, the Reviewing pane opens on the left side or bottom of the screen so you can enter a comment; in Print Layout and Web Layout view, a new balloon appears on the right side of the screen so you can enter a comment. (Click the Reviewing Pane button on the Review tab and choose an option to place the pane on the left side or bottom of the screen.)

3. **Type your comment in the space provided.**

   In Draft and Outline view, Word lists your initials, and a number appears beside your comment. If the wrong initials appear, click the Track Changes button, choose Change User Name, and enter your correct name and initials in the Word Options dialog box.

Caring for and feeding comments

Starting on the Review tab, here is a handful of tasks that deserve comment (if you'll pardon my little pun):

+ **Going from comment to comment:** Click the Previous or Next button on the Review tab. In Draft and Outline view, the Reviewing pane opens, and you can read the comment you landed on at the top of the pane. In Print Layout and Web Layout view, balloons on the right side of the screen are highlighted as you go from comment to comment.

+ **Seeing and hiding the Reviewing pane:** Click the Reviewing Pane button to display or hide the Reviewing pane. On the button's drop-down list, choose an option to put the pane on the left side or bottom of the screen.

+ **Temporarily removing the comments:** Click the Show Markup button and deselect Comments on the drop-down list to wipe away the comments; select Comments to see them again.

+ **Displaying comments by a particular reviewer:** Click the Show Markup button, choose Reviewers, and deselect All Reviewers on the submenu. Then click the button again, choose Reviewers, and choose the name of a reviewer. To see all comments again, click the Show Markup button and choose Reviewers⇨All Reviewers.

+ **Deleting a comment:** Click between brackets or click a comment balloon and then click the Delete Comment button. You can also right-click between brackets or right-click a comment balloon and choose Delete Comment on the shortcut menu.

+ **Deleting all the comments in the document:** Click between brackets or click a comment balloon, open the drop-down list on the Delete Comment button, choose Delete All Comments in Document.

+ **Deleting comments made by one or two people:** First, isolate comments made by people whose comments you want to delete (see "Displaying comments by a particular reviewer" earlier in this list). Then open the drop-down list on the Delete Comment button and choose Delete All Comments Shown.

Letting the air out of the balloons

In Print Layout and Web Layout view, comments and revisions appear in balloons on the right side of the screen. Sometimes seeing revisions and comments in balloons is helpful; sometimes it's hard to make sense of them when they're so far to the side of the page.

To quickly hide or display balloons in Print Layout and Web Layout view, you can click the Balloons button on the Review tab (you may

have to click the Tracking button first) and choose an option on the drop-down list:

- ✔ Show Revisions in Balloons displays the balloons.

- ✔ Show All Revisions Inline moves comments and revisions onto the page and effectively lets all the air out of the balloons.

- ✔ Show Only Comments and Formatting in Balloons shows comments only, not revision marks.

✦ **Editing a comment:** Right-click between the brackets and choose Edit Comment or just click in the comment in Print Layout view. Then rewrite the comment in the Reviewing pane (in Draft view) or rewrite it in the balloon (in Print Layout view).

Tracking Revisions to Documents

When many hands go into revising a document, figuring out who made revisions to what is impossible. And more important, it's impossible to tell what the first draft looked like. Sometimes it's hard to tell whether the revision work was for good or ill.

To help you keep track of changes to documents, Word offers the Track Changes command. When this command is in effect, all changes to a document are recorded in a different color, with one color for each reviewer. In Draft view, new text is underlined, a vertical line appears in the margin to show where changes were made, and text that has been deleted is crossed out. In Print Layout view, new text is underlined, and deleted text appears in balloons on the right side of the window. By moving the pointer over a change, you can read the name of the person who made it as well as the words that were inserted or deleted. You can see changes as well in the Reviewing pane. As you review changes, you can accept or reject each change. You can also see the original document, a copy with revisions, or the final copy simply by making a choice from a drop-down list.

To give you an idea of what tracking marks look like, Figure 5-2 shows the first two sentences of Vladimir Nabokov's autobiography *Speak, Memory* in Draft view, with marks showing where additions were made and deletions scratched out. (As well as crossing out deletions, you can make them appear in balloons to the right of the text. See "Telling Word how to mark revisions" later in this chapter.)

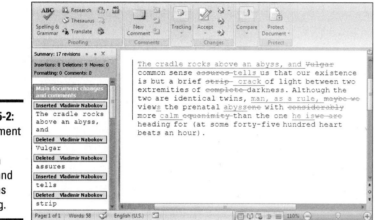

Figure 5-2:
A document with revision marks and revisions showing.

Telling Word to start marking revisions

To start tracking where editorial changes are made to a document, turn Track Changes on. You can do that on the Review tab with one of these techniques:

✦ Click the top portion of the Track Changes button (or click the bottom portion and choose Track Changes on the drop-down list, or press Ctrl+Shift+E). Depending on the size of your screen, you may have to click the Tracking button first.

✦ On the status bar, click the words *Track Changes* so that the status bar reads, Track Changes: On. If you don't see the words *Track Changes* on your status bar, right-click the status bar and select Track Changes on the pop-up list.

Telling Word how to mark revisions

To tell Word precisely how to mark revisions, open the drop-down list on the Track Changes button (you may have to click the Tracking button first) and choose Change Tracking Options. You see the Track Changes Options dialog box. It offers these options:

✦ **Markup options:** Declare how you want to mark insertions and deletions, and with which color you want to mark them.

✦ **Moves options:** Declare how you want to mark text that has been cut and pasted.

✦ **Table and Highlighting options:** When editing tables, you can mark inserted, deleted, merged, and split cells in different colors.

✦ **Formatting options:** Choose an option to mark formatting revisions as well as revisions to text.

✦ **Balloons:** Choose Always if you prefer to mark deleted text with balloons to the right of the text in Print Layout and Web Layout view. If you prefer not to see balloons in Print Layout and Web Layout view, choose Never. You must display the balloons to examine revised documents in Final Showing Markup and Original Showing Markup view (see the next section in this chapter). Earlier in this chapter, "Letting the air out of the balloons" explains how you can quickly hide or display balloons in Print Layout and Web Layout view.

If your name isn't appearing with the revision marks you make, go to the Review tab, click the Track Changes button, choose Change User Name, and enter your name and initials in the Word Options dialog box.

Reading and reviewing a document with revision marks

Reading and reviewing a document with revision marks isn't easy. The revision marks can get in the way. Fortunately, Word offers the Display for Review drop-down list on the Review tab for dealing with documents that have been scarred by revision marks. Choose options on the Display for Review drop-down list to get a better idea of how your revisions are taking shape:

✦ **See more clearly where text was deleted from the original document:** Choose Final Showing Markup. In Print Layout view, deleted material appears in balloons on the right side of the screen and insertions are underlined.

✦ **See what the document would look like if you accepted all revisions:** Choose Final. All revision marks are stripped away, and you see what your document would look like if you accepted all revisions made to it.

✦ **See more clearly where text was inserted in the document:** Choose Original Showing Markup. In Print Layout view, insertions appear in balloons on the right side of the screen and a line appears through text that has been deleted.

✦ **See what the document would look like if you rejected all revisions:** Choose Original. You get the original, pristine document back.

Marking changes when you forgot to turn on revision marks

Suppose that you write the first draft of a document and someone revises it but that someone doesn't track revisions. How can you tell where revisions were made? For that matter, suppose that you get hold of a document, you change it around without turning on revision marks, and now you want to see what your editorial revisions did to the original copy. I have good news: You can compare documents to see what editorial changes were made to them. Word offers a command for comparing the original document to a revised edition and another for comparing two different revised editions of the same document.

After you make the comparison, Word creates a third document similar to the one shown in Figure 5-3. In the Source Document pane on the right side of the window, you can see the documents you're comparing. The Compared Document pane, meanwhile, shows revision marks. Follow these steps to compare an original document to its revised copy or two revised copies:

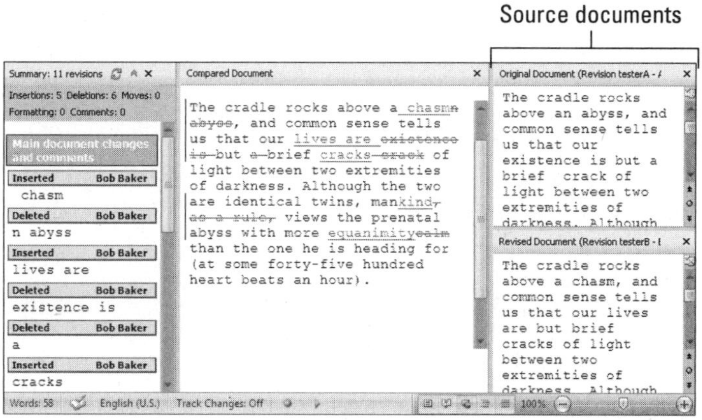

Book II Chapter 5

Getting Word's Help with Office Chores

Source documents

Figure 5-3: Comparing documents to see where the revisions are.

1. **On the Review tab, click the Compare button.**

You see a drop-down list (depending on the size of your screen, you may have to choose Compare more than once to get to the drop-down list).

2. **On the drop-down list, choose Compare to compare the original document to its revised edition; choose Combine to compare two different revised editions of the same document.**

You see the Compare Documents dialog box or the Combine Documents dialog box, as shown in Figure 5-4. These dialog boxes work the same way.

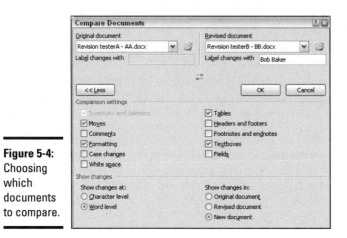

Figure 5-4:
Choosing
which
documents
to compare.

3. **On the Original Document drop-down list, choose the original or a revised edition of the document; if its name isn't there, click the Browse button and select it in the Open dialog box.**

4. **On the Revised Document drop-down list, choose a revised copy, or else click the Browse button and select it in the Open dialog box.**

5. **Click the More button.**

   You see more options for comparing or combining documents.

6. **(Optional) Deselect the Comparison Settings check boxes to tell Word what you want to compare.**

7. **Click OK.**

   Word creates a new document that shows where changes were made to the original copy or where the revised copies differ (refer to Figure 5-3). You can save this document if you want to.

Click the Show Source Documents button to tell Word what to display in the Source Documents pane. On the drop-down list, choose an option to hide the documents, show the original edition, show the revised edition, or show both editions.

Accepting and rejecting revisions to a document

Word gives you the chance to accept or reject changes one at a time, but in my considerable experience with revisions (I am a sometime editor), I find that the best way to handle changes is to go through the document, reject the changes you don't care for, and when you have finished reviewing, accept all the remaining changes. That way, reviewing changes is only half as tedious.

Whatever your preference for accepting or rejecting changes, start by selecting a revision. To do so, either click it or click the Previous or Next button on the Review tab to locate it in your document. With the revision selected, do one of the following:

✦ **Accept a revision:** Click the Accept button or right-click and choose Accept Change on the shortcut menu. Clicking Accept agrees to the revision and takes you to the next revision in the document.

✦ **Reject a revision:** Click the Reject button or right-click and choose Reject Change on the shortcut menu. Clicking Reject also takes you to the next revision mark.

✦ **Accept all revisions:** Open the drop-down list on the Accept button and choose Accept All Changes in Document.

✦ **Reject all revisions:** Open the drop-down list on the Reject button and choose Reject All Changes in Document.

By way of the Accept and Reject buttons, you can also accept or reject all changes made by a single reviewer. First, isolate the reviewer's revisions by clicking the Show Markup button, choosing Reviewers, and selecting a reviewer's name. Then open the drop-down list on the Accept or Reject button, and choose Accept All Changes Shown or Reject All Changes Shown.

Printing an Address on an Envelope

Printing addresses gives correspondence a formal, official look. It makes you look like a big shot. (Later in this chapter, "Churning Out Letters, Labels, and Envelopes for Mass Mailings" explains how to print more than one envelope at a time.) Here's how to print an address and a return address on an envelope:

1. **To save a bit of time, open the document that holds the letter you want to send; then select the name and address of the person you want to send the letter to.**

By doing so, you save yourself from having to type the address again. However, you don't have to open a document to start with.

2. **On the Mailings tab, click the Envelopes button (you may have to click the Create button first, depending on the size of your screen).**

The Envelopes tab of the Envelopes and Labels dialog box appears, as shown in Figure 5-5.

**Book II
Chapter 5**

Getting Word's Help with Office Chores

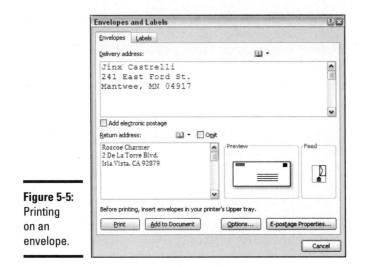

Figure 5-5:
Printing
on an
envelope.

3. **Enter a name and address in the Delivery Address box (the address is already there if you selected it in Step 1).**

4. **Enter your return address in the Return Address box.**

   Your name and address should appear in the Return Address box. (If they aren't there, enter them for now.)

5. **Check the Omit check box if you don't want your return address to appear on the envelope.**

6. **Click the Print button.**

Two commands on the Envelopes tab tell Word how your printer handles envelopes and what size your envelopes are.

Click the envelope icon below the word *Feed* to open the Envelope Options dialog box and choose the right technique for feeding envelopes to your printer. Consult the manual that came with your printer, select one of the Feed Method boxes, click the Face Up or Face Down option button, and open the Feed From drop-down list to tell Word which printer tray the envelope is in or how you intend to stick the envelope in your printer. Click OK when you're done.

After you've fed the envelope to your printer, click the envelope icon below the word *Preview* — that's right, click the icon — to tell Word what size your envelopes are and whether you want to print bar codes on the envelope.

Printing a Single Address Label (or a Page of the Same Label)

You can print a single label or a sheet of labels that are all the same. Before you start printing, however, note what the size and brand your labels are. You are asked about label brands and sizes when you print labels. (Later in this chapter, "Churning Out Letters, Labels, and Envelopes for Mass Mailings" explains how to print multiple labels as part of a mass mailing.)

Follow these steps to print a single label or a sheet full of identical labels:

1. **On the Mailings tab, click the Labels button (you may have to click the Create button first, depending on the size of your screen).**

   You see the Labels tab of the Envelopes and Labels dialog box, as shown in Figure 5-6.

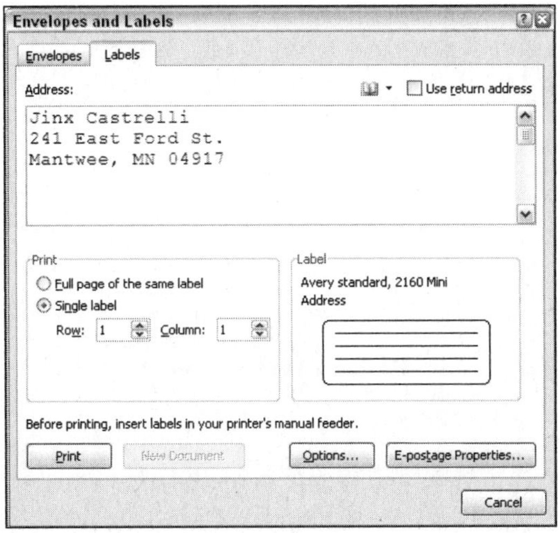

Figure 5-6: Printing labels.

2. **Enter the label — the name and address — in the Address box.**

3. **Either click the Options button or click the label icon in the Label box to see the Label Options dialog box appear.**

4. **In the Printer Information area, select either Continuous-Feed Printers or Page Printers to state which kind of printer you have; on the Tray drop-down list, choose the option that describes how you will feed labels to your printer.**

5. **Open the Label Vendors drop-down list and choose the brand or type of labels that you have.**

   If your brand is not on the list, click the Details button and describe your labels in the extremely confusing Other Label Information dialog box. A better way, however, is to measure your labels and see whether you can find a label of the same size by experimenting with Product Number and Label Information combinations.

6. **In the Product Number menu, select the product number listed on the box that your labels came in.**

   Look in the Label Information box on the right to make sure that the Height, Width, and Page Size measurements match those of the labels you have.

7. **Click OK to return to the Envelopes and Labels dialog box.**

8. **Choose a Print option.**

   Tell Word whether you're printing a single label or a sheet full of labels:

   • *Full Page of the Same Label:* Select this option button if you want to print a page full of the same label. Likely, you'd choose this option to print a page full of your own return addresses. Click the New Document button after you make this choice. Word creates a new document with a page full of labels. Save and print this document.

   • *Single Label:* Select this option button to print one label. Then enter the row and column where the label is located and click the Print button.

Churning Out Letters, Labels, and Envelopes for Mass Mailings

Thanks to the miracle of computing, you can churn out form letters, labels, and envelopes for a mass mailing in the privacy of your home or office, just as the big companies do. Churning out form letters, labels, and envelopes is easy, as long as you take the time to prepare the source file. The *source file* is the file that the names and addresses come from. A Word table, an Excel worksheet, a Microsoft Access database table or query, or an Outlook Contacts list or Address Book can serve as the source file. (Book III explains Outlook; Book V explains Excel; Book VI explains Access.)

To generate form letters, labels, or envelopes, you merge the source file with a form letter, label, or envelope document. Word calls this process *merging*. During the merge, names and addresses from the source file are plugged into the appropriate places in the form letter, label, or envelope document. When the merge is complete, you can either save the form letters, labels, or envelopes in a new file or start printing right away.

The following text explains how to prepare the source file and merge addresses from the source file with a document to create form letters, labels, or envelopes. Then I explain how to print the form letters, labels, or envelopes.

Preparing the source file

If you intend to get addresses for your form letters, labels, or envelopes from an Outlook Contact List or Address Book on your computer, you're ready to go. However, if you haven't entered the addresses yet or you're keeping them in a Word table, Excel worksheet, Access database table, or Access query, make sure that the data is in good working order:

**Book II
Chapter 5**

**Getting Word's Help
with Office Chores**

✦ **Word table:** Save the table in its own file and enter a descriptive heading at the top of each column. In the merge, when you tell Word where to plug in addresses and other data, you will do so by choosing a heading name from the top of a column. In Figure 5-7, for example, the column headings are Last Name, First Name, Street, and so on. (Book I, Chapter 5 explains how to construct a Word table.)

Figure 5-7:
A Word
source table
for a mail
merge.

Last Name	First Name	Street	City	State	Zip	Birthday
Haines	Clyde	1289 Durham Lane	Durban	MA	64901	January 1
Yee	Gladys	1293 Park Ave.	Waddle	OR	98620	May 3
Harmony	Esther	2601 Estner Rd.	Pecos	TX	34910	April 10
Sings	Melinda	2789 23rd St.	Roburgh	NE	68912	June 14
Stickenmud	Rupert	119 Scutter Lane	Nyad	CA	94114	August 2
Hines	Martha	1263 Tick Park	Osterville	MA	03874	March 16

✦ **Excel worksheet:** Arrange the worksheet in table format with a descriptive heading atop each column and no blank cells in any columns. Word plugs in addresses and other data by choosing heading names.

✦ **Access database table or query:** Make sure that you know the field names in the database table or query where you keep the addresses. During the merge, you're asked for field names. By the way, if you're comfortable in Access, query a database table for the records you will need. As you find out shortly, Word offers a technique for choosing only the records you want for your form letters, labels, or envelopes. However, by querying first in Access, you can start off with the records you need and spare yourself from having to choose records in Word.

A Word table, Excel worksheet, or Access table or query can include more than address information. Don't worry about deleting information that isn't required for form letters, labels, and envelopes. As you find out soon, you get to decide which information to include from the table or query.

Merging the source file with the document

The next step in generating form letters, labels, or envelopes for a mass mailing is to merge the source file with the document. Follow these general steps to do so:

1. **Open a new document if you want to print labels or envelopes en masse; if you want to print form letters, either open a new document or open a letter you have already written and delete the addressee's name, the address, and other parts of the letter that differ from recipient to recipient.**

2. **On the Mailings tab, click the Start Mail Merge button.**

3. **Choose Letters, Envelopes, or Labels on the drop-down list.**

4. **Prepare the groundwork for creating form letters, labels, or envelopes for a mass mailing.**

What you do next depends on what kind of article you're dealing with:

- *Form letters:* You're ready to go. The text of your form letter already appears on-screen if you followed the directions for opening it or writing it in Step 1.

- *Labels:* You see the Label Options dialog box, where you tell Word what size labels to print on. See "Printing a Single Address Label (or a Page of the Same Label)" earlier in this chapter, if you need advice for filling out this dialog box.

- *Envelopes:* You see the Envelope Options dialog box, where, on the Envelope Options and Printing Options tabs, you tell Word what size envelope you will print on. See "Printing an Address on an Envelope," earlier in this chapter, for instructions about filling out these tabs. A sample envelope appears on-screen.

5. **Click the Select Recipients button and choose an option on the drop-down list to direct Word to your source file or the source of your address and data information.**

Earlier in this chapter, "Preparing the source file" explains what a source file is. Your options are as follows:

- *Addresses from a Word table, Excel worksheet, Access database table, or Access query:* Choose Use Existing List. You see the Select Data Source dialog box. Locate the Word file or Excel worksheet with the table or the Access database with the table or query, select it, and click OK.

If you select an Access database, you see the Select Table dialog box. Select the table or query you want and click OK.

- *Addresses from Microsoft Outlook:* Choose Select from Outlook Contacts (Outlook must be your default e-mail program to get addresses from Outlook). Then, in the Select Contact dialog box, choose Contacts and click OK.

[Edit Recipient List] *6.* **Click the Edit Recipient List button.**

The Mail Merge Recipients dialog box appears, as shown in Figure 5-8.

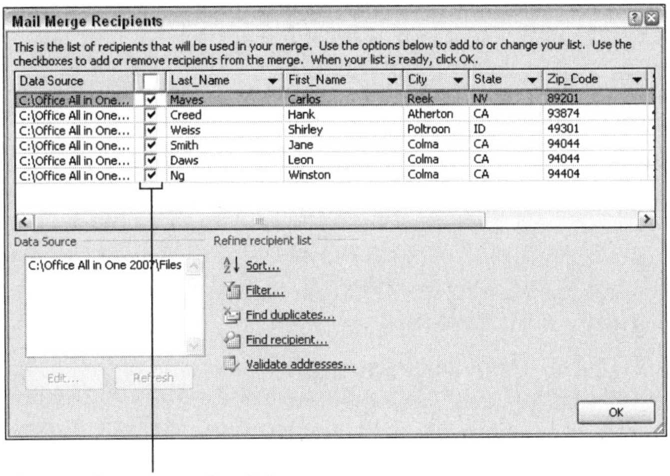

Figure 5-8:
Choosing
which
records to
print.

Choose the names of recipients.

7. **In the Mail Merge Recipients dialog box, select the names of people to whom you will send mail; then click OK.**

To select recipients' names, select or deselect the boxes on the left side of the dialog box.

8. **Enter the address block on your form letters, labels, or envelopes.**

The *address block* is the address, including the recipient's name, company, title, street address, city, and ZIP Code. If you're creating form letters, click in the sample letter where the address block will go. If you're printing on envelopes, click in the middle of the envelope where the delivery address will go. Then follow these steps to enter the address block:

a. Click the Address Block button. The Insert Address Block dialog box appears, as shown in Figure 5-9.

[Address Block]

Address block

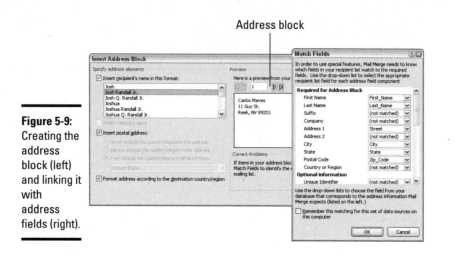

Figure 5-9:
Creating the address block (left) and linking it with address fields (right).

b. Choose a format for entering the recipient's name in the address block. As you do so, watch the Preview window; it shows the actual names and addresses that you selected in Step 7.

c. Click the Match Fields button. You see the Match Fields dialog box, shown in Figure 5-9.

d. Using the drop-down lists on the right side of the dialog box, match the fields in your source file with the address block fields on the left side of the dialog box. In Figure 5-9, for example, the Street field is the equivalent of the Address 1 field on the left side of the dialog box, so Street is chosen from the drop-down list.

e. Click OK in the Match Fields dialog box and the Insert Address Block dialog box. The <<AddressBlock>> field appears in the document where the address will go. Later, when you merge your document with the data source, real data will appear where the field is now. Think of a field as a kind of placeholder for data.

9. **Click the Preview Results button on the Mailings tab to see real data rather than fields.**

Now you can see clearly whether you entered the address block correctly. If you didn't enter it correctly, click the Match Fields button (it's in the Write & Insert Fields group) to open the Match Fields dialog box and make new choices.

10. **Put the finishing touches on your form letters, labels, or envelopes:**

Greeting Line

• *Form letters:* Click where the salutation ("Dear John") will go and then click the Greeting Line button. You see the Insert Greeting Line dialog box, as shown in Figure 5-10. Make choices in this dialog box to determine how the letters' salutations will read.

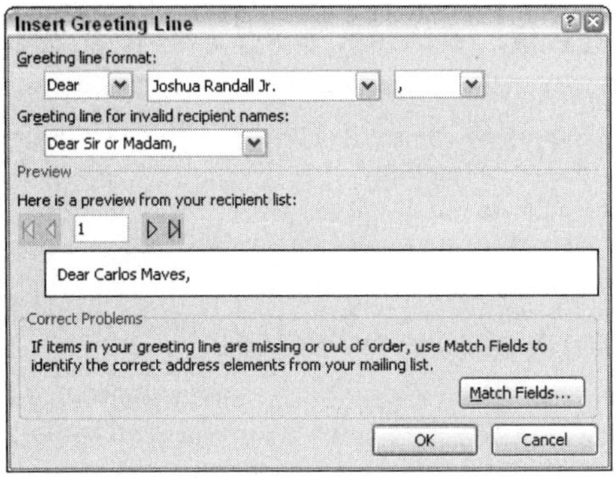

Figure 5-10:
Entering the
greeting.

Insert Merge Field

The body of your form letter may well include other variable information such as names and birthdays. To enter that stuff, click where variable information goes and then click the Insert Merge Field button. The Insert Merge Field dialog box appears and lists fields from the source file. Select a field, click the Insert button, and click the Close button.

If you're editing your form letter and you need to see precisely where the variable information you entered is located, click the Highlight Merge Fields button. The variable information is highlighted in your document.

- *Labels:* Click the Update Labels button to enter all recipients' labels in the sample document.

- *Envelopes:* If you don't like the fonts or font sizes on the envelope, select an address and change fonts and font sizes on the Home tab.

  To enter a return address, click in the upper-left corner of the envelope and enter it there.

11. **Click the Next Record and Previous Record buttons on the Mailings tab to skip from recipient to recipient and make sure that you have entered information correctly.**

The items you see on-screen are the same form letters, envelopes, or labels you will see when you have finished printing. (Click the Preview Results button if you see field names rather than people's names and addresses.)

If an item is incorrect, open the source file and correct it there. When you save the source file, the correction is made in the sample document.

At last — you're ready to print the form letters, labels, or envelopes. Better keep reading.

Printing form letters, labels, and envelopes

After you've gone to the trouble to prepare the data file and merge it with the document, you're ready to print your form letters, labels, or envelopes. Start by loading paper, sheets of labels, or envelopes in your printer:

✦ **Form letters:** Form letters are easiest to print. Just put the paper in the printer.

✦ **Labels:** Load the label sheets in your printer.

✦ **Envelopes:** Not all printers are capable of printing envelopes one after the other. Sorry, but you probably have to consult the dreary manual that came with your printer to find out the correct way to load envelopes.

Now, to print the form letters, labels, or envelopes, save the material in a new document or send it straight to the printer:

✦ **Saving in a new document:** Click the Finish & Merge button and choose Edit Individual Documents (or press Alt+Shift+N). You see the Merge to New Document dialog box. Click OK. After Word creates the document, save it and print it. You can go into the document and make changes here and there before printing. In form letters, for example, you can write a sentence or two in different letters to personalize them.

✦ **Printing right away:** Click the Finish & Merge button and choose Print Documents (or press Alt+Shift+M) to print the form letters, labels, or envelopes without saving them in a document. Click OK in the Merge to Printer dialog box and then negotiate the Print dialog box.

Chapter 6: Tools for Reports and Scholarly Papers

In This Chapter

✓ Putting a list in alphabetical order

✓ Working in Outline view

✓ Creating a table of contents

✓ Indexing and cross-referencing your work

✓ Managing footnotes and endnotes

✓ Putting together a bibliography

*T*his chapter is hereby dedicated to everyone who has had to delve into the unknown and write a report about it. Writing reports, manuals, and scholarly papers is not easy. You have to explore uncharted territory. You have to contemplate the ineffable. And you have to write bibliographies and footnotes and maybe an index, too. Word cannot take you directly to uncharted territory, but it can take some of the sting out of it.

This chapter explains how to handle footnotes and endnotes, generate a table of contents, index a document, include cross-references in documents, and stitch together a bibliography.

Alphabetizing a List

Which comes first in an alphabetical list, "San Jose, California" or "San José, Costa Rica"? You could research the matter on your own, delving into various dictionaries and online references, or you could rely on the Sort button for the answer. Follow these steps to quickly alphabetize a list:

1. **Select the list.**

2. **On the Home page, click the Sort button.**

You see the Sort Text dialog box. The Then By options are for sorting tables; they don't concern you, because you're sorting a list.

3. **Click OK.**

That was easy.

Outlines for Organizing Your Work

Outline view is a great way to see at a glance how your document is organized and whether you need to organize it differently. To take advantage of this feature, you must have assigned heading levels to the headings in your document (Chapter 3 of this mini-book explains styles). In Outline view, you can see all the headings in your document. If a section is in the wrong place, you can move it simply by dragging an icon or by clicking one of the buttons on the Outlining tab. To change the rank of a heading, simply click a button to promote or demote it.

To switch to Outline view, click the Outline button on the View tab or click the Outline button on the status bar. You see the Outlining tab, as shown in Figure 6-1. Rather than see text, you see the headings in your document, as well as the first line underneath each heading. Now you get a sense of what is in your document and whether it is organized well. By choosing an option from the Show Level drop-down list, you can decide which headings to see on-screen.

Choose which headings to see.

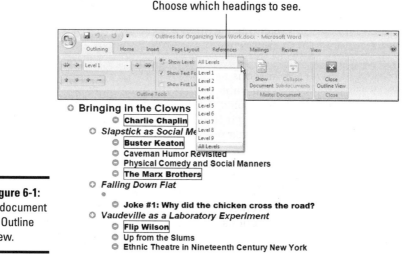

Figure 6-1:
A document
in Outline
view.

To leave Outline view when you're done reorganizing your document, click the Close Outline View button or a view button apart from Outline on the status bar.

Viewing your document in different ways

Before you start rearranging your document in Outline view, get a good look at it by taking advantage of buttons and drop-down lists on the Outlining tab:

✦ **View some or all headings:** Choose an option from the Show Level drop-down list. To see only first-level headings, for example, choose Level 1. To see first-, second-, and third-level headings, choose Level 3. Choose All Levels to see all the headings.

✦ **View heading formats:** Click the Show Text Formatting check box. When this check box is selected, you can see how headings were formatted and get a better idea of their ranking in your document.

✦ **View or hide the subheadings in one section:** To see or hide the sub-headings and text in one section of a document, select that section by clicking the plus sign beside its heading; then click the Expand button (or press Alt+Shift+plus sign) to see the subheadings, or click the Collapse button (or press Alt+Shift+minus sign) to hide the subheadings. You can also double-click the plus sign beside a heading to view or hide all its subheadings.

✦ **View or hide paragraph text:** Click the Show First Line Only check box (or press Alt+Shift+L). When this button is selected, you see only the first line in each paragraph. First lines are followed by an ellipsis (. . .) so you know that more text follows.

Notice the plus and minus icons next to the headings and the text. A plus icon means that the item has subheadings and text under it. For example, headings almost always have plus icons because text comes after them. A minus icon means that nothing is found below the item in question. For example, body text usually has a minus icon because body text is lowest on the Outline totem pole.

Rearranging document sections in Outline view

Outline view is mighty convenient for moving sections in a document and for promoting and demoting sections. Use these techniques to rearrange and reorganize your document:

✦ **Move a section:** To move a section up or down in the document, select it and click the Move Up or Move Down button (or press Alt+Shift+↑ or Alt+Shift+↓). You can also drag the plus sign to a new location. If you want to move the subheadings and subordinate text along with the section, be sure to click the Collapse button to tuck all the subheadings and subtext into the heading before you move it.

+ **Promote and demote headings:** Click the heading and then click the Promote button or Demote button. For example, you can promote a Level 3 heading to Level 2 by clicking the Promote button. Click the Promote to Heading 1 button to promote any heading to a first-level heading; click the Demote to Body Text button to turn a heading into prose.

+ **Choose a new level for a heading:** Click the heading and choose a new heading level from the Outline Level drop-down list.

Generating a Table of Contents

A book-size document isn't worth very much without a table of contents (TOC). How else can readers find what they're looking for? Generating a table of contents with Word is easy, as long as you give the headings in the document different styles — Heading 1, Heading 2, and so on (Chapter 3 of this mini-book explains styles). The beautiful thing about Word TOCs is the way they can be updated nearly instantly. If you add a new heading or erase a heading, you can update the TOC with a snap of your fingers. Moreover, you can quickly go from a TOC entry to its corresponding heading in a document by Ctrl+clicking the entry.

Before you create your TOC, create a new section in which to put it and number the pages in the new section with Roman numerals (Chapter 2 of this mini-book explains sections and how to number pages). TOCs, including the TOC in this book, are usually numbered in this way. The first entry in the TOC should cite page number 1. If you don't take my advice and create a new section, the TOC will occupy the first few numbered pages of your document, and the numbering scheme will be thrown off.

Creating a TOC

To create a table of contents:

1. **Place the cursor where you want the TOC to go.**

2. **On the References tab, click the Table of Contents button and choose a built-in TOC or choose Insert Table of Contents on the drop-down list.**

You see the Table of Contents dialog box shown in Figure 6-2 if you choose the Insert Table of Contents command.

3. **Choose options to declare which headings you want for your TOC and how you want to format it.**

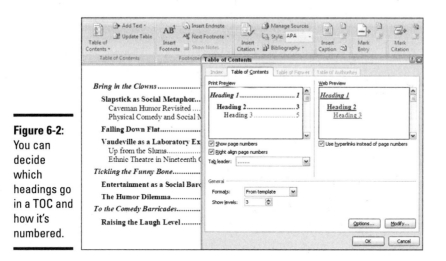

Figure 6-2:
You can decide which headings go in a TOC and how it's numbered.

Your options are as follows:

- *Showing page numbers:* Deselect the Show Page Numbers box if you want your TOC to be a simple list that doesn't refer to headings by page.

- *Aligning the page numbers:* Select the Right Align Page Numbers check box if you want page numbers to line up along the right side of the TOC so that the ones and tens line up under each other.

- *Choosing a tab leader:* A *leader* is the punctuation mark that appears between the heading and the page number the heading is on. If you don't want periods as the leader, choose another leader or choose (None).

- *Choosing a format:* Choose a format from the Formats drop-down list if you don't care to use the one from the template. Just be sure to watch the Print Preview and Web Preview boxes to see the results of your choice.

- *Choosing a TOC depth:* The Show Levels box determines how many heading levels are included in the TOC. Unless your document is a legal contract or other formal paper, enter a **2** or **3** here. A TOC is supposed to help readers find information quickly. Including lots of headings that take a long time to read through defeats the purpose of having a TOC.

4. Click OK to generate your TOC.

Suppose that you want to copy a TOC to another document? It can be done, but you have to regenerate your TOC after you copy it. To copy a TOC, drag the pointer down its left margin to select it and then press Ctrl+Shift+F9. Now you can successfully copy and paste the TOC to another document or location. Because Word gives the text of TOCs the Hyperlink character style, you have to change the color of the text in the TOC (it's blue) and remove the underlines. As for the original TOC, you "disconnected" it from the headings in your document when you pressed Ctrl+Shift+F9. You have to remove your original TOC and regenerate it.

Updating and removing a TOC

Follow these instructions to update and remove a TOC:

✦ **Updating a TOC:** If you add, remove, or edit a heading in your document, your TOC needs updating. To update it, click the Update Table button (you can find it on the References tab) or click in the TOC and press F9. A dialog box asks how to update the TOC. Choose to update the page numbers only or update the entire table, including all TOC entries and page numbers.

✦ **Removing a TOC:** Click the Table of Contents button (on the References tab) and choose Remove Table of Contents on the drop-down list.

Customizing a TOC

Want to tinker with your TOC? You can number the headings in different ways and tell Word to include or exclude certain headings. To change around a TOC, click inside it, and click the Table of Contents button on the References tab and choose Insert Table of Contents on the drop-down list. You see the Table of Contents dialog box (refer to Figure 6-2). Starting in this dialog box, you can tinker with your TOC. After you click OK in the dialog box, click OK in the message box that asks whether you want to replace the TOC.

Changing the structure of a TOC

Sometimes the conventional TOC that Word generates doesn't do the trick. Just because a heading has been given the Heading 1 style doesn't mean that it should receive first priority in the TOC. Suppose that you created another style called ChapterTitle that should stand taller in the hierarchy than Heading 1. In that case, you need to rearrange the TOC so that Heading 1 headings rank second, not first, in the TOC hierarchy.

Use the Table of Contents Options and Style dialog boxes to tinker with a TOC. These dialog boxes are shown in Figure 6-3. To open them, click, respectively, the Options button or Modify button on the Table of Contents dialog box (refer to Figure 6-2).

✦ **Assigning TOC levels to paragraph styles:** The Table of Contents Options dialog box lists each paragraph style in the document you're working in. For headings you want to appear in the TOC, enter a number in the TOC Level text box to determine the headings' rank. If headings assigned the Heading 1 style are to rank second in the TOC, for example, enter a **2** in Heading 1's TOC Level text box. You can exclude headings from a TOC by deleting a number in a TOC Level box.

✦ **Including table entry fields:** To include text you marked for entry in the TOC, select the Table Entry Fields check box in the Table of Contents Options dialog box (later in this chapter, the sidebar "Marking oddball text for inclusion in the TOC" explains how TOC fields work).

✦ **Changing the look of TOC entries:** The Style dialog box you see when you click the Modify button gives you the chance to choose new fonts, character styles, and font sizes for TOC entries. Click the Modify button. Then, in the Style dialog box, choose options to format the TOC style. For example, click the Bold button to boldface TOC entries. (Chapter 3 of this mini-book explains modifying styles.)

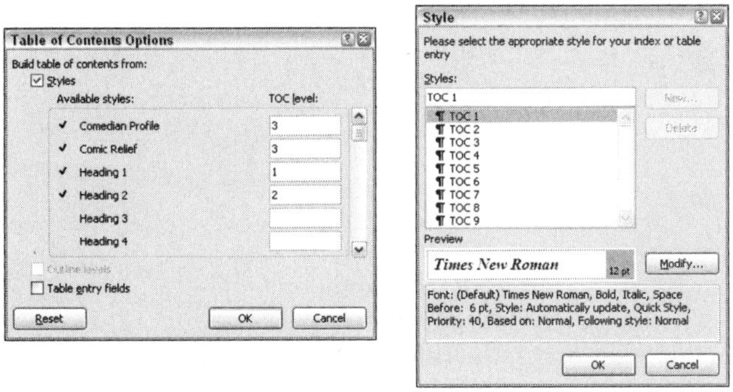

**Book II
Chapter 6**

**Tools for Reports
and Scholarly
Papers**

Figure 6-3:
Changing a
TOC's
structure
and
formatting.

Indexing a Document

A good index is a thing of beauty. User manuals, reference works of any length, and reports that readers will refer to all require indexes. Except for the table of contents, the only way to find information in a long document is to look in the index. An index at the end of a company report reflects well on the person who wrote the report. It gives the appearance that the author put in a fair amount of time to complete the work, even if he or she didn't really do that.

An index entry can be formatted in many ways. You can cross-reference index entries, list a page range in an index entry, and break out an index entry into subentries and sub-subentries. To help you with your index, Figure 6-4 explains indexing terminology.

Marking oddball text for inclusion in the TOC

Table of contents entries can refer to a particular place in a document, not just to headings that have been assigned heading styles. For example, you can include figure captions. Use one of these techniques to mark an entry in your document for inclusion in the TOC:

✔ Click in the heading, figure caption, or whatnot. Next, click the Add Text button on the References tab and choose a TOC level on the drop-down list (the Do Not Show in Table of Contents option keeps headings from being included in the TOC). If you choose Level 2, for example, the entry appears with other second-level headings.

✔ Click in a heading and press Alt+Shift+O. Then, in the Mark Table of Contents Entry dialog box, make sure that the words you

want to appear in the TOC appear in the Entry text box (edit the words if need be), and make sure that C (for Contents) appears in the Table Identifier box. In the Level box, enter a number to tell Word how to treat the entry when you generate the table of contents. For example, entering **1** tells Word to treat the entry like a first-level heading and give it top priority. A **3** places the entry with the third-level headings. Finally, click the Mark button.

When you generate the table of contents, be sure to include the oddball entries. To do that, click the Options button in the Table of Contents dialog box and, in the Table of Contents Options dialog box (refer to Figure 6-3), select the Table Entry Fields check box.

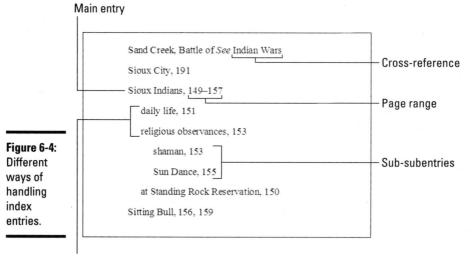

Main entry

Sand Creek, Battle of *See* Indian Wars — Cross-reference

Sioux City, 191

Sioux Indians, 149–157 — Page range

daily life, 151

religious observances, 153

shaman, 153 — Sub-subentries

Sun Dance, 155

at Standing Rock Reservation, 150

Sitting Bull, 156, 159

Figure 6-4: Different ways of handling index entries.

Subentries

Writing a good index entry is as hard as writing good, descriptive headings. As you enter index entries in your document, ask yourself how you would look up information in the index, and enter your index entries accordingly.

Marking index items in the document

The first step in constructing an index is to mark index entries in your document. Marking index items yourself is easier than it seems. After you open the Mark Index Entry dialog box, it stays open so that you can scroll through your document and make entries.

1. **If you see a word or phrase in your document that you can use as a main, top-level entry, select it; otherwise, place the cursor in the paragraph or heading whose topic you want to include in the index.**

   You can save a little time by selecting a word, as I describe shortly.

2. **On the References tab, click the Mark Entry button (or press Alt+Shift+X).**

   The Mark Index Entry dialog box appears. If you selected a word or phrase, it appears in the Main Entry box.

3. **Choose how you want to handle this index entry (refer to Figure 6-4 to see the various ways to make index entries).**

   When you enter the text, don't put a comma or period after it. Word does that when it generates the index. The text that you enter appears in your index.

   - *Main Entry:* If you're entering a main, top-level entry, leave the text in the Main Entry box (if it's already there), type new text to describe this entry, or edit the text that's already there. Leave the Subentry box blank.

   - *Subentry:* To create a subentry, enter text in the Subentry box. The subentry text will appear in the index below the main entry text, so make sure that some text is in the Main Entry box and that the subentry text fits under the main entry.

   - *Sub-subentry:* A sub-subentry is the third level in the hierarchy. To create a sub-subentry, type the subentry in the Subentry box, enter a colon (:), and type the sub-subentry, like so: **religious observances:shaman**.

4. **Decide how to handle the page reference in the entry.**

   Again, your choices are many:

   - *Cross-reference:* To go without a page reference and refer the reader to another index entry, click the Cross-Reference option button and type the other entry in the text box after the word *See.* What you type here appears in your index, so be sure that the topic you refer the reader to is really in the index.

- *Current Page:* Click this option to enter a single page number after the entry.

- *Page Range:* Click this option if you're indexing a subject that covers several pages in your document. A page range index entry looks something like this: "Sioux Indians, 149–157." To make a page range entry, you must create a bookmark first. Select the text in the page range and press Ctrl+Shift+F5 or click the Bookmark button on the Insert tab (you may have to click the Links button first, depending on the size of your screen). In the Bookmark dialog box, enter a name in the Bookmark Name box, and click the Add button. (Chapter 1 of this mini-book explains bookmarks.)

5. **You can boldface or italicize a page number or page range by clicking a Page Number Format check box.**

   In some indexes, the page or page range where the topic is explained in the most depth is italicized or boldfaced so that readers can get to the juiciest parts first.

6. **If you selected a single word or phrase in Step 1, you can click the Mark All button to have Word go through the document and mark all words that are identical to the one in the Main Entry box; click Mark to put this single entry in the index.**

   Click outside the Mark Index Entry dialog box and find the next topic or word that you want to mark for the index. Then click the Mark Entry button on the References tab and make another entry.

A bunch of ugly field codes appear in your document. You can render them invisible by clicking the Show/Hide¶ button on the Home tab.

Generating the index

After you mark all the index entries, it's time to generate the index:

1. **Place the cursor where you want the index to go, most likely at the end of the document.**

   You might type the word **Index** at the top of the page and format the word in a decorative way.

2. **On the References tab, click the Insert Index button.**

   You see the Index dialog box, as shown in Figure 6-5.

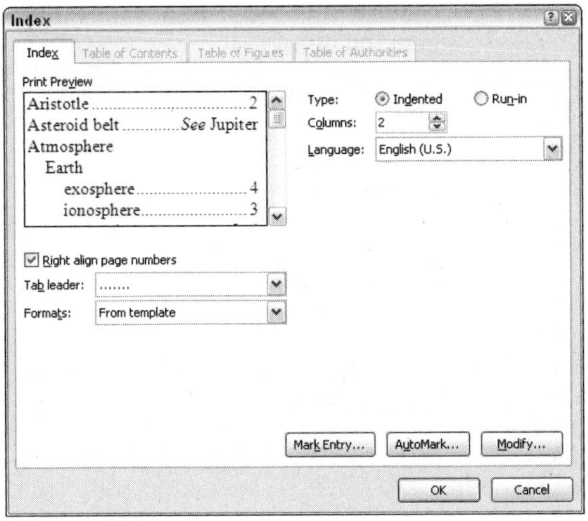

Figure 6-5:
Generating
an index.

3. Choose options in the dialog box and click OK.

As you make your choices, watch the Print Preview box to see what happens.

Here are the options in the Index dialog box:

✦ **Type:** Choose Run-in if you want subentries and sub-subentries to run together (refer to Figure 6-4); choose Indented to indent them.

✦ **Columns:** Stick with 2, unless you don't have subentries or sub-subentries and you can squeeze three columns on the page or you are working on a landscape document.

✦ **Language:** Choose a language for the table, if necessary and if you have installed a foreign language dictionary. If you have installed the dictionary, you can run the spell checker over your index and make sure that the entries are spelled correctly.

✦ **Right Align Page Numbers:** Normally, page numbers appear right after entries and are separated from entries by a comma, but you can right-align the entries so that they line up under one another with this option.

✦ **Tab Leader:** Some index formats place a leader between the entry and the page number. A *leader* is a series of dots or dashes. If you're working with a format that has a leader, you can choose a leader from the drop-down list.

✦ **Formats:** Word offers a number of attractive index layouts. You can choose one from the list.

✦ **Modify:** Click this button if you're adventurous and want to create an index style of your own (Chapter 3 explains styles).

To update an index after you create or delete entries, click it and then click the Update Index button or right-click the index and then choose Update Field on the shortcut menu.

Editing an index

After you generate an index, read it carefully to make sure that all entries are useful to readers. Inevitably, something doesn't come out right, but you can edit index entries as you would the text in a document. Index field markers are enclosed in curly brackets with the letters *XE* and the text of the index entry in quotation marks, like so: `{ XE: "Wovoka: Ghost Dance" }`. To edit an index marker, click the Show/Hide¶ button on the Home tab to see the field markers and find the one you need to edit. Then delete letters or type letters as you would do with normal text.

Here's a quick way to find index field markers: After clicking the Show/Hide¶ button, with the index fields showing, go to the Home tab, click the Editing button (if necessary), click the arrow beside the Find button, and choose Go To (or press Ctrl+G). On the Go To tab of the Find and Replace dialog box, choose Field, and type **XE** in the Enter Field Name box. Then click the Next button until you find the marker you want to edit. You can also use the Find command on the Home tab to look for index entries. Word finds these entries as well as text — if you clicked the Show/Hide¶ button and displayed index fields in your document.

Putting Cross-References in a Document

Cross-references are very handy indeed. They tell readers where to go to find more information on a topic. The problem with cross-references, however, is that the thing being cross-referenced really has to be there. If you tell readers to go to a heading called "The Cat's Pajamas" on page 93, and neither the heading nor the page exists, readers curse and tell you where to go, instead of the other way around.

Fortunately for you, Word lets you know when you make errant cross-references. You can refer readers to headings, page numbers, footnotes, endnotes, and plain-old paragraphs. And as long as you create captions for your cross-references with the Insert Caption button on the References tab, you can also make cross-references to equations, figures, graphs, listings, programs, and tables. If you delete the thing that a cross-reference refers to and render the cross-reference invalid, Word tells you about it the next time you update your cross-references. Best of all, if the page number, numbered item, or text that a cross-reference refers to changes, so does the cross-reference.

To create a cross-reference:

1. **Write the first part of the cross-reference text.**

For example, you could write **To learn more about these cowboys of the pampas, see page** and then type a blank space. The blank space separates the word *page* from the page number you're about to enter. If you're referring to a heading, write something like **For more information, see ".**Don't type a blank space this time because the heading text will appear right after the double quotation mark.

2. **On the References tab, click the Cross-Reference button.**

The Cross-Reference dialog box, as shown in Figure 6-6, appears.

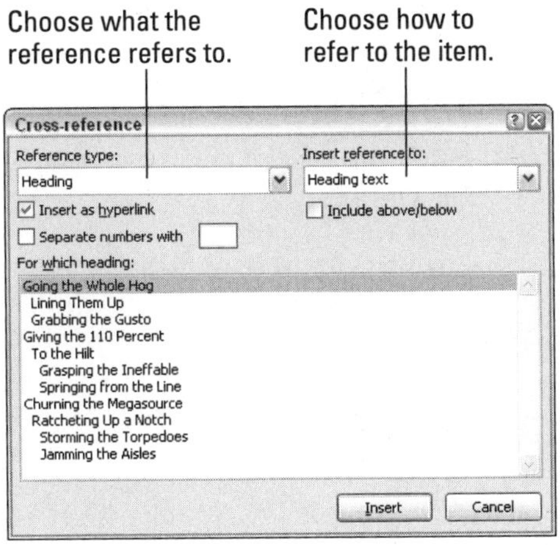

Book II
Chapter 6

Tools for Reports
and Scholarly
Papers

Choose what the reference refers to.

Choose how to refer to the item.

Cross-reference		? ⊠
Reference type:	Insert reference to:	
Heading	Heading text	
☑ Insert as hyperlink	☐ Include above/below	
☐ Separate numbers with		
For which heading:		

Going the Whole Hog
  Lining Them Up
  Grabbing the Gusto
Giving the 110 Percent
  To the Hilt
    Grasping the Ineffable
    Springing from the Line
Churning the Megasource
  Ratcheting Up a Notch
    Storming the Torpedoes
    Jamming the Aisles

[Insert] [Cancel]

Figure 6-6: Entering a cross-reference.

3. **Choose what type of item you're referring to in the Reference Type drop-down list.**

If you're referring to a plain-old paragraph, choose Bookmark. Then click outside the dialog box, scroll to the paragraph you're referring to, and place a bookmark there. (Chapter 1 of this mini-book explains bookmarks.)

4. **Make a choice in the Insert Reference To box to refer to text, a page number, or a numbered item.**

The options in this box are different, depending on what you chose in Step 3.

- *Text:* Choose this option (Heading Text, Entire Caption, and so on) to include text in the cross-reference. For example, choose Heading Text if your cross-reference is to a heading.

- *Number:* Choose this option to insert a page number or other kind of number, such as a table number, in the cross-reference.

- *Include Above/Below:* Check this box to include the word *above* or *below* to tell readers where, in relation to the cross-reference, the thing being referred to is located in your document.

5. **If you wish, leave the check mark in the Insert as Hyperlink check box to create a hyperlink as well as a cross-reference.**

   With a hyperlink, someone reading the document on-screen can Ctrl+click the cross-reference and go directly to what it refers to.

6. **In the For Which box, tell Word where the thing you're referring to is located.**

   To do so, select a heading, bookmark, footnote, endnote, equation, figure, graph, or whatnot. In long documents, you almost certainly have to click the scrollbar to find the one you want.

7. **Click the Insert button and then click the Close button.**

8. **Back in your document, enter the rest of the cross-reference text, if necessary.**

When you finish creating your document, update all the cross-references. To do that, press Ctrl+A to select the entire document. Then press F9 or right-click in the document and choose Update Field on the shortcut menu.

If the thing referred to in a cross-reference is no longer in your document, you see `Error! Reference source not found` where the cross-reference should be. To find cross-reference errors in long documents, look for the word *Error!* with the Find command (press Ctrl+F). Investigate what went wrong, and delete the cross-reference or make a new one.

Putting Footnotes and Endnotes in Documents

A *footnote* is a bit of explanation, a comment, or a reference that appears at the bottom of the page and is referred to by a number or symbol in the text. An *endnote* is the same thing, except that it appears at the end of the section, chapter, or document. If you've written a scholarly paper of any kind, you know what a drag footnotes and endnotes are.

You'll be glad to know that Word takes some of the drudgery out of footnotes and endnotes. For example, if you delete or add a note and you instruct Word to automatically number your footnotes and endnotes, all notes after the one you added or deleted are renumbered. And you don't have to worry about long footnotes because Word adjusts the page layout to make room for them. You can change the numbering scheme of footnotes and endnotes at will. When you're reviewing a document, all you have to do is move the pointer over a footnote or endnote citation. The note icon appears, as does a pop-up box with the text of the note.

Entering a footnote or endnote

To enter a footnote or endnote in a document:

1. **Place the cursor in the text where you want the note's symbol or number to appear.**

2. **On the References tab, click the Insert Footnote button (or press Alt+Ctrl+F) or the Insert Endnote button (or press Alt+Ctrl+D).**

If you're in Draft view, the Notes pane opens at the bottom of the screen with the cursor beside the number of the note you're about to enter. In Print Layout view, Word scrolls to the bottom of the page or the end of the document or section so that you can enter the note, as shown in Figure 6-7.

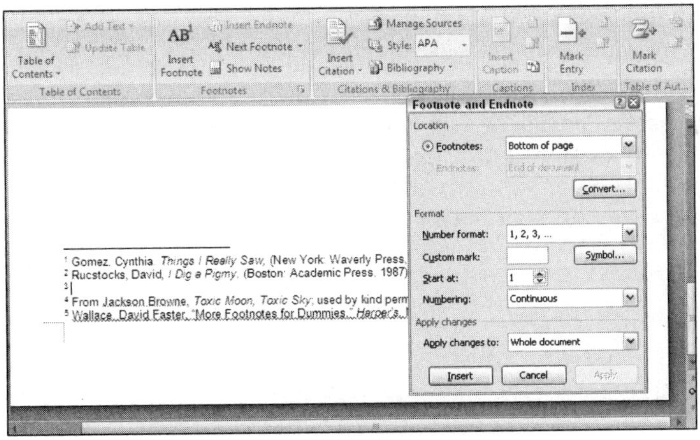

**Book II
Chapter 6**

**Tools for Reports
and Scholarly
Papers**

Figure 6-7: Entering a footnote in Print Layout view (left); the Footnote and Endnote dialog box (right).

3. **Enter your footnote or endnote.**

4. **Click the Close button in the Notes pane if you're in Draft view; in Print Layout view, scroll upward to return to the main text.**

To quickly return from writing a note to the place in your document where the footnote or endnote number citation is located, double-click the number citation at the bottom of the page (in Print Layout view) or the Notes pane (in Draft view). For example, if you just finished entering footnote 3, double-click the number 3.

Choosing the numbering scheme and position of notes

Changing the numbering scheme and positioning of endnotes and footnotes is quite easy. On the References tab, click the Footnotes group button. The Footnote and Endnote dialog box appears (see Figure 6-7). Tell Word where to place your notes:

+ **Footnotes:** Choose Bottom of Page to put footnotes at the bottom of the page no matter where the text ends; choose Below Text to put footnotes directly below the last text line on the page.

+ **Endnotes:** Choose End of Section if your document is divided into sections (such as chapters) and you want endnotes to appear at the back of sections; choose End of Document to put all endnotes at the very back of the document.

In the Format area, tell Word how to number the notes if you haven't done so already:

+ **Number Format:** Choose A B C, i ii iii, or another numbering scheme, if you want. You can also enter symbols by choosing the last option on this drop-down list.

+ **Custom Mark:** You can mark the note with a symbol by clicking the Symbol button and choosing a symbol in the Symbol dialog box. If you go this route, you have to enter a symbol each time you insert a note. Not only that, you may have to enter two or three symbols for the second and third notes on each page or document because Word can't renumber symbols.

+ **Start At:** To start numbering the notes at a place other than 1, A, or i, enter **2, B, ii,** or whatever in this box.

+ **Numbering:** To number the notes continuously from the start of your document to the end, choose Continuous. Choose Restart Each Section to begin anew at each section of your document. For footnotes, you can begin anew on each page by choosing Restart Each Page.

By the way, the Convert button in the Footnote and Endnote dialog box is for fickle scholars who suddenly decide that their endnotes should be footnotes or vice versa. Click it and choose an option in the Convert Notes dialog box to turn footnotes into endnotes, turn endnotes into footnotes, or — in documents with both endnotes and footnotes — make the endnotes footnotes and the footnotes endnotes.

Deleting, moving, and editing notes

If a devious editor tells you that a footnote or endnote is in the wrong place, that you don't need a note, or that you need to change the text in a note, all is not lost:

- ✦ **Editing:** To edit a note, double-click its number or symbol in the text. You see the note on-screen. Edit the note at this point.

- ✦ **Moving:** To move a note, select its number or symbol in the text and drag it to a new location; or you can cut and paste it to a new location.

- ✦ **Deleting:** To delete a note, select its number or symbol and press the Delete key.

Footnotes and endnotes are renumbered when you move or delete one of them.

Compiling a Bibliography

A *bibliography* is a list, usually in alphabetical order by author name, of all the books, journal articles, Web sites, interviews, and other sources used in the writing of an article, report, or book. Writing a good bibliography is a chore. Besides keeping careful track of sources, you have to list them correctly. Does the author's name or work's name come first in the citation? How do you list a Web site or magazine article without an author's name?

Word's Bibliography feature is very nice in this regard: It solves the problem of how to enter citations for the bibliography. All you have to do is enter the bare facts about the citation — the author's name, title, publication date, publisher, and so on — and Word presents this information correctly in the bibliography. You can choose among several popular bibliographical styles (APA, Chicago, and others) from the Style drop-down list, as shown in Figure 6-8. After you make your choice, Word reformats all bibliography citations. You don't have to worry about whether titles should be underlined or italicized, or how authors' names should be listed in the bibliography.

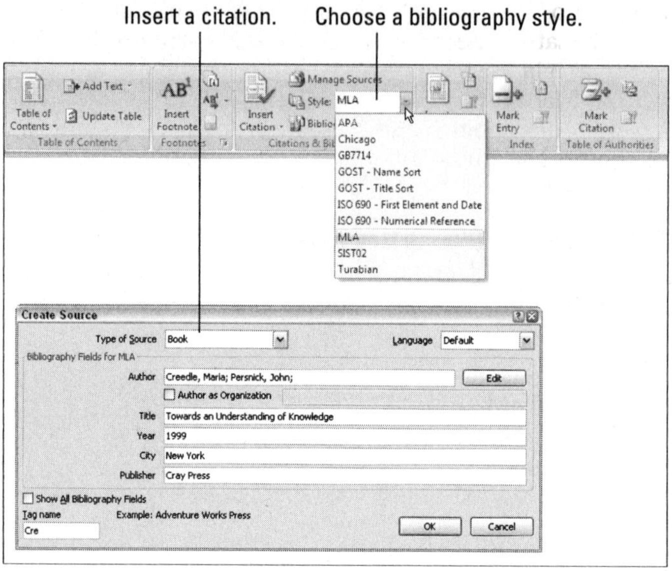

Insert a citation.   Choose a bibliography style.

Figure 6-8:
Adding a
citation
(left) and
formatting
citations
(right) for
a biblio-
graphy.

Inserting a citation for your bibliography

Abbreviated citations appear in the text of your document in between parentheses where you enter citations; the complete citation appears in the bibliography. After you enter the information about a citation, entering it a
second time is easy because Word keeps a master list of all citations you
have used in your work, both in the document you're working on and your
other documents. To enter a citation, click in your document at the place
that refers to the source, go to the References tab, and use one of these techniques to enter the citation:

✦ **Entering a citation you've already entered in your document:** Click the
Insert Citation button and choose the citation on the drop-down list. The
top of the drop-down list presents citations you've already entered.

✦ **Creating a new citation:** Click the Insert Citation button and choose Add
New Source. You see the Create Source dialog box, as shown in Figure 6-8.
Choose an option on the Type of Source drop-down list and enter particulars about the source. You can click the Show All Bibliography Fields
check box to enlarge the dialog box and enter all kinds of information
about the source. Whether clicking the check box is necessary depends
on how detailed you want your bibliography to be.

✦ **Inserting a citation placeholder:** Click the Insert Citation button and
choose Add New Placeholder if you're in a hurry and you don't currently
have all the information you need to describe the source. The Placeholder

Name dialog box appears. Enter a placeholder name for the source and click OK. Later, when you have the information for the source, either click the citation in the text and choose Edit Source on its drop-down list or click the Manage Sources button, and in the Source Manager dialog box, select the placeholder name (it has a question mark next to it) and click the Edit button. You see the Edit Source dialog box. Enter the information and click OK.

✦ **Inserting a citation you've entered in another document:** Click the Manage Sources button. You see the Source Manager dialog box. In the Master List, select the source you need and click the Copy button. Then click Close.

Your citation appears in text in parentheses. Move the pointer over it and you see an inline drop-down list that you can open to edit the citation as it appears in-text as well as edit it in the bibliography, as shown in Figure 6-9.

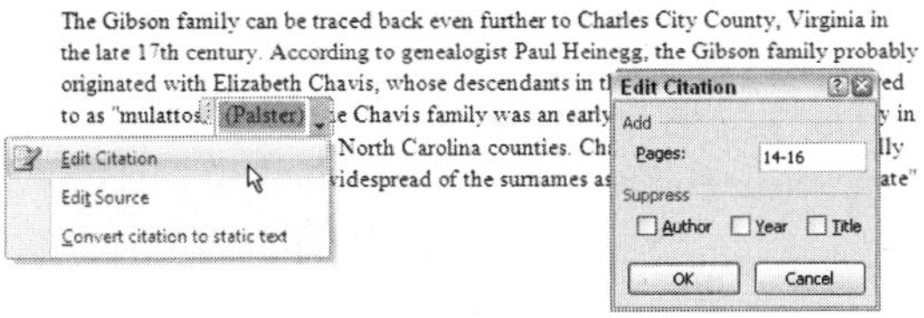

**Book II
Chapter 6**

**Tools for Reports
and Scholarly
Papers**

Figure 6-9:
In-text
citations
have drop-
down lists.

The Gibson family can be traced back even further to Charles City County, Virginia in the late 17th century. According to genealogist Paul Heinegg, the Gibson family probably originated with Elizabeth Chavis, whose descendants in th... to as "mulattos. (Palster) ...e Chavis family was an early ... North Carolina counties. Cha... ...idespread of the surnames as...

Edit Citation
Edit Source
Convert citation to static text

Edit Citation
Add
Pages: 14-16
Suppress
☐ Author ☐ Year ☐ Title
OK   Cancel

Editing a citation

Use one of these techniques to edit a citation:

✦ Open the citation's drop-down list (see Figure 6-9) and choose Edit Source. You see the Edit Source dialog box, where you can edit the citation.

✦ Click the Manage Sources button on the References tab. The Source Manager dialog box appears. Select the citation, click the Edit button, and change around the citation in the Edit Source dialog box.

Changing how citations appear in text

Citations appear in text enclosed in parentheses. Use one of these tech-niques to change how a citation appears in the text of your document:

✦ **Changing what's in parentheses:** Open the citation's drop-down list and choose Edit Citation (see Figure 6-9). You see the Edit Citation dialog box. To keep the author's name, year, or title from appearing inside parentheses, click the Author, Year, or Title check box (whether the citation in parentheses lists the author, year, or title depends on which citation style you choose). To make page numbers appear with the citation, enter page numbers in the Pages box.

✦ **Removing the in-text citation:** Swipe over the citation to select it and press Delete. Removing an in-text citation this way does not prevent the citation from appearing in the bibliography.

Generating the bibliography

Go to the References tab and follow these steps to generate your bibliography:

1. **Click in your document where you want the bibliography to appear.**

Probably that place is toward the end of the document.

2. **On the References tab, open the Style drop-down list and choose a style.**

If you're generating your bibliography for a paper you will submit to a journal or institution, ask the editors which style they prefer for bibliographies and choose that style from the list.

3. **Click the Manage Sources button.**

You see the Source Manger dialog box. Citations in the Current List box will appear in your bibliography.

4. **If necessary, address citations in the Current List box.**

If you entered any citation placeholders, their names appear in the list next to question marks. Select these placeholders, click the Edit button, and enter information in the Edit Source dialog box.

To keep a citation from appearing in the bibliography, select it and click the Delete button.

5. **Click the Close button in the Source Manager dialog box.**

6. **Click the Bibliography button and choose Insert Bibliography on the drop-down list.**

There it is — your bibliography.

Book III

Outlook 2007

The 5th Wave   By Rich Tennant

"It's your wife Mr. Dinker. Shall I have her take a seat in the closet, or do you want to schedule a meeting in the kitchen for later this afternoon?"

Contents at a Glance

Chapter 1: Getting Acquainted with Outlook

In This Chapter

✔ Getting around in Outlook

✔ Viewing folders in different ways

✔ Categorizing items so that you can locate them easily

✔ Searching in folders

✔ Deleting items

✔ Backing up your Outlook file

✔ Importing e-mail and contact information from other software programs

✔ Archiving old-and-in-the-way items

*T*his chapter pulls back the curtain and gives you a first glimpse of *Outlook*, the e-mailer and personal organizer in the Office 2007 suit of programs. Read on to find out once and for all what Outlook does, how to get from folder to folder, and the different ways to view the stuff in folders. You can find advice about keeping folders well organized, deleting stuff, backing up an Outlook file, and cleaning out items in folders that you no longer need.

What Is Outlook, Anyway?

Outlook isn't in character with the rest of the Office programs. It's a little different — you can tell as soon as you glance at the screen. The familiar Ribbon is nowhere to be found, and in its place you see a menu, the Standard toolbar, and the Advanced toolbar along the top of the window. To make things even more complicated, what you see on-screen changes when you click a Navigation Pane button on the left side of the window. Click a Navigation Pane button — Mail, Calendar, Contacts, Tasks, Notes, Folder List, or Shortcuts — and you go to a different Outlook window altogether.

Outlook can be confusing because the program serves many different purposes. To wit, Outlook is all this:

✦ **An e-mail program:** You can use it to send and receive e-mail messages and files, as well as organize e-mail messages in different folders so that you can keep track of them. (See Chapter 3 of this mini-book.)

✦ **An appointment scheduler:** Outlook is also a calendar for scheduling appointments and meetings. You can tell at a glance when and where you're expected, as well as be alerted to upcoming appointments and meetings. (See Chapter 4 of this mini-book.)

✦ **An address book:** The program can store the addresses, phone numbers, and e-mail addresses of friends, foes, clients, and family members. Looking up this information in the Contacts List is easy. (See Chapter 2 of this mini-book.)

✦ **A task reminder:** Outlook is a means of planning projects. You can tell when deadlines fall and plan your workload accordingly. (See Chapter 5 of this mini-book.)

✦ **A notes receptacle:** This part of the program is a place to jot down notes and reminders. (See Chapter 5 of this mini-book.)

Outlook is a lot of different things all rolled into one. For that reason, the program can be daunting at first. But hang in there. Soon you'll be running roughshod over Outlook and making it suffer on your behalf.

Navigating the Outlook Folders

The first thing you should know about Outlook is this: All items are kept in folders, as shown in Figure 1-1. E-mail messages when they arrive are kept in the Inbox folder. Calendar items are kept in the Calendar folder. Notes are kept in the Notes folder. All the folders, meanwhile, are kept in one big folder called Personal Folders. When you want to undertake a new task, you go to a different folder.

Here are the ways to get from folder to folder in Outlook and undertake a new task:

✦ **Navigation pane:** Click a button in the Navigation pane — Mail, Calendar, Contacts, Tasks, or Notes — to go to a folder. The Navigation pane appears on the left side of the window (see Figure 1-1).

✦ **Go menu:** Choose an option in the Go menu — Mail, Calendar, Contacts, Tasks, or Notes. You can also go to one of these folders by pressing the Ctrl key and a number 1 through 5.

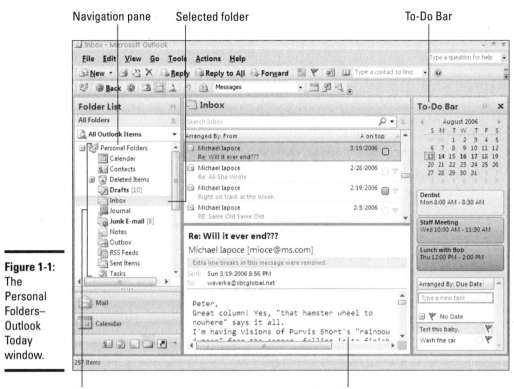

Navigation pane   Selected folder   To-Do Bar

Figure 1-1:
The
Personal
Folders–
Outlook
Today
window.

Folders   Reading pane

✦ **Folder List:** Click the Folder List button to open the Personal Folder and then select one of its subfolders in the Navigation pane. For example, to read incoming e-mail messages, select the Inbox folder (see Figure 1-1). The Folder List button is located at the bottom of the Navigation pane. You can also see the Folder List by pressing Ctrl+6 or choosing Go⇨Folder List.

✦ **Outlook Today button:** No matter where you go in Outlook, you can always click the Outlook Today button to go to Personal Folders – Outlook Today view. You can find the Outlook Today button on the Advanced toolbar.

✦ **Back, Forward, and Up One Level buttons:** Click these buttons to return to a window, revisit a window you retreated from, or climb the hierarchy of personal folders. The three buttons are found on the Advanced toolbar.

By the way, you can open a folder in a new window. To do so, right-click a Navigation Pane button and choose Open in New Window. To close a window you opened this way, click its Close button (the *X* in the upper-right corner).

Wrestling with the Navigation Pane and To-Do Bar

Outlook is designed so you can get from folder to folder without any trouble. All you have to do to open a new folder is click a button or folder icon in the Navigation pane. However, sometimes the Navigation pane gets in the way. You need the extra space for reading e-mail messages or rummaging in the Contacts folder. Here are instructions for wrestling with the Navigation pane, To-Do Bar, and Reading pane:

✦ **Hiding and displaying the Navigation pane:** As I explain earlier, the Navigation pane appears on the left side of the window and offers buttons and folder names that you can click to go to different folders (refer to Figure 1-1). Click the Expand or Maximize buttons in the Navigation pane to display or hide it. You can also choose View⇨Navigation Pane Off or Normal or keep pressing Alt+F1.

✦ **Hiding and displaying the To-Do Bar:** The *To-Do Bar* appears on the right side of the screen and shows your calendar, upcoming appointments, and tasks arranged by due date (refer to Figure 1-1). Click a calendar day to open the Calendar on that day. Double-click an appointment to open an Appointment window, or a task to open a Task window. To display or hide the To-Do Bar, click its Expand or Minimize button, choose View⇨To-Do Bar⇨Normal or Off, or keep pressing Alt+F2.

✦ **Hiding and displaying the Reading pane:** The *Reading pane* appears on the right side or bottom of the window and gives you a more detailed look at an item you selected. It comes in handy when you're reading e-mail because you can read a message and still view your message list (refer to Figure 1-1). To display or hide the Reading pane, choose View⇨Reading Pane⇨Right, Bottom, or Off. When the Reading pane is displayed, you can also hide it by dragging its border to the bottom or right side of the window.

You can decide for yourself what appears on the Navigation pane and To-Do Bar. Choose Tools⇨Options and select the Other tab in the Options dialog box. Then click the Navigation Pane button to open the Navigation Pane Options dialog box and tell Outlook which buttons to place on the Navigation pane. Click the To-Do Bar button in the Options dialog box to tell Outlook what appears on the To-Do Bar.

Getting a Better View of Items in a Folder

Because you spend so much time gazing at folders, you may as well get a good view of the items inside them. In a crowded folder, it helps to know the different ways to view items. Figure 1-2, for example, shows the Contacts folder in Business Cards view.

Select a Current View option...   ...or choose here to change views.

Figure 1-2:
Changing views of a folder's contents.

Do one of the following to change views of the items in a folder that doesn't hold e-mail:

✦ Open the Current View drop-down list on the Advanced toolbar and make a choice, as shown in Figure 1-2.

✦ Choose View➪Current View and choose a view option.

✦ Click a Current View option button in the Navigation pane, as shown in Figure 1-2. Current View option buttons are available in the Contacts, Tasks, and Notes folders.

Do one of the following to change views in a folder that holds e-mail:

✦ Choose View➪Arrange By and then choose an option for arranging items on the submenu. For example, choose From to arrange e-mail messages by sender name.

✦ Click a Sort By column name — From, Subject, Received, Size, or Categories — to arrange items by column. For example, click the Categories button to arrange e-mail messages in the window by category.

Categorizing Items

One of your biggest tasks in Outlook, if you choose to accept it, is to categorize items in folders so that you can find and deal with them. Finding items can be a chore in a folder with a lot of items, but by categorizing items, you can find the ones you're looking for. Categories are color-coded to make identifying them easier. After you assign a category to an item, you can arrange items in folders by category, and in so doing, find items. Categorizing is a great way to stay on top of all the chores you have to do.

Creating a category

Follow these steps to create a category for organizing folder items:

1. **Select an item in a folder to which you want to assign your new category.**

2. **Choose Edit⇨Categorize⇨All Categories.**

   You see the Color Categories dialog box, as shown in Figure 1-3. At this point, you can create a category from scratch or revamp one of Outlook's color-named categories:

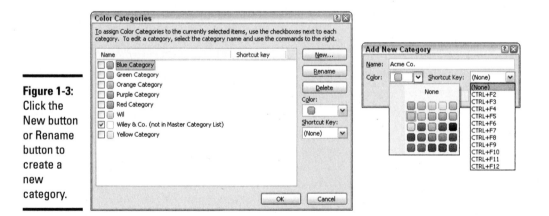

Figure 1-3: Click the New button or Rename button to create a new category.

- *Creating your own category:* Click the New button to open the Add New Category dialog box, as shown in Figure 1-3. Then enter a name for your category, choose a color from the drop-down list, and click OK. While you're at it, you can open the Shortcut Key drop-down list and choose a shortcut key combination for assigning your new category to items (see Figure 1-3). Click OK in the Color Categories dialog box.

- *Renaming a category:* In the Color Categories dialog box (see Figure 1-3), select a color category, and click the Rename button. Then enter a new name where the old one is now. You can choose a different color for your category by choosing a color in the Color drop-down list. To assign it a shortcut key, open the Shortcut Key drop-down list and choose a shortcut key combination.

To delete a category, return to the Color Categories dialog box, select the category's name, and click the Delete button. Although the category is deceased, items to which you assigned the category keep their category assignments.

Assigning items to categories

Follow these steps to assign a category to a folder item:

1. **Select the item.**

2. **Choose Edit⇨Categorize and choose a category on the submenu.**

You can also right-click, choose Categorize, and select a category on the shortcut menu, or press a Ctrl+key combination if you assigned one to the category. You can select more than one category for an item.

To remove a category assignment, right-click the item and choose Categorize⇨ Clear All Categories.

You can categorize an e-mail message you're reading in the message window by clicking the Categorize button and choosing a category on the drop-down list.

Another way to quickly categorize an e-mail message is to click the Category column of the message in a mail folder window. To tell Outlook which category to assign when you click the Category column, choose Edit⇨Categorize⇨ Set Quick Click. You see the Set Quick Click dialog box. Choose the category on the drop-down list that you want to assign by "quick-clicking" in the Category column.

Arranging items by category in folders

To arrange items by category in a folder, select the folder in the Navigation pane and follow these instructions:

✦ **In folders that hold e-mail:** Choose View⇨Arrange By⇨Categories.

✦ **In all other folders:** Open the Current View drop-down list and choose By Category.

You can also open the Categorized Mail subfolder in the Search Folders folder to display e-mail messages that you categorized.

Finding Stray Folder Items

If you can't locate an item in a folder by scrolling, changing views, or any other means, you have to resort to the Find command. Outlook offers four Find commands. From quickest to most thorough, try one of these techniques to find an item you're looking for:

✦ **Conducting a simple search in one folder:** Open the folder you want to search, enter a search term in the Search Folder box, and press Enter, as shown in Figure 1-4. If you have trouble finding the Search Folder box, choose Tools⇨Instant Search⇨Instant Search or press Ctrl+E.

✦ **Conducting a search with selected criteria in one folder:** Open the folder you want to search, click the Expand Query Builder button, and enter criteria for your search in the Search panel, as shown in Figure 1-4. You can make your search more specific by clicking the Add Criteria button and choosing more criteria from the drop-down list. (If you can't find the Expand Query Builder button, choose Tools⇨Instant Search⇨ Expand the Query Builder or press Ctrl+Alt+W.)

✦ **Searching for e-mail messages from the same person in different folders:** Select a message from the person and choose Tools⇨Instant Search⇨Messages from Sender. The Advanced Find dialog box opens with messages from the sender at the bottom.

✦ **Searching for e-mail messages in different folders:** Choose Tools⇨ Instant Search⇨Search All Mail Items (or press Ctrl+Alt+A). Then either enter a search term in the Search folder text box or click the Expand Query Builder button and enter search criteria. This search technique finds only e-mail messages; it searches in many folders, including archive folders.

✦ **Searching across many folders:** Choose Tools⇨Instant Search⇨ Advanced Find (or press Ctrl+Shift+F). You see the Advanced Find dialog box. In the Look For drop-down list, choose what you want to search for. Click the Browse button to open the Select Folder(s) dialog box, where you can select more than one folder to search in. Then choose options on the three tabs to formulate your search. Which options are available depends on which folder you're searching.

Search Folder box   Click to open the Search panel.

Saving a search so that you can run it later

If you find yourself searching for the same stuff repeatedly, save the search criteria in a file. That way, you don't have to enter the search criteria each time you run the search. Searches are saved in special files with the extension OSS (Office Saved Searches).

To save your searches, start by creating a folder for storing OSS files. Then Choose Tools➪Instant Search➪Advanced Find and conduct an advanced search for the item you often seek. After your search is complete, choose File➪Save Search in the Advanced Find dialog box, locate the folder where you save searches in the Save Search dialog box, enter a descriptive name for the search, and click OK.

Next time you want to conduct the search, choose Tools➪Instant Search➪Advanced Find to open the Advanced Find dialog box. In the dialog box, choose File➪Open Search, choose a search file in the Open Saved Search dialog box, and click OK. Then click the Find Now button in the Advanced Find dialog box.

Deleting E-Mail Messages, Contacts, Tasks, and Other Items

Outlook folders are notorious for filling quickly. E-mail messages, contacts, and tasks soon clog the folders if you spend any time in Outlook. From time to time, go through the e-mail folders, Contacts window, Task window, and Calendar to delete items you no longer need. To delete items, select them and do one of the following:

+ Click the Delete button (or press the Delete key).

+ Choose Edit⇨Delete (or press Ctrl+D).

+ Right-click and choose Delete.

Deleted items — e-mail messages, calendar appointments, contacts, or tasks — land in the Deleted Items folder in case you want to recover them. To delete items once and for all, open the Deleted Items folder and start deleting like a madman.

To spare you the trouble of deleting items twice, once in the original folder and again in the Deleted Items folder, Outlook offers these amenities:

+ **Empty the Deleted Items folder when you close Outlook:** If you're no fan of the Deleted Items folder and you want to remove deleted items without reviewing them, choose Tools⇨Options, select the Other tab in the Options dialog box, and select Empty the Deleted Items Folder Upon Exiting.

+ **Empty the Deleted Items folder yourself:** Choose Tools⇨Empty "Deleted Items" Folder to remove all the items in the Deleted Items folder. You can also right-click the Deleted Items folder in the Folder List and choose Empty "Deleted Items" Folder.

You can search for items and delete them in the Advanced Find dialog box. See "Finding Stray Folder Items," earlier in this chapter. Be sure to check out "Running the Mailbox Cleanup command" at the end of this chapter. It explains a quick way to delete Inbox messages.

Finding and Backing Up Your Outlook File

All the data you keep in Outlook — e-mail messages, names and addresses, calendar appointments and meetings — is kept in a file called Outlook.pst. Locating this file on your computer sometimes requires the services of Sherlock Holmes. The file isn't kept in a standard location. It can be any number of places, depending on the operating system on your computer and whether you upgraded from an earlier version of Office.

The all-important Outlook.pst file is hiding deep in your computer, but you need to find it. You need to know where this file is located so that you can back it up to a Zip drive, CD, or other backup medium. This file holds clients' names and the names of relatives and loved ones. It holds the e-mail messages you think are worth keeping. It would be a shame to lose this stuff if your computer failed.

Here's a quick way to find the Outlook.pst file on your computer and back it up:

1. **Choose File⇨Data File Management.**

You see the Account Settings dialog box, as shown in Figure 1-5.

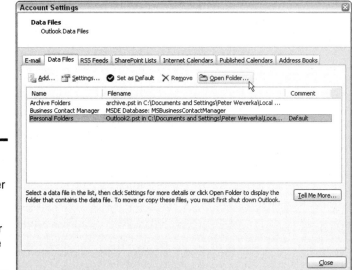

Figure 1-5:
Click the Open Folder button to find out where your Outlook file is located.

2. **Select Personal Folders and click the Open Folder button.**

Windows Explorer opens, and you see the folder where the Outlook.pst file is kept.

3. **Click the Folders button in Windows Explorer to see the folder hierarchy on your computer.**

By scrolling in the Folders pane on the left side of the window, you can determine where on your computer the elusive Outlook.pst file really is.

4. **Close Outlook.**

   Sorry, but you can't back up an `Outlook.pst` file if Outlook is running.

5. **To back up the file, right-click it in Windows Explorer, choose Send To on the shortcut menu, and choose the option on the submenu that represents where you back up files.**

   If an accident befalls your computer, copy the backup `Outlook.pst` file that you made into the folder where the `Outlook.pst` file is stored on your computer.

Importing E-Mail and Addresses from Another Program

Suppose that you've been using Outlook Express, Eudora, or Lotus Organizer to handle your e-mail and contact addresses, but now you've become a convert to Outlook. What do you do with the e-mail messages and names and addresses in the other program? You can't let them just sit there. You can, however, import them into Office and pick up where you left off.

To import e-mail and contact addresses from another program, start by choosing File➪Import and Export. You see the Import and Export Wizard. What you do next depends on where you now do your e-mailing and address tracking:

✦ **Outlook Express:** Select Import Internet Mail and Addresses and then click Next. In the Outlook Import Tool dialog box, select Outlook Express, select check boxes to decide what to import (Mail, Addresses, and/or Rules), and click the Finish button.

✦ **Eudora:** Select Import Internet Mail and Addresses and then click Next. In the Outlook Import Tool dialog box, select Eudora, choose options to decide what to do about duplicate entries, and click the Finish button. In the Browser for Folder dialog box, select the file where the Eudora data is kept and click OK.

✦ **Lotus Organizer:** Select Import from Another Program or File, click Next, select a Lotus Organizer, and click Next again. Click Next while you go along. You're asked how to handle duplicate items, to locate the Lotus Organizer data file, and to select an Outlook folder to put the data in.

Before you import e-mail and addresses from another program, weed out the e-mail messages and addresses you no longer need. Why ferry this stuff into Outlook when you no longer need it?

Cleaning Out Your Folders

Getting rid of unneeded items in folders is essential for good mental health. All that clutter can be distressing. Earlier in this chapter, "Deleting E-Mail Messages, Contacts, Tasks, and Other Items" explains how to muck out folders by emptying them. These pages explain two more techniques for removing detritus from folders — archiving and the Mailbox Cleanup command.

Archiving the old stuff

In some cases, Outlook puts e-mail messages, tasks, and appointments older than six months in the *Archive folder,* a special folder for items that Outlook thinks are stale and not worth keeping anymore. Outlook calls sending these items to the Archive folder "autoarchiving." Items that have been archived aren't lost forever. You can visit them by opening the Archive Folders folder and its subfolders on the Folders List. Archive Folders and its subfolders are created automatically the first time you archive items.

Archiving is a way of stripping your mail folders, tasks lists, and calendar of items that don't matter anymore. How and when items are archived is up to you. To archive items, you establish a default set of archiving rules that apply to all folders, and if a folder needs individual attention and shouldn't be subject to the default archiving rules, you can establish special rules for that folder. Each folder can have its own set of archiving rules or be subject to the default rules.

To tell Outlook how to archive old stuff, start by displaying an AutoArchive dialog box, as shown in Figure 1-6:

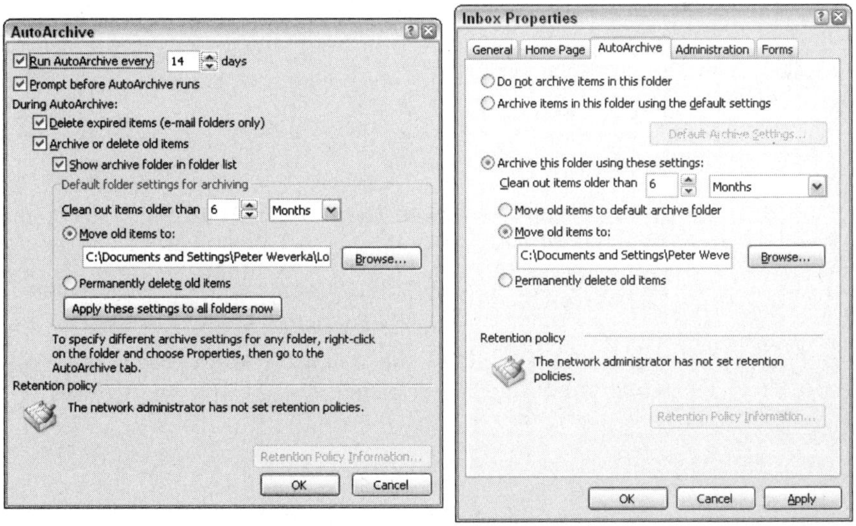

Figure 1-6: Making the default archiving rules (left) and rules for a folder (right).

Book III
Chapter 1

Getting Acquainted
with Outlook

✦ **Establishing default archiving rules:** Choose Tools⇨Options, and in the Options dialog box, select the Other tab. Then click the AutoArchive button.

✦ **Establishing rules for a specific folder:** Either right-click the folder and choose Properties or display the folder and choose File⇨Folder⇨ Properties for *Folder Name.* Then in the Properties dialog box, select the AutoArchive tab. (Because no date is connected to items in the Contacts folder, you can't autoarchive names and addresses.)

Negotiate these options to establish default archiving rules (see Figure 1-6):

✦ **Run AutoArchive Every:** Enter a number to tell Outlook how often to archive items.

✦ **Prompt Before Archive Runs:** If this check box is selected, you see a message box before archiving begins, and you can decline to archive if you want by selecting No in the message box.

✦ **Delete Expired Items (E-Mail Folders Only):** Select this check box to delete all e-mail messages when the time period has expired.

✦ **Archive or Delete Old Items:** Deselect this option if you *don't* want to archive items.

✦ **Show Archive Folder in Folder List:** Select this option if you want to keep the archived version of the folder in the Folder List. Archived items are kept in this folder so you can review them.

✦ **Clean Out Items Older Than:** Choose a cut-off time period after which to archive items.

✦ **Move Old Items To:** Click the Browse button and select a folder if you want to store the Archive file in a certain location.

✦ **Permanently Delete Old Items:** Select this option if you want to delete, not archive, old items.

Choose among these options to establish archiving rules for a specific folder (refer to Figure 1-6):

✦ **Do Not Archive Items in This Folder:** Select this option if items in the folder aren't worth archiving.

✦ **Archive Items in This Folder Using the Default Settings**: Select this option to defer to the default archiving rules for the folder.

✦ **Archive This Folder Using These Settings**: Select this option to establish archiving rules for the folder.

✦ **Clean Out Items Older Than:** Choose a cut-off time period after which to archive the items in the folder.

✦ **Move Old Items To:** Click the Browse button and select a folder if you want to store the archived items in a specific location.

✦ **Permanently Delete Old Items:** Select this option if you want to delete, not archive, items in this folder.

Besides archiving, another way to remove bric-a-brac automatically is to take advantage of the Rules Wizard to delete certain kinds of messages when they arrive. See Chapter 3 of this mini-book for more information.

Periodically compact the file in which Outlook data is stored to shrink the file and get more room on your hard disk. To compact the Outlook data file, choose File⇨Data File Management, select Personal Folders in the Outlook Data Files dialog box, and click the Settings button. In the Personal Folders dialog box, select the Compact Now button. Compacting an Outlook file can take time if the file is stuffed with data.

Running the Mailbox Cleanup command

The Mailbox Cleanup command is an all-purpose command for finding e-mail messages, archiving items, deleting items, and deleting alternate versions of items. To use the command, choose Tools⇨Mailbox Cleanup. You see the Mailbox Cleanup dialog box, as shown in Figure 1-7. The dialog box offers a speedy entrée into these different Outlook tasks:

Figure 1-7:
Mucking out the mail boxes.

✦ **Seeing how much disk space folders occupy:** Click the View Mailbox Size button and then take note of folder sizes in the Folder Size dialog box.

✦ **Finding items:** Select an option button to find items older than a certain number of days or larger than a certain number of kilobytes, enter a days or kilobytes number, and click the Find button. You land in the Advanced Find dialog box. Earlier in this chapter, "Finding Stray Folder Items" explains this dialog box. Use it to select items and delete them.

✦ **Archiving items:** Click the AutoArchive button to archive items in your folders. See "Archiving the old stuff" in this chapter for details.

✦ **Emptying the deleted items folder:** Click the Empty button to empty the Deleted Items folder. See "Deleting E-Mail Messages, Contacts, Tasks, and Other Items," earlier in this chapter.

Chapter 2: Maintaining the Contacts Folder

In This Chapter

✓ Recording information about a new contact

✓ Locating a contact in the Contacts folder

✓ Printing contact information in the Contacts folder

*I*n *pathology*, which is the study of diseases and how they're transmitted, a *contact* is a person who passes on a communicable disease, but in Outlook, a *contact* is someone about whom you keep information. Information about contacts is kept in the Contacts folder. This folder is a super-powered address book. It has places for storing people's names, addresses, phone numbers, e-mail addresses, Web pages, pager numbers, birthdays, anniversaries, nicknames, and other stuff besides. When you enter an e-mail address, you can get it straight from the Contacts folder to be sure that the address is entered correctly. As I explain in Book II, Chapter 5, you can also get addresses from the Contacts folder when you generate form letters, labels, and envelopes for mass mailings in Word.

This short but happy chapter explains how to maintain a tried-and-true Contacts folder, enter information about people in the folder, edit information, find a missing contact, and print the information in the Contacts folder.

Maintaining a Happy and Healthy Contacts Folder

A Contacts folder is only as good and as thorough as the information about contacts that you put into it. These pages explain how to enter information about a contact and update the information if it happens to change.

Don't despair if you have been using another software program to track addresses. Chapter 1 of this mini-book explains how to import those addresses into Outlook without having to re-enter them.

Entering a new contact in the Contacts folder

To place someone on the Contacts List, open the Contacts folder and start by doing one of the following:

+ Click the New Contact button.

+ Press Ctrl+N (in the Contacts Folder window) or Ctrl+Shift+C (in another window).

+ Choose File➪New➪Contact.

You see the Contact form, as shown in Figure 2-1. On this form are places for entering just about everything there is to know about a person except his or her favorite color and secret vices. Enter all the information you care to record, keeping in mind these rules of the road while you go along:

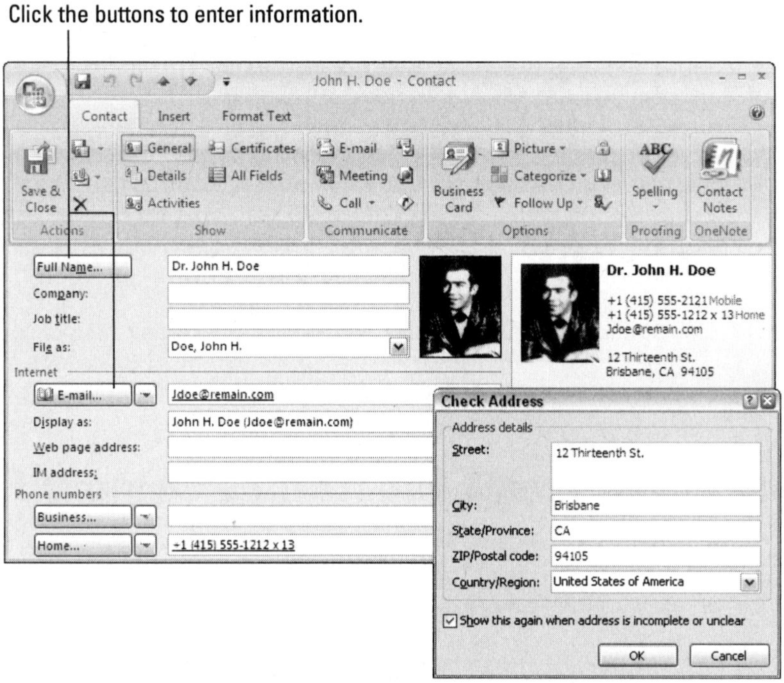

Click the buttons to enter information.

Figure 2-1:
A Contact
form.

+ **Full names, addresses, and so on:** Although you may be tempted to simply enter addresses, phone numbers, names, and so on in the text boxes, don't do it! Click the Full Name button on the General tab, for example, to enter a name (see Figure 2-1). Click the Business or Home button to enter an address in the Check Address dialog box (see Figure 2-1). By clicking these buttons and entering data in dialog boxes, you permit Outlook to separate the component parts of names, addresses, and phone numbers. As such, Outlook can use names and addresses as a source for mass mailings and mass e-mailings.

When entering information about a company, not a person, leave the Full Name field blank and enter the company's name in the Company field.

✦ **Information that matters to you:** If the form doesn't appear to have a place for entering a certain kind of information, try clicking a triangle button and choosing a new information category from the pop-up list. Click the triangle button next to the Business button and choose Home, for example, if you want to enter a home address rather than a business address.

✦ **File As:** Open the File As drop-down list and choose an option for filing the contact in the Contacts folder. Contacts are filed alphabetically by last name, first name, company name, or combinations of the three. Choose the option that best describes how you expect to find the contact in the Contacts folder.

✦ **Mailing addresses:** If you keep more than one address for a contact, display the address to which you want to send mail and select the This Is the Mailing Address check box. This way, in a mass mailing, letters are sent to the correct address.

✦ **E-mail addresses:** You can enter up to three e-mail addresses for each contact. (Click the triangle button next to the E-mail button and choose E-mail 2 or E-mail 3 to enter a second or third address.) In the Display As text box, Outlook shows you what the To: line of e-mail messages looks like when you send e-mail to a contact. By default, the To: line shows the contact's name followed by his or her e-mail address in parentheses. However, you can enter whatever you want in the Display As text box, and if entering something different helps you distinguish between e-mail addresses, enter something different. For example, enter Lydia — Personal so that you can tell when you send e-mail to Lydia's personal address as opposed to her business address.

✦ **Photos:** To put a digital photo on a Contact form, click the Add Contact Photo button, and in the Add Contact Picture dialog box, select a picture and click OK.

✦ **Details:** To keep a detailed dossier on a contact, click the Details button and enter information in the Details window. This window offers places for recording birthdays and other minutia.

Be sure to write a few words on the Notes box to describe how and where you met the contact. When the time comes to weed out contacts in the Contacts folder list, reading these descriptions helps you decide who gets weeded and who doesn't.

When you're done entering information, click the Save & Close button. If you're in a hurry to enter contact information, click the Save & New button. Doing so opens an empty form so that you can record information about another contact.

Here's a fast way to enter contact information for someone who has sent you an e-mail message: Open the message, right-click the sender's name on the From: line, and choose Add to Outlook Contacts on the shortcut menu. You see the Contact form. Enter more information about the sender if you can and then click the Save & Close button.

Changing a contact's information

Changing a contact's information is a chore if you do it by going from field to field on the General and Details windows of the Contact form. Fortunately for you, there is a faster way to update the information you have about a contact — go to the All Fields window. As Figure 2-2 shows, this window lists fields in a line-by-line fashion. Choose an option on the Select From drop-down list, scroll in the form, and update fields as necessary.

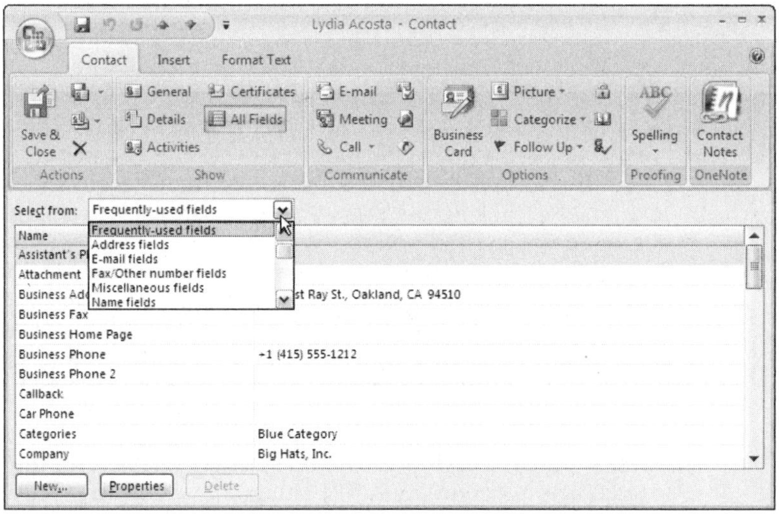

Figure 2-2: Editing data on the All Fields window.

Finding a Contact in the Contacts Folder

The Contacts folder, which is shown in Figure 2-3, can grow very large, so Outlook offers a number of ways to search it. After you find the contact you're looking for, double-click the contact's name to open the Contact window. Here are some techniques for finding a contact in the Contacts folder:

Mapping out an address

In the Communicate group in the Contact window is an obscure but very useful little button called Map that can be a great help when you need to go somewhere but aren't sure how to get there. As long as your computer is connected to the Internet and an address is on file for a contact, you can click the Map button to go online to the Windows Live Local Web site and see a map with the address at its center. You can get driving directions from this map. Double-click a contact name to open his or her Contact window. Good luck getting there!

**Book III
Chapter 2**

Maintaining the Contacts Folder

+ **Use the scrollbar:** Click the arrows or drag the scroll box to move through the list.

+ **Click a letter button:** Click a letter button on the right side of the window to move in the list to a specific letter.

+ **Change views:** Change views often helps in the search. Choose a new view in the Navigation pane or from the Current View drop-down list in the Advanced toolbar (see Figure 2-3).

Choose a view.   Conduct a search.

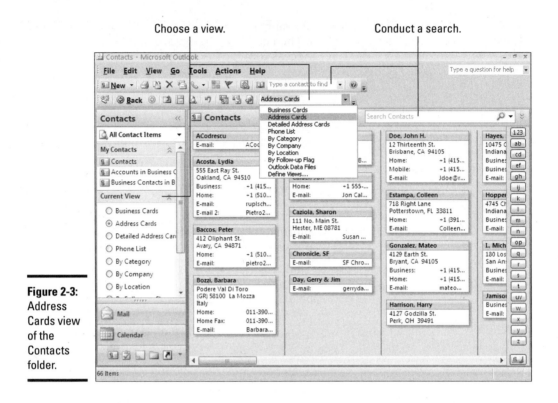

Figure 2-3:
Address
Cards view
of the
Contacts
folder.

✦ **Type a name in the Find a Contact text box:** Enter a name or e-mail address in this text box and press Enter (see Figure 2-3). The Type a Contact to Find text box is located on the Standard toolbar.

✦ **Search Contacts text box:** Enter a search term in the Search Contacts text box and open the query builder as well to conduct a thorough search (see Figure 2-3). See Chapter 1 of this mini-book for instructions about finding items in folders.

✦ **Search by category:** Categorize contacts as you enter them and switch to By Category view to arrange contacts by category. See Chapter 1 of this mini-book.

Printing the Contacts Folder

The paperless office hasn't arrived yet in spite of numerous predictions to the contrary, and sometimes it's necessary to print the Contacts folder on old-fashioned paper. For times like these, I hereby explain the different ways to print the Contacts folder and how to fiddle with the look of the printed pages.

To print information about a single contact, double-click his or her name to open the Contact window. Then click the Print button in the Contact window (you find it on the Quick Access toolbar).

Different ways to print contact information

Outlook offers several attractive ways to print contact information in the Contacts folder. Which printing options you get depends on which view of the Contacts window is showing when you give the command to print. (Open the Current View drop-down list and choose an option to change views.)

Starting in Address Cards view or Detailed Address Cards view, you can print Contact information like so:

✦ **Card Style:** Print all information on display in the Contacts window, with each contact name appearing in a gray shade.

✦ **Small Booklet Style:** Similar to Card Style, except the page is shrunk to an eighth of its size, and pages are designed to print on both sides so that they can be bound and distributed.

✦ **Medium Booklet Style:** Similar to Small Booklet Style, except pages are shrunk to a fourth of their original size.

✦ **Memo Style:** Information for each contact is printed on one page, and you get one page for each contact in the Contacts folder.

✦ **Phone Directory Style:** Similar to Card Style, except only phone numbers and fax numbers are printed.

Starting in any view apart from Address Cards and Detailed Address Cards, you can print contact information in Table Style. In Table Style, the information is printed in a simple table with column headings.

The basics of printing contact information

Follow these steps to print information about contacts in the Contacts folder:

1. **Select the contacts whose information you want to print, if you don't want to print information about everybody.**

You can select contacts by Ctrl+clicking names. Another way to select contacts is to run the Advanced Find command, as I explain in Chapter 1 of this mini-book.

2. **Click the Print button or press Ctrl+P.**

You see the Print dialog box, as shown in Figure 2-4. (In the Advanced Find dialog box, choose File➪Print.)

Choose how to print the contacts.

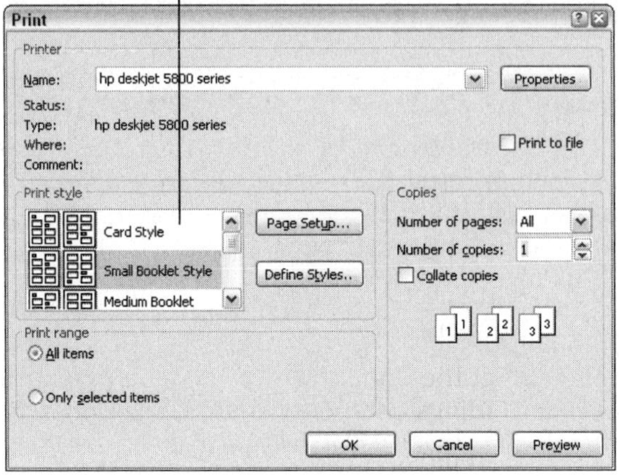

Figure 2-4:
Printing
contact
information.

3. **Under Print Style, choose an option.**

The preceding section in this chapter explains what these options are. To get another idea what the Print Styles are, select one, click the Page Setup button, and in the Page Setup dialog box, click the Print Preview button. The Print Preview window shows what the pages will look like when you print them. Click the Print button in this window to start printing right away.

If you start in a view apart from Address Cards or Detailed Address Cards, Table Style is the only Print Style option.

4. **Select Page Setup options if you want to change the number of columns that are printed, change fonts, change headers and footers, or otherwise fiddle with the printed pages.**

The next section in this chapter explains these options.

5. **If you selected contacts to print in Step 1, choose the Only Selected Items option button.**

6. **Click OK to start printing.**

Changing the look of printed pages

By default, contact information is printed in 12-, 10-, or 8-point Tahoma font. Your name, a page number, and the date and time you print the contact information appears on a footer at the bottom of the pages. To change these and other settings, click the Page Setup button in the Print dialog box (refer to Figure 2-4). You see the Page Setup dialog box. You can click the Print

Preview button in this dialog box to open the Print Preview window and see what your contacts look like when you print them (click the Page Setup button to return to the Page Setup dialog box).

Change these settings on the Format tab of the Page Setup dialog box:

+ **Where contact information is printed:** Contact information is printed alphabetically with a letter heading to mark where the As, Bs, Cs, and so on begin. To place contacts that begin with each letter on separate pages, select the Start on a New Page option button.

+ **Number of columns:** Enter a number in the Number of Columns text box to tell Outlook how many columns you want.

+ **Contact index:** Select the Contact Index on Side check box to print thumbnail letter headings on the sides of pages.

+ **Letter headings:** To remove the letter headings that mark where contacts starting with a certain letter begin, deselect the Headings for Each letter check box.

+ **Fonts and font sizes:** Click a Font button and choose a different font or font size for headings and body text.

+ **Gray shades:** Gray shades appear behind contact names, but you can remove them by deselecting the Print Using Gray Shading check box.

On the Header/Footer tab, the three boxes are for deciding what appears on the left side, middle, and right side of headers and footers. Type whatever you please into these text boxes. You can also click buttons in the dialog box to enter fields — a page number, total page number, printing date, printing time, or your name — in headers or footers.

**Book III
Chapter 2**

**Maintaining the
Contacts Folder**

Chapter 3: Handling Your E-Mail

In This Chapter

- ✓ Addressing, sending, replying to, and forwarding e-mail messages
- ✓ Creating distribution lists to send messages to groups
- ✓ Sending files and pictures with e-mail
- ✓ Understanding HTML, plain text, and rich text formats
- ✓ Receiving e-mail and files over the Internet
- ✓ Organizing and managing your e-mail
- ✓ Creating and using different folders to store e-mail
- ✓ Preventing junk e-mail

"*N*either snow nor rain nor heat nor gloom of night stays these couriers from the swift completion of their appointed rounds," reads the inscription on the Eighth Avenue New York Post Office Building. E-mailers face a different set of difficulties. Instead of snow, rain, or gloomy nights, they face junk e-mail blizzards, pesky colleagues, and the occasional co-worker who believes that all e-mail messages should be copied to everyone in the office.

This chapter explains the basics of sending and receiving e-mail, but also goes a step further to help you organize and manage your e-mail messages. This chapter unscrews the inscrutable. It shows you how to send files and pictures with e-mail messages, make a distribution list so that you can e-mail many people simultaneously, and postpone sending a message. You can also find out how to be advised when someone has read your e-mail, reorganize e-mail in the Inbox window, and be alerted to incoming messages from certain people or from people writing about certain subjects. Finally, this chapter shows you how to create folders for storing e-mail and explain what you can do to prevent junk e-mail from arriving on your digital doorstep.

Addressing and Sending E-Mail Messages

Sorry, you can't send chocolates or locks of hair by e-mail, but you can send digital pictures and computer files. These pages explain how to do it. You also discover how to send copies and blind copies of e-mail messages, reply to forwarded e-mail, create a distribution list, send e-mail from different accounts, and postpone sending a message. Better keep reading.

The basics: Sending an e-mail message

After you get the hang of it, sending an e-mail message is as easy as falling off a turnip truck. The first half of this chapter addresses everything you need to know about sending e-mail messages. Here are the basics:

1. **In the Inbox or Drafts folder, click the New E-Mail Message button or choose Ctrl+N.**

   A Message window like the one in Figure 3-1 appears.

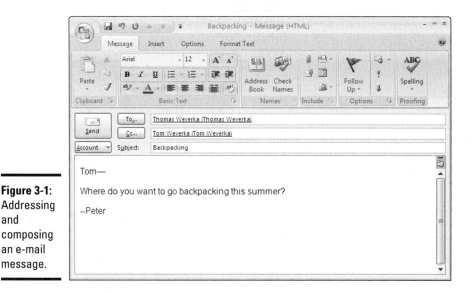

Figure 3-1:
Addressing and composing an e-mail message.

2. **Enter the recipient's e-mail address in the To text box.**

   The next section in this chapter, "Addressing an e-mail message," explains the numerous ways to address an e-mail message. You can address the same message to more than one person by entering more than one address in the To text box. For that matter, you can send copies of the message and blind copies of the message to others (see "Sending copies and blind copies of messages," later in this chapter).

3. **In the Subject text box, enter a descriptive title for the message.**

When your message arrives on the other end, the recipient sees the subject first. Enter a descriptive subject that helps the recipient decide whether to read the message right away. After you enter the subject, it appears in the title bar of the Message window.

Outlook offers different ways to get a recipient's attention. For example, you can give your message a priority rating. See "Prioritizing the messages you send," later in this chapter.

4. **Type the message.**

Whatever you do, don't forget to enter the message itself! You can spell check your message by pressing F7 or clicking the Spelling button.

As long as you compose messages in HTML format and the person receiving your e-mail messages has software capable of reading HTML, you can decorate messages to your heart's content (later in this chapter, "All about Message Formats" explains the HTML issue). Experiment with fonts and font sizes. Boldface and underline text. Throw in a bulleted or numbered list. You can find many formatting commands on the Insert, Options, and Format Text tabs. These are the same formatting commands found in Word.

5. **Click the Send button.**

As "Postponing sending a message" explains later in this chapter, you can put off sending a message. And if you have more than one e-mail account, you can choose which one to send the message with, as "Choosing which account to send messages with" explains. Messages remain in the Outbox folder if you postpone sending them or if Outlook can't send them right away because your computer isn't connected to the Internet.

If you decide in the middle of writing a message to write the rest of it later, click the Save button on the Quick Access toolbar or press Ctrl+S and close the Message window. The message lands in the Drafts folder. When you're ready to finish writing the message, open the Drafts folder and double-click your unfinished message to resume writing it.

Copies of e-mail messages you have sent are kept in the Sent Items folder. If you prefer not to keep copies of sent e-mail messages on hand, choose Tools⇨Options and on the Preferences tab of the Options dialog box, click the E-Mail Options button. You see the E-Mail Options dialog box. Deselect the Save Copies of Messages in Sent Items Folder check box.

Book III
Chapter 3

Handling Your E-Mail

Making Outlook your default e-mail program

If you switched to Outlook from Outlook Express or another e-mail program and you like Outlook, you need to tell your computer that Outlook is henceforth the e-mail program you want to use by default. The default e-mail program is the one that opens when you click an e-mail link on a Web page or give the order to send an Office file from inside an Office program. Follow these steps to make Outlook the default e-mail program on your computer:

1. **Click the Start button and choose Control Panel.**

2. **Double-click the Internet Options icon.**

   If you don't see this icon, click the Switch to Classic View link on the left side of the window. You see the Internet Properties dialog box.

3. **On the Programs tab, choose Microsoft Office Outlook on the E-Mail drop-down list and then click OK.**

Addressing an e-mail message

How do you address an e-mail message in the To text box of the Message window (refer to Figure 3-1)? Let me count the ways:

✦ **Get the address (or addresses) from the Contacts folder:** Click the To (or Cc) button to send a message to someone whose name is on file in your Contacts folder. You see the Select Names dialog box, as shown in Figure 3-2. Click or Ctrl+click to select the names of people to whom you want to send the message. Then click the To-> button (or Cc-> or Bcc-> button) to enter addresses in the To text box (or Cc or Bcc text boxes) of the Message window. Click OK to return to the Message window. This is the easiest way to address an e-mail message to several different people.

✦ **Type a person's name from the Contacts folder:** Simply type a person's name if the name is on file in the Contacts folder. (See the Tip at the end of this list to find out what to do if you aren't sure whether the name is really on file or you aren't sure whether you entered the name correctly.) To send the message to more than one person, enter a comma (,) or semicolon (;) between each name.

✦ **Type the address in the To text box:** If the address is on file in your Contacts folder or Address Book, a pop-up message with the complete address appears after you type the first couple of letters. Press Enter to enter the address without your having to type all the letters. To send the message to more than one person, enter a comma (,) or semicolon (;) between each address.

✦ **Reply to a message sent to you:** Select the message in the Inbox folder and click the Reply button. The Message window opens with the address of the person to whom you're replying already entered in the To text box. This is the most reliable way (no typos on your part) to enter an e-mail address. You can also click the Reply to All button to reply to enter the e-mail addresses of all the people to whom the original message was sent.

Select names.

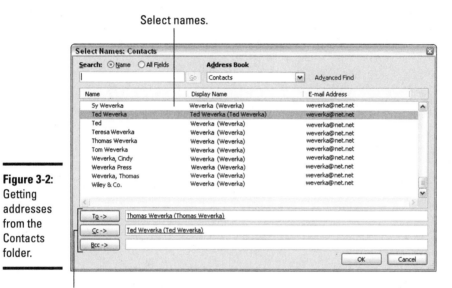

Figure 3-2:
Getting
addresses
from the
Contacts
folder.

Click a button.

Book III
Chapter 3

Handling Your
E-Mail

These days, many people have more than one e-mail address, and when you enter an e-mail address in the To text box of the Message window, it's hard to be sure whether the address you entered is the right one. To make sure that you send an e-mail address to the right address, click the Check Names button in the Names group. You see the Check Names dialog box, as shown in Figure 3-3. Select the correct name and address in the dialog box and then click OK. You can also click the Check Names button if you aren't sure whether a name was entered correctly in the To text box or you aren't sure whether a name is really on file in the Contacts folder.

Sending copies and blind copies of messages

Sending copies of messages and blind copies of messages is simple enough, but think twice before you do it. In my experience, a dysfunctional office is one where people continuously send copies of messages to one another, often to supervisors, to itemize their quarrels or document their work. However, sending copies of messages can clog mailboxes and waste everyone's time.

Sending e-mail from inside another Office program

As long as Outlook is your default e-mail program (I explain how to make it the default program earlier in this chapter), you can send e-mail messages or file attachments from other Office programs without opening Outlook. If the Word document, Excel worksheet, or Power-Point presentation needs sending right away, save it and follow these steps to send it as a file attachment to an e-mail message:

1. **With the file you want to send on-screen, click the Office button.**

2. **Choose Send➪Email.**

A message window appears with the name of your file in the subject line. Your file is ready to be sent along with the e-mail message.

3. **Enter the recipient's address in the To box and type a message in the Message box.**

4. **Click the Send button.**

That was fast! It was faster than opening Outlook and attaching the file to the e-mail message on your own. The message is sent right away if Outlook is running. Otherwise, the message is sent next time you open Outlook.

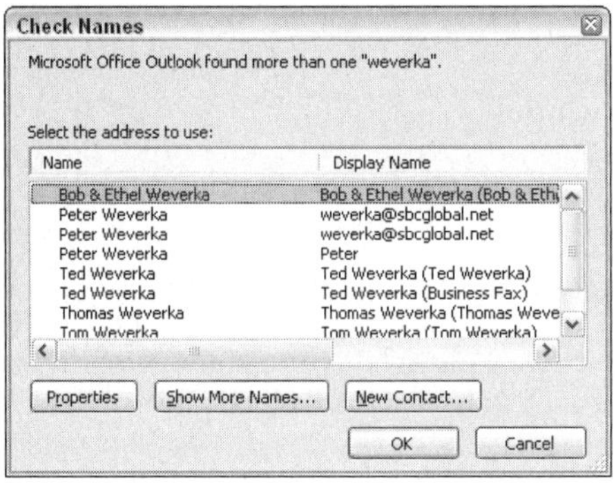

Figure 3-3:
Checking the accuracy of an e-mail address.

When you send a copy of a message, the person who receives the message knows that copies have been sent because the names of people to whom copies were sent appear at the top of the e-mail message. But when you send blind copies, the person who receives the message doesn't know that others received it.

Follow these instructions to send copies and blind copies of messages:

✦ **Send a copy of a message:** Enter e-mail addresses in the Cc text box of the Message window, or in the Select Names dialog box (refer to Figure 3-2), select names and then click the Cc->button.

✦ **Send a blind copy of a message:** On the Options tab, click the Show Bcc button, or click the To or Cc button in the Message window to open the Select Names dialog box (refer to Figure 3-2), select names, and click the Bcc-> button or else enter addresses in the Bcc-> text box.

You may well ask yourself why these buttons are called Cc and Bcc. Why the extra *C?* Actually, the Cc stands for "carbon copy" and the Bcc stands for "blind carbon copy." These terms originated in the Mesozoic era when letters were composed on the typewriter, and to make a copy of a letter, you inserted carbon paper between two paper sheets and typed away. The carbon paper turned your fingers black. You left black fingerprints on your fedora hat or angora sweater. Those were the days!

Replying to and forwarding e-mail messages

Replying to and forwarding messages is as easy as pie. For one thing, you don't need to know the recipient's e-mail address to reply to a message. In the Inbox, select the message you want to reply to or forward and do the following:

✦ **Reply to author:** Click the Reply button. The Message window opens with the sender's name already entered in the To box and the original message in the text box below. Write a reply and click the Send button.

✦ **Reply to all parties who received the message:** Click the Reply to All button. The Message window opens with the names of all parties who received the message in the To and Cc boxes and the original message in the text box. Type your reply and click the Send button. If files were attached to the original message, they aren't sent in the reply.

✦ **Forward a message:** Click the Forward button. The Message window opens with the text of the original message. Either enter an e-mail address in the To text box or click the To button to open the Select Names dialog box and then select the names of the parties to whom the message will be forwarded. Add a word or two to the original message if you like; then click the Send button.

Forwarding a message to a third party without the permission of the original author is a breach of etiquette and very bad manners. How would you like your opinions or ideas scattered hither and yon to strangers you don't know? I could tell you a story about an e-mail message of mine that an unwitting editor forwarded to a cantankerous publisher, but I'm saving that story for the soap opera edition of this book.

To find the e-mail address of someone who sent you an e-mail message, double-click the message to display it in the Message window, right-click the sender's name in the From box, and choose Outlook Properties. The e-mail address appears in the E-Mail Properties dialog box. To add a sender's name to the Contacts folder, right-click the name and choose Add to Outlook Contacts.

By default, the text of the original message appears in the Message window after you click the Reply or Reply to All button to respond to a message. However, Outlook offers the option of not displaying the original text by default. The program also offers different ways of displaying this text. To scope out these options and perhaps select one, choose Tools⇨Options, and on the Preferences tab of the Options dialog box, click the E-Mail Options button. You see the E-Mail Options dialog box. Choose an option on the When Replying to a Message drop-down list to tell Outlook how or whether to display original messages in replies.

Distribution lists for sending messages to groups

Suppose you're the secretary of the PTA at a school and you regularly send the same e-mail messages to 10 or 12 other board members. Entering e-mail addresses for the 10 or 12 people each time you want to send an e-mail message is a drag. To keep from having to enter so many e-mail addresses, you can create a *distribution list,* a list with multiple e-mail addresses. To address your e-mail message, you simply enter the name of the distribution list, not the individual names, as shown in Figure 3-4.

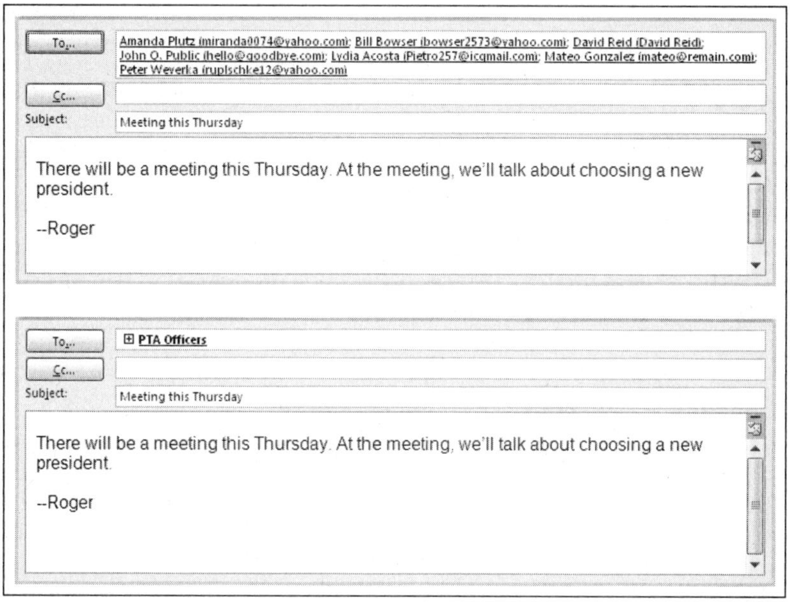

Figure 3-4:
Instead of
entering
many
addresses
(top),
enter a
distribution
list name
(bottom).

Creating a distribution list

Follow these steps to bundle e-mail addresses into a distribution list:

1. Choose File⇨New⇨Distribution List or press Ctrl+Shift+L.

You see the Distribution List window, as shown in Figure 3-5.

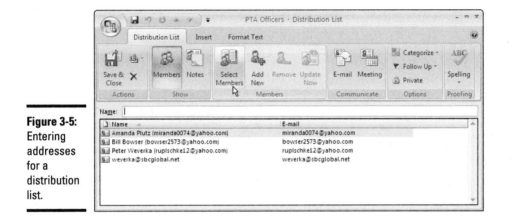

Figure 3-5: Entering addresses for a distribution list.

2. Enter a descriptive name in the Name text box.

3. Click the Select Members button to get names and addresses from the Contacts folder.

You see the Select Members dialog box.

4. Hold down the Ctrl key and select the name of each person you want to be on the list.

5. Click the Members button and then click OK.

You can find the Members button in the lower-left corner of the dialog box. The names you chose appear in the Distribution List window.

You can add the names of people who aren't in your Contacts folder by clicking the Add New button, and in the Add New Member dialog box, entering a name and e-mail address.

6. Click the Save & Close button in the Distribution List window.

Addressing e-mail to a distribution list

To address an e-mail message to a distribution list, click the New button to open a Message window, click the To button to open the Select Names dialog box, and select the distribution list name. Distribution list names appear in boldface and are marked with a Distribution List icon.

Prioritizing the messages you send

Every day, billions of e-mail messages arrive on people's computers, each one begging for the recipient's attention, each one crying out, "Read me first." With this kind of cut-throat competition, how can you give your e-mail messages a competitive advantage? How can you make yours stand out in the crowd?

The best way is to write a descriptive title in the Subject box of the Message window. The subject is the first thing people see in their Inbox. They decide whether to read a message now, later, or never on the basis of what they see on the Subject line.

Another way to (maybe) get other's attention is to assign a high priority rating to your message. If the recipient reads his or her e-mail with Outlook or Outlook Express, a red exclamation point appears beside the message in the Inbox folder. Conversely, you can assign a low priority to messages as well, in which case a downward-pointing arrow appears next to the message heading in the Inbox folder. However, prioritizing this way is only worthwhile if the recipient runs Outlook or Outlook Express because other e-mail programs don't know what to make of the exclamation point or the arrow.

To assign a priority to a message, click the High Importance or Low Importance button in the Message window (you can find these buttons in the Options group). In the Inbox folder, click the Sort by Importance button, the leftmost sorting button, to arrange messages by their priority ratings.

!	D	@	From	Subject	Received	Size	Categ...	⚑
				Sort by: Importance				
⊟ Importance: High (1 item)								
!			HomeLoans@ookk.fsnet....	Home Loans & Refinancing Av...	Fri 9/8/2000 5:33 PM	8 KB		⚑
!		@	IJRogers@wiley.com	Re: Office AIO Status	Mon 8/14/2006 11:56 AM	37 KB		⚑
!			Michael Taylor	roll 'em	Sun 8/13/2006 8:03 PM	6 KB		⚑
!			Netflix Shipping	For Tue: The Three Burials of ...	Mon 6/5/2006 6:31 PM	11 KB		⚑
!		@	Susan Christophersen	Book 5, Chs. 2 and 3 To AR bef...	Wed 4/19/2006 8:56 AM	163 KB		⚑
!			Alan L. Rubin, M. D.	For Dummies Authors' Unconf...	Tue 4/18/2006 2:40 PM	8 KB		⚑

Search Inbox

Inbox

Editing a distribution list

The names of distribution lists appear in the Contacts folder, where they are boldfaced and marked with an icon showing two heads in profile. You can treat the lists like regular contacts. In the Contacts folder, double-click a distribution list name to open the Distribution List window (refer to Figure 3-5). From there, you can add names to the list, remove names from the list, or select new names for the list.

Sending a file along with a message

Sending a file along with an e-mail message is called *attaching* a file in Outlook lingo. Yes, it can be done. You can send a file or several files along with an e-mail message by following these steps:

1. **With the Message window open, click the Attach File button.**

You see the Insert File dialog box.

2. **Locate and select the file that you want to send along with your e-mail message.**

Ctrl+click filenames to select more than one file.

3. **Click the Insert button.**

The name of the file (or files) appears in the Attached text box in the Message window. Address the message and type a note to send along with the file. You can right-click a filename in the Attach text box and choose Open on the shortcut menu to open a file you're about to send. Or, if you change your mind about sending the file, you can click Remove.

TIP

Here's a fast way to attach a file to a message: Find the file in Windows Explorer or My Computer and drag it into the Message window. The file's name appears in the Attach box as though you placed it there by clicking the Attach File button.

Including a picture in an e-mail message

As shown in Figure 3-6, you can include a picture in the body of an e-mail message, but in order to see it, the recipient's e-mail software must display messages by using HTML. As "All about Message Formats" explains later in this chapter, not everyone has software that displays e-mail by using HTML. People who don't have HTML e-mail software get the picture anyhow, but it doesn't appear in the body of the e-mail message; it arrives as an attached file (see "Handling Files That Were Sent to You," later in this chapter, to find out about receiving files by e-mail). To view the attached file, the recipient has to open it with a graphics software program, such as Paint or Windows Picture and Fax Viewer.

Follow these steps to adorn an e-mail message with a picture:

1. **In the Message window, click the Insert tab.**

2. **Click in the body of the e-mail message where you want the picture to go.**

3. **Click the Insert Picture button.**

You see the Insert Picture dialog box.

Figure 3-6:
Inserting a
picture in
an e-mail
message.

4. **Locate and select the digital picture you want to send; then click the Insert button.**

   The picture lands in the Message window. Select the picture, go to the (Picture Tools) Format tab, open the drop-down list on the Text Wrapping button, and choose an option to decide how text behave nearby the picture. Book VIII, Chapter 3 explains graphics in detail; Book I, Chapter 8 explains how to manipulate graphic images.

Want to remove a picture from an e-mail message? Select it and press the Delete key.

Choosing which account to send messages with

If you've set up more than one e-mail account, you can choose which one to send an e-mail message with. Follow these instructions to choose an account for sending e-mail messages:

✦ **Choosing the default account for sending messages:** When you click the Send button in the Message window, the e-mail message is sent by way of the default e-mail account. To tell Outlook which account that is, choose Tools⇨Account Settings. You see the Account Settings dialog box. Select the account that you want to be the default and click the Set as Default button.

+ **Sending an individual message:** To bypass the default e-mail account and send a message with a different account, click the Account button in the Message window, and choose an account name from the drop-down list. Then click the Send button.

Postponing sending a message

As you probably know, e-mail messages are sent immediately when you click the Send button in the Message window if your computer is connected to the Internet. If it isn't connected, the message lands in the Outbox folder, where it remains until you connect to the Internet.

But suppose you want to postpone sending a message? Outlook offers two techniques for putting off sending a message:

+ **Moving messages temporarily to the Drafts folder:** Compose your message, click the Save button in the Message window (or press Ctrl+S), and close the Message window. Your e-mail message goes to the Drafts folder. When you're ready to send it, open the Drafts folder, double-click your message to open it, and click the Send button in the Message window.

Delay Delivery

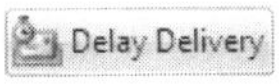

+ **Postponing the send date:** Click the Options tab in the Message window. On the Options tab, click the Delay Delivery button. You see the Message Options dialog box, as shown in Figure 3-7. Select the Do Not Deliver Before check box, enter a date on the calendar, and if you so desire, select a time from the drop-down list. Then click the Close button. In the Message window, click the Send button. Your message goes to the Outbox folder, where it remains until the time arrives to send it and you open Outlook.

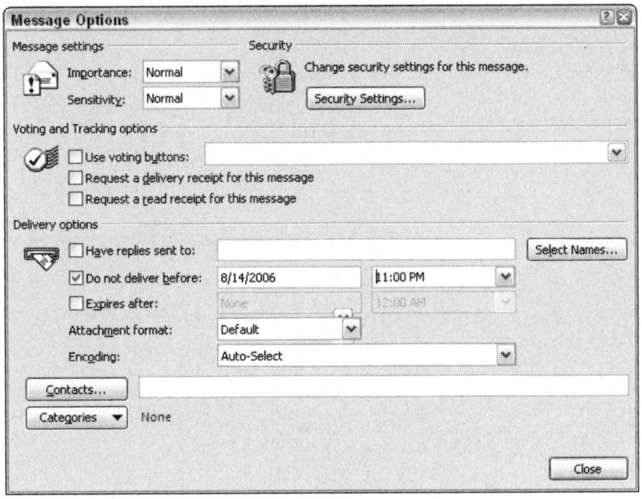

Figure 3-7: Putting off sending an e-mail message.

Being Advised When Someone Has Read Your E-Mail

Outlook offers a command whereby you can be informed when someone has received or read an e-mail message you sent. You can even send a mini-ballot to someone else, solicit their vote, and have the vote sent to you by e-mail. To perform this magic trick, start in the Message window and click the Options tab. In the Tracking group, select one or more of these options:

✦ **Use Voting Buttons:** Voting buttons are included on a drop-down list in the e-mail message you send. Choose a set of buttons from the drop-down list, as shown in Figure 3-8. The recipient clicks the Vote button, chooses an option on a drop-down list, and the response is sent to you in the form of an e-mail message with the word Approve, Reject, Yes, No, or Maybe in the subject line.

The Receipt Read message box

Voting buttons

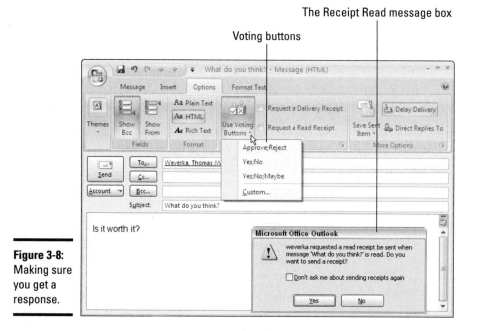

Figure 3-8: Making sure you get a response.

✦ **Request a Delivery Receipt:** You're informed by e-mail after the message is delivered. Select the Request a Delivery Receipt check box. To be informed, however, you and the recipient must use the same Exchange Server, and the recipient must choose to inform you that the message was delivered. Don't count on this one really working.

✦ **Request a Read Receipt:** The message box appears, as shown in Figure 3-8. If the recipient clicks the Yes button, a Message window appears immediately so that he or she can send an e-mail informing you that the message was read. The message, when it arrives on your end, lists the date and time that the response message was sent. Select the Request a Read Receipt check box.

All about Message Formats

Outlook offers three formats for sending e-mail messages: HTML, plain text, and rich text. What are the pros and cons of the different formats?

✦ **HTML format:** These days, almost all e-mail is transmitted in HTML format, the same format with which Web pages are made. If HTML is the default format you use for creating messages in Outlook — and it is unless you tinkered with the default settings — the e-mail messages you send are, in effect, little Web pages. HTML gives you the most opportunities for formatting text and graphics. In HTML format, you can place pictures in the body of an e-mail message, use a background theme, and do any number of sophisticated formatting tricks.

However, the HTML format has it share of detractors. First, the messages are larger because they include sophisticated formatting instructions, and being larger, they take longer to transmit over the Internet. Some e-mail accounts allocate a fixed amount of disk space for incoming e-mail messages and reject messages when the disk space allocation is filled. Because they're larger than other e-mail messages, HTML messages fill the disk space quicker. Finally, some e-mail software can't handle HTML messages. In this software, the messages are converted to plain text format.

✦ **Plain text format:** In plain text format, only letters and numbers are transmitted. The format doesn't permit you to format text or align paragraphs in any way, but you can rest assured that the person who receives the message can read it exactly as you wrote it.

✦ **Rich text format:** The third e-mail message format, rich text, is proprietary to Microsoft e-mailing software. Only people who use Outlook and Outlook Express can see rich text formats. I don't recommend choosing the rich text format. If formatting text in e-mail messages is important to you, choose the HTML format because more people can read your messages.

When someone sends you an e-mail message, you can tell which format it was transmitted in by looking at the title bar, where *HTML, Plain Text,* or *Rich Text* appears in parentheses after the subject of the message. Outlook is smart enough to transmit messages in HTML, plain text, or rich text format when you reply to a message that was sent to you in that format.

Follow these instructions if you need to change the format in which your e-mail messages are transmitted:

✦ **Changing the default format:** Choose Tools➪Options, and in the Options dialog box, select the Mail Format tab. From the Compose in This Message Format drop-down list, choose HTML, Plain Text, or Rich Text.

✦ **Changing the format for a single e-mail message:** In the Message window, click the Options tab. Then click the Plain Text, HTML, or Rich Text button.

✦ **Always using the plain text or rich text format with a contact:** To avoid transmitting in HTML with a contact, start in the Contacts folder, double-click the contact's name, and in the Contact form, double-click the contact's e-mail address. You see the E-Mail Properties dialog box. In the Internet Format drop-down list, choose Send Plain Text Only or Send Using Outlook Rich Text Format.

Devising a signature for your e-mail messages

An *e-mail signature* is an address, word, phrase, or pithy saying that appears at the bottom of all the e-mail messages you send. Sometimes signatures list company information or instructions for reaching the sender. You can create more than one signature and then choose different signatures for different e-mail messages.

Follow these steps to create an e-mail signature:

1. **Choose Tools➪Options, select the Mail Format tab in the Options dialog box, and click the Signatures button.**

   You see the Signatures and Stationery dialog box.

2. **Click the New button.**

   The New Signature dialog box appears.

3. **Enter a descriptive name for the signature and click OK.**

4. **In the Edit Signature box, type your signature.**

5. **Choose a font and font size for the signature.**

   You can also choose alignment options.

6. **Click OK twice to return the Options dialog box and then to Outlook.**

If you change your mind about putting a signature in your e-mail messages, return to the E-Mail Signature tab of the Signatures and Stationery dialog box and choose (None) in the New Messages drop-down list.

To choose which signature to use if you create more than one, click the Signature button on the Message tab in the Message window and choose a signature from the drop-down list.

Receiving E-Mail Messages

Let's hope that all the e-mail messages you receive carry good news. These pages explain how to collect your e-mail and all the different ways that Outlook notifies you when e-mail has arrived. You can find several tried-and-true techniques for reading e-mail messages in the Inbox window. Outlook offers a bunch of different ways to rearrange the window as well as the messages inside it.

Getting your e-mail

Here are all the different ways to collect e-mail messages that were sent to you:

✦ **Collect the e-mail:** Press F9 or choose Tools⊏>Send/Receive⊏>Send/Receive All.

✦ **Collect e-mail from a single account (if you have more than one):** Choose Tools⊏>Send/Receive, and on the submenu, choose the name of an e-mail account or group. (See "Groups for handling e-mail from different accounts," later in this chapter to find out what groups are.)

✦ **Collect e-mail automatically every few minutes:** Press Ctrl+Alt+S or choose Tools⊏>Send/Receive⊏>Send/Receive Settings⊏>Define Send/Receive Groups. You see the Send/Receive Groups dialog box, as shown in Figure 3-9. Select a group (groups are explained in "Groups for handling e-mail from different accounts"), select the Schedule an Automatic Send/Receive Every check box, and enter a minute setting. To temporarily suspend automatic e-mail collections, choose Tools⊏>Send/Receive⊏>Send/Receive Settings⊏>Disable Scheduled Send/Receive.

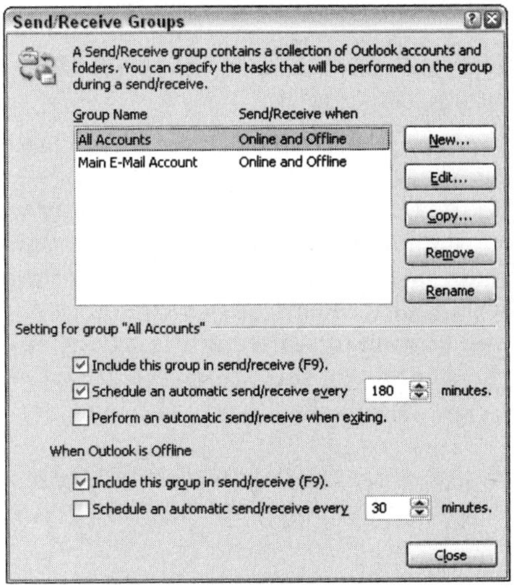

**Book III
Chapter 3**

**Handling Your
E-Mail**

Figure 3-9:
Handling
group
settings.

If you're not on a network or don't have a DSL or cable Internet connection, you shortly see the Connection dialog box. Enter your password, if necessary, and click the Connect button. The Outlook Send/Receive dialog box appears to show you the progress of messages being sent and received.

Being notified that e-mail has arrived

Take the e-mail arrival quiz. Winners get the displeasure of knowing that they understand far more than is healthy about Outlook. You can tell when e-mail has arrived in the Inbox folder because:

A) You hear this sound: *ding.*

B) The mouse cursor briefly changes to a little envelope.

C) A little envelope appears in the system tray to the left of the Windows clock. (You can double-click the envelope to open the Inbox folder.)

D) A pop-up *desktop alert* with the sender's name, the message's subject, and the text of the message appears briefly on your desktop.

E) All of the above.

The answer is E, "All of the above," but if four arrival notices strike you as excessive, you can eliminate one or two. Choose Tools⇨Options and on the Preferences tab of the Options dialog box, click the E-Mail Options button. Then, in the E-Mail Options dialog box, click the Advanced E-Mail Options button. At long last, in the Advanced E-Mail Options dialog box, select or deselect the four When New Items Arrive in My Inbox options. To make desktop alerts stay longer on-screen, click the Desktop Alert Settings button and drag the duration slider in the Desktop Alert Settings dialog box. While you're at it, click the Preview button to see what the alerts look like.

Reading your e-mail in the Inbox window

Messages arrive in the Inbox window, as shown in Figure 3-10. Unread messages are shown in boldface type and have envelope icons next to their names; messages that you've read (or at least opened to view) are shown in Roman type and appear beside open envelope icons. To read a message, select it and look in the Reading pane, or to focus more closely on a message, double-click it to open it in a Message window, as shown in Figure 3-10. In the Folder List, a number in parentheses beside the Inbox folder and Deleted Items folder tells you how many unread messages are in those folders. (The number in square brackets beside the Drafts and Junk E-Mail folders tells you how many items, read and unread, are in those folders.)

Later in this chapter, "Techniques for Organizing E-Mail Messages," explains how to organize messages in the Inbox folder. Meanwhile, here are some

Groups for handling e-mail from different accounts

Groups are meant to help people who have more than one e-mail account handle their e-mail. To begin with, all e-mail accounts belong to a group called All Accounts. Unless you change the default settings, all your e-mail accounts belong to the All Accounts group, and e-mail is sent by and received from all your e-mail accounts at the same time. If you want to change these default settings, press Ctrl+Alt+S or choose Tools⇨Send/Receive⇨Send/Receive Settings⇨Define Send/Receive Groups. You see the Send/Receive Groups dialog box (see Figure 3-9) Follow these instructions in the dialog box to change how you handle e-mail from different accounts:

✔ **Excluding an account from the All Accounts group:** Exclude an account if you don't want to collect its e-mail on a regular basis. Maybe you want to collect mail from this account sporadically. To exclude an account, select the All Accounts group in the Send/Receive Groups dialog box and click the Edit button. You land in the Send/Receive Settings – All Accounts dialog box. In the Accounts list, select the account you want to exclude and deselect the Include the Selected Account in this Group check box.

✔ **Creating a new group:** Create a new group if you want to establish settings for a single e-mail account or group of accounts. Click the New button in the Send/Receive Groups dialog box, enter a name in the Send/Receive Group Name dialog box, and click OK. You see the Send/Receive Settings dialog box. For each account you want to include in your new group, select an account name and then select the Include the Select Account in This Group check box.

✔ **Choosing settings for a group:** In the Send/Receive Groups dialog box, select the group whose settings you want to establish. At the bottom of the dialog box (see Figure 3-9), select whether to send and receive e-mail when you press F9, whether to send and receive automatically every few minutes, and whether to send and receive when you exit Outlook.

simple techniques you can use to unclutter the Inbox folder and make it easier to manage:

✦ **Hiding and displaying the Reading pane:** Click the Reading Pane button to make the Reading pane appear or disappear. The Reading pane gives you an opportunity to read messages without opening them in a Message window. However, with the Reading pane gone, column headings — From, Subject, Received, Size, Flagged, and Category — appear in the Inbox window, and you can click a column heading name to sort messages in different ways, as shown in Figure 3-11. For example, click the From column name to arrange messages by sender name; click the Received column name to arrange messages according to the date you received them.

Double-click a message to read it in a Message window.

Reading pane

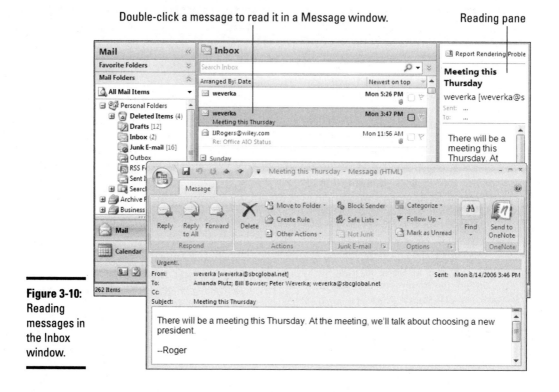

Figure 3-10:
Reading
messages in
the Inbox
window.

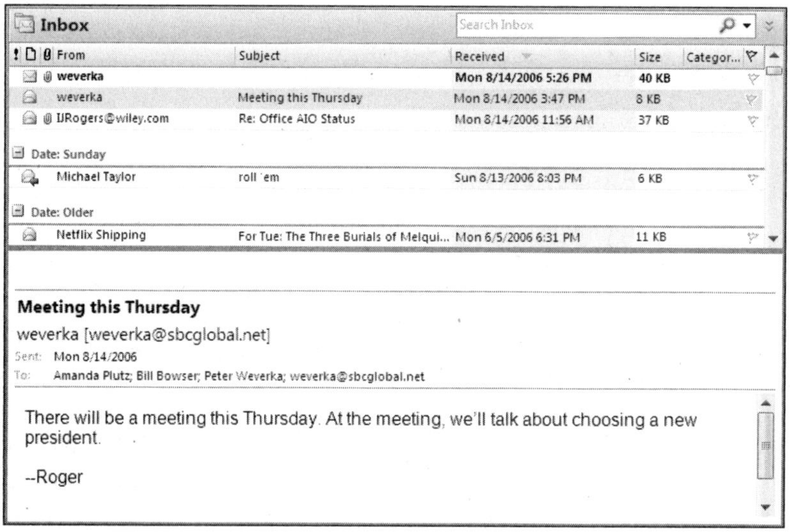

Figure 3-11:
Another
way to look
at the Inbox,
with the
Reading
pane on the
bottom.

You can eat your cake and have it too by displaying column names *and* the Reading pane, as shown in Figure 3-11. To do so, choose View⇨Reading Pane⇨Bottom on the submenu. This command places the Reading pane below the e-mail message list.

✦ **Hiding and displaying the Navigation pane:** Choose View⇨Navigation Pane⇨Normal or Minimized, or press Alt+F1. By hiding the Navigation pane, you get even more room to display messages.

✦ **Autopreviewing messages:** Click the AutoPreview button or choose View⇨AutoPreview to read the text of all on-screen messages in small type. The message text appears below the subject heading of each message.

✦ **Changing views:** Choose an option on the Current View drop-down list to reduce the number of messages in the window. For example, you can see only unread messages or messages that arrived in the past week.

Suppose you open an e-mail message but you regret doing so because you want the unopened envelope icon to appear beside the message's name. In other words, you want to handle the message later on. To make a message in the Inbox window appear as if it has never been opened, right-click it and choose Mark as Unread.

Handling Files That Were Sent to You

You can tell when someone sends you files along with an e-mail message because the paper clip icon appears in the Attachment column of the Inbox window (if column headings are displayed), as shown in Figure 3-12. If you display the Reading pane, the name of the file that was sent to you appears in the Reading pane. If you double-click the message to open it in a window, the name of the file appears there as well.

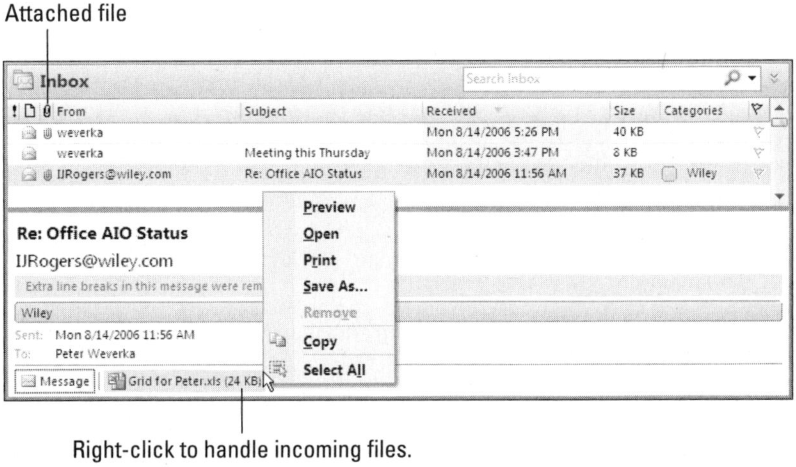

Attached file

!	🗅	📎	From	Subject	Received ▾	Size	Categories	▽
		📎	weverka		Mon 8/14/2006 5:26 PM	40 KB		▽
			weverka	Meeting this Thursday	Mon 8/14/2006 3:47 PM	8 KB		▽
		📎	IJRogers@wiley.com	Re: Office AIO Status	Mon 8/14/2006 11:56 AM	37 KB	☐ Wiley	▽

🔍 Inbox   Search Inbox

Re: Office AIO Status
IJRogers@wiley.com

Extra line breaks in this message were rem

Wiley

Sent: Mon 8/14/2006 11:56 AM
To: Peter Weverka

📄 Message   📊 Grid for Peter.xls (24 KB)

Preview
Open
Print
Save As...
~~Remove~~
📋 Copy
🔲 Select All

Figure 3-12:
Receiving
a file.

Right-click to handle incoming files.

Preventing computer viruses from spreading by e-mail

Outlook doesn't permit you to receive these kinds of files because they may contain computer viruses: batch program files (.bat), executable program files (.exe), JavaScript source files (.js), Microsoft Access Application files (.mdb), and Visual Basic Scripts (.vbs). If someone attempts to send you one of these files and, more-over, your Internet service provider (ISP) permits it to be sent, you get this message: *Outlook blocked access to the following potentially* *unsafe attachments*. Because computer viruses can be hidden in macros, any file that can conceivably contain a macro is screened. When you try to open one of these files, a dialog box warns you to open files only from trustworthy sources. If you suspect that a file has a virus, don't open it. Save it to your hard disk and scan it for viruses with your antivirus software. You do have antivirus software, don't you?

Opening Mail Attachment

? You should only open attachments from a trustworthy source.

Attachment: Grid for Peter.xls from Re: Office AIO Status - Message (Plain Text)

Would you like to open the file or save it to your computer?

[Open] [Save] [Cancel]

☑ Always ask before opening this type of file

Files that are sent to you over the Internet land deep inside your computer in a subfolder of the Temporary Internet Files folder. This is the same obscure folder where Web pages you encounter when surfing the Internet are kept. The best way to handle an incoming file is to open it or save it right away to a folder where you're likely to find it when you need it.

Saving a file you received

To save a file that was sent to you in a new folder:

✦ Double-click the filename and click the Save button in the Opening File Attachment dialog box.

✦ Right-click the filename and choose Save As, as shown in Figure 3-12.

✦ Choose File⇨Save Attachments⇨*Filename*.

✦ Click the Other Actions button in the Message window and choose Save Attachments.

Opening a file you received

To open a file that was sent to you:

+ Double-click the filename in the Reading pane or Message window and then click the Open button in the Opening Mail Attachment dialog box.

+ Right-click the filename and choose Open, as shown in Figure 3-12.

+ Right-click the paper clip icon in the Inbox window and choose View Attachments⇨*Filename*.

As long as the file being sent to you is a Word, PowerPoint, or Excel file, you can preview it inside the Message window or Reading pane. To do so, right-click the filename and choose Preview on the shortcut menu (refer to Figure 3-12). After you preview the file, you can decide whether to open or save it.

Techniques for Organizing E-Mail Messages

If you're one of those unfortunate souls who receives 20, 30, 40 or more e-mail messages daily, you owe it to yourself and your sanity to figure out a way to organize e-mail messages such that you keep the ones you want, you can find e-mail messages easily, and you can quickly eradicate the e-mail messages that don't matter to you. Outlook offers numerous ways to manage and organize e-mail messages. Pick and choose the techniques that work for you.

In a nutshell, here are all the techniques for organizing e-mail messages:

+ **Change views in the Inbox window:** Open the Current View drop-down list on the Advanced toolbar and choose Last Seven Days, Unread Messages in This Folder, or another view to shrink the number of e-mail messages in the Inbox window.

+ **Rearrange, or sort, messages in the Inbox window**: If necessary, click the Reading Pane button to remove the Reading pane and see column heading names in the Inbox window. Then click a column heading name to rearrange, or sort, messages by sender name, subject, receipt date, size, or flagged status. See "Reading your e-mail in the Inbox window," earlier in this chapter, for details.

+ **Delete the messages that you don't need:** Before they clutter the Inbox, delete messages that you're sure you don't need as soon as you get them. To delete a message, select it and then click the Delete button, press the Delete key, or choose Edit⇨Delete.

+ **Move messages to different folders:** Create a folder for each project you're involved with, and when an e-mail message about a project arrives, move it to a folder. See "All about E-Mail Folders," later in this chapter.

✦ **Move messages automatically to different folders as they arrive:** Instead of moving messages yourself after they arrive, you can tell Outlook to move messages automatically to different folders. See "Earmarking messages as they arrive," later in this chapter.

✦ **Destroy junk mail as it arrives:** You can delete junk mail automatically. See "Yes, You Can Prevent Junk Mail (Sort of)," later in this chapter.

✦ **Flag messages:** Flag a message with a color-coded flag to let you know to follow up on it. See "Flagging e-mail messages," the next section in this chapter.

✦ **Categorize messages:** Assign e-mail messages to categories; then, arrange e-mail messages by category in the Inbox window by choosing View➪Arrange By➪Categories. See Chapter 1 of this mini-book for info about categorizing items in a folder.

✦ **Have Outlook remind you to reply to a message:** Instruct Outlook to make the Reminder message box appear at a date and time in the future so that you know to reply to a message. See "Being reminded to take care of e-mail messages," later in this chapter.

✦ **Make liberal use of the Search commands:** You can always find a stray message with the Search commands. (See Chapter 1 of this mini-book to know more about finding items in folders.) To quickly find all the messages from one person, right-click an e-mail message from that person and choose Find All➪Messages from Sender. Choose Find All➪Related Messages to find messages that are part of the same conversation (the original message and all replies).

✦ **Archive messages you no longer need:** Archiving is a good way to strip the Inbox folder of items that you don't need. See Chapter 1 of this mini-book for more about archiving.

✦ **Use the Mailbox Cleanup command:** This handy command archives messages, deletes them, and deletes alternate versions of messages. See Chapter 1 of this mini-book for more about this command.

Flagging e-mail messages

One way to call attention to e-mail messages is to flag them. As shown in Figure 3-13, you can make color-coded flags appear in the Inbox window. You can use red flags, for example, to mark urgent messages and green flags to mark the not-so-important ones. Which color you flag a message with is up to you. Outlook offers six colors. As Figure 3-13 shows, you can click the Sort by Flag Status button in the Inbox window to arrange messages in color-coded flag order.

Flag a message.   Click to sort messages by flag.

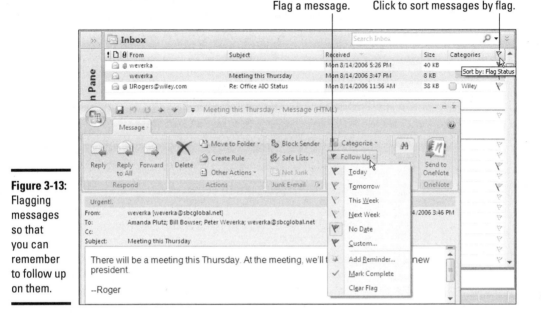

Figure 3-13:
Flagging
messages
so that
you can
remember
to follow up
on them.

Follow these instructions to flag an e-mail message:

◆ **Starting in the Message window:** Click the Follow Up button and choose a flag (see Figure 3-13). If the color you prefer isn't showing, choose Custom. You see the Custom dialog box. From the Flag To drop-down list, choose a follow-up notice, or else type one of your own in the text box. The notice appears across the top of the e-mail message in the Message window.

◆ **Starting in the Inbox folder:** Select the message, click the Follow Up button, and choose a flag color. You can also right-click, choose Follow Up, and choose a flag color.

To "unflag" a message, right-click it and choose Follow Up➪Clear Flag. You can also right-click and choose Follow Up➪Mark Complete to put a checkmark where the flag used to be and remind yourself that you're done with the message. Later in this chapter, "Earmarking messages as they arrive," explains how you can flag messages automatically as they arrive.

Being reminded to take care of e-mail messages

If you know your way around the Calendar and Tasks windows, you know that the Reminder message box appears when an appointment or meeting is about to take place or a task deadline is about to fall. What you probably don't know, however, is that you can put the Reminders dialog box to work in regard to e-mail messages by following these steps:

1. **Select the message.**

2. **Click the Follow Up button and choose Add Reminder.**

You see the Custom dialog box, as shown in Figure 3-14. You can also right-click a message and choose Follow Up⇨Add Reminder to see the dialog box.

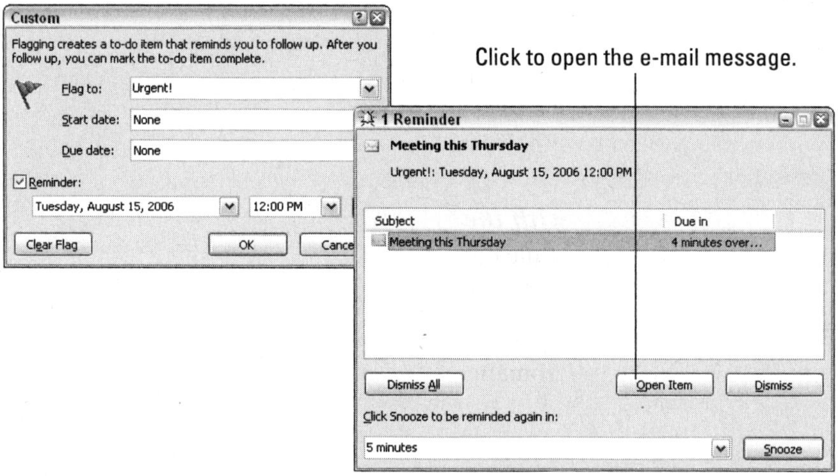

Click to open the e-mail message.

Figure 3-14:
Reminding
yourself to
take care of
an e-mail
message.

3. **On the Flag To drop-down list, choose an option that describes why the e-mail message needs your attention later, or if none of the options suits you, enter a description in the Flag To text box.**

The description you choose or enter appears above the message in the Reading pane, and message window, as well in the Reminder message box, as shown in Figure 3-14.

4. **Choose the date and time that you want the Reminder message box to appear.**

As Chapter 5 of this mini-book explains in detail, the Reminder message box appears 15 minutes before the date and time you enter.

5. **Click OK.**

When the reminder falls due, you see the Reminder message box, as shown in Figure 3-14, where you can click the Open Item button to open the e-mail message. See Chapter 5 of this mini-book if you need to find out how the Reminder message box works.

Earmarking messages as they arrive

To help you organize messages better, Outlook gives you the opportunity to mark messages in various ways and even move messages as they arrive automatically to folders apart from the Inbox folder. Being able to move messages immediately to a folder is a great way to keep e-mail concerning different projects separate. If you belong to a newsgroup that sends many messages per day, being able to move those messages instantly into their own folder is a real blessing because newsgroup messages have a habit of cluttering the Inbox folder.

To earmark messages for special treatment, Outlook has you create so-called rules. To create a rule, start by trying out the Create Rule command, and if that doesn't work, test-drive the more powerful Rules Wizard.

Simple rules with the Create Rule command

Use the Create Rule command to be alerted when e-mail arrives from a certain person or the Subject line of a message includes a certain word. You can make the incoming message appear in the New Item Alerts window (as shown at the top of Figure 3-15), play a sound when the message arrives, or move the message automatically to a certain folder.

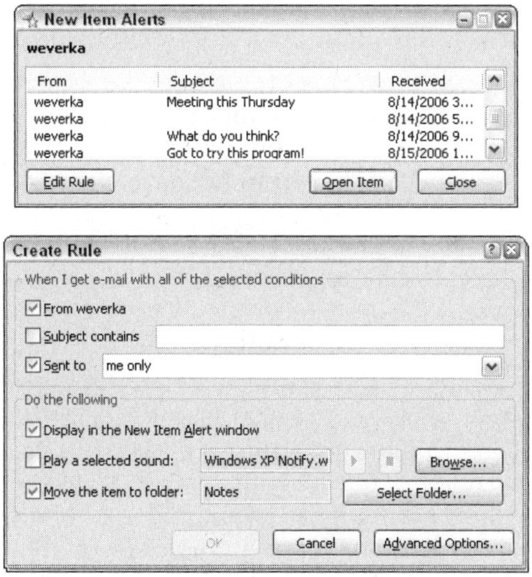

Book III Chapter 3

Handling Your E-Mail

Figure 3-15: The New Item Alerts window (top) and Create Rule dialog box (bottom).

New Item Alerts

weverka

From	Subject	Received
weverka	Meeting this Thursday	8/14/2006 3...
weverka		8/14/2006 5...
weverka	What do you think?	8/14/2006 9...
weverka	Got to try this program!	8/15/2006 1...

Edit Rule   Open Item   Close

Create Rule

When I get e-mail with all of the selected conditions

☑ From weverka
☐ Subject contains
☑ Sent to   me only

Do the following

☑ Display in the New Item Alert window
☐ Play a selected sound: Windows XP Notify.w   Browse...
☑ Move the item to folder: Notes   Select Folder...

OK   Cancel   Advanced Options...

Follow these steps to create a simple rule:

1. If you want to be alerted when e-mail arrives from a certain person, find an e-mail message from the person, right-click it, and choose Create Rule; otherwise, click the Create Rule button.

You see the Create Rule dialog box, as shown at the bottom of Figure 3-15.

2. Fill in the dialog box and click OK.

These commands are self-explanatory.

Another way to create a simple rule is to choose Tools⇨Organize. The Ways to Organize Inbox panel appears. Starting here, you can move messages from a certain person to a folder or color-code messages as they arrive from a certain person.

Creating complex rules with the Rules Wizard

Use the Rules Wizard to create complex rules that earmark messages with words in the message body or earmark messages sent to distribution lists. You can also create a rule to flag messages automatically or delete a conversation (the original message and all replies).

To run the Rules Wizard, choose Tools⇨Rules and Alerts. You see the Rules and Alerts dialog box. Click the New Rule button and keep clicking Next in the Rules Wizard dialog boxes as you complete the two steps to create a rule:

+ **Step 1:** Choose the rule you want to create or how you want to be alerted in the New Item Alerts window (refer to Figure 3-15).

+ **Step 2:** Click a hyperlink to open a dialog box and describe the rule. For example, click the Specific Words link to open the Search Text dialog box and enter the words that earmark a message. Click the Specified link to open the Rules and Alerts dialog box and choose a folder to move the messages to. You must click each link in the Step 2 box to describe the rule.

To edit a rule, double-click it in the Rules and Alerts dialog box and complete Steps 1 and 2 all over again.

All about E-Mail Folders

Where Outlook e-mail is concerned, everything has its place and everything has its folder. E-mail messages land in the Inbox folder when they arrive. Messages you write go to the Outbox folder until you send them. Copies of e-mail messages you send are kept in the Sent Items folder. And you can create folders of your own for storing e-mail.

If you're one of those unlucky people who receive numerous e-mail messages each day, you owe it to yourself to create folders in which to organize e-mail messages. Create one folder for each project you're working on. That way, you know where to find e-mail messages when you want to reply to or delete them. These pages explain how to move e-mail messages between folders and create folders of your own for storing e-mail.

Moving e-mail messages to different folders

Click to select the message you want to move and use one of these techniques to move an e-mail message to a different folder:

+ **With the Move to Folder button:** Click the Move to Folder button, and on the drop-down list, select a folder. The Move to Folder button is located on the Standard toolbar to the right of the Print button.

+ **With the Move to Folder command:** Choose Edit➪Move to Folder, press Ctrl+Shift+V, or right-click and choose Move to Folder. You see the Move Items dialog box. Select a folder and click OK.

+ **By dragging:** Click the Folder List button, if necessary, to see all the folders; then drag the e-mail message into a different folder.

Earlier in this chapter, "Earmarking messages as they arrive" explains how to move e-mail messages automatically to folders as they are sent to you.

Creating a new folder for storing e-mail

Follow these steps to create a new folder:

1. **Choose File➪New➪Folder.**

   You see the Create New Folder dialog box, as shown in Figure 3-16. You can also open this dialog box by pressing Ctrl+Shift+E or right-clicking a folder in the Folder List and choosing New Folder.

2. **Select the folder that the new folder will go inside.**

   For example, to create a first-level folder, select Personal Folders.

3. **Enter a name for the folder.**

4. **Click OK.**

To delete a folder you created, select it and click the Delete button. Items in the folder are deleted along with the folder itself. To rename a folder, right-click it, choose Rename, and enter a new name.

**Book III
Chapter 3**

**Handling Your
E-Mail**

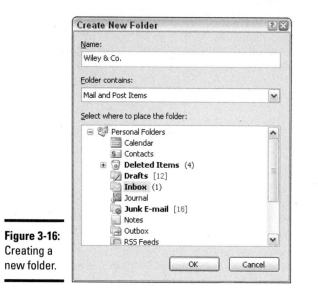

Figure 3-16:
Creating a
new folder.

Yes, You Can Prevent Junk Mail (Sort of)

Outlook maintains a folder called Junk E-Mail especially for storing junk
e-mail, or *spam* as the digital variety is sometimes called. E-mail messages
with certain words or phrases in the Subject line — *for free!*, *money-back
guarantee*, *order now* — are routed automatically to the Junk E-Mail folder,
where they needn't bother you. What's more, you can add senders' names to
the Blocked Senders list and route mail from those senders straight into the
Junk E-Mail folder.

As nice as it is, the Junk E-Mail folder has one fatal flaw — sometimes a legitimate e-mail message finds its way into the folder. From time to time, you
have to look in the Junk E-Mail folder to see whether something of value is in
there — and that sort of defeats the purpose of routing messages automatically to the Junk E-Mail folder. You still have to look through all that junk
e-mail!

Realistically, the only way to prevent getting junk e-mail is to safeguard your
e-mail address. These pages explain the two ways to handle junk e-mail by
using the features inside Outlook and by taking preventative measures to
keep your e-mail address from falling into the wrong hands.

Getting Outlook's help to prevent junk e-mail

Outlook maintains a *Safe Senders* and *Blocked Senders list* to help distinguish e-mail from junk e-mail. To help Outlook recognize junk e-mail and route it to the Junk E-Mail folder, you can take these measures to add addresses to the lists:

✦ **Add a sender to the Safe Senders list:** Senders on this list are deemed legitimate, and their e-mail messages are always routed to the Inbox folder. In the Message window, click the Safe Lists button and choose Add Sender to Safe Senders List on the drop-down list. In a folder, right-click and choose Junk E-Mail⇨Add Sender to Safe Senders List. Choose this option if you find a legitimate e-mail message in the Junk E-Mail folder.

✦ **Add a domain name to the Safe Senders list:** A *domain* is the server from which e-mails are sent or Web sites are hosted. In an e-mail address, the domain name is the part of the address after the at (@) symbol. If you trust e-mail messages from a certain domain, you can accept all messages sent from it. In the Message window, click the Safe Lists button and choose Add Sender's Domain to Safe Senders List on the drop-down list. In a folder, right-click and choose Junk E-Mail⇨Add Sender's Domain to Safe Senders List. In my opinion, this command is useless, as junk e-mailers can commandeer people's e-mail addresses in any domain.

✦ **Add an address to the Blocked Senders list:** E-mail from senders on the Blocked Senders list goes straight to the Junk E-Mail folder. In the Message window, click the Blocked Sender button. In a folder, right-click and choose Junk E-Mail⇨Add Sender to Blocked Senders List.

If you accidentally add an address to the Safe Senders or Blocked Senders list, you can remove it from the list. Choose Tools⇨Options and click the Junk E-Mail button on the Preferences tab of the Options dialog box. You land in the Junk E-Mail Options dialog box. On the Safe Senders or Blocked Senders tab, select the address and click the Remove button.

Follow these steps to tell Outlook how carefully to look for incoming junk e-mail:

1. **Choose Tools⇨Options to open the Options dialog box.**

2. **On the Preferences tab, click the Junk E-Mail button.**

You see the Junk E-Mail Options dialog box.

3. **On the Options tab, choose options to tell Outlook how diligently to look for junk e-mail.**

4. **Click OK.**

Preventative medicine for junk e-mail

As zealous as Outlook is about preventing junk e-mail, the program can't really do the job. Junk e-mailers change addresses frequently. They are clever about putting words in the subject lines of their messages so that the messages aren't recognized as spam. The only foolproof way to keep your e-mail address free of junk e-mail is to safeguard your address. These pages explain how junk e-mailers obtain addresses and show you how to keep your address out of their hands.

How junk e-mailers obtain e-mail addresses

Junk e-mailers can't send spam unless they have e-mail addresses and lots of them. They obtain addresses in different ways. Knowing how they get e-mail addresses can help you keep your address from falling into their clutches. Here are the ways that spammers acquire addresses:

+ **Purchasing e-mail address lists:** These lists are for sale on the Internet. Try searching for "bulk e-mail list" to see what I mean. The people who sell the lists claim that the addresses are "opt-in," meaning that addressees opted, or chose, to make their e-mail addresses available to others. If you ever signed up for something on the Internet and checked the box that said, "I agree to receive offers and opportunities via e-mail from our advertisers," your address is on at least one junk e-mail address list.

+ **Running spamware:** *Spamware* is software designed to assist spammers. Some kinds of spamware can gather addresses from Web sites, newsgroups, and message boards. This software looks for the at symbol (@) on Web pages, copies the words on either side of the at symbol, and in so doing collects e-mail addresses.

+ **Collecting addresses on the Internet:** Some Web sites are actually traps meant to collect e-mail addresses. If you voted for something online, entered a contest or sweepstakes, or took a quiz that required entering your e-mail address, you made your address available to spammers.

+ **Mounting a dictionary attack:** In a *dictionary attack,* names and randomly generated numbers are combined with msn.com, compuserve.com, or another e-mail domain name to form e-mail addresses, and the addresses are sent a test message. If the test message is returned as undeliverable — if it *bounces,* to use e-mail terminology — the address is discarded. But if the test message is delivered, the address is known to be "live." Spam messages are then sent to all live addresses at the e-mail domain.

Preventing junk e-mail from reaching your Inbox

By following the simple rules I describe here, you can keep spammers from discovering your e-mail address and prevent junk-mail from arriving in your

Inbox. These rules are easy to follow. All you have to do is remember them and stick to them:

✦ **Use a secondary e-mail address:** Create a secondary e-mail account and give its e-mail address to businesses and merchants on the Internet who might sell your address to spammers or might themselves be spammers. The Internet offers many places to create free Web-based e-mail accounts. For example, check out Gmail (`http://gmail.google.com`), Hotmail (`www.hotmail.com`), and Yahoo! Mail (`http://mail.yahoo.com`). Never give your primary e-mail address to strangers.

✦ **Don't reply to spam:** Don't reply to junk e-mail messages under any circumstances. By replying, all you do is alert the spammer to the fact that your e-mail address is legitimate, and that makes you a target of even more spam.

✦ **Don't unsubscribe to junk e-mail messages:** Some spam messages contain an Unsubscribe link that you can click to prevent more messages from coming. The links are a ruse. All you do by clicking them is make spammers aware that your e-mail address is live and therefore, worth targeting with more spam.

✦ **Don't buy anything advertised by spam:** Even if the message is selling what looks to be a terrific bargain, resist the temptation. By buying, you expose yourself to all the risks of replying to junk e-mail.

✦ **Don't be fooled by sneaky spam:** Junk e-mailers are very good about disguising what they do. They have to be because spam-filtering software is good at recognizing it. When certain words — *sale, free, bargain,* and others — appear in the subject line of messages or in the messages themselves, Outlook flags them automatically as junk e-mail. To get around this obstacle, spammers sometimes write business-like message headings to trick you into opening messages: *This Needs Your Attention, Urgent and Confidential, Meeting Agenda.* Some message headings play on the fact that many people order items online: *Your Order #31334, Confirmation of Purchase.*

✦ **Be careful where (and how) you post your e-mail address:** Spammers gather e-mail addresses from the Internet. They get the addresses from Web pages, newsgroups, chat rooms, and message boards. Harvestware, a variety of spamware, can scour the Internet for the tell-tale at symbol (@) found in e-mail addresses and copy those addresses back to a spammer's computer. If you have to post your e-mail address on the Internet, get around the problem by putting blank spaces between the letters in your address, or spell out the address like so:

```
johndoe at earthlink dot net
```

+ **Try to choose an address that's not subject to dictionary attacks:** As I explain earlier in this chapter, a dictionary attack is a technique spammers use to generate e-mail addresses. To generate them, common names are randomly assigned number combinations and then joined to a domain name. To keep your e-mail address from being subjected to dictionary attacks, choose an uncommon name for your address.

Chapter 4: Managing Your Time and Schedule

In This Chapter

✔ Understanding how the Calendar works

✔ Going to different dates in the Calendar

✔ Scheduling appointments and events

✔ Rescheduling an activity

✔ Getting different views of your schedule

✔ Customizing the Calendar window

The purpose of the Outlook Calendar is to keep you from arriving a day late and a dollar short. Use the Calendar to schedule meetings and appointments. Use it to make the most of your time. This chapter explains how to go from day to day, week to week, and month to month in the Calendar window. It shows you how to schedule and reschedule appointments and meetings, look at your schedule in different ways, and customize the Calendar.

Introducing the Calendar

Use the Calendar to juggle appointments and meetings, remind yourself where you're supposed to be, and get there on time. Surveying your schedule in the Calendar window is easy. Merely by clicking a button, you can tell where you're supposed to be today, any given day, this week, this work week, this month, or any month. Figure 4-1 shows, for example, someone's schedule during the work week of August 14–18 (a work week comprises Monday through Friday, not Monday through Sunday). All you have to do to find out how busy you are on a particular day, week, or month is gaze at the Calendar window. Whether someone invites you to a meeting or wants to schedule an appointment, you can open the Calendar and see right away if your schedule permits you to attend the meeting or make the appointment.

Date Navigator   Click to change views.

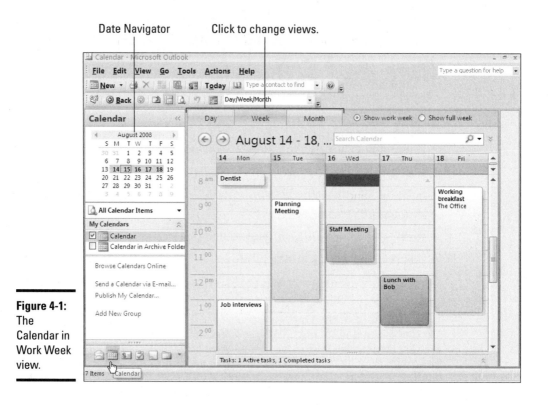

Figure 4-1:
The
Calendar in
Work Week
view.

Outlook gives you opportunities to categorize meetings and appointments so that you can tell at a glance what they're all about. Moving a meeting or appointment is simply a matter of dragging it elsewhere in the Calendar window. By double-clicking a meeting or appointment in the Calendar window, you can open a window to find out where the meeting takes place or read notes you jotted down about the meeting. You can even make a bell ring and the Reminder message box appear when a meeting or appointment is forthcoming.

To make the Task List, an abbreviated Tasks window, appear below the Calendar window, choose View➪Daily Task List➪Normal. Chapter 5 of this mini-book explains how to schedule tasks in the Tasks window.

The Different Kinds of Activities

For scheduling purposes, Outlook makes a distinction between appointments, events, and meetings. Meetings, however, aren't everybody's concern. If your computer is connected to a network and the network uses the Microsoft Exchange Server, you can use Outlook to invite colleagues on the network to come to meetings. But if your computer isn't on a network, don't bother with meetings. Schedule appointments and events instead. You can schedule the following activities:

✦ **Appointment:** An activity that occupies a certain time period on a certain day. For example, a meeting that takes place between 11 a.m. and 12 p.m. is an appointment.

✦ **Recurring appointment:** An appointment that takes place daily, weekly, or monthly on the same day and same time each day, week, or month. A weekly staff meeting is a recurring appointment. The beauty of recurring appointments is that Outlook enters them weeks and months in advance in the Calendar window. You don't have to re-enter these appointments over and over.

✦ **Event:** An activity that lasts all day. A trade show, for example, is an event. A birthday is an event. A day spent on vacation is also an event (is it ever!). On the Calendar, events and recurring events appear first.

✦ **Recurring event:** An all-day activity that takes place each week, month, or year. Unromantic (or forgetful) users of Outlook are hereby advised to schedule these recurring events in the Calendar: Valentine's Day, their significant other's birthday, and first-date and wedding anniversaries. Thanks to Outlook, no one will ever accuse you again of being cold-hearted or indifferent.

✦ **Meeting:** Same as an appointment except that you can invite others to attend. Scheduling meetings isn't covered in this book. See your network administrator for details.

Going to a Different Day, Week, or Month

Days on which meetings or appointments are scheduled appear in boldface in the *Date Navigator,* the calendar in the upper-left corner of the window (refer to Figure 4-1). Here are all the different ways to go to different days, weeks, or months in the Calendar window:

✦ **To today:** Click the Today button on the Standard toolbar.

✦ **To a specific day:** Click a day in the Date Navigator. You can also press Ctrl+G and select a day in the Go To Date dialog box. In some views, you can press Alt+Page Up or Alt+Page Down to go backward or forward by a month.

✦ **To a different month:** Click an arrow beside the month name in the Date Navigator to go backward or forward by a month. Here's a quick way to go from month to month in the Calendar: Click the month name in the Date Navigator and hold down the mouse button. You see a list of month names. Drag the pointer to the name of the month you want to go to.

Reconfiguring the Calendar

Unless you change settings, the Calendar work week begins on Monday; in Day view and Week view, the earliest timeslot you see before you begin scrolling is 8:00 a.m. If these settings don't accurately reflect the days and hours in which you work, you can change them by following these steps:

1. **Choose Tools⇨Options.**

   You see the Options dialog box.

2. **On the Preferences tab, click the Calendar Options button.**

The Calendar Options dialog box appears.

3. **Under Calendar Work Week, select the day of the week on which your work week starts, what you consider the first day of the week, and what time you want the Calendar to list first in Day view and Week view.**

4. **Click OK in the Calendar Options dialog box and then click OK in the Options dialog box.**

Calendar Options   ? ✕

Calendar work week

☐ Sun   ☑ Mon   ☑ Tue   ☑ Wed   ☑ Thu   ☑ Fri   ☐ Sat

First day of week: Sunday ▾   Start time: 8:00 AM ▾

First week of year: Starts on Jan 1 ▾   End time: 12:01 AM ▾

Calendar options

☑ Show "click to add" prompts on the calendar

☐ Show week numbers in the Month View and Date Navigator

☑ Allow attendees to propose new times for meetings you organize

Use this response when you propose new meeting times: Tentative ▾

Default color: ▾   Planner Options...   Add Holidays...

☐ Use selected color on all calendars

Advanced options

☑ Enable alternate calendar: English ▾   Gregorian ▾   Options...

☑ When sending meeting requests over the Internet, use iCalendar format

Free/Busy Options...   Resource Scheduling...   Time Zone...

OK   Cancel

Use the scroll bar on the right side of the window to travel from hour to hour in Day view and Work Week view. In Week view and Month view, manipulating the scroll bar takes you from week to week.

Scheduling an Activity

Now that you know how the Calendar works, the next step is to fill the pages of the Calendar with all kinds of busywork. These pages explain how to schedule activities, schedule recurring activities, and magically transform an e-mail message into a Calendar item. You can find many intriguing shortcuts on these pages.

Scheduling an activity: The basics

Follow these basic steps to schedule an appointment, recurring appointment, event, or recurring event:

1. **Select the day in which you want to schedule the activity.**

If the activity occupies a certain time period, you can select the time period in Day or Week view and save yourself the trouble of entering a time period in the Appointment dialog box. To select a time period, drag downward in the Calendar window. To create a half-hour appointment, simply double-click a half-hour slot in Day or Week view. The Appointment dialog box opens with the Start and End time entered already.

2. **Click the New Appointment button, press Ctrl+N, or choose Actions⇨New Appointment.**

As shown in Figure 4-2, you see the Appointment window for naming the activity, stating its starting and ending time, and choosing whether you want to be alerted to its occurrence. When you double-click an appointment or event in the Calendar window, this is the window you see.

3. **Enter information in the form.**

Enter a subject, location (you can open the drop-down list and choose one you've entered before), start date and time, and end date and time. To enter a recurring event or appointment, click the Recurrence button. To enter an event instead of an appointment, click the All Day Event check box.

If the appointment time you enter conflicts with an appointment you've already scheduled, the Appointment window tells you as much. You can click the Calendar button to view the calendar and look for open timeslots.

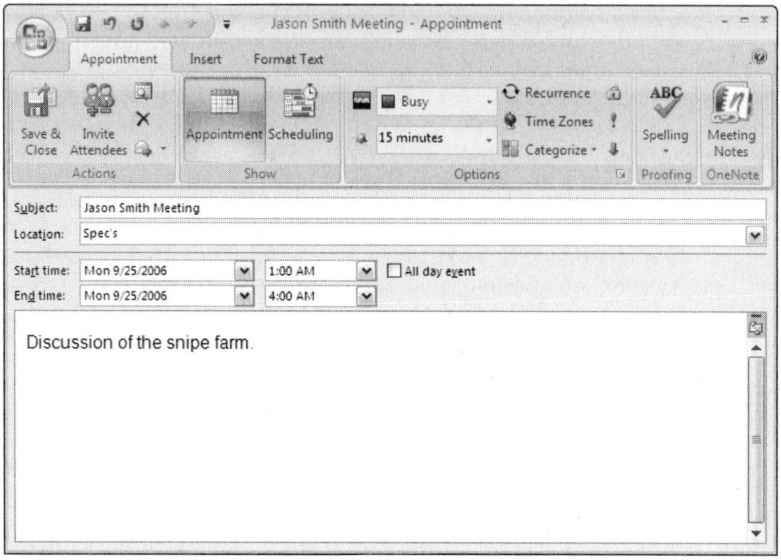

Figure 4-2:
The window
for
scheduling
activities.

4. **Open the Reminder drop-down list and choose an option if you want to be reminded when the activity is imminent (or choose None if you don't care to be reminded).**

   Choose an option from the drop-down list to make the Reminder message box appear before the activity begins. Chapter 5 of this mini-book explains how reminders work.

5. **Click the Save & Close button when you're finished describing the appointment or event.**

   The appointment or event is entered in the Calendar window.

Scheduling a recurring appointment or event

To enter a recurring appointment or event, click the Recurrence button in the Appointment window (refer to Figure 4-2). You see the Appointment Recurrence dialog box, as shown in Figure 4-3. Describe how persistent the activity is and click OK:

✦ **Appointment Time:** Enter the starting and ending time, if you didn't do so already in the Appointment form.

✦ **Recurrence Pattern:** Use the options and drop-down lists to describe how often the activity recurs.

✦ **Range of Recurrence:** Describe when the recurring events will cease recurring. Choose the No End Date option button if the activity occurs *ad infinitum, ad nauseum* (that's Latin for "unto infinity, most nauseously").

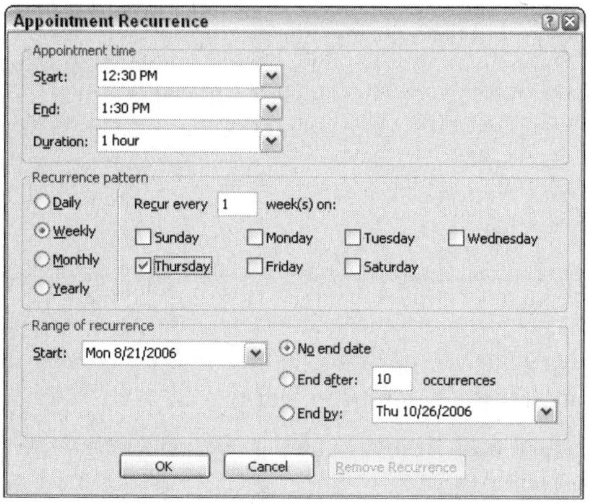

Figure 4-3:
My, this appointment is persistent!

In the Calendar window, recurring activities are marked by the arrow chasing its tail icon. To change a recurring activity into a one-time activity, click the Recurrence button, and in the Appointment Recurrence dialog box, click the Remove Recurrence button.

Scheduling an event

Select the All Day Event check box in the Appointment window (refer to Figure 4-2) to schedule an event, not an appointment. As I explain earlier, an event is an activity that lasts all day. You can choose Actions➪New All Day Event to open the Event dialog box straightaway.

Canceling, Rescheduling, and Altering Activities

Canceling, rescheduling, and altering appointments and events are pretty easy. You can always double-click an activity to open an Appointment or Event window and change the particulars there. And you can take advantage of these shortcuts:

✦ **Canceling:** Select an activity and click the Delete button. When you cancel a recurring activity, a dialog box asks whether you want to delete all occurrences of the activity or just the activity on the day you selected. Click an option button and click OK.

Using an e-mail message to schedule an appointment

Here's a neat little trick that can save you time when e-mail correspondence has to do with scheduling an appointment. To get a head start on scheduling, drag the e-mail message from the Inbox window over the Calendar button on the Navigation pane. On the theory that you want to schedule an appointment around the information in the e-mail message, the Appointment window appears on-screen. For the subject of the appointment, Outlook enters the subject of the e-mail message. The text of the e-mail message appears in the window as well. Fiddle with the particulars of the appointment and click the Save & Close button.

   ✦ **Rescheduling:** Drag the activity to a new location on the schedule. Release the mouse button when the activity is in the new timeslot.

   ✦ **Changing start and end times:** In Day or Work Week view, move the pointer over the top or bottom of the activity and start dragging when you see the double arrow.

   ✦ **Changing the description:** Click in the activity's box and start typing or editing.

Getting a Better View of Your Schedule

Here are the various and sundry ways to organize and view the activities you so patiently entered in the Calendar window:

   ✦ **Change Calendar views:** Click one of the three View buttons — Day, Week (work week or full week), or Month — to read the fine print or get the bird's-eye view of activities you've scheduled in the Calendar window.

   ✦ **Change views of the Calendar window:** Open the Current View drop-down list and choose Events, Recurring Appointments, or another view to isolate certain kinds of activities.

   ✦ **Categorize messages:** Assign activities to categories and then arrange activities by category in the Calendar window. To do so, choose By Category in the Current View drop-down list. Chapter 1 of this mini-book explains categorizing.

Customizing the Outlook Calendar Window

In case you're in the mood to redecorate, here are a couple of ways to customize Outlook:

✦ **Changing fonts and font sizes:** To change the look of the letters in the Calendar window, right-click an empty spot in the window and choose Other Settings. You see the Format dialog box. Starting here, you can click font buttons to change fonts and font sizes in different parts of the Calendar window.

✦ **Changing the background color:** To choose a background color for the Calendar window, choose Tools➪Options, and on the Preferences tab of the Options dialog box, click the Calendar Options button. You see the Calendar Options dialog box. Choose a new color from the Default Color drop-down list.

**Book III
Chapter 4**

**Managing Your
Time and Schedule**

Chapter 5: Tasks, Reminders, and Notes

In This Chapter

✓ Creating, handling, and managing tasks

✓ Being reminded when deadlines and activities are forthcoming

✓ Jotting down digital notes

*T*his short chapter describes some Outlook goodies that were neglected in the other chapters of this mini-book. It explains how the Tasks window can help you meet your deadlines and how to be alerted when an activity is looming, a task deadline is arriving, an e-mail needs your attention, or someone in your Contacts folder needs love and attention. Finally, it explains Outlook's digital stick 'em notes.

Tasks: Seeing What Needs to Get Done

As shown in Figure 5-1, use the Tasks window to see what needs to be done, when it's due, and whether it's overdue. On this list, due dates clearly show how smartly the whip is being cracked and how close you are to meeting or missing deadlines. A gray line appears across tasks that are done. Tasks that are overdue appear in red. Read on if you want to find out how to enter a task, attach a file to a task, and manage tasks in the Tasks window.

The best way to examine tasks is to display the Reading pane and move it to the bottom of the Tasks window. This way, you can select a task and read notes you've made about it, as shown in Figure 5-1. To display the Reading pane along the bottom of the Tasks window, choose View⇨Reading Pane⇨ Bottom.

Select a task.

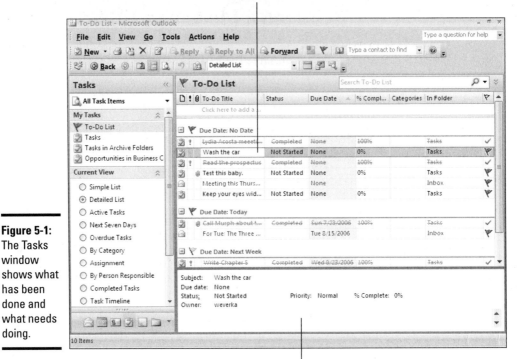

Figure 5-1:
Figure 5-1:
The Tasks
window
shows what
has been
done and
what needs
doing.

Examine it in the Reading pane.

Entering a task in the Tasks window

Outlook offers two ways to enter a task in the Tasks window:

✦ **The fast way:** Click at the top of the window where it says "Click here to add a new Task," type a few words to describe the task, press the Tab key to go to the Due Date box, and enter the due date there. To enter the date, type it or open the drop-down calendar and choose a date there.

✦ **The slow but thorough way:** Click the New button, press Ctrl+N, or choose Actions⇨New Task. You see the Task window, as shown in Figure 5-2. On this window are places for describing the task, entering start and due dates, describing the task's status, prioritizing the task, and jotting down notes about it. Click the Save & Close button when you're finished describing the task.

Attaching a file to a task

Attaching a file to a task is a neat way to get down to work quickly. Instead of fumbling in your computer for a Word document, Excel worksheet, or other type of file to work on, you can open it merely by double-clicking its name in the Tasks window or Reading pane of the Tasks folder. To attach a file to a task, go to the Insert tab in the Task window and click the Attach File button. Then, in the Insert File dialog box, select the file and click the Insert button.

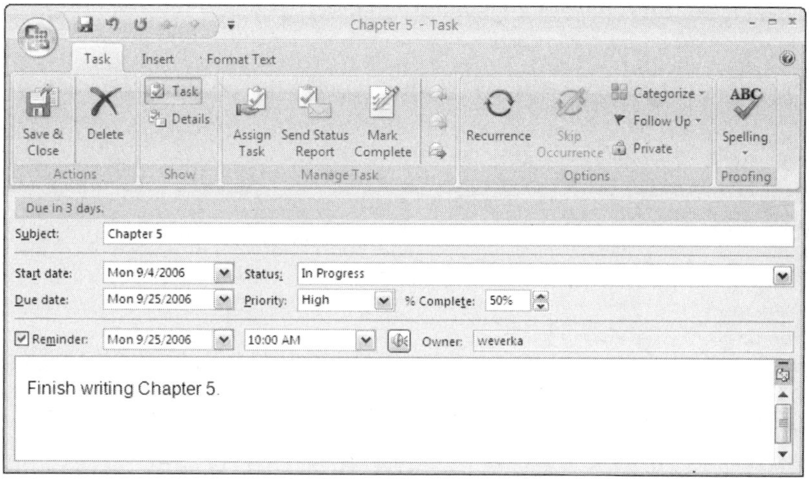

Figure 5-2:
Describing
a task.

**Book III
Chapter 5**

**Tasks, Reminders,
and Notes**

By clicking the Recurrence button in the Task window, you can enter a Sisyphean task that gets repeated over and over again. In the Task Recurrence dialog box, describe how often the task recurs. Recurring tasks are marked in the Tasks window with an unusual icon. What is that? Looks to me like a clipboard with a piece of toilet paper stuck to it.

Click the Details button in the Task window to track the hours you worked on a project, the companies you worked for, and how many miles you logged going to and fro in your work.

Examining tasks in the Tasks window

Juggling many different tasks is a high art, and to help you get better at it, the Tasks window offers these techniques for examining tasks that need doing:

✦ **Choose To-Do List or Tasks in the Tasks pane:** Under My Tasks in the upper-left corner of the Tasks window, choose To-Do List to examine all tasks, including those you fashioned from e-mail messages and Calendar appointments; choose Tasks to see only the tasks you set for yourself in the Tasks folder.

✦ **Change views:** In the Tasks pane or on the Current View drop-down list, choose a View option. For example, choose Overdue Tasks or Next Seven Days to focus on the tasks that *really* need doing.

Handling and managing tasks

When the time comes to manage the tasks in the Tasks window, I hope you are a stern taskmaster. Here's advice for handling and managing tasks:

✦ **Marking a task as complete:** Click the check box beside the task name in the Tasks window. Outlook draws a line through completed tasks.

 ✦ **Deleting a task:** Select the task and then click the Delete button or press Ctrl+D.

✦ **Editing a task:** Double-click a task in the Tasks window to open the Task window and change the particulars there.

Reminders for Being Alerted to Activities and Tasks

Outlook offers the Reminder message box to alert you when an appointment or event from the Calendar is about to take place (see Chapter 4 of this mini-book), when a task deadline is looming (see the preceding section in this chapter), when an e-mail message needs a reply (see Chapter 3 of this mini-book), or when someone whose name is in your Contacts folder needs attention (see Chapter 2 of this mini-book). Figure 5-3 shows the Reminder message box. When Outlook is running and you least expect it, a Reminder message box similar to the one in the figure may appear to keep you on your toes.

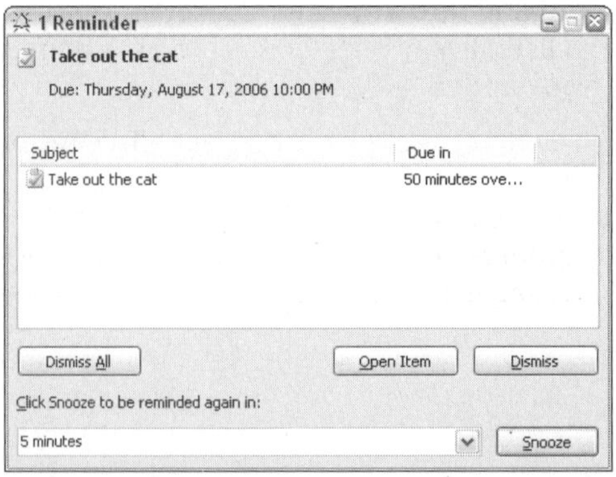

Figure 5-3: The Reminder message box.

Do the following in the Reminder message box to handle a reminder:

✦ **Dismiss it:** Click the Dismiss button to shelve the reminder notice. If more than one notice appears in the Reminder message box and you want to erase them all, click the Dismiss All button.

✦ **Be reminded later:** Click the Snooze button. The Click Snooze to Be Reminded Again In text box tells you when the next reminder message will arrive. To change this setting, open the drop-down list and choose a different time period.

✦ **Open the item:** Click the Open Item button to examine the appointment, task, e-mail message, or contact to which the reminder pertains.

✦ **Procrastinate:** Click the Close button (the *X*) in the Reminder message box to make it disappear. To open the message box later, choose View⇨Reminders Window.

Reminders work only for items that are stored in these folders: Tasks, Calendar, Inbox, and Contacts. Store an item in another folder or a subfolder of one of the folders I just named, and you won't see the Reminder message box when the reminder is due. To make sure you get reminded, store items in these folders: Tasks, Calendar, Inbox, or Contacts.

Scheduling a reminder message

Follow these instructions to schedule a reminder message:

✦ **Calendar appointment or event:** In the Appointment or Event window, open the Reminder drop-down list and choose how many minutes, hours, or weeks in advance to make the reminder appear.

✦ **Task deadline:** In the Task window (refer to Figure 5-2), select the Reminder check box and choose a time period in the drop-down list.

✦ **E-mail message:** If you're in the Message window, click the Follow Up button and choose Add Reminder on the drop-down list; in the Inbox window, right-click the message and choose Follow Up⇨Add Reminder. You see the Custom dialog box. Choose a date and time in the Start and Due Date drop-down lists. If you enter a date but not a time, the Reminder message box appears at 5:00 p.m.

✦ **Contacts name:** In a Contact window, click the Follow Up button and choose Add Reminder on the drop-down list; in the Contacts window, right-click a contact name and choose Follow Up⇨Add Reminder. The Custom dialog box appears. Treat this dialog box the same way you treat the one for e-mail messages (see the preceding item in this list).

Making reminders work your way

You can do two or three things to make reminders work your way:

+ **Changing the reminder time for appointments and events:** By default, the Reminder message box appears 15 minutes before appointments and events start. To change this setting, choose Tools⇨Options, and on the Preferences tab of the Options dialog box, enter a new setting in the Default Reminder drop-down list.

+ **Changing the default time for task reminders:** When a task's deadline arrives, the Reminders dialog box lets you know at 8:00 a.m. (or when you start Outlook, if you start the program after 8:00 a.m.). To change this default setting, choose Tools⇨Options, and in the Preferences tab of the Options dialog box, choose a new time from the Reminder Time drop-down list.

+ **Play a different sound (or no sound):** By default, you hear a little chime when the Reminder message box appears on-screen. To hear a different sound or no sound at all, choose Tools⇨Options and then select the Other tab in the Options dialog box. Next, click the Advanced Options button, and in the Advanced Options dialog box, click the Reminder Options button. You arrive — at last — at the Reminder Options dialog box. To play no sound, deselect the Play Reminder Sound check box. To play a different sound, click the Browse button and then select a .wav sound file in the Reminder Sound File dialog box.

Making Notes to Yourself

As shown in Figure 5-4, notes resemble the yellow stick 'em notes that you often see affixed to manuscripts and refrigerator doors. Click the Notes button on the Navigation pane to go to the Notes window. Write a note to mark down a deadline, for example, or remind you to take out the cat. Here are instructions for doing all and sundry with notes:

+ **Creating a note:** Click the New Note button and then type the note in the Note window. Then click outside the window.

+ **Opening a note:** Double-click a note to read it in its Note window.

+ **Forwarding a note:** To forward a note to someone in an e-mail message, right-click the note and choose Forward. A Message window opens so that you can address the message. The note arrives in the form of a file attachment, and the recipient must have Outlook in order to read it.

+ **Deleting a note:** Select the note and click the Delete button or press the Delete key.

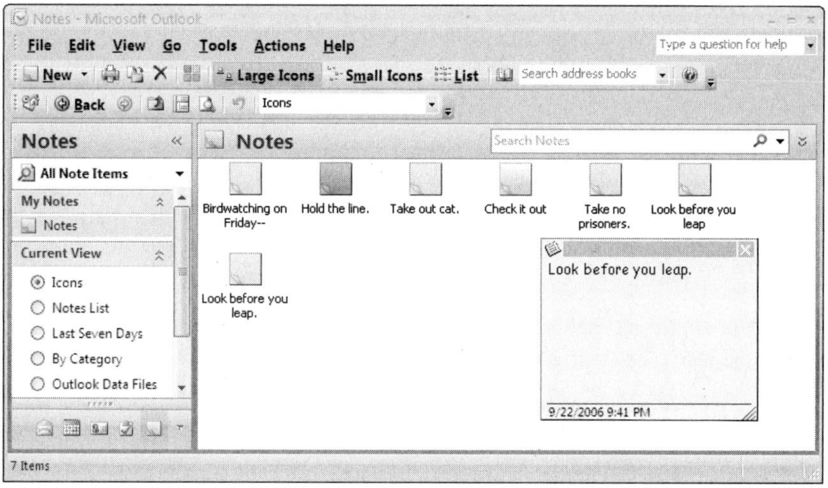

Figure 5-4:
Notes, notes, and more notes.

Book IV

PowerPoint 2007

The 5th Wave   By Rich Tennant

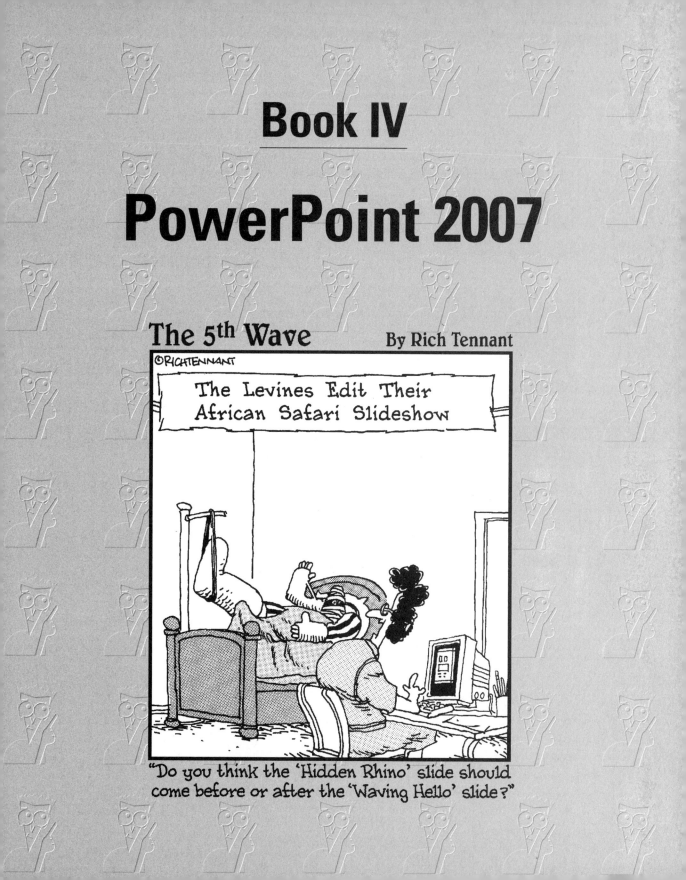

"Do you think the 'Hidden Rhino' slide should come before or after the 'Waving Hello' slide?"

Contents at a Glance

Chapter 1: Getting Started in PowerPoint

In This Chapter

✔ **Introducing PowerPoint**

✔ **Finding your way around the screen**

✔ **Understanding what creating a presentation is all about**

✔ **Creating a presentation**

✔ **Inserting the slides**

✔ **Changing views of the screen**

✔ **Rearranging the Slides and Notes panes**

✔ **Manipulating slides**

✔ **Creating a photo album**

✔ **Hiding slides for use in a presentation**

*I*t's impossible to sit through a conference, seminar, or trade show these days without seeing at least one PowerPoint presentation. PowerPoint has found its way into nearly every office and boardroom. I've heard of a man — a very unromantic man — who proposed to his wife by way of a PowerPoint presentation.

As nice as PowerPoint can be, it has its detractors. If the software isn't used properly, it can come between the speaker and the audience. In an article in the May 28, 2001, *New Yorker* titled "Absolute PowerPoint: Can a Software Package Edit Our Thoughts?," Ian Parker argued that PowerPoint may actually be more of a hindrance than a help in communicating. PowerPoint, Parker wrote, is "a social instrument, turning middle managers into bullet-point dandies." The software, he added, "has a private, interior influence. It edits ideas . . . . It helps you make a case, but also makes its own case about how to organize information, how to look at the world."

To make sure that you use PowerPoint wisely, this chapter shows what creating a PowerPoint presentation entails. After a brief tour of PowerPoint, you find out how to create presentations, get a better view of your work, insert slides, put together a photo album, and hide slides.

Getting Acquainted with PowerPoint

Figure 1-1 (top) shows the PowerPoint window. That thing in the middle is a *slide,* the PowerPoint word for an image that you show your audience. Surrounding the slide are many tools for entering text and decorating slides. When the time comes to show your slides, you dispense with the tools and make the slide fill the screen, as shown in Figure 1-1 (bottom).

To make PowerPoint do your bidding, you need to know a little jargon:

✦ **Presentation:** All the slides, from start to finish, that you show your audience. Sometimes presentations are called *slides shows.* Presentations are saved in presentation files (`.pptx` files).

✦ **Slides:** The images you create with PowerPoint. During a presentation, slides appear on-screen one after the other. Don't be put off by the word *slide* and dreary memories of sitting through your uncle's slide show vacation memories. You don't need a slide projector to show these slides. You can now plug a laptop or other computer into special monitors that display PowerPoint slides.

✦ **Notes:** Printed pages that you, the speaker, write and print so that you know what to say during a presentation. Only the speaker sees notes. Chapter 5 in this mini-book explains notes.

✦ **Handout:** Printed pages that you may give to the audience along with a presentation. A handout shows the slides in the presentation. Handouts are also known by the somewhat derogatory term *leave-behinds.* Chapter 5 of this mini-book explains handouts.

A Brief Geography Lesson

Here is a brief geography lesson about the different parts of a PowerPoint screen. I'd hate for you to get lost in PowerPoint Land. Figure 1-2 shows the different parts of the screen. Fold down the corner of this page so that you can return here if screen terminology confuses you:

✦ **Office button:** The round button you can click to open a menu with commands for creating, opening, and saving PowerPoint presentations, as well as doing other file-management tasks.

✦ **Quick Access toolbar:** A toolbar with four buttons — Save, Undo, Repeat, and Print. You see this toolbar wherever you go in PowerPoint.

✦ **Ribbon:** The place where the tabs are located. Click a tab — Home, Insert, Design, Animations, Slide Show, Review, or View — to start a task.

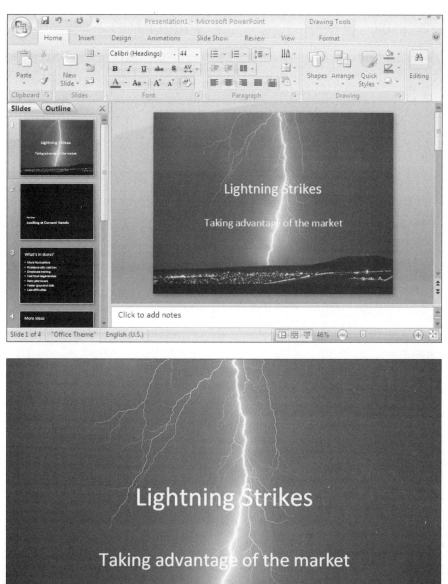

Figure 1-1:
The
PowerPoint
window
(top) and a
slide as it
looks in a
presentation
(bottom).

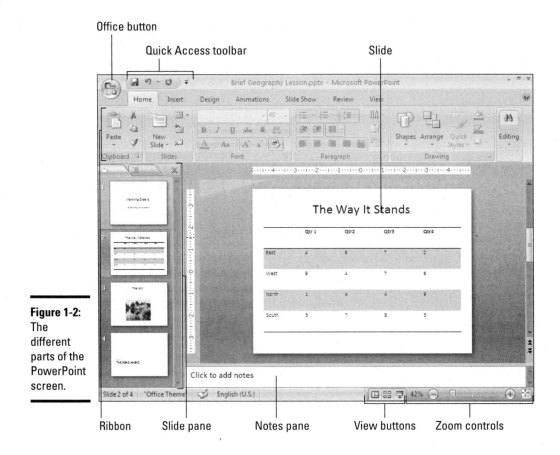

Office button

Quick Access toolbar

Slide

Figure 1-2:
The different parts of the PowerPoint screen.

Ribbon   Slide pane   Notes pane   View buttons   Zoom controls

✦ **Slides pane:** In Normal view, the place on the left side of the screen where you can see the slides or the text on the slides in your presentation. Scroll in the Slides pane to move backward and forward in a presentation.

✦ **Slide window:** Where a slide (in Normal view) or slides (in Slide Sorter view) are displayed. Scroll to move backward or forward in your presentation.

✦ **Notes pane:** Where you type notes (in Normal view) that you can refer to when giving your presentation. The audience can't see these notes — they're for you and you alone. See Chapter 5 of this mini-book for details.

✦ **View buttons:** Buttons you can click to switch to (from left to right) Normal, Slide Sorter, and Slide Show view. See "Getting a Better View of Your Work" later in this chapter.

✦ **Zoom controls:** Tools for enlarging or shrinking a slide (in Normal view).

A Whirlwind Tour of PowerPoint

To help you understand what you're getting into, you're invited on a whirlwind tour of PowerPoint. Creating a PowerPoint presentation entails completing these basic tasks:

✦ **Creating the slides:** After you create a new presentation, your next task is to insert the slides. PowerPoint offers many preformatted slide layouts, each one designed for presenting information a certain way.

✦ **Notes:** As you create slides, you can jot down notes in the Notes pane. You can use these notes later to formulate your presentation and decide what you're going to say to your audience while each slide is on-screen (see Chapter 5 of this mini-book).

✦ **Designing your presentation**: After you create a presentation, the next step is to think about its appearance. You can change slides' colors and backgrounds, as well as choose a *theme* for your presentation — an all-encompassing design that applies to all (or most of) the slides (see Chapter 2 of this mini-book).

✦ **Inserting tables, charts, diagrams, and shapes:** A PowerPoint presentation should be more than a loose collection of bulleted lists. Starting on the Insert tab, you can place tables, charts, and diagrams on slides, as well as adorn your slides with text boxes, WordArt images, and shapes (see Chapter 4 of this mini-book).

✦ **"Animating" your slides:** PowerPoint slides can play video and sound, as well as be "animated" (see Chapter 4 of this mini-book). You can make the items on a slide move on the screen. As a slide arrives, you can make it spin or flash.

✦ **Delivering your presentation:** During a presentation, you can draw on the slides. You can also blank the screen and show slides out of order. In case you can't be there in person, PowerPoint gives you the opportunity to create self-running presentations and presentations that others can run on their own. You can also distribute presentations on CDs and post them on the Internet (see Chapter 5 of this mini-book).

Creating a New Presentation

When you start PowerPoint, the program creates a new, blank presentation just for you. You can make this bare-bones presentation the starting point for constructing your presentation, or you can get a more sophisticated, fully realized layout and design by starting with a template. Templates are a mixed blessing. They're designed by artists and they look very good. Some templates come with *boilerplate text* — already written material that you can recycle into your presentation. However, presentations made from templates are harder to modify. Sometimes the design gets in the way. As well, a loud or intricate background may overwhelm the diagram or chart you want to put on a slide.

 No matter what kind of presentation you want, you can start creating it by clicking the Office button and choosing New on the menu (or pressing Ctrl+N). You see the New Presentation dialog box, as shown in Figure 1-3. Use one of these techniques to create a presentation:

✦ **Blank presentation:** Double-click the Blank Presentation icon. A new presentation appears. Try visiting the Design tab and choosing a theme or background style to get a taste of all the things you can do to decorate a presentation.

✦ **Presentation from a template:** You have considerably more choices if you want to create your presentation from a template:

Find a template.   Go forward or backward in your search.

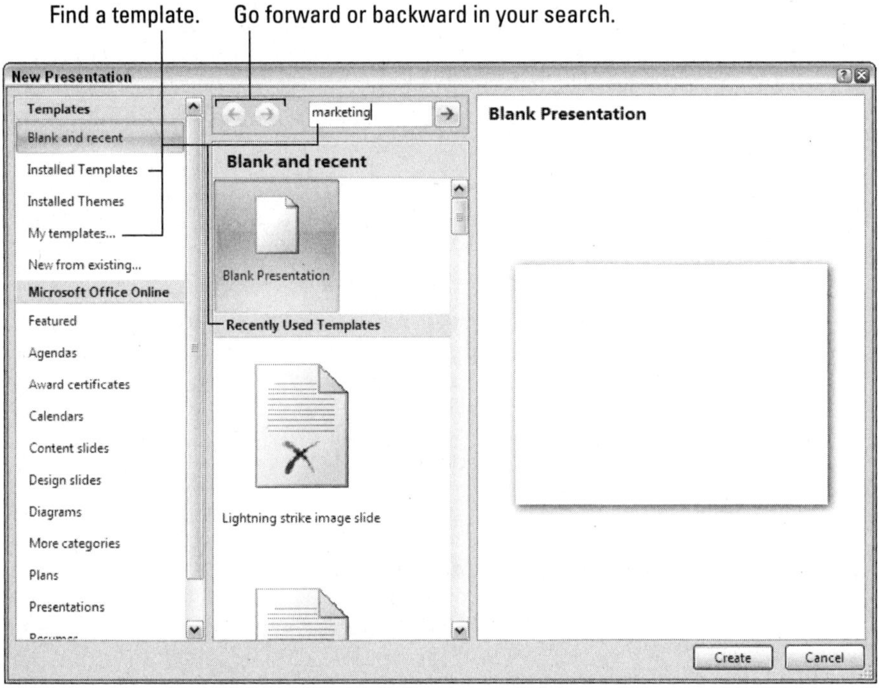

Figure 1-3:
The New Presentation dialog box is the starting point for creating a presentation.

- *Use a template on your computer:* Click Installed Templates (you can find this button under Templates in the upper-right corner of the dialog box). Templates that you loaded on your computer when you installed PowerPoint appear in the dialog box. Double-click a template to create a presentation.

- *Search for a template online at Microsoft:* Enter a search term in the Search box, make sure your computer is connected to the Internet, and click the Start Searching button. Templates appear in the dialog box. Click a template to examine it. Double-click a template to download and use it to create a presentation.

- *Use a template you created (or downloaded earlier from Microsoft):* Click the My Templates button. The New Presentation dialog box appears. Select a template and click OK.

- *Select a recently used template:* Click a template name in the middle of the dialog box if you want to use a template listed there.

✦ **Recycle another presentation:** If you can use another presentation as the starting point for creating a new presentation, nab slides from the other presentation. Click the New from Existing button. In the New from Existing Presentation dialog box, select the presentation and click the Create New button.

If you intend to create a presentation from photos you took of a vacation or family reunion, consider creating a photo album. See "Putting Together a Photo Album" later in this chapter.

Advice for Building Persuasive Presentations

Before you create any slides, think about what you want to communicate to your audience. Your goal isn't to dazzle the audience with your PowerPoint skills, but communicate something — a company policy, the merits of a product, the virtues of a strategic plan. Your goal is to bring the audience around to your side. To that end, here is some practical advice for building persuasive presentations:

✦ **Start by writing the text in Word:** Start in Microsoft Word — not PowerPoint — so you can focus on the words. In Word, you can clearly see how a presentation develops. You can make sure that your presentation builds to its rightful conclusion. PowerPoint has a special command for getting headings from a Word file. (See "Conjuring slides from Word document headings" later in this chapter.)

✦ **When choosing a design, consider the audience:** A presentation to the American Casketmakers Association calls for a mute, quiet design; a

Book IV
Chapter 1

Getting Started in
PowerPoint

presentation to the Cheerleaders of Tomorrow calls for something bright and splashy. Select a slide design that sets the tone for your presentation and wins the sympathy of the audience.

✦ **Keep it simple:** To make sure that PowerPoint doesn't upstage you, keep it simple. Make use of the PowerPoint features, but do so judiciously. An animation in the right place at the right time can serve a valuable purpose. It can highlight an important part of a presentation and grab the audience's attention. But stuffing a presentation with too many gizmos turns a presentation into a carnival sideshow and distracts from your message.

✦ **Follow the one-slide-per-minute rule:** At the very minimum, a slide should stay on-screen for at least one minute. If you have 15 minutes to speak, you're allotted no more than 15 slides for your presentation, according to the rule.

✦ **Beware the bullet point:** Terse bullet points have their place in a presentation, but if you put them there strictly to remind yourself what to say next, you're doing your audience a disfavor. Bullet points can cause drowsiness. They can be a distraction. The audience skims the bullets when it should be attending to your voice and the argument you're making. When you're tempted to use a bulleted list, consider using a table, chart, or diagram instead. Figure 1-4 demonstrates how a bulleted list can be presented instead in a table, chart, or diagram.

✦ **Take control from the start:** Spend the first minute introducing yourself to the audience without running PowerPoint (or, if you do run PowerPoint, put a simple slide with your company name or logo on-screen). Make eye contact with the audience. This way, you establish your credibility. You give the audience a chance to get to know you.

✦ **Make clear what you're about:** In the early going, state very clearly what your presentation is about and what you intend to prove with your presentation. In other words, state the conclusion at the beginning as well as the end. This way, your audience knows exactly what you're driving at and can judge your presentation according to how well you build your case.

✦ **Personalize the presentation:** Make the presentation a personal one. Tell the audience what *your* personal reason for being there is or why *you* work for the company you work for. Knowing that you have a personal stake in the presentation, the audience is more likely to trust you. The audience understands that you're not a spokesperson, but a *speaker* — someone who has come before them to make a case for something that you believe in.

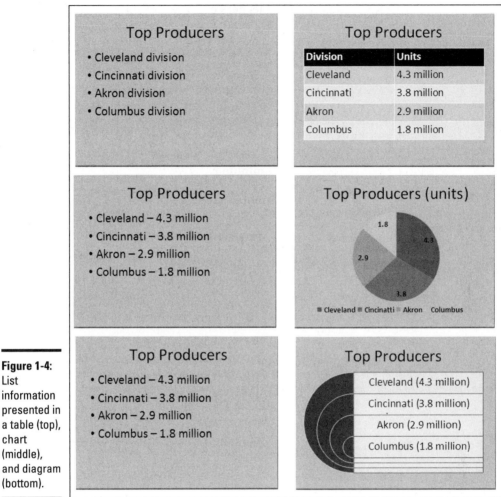

Figure 1-4:
List information presented in a table (top), chart (middle), and diagram (bottom).

✦ **Tell a story:** Include an anecdote in the presentation. Everybody loves a pertinent and well-delivered story. This piece of advice is akin to the previous one about personalizing your presentation. Typically, a story illustrates a problem for *people* and how *people* solve the problem. Even if your presentation concerns technology or an abstract subject, make it about people. "The people in Shaker Heights needed faster Internet access," not, "the data switches in Shaker Heights just weren't performing fast enough."

**Book IV
Chapter 1**

Getting Started in PowerPoint

✦ **Rehearse and then rehearse some more:** The better you know your material, the less nervous you are. To keep from getting nervous, rehearse your presentation until you know it backward and forward. Rehearse it out loud. Rehearse it while imagining you're in the presence of an audience.

✦ **Use visuals, not only words, to make your point:** You really owe it to your audience to take advantage of the table, chart, diagram, and picture capabilities of PowerPoint. People understand more from words and pictures than they do from words alone. It's up to you — not the slides — as the speaker to describe topics in detail with words.

Want to see just how PowerPoint can suck the life and drama out of a dramatic presentation? Try visiting the Gettysburg PowerPoint Presentation, a rendering of Lincoln's Gettysburg Address in PowerPoint. Yikes! You can find it here: www.norvig.com/Gettysburg.

Creating New Slides for Your Presentation

After you create a presentation, your next step on the path to glory is to start inserting the slides. As shown in Figures 1-5 and 1-6, you can choose among several different *slide layouts,* the preformatted slide designs that help you enter text, graphics, and other things. Some layouts have *text placeholder frames* for entering titles and text; some come with *content placeholder frames* designed especially for inserting a table, chart, diagram, picture, clip-art image, or video. When you insert a new slide, select the layout that best approximates the slide you have in mind for your presentation. These pages explain how to insert slides and harvest them from Word document headings.

Inserting a new slide

Follow these steps to insert a new slide in your presentation:

1. **Select the slide that you want the new slide to go after.**

In Normal view, select the slide on the Slides pane. In Slide Sorter view, select the slide in the main window.

2. **Click the Home tab.**

3. **Click the bottom half of the New Slide button.**

You see a drop-down list of slide layouts. (If you click the top half of the Add Slide button, you insert a slide with the same layout as the one you selected in Step 1.) Figures 1-5 and 1-6 show you what the slide layouts look like (left), what a slide looks like right after you insert it (middle), and finished slides (right).

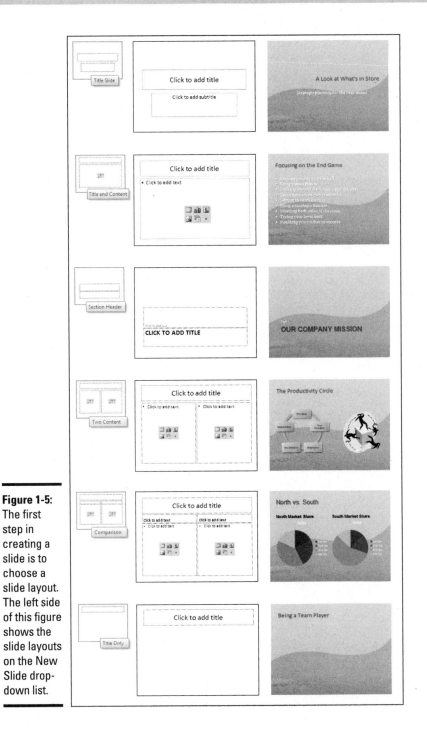

Figure 1-5:
The first step in creating a slide is to choose a slide layout. The left side of this figure shows the slide layouts on the New Slide drop-down list.

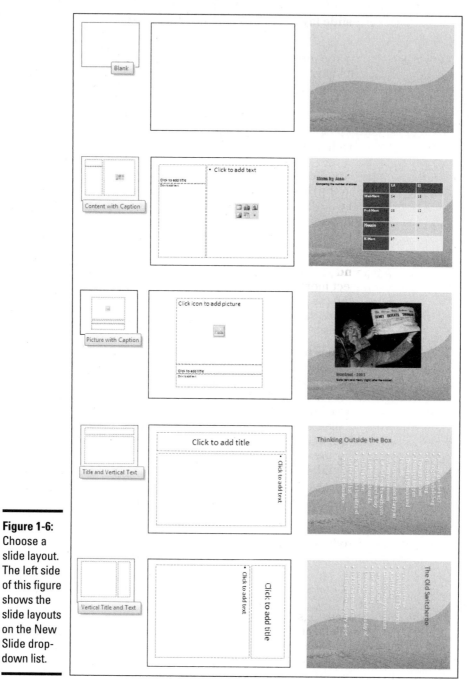

Figure 1-6:
Choose a slide layout. The left side of this figure shows the slide layouts on the New Slide drop-down list.

4. **Select the slide layout that best approximates the slide you want to create.**

   Don't worry too much about selecting the right layout. You can change slide layouts later, as "Selecting a different layout for a slide" explains later in this chapter.

Speed techniques for inserting slides

When you're in a hurry, use these techniques to insert a slide:

✦ **Creating a duplicate slide:** Select the slide or slides you want to duplicate, and on the Home tab, open the drop-down list on the New Slide button and choose Duplicate Selected Slides (or press Ctrl+M). You can also right-click the space between two slides and choose New Slide on the shortcut menu to create a duplicate of the slide above the place where you right-clicked.

✦ **Copying and pasting slides:** Click the slide you want to copy (or Ctrl+ click to select more than one slide) and then click the Copy button on the Home tab (or press Ctrl+C). Next, click to select the slide that you want the copied slide (or slides) to appear after and click the Paste button (or press Ctrl+V).

✦ **Recycling slides from other presentations:** Select the slide that you want the recycled slides to follow in your presentation, and on the Home tab, open the drop-down list on the New Slide button and then choose Reuse Slides. The Reuse Slides task pane opens. Open the drop-down list on the Browse button, choose Browse File, and select a presentation in the Browse dialog box. The Reuse Slides task pane shows thumbnail versions of slides in the file you selected. One at a time, click slides to add them to your presentation. You can right-click a slide and choose Insert All Slides to grab all the slides in the presentation.

Conjuring slides from Word document headings

If you think about it, Word headings are similar to slide titles. Headings, like slide titles, introduce a new topic. If you know your way around Word and you want to get a head start creating a PowerPoint presentation, you can borrow the headings in a Word document for your PowerPoint slides. When you import the headings from Word, you get one slide for each *Level 1 heading* (headings given the Heading 1 style). Level 1 headings form the title of the slides, Level 2 headings form first-level bullets, Level 3 headings form second-level bullets, and so on. Paragraph text isn't imported. Figure 1-7 shows what the headings from a Word document look like after they land in a PowerPoint presentation.

Each Level 1 heading in the Word document becomes a slide title in PowerPoint.

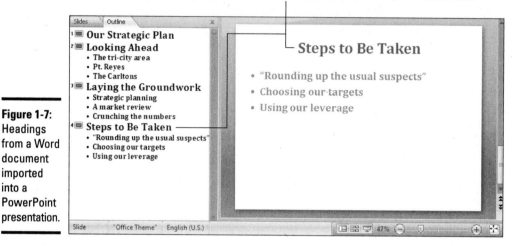

Figure 1-7:
Headings
from a Word
document
imported
into a
PowerPoint
presentation.

Follow these steps to use headings in a Word document to create slides in a PowerPoint presentation:

Outline

1. In Normal view, click the Outline tab in the Slides pane.

The Outline tab displays slide text (see Figure 1-7). You get a better sense of how headings from the Word document land in your presentation by viewing your presentation from the Outline tab.

2. Select the slide that the new slides from the Word document will follow.

3. Click the Home tab.

4. Open the drop-down list on the New Slide button and choose Slides from Outline.

You see the Insert Outline dialog box.

5. Select the Word document with the headings you want for your presentation; then click the Insert button.

Depending on how many first-level headings are in the Word document, you get a certain number of new slides. These slides probably need work. The *capitalization scheme* — the way in which headings are capitalized — in the Word document and your PowerPoint presentation may be different. The Word text may need tweaking to make it suitable for a PowerPoint presentation.

Selecting a different layout for a slide

If you mistakenly choose the wrong layout for a slide, all is not lost. You can start all over. You can graft a new layout onto your slide with one of these techniques:

+ On the Home tab, click the Layout button and then choose a layout on the submenu.

+ Right-click the slide (being careful not to right-click a frame or object), choose Layout on the drop-down list, and choose a layout on the submenu.

TIP

PowerPoint also offers the Reset command for giving a slide its original layout after you've fiddled with it. If you've pushed a slide all out of shape and you regret doing so, select your slide and click the Reset button on the Home tab.

Getting a Better View of Your Work

Depending on the task at hand, some views are better than others. These pages explain how to change views and the relative merits of Normal, Slide Sorter, Notes Page, Slide Show, Slide Master, Handout Master, and Notes Master view.

Changing views

PowerPoint offers two places to change views:

+ **View buttons on the status bar:** Click a View button — Normal, Slide Sorter, or Slide Show — on the status bar to change views, as shown in Figure 1-8.

+ **View tab:** Click the View tab and then click a button on the Presentation Views group to change views, as shown in Figure 1-8.

Looking at the different views

Here is a survey of the different views with notes about when to use each one:

Outline

+ **Normal/Outline view for fiddling with text:** Switch to Normal view and select the Outline tab in the Slides pane (refer to Figure 1-7) when you're entering or reading text. You can find the Outline tab at the top of the Slides pane. The words appear in outline form. Normal/Outline view is ideal for focusing on the words in a presentation.

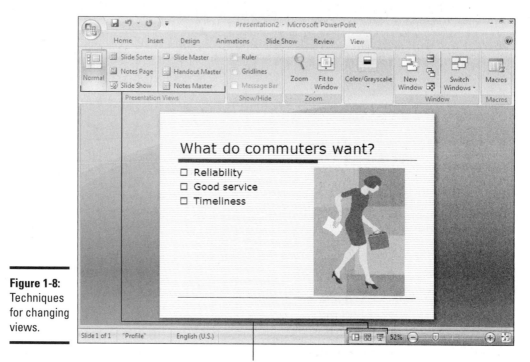

Figure 1-8:
Techniques
for changing
views.

Click a View button on the View tab or status bar.

✦ **Normal/Slides view for examining slides:** Switch to Normal view and select the Slides tab in the Slides pane when you want to examine a slide. In this view, thumbnail slides appear in the Slides pane, and you can see your slide in all its glory in the middle of the screen.

✦ **Slide Sorter view for moving and deleting slides:** In Slide Sorter view, you see thumbnails of all the slides in the presentation. From here, moving slides around is easy, and seeing many slides simultaneously gives you a sense of whether the different slides are consistent with one another and how the whole presentation is shaping up. The slides are numbered so that you can see where they appear in a presentation.

✦ **Notes Page view for reading your speaker notes:** In Notes Page view, you see notes you've written to aid you in your presentation — if you've written any. You can write notes in this view as well as in the Notes pane in Normal view. Chapter 5 of this mini-book explains notes pages.

✦ **Slide Show view for giving a presentation:** In Slide Show view, you see a single slide. Not only that, but the slide fills the entire screen. This is what your presentation looks like when you show it to an audience.

+ **The master views for a consistent presentation:** The master views — Slide Master, Handout Master, and Notes Master — are for handling *master styles,* the formatting commands that pertain to all the slides in a presentation, handouts, and notes. To switch to these views, visit the View tab and click the appropriate button. Chapter 2 of this mini-book looks into master slides and master styles.

Hiding and Displaying the Slides Pane and Notes Pane

In Normal view, the Slides pane with its slide thumbnails appears on the left side of the screen, and the Notes pane appears on the bottom of the screen so that you can scribble notes about presentations. Sometimes these panes just take up valuable space. They clutter the screen and occupy real estate that could be better used for formatting slides. Follow these instructions to temporarily remove the Slides and Notes pane:

+ **Removing the Notes pane:** Move the pointer over the border between the pane and the rest of the screen, and after the pointer changes to a two-headed arrow, drag the border to the bottom of the screen.

+ **Removing the Slides pane (and the Notes pane):** Click the Close button on the Slides pane. This button is located to the right of the Outline tab. Clicking it removes the Notes pane as well as the Slides pane.

 + **Restoring the Slides and Notes pane:** On the View tab, click the Normal button. You can also move the pointer to the left side or bottom of the screen, and when you see the double-headed arrow, click and start dragging toward the center of the screen.

You can change the size of either pane by moving the pointer over its border and then clicking and dragging.

Selecting, Moving, and Deleting Slides

As a presentation takes shape, you have to move slides forward and backward. Sometimes you have to delete a slide. And you can't move or delete slides until you select them first. Herewith are instructions for selecting, moving, and deleting slides.

Selecting slides

The best place to select slides is Slide Sorter view (if you want to select several at a time). Use one of these techniques to select slides:

✦ **Select one slide:** Click the slide.

✦ **Select several different slides**: Hold down the Ctrl key and click each slide in the Slides pane or in Slide Sorter view.

✦ **Select several slides in succession:** Hold down the Shift key and click the first slide and then the last one.

✦ **Select a block of slides:** Drag across the slides you want to select. Be sure when you click and start dragging that you don't click a slide.

Moving slides

To move or rearrange slides, you're advised to go to Slide Sorter view. Select the slide or slides you want to move and use one of these techniques to move slides:

✦ **Dragging and dropping:** Click the slides you selected and drag them to a new location. You see the drag pointer, and in Slide Sorter view, a vertical line shows you where the slide or slides will land when you release the mouse button. On the Slides pane, a horizontal line appears between slides to show you where the slide or slides will land when you release the mouse button.

✦ **Cutting and pasting:** On the Home tab, cut the slide or slides to the Windows Clipboard (click the Cut button, press Ctrl+X, or right-click and choose Cut). Then select the slide that you want the slide or slides to appear after and give the Paste command (click the Paste button, press Ctrl+V, or right-click and choose Paste). You can right-click between slides and paste with precision.

Deleting slides

Before you delete a slide, think twice about deleting. Short of using the Undo command, you can't resuscitate a deleted slide. Select the slide or slides you want to delete and use one of these techniques to delete slides:

| Delete |

✦ On the Home tab, click the Delete button.

✦ Press the Delete key.

✦ Right-click and choose Delete Slide on the shortcut menu.

Putting Together a Photo Album

Photo album is just the PowerPoint term for inserting many photographs into a presentation all at once. You don't necessarily have to stuff the photo album with travel or baby pictures for it to be a proper photo album. The Photo Album is a wonderful feature because you can use it to dump a bunch of photos in a PowerPoint presentation without having to create slides one at a time, insert the photos, and endure the rest of the rigmarole. Create a photo album to quickly place a bunch of photos on PowerPoint slides.

Creating your photo album

PowerPoint creates a new presentation for you when you create a photo album. To start, take note of where on your computer the photos you want for the album are. Then go to the Insert tab and click the Photo Album button. You see the Photo Album dialog box, as shown in Figure 1-9. For such a little thing, the Photo Album dialog box offers many opportunities for constructing a PowerPoint presentation. Your first task is to decide which pictures you want for your album. Then you choose a slide layout for the pictures.

Insert photos.   Change the order of slides.

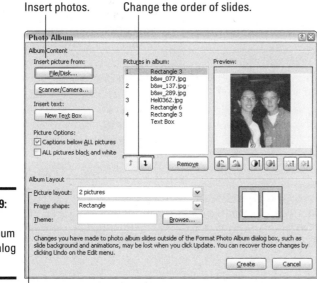

Figure 1-9: Create a photo album in this dialog box.

Choose a layout.

Inserting pictures and creating slides

Here is the lowdown on choosing pictures for your photo album:

✦ **Inserting photos:** Click the File/Disk button and choose photos in the Insert New Pictures dialog box. You can select more than one photo at a time by Ctrl+clicking in the dialog box. The filenames of photos you selected appear in the Pictures in Album box. Slide numbers appear as well so that you know which photos are on which slides.

✦ **Inserting photos from a scanner or digital camera:** Click the Scanner/Camera button. You see the Insert Picture from Scanner or Camera dialog box. See Book VIII, Chapter 3 for details.

✦ **Inserting a text box:** Insert a text box if you want to enter commentary in your photo album. In the Pictures in Album box, select the picture or text box that you want your new text box to go after and then click the New Text Box button. Later, you can go into your presentation and edit the placeholder text, which PowerPoint aptly enters as *Text Box*.

✦ **Providing captions for all pictures:** To place a caption below all the pictures in your photo album, select the Captions Below ALL Pictures check box. PowerPoint initially places the picture filename in the caption, but you can delete this caption and enter one of your own. (To select this option, you must choose any picture layout except Fit to Slide.)

✦ **Changing the order of pictures:** Select a picture in the Pictures in Album box and then click an arrow button to move it forward or backward in the presentation.

✦ **Changing the order of slides:** Ctrl+click to select each picture on a slide. Then click an arrow as many times as necessary to move the slide forward or backward in the presentation.

✦ **Removing a picture:** Select a picture in the Pictures in Album box and click the Remove button to remove it from your photo album. You can Ctrl+click pictures to select more than one.

Choosing a layout for slides

Your next task is to go to the bottom of the Photo Album dialog box (refer to Figure 1-9) to choose a layout for the slides in the presentation. Open the Picture Layout drop-down list to choose one of the seven picture layouts for your slides:

✦ Choose Fit to Slide for a presentation in which each picture occupies an entire slide.

✦ Choose a "pictures" option to fit 1, 2, or 4 pictures on each slide.

✦ Choose a "pictures with" option to fit 1, 2, or 4 pictures as well as a text title frame on each slide.

Changing the look of pictures

The Photo Album dialog box (refer to Figure 1-9) offers a handful of tools for changing the look of the pictures. When you use these tools, keep your eye on the Preview box — it shows you what you're doing to your picture.

✦ **Making all photos black and white:** Select the ALL Pictures Black and White check box.

✦ **Rotating pictures:** Click a Rotate button to rotate the picture clockwise or counterclockwise.

✦ **Changing the contrast:** Click a Contrast button to sharpen or mute the light and dark colors or shades in the picture.

✦ **Changing the brightness**: Click a Brightness button to make the graphic brighter or more somber.

✦ **Choosing a frame shape for pictures:** If you opted for a "picture" or "picture with" slide layout, you can choose a shape — Beveled, Oval, or others — for your pictures on the Frame Shape drop-down list. The preview slide in the dialog box shows what your choice means in real terms.

✦ **Choosing a theme for your photo album:** If you selected a "picture" or "picture with" slide layout, you can choose a theme for your slide presentation. Click the Browse button and choose a theme in the Choose Theme dialog box.

At last, click the Create button when you're ready to create the photo album. PowerPoint attaches a title slide to the start of the album that says, *Photo Album* with your name below.

Putting on the final touches

Depending on the options you chose for your photo album, it needs all or some of these final touches:

✦ **Fix the title slide:** Your title slide should probably say more than the words *Photo Album* and your name.

✦ **Fill in the text boxes:** If you entered text boxes in your album, by all means, replace PowerPoint's generic text with meaningful words of your own.

✦ **Write the captions:** If you asked for photo captions, PowerPoint entered photo filenames below photos. Replace those filenames with something more descriptive.

Editing your photo album

To go back into the Photo Album dialog box and rearrange the photos in your album, go to the Insert tab, open the drop-down list on the Photo Album button, and choose Edit Photo Album on the drop-down list. You see the Edit Photo Album dialog box. It looks and works exactly like the Photo Album dialog box (refer to Figure 1-9). Of course, you can also edit your photo album by treating it like any other PowerPoint presentation. Change the theme, fiddle with the slides, and do what you will to torture your photo album into shape.

Hidden Slides for All Contingencies

Hide a slide when you want to keep it on hand "just in case" during a presentation. Hidden slides don't appear in slide shows unless you shout *Ollie ollie oxen free!* and bring them out of hiding. Although you, the presenter, can see hidden slides in Normal view and Slide Sorter view, where their slide numbers are crossed through, the audience doesn't see them in the course of a presentation unless you decide to show them. Create hidden slides if you anticipate having to turn your presentation in a different direction — to answer a question from the audience, prove your point more thoroughly, or revisit a topic in more depth. Merely by right-clicking and choosing a couple of commands, you can display a hidden slide in the course of a slide show.

Hiding a slide

The best place to put hidden slides is the end of a presentation where you know you can find them. Follow these steps to hide slides:

1. **Select the slide or slides that you want to hide.**

2. **On the Slide Show tab, click the Hide Slide button.**

You can also right-click the slide and choose Hide Slide. Hidden slides' numbers are boxed in the Slides pane and Slide Sorter window.

To unhide a slide, click the Hide Slide button again or right-click the slide in the Slides pane or Slide Sorter window and choose Hide Slide on the shortcut menu.

Showing a hidden slide during a presentation

Hidden slides don't appear during the course of a presentation, but suppose that the need arises to show one. Before showing a hidden slide, take careful note of which slide you're viewing now. You have to return to this slide after viewing the hidden slide. Follow these steps to view a hidden slide during a presentation:

1. **Right-click the screen and choose Go to Slide.**

You see a submenu with the titles of slides in your presentation. You can tell which slides are hidden because their numbers are enclosed in parentheses.

2. **Select a hidden slide so that the audience can view it.**

How do you resume your presentation after viewing the hidden slide? If you look at only one hidden slide, you can right-click and choose Last Viewed on the shortcut menu to return to the slide you saw before the hidden slide. If you've viewed several hidden slides, right-click the screen, choose Go to Slide, and select a slide to pick up where you left off.

Chapter 2: Fashioning a Look for Your Presentation

In This Chapter

✔ **Introducing themes and background styles**

✔ **Selecting and tweaking slide themes**

✔ **Creating a solid color, gradient, clip-art, picture, and texture slide background**

✔ **Selecting a theme or background for specific slides**

✔ **Redesigning your presentation with master slides**

*F*rom your audience's point of view, this chapter is the most important in this mini-book. What your presentation looks like — which theme and background style you select for the slides in your presentation — sets the tone. The audience judges your presentation right away by the first slide it sees. Seeing that first slide, audience members make a snap judgment as to what your presentation is about and whether your presentation is worth watching closely. When you fashion a look for your presentation, what you're really doing is declaring what you want to communicate to your audience.

This chapter explains how to fashion the appearance of slide backgrounds. It examines what you need to consider when you select colors and designs for backgrounds. You also discover how to select and customize a theme, and how to create your own slide backgrounds with a solid (or transparent) color, a two-color gradient blend, a clip-art image, or a picture. In this chapter, I look into how to change the background of some but not all of the slides in a presentation. I show you how to use master slides and master styles to make sure that slides throughout your presentation are consistent with one another.

Looking at Themes and Background Styles

What a presentation looks like is mostly a matter of slide backgrounds, and when you select a background for slides, you start by selecting a theme. A *theme* is a "canned" slide design. Themes are designed by graphic artists. Most themes include sophisticated background patterns and colors. For each theme, PowerPoint offers several alternative theme colors, fonts, and background styles. As well, you can create a background of your own from a single color, a gradient mixture of two colors, or a picture.

Figure 2-1 shows examples of themes. Themes range from the fairly simple to the quite complex. When you installed PowerPoint on your computer, you also installed a dozen or more themes, and you can acquire more themes online from Microsoft and other places. After you select a theme for your presentation, you can tweak it a little bit. You can do that by choosing a background style or by creating an entirely new background of your own. Figure 2-2 shows examples of backgrounds you can create yourself. Self-made backgrounds are not as intrusive as themes. The risk of the background overwhelming the lists, tables, charts, and other items in the forefront of slides is less when you fashion a background style yourself.

Figure 2-1:
Examples of themes.

More than any other design decision, what sets the tone for a presentation are the colors you select for slide backgrounds. If the purpose of your presentation is to show photographs you took on a vacation to Arizona's Painted Desert, select light-tone, hot colors for the slide backgrounds. If your presentation is an aggressive sales pitch, consider a black background. There is no universal color theory for selecting the right colors in a design because everyone is different. Follow your intuition. It will lead you to the right background color choices.

Figure 2-2:
Examples of background styles (clockwise from upper-left): plain style, gradient, solid color, customized radial gradient, clip art, and picture.

Choosing a Theme for Your Presentation

After you initially select a theme, you can do one or two things to customize it. These pages explain how to find and select a theme for your presentation and diddle with a theme after you've selected it. By the way, you can find the name of the theme that is currently in use on the left side of the status bar, in case you're curious about a theme you want to replace.

Selecting a theme

Use one of these techniques to select a new theme for your presentation:

✦ **Selecting a theme in the Themes gallery:** On the Design tab, open the Themes gallery and move the pointer over different themes to "live-preview" them, as shown in Figure 2-3. Click a theme to select it.

✦ **Borrowing a theme from another presentation:** On the Design tab, open the Themes gallery and click Browse for Themes (see Figure 2-3). You see the Choose Theme or Themed Document dialog box. Locate and select a presentation with a theme you can commandeer for your presentation and click the Apply button.

Tweaking a theme

Starting on the Design tab, you can customize a theme with these techniques:

**Book IV
Chapter 2**

**Fashioning a
Look for Your
Presentation**

✦ **Choosing a new set of colors:** The easiest and best way to experiment with customizing a theme is to select a different color set. Click the Theme Colors button, slide the pointer over the different color sets on the drop-down list, and see what effect they have on your slide.

✦ **Change the fonts:** Click the Theme Fonts button and then choose a combination of fonts on the drop-down list. The first font in each pair applies to slide titles and the second to slide text. You can also choose Create New Theme Fonts on the list and select theme fonts of your own.

✦ **Change theme effects:** Click the Theme Effects button and choose a theme effect on the drop-down list. A *theme effect* is a slight refinement to a theme.

✦ **Choosing background style variation:** Most themes offer background style variations. Click the Background Styles button to open the Background Styles gallery and select a style. The next section in this chapter, "Creating Slide Backgrounds on Your Own," explains how you can create backgrounds similar to these, as well as how to create a single-color, gradient, clip-art, picture, and texture background.

Suppose you regret customizing a theme. To get the original theme back, select it again. Make like you were selecting a theme for the first time and select it in the Themes gallery.

Move the pointer over a theme to "live-preview" it.

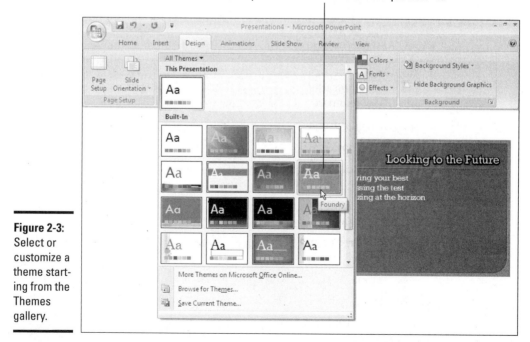

Figure 2-3: Select or customize a theme starting from the Themes gallery.

Creating Slide Backgrounds on Your Own

Besides a theme or background style, your other option for creating slide backgrounds is to do it on your own. For a background, you can have a solid color, a transparent color, a gradient blend of two colors, a picture, or a clip-art image.

+ **Solid color:** A single, uniform color. You can adjust a color's transparency and in effect "bleach out" the color to push it farther into the background.

+ **Gradient:** A mixture of two colors with the colors blending into one another.

+ **Clip art:** A clip-art image from the Microsoft Clip Organizer.

+ **Picture:** A photograph or graphic.

+ **Texture:** A uniform pattern that gives the impression that the slide is displayed on a material such as cloth or stone.

How to create these kinds of slide backgrounds on your own is the subject of the next several pages.

Using a solid (or transparent) color for the slide background

Using a solid or transparent color for the background gives your slides a straightforward, honest look. Because all the slides are the same color or transparent color, the audience can focus better on the presentation itself rather than the razzle-dazzle. Follow these steps to use a solid or transparent color as the background:

Background Styles ▾

1. **On the Design tab, click the Background Styles button and choose Format Background on the drop-down list.**

   You see the Format Background dialog box.

2. **Select the Solid Fill option button.**

3. **Click the Color Picker button and choose a color on the drop-down list.**

   The muted theme colors are recommended because they look better in the background, but you can select a standard color or click the More Colors button and select a color in the Colors dialog box.

4. **Drag the Transparency slider if you want a "bleached out" color rather than a slide color.**

   At 0% transparency, you get a solid color; at 100%, you get no color at all.

5. **Click the Apply to All button and then the Close button.**

   I sincerely hope you like your choice of colors, but if you don't, try, try, try again.

Selecting a gradient blend of two colors for the slide background

Gradient refers to how and where two or more colors grade, or blend, into one another on a slide. As well as the standard linear gradient direction, you can opt for a radial, rectangular, or path gradient direction, as shown in Figure 2-4. Gradient backgrounds look terribly elegant. Using a gradient is an excellent way to create an original background that looks different from all the other presenter's slide backgrounds.

[Background Styles ~]

To create a gradient background for slides, start on the Design tab, click the Background Styles button, and choose Format Background on the drop-down list. Then, in the Format Background dialog box, click the Gradient Fill option button. You get a different set of options in the Format Background dialog box:

✦ The *Type drop-down list* tells PowerPoint what type of gradient you want — Linear, Radial, Rectangular, or Path (see Figure 2-4). If you choose the Linear option, you can select the angle at which the colors blend.

✦ *Stops* indicate where on the slide colors blend. You choose one gradient stop for each color you want.

Figure 2-4: The Gradient Direction options (clockwise from upper-left): Linear (at 180 degrees), Radial, Rectangular, and Path (all shown at 50-50 percent blend).

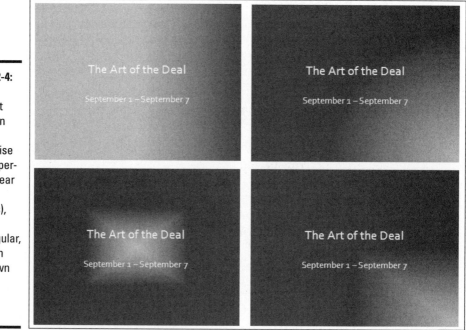

Before you experiment with gradients, try opening the Preset Colors drop-down list to see whether one of the ready-made gradient options does the job for you.

Drag the Format Background dialog box to the left side of the screen so that you can see your slide better and then follow these steps to create a gradient blend of the different colors:

1. **Select Stop 1 on the Stops drop-down list; then click the Color button and choose a color; then click the Add button.**

2. **Select Stop 2 on the Stops drop-down list, choose a color for it as well, and click the Add button.**

Now you've selected the two gradient colors. You can select more colors if you want. Your next task is to tell PowerPoint where to blend the colors.

3. **Select Stop 1 on the Stop drop-down list and then drag the Stop Position slider.**

Watch how the slide on your screen changes as you drag.

4. **Select Stop 2 on the Gradient Stops drop-down list and drag the Stop Position slider.**

Notice how the two colors blend on your slide. For Figure 2-4, I dragged the slider to 50% for each stop color. I'll wager you have to repeat Steps 3 and 4 several times until you find the right blend.

5. **Open the Type drop-down list and choose a Gradient Direction option: Linear, Radial, Rectangular, Path, or Shade from Title.**

Refer to Figure 2-4 to see how these options look. If you choose Linear, you can enter a degree measurement in the Angle box to change the angle at which the colors blend. At 90 degrees, for example, they blend horizontally across the slide; at 180 degrees, they blend vertically across the slide.

6. **Drag the Transparency slider to make the colors more or less transparent.**

At 0% transparency, you get solid colors (except where they blend); at 100%, you get no color at all.

7. **Click the Apply to All button.**

Very likely, you have to experiment with stop colors and stop positions until you blend the colors to your satisfaction. Good luck.

**Book IV
Chapter 2**

**Fashioning a
Look for Your
Presentation**

Placing a clip-art image in the slide background

As long as they're on the pale side or you've made them semi-transparent, clip-art images do fine for slide backgrounds. They look especially good in title slides. Figure 2-5 shows examples of clip-art images as backgrounds. As Book VIII, Chapter 4 explains, PowerPoint comes with numerous clip-art images. You're invited to place one in the background of your slides by following these steps:

1. **On the Design tab, click the Background Styles button and choose Format Background on the drop-down list.**

   The Format Background dialog box appears.

2. **Click the Picture or Texture Fill option button.**

3. **Click the Clip Art button.**

   You see the Select Picture dialog box.

4. **Find and select a clip-art image that you can use in the background of your slides.**

   You can scroll through the clip-art images until you find a good one, enter a search term in the Search Text box and click the Go button, or click the Include Content from Office Online check box to search online at Microsoft for a clip-art image. You can get hundreds of clip-art images this way.

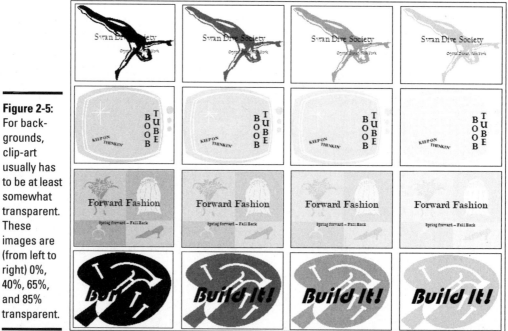

Figure 2-5: For backgrounds, clip-art usually has to be at least somewhat transparent. These images are (from left to right) 0%, 40%, 65%, and 85% transparent.

5. **In the Format Background dialog box, enter a Transparency measurement.**

    Drag the Transparency slider or enter a measurement in the box. The higher the measurement, the more transparent the image is (see Figure 2-5).

6. **Enter measurements in the Offsets boxes to make your clip-art image fill the slide.**

7. **Click the Apply to All button and then click Close.**

    There you have it. The clip-art image you selected lands in the slides' backgrounds.

Using a graphic for a slide background

Figure 2-6 shows examples of graphics being used as slide backgrounds. Select your graphic carefully. A graphic with too many colors — and that includes the majority of color photographs — obscures the text and makes it difficult to read. You can get around this problem by "recoloring" a graphic to give it a uniform color tint, selecting a grayscale photograph, selecting a photo with colors of a similar hue, or making the graphic semi-transparent, but all in all, the best way to solve the problem of a graphic that obscures the text is to start with a quiet, subdued graphic. (Book VIII, Chapter 3 explains all the ins and outs of using graphics in Office 2007.)

Figure 2-6: Examples of graphics used as slide backgrounds.

Book IV Chapter 2

Fashioning a Look for Your Presentation

One more thing: Select a landscape-style graphic that is wider than it is tall. PowerPoint expands graphics to make them fill the entire slide background. If you select a skinny, portrait-style graphic, PowerPoint has to do a lot of expanding to make the graphic fit on the slide, and you end up with a distorted background image.

Follow these steps to use a graphic as a slide background:

[Background Styles button icon] **1.** **On the Design tab, click the Background Styles button and choose Format Background on the drop-down list.**

You see the Format Background dialog box.

2. **Click the Picture or Texture Fill option button.**

3. **Click the File button.**

The Insert Picture dialog box appears.

4. **Locate the graphic you want, select it, and click the Insert button.**

The graphic lands on your slide.

5. **Enter a Transparency measurement to make the graphic fade a bit into the background.**

Drag the slider or enter a measurement in the Transparency box. The higher percentage measurement you enter, the more "bleached out" the graphic is.

6. **Using the Offsets text boxes, enter measurements to make your graphic fit on the slides.**

7. **Click the Apply to All button.**

How do you like your slide background? You may have to open the Format Background dialog box again and play with the transparency setting. Only the very lucky and the permanently blessed get it right the first time.

Using a texture for a slide background

Yet another option for slide backgrounds is to use a texture. As shown in Figure 2-7, a *texture* gives the impression that the slide is displayed on a material such as cloth or stone. A texture can make for a very elegant slide background. Follow these steps to use a texture as a slide background:

[Background Styles button icon] **1.** **On the Design tab, click the Background Styles button and choose Format Background on the drop-down list.**

The Format Background dialog box appears.

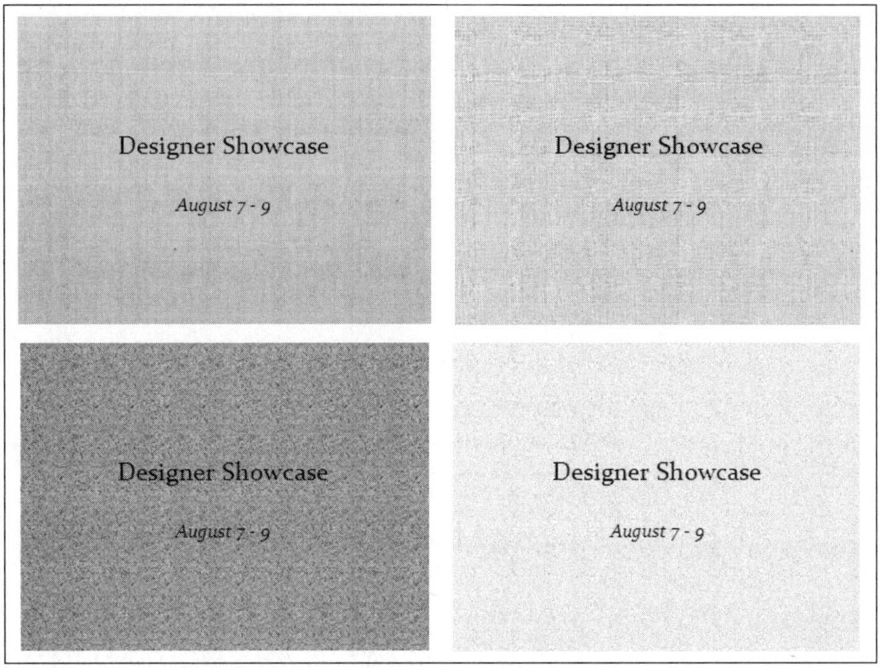

Figure 2-7:
Different textures (clockwise from upper-left): Papyrus, Canvas, Newsprint, and Cork.

2. **Click the Picture or Texture Fill option button.**

3. **Click the Texture button and choose a texture on the drop-down list.**

4. **Enter a Transparency measurement to make the texture less imposing.**

Drag the slider or enter a measurement in the Transparency box.

5. **Click the Apply to All button and then click Close.**

Changing the Background of a Single or Handful of Slides

To make a single slide (or a handful of slides) stand out in a presentation, change their background style or theme. A different background tells your audience that the slide being presented is a little different from the one before it. Maybe it imparts important information. Maybe it introduces another segment of the presentation. Use a different background style or theme to mark a transition, indicate that your presentation has shifted gears, or mark a milestone in your presentation.

**Book IV
Chapter 2**

**Fashioning a
Look for Your
Presentation**

Follow these steps to change the background of one or several slides in your presentation:

1. **In Slide Sorter view, select the slides that need a different look.**

You can select more than one slide by Ctrl+clicking slides.

2. **On the Design tab, choose a different theme or background for the slides you selected.**

How you do this depends on whether you're working with a theme or a slide background:

- *Theme:* In the Themes Gallery, select a different theme. (See "Choosing a Theme for Your Presentation" earlier in this chapter for details.)

- *Slide background:* Make like you're creating a background style for all the slides (see "Creating Slide Backgrounds on Your Own" earlier in this chapter) but click the Close button, not the Apply to All button, in the Format Background dialog box.

When you assign a different theme to some of the slides in a presentation, PowerPoint creates another Slide Master. You may be surprised to discover that when you insert a new slide in your presentation, a second, third, or fourth set of slide layouts appear on the Add Slide drop-down list. These extra layouts appear because your presentation has more than one Slide Master. The next section in this chapter, "Using Master Slides and Master Styles for a Consistent Design," explains what Slide Masters are.

Using Master Slides and Master Styles for a Consistent Design

Consistency is everything in a PowerPoint design. Consistency of design is a sign of professionalism and care. In a consistent design, the fonts and font sizes on slides are consistent from one slide to the next, the placeholder text frames are in the same positions, and the text is aligned the same way across different slides. In the bulleted lists, each entry is marked with the same bullet character. If the corner of each slide shows a company logo, the logo appears in the same position.

It would be torture to have to examine every slide to make sure it's consistent with the others. In the interest of consistency, PowerPoint offers master styles and master slides. A *master slide* is a model slide from which the slides in a presentation inherit their formats. A *master style* is a format that applies to many different slides. Starting from a master slide, you can change a master style and in so doing, reformat many slides the same way. These pages explain how master slides can help you quickly redesign a presentation.

Switching to Slide Master view

To work with master slides, switch to *Slide Master view,* as shown in Figure 2-8. From this view, you can start working with master slides:

1. **Click the View tab.**

2. **Click the Slide Master button.**

In Slide Master view, you can select a master slide in the Slides pane, format styles on a master slide, and in this way reformat many different slides. (Click the Close Master View, Normal, or Slide Sorter button when you want to leave Slide Master view.)

Select the Slide Master...

...or a layout.

Change a master style.

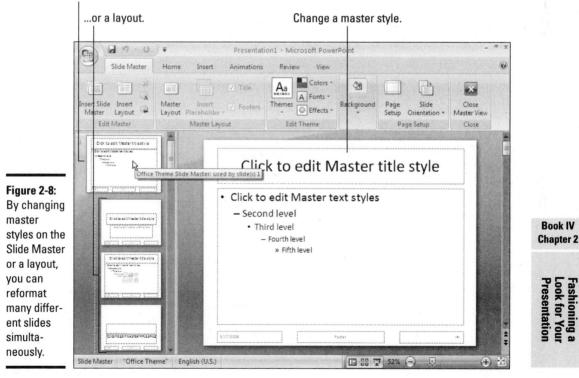

Figure 2-8:
By changing master styles on the Slide Master or a layout, you can reformat many different slides simulta-neously.

Understanding master slides and master styles

Master slides are special, high-powered slides. Use master slides to deliver the same formatting commands to many different slides. Whether the commands affect all the slides in your presentation or merely a handful of slides depends on whether you format the Slide Master (the topmost slide in Slide Master view) or a layout (one of the other slides):

✦ **The Slide Master:** The *Slide Master* is the first slide in the Slides pane in Slide Master view (see Figure 2-8). It's a little bigger than the master slides, as befits its status as Emperor of All Slides. Formatting changes you make to the Slide Master affect all the slides in your presentation. When you select a theme for your presentation, what you're really doing is assigning a theme to the Slide Master. Because formatting commands given to the Slide Master apply throughout a presentation, the theme design and colors are applied to all slides. If you want a company logo to appear on all your slides, place the logo on the Slide Master.

✦ **Layouts:** As you probably know, you choose a slide layout — Title and Content, for example — on the New Slide drop-down list to create a new slide. PowerPoint provides one *layout* for each type of slide layout in your presentation. By selecting and reformatting a layout in Slide Master view, you can reformat all slides in your presentation that were created with the same slide layout. For example, to change fonts, alignments, and other formats on all slides that you created with the Title and Content slide layout, select the Title and Content layout in Slide Master view and then change master styles on the slide. Each layout controls its own little fiefdom in a PowerPoint presentation — a fiefdom comprised of slides created with the same slide layout.

✦ **Master styles:** Each master slide — the Slide Master and each layout — offers you the opportunity to click to edit master styles (refer to Figure 2-8). The master style governs how text is formatted on slides. By changing a master style on a master slide, you can change the look of slides throughout a presentation. For example, by changing the Master Title Style font, you can change fonts in all the slide titles in your presentation.

The PowerPoint Slide Master–layouts–slides system is designed on the "trickle down" theory. When you format a master style on the Slide Master, formats trickle down to layouts and then to slides. When you format a master style on a layout, the formats trickle down to slides you created using the same slide layout. This chain-of-command relationship is designed to work from the top down, with the master slide and layouts barking orders to the slides below. In the interest of design consistency, slides take orders from layouts, and layouts take orders from the Slide Master.

In Slide Master view, you can move the pointer over a layout thumbnail in the Slides pane to see a pop-up box that tells you the layout's name and which slides in your presentation "use" the layout. For example, a pop-up box that reads "Title and Content Layout: used by slide(s) 2-3, 8" tells you that slides 2 through 3 and 8 in your presentation are governed by the Title and Content layout.

Editing a master slide

Now that you know the relationship among the Slide Master, layouts, and slides, you're ready to start editing master slides. To edit a master slide, switch to Slide Master view, select a master slide, and change a master style. To insert a graphic on a master slide, visit the Insert tab. On the Edit Master tab, you can find commands for changing fonts, formatting paragraphs, and aligning text.

Changing a master slide layout

Changing the layout of a master slide entails changing the position and size of text frames and content frames as well as removing these frames:

+ **Changing size of frames:** Select the frame you want to change, and then move the pointer over a frame handle on the corner, side, top or bottom of the frame and drag when you see the double-headed arrow.

+ **Moving frames:** Move the pointer over the perimeter of a frame, click when you see the four-headed arrow, and drag.

+ **Removing a frame from the Slide Master:** Click the perimeter of the frame to select it and then press Delete.

+ **Adding a frame to the Slide Master:** On the Slide Master tab, click the Master Layout button. You see the Master Layout dialog box. Select the check box beside the name of each frame you want to add and click OK.

Chapter 3: Entering the Text

In This Chapter

✓ Entering and changing the font, size, and color of text

✓ Creating text boxes and text box shapes

✓ Handling overflow text in text boxes and frames

✓ Aligning the text in text boxes and text frames

✓ Creating bulleted and numbered lists

✓ Placing footers on slides

This chapter explains how to change the appearance of text, create text boxes, and create text box shapes. I solve the riddle of what to do when text doesn't fit in a text box or text placeholder frame. You also discover how to align text, handle bulleted and numbered lists, and put a footer on all or some of the slides in your presentation.

By the time you finish reading this chapter, if you read it all the way through, you will be one of those people others turn to when they have a PowerPoint question about entering text on slides. You'll become a little guru in your own right.

Entering Text

No presentation is complete without a word or two at least, which is why the first thing you see when you add a new slide to a presentation are the words "Click to add text." As soon as you "click here," those words of instruction disappear, and you're free to enter a title or text of your own. Most slides include a text placeholder frame at the top for entering a slide title; many slides also have another, larger text placeholder frame for entering a bulleted list.

As shown in Figure 3-1, the easiest way to enter text on slides is to click in a text placeholder frame and start typing. The other way is to switch to Normal view, select the Outline tab in the Slides pane (see Figure 3-1), and enter text there. Text that you type next to a slide icon in the Outline pane is then made the title of the slide.

On the Slides pane in Normal/Outline view   In a text placeholder frame

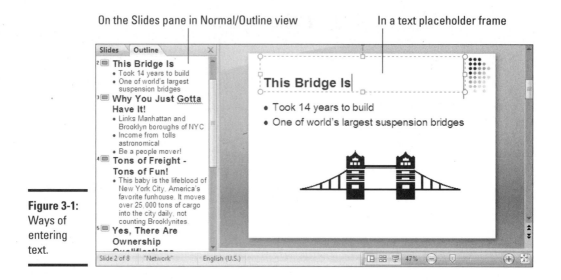

Figure 3-1:
Ways of
entering
text.

Enter text on slides the same way you enter text in a Word document — by wiggling your fingers over the keyboard. While you're at it, you can change fonts, the font size of text, and the color of text, as the following pages explain. (Chapter 1 of this mini-book describes how to get the text for slides from the headings in a Word document; Book I, Chapter 2 explains everything a sane person needs to know about handling fonts.)

Choosing fonts for text

If you aren't happy with the fonts in your presentation, you have three ways to remedy the problem:

✦ **Dig in and choose new fonts on a slide-by-slide basis.** Select the text, go to the Home tab, and choose a font from the Font drop-down list or the Font dialog box. You can also choose fonts on the Mini Toolbar.

✦ **Select new theme fonts for your presentation.** Theme fonts are combinations of fonts that the designers of PowerPoint themes deem appropriate for the theme you're working in. To change theme fonts, go to the Design tab, click the Theme Fonts button, and select a new font combination.

✦ **Choose a new font on a master slide to change fonts throughout your presentation.** Chapter 2 of this mini-book explains master slides and how you can use them to change formats simultaneously on many slides. In Slide Master view, select a master slide and change its fonts on the Edit Master tab.

Changing the font size of text

For someone in the back row of an audience to be able to read text in a PowerPoint presentation, the text should be no smaller than 28 points. Try this simple test to see whether text in your presentation is large enough to read: Stand five or so feet from your computer and see whether you can read the text. If you can't read it, make it larger.

Go to the Home tab and click in or select the text whose size you want to change. Then use one of these techniques to change font sizes:

✦ **Font Size drop-down list:** Open this list and choose a point size. To choose a point size that isn't on the list, click in the Font Size text box, enter a point size, and press Enter.

✦ **Font dialog box:** Click the Font group button to open the Font dialog box. Then either choose a point size from the Size drop-down list or enter a point size in the Size text box and click OK.

✦ **Increase Font Size and Decrease Font Size buttons:** Click these buttons (or press Ctrl+] or Ctrl+[) to increase or decrease the point size by the next interval on the Font Size drop-down list. Watch the Font Size list or your text and note how the text changes size. This is an excellent technique when you want to "eyeball it" and you don't care to fool with the Font Size list or Font dialog box.

Changing the color of text

Before you change the color of text, peer into your computer screen and examine the background theme or color you selected for your slides. Unless the color of the text is different from the theme or color, the audience can't read the text. Besides choosing a color that contributes to the overall tone of the presentation, select a color that's easy to read.

Select the text that needs touching up and then use one of these techniques to change the color of text:

✦ On the Mini Toolbar, open the drop-down list on the Font Color button and choose a color.

✦ On the Home tab, open the drop-down list on the Font Color button and choose a color.

✦ On the Home tab, click the Font group button to open the Font dialog box, click the Font Color button in the dialog box, and choose a color on the drop-down list.

**Book IV
Chapter 3**

Entering the Text

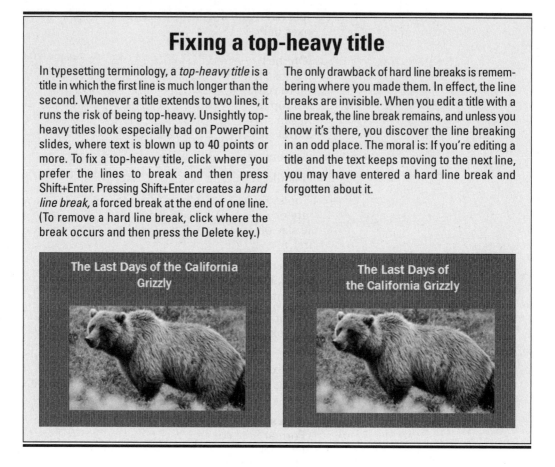

Fixing a top-heavy title

In typesetting terminology, a *top-heavy title* is a title in which the first line is much longer than the second. Whenever a title extends to two lines, it runs the risk of being top-heavy. Unsightly top-heavy titles look especially bad on PowerPoint slides, where text is blown up to 40 points or more. To fix a top-heavy title, click where you prefer the lines to break and then press Shift+Enter. Pressing Shift+Enter creates a *hard line break,* a forced break at the end of one line. (To remove a hard line break, click where the break occurs and then press the Delete key.)

The only drawback of hard line breaks is remembering where you made them. In effect, the line breaks are invisible. When you edit a title with a line break, the line break remains, and unless you know it's there, you discover the line breaking in an odd place. The moral is: If you're editing a title and the text keeps moving to the next line, you may have entered a hard line break and forgotten about it.

The Font Color drop-down list offers theme colors and standard colors. You are well advised to choose a theme color. These colors jive with the theme you choose for your presentation.

Fun with Text Boxes and Text Box Shapes

Text boxes give you an opportunity to exercise your creativity. They add another element to slides. Use them to position text wherever you want, annotate a chart or equation, or place an announcement on a slide. You can even create a vertical text box in which the text reads from top to bottom instead of left to right, or turn a text box into a circle, arrow, or other shape. Figure 3-2 shows examples of text boxes and text box shapes.

In Office 2007 terminology, a PowerPoint text box is an object. Book I, Chapter 8 explains all the different techniques for handling objects, including how to make them overlap and change their sizes. Here are the basics of handling text boxes in PowerPoint:

✦ **Creating a text box:** On the Insert tab, open the drop-down list on the Text Box button and choose Horizontal or Vertical. Text in a *horizontal text box* reads from left to right; in a *vertical text box,* text reads from top to bottom or bottom to top (see Figure 3-2). Move the pointer to a part of the slide where you can see the *text box pointer,* a downward-pointing arrow. Click and start dragging to create your text box.

✦ **Rotating a text box:** Use one of these techniques to rotate a text box:

- Drag the rotation handle, the green circle above the text box.

- On the (Drawing Tools) Format tab, click the Rotate button and choose a Rotate or Flip command on the drop-down list. (Depending on the size of your screen, you may have to click the Arrange button first.)

- On the (Drawing Tools) Format tab, click the Size group button (you may have to click the Size button first), and in the Size and Position dialog box, enter a measurement in the Rotation box.

✦ **Changing the direction of text:** Select the text in the text box, and on the Home tab, click the Text Direction button and then choose an option on the drop-down list.

✦ **Turning a shape into a text box:** Create the shape, and then click in the shape and start typing. (Book I, Chapter 8 explains how to create a shape.)

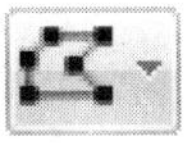

✦ **Turning a text box into a shape:** Right-click the text box and choose Format Shape. In the Format Shape dialog box, click the Text Box category, and under AutoFit, click the Do Not AutoFit option button. Then close the dialog box, click the (Drawing Tools) Format tab, click the Edit Shape button, choose Change Shape on the drop-down list, and choose a shape on the Change Shape submenu.

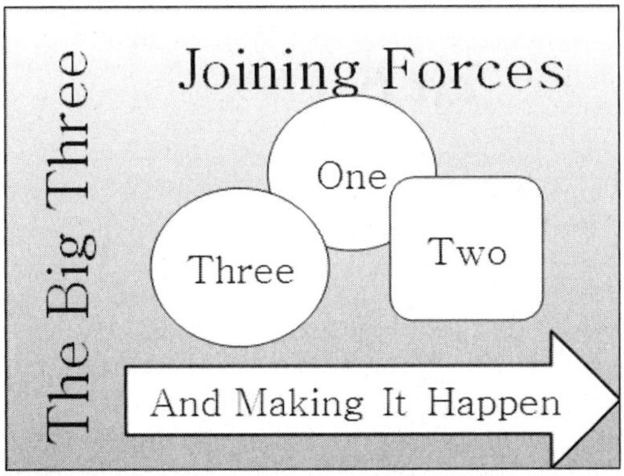

Figure 3-2: Examples of text boxes and text box shapes.

Many people object to the small text boxes that appear initially when you create a text box. If you prefer to establish the size of text boxes when you create them, not when you enter text, change the AutoFit setting and then create a default text box with the new setting. The next section in this chapter explains how to change the AutoFit settings.

Controlling How Text Fits in Text Frames and Text Boxes

When text doesn't fit in a text placeholder frame or text box, PowerPoint takes measures to make it fit. In a text frame, PowerPoint shrinks the amount of space between lines and then it shrinks the text itself. When text doesn't fit in a text box, PowerPoint enlarges the text box to fit more text. PowerPoint handles overflow text as part of its AutoFit mechanism.

How AutoFit works is up to you. If, like me, you don't care for how PowerPoint enlarges text boxes when you enter the text, you can tell PowerPoint not to "AutoFit" text, but instead to make text boxes large from the get-go. And if you don't care for how PowerPoint shrinks text in placeholder text frames, you can tell PowerPoint not to shrink text. These pages explain how to choose AutoFit options for overflow text in your text frames and text boxes.

Choosing how PowerPoint "AutoFits" text in text frames

When text doesn't fit in a text placeholder frame and PowerPoint has to "AutoFit" the text, you see the AutoFit Options button. Click this button to open a drop-down list with options for handling overflow text, as shown in Figure 3-3. The AutoFit options — along with a couple of other techniques, as I explain shortly — represent the "one at a time" way of handling overflow text. You can also change the default AutoFit options for handling overflow text, as I also explain if you'll bear with me a while longer and quit your yawning.

"AutoFitting" the text one frame at a time

When text doesn't fit in a text placeholder frame, especially a title frame, the first question to ask is, "Do I want to fool with the integrity of the slide design?" Making the text fit usually means shrinking the text, enlarging the text frame, or compromising the slide design in some way, but audiences notice design inconsistencies. Slides are shown on large screens where design flaws are easy to see.

Making text fit in a text frame usually means making a compromise. Here are different ways to handle the problem of text not fitting in a text frame. Be prepared to click the Undo button when you experiment with these techniques:

✦ **Edit the text:** Usually when text doesn't fit in a frame, the text needs editing. It needs to be made shorter. A slide is not a place for a treatise.

Editing the text is the only way to make it fit in the frame without compromising the design.

✦ **Enlarge the frame:** Click the AutoFit Options button and choose Stop Fitting Text to This Placeholder on the shortcut menu (see Figure 3-3). Then select the frame and drag the bottom or top selection handle to enlarge it.

✦ **Decrease the font size:** Select the text, go to the Home tab, and choose a smaller Font Size measurement. You can also click the Decrease Font Size button to decrease the font size.

✦ **Decrease the amount of spacing between lines:** Click the Paragraph group button on the Home tab to open the Paragraph dialog box and decrease the After measurement under Spacing.

✦ **Change the frame's internal margins:** Similar to a page, text frames have internal margins to keep text from getting too close to a frame border. By shrinking these margins, you can make more room for text. Right-click the text frame and choose Format Shape. Then, in the Text Box category of the Format Shape dialog box, enter smaller measurements for the Internal Margin boxes.

✦ **Create a new slide for the text:** If you're dealing with a list or paragraph text in a body text frame, the AutoFit Options drop-down list offers two ways to create a new slide (see Figure 3-3). Choose Continue on a New Slide to run the text onto another slide; choose Split Text between Two Slides to divide the text evenly between two slides. I don't recommend either option, though. If you need to make a new slide, do it on your own and then rethink how to present the material. Inserting a new slide to accommodate a long list throws a presentation off-track.

The AutoFit Options button appears when text doesn't fit in a text frame.

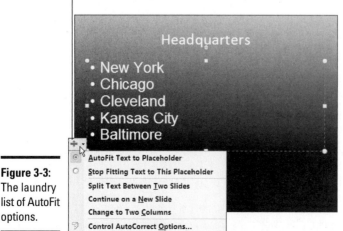

Figure 3-3:
The laundry list of AutoFit options.

Choosing default AutoFit options for text frames

Unless you change the default AutoFit options, PowerPoint shrinks the amount of space between lines and then shrinks the text itself to make text fit in text placeholder frames. Follow these steps if you want to decide for yourself whether PowerPoint "AutoFits" text in text frames:

1. **Open the AutoFormat As You Type tab in the AutoCorrect dialog box.**

Here are the two ways to get there:

- Click the AutoFit Options button (refer to Figure 3-3) and choose Control AutoCorrect Options on the drop-down list.

- Click the Office button and choose PowerPoint Options to open the PowerPoint Options dialog box. In the Proofing category, click the AutoCorrect Options button.

2. **Deselect the AutoFit Title Text to Placeholder check box to prevent AutoFitting in title text placeholder frames.**

3. **Deselect the AutoFit Body Text to Placeholder check box to prevent Autofitting in text placeholder frames apart from title frames.**

4. **Click OK.**

Choosing how PowerPoint "AutoFits" text in text boxes

PowerPoint offers three options for handling overflow text in text boxes:

✦ **Do Not AutoFit:** Doesn't fit text in the text box but lets text spill out.

✦ **Shrink Text on Overflow:** Shrinks the text to make it fit in the text box.

✦ **Resize Shape to Fit Text:** Enlarges the text box to make the text fit inside it.

Follow these steps to tell PowerPoint how or whether to fit text in text boxes:

1. **Select the text box.**

2. **Right-click the text box and choose Format Shape.**

You see the Format Shape dialog box.

3. **Click the Text Box category.**

4. **Choose an AutoFit option: Do Not AutoFit, Shrink Text on Overflow, or Resize Shape to Fit Text.**

5. **Click the Close button.**

Some people find it easier to dispense with "AutoFitting." If you're one of those people, go to the Text Box category of the Format Shape dialog box, and under AutoFit, choose the Do Not AutoFit option or the Shrink Text on Overflow option. To make your AutoFit setting applicable to all the text boxes you create in your presentation, right-click the text box and choose Set As Default Text Box on the shortcut menu.

Positioning Text in Frames and Text Boxes

How text is positioned in text frames and text boxes is governed by two sets of commands: the Align Text commands and the Align commands. By choosing combinations of Align and Align Text commands, you can land text where you want it in a text frame or text box. Just wrestle with these two commands until you land your text where you want it to be in the text frame or box:

✦ **Align commands** control horizontal (left-to-right) alignments. On the Home tab, click the Align Left, Center, Align Right, or Justify button.

✦ **Align Text commands** control vertical (up-and-down) alignments. On the Home tab, click the Align Text button and choose Top, Middle, or Bottom on the drop-down list, as shown in Figure 3-4.

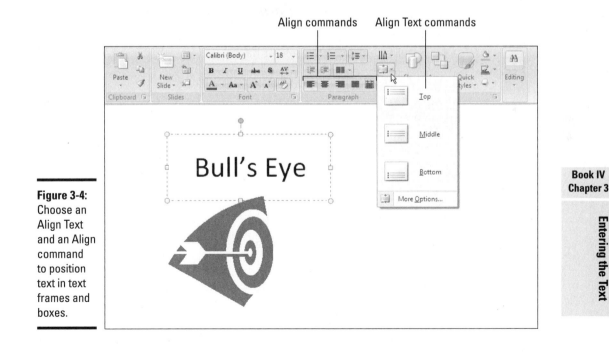

Figure 3-4:
Choose an Align Text and an Align command to position text in text frames and boxes.

**Book IV
Chapter 3**

Entering the Text

Distributing a title means to stretch it across a text frame or text box, from the left to the right margin. As long as enough words are in the title to distribute it without making the title a shambles, a distributed title looks rather interesting. To distribute a title, select it and click the Distributed button on the Home tab.

Handling Bulleted and Numbered Lists

What is a PowerPoint presentation without a list or two? It's like an emperor without any clothes on. This part of the chapter explains everything there is to know about bulleted and numbered lists.

These lists can be as simple or complex as you want them to be. PowerPoint offers a bunch of different ways to format these lists, but if you're in a hurry or you don't care whether your lists look like everyone else's, you can take advantage of the Numbering and Bullets buttons and go with standard lists. Nonconformists and people with nothing else to do, however, can try their hand at making fancy lists. The following pages cover that topic, too.

Creating a standard bulleted or numbered list

In typesetting terms, a *bullet* is a black, filled-in circle or other character that marks an item on a list. Many slide layouts include text frames that are already formatted for bulleted lists. All you have to do in these text frames is "click to add text" and keep pressing the Enter key while you enter items for your bulleted list. Each time you press Enter, PowerPoint adds another bullet to the list. Bulleted lists are useful when you want to present the reader with alternatives or present a list in which the items aren't ranked in any order. Use a numbered list to rank items in a list or present step-by-step instructions.

Follow these instructions to create a standard bulleted or numbered list:

 ✦ **Creating a bulleted list:** Select the list if you've already entered the list items, click the Home tab, and click the Bullets button (or click the Bullets button on the Mini Toolbar). You can also right-click, choose Bullets on the shortcut menu, and choose a bullet character on the submenu if you don't care for the standard, black, filled-in circle.

 ✦ **Creating a numbered list:** Select the list if you've already entered the list items, click the Home tab, and click the Numbering button. You can also right-click, choose Numbering on the shortcut menu, and select a numbering style on the submenu.

✦ **Converting a numbered to a bulleted list (or vice versa):** Drag over the list to select it, click the Home tab, and then click the Bullets or Numbering button.

To remove the bullets or numbers from a list, select the list, right-click it, choose Bullets or Numbering on the shortcut menu, and choose None on the submenu.

Choosing a different bullet character, size, and color

As Figure 3-5 demonstrates, the black filled-in circle isn't the only character you can use to mark items in a bulleted list. You can also opt for what PowerPoint calls *pictures* (colorful bullets of many sizes and shapes) or symbols from the Symbol dialog box. While you're at it, you can change the bullet color and size.

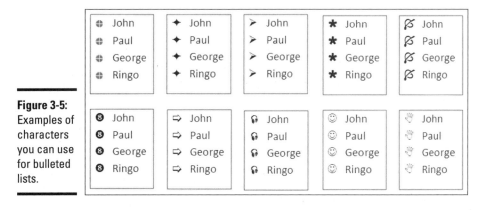

Figure 3-5: Examples of characters you can use for bulleted lists.

If you decide to change the bullet character in your lists, be consistent from slide to slide. Unless you want to be goofy, select the same bullet character throughout the lists in your presentation for the sake of consistency. You don't want to turn your slide presentation into a showcase for bullets, do you?

To use pictures or unusual symbols for bullets, start by selecting your bulleted list (if you already entered the list items), clicking the Home tab, and opening the drop-down list on the Bullets button. Do any of the bullets on the drop-down list tickle your fancy? If one does, choose it; otherwise, click the Bullets and Numbering option at the bottom of the drop-down list. You see the Bulleted tab of the Bullets and Numbering dialog box. Starting there, you can customize your bullets:

✦ **Using a picture for bullets:** Click the Picture button and select a bullet in the Picture Bullet dialog box.

✦ **Using a symbol for bullets:** Click the Customize button and select a bullet in the Symbol dialog box. By opening the Font drop-down list and choosing a Wingdings font, you can choose an oddball character for bullets.

✦ **Changing bullets' color:** Click the Color button in the Bullets and Numbering dialog box and choose an option on the drop-down list. Theme colors are considered most compatible with the theme design you choose for your presentation.

✦ **Changing bullets' size:** Enter a percentage figure in the Size % of Text box. For example, if you enter 200, the bullets are twice as big as the font size you choose for the items in your bulleted list.

Choosing a different list-numbering style, size, and color

PowerPoint offers seven different ways of numbering lists. As well as choosing a different numbering style, you can change the size of numbers relative to the text and change the color of numbers. To select a different list-numbering style, size, or color, begin by selecting your list (if you already entered the list items), clicking the Home tab, and opening the drop-down list on the Numbering button. If you like one of the numbering-scheme choices, select it; otherwise choose Bullets and Numbering to open the Numbered tab of the Bullets and Numbering dialog box. In this dialog box, you can customize list numbers:

✦ **Choosing a numbering scheme:** Select a numbering scheme and click OK.

✦ **Changing the numbers' color:** Click the Color button and choose a color on the drop-down list. Theme colors are more compatible with the theme design you choose than the other colors are.

✦ **Changing the numbers' size:** Enter a percentage figure in the Size % of Text box. For example, if you enter 50, the numbers are half as big as the font size you choose for the items in your numbered list.

Putting Footers (and Headers) on Slides

A *footer* is a line of text that appears at the foot, or bottom, of a slide. Figure 3-6 shows a footer. Typically, a footer includes the date, a company name, and/or a slide number, and footers appear on every slide in a presentation if they appear at all. That doesn't mean you can't exclude a footer from a slide or put footers on some slides, as I explain shortly. For that matter, you can move slide numbers, company names, and dates to the top of slides, in which case they become *headers*. When I was a kid, "header" meant crashing your bike and falling headfirst over the handlebars. How times change.

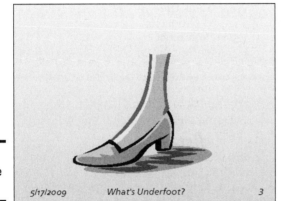

5/17/2009   *What's Underfoot?*   3

Figure 3-6:
An example
of a footer.

These pages explain everything a body needs to know about footers and headers — how to enter them, make them appear on all or some slides, and exclude them from slides.

Some background on footers and headers

PowerPoint provides the Header & Footer command to enter the date, a word or two, and/or a slide number on the bottom of all slides in your presentation. This command is really just a convenient way for you to enter a footer on the Slide Master without having to switch to Slide Master view. As Chapter 2 in this mini-book explains, the Slide Master governs the formatting and layout of all slides in your presentation. The Slide Master includes text placeholder frames for a date, some text, and a slide number. Anything you enter on the Slide Master, including a footer, appears on all your slides.

If a date, some text, and/or a slide number along the bottom of all the slides in your presentation is precisely what you want, you've got it made. You can enter a footer on every slide in your presentation with no trouble at all by using the Header & Footer command. However, if you're a maverick and you want your footers and headers to be a little different from the next guy's — if you want the date, for example, to be in the upper-right corner of slides or you want footers to appear on some slides but not others — you have some tweaking to do. You may have to create a nonstandard footer or remove the footer from some of the slides.

Putting a standard footer on all your slides

A standard footer includes the date, some text, and/or the page number. To put a standard footer on all the slides in your presentation, click the Insert tab and then click the Header & Footer button. You see the Header and Footer dialog box. Choose some or all of these options to enter a footer:

+ **Date and Time:** Select this check box to make the date appear in the lower-left corner of all your slides. Then tell PowerPoint whether you want a current or fixed date:

  • *Update Automatically:* Select this option button to make the day's date (or date and time) appear in the footer and then open the drop-down list to choose a date (or date and time) format. With this option, the date you give your presentation always appears on slides.

  • *Fixed:* Select this option button and enter a date in the text box. For example, enter the date you created the presentation. With this option, the date remains the same no matter when or where you give the presentation.

+ **Slide Number:** Select this check box to make slide numbers appear in the lower-right corner of all slides.

+ **Footer:** Select this check box, and in the text box, enter the words that you want to appear in the bottom, middle of all the slides.

Creating a nonstandard footer

As "Some background on footers and headers" explains earlier in this chapter, you have to look elsewhere than the Header and Footer dialog box if you want to create something besides the standard footer. Suppose you want to move the slide number from the lower-right corner of slides to another position? Or you want to fool with the fonts in headers and footers?

Follow these steps to create a nonstandard footer:

1. **Create a standard footer if you want your nonstandard footer to include today's date and/or a slide number.**

   If you want to move the slide number into the upper-right corner of slides, for example, create a standard footer first (see the preceding section in this chapter). Later, you can move the slide number text frame into the upper-right corner of slides.

2. **On the View tab, click the Slide Master button.**

   You switch to Slide Master view. Chapter 2 in this mini-book explains this view and how to format many slides at once with master slides.

3. Select the Slide Master, the first slide in the Slides pane.

4. Adjust and format the footer text boxes to taste (as they say in cookbooks).

For example, move the slide number text frame into the upper-right corner to put slide numbers there. Or change the font in the footer text boxes. Or place a company logo on the Slide Master to make the logo appear on all your slides.

5. Click the Close button to return to Normal view.

You can always return to Slide Master view and adjust your footer.

Removing a footer from a single slide

On a crowded slide, the items in the footer — the date, footer text, and page number — can get in the way or be a distraction. Fortunately, removing one or all of the three footer text frames from a slide is easy:

1. Switch to Normal view and display the slide with the footer that needs removing.

2. Select the Insert tab.

3. Click the Header & Footer button.

The Header and Footer dialog box appears.

4. Deselect check boxes — Date and Time, Slide Number, and Footer — to tell PowerPoint which parts of the footer you want to remove.

5. Click the Apply button.

Be careful not to click the Apply to All button. Clicking this button removes footers throughout your slide presentation.

Chapter 4: Making Your Presentations Livelier

In This Chapter

✔ **Looking at ways to make a presentation livelier**

✔ **Slapping a transition or animation on a slide**

✔ **Making sound a part of your presentation**

✔ **Playing video during a presentation**

The purpose of this chapter is to make your presentation stand out in a crowd. I suggest ways to enliven your presentation with pictures, charts, slides, and tables. I show how transitions and animations can make a presentation spicier. Finally, you discover how to play sound and video during a presentation.

Suggestions for Enlivening Your Presentation

Starting on the Insert tab, you can do a lot to make a presentation livelier. The Insert tab offers buttons for inserting pictures, tables, charts, diagrams, shapes, and clip-art images on slides:

✦ **Photos:** Everyone likes a good photo, but more than that, audiences understand more from words and pictures than they do from words alone. A well-chosen photo reinforces the ideas that you're trying to put across in your presentation. (See Book VIII, Chapter 3.)

✦ **Tables:** A table is a great way to plead your case or defend your position. Raw table data is irrefutable — well, most of the time, anyway. Create a table when you want to demonstrate how the numbers back you up. (See Book I, Chapter 5.)

✦ **Charts:** Nothing is more persuasive than a chart. The bars, pie slices, or columns show the audience instantaneously that production is up or down, or that sector A is outperforming sector B. The audience can compare the data and see what's what. (See Book I, Chapter 6.)

✦ **Diagrams:** A diagram is an excellent marriage of images and words. Diagrams allow an audience to literally visualize a concept, idea, or relationship. You can present an abstract idea such that the audience understands it better. (See Book I, Chapter 7.)

✦ **Shapes:** Lines and shapes can also illustrate ideas and concepts. You can also use them as slide decorations. (See Book I, Chapter 8.)

✦ **Clip-art images:** Clip-art images bring a little more color to presentations. They make presentations friendlier and easier to look at. (See Book VIII, Chapter 4.)

The grid and drawing guides

The *grid* is an invisible set of horizontal and vertical lines to which objects — clip-art images, pictures, and shapes — cling when you move them on a slide. The grid is meant to help objects line up squarely with one another. When you drag an object, it sticks to the nearest grid line. Besides the grid, PowerPoint offers the drawing guides for aligning objects. These guides divide a slide into vertical and horizontal planes.

When you want to align or place objects with precision, display the grid and the drawing guides:

✔ **Displaying (and hiding) the grid:** Press Shift+F9 or go to the View tab and click the Gridlines check box.

✔ **Displaying (and hiding) the drawing guides:** Press Alt+F9 or right-click (but not on an object or frame), choose Grid and Guides, and in the Grid and Guides dialog box, select the Display Drawing Guides on Screen check box.

Even if the Snap Objects to Grid check box in the Grid and Guides dialog box is selected, you can move objects without them snapping to a gridline by holding down the Alt key while you drag.

Select the Snap Objects to Other Objects check box if you want shapes to abut each other or fall along a common axis.

Hitting the Target

Transitions and Animations

In PowerPoint-speak, a *transition* is a little bit of excitement that occurs as one slide leaves the screen and the next slide climbs aboard. An *animation* is movement on the slide. For example, you can animate bulleted lists such that the bullet points appear on a slide one at a time when you click the mouse rather than all at once.

Before you know anything about transitions and animations, you should know that they can be distracting. The purpose of a presentation is to communicate with the audience, not display the latest, busiest, most dazzling presentation technology. For user-run, kiosk-style presentations, however, eye-catching transitions and animations can be useful because they draw an audience. (A user-run presentation plays on its own, as I explain in Chapter 5 of this mini-book.) For audiences that enjoy high-tech wizardry, transitions and animations can be a lot of fun and add to a presentation.

Showing transitions between slides

Transitions include the Dissolve, the Wipe Up, and the Cover Down. Figure 4-1 shows how a transition works. For the figure, I chose the News Flash transition. This slide doesn't so much arrive on-screen as it does spin onto the screen. Don't worry, you get a chance to test-drive these transitions before you attach them to slides. Follow these steps to show transitions between slides:

Figure 4-1: The News Flash transition in action.

1. **Click the Animations tab.**

2. **Select the slides that need a transition.**

If you need to select more than one slide or you don't want to assign the same transition to all your slides, switch to Slide Sorter view to make selecting slides easier.

To apply the same transition to all the slides in the presentation, skip this step and click the Apply to All button after you select a transition.

3. **In the Transition Scheme gallery, choose a transition (you may have to click the Transition Scheme button first, depending on the size of your screen).**

The names and images on the drop-down list give you an idea of what the transitions are, but the only sure way to tell what a transition does is to watch a slide after you make your choice. However fleetingly, you see the transition you chose on a slide.

4. **If you care to, open the Transition Sound drop-down list and choose a sound to accompany the transition.**

Hold the pointer over sound names to hear the different sounds. The Loop until Next Sound option at the bottom of the drop-down list plays a sound continuously until the next slide in the presentation appears.

5. **On the Transition Speed drop-down list, choose Slow, Medium, or Fast to declare how quickly or slowly you want the transition to occur.**

As I mention in Step 2, you can click the Apply to All button to assign the same transition to all the slides in your presentation.

If you can't recall which transition you assigned to a slide, click the slide's Play Animations symbol (a flying star) or click the Preview button on the Animations tab. You see a transition and hear an accompanying sound if you chose one.

Animating parts of a slide

When it comes to animations, you can choose between *animation schemes,* the pre-built special effects made by the elves of Microsoft, or *customized animations* that you build on your own. Only fans of animation and people with a lot of time on their hands go the second route.

Choosing a ready-made animation scheme

Follow these steps to preview and choose an animation scheme for slides:

1. **Go to the Animations tab.**

2. **Click to select the element on the slide that you want to animate.**

You can tell when you've selected an element because a selection box appears around it.

3. **Open the Animate drop-down list and choose an animation effect, as shown in Figure 4-2.**

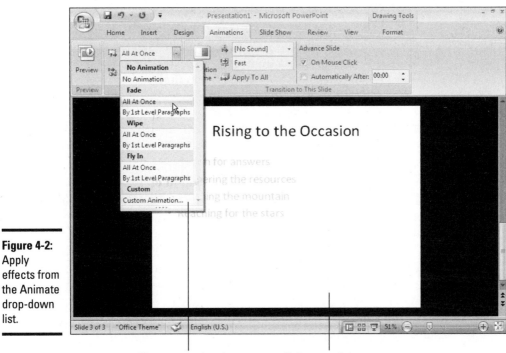

Choose an animation.   Select an element.

Figure 4-2:
Apply effects from the Animate drop-down list.

Your choices are Fade, Wipe, and Fly In.

If you choose a text-box or text-frame element with more than one paragraph in Step 1, tell PowerPoint whether to animate all the text or animate each paragraph separately from the others:

- *All at Once:* All the text is animated at the same time.

- *By 1st Level Paragraphs:* Each paragraph is treated separately and is animated on its own. For example, each item in a bulleted list is treated as a separate element — each item fades, wipes, or flies in after the one before it, not at the same time as the one before it.

Very briefly, you see a preview of the animation choice you made. To get a good look at the animation you just chose for your slide, click the Preview button on the Animation tab.

To remove an animation, return to the Animate drop-down list and choose No Animation.

**Book IV
Chapter 4**

**Making Your
Presentations
Livelier**

Fashioning your own animation scheme

To fashion your own animation scheme, click the Custom Animation button. You see the Custom Animation task pane. Select an element on the slide and follow these general instructions to animate it:

✦ Click the Add Effect button and choose an animation on one of the submenus.

✦ On the Start drop-down list, declare whether the animation begins when you click your slide, at the same time as the previous animation, or after the previous animation.

✦ Open the Speed drop-down list and choose a speed setting.

✦ Select an animation in the task pane and click a Re-Order button to change the order in which animations occur, if more than one slide element is animated on your slide.

Sounding Off on Slides

Especially in user-run, kiosk-style presentations, sound can be a welcome addition. Sound gives presentations an extra dimension. Sound attracts an audience. PowerPoint offers two ways to make sound a part of a presentation:

✦ **As part of slide transitions:** The sound is heard as a new slide arrives on-screen. On the Animations tab, open the Transition Sound drop-down list and choose a sound. (See "Showing transitions between slides" earlier in this chapter.)

✦ **On the slide itself:** The means of playing the sound appears on the slide in the form of a Sound icon, as shown in Figure 4-3. By clicking the Sound icon, you can play the sound. You can also make the sound play as soon as the slide arrives on-screen.

Figure 4-3: Making sound part of a pres- entation.

Table 4-1 describes the sound files you can use in PowerPoint presentations, whether each file type is a wave or MIDI sound, and whether the file can be used in slide transitions. To find out what kind of sound file you're dealing with, note the file's three-letter extension; or open Windows Explorer or My Computer, find the sound file, switch to Details view, and look in the Type column. To switch to Details view in Windows Explorer or My Computer, click the View button and choose Details on the drop-down list.

Table 4-1	Sound File Formats		
File Type	*Extension*	*Wave/MIDI*	*In Transitions*
MIDI Sequence	`.midi, .mid`	MIDI	Yes
MP3 audio file	`.mp3`	Wave	No
Wave sound	`.wav`	Wave	Yes
Windows Media Audio File	`.wma`	Wave	No

Playing sounds: A precautionary tale

Before you consider making sound a part of your presentation, consider how PowerPoint handles sound files. Unless a sound file is a WAV file and is less than 100 KB in size, it isn't made a part of a presentation. The sound file isn't *embedded.* To play a sound file larger than 100 KB, PowerPoint reaches into the folder on your computer where the sound file is located and plays the file from there. Keeping large sound files separate from the PowerPoint presentation in which they're played can cause problems if you move a sound file, load your presentation on a different computer, or send your presentation to someone else because your PowerPoint presentation gets separated from the sound file.

If you intend to move your PowerPoint presentation to a different computer, consider these precautions to make sure that the sound files in the presentation still play:

✦ **Keep sound files in the same folder as your presentation file:** Move the sound files you need for your presentation into the same folder as the presentation, insert the sound files, and send the sound files along with the presentation file to the other computer. This way, the relationship between the presentation and the sound files remains intact. When your presentation calls on a sound file to play, the sound file is ready and waiting.

✦ **Package your presentation for a CD:** Packaging folds all the files associated with a PowerPoint presentation — the sound and video files — into one large file so that the presentation can be taken on the road. Chapter 5 of this mini-book describes the Package for CD command.

✦ **Change the WAV-file-size-link setting:** You can change the 100 KB cutoff point for storing WAV files inside slides. Click the Office button and choose PowerPoint Options to open the PowerPoint Options dialog box, select the Advanced category, and under Save (you may have to scroll to get there), enter a new KB measurement in the Link Sounds with File Size Greater Than box.

Inserting a sound file on a slide

Before you insert your sound file on a slide, ask yourself, "Do I want the sound file to start playing when the slide appears or when I click the Sound icon?" Clicking the Sound icon gives you more control over when the sound is heard, but you have to remember to click the icon to start playing the sound. You can hide the Sound icon or leave it on a slide to remind yourself to click to start playing sounds.

Follow these steps to insert a sound file in a slide:

1. **Click the Insert tab.**

2. **Click the Sound button.**

You see the Insert Sound dialog box.

3. **Locate and select a sound file and then click OK.**

Earlier in this chapter, Table 4-1 lists the type of sound files that you can play in presentations.

4. **Choose Automatically or When Clicked in the dialog box that asks how you want the sound to start playing.**

Here are your choices:

- *Automatically:* Click this button to make the sound play automatically as soon as the slide appears.

- *When Clicked:* Click this button to play the sound when you click the Sound icon on your slide.

Don't worry about choosing right now. You can always change your mind about when a sound plays, as "Telling PowerPoint when and how to play a sound file" explains later in this chapter.

A Sound icon appears on the slide to remind you that sounds are supposed to play when your slide is on-screen. You can change the size of this icon by selecting it and dragging a corner handle or going to the (Sound Tools) Options tab and entering new Height and Width measurements. You can also drag the icon into an out-of-the-way corner of your slide.

To quit playing a sound file on a slide, select the Sound icon and then press the Delete key.

Telling PowerPoint when and how to play a sound file

To tell PowerPoint when and how to play a sound file, start by selecting the Sound icon and going to the (Sound Tools) Options tab, as shown in Figure 4-4. From there, you can select options on the tab or click the Sound Options group button to open the Sound Options dialog box and select options there. Here are your choices for telling PowerPoint when and how to play a sound file:

✦ **Controlling the volume:** Click the Slide Show Volume button (on the tab) or the Sound Volume icon (in the dialog box) to control how loud the sound is. The tab offers Low, Medium, High, and Mute settings; the dialog box offers a slider.

✦ **Hiding and unhiding the Sound icon:** Select the Hide during Show check box (on the tab) or the Hide Sound Icon during Slide Show check box (in the dialog box). If you hide the Sound icon, the sound file must play automatically; otherwise, you won't see the Sound icon and be able to click it and make the file play.

✦ **Continuously playing a sound:** Select the Loop until Stopped check box (on the tab or the dialog box) to play the sound file over and over again or until you move on to the next slide.

✦ **Changing the Automatically or When Clicked status:** Open the Play Sound drop-down list on the Options tab and choose Automatically or When Clicked to tell PowerPoint when to start playing sound.

Figure 4-4: Visit the (Sound Tools) Options tab or Sound Options dialog box to control when and how sounds play.

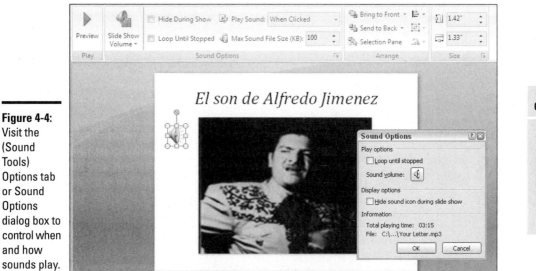

Starting, pausing, and resuming a sound file

While a sound file is playing during a presentation, you can pause and resume playing it as long as the Sound icon appears on your slide. (If you've hidden the Sound icon, you're out of luck because you have to click it to pause a sound file.) Follow these instructions to start, pause, and resume a sound recording during a presentation:

✦ **Starting a sound file:** Click the Sound icon.

✦ **Pausing and resuming a sound file:** Click the Sound icon to pause. To resume playing, click the Sound icon again. Be careful to click the Sound icon and not another part of your slide when you start, pause, or resume playing a sound file. Clicking another part of the slide advances your presentation to the next slide.

Playing Video on Slides

If a picture is worth a thousand words, what is a moving picture worth? Ten thousand? To give your presentation more cachet, you can play video on slides and in so doing, turn your presentation into a mini-movie theater.

To play video, PowerPoint relies on *Windows Media Player,* the media player that comes with Windows. Therefore, to play video on a slide, stick to formats that Windows Media Player can handle: AVI (Audio Visual Interleaved), MPEG (Motion Picture Experts Group), MPG (Media Planning Group), WMV (Windows Media Video), and ASF (Advanced Systems Format). Avoid video files in these formats: MOV (QuickTime Video), RM (RealVideo), and VCD (Video Compact Disc).

Inserting a video on a slide

Follow these steps to insert a video on a slide:

1. **Open the Insert Movie dialog box.**

You can open the dialog box with one of these techniques:

- Click the Movie icon in a content placeholder frame.

- On the Insert tab, click the Movie button.

2. **Select a video file in the Insert Movie dialog box and click OK (or Open).**

3. **In the dialog box that asks how you want the video to start playing, select Automatically or When Clicked.**

Automatically makes the video play automatically when the slide appears; When Clicked plays the video after you or another presenter clicks it. Don't waste too much time deciding because changing your mind is easy enough, as "Fine-tuning a video presentation" explains shortly.

The video appears on your slide. If I were you, I would find out how (or whether) the video plays. To do that, right-click the video and choose Preview on the shortcut menu or go to the (Movie Tools) Options tab and click the Preview button.

Unlike photos, videos aren't made a part of a slide when you place a video on a slide. To use a technical term, videos aren't *embedded* in slides. To play a video, PowerPoint notes the address of the video file on your computer, reaches into the folder where the video is stored, and plays the video file from there. How PowerPoint plays videos on slides needn't concern you if you never have to move your presentation to a different computer or give your presentation to someone else. But if your presentation will travel, either keep video files in the same folder as your presentation file and move the video files along with your presentation file to the other computer, or use the Package for CD command to fold video files into your presentation and embed them there. (Chapter 5 of this mini-book explains the Package for CD command.)

Fine-tuning a video presentation

As shown in Figure 4-5, select the video and go to the (Movie Tools) Options tab to fine-tune a video presentation. The Options tab and the Movie Options dialog box offer all kinds of commands for making a video play the way you want it to play. Click the Movie Options group button (see Figure 4-5) to open the Movie Options dialog box. Here are different ways you can fine-tune a video presentation:

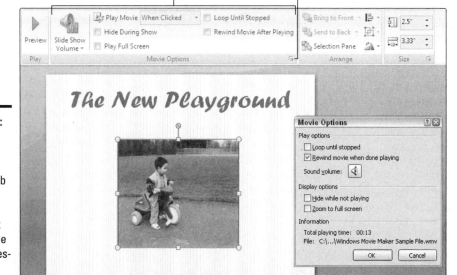

Figure 4-5: Visit the (Movie Tools) Options tab or Movie Options dialog box to fine-tune a video presentation.

+ **Controlling the volume:** Click the Slide Show Volume button (on the Options tab) or the Sound Volume icon (in the Movie Options dialog box) to control how loud the video sound is.

+ **Playing the video automatically or when you click:** Open the Play Movie drop-down list on the Options tab and choose Automatically or When Clicked to tell PowerPoint when to start playing the video.

+ **Hiding the video until you give the order to start playing:** You can hide the video until you start playing it by selecting the Hide during Show check box (on the Options tab) or the Hide While Not Playing check box (in the Movie Options dialog box).

+ **Continuously playing, or looping, the video:** Play a movie continuously or until you go to the next slide by selecting the Loop until Stopped check box (on the Options tab or Movie Options dialog box).

+ **Playing the video at full-screen:** Make a video fill the entire screen by selecting the Play Full Screen check box (on the Options tab) or the Zoom to Full Screen check box (in the Movie Options dialog box). Be careful of this one. Videos can look terribly grainy when they appear on the big screen.

+ **Rewinding the video when it's finished playing:** Rewind a video if you want to see the first frame, not the last, when the video finishes playing. Select the Rewind Movie After Playing check box (on the Options tab) or the Rewind Movie When Done Playing check box (in the Movie Options dialog box) to make the start of the video appear after the video plays; deselect this option to freeze frame on the end of the video when it finishes playing.

Chapter 5: Delivering a Presentation

In This Chapter

✔ **Writing, editing, and printing speaker notes**

✔ **Rehearsing a presentation to see how long it is**

✔ **Going from slide to slide in a live presentation**

✔ **Drawing on slides during a presentation**

✔ **Delivering a presentation when you can't be there in person**

*A*t last, the big day has arrived. It's time to give the presentation. "Break a leg," as actors say before they go on stage. This chapter explains how to rehearse your presentation to find out how long it is and show your presentation. You discover some techniques to make your presentation livelier, including how to draw on slides with a pen or highlighter and blank out the screen to get the audience's full attention. The chapter describes how to handle the speaker notes and print handouts for your audience. In case you can't be there in person to deliver your presentation, this chapter shows you how to create a user-run presentation, a self-running presentation, and a presentation designed to be viewed from a CD.

All about Notes

Notes are strictly for the speaker. They aren't for the unwashed masses. Don't hesitate to write notes to yourself when you put together your presentation. The notes will come in handy when you're rehearsing and giving your presentation. They give you ideas for what to say and help you communicate better. Here are instructions for entering, editing, and printing notes:

> ✦ **Entering a note:** To enter a note, start in Normal view, click in the Notes pane, and start typing. Treat the Notes pane like a page in a word processor. For example, press Enter to go to the next line and press the

Tab key to indent text. You can drag the border above the Notes pane up or down to make the pane larger or smaller.

+ **Editing notes in Notes Page view:** After you've jotted down a bunch of notes, switch to Notes Page view and edit them. To switch to Notes Page view, click the View tab and then click the Notes Page button. Notes appear in a text frame below a picture of the slide to which they refer. You may have to zoom in to read them.

+ **Printing your notes:** Click the Office button and choose Print⇨Print (or press Ctrl+P). You see the Print dialog box. In the Print What drop-down list, choose Notes Pages, and click OK.

Rehearsing and Timing Your Presentation

Slide presentations and theatrical presentations have this in common: They are as good as the number of times you rehearse them. Be sure to rehearse your presentation many times over. The more you rehearse, the more comfortable you will be giving your presentation. Follow these steps to rehearse a presentation, record its length, and record how long each slide is displayed:

1. **Select the first slide in your presentation.**

2. **Click the Slide Show tab.**

3. **Click the Rehearse Timings button.**

The Rehearsal toolbar appears, as shown in Figure 5-1, and you switch to Slide Show view.

Note how long your presentation is.

Figure 5-1:
Timing the
rehearsal.

Advance to the next side.

4. **Give your presentation one slide at a time and click the Next button on the Rehearsal toolbar to go from slide to slide.**

When each slide appears, imagine that you're presenting it to an audience. Say what you intend to say during the real presentation. If you anticipate audience members asking questions, allot time for questions.

The Rehearsal toolbar tells you how long each slide has been displayed and how long your presentation is so far. You can do these tasks from the Rehearsal toolbar:

- *Go to the next slide:* Click the Next button.

- *Pause recording:* Temporarily stop the recording so that you can feed the dog or take a phone call. Click the Pause button a second time to resume recording.

- *Repeat a slide:* Click the Repeat button if you get befuddled and want to start over with a slide. The slide timing returns to 0:00:00.

5. **In the dialog box that asks whether you want to keep the slide timings, note how long your presentation is (see Figure 5-1).**

Is your presentation too long or too short? I hope, like baby bear's porridge, your presentation is "just right." But if it's too long or short, you have some work to do. You have to figure out how to shorten or lengthen it.

6. **In the dialog box that asks whether you want to keep the slide timings, click Yes if you want to see how long each slide stayed on-screen during the rehearsal.**

By clicking Yes, you can see how long each slide remained on-screen in Slide Sorter view.

If you save the slide timings, PowerPoint assumes that, during a presentation, you want to advance to the next slide manually or after the recorded time, whichever comes first. For example, suppose the first slide in your presentation remained on-screen for a minute during the rehearsal. During your presentation, the first slide will remain on-screen for a minute and automatically yield to the second slide unless you click to advance to the second slide before the minute has passed. If you recorded slide timings strictly to find out how long your presentation is, you need to tell PowerPoint not to advance automatically to the next slide during a presentation after the recorded time period elapses. On the Slide Show tab, deselect the Use Rehearsed Timings check box.

Showing Your Presentation

Compared to the preliminary work, giving a presentation can seem kind of anticlimactic. All you have to do is go from slide to slide and woo your audience with your smooth-as-silk voice and powerful oratory skills. Well, at least the move-from-slide-to-slide part is pretty easy. These pages explain how to start and end a presentation, all the different ways to advance or retreat from slide to slide, and how to jump to different slides.

Starting and ending a presentation

Here are the different ways to start a presentation from the beginning:

+ On the Slide Show tab, click the From Beginning button.
+ Select the first slide and then click the Slide Show view button.

You can start a presentation in the middle by selecting a slide in the middle and then clicking the Slide Show view button or going to the Slide Show tab and clicking the From Current Slide button.

Here are the different ways to end a presentation prematurely:

+ Press Esc, Ctrl+Break, or – (the Hyphen key).
+ Click the Slide button and choose End Show on the pop-up list. This button is located in the lower-left corner of the screen.
+ Right-click and choose End Show in the shortcut menu.

Going from slide to slide

In a nutshell, PowerPoint offers four ways to move from slide to slide in a presentation. Table 5-1 describes techniques for navigating a presentation using the four different ways:

+ **Use the slide control buttons:** Click a slide control button — Previous and Next — in the lower-left corner of the screen, as shown in Figure 5-2. If you don't see the slide control buttons, jiggle the mouse.
+ **Click the Slide button:** Click this button and make a choice on the pop-up list (see Figure 5-2).
+ **Right-click on-screen:** Right-click and choose a navigation option on the shortcut menu.
+ **Press a keyboard shortcut:** Press one of the numerous keyboard shortcuts that PowerPoint offers for going from slide to slide (see Table 5-1).

Table 5-1	Techniques for Getting from Slide to Slide			
To Go Here	*Slide Control Button*	*Click the Slide Button and Choose. . .*	*Right-click and Choose. . .*	*Keyboard Shortcut*
Next slide*	Next	Next	Next	Enter, spacebar, N, Page Down, ↓, or →
Previous slide	Previous	Previous	Previous	Backspace, P, Page Up, ↑, or ←
Specific slide		Go To Slide⇨ Slide number and title	Go to Slide⇨ Slide number and title	Slide number+Enter; Ctrl+S and then select Slide number and title
Last viewed slide		Last Viewed	Last Viewed	

If animations are on a slide, commands for going to the next slide instead make animations play in sequence. To bypass animations and go to the next slide, use a command for going forward across several slides. (See "Jumping forward or backward to a specific slide.")

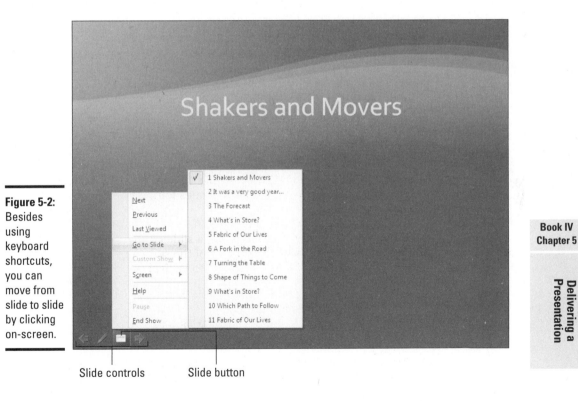

Figure 5-2: Besides using keyboard shortcuts, you can move from slide to slide by clicking on-screen.

Slide controls   Slide button

Going forward (or backward) from slide to slide

To go forward from one slide to the following slide in a presentation, click on-screen. After you click, the next slide appears. If all goes well, clicking is the only technique you need to know when giving a presentation to go from slide to slide, but Table 5-1 lists other ways to go to the next slide in a presentation as well as techniques for going backward to the previous slide.

To go to the first slide in a presentation, press Home; to go to the last slide, press End.

Jumping forward or backward to a specific slide

If you find it necessary to jump forward or backward across several slides in your presentation to get to the slide you want to show, it can be done with these techniques:

✦ Either click the Slide button or right-click, choose Go to Slide, and then choose a slide in your presentation on the submenu (refer to Figure 5-2).

✦ Press Ctrl+S. You see the All Slides dialog box. It lists all slides in your presentation. Select the slide you want to show and click the Go To button.

✦ Press the slide number you want on your keyboard (if you can remember the slide's number) and then press the Enter key. For example, to show the third slide in your presentation, press 3 and then press Enter.

If you need to return to where you started after you make the jump to a different slide, you can do so by right-clicking and choosing Last Viewed on the shortcut menu. You can also click the Slide button and choose Last Viewed (refer to Figure 5-2). The Last Viewed command takes you to the last slide you showed, wherever it is in your presentation.

Tricks for Making Presentations a Little Livelier

To make presentations a little livelier, whip out a pen and draw on a slide or blank the screen. Draw to underline words or draw check marks as you hit the key points, as shown in Figure 5-3. Drawing on slides is an excellent way to add a little something to a presentation. Blank the screen when you want the audience's undivided attention.

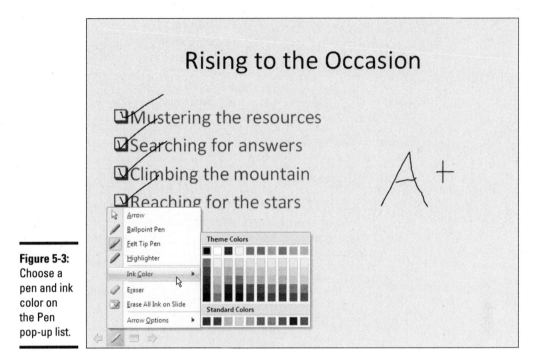

Figure 5-3:
Choose a pen and ink color on the Pen pop-up list.

Wielding a pen or highlighter in a presentation

Follow these instructions so you can draw on a slide:

+ **Selecting a pen or highlighter:** PowerPoint offers the Ballpoint Pen (thin) and Felt Tip Pen (thicker), as well as the Highlighter for highlighting text on a slide. To select a pen or the Highlighter, click the Pen button and choose a pen or the Highlighter (see Figure 5-3). You can also right-click, choose Pointer Options, and make a selection on the submenu.

+ **Choosing a color for drawing:** After you select a pen or the Highlighter, click the Pen button, choose Ink Color, and choose a color on the submenu (see Figure 5-3). You can also right-click to choose a color for drawing.

Press Esc when you're finished using the pen. (Just be careful not to press Esc twice because the second press tells PowerPoint to end the presentation.)

Erasing pen and highlighter drawings

Follow these instructions to erase pen and highlighter drawings:

✦ **Erasing lines one at a time:** Click the Pen button and choose Eraser (or right-click and choose Pointer Options⇨Eraser). The Eraser appears. Drag it to a line and click to erase the line. Press Esc after you're finished using the Eraser.

✦ **Erasing all the lines on a slide:** Press E or click the Pen button and choose Erase All Ink on Slide (refer to Figure 5-3).

✦ **Erasing lines you told PowerPoint to keep:** As I explain shortly, PowerPoint asks at the end of a presentation that you drew on whether you want to keep the lines. If you elect to keep them, the lines become part of your presentation, and you can't delete them by clicking with the Eraser or by choosing the Erase All Ink on Slide command. To discard these lines later, go to the Review tab, open the drop-down list on the Delete button, and choose one of these options:

   • *Delete All Markup on the Current Slide:* Deletes lines you drew on a slide you selected

   • *Delete All Markup in This Presentation:* Deletes lines you drew on all the slides in your presentation

Pen marks aren't permanent, although you can keep them. At the end of a presentation in which you have drawn on slides, a dialog box asks whether you want to keep or discard your scribblings. Click the Keep or Discard button. (If you prefer not to see this dialog box because you intend never to keep your drawings, click the Office button and choose PowerPoint Options. In the PowerPoint Options dialog box, select the Advanced category and then deselect the Prompt to Keep Ink Annotations When Exiting check box.)

Blanking the screen

Here's a technique for adding a little drama to a presentation: When you want the audience to focus on you, not the PowerPoint screen, blank the screen. Make an all-black or all-white screen appear where a PowerPoint slide used to be. Every head in the audience will turn your way and listen keenly to what you have to say next. I sure hope you have something important to say.

Follow these instructions to blank out the screen during a presentation:

✦ **Black screen:** Press B, the period key, or right-click and choose Screen⇨Black Screen.

✦ **White screen:** Press W, the comma key, or right-click and choose Screen⇨White Screen.

To see a PowerPoint slide again, click on-screen or press any key on the keyboard.

Delivering a Presentation When You Can't Be There in Person

PowerPoint offers numerous ways to deliver a presentation when you can't be there in person. You can deliver your presentation in the form of a *handout,* a printed version of the presentation with thumbnail slides; create a self-running presentation; or create a user-run presentation with action buttons that others can click to get from slide to slide. The rest of this chapter explains how to do all that as well as package your presentation so that people who don't have PowerPoint can view it.

Book VIII, Chapter 2 describes two more ways to distribute PowerPoint presentations — by saving them as PDF files and publishing them on the Internet.

Providing handouts for your audience

Handouts are thumbnail versions of slides that you print and distribute to the audience. Figure 5-4 shows examples of handouts. Handouts come in one, two, three, four, six, or nine slides per page. If you select three slides per page, the handout includes lines that your audience can take notes on (see Figure 5-4); the other sizes don't offer these lines.

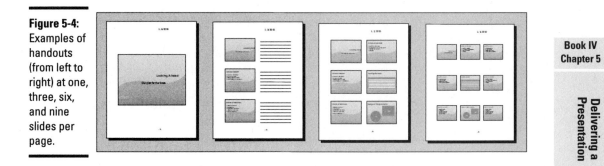

Figure 5-4: Examples of handouts (from left to right) at one, three, six, and nine slides per page.

To tell PowerPoint how to construct handouts, click the View tab and then click the Handout Master button. In Handout Master view, on the Handout Master tab, you can do a number of things to make your handouts more useful and attractive. As you make your choices, keep your eye on the sample handout page; it shows what your choices mean in real terms.

+ **Handout Orientation:** Select Portrait or Landscape. In landscape mode, the page is turned on its side and is longer than it is tall.

+ **Slide Orientation:** Select Portrait or Landscape, although I can't think of a good reason to choose Portrait.

+ **Slides-Per-Page:** Open the drop-down list and choose how many slides appear on each page. Figure 5-4 shows what some of the choices are.

+ **Header:** Select the Header check box and enter a header in the text frame to make a header appear in the upper-left corner of all handout pages. Candidates for headers include your name, your company name, and the location of a conference or seminar. The point is to help your audience identify the handout.

+ **Footer:** Select the Footer check box and enter a footer in the text frame in the lower-left corner of handout pages. Candidates for footers are the same as candidates for headers.

+ **Page Number:** Select this check box if you want page numbers to appear on the handout pages.

+ **Date:** Select this check box if you want the date you print the handout to appear on the handout pages.

+ **Background Styles**: Open the Background Styles drop-down list and choose a gradient or color, if you're so inclined. Chapter 2 of this mini-book explains background styles. Make sure that the background doesn't obscure the slide thumbnails or put too much of a burden on your printer.

To print handouts, click the Office button and choose Print⇨Print (or press Ctrl+P). You see the Print dialog box. Choose Handouts on the Print What drop-down list, enter how many handout copies you need in the Number of Copies text box, and click OK.

Creating a self-running, kiosk-style presentation

A self-running, kiosk-style presentation is one that plays on its own. You can make it play from a kiosk or simply send it to co-workers so that they can play it. In a self-running presentation, slides appear on-screen one after the other without you or anyone else having to advance the presentation from slide to slide. When the presentation finishes, it starts all over again from Slide 1.

Telling PowerPoint how long to keep slides on-screen

PowerPoint offers two ways to indicate how long you want each slide to stay on-screen:

✦ **Entering the time periods yourself:** Switch to Slide Sorter view and click the Animations tab. Then deselect the On Mouse Click check box and select the Automatically After check box, as shown in Figure 5-5. Next, tell PowerPoint to keep all slides on-screen the same amount of time or choose a different time period for each slide:

Enter a time period.

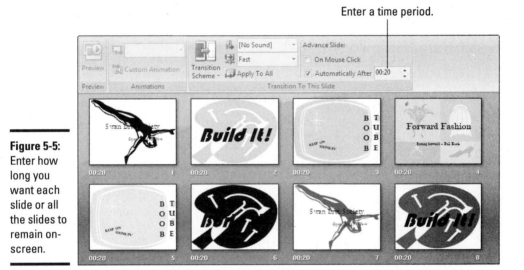

Figure 5-5: Enter how long you want each slide or all the slides to remain on-screen.

- *All slides the same time:* Enter a time period in the Automatically After text box and click the Apply to All button.

- *Each slide a different time:* One by one, select each slide and enter a time period in the Automatically After text box.

✦ **Rehearsing the presentation:** Rehearse the presentation and save the timings. (See "Rehearsing and Timing Your Presentation" earlier in this chapter.) Be sure to save the slide timings after you're finished rehearsing.

In Slide Sorter view, you can see how long each slide will stay on-screen (see Figure 5-5).

**Book IV
Chapter 5**

**Delivering a
Presentation**

Telling PowerPoint that your presentation is self-running

Before you can "self-run" a presentation, you have to tell PowerPoint that you want it to do that. Self-running presentations don't have the control buttons in the lower-left corner. You can't click the screen or press a key to move forward or backward to the next or previous slide. The only control you have over a self-running presentation is pressing the Esc key (pressing Esc ends the presentation).

Follow these steps to make yours a kiosk-style, self-running presentation:

1. **Click the Slide Show tab.**

2. **Click the Set Up Slide Show button.**

   You see the Set Up Slide Show dialog box.

3. **Under Show Type, select the Browsed at a Kiosk (Full Screen) option.**

   When you select this option, PowerPoint automatically selects the Loop Continuously Until 'Esc' check box.

4. **Make sure that the Using Timings, If Present option button is selected.**

5. **Click OK.**

   That's all there is to it.

Creating a user-run presentation

A *user-run,* or *interactive,* presentation is one that the viewer gets to control. The viewer decides which slide appears next and how long each slide remains on-screen. User-run presentations are similar to Web sites. Users can browse from slide to slide at their own speed. They can pick and choose what they want to investigate. They can backtrack and view slides they saw previously or return to the first slide and start anew.

The slide controls — the Previous and Next buttons — that you normally see during a presentation in the lower-left corner of slides don't appear in user-run presentations. You have to supply the means for viewers to get from slide to slide, and to do that, you create action buttons. An *action button* is a button that you can click to go to another slide in your presentation or the previous slide you viewed, whatever that slide was. PowerPoint provides 11 action buttons in the Shapes gallery. Figure 5-6 shows some action buttons and the dialog box you use to create them.

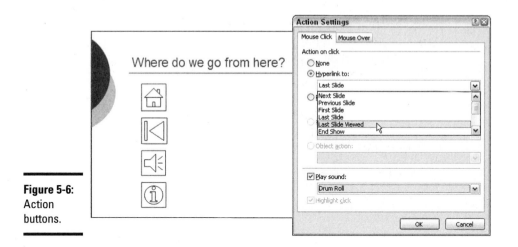

Figure 5-6:
Action
buttons.

Drawing an action button

After you draw an action button from the Shapes gallery, the Action Settings
dialog box, as shown in Figure 5-6, appears so you can tell PowerPoint which
slide to go to when the button is clicked. Select the slide (or master slide)
that needs action and follow these steps to adorn it with an action button:

**1. On the Home or Insert tab, open the Shapes gallery and scroll to the
Action Buttons category at the bottom.**

2. Click an action button to select it.

Choose the button that best illustrates which slide will appear when the
button is clicked.

3. Draw the button on the slide.

To do so, drag the pointer in a diagonal fashion. (As far as drawing them
is concerned, action buttons work the same as all other shapes and
other objects. Book I, Chapter 8 explains how to manipulate objects.)
The Action Settings dialog box, as shown in Figure 5-6, appears after you
finish drawing your button.

**4. Select the Mouse Over tab if you want users to activate the button by
moving the mouse pointer over it, not clicking it.**

5. Select the Hyperlink To option button.

6. On the Hyperlink To drop-down list, choose an action for the button.

You can go to the next slide, the previous slide, the first or last slide in a presentation, the last slide you viewed, or a specific slide.

To make clicking the action button take users to a specific slide, choose Slide on the list. You see the Hyperlink to Slide dialog box, which lists each slide in your presentation. Select a slide and click OK.

7. To play a sound when your action button is activated, select the Play Sound check box and select a sound on the drop-down list.

"Mouse-over" hyperlinks can do with sound accompaniment so users understand when they've activated an action button.

8. Click OK in the Actions Settings dialog box.

To test your button, you can right-click it and choose Open Hyperlink.

To change a button's action, select it and then click the Action button on the Insert tab, or right-click your action button and choose Edit Hyperlink. In the Action Settings dialog box, choose a new action and click OK.

Making yours a user-run presentation

Follow these steps to declare your presentation a user-run presentation and allow users to navigate from slide to slide with the scrollbar as well as by clicking action buttons:

1. Select the Slide Show tab.

2. Click the Set Up Slide Show button.

You see the Set Up Show dialog box.

3. Select the Browsed by an Individual (Window) option button.

4. (Optional) Click the Show Scrollbar check box.

If you choose this option, a scrollbar appears on the right side of the presentation so that users can go from slide to slide by scrolling.

5. Click OK.

Your presentation is no longer quite yours. It also belongs to all the people who view it in your absence.

Packaging your presentation

The Package for CD command copies a presentation to a CD so that you can take a presentation on the road or distribute it to others on CDs. By using the Package for CD command, you can even distribute a presentation to people who don't have PowerPoint on their computers. Along with the presentation, the command copies a program called PowerPoint Viewer to the CD. *PowerPoint Viewer* is an abridged version of PowerPoint. It has all the PowerPoint slide-show commands but none of the slide-creation commands. After someone pops the CD in a computer, PowerPoint Viewer opens, and the presentation you copied starts playing in PowerPoint Viewer. With the Package for CD command, you don't have to be concerned when you go on the road whether PowerPoint is installed on the computer where you're expected to give your presentation.

The Package for CD command offers another important benefit. As Chapter 4 of this mini-book (about sound and video) explains, video files and most sound files aren't embedded in presentations. To play a video or sound, PowerPoint reaches into the folder on your computer where the video or sound file is kept, and it plays the video or sound file from that location. If your presentation will travel and it includes sound and video, you have to consider how to transport the sound and video files along with your presentation file. The easiest way to transport these files is to bundle the files with your PowerPoint presentation by using the Package for CD command.

These pages explain the ins and outs of the Package for CD command. You find out how to copy a presentation (and PowerPoint Viewer) to a CD or folder and play a presentation in PowerPoint Viewer.

Packaging a presentation on a CD

Follow these steps to copy your presentation along with all its attendant files and the PowerPoint Viewer to a CD or a folder:

1. **Open the presentation you want to package.**

2. **Click the Office button and choose Publish⇨Package for CD.**

   You see the Package for CD dialog box, as shown in Figure 5-7.

Figure 5-7: The Package for CD command assembles all files needed to play a presentation.

> **Package for CD**
>
> Copy presentations to a CD that will play on computers running Microsoft Windows 2000 or later, even without PowerPoint.
>
> Name the CD: Marketing Plan
>
> Files to be copied:
>
> Marketing Plan.pptx   Add Files...
>
> Linked files and the PowerPoint Viewer are included by default. To change this, click Options.   Options...
>
> Copy to Folder...   Copy to CD   Close

3. **Enter a name for the CD or folder in the Name the CD text box.**

   The name you enter will appear as the name of the CD if you view the CD in Windows Explorer or My Computer; if you're copying your presentation to a folder, the name you enter will be given to the folder PowerPoint creates when it creates the packaged presentation file.

4. **Create the packaged presentation and copy it to a CD or to a folder on your computer.**

   Copy the presentation to a folder if you want to send the presentation by e-mail rather than distribute it by CD.

   • *Copying to a CD:* Click the Copy to CD button.

   • *Copying to a folder:* Click the Copy to Folder button. In the Copy to Folder dialog box, click the Browse button, and in the Choose Location dialog box, select a folder for storing the folder where you will keep your packaged presentation. Then click the Select button and click OK in the Copy to Folder dialog box.

5. **Click Yes in the message box that asks if you want to include linked content in the presentation.**

   It can take PowerPoint several minutes to assemble the files and copy them to the CD or folder. Besides the files, PowerPoint needs to copy the PowerPoint Viewer program (`pptview.exe`).

   If you're copying your presentation to a CD, PowerPoint asks whether you want to copy the same presentation to another CD. Either insert a fresh CD and click Yes, or click the No button.

Distributing your presentation to people who don't have PowerPoint

Not everyone has PowerPoint. Not everyone is so blessed. Some people live along in ignorant bliss without knowing anything about PowerPoint and its slide-show capabilities.

Don't be discouraged if you want to send your PowerPoint presentation to someone who doesn't have or may not have PowerPoint. Someone who doesn't have PowerPoint on his or her computer can still play a PowerPoint presentation by way of *PowerPoint Viewer,* a software program you can download for free from Microsoft starting at this Web page (enter **PowerPoint Viewer** in the Search text box and click the Go button):

    www.microsoft.com/downloads

Playing a packaged presentation in PowerPoint Viewer

If you distribute your presentation on a CD, tell the people to whom you give the CD that the CD plays automatically after you put it in the computer's CD drive.

Distributing a packaged presentation by e-mail can be difficult because you have to send several files, and moreover, many e-mail programs don't permit you to send program (.exe) files, including pptview.exe, the PowerPoint Viewer program file. To get around this problem, compress the files before sending them. In Windows Explorer or My Computer, select all the files in the folder you created for your packaged presentation (choose Edit⇨Select All), right-click the files, and choose Send To⇨Compress (Zipped) Folder. Make sure the people to whom you send the compressed file know how to decompress it (right-click it and choose Extract All).

Here are instructions for running a presentation in PowerPoint Viewer:

✦ **Getting from slide to slide:** Click on-screen or right-click and choose Next on the shortcut menu.

✦ **Retreating:** Right-click and choose Previous or Last Viewed.

✦ **Going to a specific slide:** Right-click, choose Go to Slide, and select a slide on the submenu.

✦ **Ending the show:** Press Esc or right-click and choose End Show.

If your presentation includes video or sound, inform users that they may have to click the sound icon or video screen to hear the sound or watch the video. Whether users have to click or whether the sound or video plays automatically depends on which option you choose when you insert the sound or video on your slides.

Book V

Excel 2007

The 5th Wave   By Rich Tennant

"I've used several spreadsheet programs, but this is the best one for designing quilt patterns."

Contents at a Glance

Chapter 1: Up and Running with Excel

In This Chapter

✔ **Creating an Excel worksheet**

✔ **Understanding what a worksheet is**

✔ **Entering text, as well as numeric, date, and time data**

✔ **Using the AutoFill command to enter lists and serial data**

✔ **Establishing conditional formats for text**

✔ **Setting up data-validation rules**

This chapter introduces *Excel,* the official number cruncher of Office 2007. The purpose of Excel is to track, analyze, and tabulate numbers. Use the program to project profits and losses, formulate a budget, or analyze Elvis sightings in North America. Doing the setup work takes time, but after you enter the numbers and tell Excel how to tabulate them, you're on Easy Street. Excel does the math for you. All you have to do is kick off your shoes, sit back, and see how the numbers stack up.

This chapter explains what a workbook and a worksheet is, and how rows and columns on a worksheet determine where cell addresses are. You also discover tips and tricks for entering data quickly in a worksheet, and how to construct data-validation rules to make sure that data is entered accurately.

Creating a New Excel Workbook

When you start Excel, the program greets you with a brand-new workbook with the generic name "Book1" on the title bar. *Workbook* is just the Excel term for the files you create with the program. You can start working right away on the generic workbook or you can take advantage of one of Excel's templates. A *template* is a preformatted workbook designed for a specific purpose, such as budgeting, tracking inventories, or tracking purchase orders. Creating a workbook from a template is mighty convenient if you happen to find a template that suits your purposes, but in my experience, you almost always have to start from a generic, blank workbook because your data is your own. You need a workbook you create yourself — not one created from a template by someone else.

 Whether you want to create a new workbook from a template or from scratch, start by clicking the Office button and choosing New on the drop-down list. You see the New Workbook dialog box, as shown in Figure 1-1. Create your workbook with one of these techniques:

✦ **Blank workbook:** Double-click the Blank Workbook icon. (By pressing Ctrl+N, you can create a new, blank workbook without opening the New Workbook dialog box.)

✦ **Workbook from a template:** Take your pick from these techniques to create a workbook from a template:

  • *Use a template on your computer:* Click Installed Templates (you can find this button under Templates). Templates that you loaded on your computer when you installed Office appear in the dialog box. Double-click a template to create a workbook.

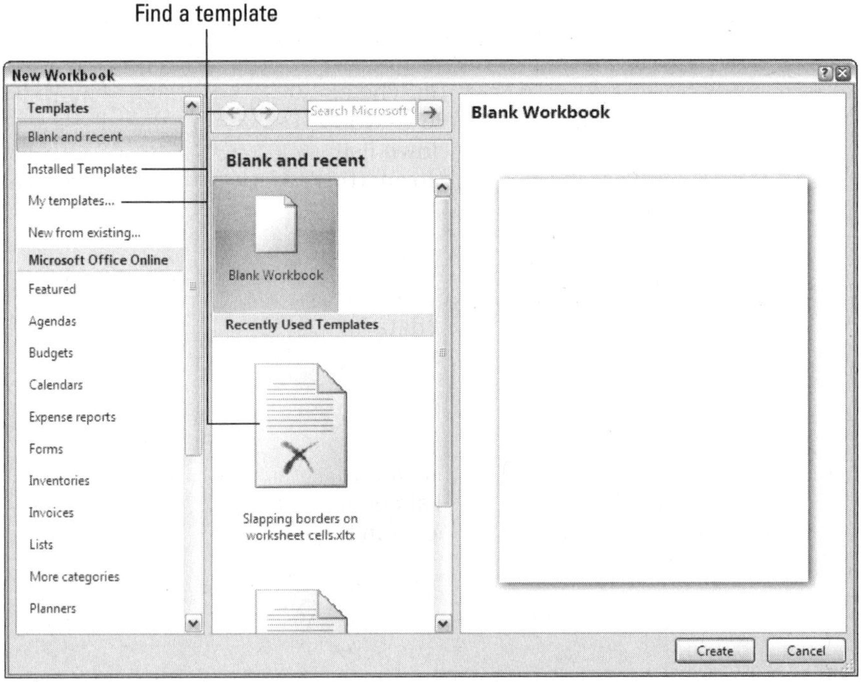

Find a template

New Workbook

Templates	Search Microsoft	**Blank Workbook**
Blank and recent		
Installed Templates	**Blank and recent**	
My templates...		
New from existing...	Blank Workbook	
Microsoft Office Online		
Featured	**Recently Used Templates**	
Agendas		
Budgets		
Calendars		
Expense reports		
Forms	Slapping borders on worksheet cells.xltx	
Inventories		
Invoices		
Lists		
More categories		
Planners		

Create | Cancel

Figure 1-1: Create a workbook by starting in the New Workbook dialog box.

- *Search for a template online at Microsoft:* Enter a search term in the Search Microsoft box, make sure your computer is connected to the Internet, and click the Start Searching button. Templates appear in the dialog box. Double-click a template to download and use it to create a workbook.

- *Use a template you created (or downloaded earlier from Microsoft):* Click My Templates. The New dialog box appears. Select a template and click OK. (If you have created your own template, its name appears in this dialog box.)

- *Select a recently used template:* Double-click a template name in the middle of the dialog box under Blank and Recent.

✦ **Recycle another workbook:** If you can use another workbook as the starting point for creating a new one, click New from Existing. In the New from Existing Workbook dialog box, select the workbook and click the Create New button.

Book I, Chapter 1 explains how to save a workbook after you create it as well as how to open a workbook that you want to work on.

Getting Acquainted with Excel

If you've spent any time in an Office program, much of the Excel screen should look familiar to you. The buttons on the Home tab — the Bold and Align buttons, for example — work the same in Excel as they do in Word. The Font and Font Size drop-down lists work the same as well. Any command in Excel that has to do with formatting text and numbers works the same in Excel and Word.

As I mention earlier, an Excel file is a *workbook*. Each workbook comprises one or more worksheets. A *worksheet,* also known as a *spreadsheet,* is a table where you enter data and data labels. Figure 1-2 shows a worksheet with data about rainfall in different counties. A worksheet works like an accountant's ledger — only it's much easier to use. Notice how the worksheet is divided by gridlines into columns (A, B, C, and so on) and rows (1, 2, 3, and so on). The rectangles where columns and rows intersect are *cells,* and each cell can hold one data item, a formula for calculating data, or nothing at all. At the bottom of the worksheet are tabs — Sheet1, Sheet2, and Sheet3 — for visiting the other worksheets in the workbook.

Each cell has a different cell address. In Figure 1-2, cell B7 holds 13, the amount of rain that fell in Sonoma County in the winter. Meanwhile, as the Formula bar at the top of the screen shows, cell F7, the *active cell,* holds the formula =B7+C7+D7+E7, the sum of the numbers in cells — you guessed it — B7, C7, D7, and E7.

Active cell address   Formula bar   Cells

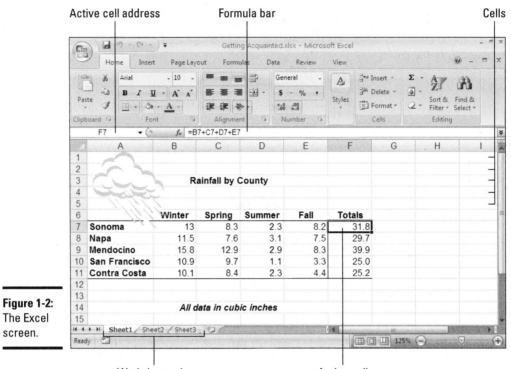

Figure 1-2:
The Excel
screen.

Worksheet tabs   Active cell

The beauty of Excel is that the program does all the calculations and recalculations for you after you enter the data. If I were to change the number in cell B7, Excel would instantly recalculate the total amount of rainfall in Sonoma County in cell F7. People like me who struggled in math class will be glad to know that you don't have to worry about the math because Excel does it for you. All you have to do is make sure that the data and the formulas are entered correctly.

After you enter and label the data, enter the formulas, and turn your worksheet into a little masterpiece, you can start analyzing the data. You can also generate charts like the one in Figure 1-3. Do you notice any similarities between the worksheet in Figure 1-2 and the chart in Figure 1-3? The chart is fashioned from data in the worksheet, and it took me about a half minute to create that chart. (Book I, Chapter 6 explains how to create charts in Excel, Word, and PowerPoint.)

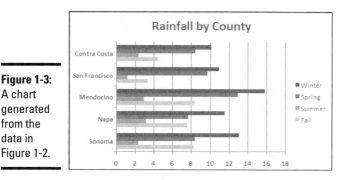

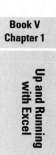

Figure 1-3:
A chart
generated
from the
data in
Figure 1-2.

Rows, columns, and cell addresses

Not that anyone except an Enron accountant needs all of them, but an Excel worksheet has numerous columns and over 1 million rows. The rows are numbered, and columns are labeled A to Z, then AA to AZ, then BA to BZ, and so on. The important thing to remember is that each cell has an address whose name comes from a column letter and a row number. The first cell in row 1 is A1, the second is B1, and so on. You need to enter cell addresses in formulas to tell Excel which numbers to compute.

To find a cell's address, either make note of which column and row it lies in, or click the cell and glance at the Formula bar (see Figure 1-2). The left side of the Formula bar lists the address of the *active cell,* the cell you click in the worksheet. In Figure 1-2, cell F7 is the active cell.

Workbooks and worksheets

When you create a new Excel file, you open a *workbook,* a file with three worksheets in it. The worksheets are called Sheet1, Sheet2, and Sheet3 (you can change their names and add more worksheets). To get from worksheet to worksheet, click tabs along the bottom of the Excel window. Why three worksheets? Because you might need more than one worksheet for a single project. Think of a workbook as a stack of worksheets. Besides calculating the numbers in cells across the rows or down the columns of a worksheet, you can make calculations throughout a workbook by using numbers from different worksheets in a calculation.

Entering Data in a Worksheet

Entering data in a worksheet is an irksome activity. Fortunately, Excel offers a few shortcuts to take the sting out of it. These pages explain how to enter data in a worksheet, the different types of data, and how to enter text labels, numbers, dates, and times.

The basics of entering data

What you can enter in a worksheet cell falls in one of four categories:

✦ Text

✦ A value (numeric, date, or time)

✦ A logical value (True or False)

✦ A formula that returns a value, logical value, or text

Still, no matter what type of data you're entering, the basic steps are the same:

1. **Click the cell where you want to enter the data or text label.**

As shown in Figure 1-4, a square appears around the cell to tell you that the cell you clicked is now the active cell. Glance at the left side of the Formula bar if you're not sure of the address of the cell you're about to enter data in. The Formula bar lists the cell address.

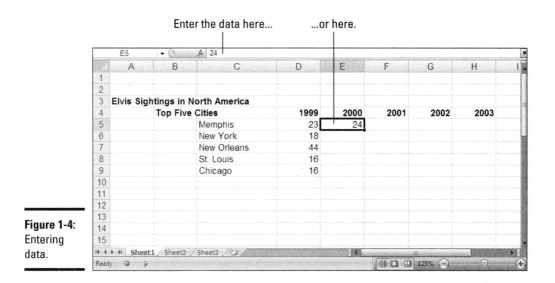

Figure 1-4: Entering data.

2. **Type the data in the cell.**

If you find typing in the Formula bar easier, click and start typing there. As soon as you type the first character, the Cancel button (an *X*) and Enter button (a check mark) appear beside the Insert Function button (labeled *fx*) on the Formula bar.

3. Press the Enter key to enter the number or label.

Besides pressing the Enter key, you can also press an arrow key ($\leftarrow$, $\uparrow$, $\rightarrow$, $\downarrow$), press Tab, or click the Enter button (the check mark) on the Formula bar.

If you change your mind about entering data, click the Cancel button or press Esc to delete what you entered and start over.

Chapter 3 in this mini-book explains how to enter logical values and formulas. The next several pages describe how to enter text labels, numeric values, date values, and time values.

The Paste Special command can come in very handy with worksheet data. As numbers are updated in the source file, they can be updated automatically in an Excel worksheet as well. Consider linking worksheets if your adventures in Excel enable you to keep source data in one place. Book VIII, Chapter 8 explains linking files.

Entering text labels

Sometimes a text entry is too long to fit in a cell. How Excel accommodates text entries that are too wide depends on whether data is in the cell to the right of the one you entered the text in:

- ✦ If the cell to the right is empty, Excel lets the text spill into the next cell.

- ✦ If the cell to the right contains data, the entry gets cut off. Nevertheless, the text you entered is in the cell. Nothing gets lost when it can't be displayed on-screen. You just can't see the text or numbers except by glancing at the Formula bar, where the contents of the cell can be seen in their entirety.

To solve the problem of text that doesn't fit in a cell, widen the column, shorten the text entry, reorient the text (Chapter 4 of this mini-book explains aligning numbers and text in columns and rows), or wrap the contents of the cell. *Wrapping* runs the text down to the next line, much the way the text in this paragraph runs to the next line when it reaches the right margin. Excel makes rows taller to accommodate wrapped text in a cell. To wrap text in cells, select the cells, go to the Home tab, and click the Wrap Text button (you can find it in the Alignment group).

Entering numeric values

When a number is too large to fit in a cell, Excel displays pounds signs (###) instead of a number or displays the number in scientific notation. You can always glance at the Formula bar, however, to see a number in its entirety. As well, you can always widen the column to display the entire number.

To enter a fraction in a cell, enter a 0 or a whole number, a blank space, and the fraction. For example, to enter ⅜, type a **0**, press the spacebar, and type **3/8**. To enter 5⅜, type the **5**, press the spacebar, and type **3/8**. For its purposes, Excel converts fractions to decimal numbers, as you can see by looking in the Formula bar after you enter a fraction. For example, 5⅜ displays as 5.375 in the Formula bar.

Here's a little trick for entering numbers with decimals quickly. To spare yourself the trouble of pressing the period key (.), you can tell Excel to enter the period automatically. Instead of entering 12.45, for example, you can simply enter 1245. Excel enters the period for you: 12.45. To perform this trick, click the Office button, choose Excel Options, click the Advanced category in the Excel Options dialog box, click the Automatically Insert a Decimal Point check box, and in the Places text box, enter the number of decimal places you want for numbers. Deselect this option when you want to go back to entering numbers the normal way.

Entering date and time values

Dates and times can be used in calculations, but entering a date or time value in a cell can be problematic because these values must be entered in such a way that Excel can recognize them as dates or times, not text.

Not that you need to know it especially, but Excel converts dates and times to serial values for the purpose of being able to use dates and times in calculations. For example, July 31, 2004, is the number 38199. July 31, 2004, at Noon is 38199.5. These serial values represent the number of whole days since January 1, 1900. The portion of the serial value to the right of the decimal point is the time, represented as a portion of a full day.

Entering date values

You can enter a date value in a cell in just about any format you choose, and Excel understands that you're entering a date. For example, enter a date in any of the following formats and you'll be all right:

m/d/yy	7/31/07
m-d-yyyy	7-31-2007
d-mmm-yy	31-Jul-07

Here are some basic things to remember about entering dates:

+ **Date formats**: You can quickly apply a format to dates by selecting cells and using one of these techniques:

   • On the Home tab, open the Number Format drop-down list and choose Short Date (*m/d/yyyy*; 7/31/2007) or Long Date (*day-of-the-week, month, day, year*; Tuesday, July 31, 2007), as shown in Figure 1-5.

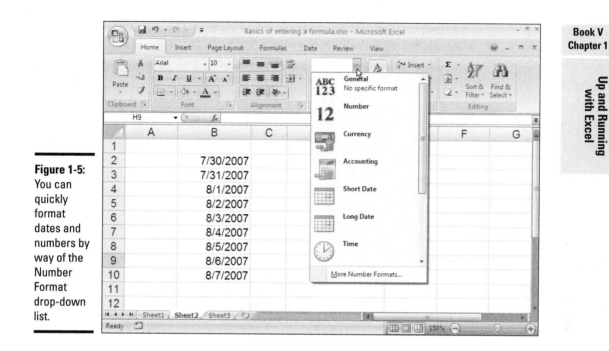

Figure 1-5:
You can quickly format dates and numbers by way of the Number Format drop-down list.

- On the Home tab, click the Number group button to open the Number tab of the Format Cells dialog box. As shown in Figure 1-6, choose the Date category and then choose a date format.

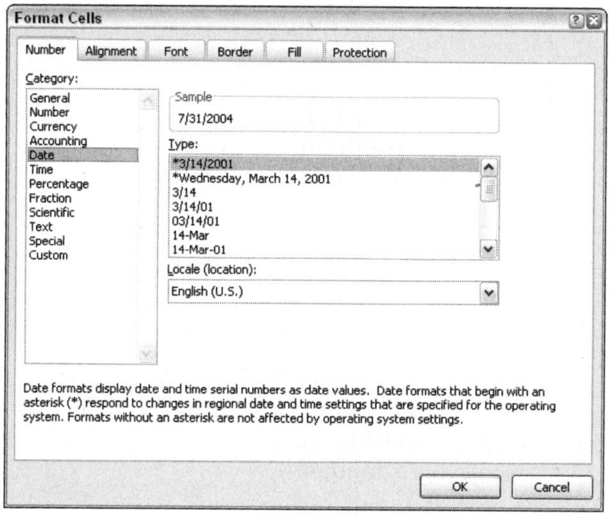

Figure 1-6:
You can also choose a date format in the Format Cells dialog box.

✦ **Current date:** Press Ctrl+; (semicolon) and press Enter to enter the current date.

✦ **Current year's date:** If you don't enter the year as part of the date, Excel assumes that the date you entered is in the current year. For example, if you enter a date in the *m/d* (7/31) format during the year 2007, Excel enters the date as 7/31/07. As long as the date you want to enter is the current year, you can save a little time when entering dates by not entering the year, as Excel enters it for you.

✦ **Dates on the Formula bar:** No matter which format you use for dates, dates are displayed in the Formula bar in the format that Excel prefers for dates: *m/d/yyyy* (7/31/2007). How dates are displayed in the worksheet is up to you.

✦ **20th and 21st century two-digit years:** When it comes to entering two-digit years in dates, the digits 30 through 99 belong to the 20th century (1930–1999), but the digits 00 through 29 belong to the 21st century (2000–2029). For example, 7/31/07 refers to July 31, 2007, not July 31, 1907. To enter a date in 1929 or earlier, enter four digits instead of two to describe the year: **7-31-1929**. To enter a date in 2030 or later, enter four digits instead of two: **7-31-2030**.

✦ **Dates in formulas:** To enter a date directly in a formula, enclose the date in quotation marks. (Make sure that the cell where the formula is entered has been given the Number format, not the Date format.) For example, the formula =today( )-"1/1/2003" calculates the number of days that have elapsed since January 1, 2003. Formulas are the subject of Chapter 3 of this mini-book.

Entering time values

Excel recognizes time values that you enter in the following ways:

h:mm AM/PM	3:31 AM
h:mm:ss AM/PM	3:31:45 PM

Here are some things to remember when entering time values:

✦ **Use colons:** Separate hours, minutes, and seconds with a colon (:).

✦ **Time formats:** To change to the *h:mm:ss* AM/PM time format, select the cells, go to the Home tab, and choose Time on the Number Format drop-down list. You can also change time formats by clicking the Number group button on the Home tab and selecting a time format on the Number tab of the Format Cells dialog box.

✦ **AM or PM time designations:** Unless you enter AM or PM with the time, Excel assumes that you're operating on military time. For example, 3:30 is considered 3:30 a.m.; 15:30 is 3:30 p.m. Don't enter periods after the letters am or pm (don't enter a.m. or p.m.).

✦ **Current time:** Press Ctrl+Shift+; (semicolon) and press Enter to enter the current time.

✦ **Dates on the Formula bar:** On the Formula bar, times are displayed in this format: *hours:minutes:seconds,* followed by the letters AM or PM. However, the time format used in cells is up to you.

Combining date and time values

You can combine dates and time values by entering the date, a blank space, and the time:

✦ 7/31/04 3:31 am

✦ 7-31-04 3:31:45 pm

Quickly Entering Lists and Serial Data with the AutoFill Command

Data that falls in the "serial" category — month names, days of the week, and consecutive numbers and dates, for example — can be entered quickly with the AutoFill command. Believe it or not, Excel recognizes certain kinds of serial data and enters it for you as part of the AutoFill feature. Instead of laboriously entering this data one piece at a time, you can enter it all at once by dragging the mouse. Follow these steps to "autofill" cells:

1. **Click the cell that is to be first in the series.**

For example, if you intend to list the days of the week in consecutive cells, click where the first day is to go.

2. **Enter the first number, date, or list item in the series.**

3. **Move to the adjacent cell and enter the second number, date, or list item in the series.**

If you want to enter the same number or piece of text in adjacent cells, it isn't necessary to take this step, but Excel needs the first and second items in the case of serial dates and numbers so that it can tell how much to increase or decrease the given amount or time period in each cell. For example, entering **5** and **10** tells Excel to increase the number by 5 each time so that the next serial entry is 15.

Creating your own AutoFill list

As you probably know, Excel is capable of completing lists on its own with the AutoFill feature. You can enter the days of the week or month names simply by entering one day or month and dragging the AutoFill handle to enter the others. Here's some good news: The AutoFill command can also reproduce the names of your co-workers, the roster of a softball team, street names, or any other list that you care to enter quickly in a worksheet.

Follow these steps to enter items for a list so that you can enter them in the future by dragging the AutoFill handle:

1. **Click the Office button and choose Excel Options to open the Excel Options dialog box.**

2. **Select the Popular category.**

3. **Click the Edit Custom Lists button.**

   You see the Custom Lists dialog box.

4. **In the List Entries box, enter items for the list, and enter a comma after each item.**

   You can see how it's done by glancing at the Custom Lists box.

5. **Click OK.**

4. Select the cell or cells you just entered data in.

To select a single cell, click it; to select two, drag over the cells. Chapter 2 of this mini-book describes all the ways to select cells in a worksheet.

5. **Click the AutoFill handle and start dragging in the direction in which you want the data series to appear on your worksheet.**

The *AutoFill handle* is the little black square in the lower-right corner of the cell. Finding it can be difficult. Carefully move the mouse pointer over the lower-right corner of the cell, and when you see the mouse pointer change into a black cross, click and start dragging. As you drag, the serial data appears in a pop-up box, as shown in Figure 1-7.

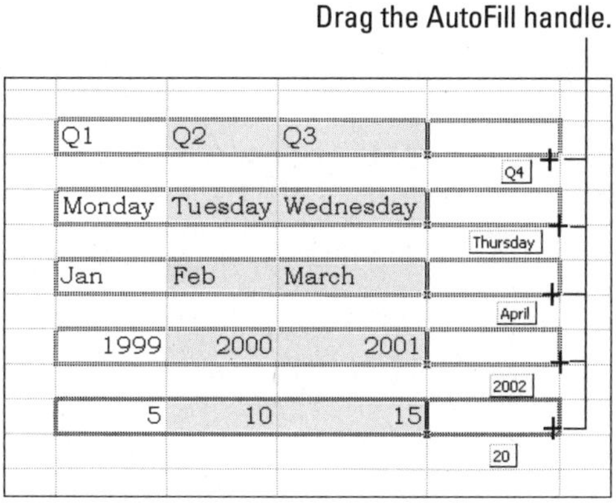

Drag the AutoFill handle.

Q1	Q2	Q3	Q4
Monday	Tuesday	Wednesday	Thursday
Jan	Feb	March	April
1999	2000	2001	2002
5	10	15	20

Figure 1-7:
Entering serial data and text.

The AutoFill Options button appears after you enter the serial data. Click it and choose an option if you want to copy cells or fill the cells without carrying along their formats.

To enter the same number or text in several empty cells, drag over the cells to select them or select each cell by holding down the Ctrl key as you click. Then type a number or some text and press Ctrl+Enter.

Formatting Numbers, Dates, and Time Values

When you enter a number that Excel recognizes as belonging to one of its formats, Excel assigns the number format automatically. Enter **45%**, for example, and Excel assigns the Percentage Style format. Enter **$4.25**, and Excel assigns the Currency Style format. Besides assigning formats by hand, however, you can assign them to cells from the get-go and spare yourself the trouble of entering dollar signs, commas, percent signs, and other extraneous punctuation. All you have to do is enter the raw numbers. Excel does the window dressing for you.

Excel offers five number-formatting buttons on the Home tab — Accounting Number Format, Percent Style, Comma Style, Increase Decimal, and Decrease Decimal. Select cells with numbers in them and click one of these buttons to change how numbers are formatted:

✦ **Accounting Number Format:** Places a dollar sign before the number and gives it two decimal places. You can open the drop-down list on this button and choose a currency symbol apart from the dollar sign.

✦ **Percent Style:** Places a percent sign after the number and converts the number to a percentage.

✦ **Comma Style:** Places commas in the number.

✦ **Increase Decimal:** Increases the number of decimal places by one.

✦ **Decrease Decimal:** Decreases the number of decimal places by one.

To choose among many formats and to format dates and time values as well as numbers, click the Number group button on the Home tab. Then make your selections on the Number tab of the Format Cells dialog box. Figure 1-8 shows this dialog box. Choose a category and select options to describe how you want numbers or text to appear.

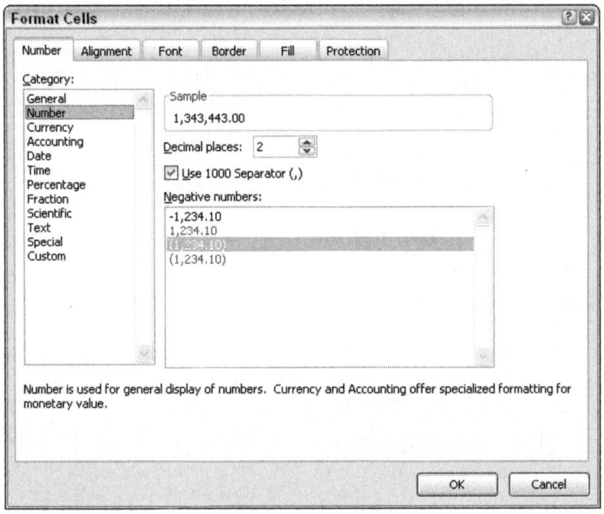

Figure 1-8:
The Number category of the Format Cells dialog box.

To strip formats from the data in cells, select the cells, go to the Home tab, click the Clear button, and choose Clear Formats.

TIP

Entering ZIP codes can be problematic because Excel strips the initial zero from the number if it begins with a zero. To get around that problem, visit the Number tab of the Format Cells dialog box (see Figure 1-8), choose Special in the Category list, and select a ZIP Code option.

Conditional Formats for Calling Attention to Data

A *conditional format* is one that applies when data meets certain conditions. To call attention to numbers greater than 10,000, for example, you can tell Excel to highlight those numbers automatically. To highlight negative numbers, you can tell Excel to display them in bright red. Conditional formats help you analyze and understand data better.

Select the cells that are candidates for conditional formatting and follow these steps to tell Excel when and how to format the cells:

![Conditional Formatting]

1. **On the Home tab, click the Conditional Formatting button (you may have to click the Styles button first, depending on the size of your screen).**

2. **Choose Highlight Cells Rules or Top/Bottom Rules on the drop-down list.**

   You see a submenu with choices about establishing the rule for whether values in the cells are highlighted or otherwise made more prominent:

   • *Highlight Cells Rules:* These rules are for calling attention to data if it falls in a numerical or date range, or it's greater or lesser than a specific value. For example, you can highlight cells that are greater than 400.

   • *Top/Bottom Rules:* These rules are for calling attention to data if it falls within a percentage range relative to all the cells you selected. For example, you can highlight cells with data that falls in the bottom 10-percent range.

3. **Choose an option on the submenu.**

   You see a dialog box similar to the ones in Figure 1-9.

4. **On the left side of the dialog box, establish the rule for flagging data.**

5. **On the With drop-down list, choose how you want to call attention to the data.**

   For example, you can display the data in red or yellow. If you choose Custom Format on the drop-down list, you can open the Format Cells dialog box, where you can choose a font style or color for the text.

6. **Click OK.**

Establish the rule.

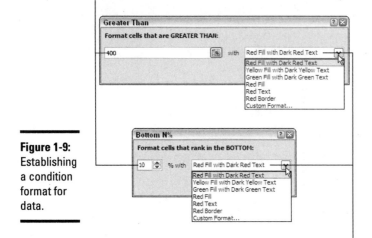

Figure 1-9:
Establishing
a condition
format for
data.

Choose how to call attention to data.

To remove conditional formats, select the cells with the formats, click the Conditional Formatting button, and choose Clear Rules➪Clear Rules from Selected Cells.

Establishing Data-Validation Rules

By nature, people are prone to enter data incorrectly because the task of entering data is so dull. This is why data-validation rules are invaluable. A *data-validation rule* is a rule concerning what kind of data can be entered in a cell. When you select a cell that has been given a rule, an input message tells you what to enter, as shown in Figure 1-10. And if you enter the data incorrectly, an error alert tells you as much, also shown in Figure 1-10.

Data-validation rules are an excellent defense against sloppy data entry and that itchy feeling you get when you're in the middle of an irksome task. In a cell that records date entries, you can require dates to fall in a certain time frame. In a cell that records text entries, you can choose an item from a list instead of typing it yourself. In a cell that records numeric entries, you can require the number to fall within a certain range. Table 1-1 describes the different categories of data-validation rules.

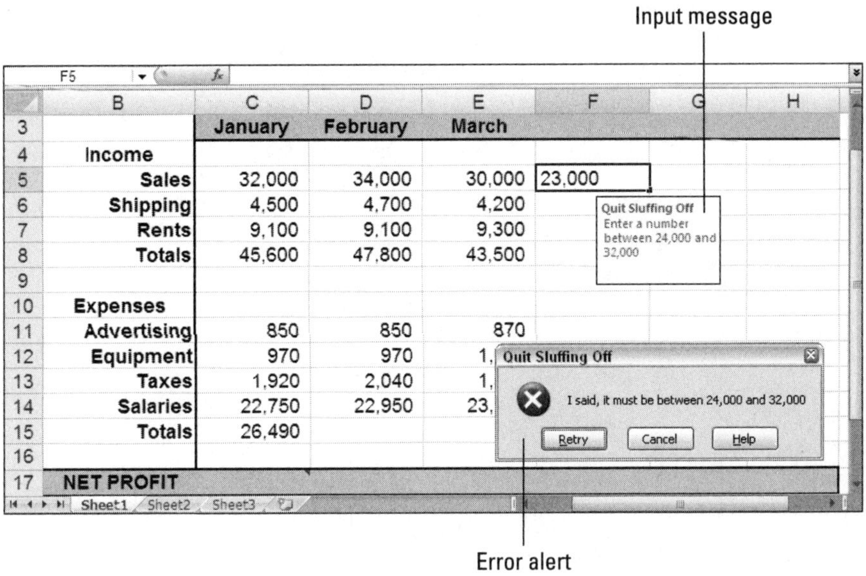

Input message

Figure 1-10:
A data-
validation
rule in
action.

Error alert

Table 1-1	Data-Validation Rule Categories
Rule	*What Can Be Entered*
Any Value	Anything whatsoever. This is the default setting.
Whole Number	Whole numbers (no decimal points allowed). Choose an operator from the Data drop-down list and values to describe the range of numbers that can be entered.
Decimal	Same as the Whole Number rule except numbers with decimal points are permitted.
List	Items from a list. Enter the list items in cells on a worksheet, either the one you're working in or another. Then reopen the Data Validation dialog box, click the Range Selector button (you can find it on the right side of the Source text box), and select the cells that hold the list. The list items appear in a drop-down list on the worksheet.
Date	Date values. Choose an operator from the Data drop-down list and values to describe the date range. Earlier in this chapter, "Entering date and time values" describes the correct way to enter date values.
Time	Time values. Choose an operator from the Data drop-down list and values to describe the date and time range. Earlier in this chapter, "Entering date and time values" describes the correct way to enter a combination of date and time values.
Text Length	A certain number of characters. Choose an operator from the Data drop-down list and values to describe how many characters can be entered.
Custom	A logical value (True or False). Enter a formula that describes what constitutes a true or false data entry.

Follow these steps to establish a data-validation rule:

1. **Select the cell or cells that need a rule.**

2. **On the Data tab, click the Data Validation button.**

As shown in Figure 1-11, the Data Validation dialog box appears.

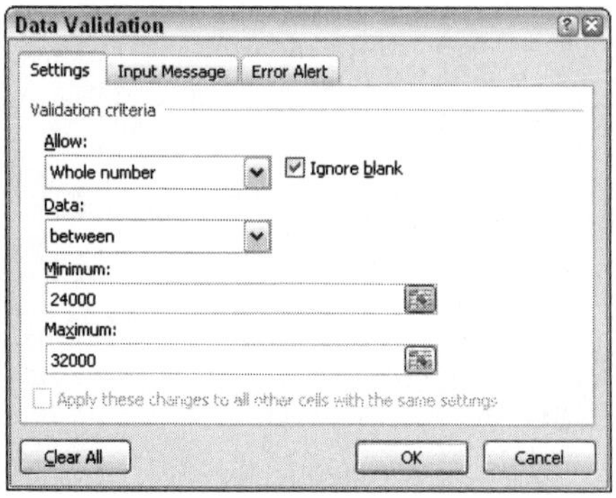

Figure 1-11:
Creating a
data-
validation
rule.

3. **On the Allow drop-down list, choose the category of rule you want.**

Table 1-1, earlier in this chapter, describes these categories.

4. **Enter the criteria for the rule.**

What the criteria is depends on what rule category you're working in. Table 1-1 describes how to enter the criteria for rules in each category. You can refer to cells in the worksheet by selecting them. To do that, either select them directly or click the Range Selector button and then select them.

5. **Click the Input Message tab and enter a title and input message.**

You can see a title ("Quit Sluffing Off") and input message ("Enter a number between 24,000 and 32,000") in Figure 1-10. The title appears in boldface. Briefly describe what kind of data belongs in the cell or cells you selected.

6. **Select the Error Alert tab, choose a style for the symbol in the Message Alert dialog box, enter a title for the dialog box, and enter a warning message.**

In the error message in Figure 1-10, the Stop symbol was chosen. The title you enter appears across the top of the dialog box, and the message appears beside the symbol.

7. **Click OK.**

To remove data-validation rules from cells, select the cells, click the Data Validation button, and on the Settings tab of the Data Validation dialog box, click the Clear All button, and click OK.

Chapter 2: Refining Your Worksheet

In This Chapter

✔ **Changing worksheet data**

✔ **Going here and there in a worksheet**

✔ **Freezing and splitting columns and rows to make data entry easier**

✔ **Documenting a worksheet with comments**

✔ **Selecting cells**

✔ **Copying and moving data**

✔ **Moving among, deleting, and renaming worksheets**

✔ **Hiding and protecting worksheets so they can't be altered**

This chapter delves into the workaday world of worksheets (say that three times fast). It explains how to edit worksheet data and move quickly here and there in a worksheet. You also discover a couple of techniques for entering data quickly, how to select cells, and how to copy and move data in cells. This chapter describes how to move, delete, and rename worksheets, as well as protect them from being edited or altered.

Editing Worksheet Data

Not everyone enters data correctly the first time. To edit data you entered in a cell, do one of the following:

+ **Double-click the cell.** Doing so places the cursor squarely in the cell, where you can start deleting or entering numbers and text.

+ **Click the cell and press F2.** This technique also lands the cursor in the cell.

+ **Click the cell you want to edit.** With this technique, you edit the data on the Formula bar.

If nothing happens when you double-click, or if pressing F2 lands the cursor in the Formula bar, not a cell, somebody has been fooling with the Options settings. Click the Office button, choose Excel Options, select the Advanced category in the Excel Options dialog box, and click the Allow Editing Directly in Cells check box.

Moving Around in a Worksheet

Going from place to place gets progressively more difficult as a worksheet gets larger. Luckily for you, Excel offers keyboard shortcuts for jumping around. Table 2-1 describes these keyboard shortcuts. (If the keyboard shortcuts in Table 2-1 don't work on your machine, someone has told Excel to adopt the keyboard shortcuts of Lotus 1-2-3, another spreadsheet program. To remedy the problem, click the Office button, choose Excel Options, select the Advanced category in the Excel Options dialog box, and deselect the Transition Navigation Keys check box near the bottom of the screen.)

Table 2-1	Keyboard Shortcuts for Getting Around in Worksheets
Press. . .	*To Move the Selection. . .*
Home	To column A
Ctrl+Home	To cell A1, the first cell in the worksheet
Ctrl+End	To the last cell in the last row with data in it
←, →, ↑, ↓	To the next cell
Ctrl+←, →, ↑, ↓	In one direction toward the nearest cell with data in it or to the first or last cell in the column or row
Page Up *or* Page Down	Up or down one screen's worth of rows
Alt+Page Up *or* Alt+Page Down	Left or right one screen's worth of columns
Ctrl+Page Up *or* Ctrl+Page Down	Backward or forward through the workbook, from worksheet to worksheet

In addition to pressing keys, you can use these techniques to get from place to place in a worksheet:

✦ **Scroll bars:** Use the vertical and horizontal scroll bars to move to different areas. Drag the scroll box to cover long distances. To cover long distances very quickly, hold down the Shift key as you drag the scroll box on the vertical scroll bar.

✦ **Scroll wheel on the mouse:** If your mouse is equipped with a scroll wheel, turn the wheel to quickly scroll up and down.

✦ **Name box:** Enter a cell address in the Name box and press Enter to go to the cell. As shown in Figure 2-1, the Name box is found to the left of the Formula bar.

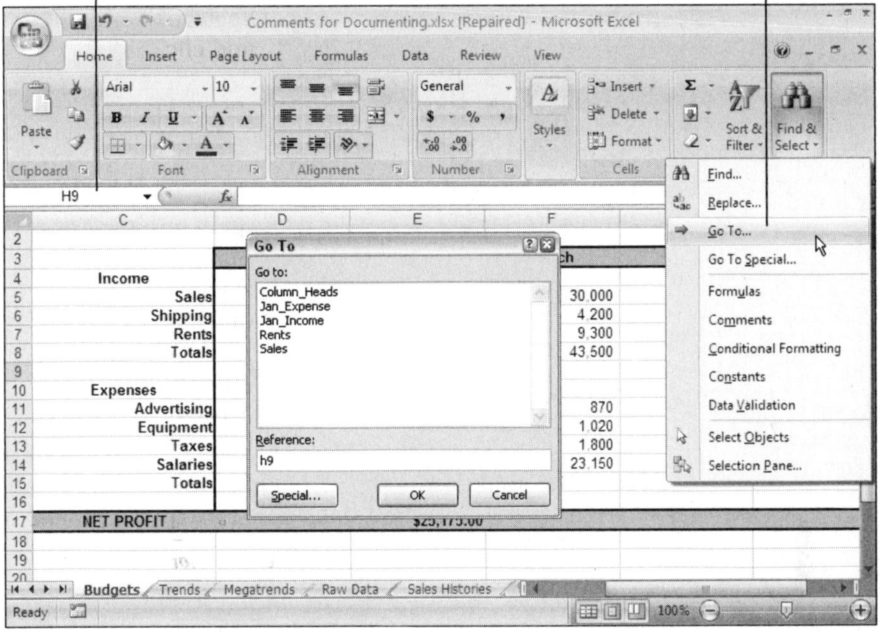

Enter an address in the Name box.　　　　Choose the Go To command.

Figure 2-1:
Going to a
specific cell.

+ **The Go To command:** On the Home tab, click the Find & Select button, and choose Go To on the drop-down list (or press Ctrl+G or F5). As shown in Figure 2-1, you see the Go To dialog box. Enter a cell address in the Reference box and click OK. Cell addresses you've already visited with the Go To command are already listed in the dialog box. Click the Special button to open the Go To Special dialog box and visit a formula, comment, or other esoteric item.

+ **The Find command:** On the Home tab, click the Find & Select button, and choose Find on the drop-down list. Enter the data you seek in the Find What box and click the Find Next button.

To scroll to the active cell if you no longer see it on-screen, press Ctrl+ Backspace.

Getting a Better Look at the Worksheet

Especially when you're entering data, it pays to get a good look at the worksheet. You need to know which column and row you're entering data in. These pages explain techniques for changing your view of a worksheet so you always know where you are. Read on to discover how to freeze, split, and hide columns and rows. (On the subject of changing views, Book I, Chapter 3 explains an essential technique for changing views: zooming in and zooming out.)

Freezing and splitting columns and rows

Sometimes your adventures in a worksheet take you to a faraway cell address, such as X31 or C39. Out there in the wilderness, it's hard to tell where to enter data because you can't see the data labels in the first column or first row that tell you where to enter data on the worksheet.

To see one part of a worksheet no matter how far you stray from it, you can *split* the worksheet or *freeze* columns and rows on-screen. In Figure 2-2, I split the worksheet so that column A, Property, always appears on-screen, no matter how far I scroll to the right; similarly, row 1 also appears at the top of the worksheet no matter how far I scroll down. Notice how the row numbers and column letters are interrupted in Figure 2-2. Because I split the screen, I always know what data to enter in a cell because I can clearly see property names in the first column and the column headings along the top of the worksheet.

Drag to adjust the split. Double-click to remove a split line.   Split bar

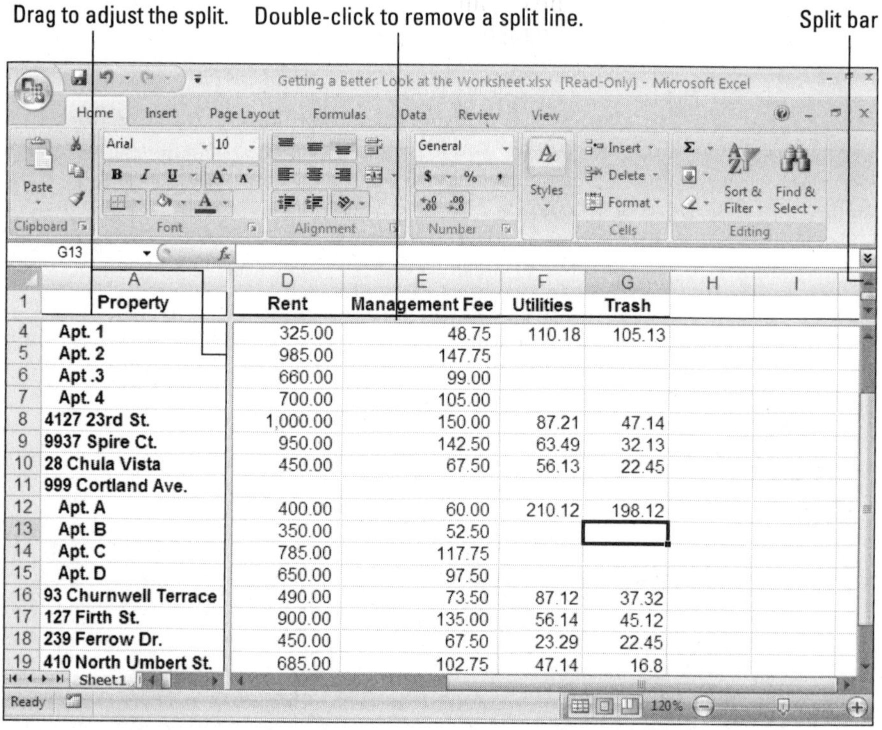

Figure 2-2: Splitting a worksheet.

Freezing columns or rows on a worksheet works much like splitting except that lines instead of gray bars appear on-screen to show which columns and rows are frozen, and you can't adjust where the split occurs by dragging the boundary where the worksheet is split.

Splitting the worksheet is superior to freezing columns or rows because, for one, you can drag the split lines to new locations when you split the worksheet, and moreover, you can remove a horizontal or vertical split simply by double-clicking it. However, if your goal is simply to freeze the topmost row or leftmost column in your worksheet, use a Freeze Panes command because all you have to do is click the Freeze Panes button on the View tab and choose Freeze Top Row or Freeze First Column.

Giving the Split or Freeze Panes command

Follow these steps to split or freeze columns and rows on-screen:

1. **Click the cell directly below the row you want to freeze or split, and click in the column to the right of the column that you want to freeze or split.**

In Figure 2-2, for example, I clicked cell B2, row 2 being below row 1, the row with the column labels (Property, Management Fee, and so on), and column B being to the right of column A, the column with the row labels (the property addresses).

2. **On the View tab, split or freeze the columns and rows.**

Go to the View tab and use one of these techniques:

- *Splitting:* Click the Split button. The other way to split a worksheet is to grab hold of a *split bar,* the little division markers directly above the vertical scroll bar (refer to Figure 2-2) and directly to the left of the horizontal scroll bar. You can tell where split bars are because the pointer turns into a double arrow when it's over a split bar. Click and drag a split bar to split the screen vertically or horizontally.

- *Freezing:* Click the Freeze Panes button and choose one of three Freeze options on the drop-down list. The second and third options, respectively, freeze the top row or first column. The first option, Freeze Panes, freezes the column(s) to the left and the row(s) above the cell you select in Step 1.

Bars or lines appear on-screen to show which row(s) and column(s) have been frozen or split. Move where you will in the worksheet. The column(s) and row(s) you froze or split stay on-screen.

Your own customized views

After you go to the trouble of freezing the screen or zooming in to a position you're comfortable with, you may as well save your view of the screen as a customized view. That way, you can call upon the customized view whenever you need it. View settings, the window size, the position of the grid on-screen, and cells that are selected can all be saved in a customized view.

Follow these steps to create a customized view:

1. **On the View tab, click the Custom Views button.**

You see the Custom Views dialog box. It lists views you've already created, if you've created any.

2. **Click the Add button.**

The Add View dialog box appears.

3. **Enter a name for the view and click OK.**

To switch to a customized view, click the Custom Views button, select a view in the Custom Views dialog box, and click the Show button.

Custom Views	? ⨯
Vie_w_s:	
Splitsville	Show
	Close
	Add...
	Delete

Add View	? ⨯
_N_ame: Freezer	
Include in view	
☑ Print settings	
☑ Hidden _r_ows, columns and filter settings	
OK Cancel	

Unsplitting and unfreezing

Use one of these techniques to keep your worksheet from splitting or freezing to death:

✦ **Unsplitting:** Click the Split button again; double-click one of the split bars to remove it; or drag a split bar into the top or left side of the worksheet window.

+ **Unfreezing:** Click the Freeze Panes button on the View tab and choose Unfreeze Panes on the drop-down list.

Hiding columns and rows

Another way to take the clutter out of a worksheet is to temporarily hide columns and rows:

+ **Hiding columns or rows:** Drag over the column letters or row numbers of the columns or rows that you want to hide. Dragging this way selects entire columns or rows. Then click the Format button on the Home tab, choose Hide & Unhide, and choose Hide Columns or Hide Rows.

+ **Unhiding columns and rows:** Select columns to the right and left of the hidden columns, or select rows above and below the hidden rows. To select columns or rows, drag over their letters or numbers. Then click the Format button on the Home tab, choose Hide & Unhide, and choose Unhide Columns or Unhide Rows.

It's easy to forget where you hid columns or rows. To make sure all columns and rows in your worksheet are displayed, click the Select All button (or press Ctrl+A) to select your entire worksheet. Then click the Format button and choose Hide & Unhide⇨Unhide Columns; click the Format button again and choose Hide & Unhide⇨Unhide Rows.

Comments for Documenting Your Worksheet

It may happen that you return to your worksheet days or months from now and discover to your dismay that you don't know why certain numbers or formulas are there. For that matter, someone else may inherit your worksheet and be mystified as to what the heck is going on. To take the mystery out of a worksheet, document it by entering comments here and there. A *comment* is a note that describes part of a worksheet. Each comment is connected to a cell. You can tell where a comment is because a small red triangle appears in the corner of cells that have been commented on. Move the pointer over one of these triangles and you see the pop-up box, a comment, and the name of the person who entered the comment, as shown in Figure 2-3. Click the Show All Comments button on the Review tab to see every comment in a worksheet.

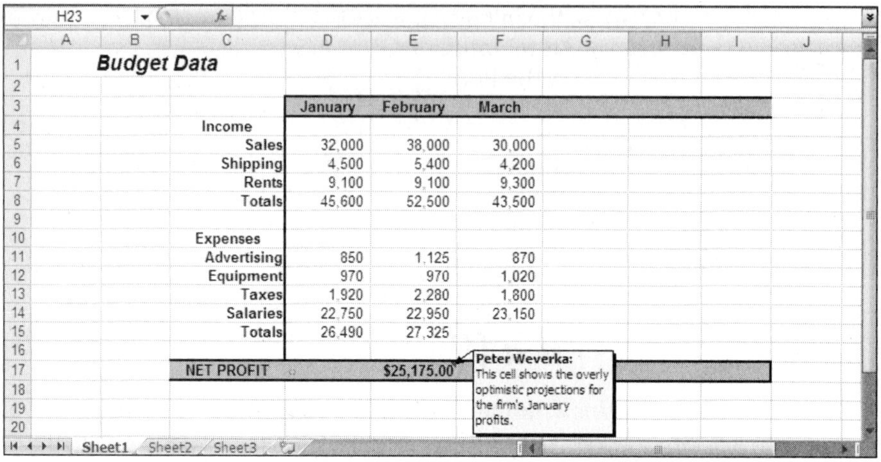

H23			⏷		*fx*						
	A	B	C	D	E	F	G	H	I	J	
1			**Budget Data**								
2											
3				January	February	March					
4			Income								
5			Sales	32,000	38,000	30,000					
6			Shipping	4,500	5,400	4,200					
7			Rents	9,100	9,100	9,300					
8			Totals	45,600	52,500	43,500					
9											
10			Expenses								
11			Advertising	850	1,125	870					
12			Equipment	970	970	1,020					
13			Taxes	1,920	2,280	1,800					
14			Salaries	22,750	22,950	23,150					
15			Totals	26,490	27,325						
16							Peter Weverka:				
17			NET PROFIT		$25,175.00		This cell shows the overly optimistic projections for				
18							the firm's January profits.				
19											
20											

Sheet1 Sheet2 Sheet3

Figure 2-3:
Comments explain what's what in a worksheet.

Here's everything a mere mortal needs to know about comments:

✦ **Entering a comment:** Click the cell that deserves the comment, go to the Review tab, and click the New Comment button (or press Shift+F2). Enter your comment in the pop-up box. Click in a different cell when you're done entering your comment.

✦ **Reading a comment:** Move the pointer over the small red triangle and read the comment in the pop-up box.

✦ **Finding comments**: On the Review tab, click the Previous or Next button to go from comment to comment.

✦ **Editing a comment:** Select the cell with the comment, click the Edit Comment button on the Review tab and edit the comment in the pop-up box.

✦ **Deleting comments:** Click a cell with a comment and then click the Delete button on the Review tab or right-click the cell and choose Delete Comment. To delete several comments, select them by Ctrl+clicking and then click the Delete button.

✦ **Deleting all comments in a worksheet:** Select all comments and then click the Delete button on the Review tab. You can select all comments by clicking the Find & Select button on the Home tab, choosing Go To, and in the Go To dialog box, clicking the Special button and choosing Comments in the Go to Special dialog box.

If your name doesn't appear in the pop-up box after you enter a comment and you want it to appear there, click the Office button, choose Excel Options, select the Popular category in the Excel Options dialog box, and enter your name in the User Name text box.

You can print the comments in a worksheet. On the Page Layout tab, click the Page Setup group button, and on the Sheet tab of the Page Setup dialog box, open the Comments drop-down list and choose At End of Sheet or As Displayed on Sheet.

Selecting Cells in a Worksheet

To copy, move, delete, and format numbers and words in a worksheet, you have to select the cells in which the numbers and words are found. Here are ways to select cells and the data inside them:

✦ **A block of cells:** Drag diagonally across the worksheet from one corner of the block of cells to the opposite corner. You can also click in one corner and Shift+click the opposite corner.

✦ **Adjacent cells in a row or column:** Drag across the cells.

✦ **Cells in various places:** While holding down the Ctrl key, click different cells.

✦ **A row or rows:** Click a row number to select an entire row. Click and drag down the row numbers to select several adjacent rows.

✦ **A column or columns:** Click a column letter to select an entire column. Click and drag across letters to select several adjacent columns.

✦ **Entire worksheet:** Click the Select All button, the square to the left of the column letters and above the row numbers; press Ctrl+A; or press Ctrl+Shift+Spacebar.

Press Ctrl+Spacebar to select the column that the active cell is in; press Shift+Spacebar to select the row where the active cell is.

You can enter the same data item in several different cells by selecting cells and then entering the data in one cell and pressing Ctrl+Enter. This technique comes in very handy, for example, when you want to enter a placeholder zero (0) in several different cells.

Deleting, Copying, and Moving Data

In the course of putting together a worksheet, it is sometimes necessary to delete, copy, and move cell contents. Here are instructions for doing these chores:

✦ **Deleting cell contents:** Select the cells and then press the Delete key, click the Clear button on the Home tab and choose Clear Contents, or right-click and choose Clear Contents. (Avoid the Delete button on the Home tab for deleting cell contents. Clicking that button deletes cells as well as their contents.)

✦ **Copying and moving cell contents:** Select the cells and use one of these techniques:

  • *Cut or Copy and Paste commands:* When you paste the data, click where you want the first cell of the block of cells you're copying or moving to go. (Book I, Chapter 2 explains copying and moving data in detail.) Be careful not to overwrite cells with data in them when you copy or move data. After you paste data, you see the Paste Options button. Click this button and choose an option from the drop-down list to format the data in different ways.

  • *Drag and drop:* Move the pointer to the edge of the cell block, click when you see the four-headed arrow, and start dragging. Hold down the Ctrl key to copy the data.

Handling the Worksheets in a Workbook

As a glance at the bottom of the worksheet tells you, each workbook comes with three worksheets named — not very creatively — Sheet1, Sheet2, and Sheet3. Follow these instructions to move among worksheets or to add, delete, rename and change the order of worksheets:

✦ **Moving among worksheets:** To go from one worksheet to another, click a worksheet tab along the bottom of the screen. If you can't see a tab, click one of the scroll arrows to the left of the worksheet tabs.

✦ **Renaming a worksheet:** Right-click the worksheet tab, choose Rename on the shortcut menu, type a new name, and press Enter. You can also click the Format button on the Home tab, choose Rename Sheet on the drop-down list, and enter a new name. Spaces are allowed in names, and names can be 31 characters long. Brackets ([]) are allowed in names, but you can't use these symbols: / \ : ? and *.

✦ **Selecting worksheets:** Click the worksheet's tab to select it. To select several worksheets, Ctrl+click their tabs or click the first tab and then Shift+click the last tab in the set. To select all the worksheets, right-click a tab and choose Select All Sheets on the shortcut menu.

✦ **Rearranging worksheets:** Drag the worksheet tab to a new location. As you drag, a tiny black arrow and a page icon appear to show you where the worksheet will land after you release the mouse button. You can also select a sheet, click the Format button on the Home tab, and choose Move or Copy Sheet on the drop-down list. The Move or Copy dialog box appears, as shown in Figure 2-4. Click the sheet in the Before Sheet list where you want the worksheet to go and click OK.

Figure 2-4: Besides dragging it, you can move a worksheet in this dialog box.

Move or Copy

Move selected sheets
To book:
Comments for Documenting.xlsx
Before sheet:

Budgets
Projections
Trends
Megatrends
Raw Data
Sales Histories
(move to end)

☐ Create a copy

☑ Match destination theme

OK   Cancel

✦ **Inserting a new worksheet:** On the Home tab, open the drop-down list on the Insert button and choose Insert Sheet; click the Insert Sheet button (you can find it to the right of the worksheet tabs); or press Shift+F11.

✦ **Deleting a worksheet:** Select the sheet, and on the Home tab, open the drop-down list on the Delete button and choose Delete Sheet. You can also right-click a worksheet tab and choose Delete.

✦ **Copying a worksheet:** Hold down the Ctrl key and drag the worksheet tab to a new location.

✦ **Color-coding a worksheet:** Right-click a worksheet tab and choose Tab Color. Then select a color on the submenu, or choose More Colors and select a color in the Colors dialog box. You can also select a worksheet tab, click the Format button on the Home tab, choose Tab Color on the drop-down list, and choose a color on the submenu.

You can change the size of columns or apply numeric formats to the same addresses in different worksheets by selecting all the sheets first and then formatting one worksheet. The formats apply to all the worksheets that you select. Being able to format several different worksheets simultaneously comes in handy, for example, when your workbook tracks monthly data and each worksheet pertains to one month. Of course, another way to handle worksheets with similar data is to create the first worksheet and copy it to the second, third, and fourth worksheets with the Copy and Paste commands.

Keeping Others from Tampering with Worksheets

People with savvy and foresight sometimes set up workbooks so that one worksheet holds raw data and the other worksheets hold formulas that calculate the raw data. This technique prevents others from tampering with the raw data. Furthermore, if the worksheet with raw data is hidden, the chance it will be tampered with is lower; and if the worksheet is protected, no one can tamper with it unless they have a password. These pages explain how to hide a worksheet so others are less likely to find it and how to protect a worksheet from being edited.

Hiding a worksheet

Follow these instructions to hide and unhide worksheets:

✦ **Hiding a worksheet:** Right-click the worksheet's tab and choose Hide on the shortcut menu. You can also display the worksheet, click the Format button on the Home tab, and choose Hide & Unhide⇨Hide Sheet.

✦ **Unhiding a worksheet:** Right-click any worksheet tab and choose Unhide, or click the Format button on the Home tab and choose Hide & Unhide⇨ Unhide Sheet. You see the Unhide dialog box. Select the name of the worksheet you want to unhide and click OK.

Protecting a worksheet

Protecting a worksheet means to restrict others from changing it — from formatting it, inserting new rows and columns, or deleting rows and columns, among other tasks. You can also prevent any editorial changes whatsoever from being made to a worksheet. Follow these steps to protect a worksheet from tampering by others:

1. **Select the worksheet that needs protection.**

2. **On the Review tab, click the Protect Sheet button.**

You see the Protect Sheet dialog box, as shown in Figure 2-5. You can also open this dialog box by clicking the Format button on the Home tab and choosing Protect Sheet.

Protect Sheet

☑ Protect worksheet and contents of locked cells

Password to unprotect sheet:

Allow all users of this worksheet to:

☐ Select locked cells
☐ Select unlocked cells
☐ Format cells
☑ Format columns
☑ Format rows
☐ Insert columns
☐ Insert rows
☐ Insert hyperlinks
☐ Delete columns
☐ Delete rows

OK   Cancel

Figure 2-5:
Select what
you want
others to be
able to do.

3. **Enter a password in the Password to Unprotect Sheet box if you want only people with the password to be able to unprotect the worksheet after you protect it.**

4. **On the Allow All Users of This Worksheet To list, select the check box next to the name of each task that you want to permit others to do.**

   For example, click the Format Cells check box if you want others to be able to format cells.

   Deselect the Select Locked Cells check box to prevent any changes from being made to the worksheet. By default, all worksheet cells are locked, and by preventing others from selecting locked cells, you effectively prevent them from editing any cells.

5. **Click OK.**

   If you entered a password in Step 3, you must enter it again in the Confirm Password dialog box and click OK.

To unprotect a worksheet that you protected, click the Unprotect Sheet button on the Review tab. You must enter a password if you elected to require others to have a password before they can unprotect a worksheet.

Chapter 3: Formulas and Functions for Crunching Numbers

In This Chapter

- ✓ **Constructing a formula**
- ✓ **Using cell ranges in formulas**
- ✓ **Naming cell ranges**
- ✓ **Referring to cells in other worksheets**
- ✓ **Copying formulas to other columns and rows**
- ✓ **Preventing errors in formulas**
- ✓ **Using functions in formulas**

*F*ormulas are where it's at as far as Excel is concerned. After you know how to construct formulas — and constructing them is pretty easy — you can put Excel to work. You can make the numbers speak to you. You can turn a bunch of unruly numbers into meaningful figures and statistics.

This chapter explains what a formula is, how to enter a formula, and how to enter a formula quickly. You also discover how to copy formulas from cell to cell and how to keep formula errors from creeping into your workbooks. Finally, this chapter explains how to make use of the hundred or so functions that Excel offers.

How Formulas Work

A *formula,* you may recall from the sleepy hours you spent in the back of math class, is a way to calculate numbers. For example, 2+3=5 is a formula. When you enter a formula in a cell, Excel computes the formula and displays its results in the cell. Click in cell A3 and enter **=2+3**, for example, and Excel displays the number 5 in cell A3.

Referring to cells in formulas

As well as numbers, Excel formulas can refer to the contents of different cells. When a formula refers to a cell, the number in the cell is used to compute the formula. In Figure 3-1, for example, cell A1 contains the number 2;

cell A2 contains the number 3; and cell A3 contains the formula =A1+A2. As shown in cell A3, the result of the formula is 5. If I change the number in cell A1 from 2 to 3, the result of the formula in cell A3 (=A1+A2) becomes 6, not 5. When a formula refers to a cell and the number in a cell changes, the result of the formula changes as well.

Formula in the Formula bar

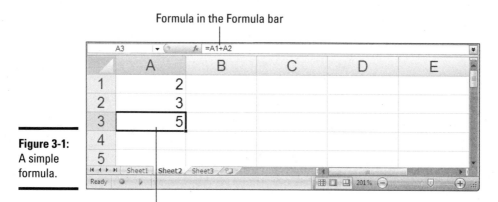

Figure 3-1:
A simple
formula.

Results of the formula

To see the value of using cell references in formulas, consider the worksheet shown in Figure 3-2. The purpose of this worksheet is to track the budget of a school's Parent Teacher Association (PTA):

Figure 3-2:
Using
formulas
in a
worksheet.

	A B	C	D	E
1				
2	Income	Actual Income	Projected Income	Over/Under Budget
3	Book Fair	4,876.40	5,500.00	-623.60
4	Dances	1,476.95	1,800.00	-323.05
5	Fundraising	13,175.00	5,000.00	8,175.00
6	Merchandise Sales	5,888.50	7,000.00	-1,111.50
7	Membership Fees	3,918.00	3,000.00	918.00
8	Total Income	$ 29,334.85	$ 22,300.00	$ 7,034.85

✦ Column C, Actual Income, lists income from different sources.

✦ Column D, Projected Income, shows what the PTA members thought income from these sources would be.

✦ Column E, Over/Under Budget, shows how actual income compares to projected income from the different sources.

As the figures in the Actual Income column (column C) are updated, figures in the Over/Under Budget column (column E) and the Total Income row (row 8) change instantaneously. These figures change instantaneously because the formulas refer to the numbers in cells, not to unchanging numbers (known as *constants*).

Figure 3-3 shows the formulas used to calculate the data in the worksheet in Figure 3-2. In column E, formulas deduct the numbers in column D from the numbers in column C to show where the PTA over- or under-budgeted for the different sources of income. In row 8, you can see how the SUM function is used to total cells in rows 3 through 7. The end of this chapter explains how to use functions in formulas.

Figure 3-3:
The
formulas
used to
generate
the numbers
in Figure 3-2.

	A	B	C	D	E
1					
2	Income		Actual Income	Projected Income	Over/Under Budget
3		Book Fair	4876.4	5500	=C3-D3
4		Dances	1476.95	1800	=C4-D4
5		Fundraising	13175	5000	=C5-D5
6		Merchandise Sales	5888.5	7000	=C6-D6
7		Membership Fees	3918	3000	=C7-D7
8	Total Income		=SUM(C3:C7)	=SUM(D3:D7)	=SUM(E3:E7)
9					

Excel is remarkably good about updating cell references in formulas when you move cells. To see how good Excel is, consider what happens to cell addresses in formulas when you delete a row in a worksheet. If a formula refers to cell C1 but you delete row B, row C becomes row B, and the value in cell C1 changes addresses from C1 to B1. You would think that references in formulas to cell C1 would be out of date, but you would be wrong. Excel automatically adjusts all formulas that refer to cell C1. Those formulas now refer to cell B1 instead.

In case you want to know, you can display formulas in worksheet cells instead of the results of formulas, as was done in Figure 3-3, by pressing Ctrl+' or clicking the Show Formulas button on the Formulas tab (you may have to click the Formula Auditing button first, depending on the size of your screen). Click the Show Formulas button a second time to see formula results again.

Referring to formula results in formulas

Besides referring to cells with numbers in them, you can refer to formula results in a cell. Consider the worksheet shown in Figure 3-4. The purpose of this worksheet is to track scoring by the players on a basketball team:

Averages returned from the formula results in column E

	A	B	C	D	E	F
2		Game 1	Game 2	Game 3	Totals	Average
3	Jones	4	3	7	14	4.7
4	Sacharsky	2	1	0	3	1.0
5	Mellon	11	13	8	32	10.7
6	Gomez	8	11	6	25	8.3
7	Riley	2	0	0	2	0.7
8	Pealer	3	8	4	15	5.0
9	Subrata	13	18	18	49	16.3

	A	B	C	D	E	F
2		Game 1	Game 2	Game 3	Totals	Average
3	Jones 4	3	7		=B3+C3+D3	=E3/3
4	Sacharsky 2	1	0		=B4+C4+D4	=E4/3
5	Mellon 11	13	8		=B5+C5+D5	=E5/3
6	Gomez 8	11	6		=B6+C6+D6	=E6/3
7	Riley 2	0	0		=B7+C7+D7	=E7/3
8	Pealer 3	8	4		=B8+C8+D8	=E8/3
9	Subrata 13	18	18		=B9+C9+D9	=E9/3

Figure 3-4: Using formula results as other formulas.

✦ The Totals column (column E) shows the total points each player has scored in the three games.

✦ The Average column (column F), using the formula results in the Totals column, determines how much each player has scored on average. The Average column does that by dividing the results in column E by 3, the number of games played.

In this case, Excel uses the results of the total-calculation formulas in column E to compute average points per game in column F.

Operators in formulas

Addition, subtraction, and division aren't the only operators you can use in formulas. Table 3-1 explains the arithmetic operators you can use and the key you press to enter each operator. In the table, operators are listed in the order of precedence.

Table 3-1	Arithmetic Operators for Use in Formulas	
Operator	*Symbol*	*Example Formula*
Percent	%	=50%, 50 percent, or 0.5
Exponentiation	^	=50^2, 50 to the second power, or 2500
Division	/	=E2/3, the number in cell E2 divided by 3
Multiplication	*	=E2*4, the number in cell E2 multiplied by 4
Addition	+	=F1+F2+F3, the sum of the numbers in those cells
Subtraction	–	=G5–8, the number in cell G5 minus 8

Another way to compute a formula is to make use of a function. As "Working with Functions" explains later in this chapter, a function is a built-in formula that comes with Excel. SUM, for example, adds the numbers in cells. AVG finds the average of different numbers.

The order of precedence

When a formula includes more than one operator, the order in which the operators appear in the formula matters a lot. Consider this formula:

    =2+3*4

Does this formula result in 14 (2+[3*4]) or 20 ([2+3]*4)? The answer is 14 because Excel performs multiplication before addition in formulas. In other words, multiplication takes precedence over addition. The order in which calculations are made in a formula that includes different operators is called the *order of precedence*. Be sure to remember the order of precedence when you construct complex formulas with more than one operator:

 1. Percent (%)

 2. Exponentiation (^)

 3. Multiplication (*) and division (/); leftmost operations are calculated first

 4. Addition (+) and subtraction (-); leftmost operations are calculated first

 5. Concatenation (&)

 6. Comparison (+, <, <=, >,>=, and <>)

To get around the order of precedence problem, enclose parts of formulas in parentheses. Operations in parentheses are calculated before all other parts of a formula. For example, the formula =2+3*4 equals 20 when it is written this way: =(2+3)*4.

The Basics of Entering a Formula

No matter what kind of formula you enter, no matter how complex the formula is, follow these basic steps to enter it:

1. **Click the cell where you want to enter the formula.**

2. **Click in the Formula bar.**

3. **Enter the equals sign (=).**

You must be sure to enter the equals sign before you enter a formula. Without it, Excel thinks you're entering text or a number, not a formula.

4. **Enter the formula.**

For example, enter **=B1*.06**. Make sure that you enter all cell addresses correctly. By the way, you can enter lowercase letters in cell references. Excel changes them to uppercase after you finish entering the formula. The next section in this chapter explains how to enter cell addresses quickly in formulas.

5. **Press Enter or click the Enter button (the check mark).**

The result of the formula appears in the cell.

Speed Techniques for Entering Formulas

Entering formulas and making sure that all cell references are correct is a tedious activity, but fortunately for you, Excel offers a few techniques to make entering formulas easier. Read on to find out how ranges make entering cell references easier and how you can enter cell references in formulas by pointing and clicking. You also find instructions here for copying formulas.

Clicking cells to enter cell references

The hardest part about entering a formula is entering the cell references correctly. You have to squint to see which row and column the cell you want to refer to is in. You have to carefully type the right column letter and row number. However, instead of typing a cell reference, you can click the cell you want to refer to in a formula.

In the course of entering a formula, simply click the cell on your worksheet that you want to reference. As shown in Figure 3-5, shimmering marquee lights appear around the cell that you clicked so that you can clearly see which cell you're referring to. The cell's reference address, meanwhile, appears in the Formula bar. In Figure 3-5, I clicked cell F3 instead of entering its reference address on the Formula bar. The reference F3 appears on the Formula bar, and the marquee lights appear around cell F3.

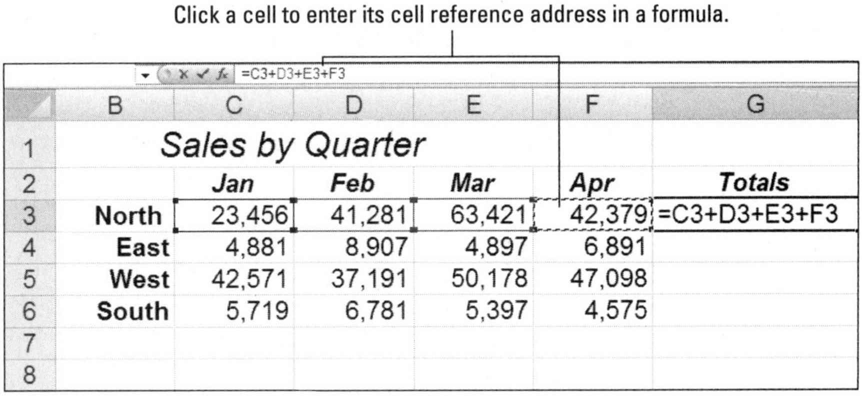

Click a cell to enter its cell reference address in a formula.

	B	C	D	E	F	G
	▼ ⊘ ✕ ✓ *fx*	=C3+D3+E3+F3				
1		Sales by Quarter				
2		*Jan*	*Feb*	*Mar*	*Apr*	*Totals*
3	North	23,456	41,281	63,421	42,379	=C3+D3+E3+F3
4	East	4,881	8,907	4,897	6,891	
5	West	42,571	37,191	50,178	47,098	
6	South	5,719	6,781	5,397	4,575	
7						
8						

Figure 3-5:
Clicking to
enter a cell
reference.

Get in the habit of pointing and clicking cells to enter cell references in
formulas. Clicking cells is easier than typing cell addresses, and the cell references
are entered more accurately.

Entering a cell range

A *cell range* is a line or block of cells in a worksheet. Instead of typing cell reference
addresses one at a time, you can simply select cells on your worksheet.
In Figure 3-6, I selected cells C3, D3, E3, and F3 to form cell range C3:F3. This
spares me the trouble of entering the cell addresses one at a time: C3, D3, E3,
and F3. The formula in Figure 3-6 uses the SUM function to total the numeric
values in cell range C3:F3. Notice the marquee lights around the range C3:F3.
The lights show precisely which range you're selecting. Cell ranges come in
especially handy where functions are concerned (see "Working with
Functions" later in this chapter).

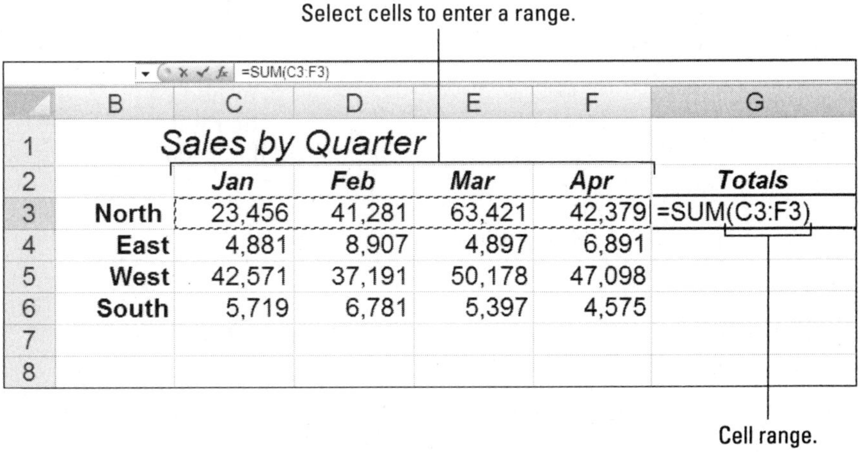

Select cells to enter a range.

	B	C	D	E	F	G
	▼ ⊘ ✕ ✓ *fx*	=SUM(C3:F3)				
1		Sales by Quarter				
2		*Jan*	*Feb*	*Mar*	*Apr*	*Totals*
3	North	23,456	41,281	63,421	42,379	=SUM(C3:F3)
4	East	4,881	8,907	4,897	6,891	
5	West	42,571	37,191	50,178	47,098	
6	South	5,719	6,781	5,397	4,575	
7						
8						

Figure 3-6:
Using a cell
range in a
formula.

Cell range.

To identify a cell range, Excel lists the outermost cells in the range and places a colon (:) between cell addresses:

✦ A cell range comprising cells A1, A2, A3, and A4 is listed this way: A1:A4.

✦ A cell range comprising a block of cells from A1 to D4 is listed this way: A1:D4.

You can enter cell ranges on your own without selecting cells. To do so, type the first cell in the range, enter a colon, and type the last cell.

Naming cell ranges so that you can use them in formulas

Whether you type cell addresses yourself or drag across cells to enter a cell range, entering cell address references is a chore. Entering =C1+C2+C3+C4, for example, can cause a finger cramp; entering =SUM(C1:C4) is no piece of cake, either. To take the tedium out of entering cell ranges in formulas, you can name cell ranges. Then, to enter a cell range in a formula, all you have to do is select a name in the Paste Name dialog box or click the Use in Formula button on the Formulas tab, as shown in Figure 3-7. Naming cell ranges has an added benefit. You can choose a name from the Name Box drop-down list and go directly to the cell range whose name you choose, as shown in Figure 3-7.

Choose a name to move there.   Enter a named cell range in a formula.

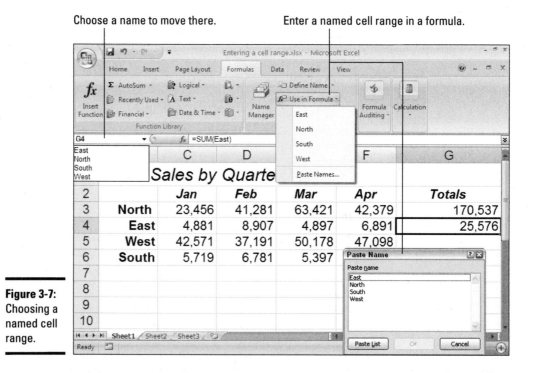

Figure 3-7: Choosing a named cell range.

Naming cell ranges has one disadvantage, and it's a big one. Excel doesn't adjust cell references when you copy a formula with a range name from one cell to another. A range name always refers to the same set of cells. Later in this chapter, "Copying Formulas from Cell to Cell" explains how to copy formulas.

Creating a cell range name

Follow these steps to create a cell range name:

1. **Select the cells that you want to name.**

2. **On the Formulas tab, click the Define Name button.**

You see the New Name dialog box.

3. **Enter a descriptive name in the Name box.**

Names can't begin with a number or include blank spaces.

4. **On the Scope drop-down list, choose Workbook or a worksheet name.**

Choose a worksheet name if you intend to use the range name you're creating only in formulas that you construct in a single worksheet. If your formulas will refer to cell range addresses in different worksheets, choose Workbook so that you can use the range name wherever you go in your workbook.

5. **Enter a comment to describe the range name, if you want.**

Enter a comment if doing so will help you remember where the cells you're naming are located or what type of information they hold. As I explain shortly, you can read comments in the Name Manager dialog box, the place where you go to edit and delete range names.

6. **Click OK.**

In case you're in a hurry, here's a fast way to enter a cell range name: Select the cells for the range, click in the Name Box (you can find it to the left of the Formula bar, as shown in Figure 3-7), enter a name for the range, and press the Enter key.

Entering a range name as part of a formula

To include a cell range name in a formula, click in the Formula bar where you want to enter the range name and then use one of these techniques to enter the name:

✦ On the Formulas tab, click the Use in Formula button and choose a cell range name on the drop-down list (refer to Figure 3-7).

✦ Press F3 or click the Use in Formula button and choose Paste Names on the drop-down list. You see the Paste Name dialog box (refer to Figure 3-7). Select a cell range name and click OK.

Quickly traveling to a cell range that you named

To go quickly to a cell range you named, open the Name Box drop-down list and choose a name (refer to Figure 3-7). The Name Box drop-down list is located to the left of the Formula bar.

To make this trick work, the cursor can't be in the Formula bar. The Name Box drop-down list isn't available when you're constructing a formula.

Managing cell range names

To rename or delete cell range names, click the Name Manager button on the Formulas tab. You see the Name Manager dialog box, as shown in Figure 3-8. This dialog box lists names, cell values in names, the worksheet on which the range name is found, and whether the range name can be applied throughout a workbook or only in one worksheet. To rename or delete a cell range name, select it in the dialog box and use these techniques:

✦ **Renaming:** Click the Edit button and enter a new name in the Edit Name dialog box.

✦ **Deleting:** Click the Delete button and click OK in the confirmation box.

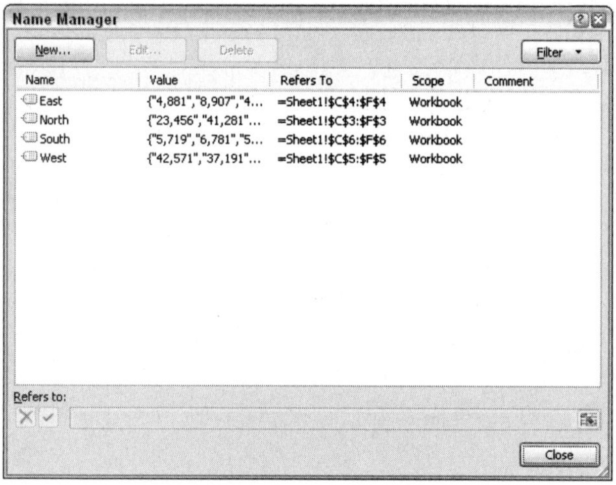

Figure 3-8: The Name Manager dialog box.

Name	Value	Refers To	Scope	Comment
East	{"4,881","8,907","4...	=Sheet1!$C$4:$F$4	Workbook	
North	{"23,456","41,281"...	=Sheet1!$C$3:$F$3	Workbook	
South	{"5,719","6,781","5...	=Sheet1!$C$6:$F$6	Workbook	
West	{"42,571","37,191"...	=Sheet1!$C$5:$F$5	Workbook	

Name Manager

New...   Edit...   Delete   Filter ▾

Refers to:

Close

Referring to cells in different worksheets

Excel gives you the opportunity to use data from different worksheets in a formula. If one worksheet lists sales figures from January and the next lists sales figures from February, you can construct a "grand total" formula in either worksheet to tabulate sales in the two-month period. A reference to a cell on a different worksheet is called a *3D reference*.

Construct the formula as you normally would, but when you want to refer to a cell or cell range in a different worksheet, click a worksheet tab to move to the other worksheet and select the cell or range of cells there. Without returning to the original worksheet, complete your formula in the Formula bar and press Enter. Excel returns you to the original worksheet, where you can see the results of your formula.

The only things odd about constructing formulas across worksheets are the cell references. As a glance at the Formula bar tells you, cell addresses in cross-worksheet formulas list the sheet name and an exclamation point (!) as well as the cell address itself. For example, this formula in Worksheet 1 adds the number in cell A4 to the numbers in cells D5 and E5 in Worksheet 2:

```
=A4+Sheet2!D5+Sheet2!E5
```

This formula in Worksheet 2 multiplies the number in cell E18 by the number in cell C15 in Worksheet 1:

```
=E18*Sheet1!C15
```

This formula in Worksheet 2 finds the average of the numbers in the cell range C7:F7 in Worksheet 1:

```
=AVERAGE(Sheet1!C7:F7)
```

Copying Formulas from Cell to Cell

Often in worksheets, the same formula but with different cell references is used across a row or down a column. For example, in the worksheet shown in Figure 3-9, column F totals the rainfall figures in rows 7 through 11. To enter formulas for totaling the rainfall figures in column F, you could laboriously enter formulas in cells F7, F8, F9, F10, and F11. But a faster way is to enter the formula once in cell F7 and then copy the formula in F7 down the column to cells F8, F9, F10, and F11.

Drag the AutoFill handle.

F7	fx =B7+C7+D7+E7				
	A	B	C	D	E	F
5						
6		Winter	Spring	Summer	Fall	Totals
7	Sonoma	13	8.3	2.3	8.2	31.8
8	Napa	11.5	7.6	3.1	7.5	
9	Mendocino	15.8	12.9	2.9	8.3	
10	San Francisco	10.9	9.7	1.1	3.3	
11	Contra Costa	10.1	8.4	2.3	4.4	+

F11	fx =B11+C11+D11+E11				
	A	B	C	D	E	F
5						
6		Winter	Spring	Summer	Fall	Totals
7	Sonoma	13	8.3	2.3	8.2	31.8
8	Napa	11.5	7.6	3.1	7.5	29.7
9	Mendocino	15.8	12.9	2.9	8.3	39.9
10	San Francisco	10.9	9.7	1.1	3.3	25
11	Contra Costa	10.1	8.4	2.3	4.4	25.2

Figure 3-9:
Copying a
formula.

REMEMBER

When you copy a formula to a new cell, Excel adjusts the cell references in the formula so that the formula works in the cells to which it has been copied. Astounding! Opportunities to copy formulas abound on most worksheets. And copying formulas is the fastest and safest way to enter formulas in a worksheet.

Follow these steps to copy a formula:

1. **Select the cell with the formula you want to copy down a column or across a row.**

2. **Drag the AutoFill handle across the cells to which you want to copy the formula.**

This is the same AutoFill handle you drag to enter serial data (see Chapter 1 of this mini-book about entering lists and serial data with the AutoFill command). The AutoFill handle is the small black square in the lower-right corner of the cell. When you move the mouse pointer over it, it changes to a black cross. Figure 3-9 shows a formula being copied.

3. **Release the mouse button.**

If I were you, I would click in the cells to which you copied the formula and glance at the Formula bar to make sure that the formula was copied correctly. I'd bet you it was.

You can also copy formulas with the Copy and Paste commands. Just make sure that cell references refer correctly to the surrounding cells.

Detecting and Correcting Errors in Formulas

It happens. Everyone makes an error from time to time when entering formulas in cells. Especially in a worksheet in which formula results are calculated into other formulas, a single error in one formula can spread like a virus and cause miscalculations throughout a worksheet. To prevent that from happening, Excel offers several ways to correct errors in formulas. You can correct them one at a time, run the error checker, and trace cell references, as the following pages explain.

 By the way, if you want to see formulas in cells instead of formula results, click the Show Formulas button on the Formulas tab (you may have to click the Formula Auditing button first, depending on the size of your screen). Sometimes seeing formulas this way helps to detect formula errors.

Correcting errors one at a time

When Excel detects what it thinks is a formula that has been entered incorrectly, a small green triangle appears in the upper-left corner of the cell where you entered the formula. And if the error is especially egregious, an *error message* — three or four cryptic letters preceded by a pound sign (#) — appears in the cell. Table 3-2 explains common error messages.

Table 3-2	Common Formula Error Messages
Message	*What Went Wrong*
#DIV/0!	You tried to divide a number by a zero (0) or an empty cell.
#NAME	You used a cell range name in the formula, but the name isn't defined. Sometimes this error occurs because you type the name incorrectly. (Earlier in this chapter, "Naming cell ranges so that you can use them in formulas" explains how to name cell ranges.)
#N/A	The formula refers to an empty cell, so no data is available for computing the formula. Sometimes people enter N/A in a cell as a placeholder to signal the fact that data isn't entered yet. Revise the formula or enter a number or formula in the empty cells.
#NULL	The formula refers to a cell range that Excel can't understand. Make sure that the range is entered correctly.
#NUM	An argument you use in your formula is invalid.
#REF	The cell or range of cells that the formula refers to isn't there.
#VALUE	The formula includes a function that's used incorrectly, takes an invalid argument, or is misspelled. Make sure that the function uses the right argument and is spelled correctly.

To find out more about a formula error and perhaps correct it, select the cell with the green triangle and then click the Error button. This small button appears beside a cell with a formula error after you click the cell. The drop-down list on the Error button offers opportunities for correcting the formula error and finding out more about it, as shown in Figure 3-10.

	D	E	F	G	H	I	J	K
E37		fx	=SUM(E32:E35)					
35	4,487	55,572.38	0.05	2,778.62				
36	3,982	50,175.66	0.05	2,508.78				
37	17,	242,700.91		17,914.27				
38		Formula Omits Adjacent Cells						
39	Sales	Update Formula to Include Cells	oyalty					
40	8,	Help on this error						
41	1,	Ignore Error		Error Checking				
42		Edit in Formula Bar		Error in cell E37		Update Formula to Include Cells		
43	12,	Error Checking Options...		=SUM(E32:E35)		Help on this error		
44	1	1.00	0	Formula Omits Adjacent Cells				
45	23,101	305,483.33		The formula in this cell refers to a range that has additional numbers adjacent to it.		Ignore Error		
46						Edit in Formula Bar		
47	Sales	Pub	Rate	Options...		Previous	Next	
48	6,805	100,075.72	0.07	7,005.30	Domestic	6,805	100,075	

Figure 3-10: Correcting errors one at a time (left) and running the error checker (right).

Running the error checker

Error Checking — Another way to tackle formula errors is to run the error checker. When the checker encounters what it thinks is an error, the Error Checking dialog box tells you what the error is, as shown in Figure 3-10. To run the error checker, go to the Formulas tab and click the Error Checking button (you may have to click the Formula Auditing button first, depending on the size of your screen).

If you see clearly what the error is, click the Edit in Formula Bar button, repair the error in the Formula bar, and click the Resume button in the dialog box (you find this button at the top of the dialog box). If the error isn't one that really needs correcting, either click the Ignore Error button or click the Next button to send the error checker in search of the next error in your worksheet.

Tracing cell references

In a complex worksheet in which formulas are piled on top of one another and the results of some formulas are computed into other formulas, it helps to be able to trace cell references. By tracing cell references, you can see how the data in a cell figures into a formula in another cell, or if the cell contains a formula, which cells the formula gathers data from to make its computation. You can get a better idea of how your worksheet is constructed, and in so doing, find structural errors more easily.

Figure 3-11 shows how cell tracers describe the relationships between cells. A *cell tracer* is a blue arrow that shows the relationships between cells used in formulas. You can trace two types of relationships:

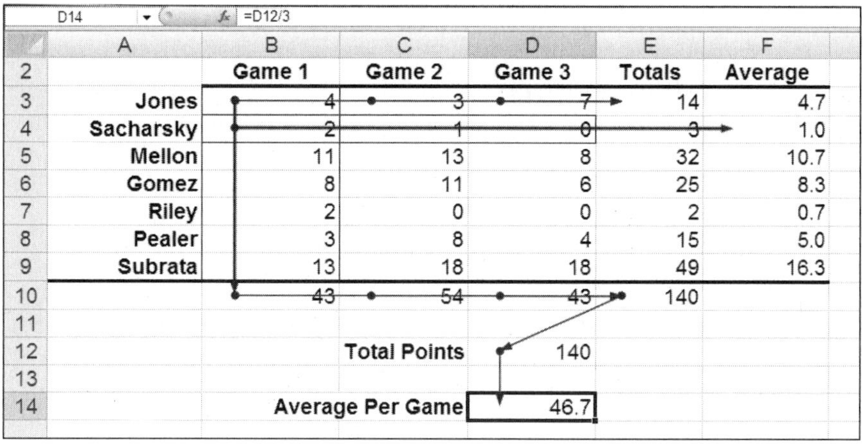

	A	B	C	D	E	F
		Game 1	Game 2	Game 3	Totals	Average
3	Jones	4	3	7	14	4.7
4	Sacharsky	2	1	0	3	1.0
5	Mellon	11	13	8	32	10.7
6	Gomez	8	11	6	25	8.3
7	Riley	2	0	0	2	0.7
8	Pealer	3	8	4	15	5.0
9	Subrata	13	18	18	49	16.3
10		43	54	43	140	
11						
12			Total Points	140		
13						
14			Average Per Game	46.7		

D14 = D12/3

Figure 3-11: Tracing the relationships between cells.

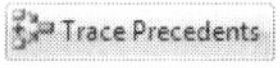

✦ **Tracing precedents:** Select a cell with a formula in it and trace the formula's *precedents* to find out which cells are computed to produce the results of the formula. Trace precedents when you want to find out where a formula gets its computation data. Cell tracer arrows point from the referenced cells to the cell with the formula results in it.

To trace precedents, click the Trace Precedents button on the Formulas tab (you may have to click the Formula Auditing button first, depending on the size of your screen).

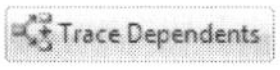

✦ **Tracing dependents:** Select a cell and trace its *dependents* to find out which cells contain formulas that use data from the cell you selected. Cell tracer arrows point from the cell you selected to cells with formula results in them. Trace dependents when you want to find out how the data in a cell contributes to formulas elsewhere in the worksheet. The cell you select can contain a constant value or a formula in its own right (and contribute its results to another formula).

To trace dependents, click the Trace Dependents button on the Formulas tab (you may have to click the Formula Auditing button first, depending on the size of your screen).

To remove the cell tracer arrows from a worksheet, click the Remove Arrows button. You can open the drop-down list on this button and choose Remove Precedent Arrows or Remove Dependent Arrows to remove only cell-precedent or cell-dependent tracer arrows.

Working with Functions

A *function* is a canned formula that comes with Excel. Excel offers hundreds of functions, some of which are very obscure and fit only for use by rocket scientists or securities analysts. Other functions are very practical. For example, you can use the SUM function to quickly total the numbers in a range of cells (earlier in this chapter, "Entering a cell range" describes cell ranges). Instead of entering =C2+C3+C4+C5 on the Formula bar, you can enter =SUM(C2:C5), which tells Excel to total the numbers in cell C2, C3, C4, and C5. To obtain the product of the number in cell G4 and .06, you can use the PRODUCT function and enter =PRODUCT(G4,.06) on the Formula bar.

Table 3-3 lists the most common functions. To get an idea of the numerous functions that Excel offers, go to the Formulas tab and click the Insert Function button. You see the Insert Function dialog box, as shown in Figure 3-12. (Later in this chapter, I show you how you can use this dialog box to use functions in formulas.) Choose a function category in the dialog box, choose a function name, and read the description. You can click the Help on This Function link to open the Excel Help window and get a thorough description of the function and how it's used.

Table 3-3	Common Functions and Their Use
Function	*Returns*
AVERAGE(*number1,number2,. . .*)	The average of the numbers in the cells listed in the arguments.
COUNT(*value1,value2,. . .*)	The number of cells that contain the numbers listed in the arguments.
MAX(*number1,number2,. . .*)	The largest value in the cells listed in the arguments.
MIN(*number1,number2,. . .*)	The smallest value in the cells listed in the arguments.
PRODUCT(*number1,number2,. . .*)	The product of multiplying the cells listed in the arguments.
STDEV(*number1,number2,. . .*)	An estimate of standard deviation based on the sample cells listed in the argument.
STDEVP(*number1,number2,. . .*)	An estimate of standard deviation based on the entire sample cells listed in the arguments.
SUM(*number1,number2,. . .*)	The total of the numbers in the arguments.
VAR(*number1,number2,. . .*)	An estimate of the variance based on the sample cells listed in the arguments.
VARP(*number1,number2,. . .*)	A variance calculation based on all cells listed in the arguments.

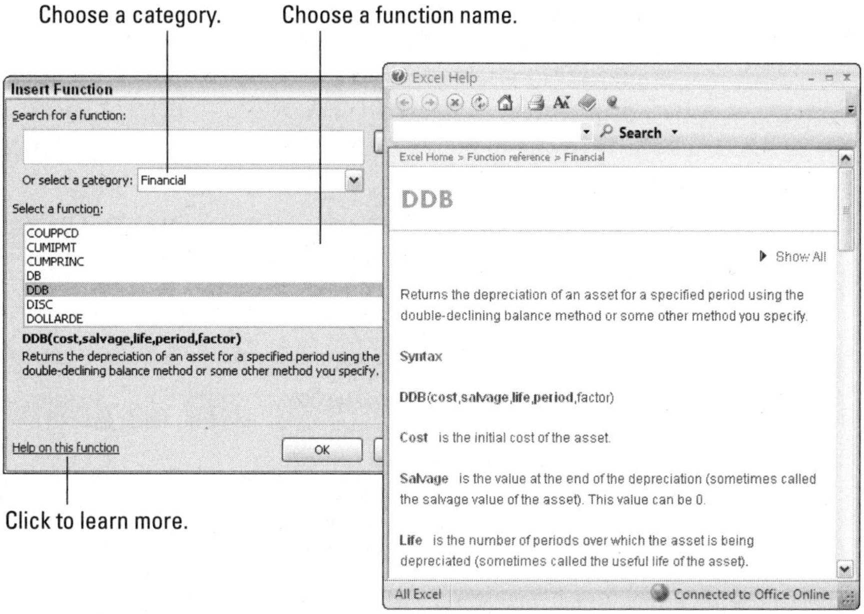

Choose a category. Choose a function name.

Insert Function

Search for a function:

Or select a category: Financial

Select a function:

COUPPCD
CUMIPMT
CUMPRINC
DB
DDB
DISC
DOLLARDE

DDB(cost,salvage,life,period,factor)
Returns the depreciation of an asset for a specified period using the
double-declining balance method or some other method you specify.

Help on this function   OK

Excel Help

Search

Excel Home > Function reference > Financial

DDB

▶ Show All

Returns the depreciation of an asset for a specified period using the
double-declining balance method or some other method you specify.

Syntax

DDB(cost,salvage,life,period,factor)

Cost   is the initial cost of the asset.

Salvage   is the value at the end of the depreciation (sometimes called
the salvage value of the asset). This value can be 0.

Life   is the number of periods over which the asset is being
depreciated (sometimes called the useful life of the asset).

All Excel   Connected to Office Online

Figure 3-12:
The Insert
Function
dialog box.

Click to learn more.

Using arguments in functions

Every function takes one or more *arguments* — the cell references or
numbers, enclosed in parentheses, that the function acts upon. For example,
=AVERAGE(B1:B4) returns the average of the numbers in the cell range B1
through B4; =PRODUCT(6.5,C4) returns the product of multiplying the number
6.5 by the number in cell C4. When a function requires more than one argument,
enter a comma between the arguments (enter a comma without a space).

Entering a function in a formula

To enter a function in a formula, you can enter the function name by typing it
in the Formula bar, or you can rely on Excel to enter it for you. Enter function
names yourself if you're well acquainted with a function and comfortable
using it.

No matter how you want to enter a function as part of a formula, start this way:

1. **Select the cell where you want to enter the formula.**

2. **In the Formula bar, type an equals sign (=).**

   Please, please, please be sure to start every formula by entering an
   equals sign (=). Without it, Excel thinks you're entering text or a number
   in the cell.

3. Start constructing your formula, and when you come to the place where you want to enter the function, type the function's name or call upon Excel to help you enter the function and its arguments.

Later in this chapter, "Manually entering a function" shows you how to type in the function yourself; "Getting Excel's help to enter a function" shows you how to get Excel to do the work.

If you enter the function on your own, it's up to you to type the arguments correctly; if you get Excel's help, you also get help with entering the cell references for the arguments.

Quickly entering a function and its arguments

To quickly total the numbers in cells, click your worksheet where you want the total to appear, and then click the AutoSum button on the Home or Formulas tab. Excel takes an educated guess as to which cells need totaling, and the program highlights those cells. If Excel guesses correctly and highlights the cells you want to total, click the Enter button and be done with it. Otherwise, select the cells you want to add up and then press Enter.

Similarly, you can use the drop-down list on the AutoSum button to quickly obtain the average, count of, minimum amount, or maximum amount of cells by clicking in a nearby cell, opening the drop-down list on the AutoSum button, and choosing Average, Count Numbers, Max, or Min.

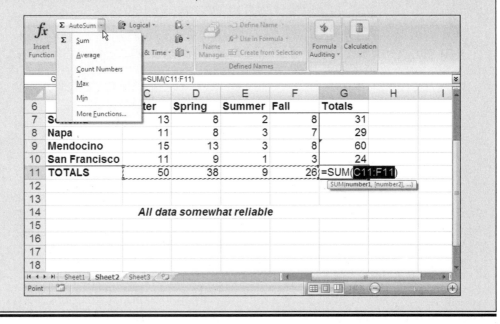

Manually entering a function

Be sure to enclose the function's argument or arguments in parentheses. Don't enter a space between the function's name and the first parenthesis. Likewise, don't enter a comma and a space between arguments; enter a comma, nothing more:

=SUM(F11,F14,23)

You can enter function names in lowercase. Excel converts function names to uppercase after you click the Enter button or press Enter to complete the formula. Entering function names in lowercase is recommended because doing so gives you a chance to find out whether you entered a function name correctly. If Excel doesn't convert your function name to uppercase, you made a typing error when you entered the function name.

Getting Excel's help to enter a function

Besides entering a function by typing it, you can do it by way of the Function Arguments dialog box, as shown in Figure 3-13. The beauty of using this dialog box is that it warns you if you enter arguments incorrectly, and it spares you the trouble of typing the function name without making an error. What's more, the Function Arguments dialog box shows you the results of the formula as you construct it so that you get an idea whether you're using the function correctly.

Enter arguments.   Formula result.

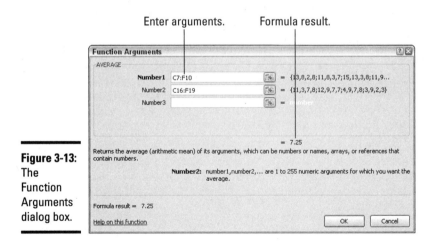

Figure 3-13:
The
Function
Arguments
dialog box.

Follow these steps to get Excel's help with entering a function as part of a formula:

1. **On the Formulas tab, tell Excel which function you want to use.**

You can do that with one of these techniques:

- *Clicking a Function Library button:* Click the button whose name describes what kind of function you want and choose the function's name on the drop-down list. You can click the Financial, Logical, Text, Date & Time, Lookup & Reference, Math & Trig, or More Functions buttons.

- *Clicking the Recently Used button:* Click this button and choose the name of a function you used recently.

- *Clicking the Insert Function button:* Clicking this button opens the Insert Function dialog box (refer to Figure 3-12). Find and choose the name of a function. You can search for functions or choose a category and then scroll the names until you find the function you want.

You see the Function Arguments dialog box (refer to Figure 3-13). It offers boxes for entering arguments for the function to compute.

2. **Enter arguments in the spaces provided by the Function Arguments dialog box.**

To enter cell references or ranges, you can click or select cells in your worksheet. If necessary, click the Range Selector button (you can find it to the right of an argument text box) to shrink the Function Arguments dialog box and get a better look at your worksheet.

3. **Click OK when you finish entering arguments for your function.**

I hope you didn't have to argue too strenuously with the Function Arguments dialog box.

Chapter 4: Making a Worksheet Easier to Read and Understand

In This Chapter

✔ Aligning numbers and text

✔ Changing column and row sizes

✔ Applying cell styles to data in cells

✔ Splashing color on a worksheet

✔ Drawing borders between cells and titles

✔ Making worksheets fit well on the page

✔ Preparing a worksheet before you print it

This short and pithy chapter explains how to dress a worksheet in its Sunday best in case you want to print and present it to others. It explains how to align numbers and text, insert rows and columns, as well as change the size of rows and columns. You find out how to decorate a worksheet with colors and borders, as well as create and apply styles to make formatting tasks go more quickly. Finally, this chapter describes everything you need to know before you print a worksheet, including how to make it fit on one page and repeat row labels and column names on all pages.

Laying Out a Worksheet

Especially if you intend to print your worksheet, you may as well dress it in its Sunday best. And you can do a number of things to make worksheets easier to read and understand. You can change character fonts. You can draw borders around or shade important cells. You can also format the numbers so that readers know, for example, whether they're staring at dollar figures or percentages. This part of this chapter is dedicated to the proposition that a worksheet doesn't have to look drab and solemn.

Aligning numbers and text in columns and rows

To start with, numbers in worksheets are right-aligned in cells, and text is left-aligned. Numbers and text sit squarely on the bottom of cells. You can, however, change the way that data is aligned. For example, you can make data float at the top of cells rather than rest at the bottom, and you can center or justify data in cells. Figure 4-1 illustrates different ways to align text and numbers. How text is aligned helps people make sense of your worksheets. In Figure 4-1, for example, Income and Expenses are left-aligned so they stand out and make it clearer what the right-aligned column labels below are all about.

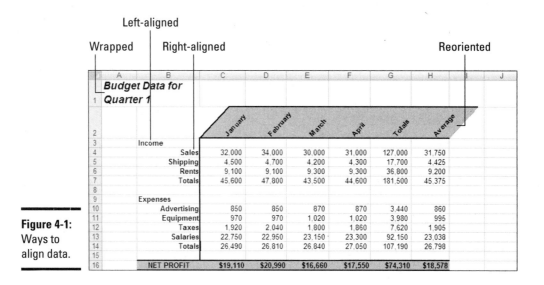

Figure 4-1:
Ways to
align data.

Select the cells whose alignment needs changing and follow these instructions to realign data in the cells:

+ **Changing the horizontal (side-to-side) alignment:** On the Home tab, click the Align Text Left, Center, or Align Text Right button. You can also click the Alignment group button, and on the Alignment tab of the Format Cells dialog box, choose an option on the Horizontal drop-down list. Figure 4-2 shows the Format Cells dialog box.

+ **Changing the vertical (top-to-bottom) alignment:** On the Home tab, click the Top Align, Middle Align, or Bottom Align button. You can also click the Alignment group button to open the Format Cells dialog box (see Figure 4-2) and choose an option on the Vertical drop-down list. The Justify Distributed option makes all the letters or numbers fit in a cell, even if it means wrapping text to two or more lines.

+ **Reorienting the cells:** On the Home tab, click the Orientation button and choose an option on the drop-down list. (For Figure 4-2, I chose the Angle Counterclockwise option.) You can also click the Alignment group button, and on the Alignment tab of the Format Cells dialog box (see Figure 4-2), drag the diamond in the Orientation box or enter a number in the Degrees text box.

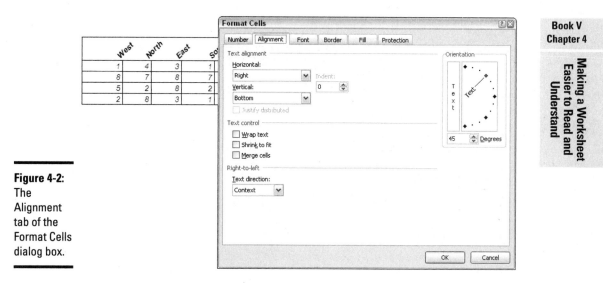

Figure 4-2:
The
Alignment
tab of the
Format Cells
dialog box.

Changing the orientation of text in cells is an elegant solution to the problem of keeping a worksheet from getting too wide. Numbers are usually a few characters wide, but heading labels can be much wider than that. By changing the orientation of a heading label, you make columns narrower and keep worksheets from growing too fat to fit on the screen or page.

Inserting and deleting rows and columns

At some point, everybody has to insert new columns and rows and delete ones that are no longer needed. Make sure before you delete a row or column that you don't delete data that you really need. Do the following to insert and delete rows and columns:

+ **Deleting rows or columns:** Drag across the row numbers or column letters of the rows or columns you want to delete; then right-click and choose Delete or click the Delete button on the Home tab and select Delete Sheet Rows or Delete Sheet Columns on the drop-down list.

+ **Inserting rows:** Select the row below the row you want to insert; then click the Insert button and choose Insert Sheet Rows, or right-click the row you selected and choose Insert on the shortcut menu. For example, to insert a new row above row 11, select the current row 11 before choosing Insert.

+ **Inserting columns:** Select the column to the right of where you want the new column to be; then click the Insert button and choose Insert Sheet Columns, or right-click the column you selected and choose Insert on the shortcut menu.

Merging and centering text across several cells

In the illustration shown here, "Sales Totals by Regional Office" is centered across four different cells. Normally, text is left-aligned, but if you want to center it across several cells, drag across the cells to select them and then click the Merge & Center button on the Home tab. Merging and centering allows you to display text across several columns.

To "unmerge and uncenter" cells, select the text that you merged and centered, open the drop-down list on the Merge & Center button, and choose Unmerge Cells. You can also deselect the Merge Cells check box in the Format Cells dialog box (refer to Figure 4-2).

B	C	D	E	F	G
	Sales Totals by Regional Office				
	North	**West**	**East**	**South**	

A fast way to insert several rows or columns is to insert one and keep pressing F4 (the Repeat command) until you insert all the rows or columns you need.

After you insert rows or columns, the Insert Options button appears. Click it and choose an option from the drop-down list if you want your new row or column to have the same or different formats as the row or column you selected to start the Insert operation.

To insert more than one row or column at a time, select more than one row number or column letter before giving the Insert command.

Changing the size of columns and rows

By default, columns are 8.43 characters wide. To make columns wider, you have to widen them yourself. Rows are 12.75 points high, but Excel makes them higher when you enter letters or numbers that are taller than 12.75 points (72 points equals one inch). Excel offers a bunch of different ways to change the size of columns and rows. You can start on the Home tab and choose options on the Format button drop-down list, as shown in Figure 4-3, or you can rely on your wits and change sizes manually by dragging or double-clicking the boundaries between row numbers or column letters.

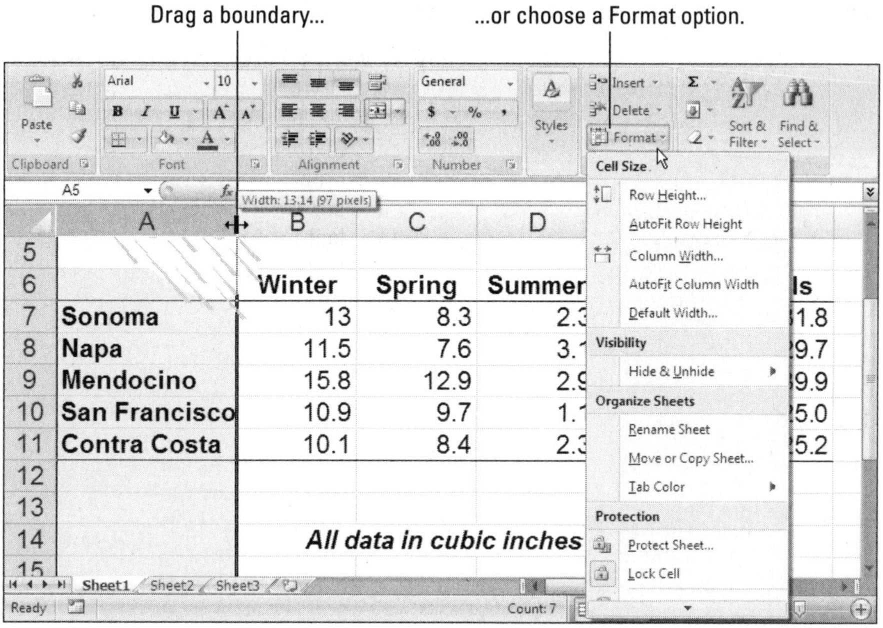

Drag a boundary...   ...or choose a Format option.

Figure 4-3:
Ways to
change the
size of
columns
and rows.

Before you change the size of columns or rows, select them (Chapter 2 of
this mini-book explains how). Click or drag across row numbers to select
rows; click or drag across column letters to select columns.

Adjusting the height of rows

Here are ways to change the height of rows:

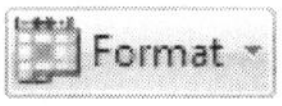

✦ **One at a time:** Move the mouse pointer onto the boundary between row
numbers and, when the pointer changes to a cross, drag the boundary
between rows up or down. A pop-up box tells you how tall the row will
be after you release the mouse button.

✦ **Several at a time:** Select several rows and drag the boundary between
one of the rows; all rows change height. You can also click the Format
button on the Home tab, choose Row Height, and enter a measurement
in the Row Height dialog box.

✦ **Tall as the tallest entry:** To make a row as tall as its tallest cell entry,
double-click the border below a row number (after you've selected a
row), or click the Format button on the Home tab and choose AutoFit
Row Height.

Adjusting the width of columns

Here are ways to make columns wider or narrower:

Format ▾

✦ **One at a time:** Move the mouse pointer onto the boundary between column letters, and when the pointer changes to a cross, drag the border between the columns. A pop-up box tells you what size the column is.

✦ **Several at a time:** Select several columns and drag the boundary between one of the columns; all columns adjust to the same width. You can also click the Format button on the Home tab, choose Column Width, and enter a measurement in the Column Width dialog box.

✦ **As wide as their entries:** To make columns as wide as their widest entries, select the columns, click the Format button on the Home tab, and choose AutoFit Column Width on the drop-down list. You can also double-click the right border of a column letter. By "autofitting" columns, you can be certain that the data in each cell in a column appears on-screen.

To change the 8.43-character standard width for columns in a worksheet, click the Format button on the Home tab, choose Default Width on the drop-down list, and enter a new measurement in the Standard Width dialog box.

Decorating a Worksheet with Borders and Colors

The job of gridlines is simply to help you line up numbers and letters in cells. Gridlines aren't printed when you print a worksheet, and because gridlines aren't printed, drawing borders on worksheets is absolutely necessary if you intend to print your worksheet. Use borders to steer the reader's eye to the most important parts of your worksheet — the totals, column labels, and heading labels. You can also decorate worksheets with colors. This part of the chapter explains how to put borders and colors on worksheets.

Cell styles for quickly formatting a worksheet

A *style* is a collection of formats — boldface text, a background color, or a border around cells — that can be applied all at once to cells without having to visit a bunch of different dialog boxes or give a bunch of different commands. Styles save time. If you find yourself choosing the same formatting commands time and time again, consider creating a style. That way, you can apply all the formats simultaneously and go to lunch earlier. Excel comes with many built-in styles, and you can create styles of your own, as the following pages explain.

Applying a built-in cell style

By way of the Cell Styles gallery, you can choose from any number of attractive styles for cells in a worksheet. Excel offers styles for titles and headings, styles for calling attention to what kind of data is in cells, and styles to accent cells. Follow these steps to reformat cells by choosing a cell style:

1. **Select the cells that need a new look.**

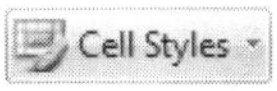

2. **On the Home tab, click the Cell Styles button.**

As shown in Figure 4-4, the Cell Styles gallery opens. (Depending on the size of your screen, you may have to click the Style button and then click the More button to open the Cell Styles gallery.)

Good, Bad and Neutral			
Normal	Bad	Good	Neutral
Data and Model			
Calculation	Check Cell	Explanatory T...	Hyperlink	Input	Linked Cell
Note	Output	Warning Text			
Titles and Headings			
Headin...	Heading 2	Heading 3	Heading 4	Title	Total
Themed Cell Styles			
20% - Accent1	20% - Accent2	20% - Accent3	20% - Accent4	20% - Accent5	20% - Accent6
40% - Accent1	40% - Accent2	40% - Accent3	40% - Accent4	40% - Accent5	40% - Accent6
60% - Accent1	60% - Accent2	60% - Accent3	60% - Accent4	60% - Accent5	60% - Accent6

New Cell Style...

Merge Styles...

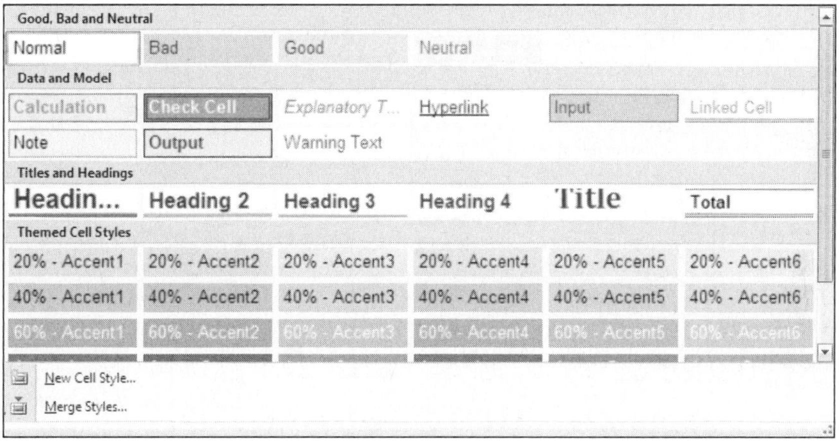

Figure 4-4: Choosing a new style from the Cell Styles gallery.

3. **Select a cell style.**

The Cell Styles gallery is divided into categories. Scroll through the categories until you find a style that suits your purposes.

To remove a style from cells, select the cells, open the Cell Styles gallery, and choose Normal. (You find Normal in the "Good, Bad, and Neutral" category.)

Creating your own cell style

The names of cell styles you create on your own are placed at the top of the Cell Styles gallery under the Custom heading. Create a cell style if you're the creative type or if no built-in style meets your high standards. Follow these steps to create a cell style:

1. **Apply the formatting commands you want for your style to a single cell.**

For example, left-align cell data. Or apply a fill color to the cells (see "Decorating worksheets with colors" later in this chapter). Or change fonts and font sizes. Knock yourself out. Choose all the formatting commands you want for your new style.

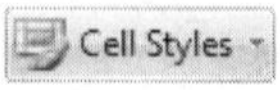

Cell Styles

2. Click the Cell Styles button on the Home tab to open the Cell Styles gallery.

Depending on the size of your screen, you may have to click the Style button and then click the More button first.

3. Choose New Cell Style at the bottom of the gallery.

You see the Style dialog box, as shown in Figure 4-5. It lists formatting specifications you chose for the cell you selected in Step 1. If these specifications aren't what you're after, or if you want to change a specification, you can click the Format button and describe your new style in the Format Cells dialog box.

Figure 4-5:
Creating a
new style
for the Cell
Styles
gallery.

Style	? ✗
Style name:	My Style
	Format...
Style Includes (By Example)	
☑ Number	General
☑ Alignment	General, Bottom Aligned
☑ Font	Baskerville Old Face 18, Red
☐ Border	
☑ Fill	No Shading
☑ Protection	Locked
	OK Cancel

4. Enter a descriptive name for your style in the Style Name text box.

5. Click OK.

Next time you open the Cell Styles gallery, you see the name of your style at the top under Custom.

To remove a style you created from the Cell Styles gallery, right-click its name in the gallery and choose Delete on the shortcut menu.

Slapping borders on worksheet cells

Put borders on worksheet cells to box in cells, draw lines beneath cells, or draw lines along the side of cells. Borders can direct people who review your worksheet to its important parts. Typically, for example, a line appears above the Totals row of a worksheet to separate the Totals row from the rows above and help readers locate cumulative totals.

To draw borders on a worksheet, start by selecting the cells around which or through which you want to place borders. Then do one of the following to draw the borders:

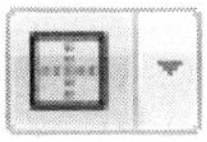

✦ **Borders button:** On the Home tab, open the drop-down list on the Borders button and choose a border, as shown in Figure 4-6.

✦ **Format Cells dialog box:** As shown in Figure 4-7, the Border tab of the Format Cells dialog box offers different lines for borders and colors for borderlines as well. To open this dialog box, click the Format button on the Home tab and choose Format Cells, or choose More Borders on the Borders button drop-down list. Select a border style and either click in the Border box to tell Excel where to draw the border or click a Preset button.

To remove the border from cells, select the cells, open the drop-down list on the Borders button, and choose No Border.

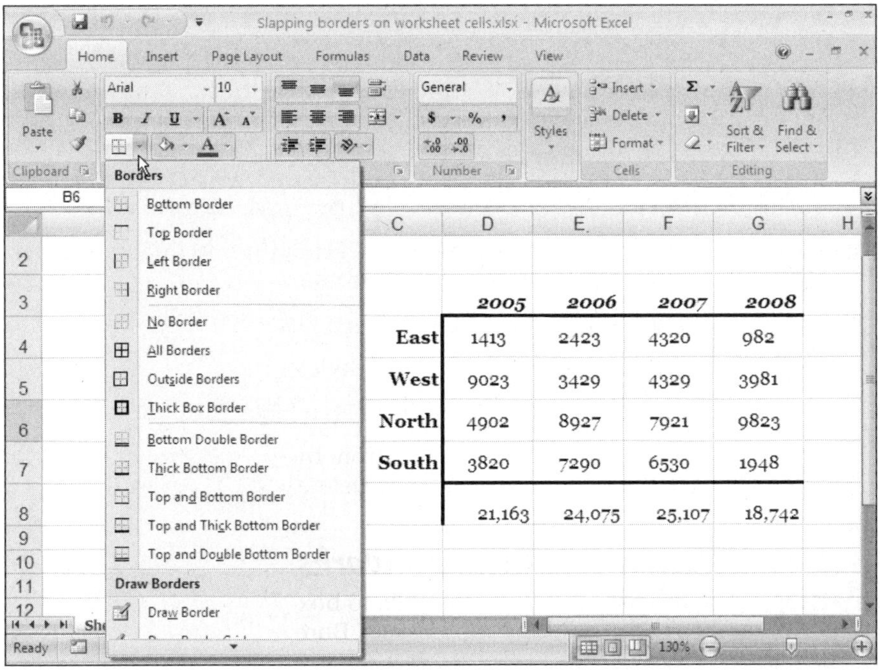

Figure 4-6: Drawing a border with the Borders button.

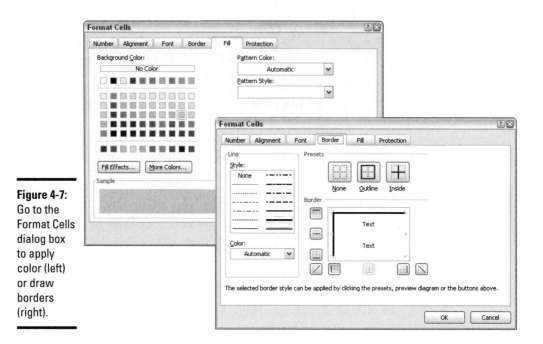

Figure 4-7:
Go to the Format Cells dialog box to apply color (left) or draw borders (right).

Decorating worksheets with colors

Apply background colors to cells to make them stand out or help the people who review your worksheets understand how they are laid out. Follow these steps to splash color on your worksheet:

1. **Select the cells that need a background color.**

2. **On the Home tab, click the Format button and choose Format Cells on the drop-down list.**

You see the Format Cells dialog box.

3. **Click the Fill tab.**

Figure 4-7 shows what the Fill tab looks like.

4. **Select a color and click OK.**

To remove colors from cells, select them, open the Fill tab of the Format Cells dialog box, and select No Color.

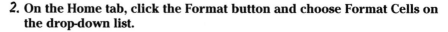

You can also apply fill colors opening the drop-down list on the Fill Color button on the Home tab and selecting a color.

Getting Ready to Print a Worksheet

Printing a worksheet isn't simply a matter of giving the Print command. A worksheet is a vast piece of computerized sprawl. Most worksheets don't fit neatly on a single page. If you simply click the Print button to print your worksheet, you wind up with page breaks in unexpected places, both on the right side of the page and the bottom. Read on to discover how to set up a worksheet so that the people you hand it to can read and understand it easily.

Making a worksheet fit on a page

Unless you tell it otherwise, Excel prints everything from cell A1 to the last cell with data in it in the southeast corner of the worksheet. Usually, it isn't necessary to print all those cells because some of them are blank. And printing an entire worksheet often means breaking the page up in all kinds of awkward places. To keep that from happening, here are some techniques for making a worksheet fit tidily on one or two pages.

As you experiment with the techniques described here, switch occasionally to Page Layout view. In this view, you get a better idea of what your worksheet will look like when you print it. To switch to Page Layout view, click the Page Layout View button on the status bar or View tab.

Printing part of a worksheet

To print part of a worksheet, select the cells you want to print, go to the Page Layout tab, click the Print Area button, and choose Set Print Area on the drop-down list. This command tells Excel to print only the cells you selected. On the worksheet, a dotted line appears around cells in the print area. To remove the dotted lines from your worksheet, click the Print Area button and choose Clear Print Area on the drop-down list.

Printing a landscape worksheet

If your worksheet is too wide to fit on one page, try turning the page on its side and printing in landscape mode. In landscape mode, pages are wider than they are tall. Landscape mode is often the easiest way to fit a worksheet on a page.

To make yours a landscape worksheet instead of a portrait worksheet, go to the Page Layout tab, click the Orientation button, and choose Landscape on the drop-down list.

Seeing and adjusting the page breaks

Reading a worksheet is extremely difficult when it's broken awkwardly across pages. Where one page ends and the next begins is a *page break*. Use these techniques to see where page breaks occur, adjust the position of page breaks, and insert and remove page breaks:

✦ **Viewing where pages break occur:** Click the Page Break Preview button on the status bar or View tab. As shown in Figure 4-8, you switch to Page Break Preview view. In this view, page numbers appear clearly on the worksheet and dashed lines show you where Excel wants to break the pages.

✦ **Adjusting page break positions:** In Page Break Preview view, drag a dashed line to adjust the position of a page break. After you drag a dashed line, it ceases being a default page break and becomes a manual page break. Manual page breaks are marked by solid lines, not dashed lines (see Figure 4-8). You can drag them, too. Excel shrinks the numbers and letters on your worksheet if you try to squeeze too much data on a worksheet by dragging a page break.

Insert and remove page breaks.

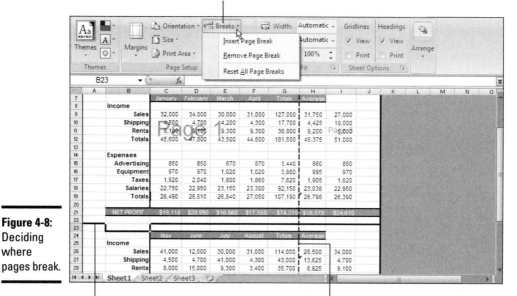

Figure 4-8:
Deciding
where
pages break.

Manual page break

Default page break; drag to change a page break position.

Breaks ▾

✦ **Inserting a page break:** Select the cell directly below where you want the horizontal break to occur and directly to the right of where you want the vertical break to be, click the Breaks button on the Page Layout tab, and choose Insert Page Break (see Figure 4-8). Drag a page break to adjust its position.

✦ **Removing a page break:** Select a cell directly below or directly to the right of the page break, click the Breaks button in the Page Layout tab, and choose Remove Page Break (see Figure 4-8).

✦ **Removing all manual page breaks:** To remove all manual page breaks you inserted, go to the Page Layout tab, click the Breaks button, and choose Reset All Page Breaks.

Switch to Page Layout or Normal view after you're done fooling with page breaks. You can clearly see page breaks in Page Layout view. In Normal view, page breaks are marked by a dotted line. (If you don't care to see these dotted lines on your worksheet in Normal view, click the Office button, choose Excel Options, click the Advanced category in the Excel Options dialog box, and deselect the Show Page Breaks check box.)

"Scaling to fit" a worksheet

To scale the numbers and letters in a worksheet and make them a bit smaller so they fit on a page, you can experiment with the Scale to Fit options. These options are located on the Page Layout tab. Start in Page Layout view, go to the Page Layout tab, and test-drive these options to make your worksheet fit on a single page or a certain number of pages:

✦ **Scaling by width:** Open the Width drop-down list and choose an option to make your worksheet fit across one or more pages. Choose the 1 Page option, for example, to squeeze a worksheet horizontally so it fits on one page.

✦ **Scaling by height:** Open the Height drop-down list and choose an option to make your worksheet fit across on a select number of pages. For example, choose the 2 Pages option to shrink a worksheet vertically so it fits on two pages.

✦ **Scaling by percentage:** Enter a percentage measurement in the Scale box to shrink a worksheet vertically and horizontally. In order to scale this way, you must choose Automatic in the Width and Height drop-down lists.

You can also fit a worksheet on a select number of pages by going to the Page Setup dialog box, as shown in Figure 4-9. With this technique, you get a chance to "print-preview" your worksheet and get a better look at it after you change the scale. On the Page Layout tab, click the Page Setup group button to open the Page Setup dialog box. On the Page tab, select the Fit To option button and enter the ideal number of pages you want for your worksheet in the Page(s) Wide By and Tall text boxes. Excel shrinks the data as much as is necessary to make it fit on the number of pages you asked for. Click the Print Preview button to look at the Print Preview screen and find out whether shrinking your worksheet this way helps.

Adjusting the margins

Another way to stuff all the data onto one page is to narrow the margins a bit. Go to the Page Layout tab and use either of these techniques to adjust the size of the margins:

✦ Click the Margins button and choose Narrow on the drop-down list.

✦ Click the Page Setup group button, and on the Margins tab of the Page Setup dialog box, change the size of the margins, as shown in Figure 4-9. By clicking the Print Preview button, you can go to the Print Preview screen and adjust margins there by dragging them. Select the Show Margins check box to display the margins.

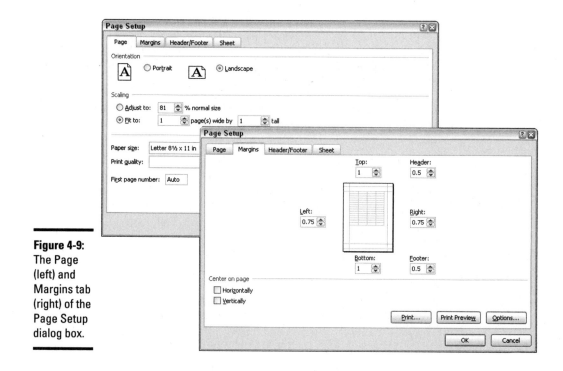

Figure 4-9:
The Page (left) and Margins tab (right) of the Page Setup dialog box.

Making a worksheet more presentable

Before you print a worksheet, visit the Page Setup dialog box and see what you can do to make your worksheet easier for others to read and understand. To open the Page Setup dialog box, go to the Page Layout tab and click the Page Setup group button or click the Page Setup button on the Print Preview screen. Here are your options:

✦ **Including page numbers on worksheets:** On the Page tab of the Page Setup dialog box (refer to Figure 4-9), enter **1** in the First Page Number text box. Then, on the Header/Footer tab, open the Header or Footer drop-down list and choose an option that includes a page number. Choosing the Page 1 of ? option, for example, enters the page number and the total number of pages in the worksheet in your header or footer.

✦ **Putting headers and footers on pages:** On the Header/Footer tab of the Page Setup dialog box, choose options from the Header and Footer drop-down lists. You'll find options for listing the filename, page numbers, the date, and your name. By clicking the Custom Header or Custom Footer button, you can open the Header or Footer dialog box and construct a header or footer there. Figure 4-10 shows the Header dialog box.

✦ **Centering worksheet data on the page:** On the Margins tab, select Horizontally or Vertically to center the worksheet relative to the top or bottom or sides of the page. You can select both check boxes. The preview screen shows what your choices mean in real terms.

✦ **Printing gridlines, column letters, and row numbers:** By default, the gridlines, column letters, and row numbers that you know and love in a worksheet aren't printed, but you can print them by selecting the Gridlines check box as well as the Row and Column Headings check box in the Sheet tab of the Page Setup dialog box.

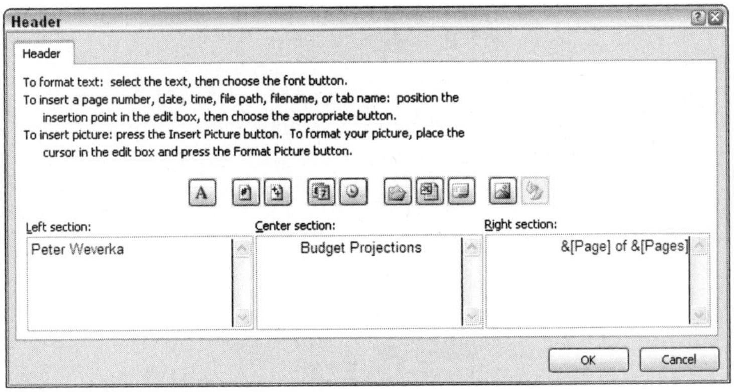

Figure 4-10:
Constructing
a fancy
header.

Repeating row and column headings on each page

If your worksheet is a big one that stretches beyond one page, you owe it to the people who view your worksheet to repeat row and column headings from page to page. Without these headings, no one can tell what the data in the worksheet means. Follow these steps to repeat row and column headings from page to page:

Print Titles

1. **On the Page Layout tab, click the Print Titles button.**

You see the Sheet tab of the Page Setup dialog box.

2. **Select the Row and Column Headings check box.**

You can find this check box under Print.

3. **To repeat rows, click the Range Selector button next to the Rows to Repeat at Top text box; to repeat columns, click the Range Selector button next to the Columns to Repeat at Left text box.**

These buttons are located on the right side of the dialog box. The dialog box shrinks so that you can get a better look at your worksheet.

4. **Click the row or column with the labels or names you need.**

As long as they're next to each other, you can select more than one row or column by dragging over the row numbers or column letters.

5. **Click the Range Selector button to enlarge the dialog box and see it again.**

The text box now lists a cell range address.

6. **Repeat Steps 3 through 5 to select column or row headings.**

7. **Click OK to close the Page Setup dialog box.**

If I were you, I would click the Print Preview button in the Page Setup dialog box first to make sure that row and column headings are indeed repeating from page to page.

To remove row and column headings, return to the Sheet tab of the Page Setup dialog box and delete the cell references in the Rows to Repeat at Top text box and the Columns to Repeat at Left text box. You can also press Ctrl+F3 and delete Print_Titles in the Name Manager dialog box.

Chapter 5: Analyzing Data

In This Chapter

✔ Sorting information in a worksheet list

✔ Filtering a list to find the information you need

✔ Using the Goal Seek command to produce formula results

✔ Performing what-if analyses with data tables

*T*his chapter offers a handful of tricks for analyzing the data that you so carefully and lovingly enter in a worksheet. Delve into this chapter to find out how to manage, sort, and filter worksheet lists. You also discover how the Goal Seek command can help you target values in different kinds of analysis, and how you can map out different scenarios with data by using one- and two-input data tables.

Managing Information in Lists

Although Excel is a spreadsheet program, many people use it to keep and maintain lists — address lists, product lists, employee lists, and inventory lists, among other types of lists. These pages deal with all the different things you can do with a worksheet list. They explain the difference between a conventional worksheet and a list, constructing a list, sorting a list, and filtering a list.

Constructing a list

To sort and filter data in a worksheet, your worksheet must be constructed like a list. Make sure that your worksheet has these characteristics:

✦ **Column labels:** Enter column labels along the top row, as shown in Figure 5-1. Excel needs these labels to identify and be able to filter the data in the rows below. Each label must have a different name. The row along the top of the worksheet where the column labels are is called the *header row*.

✦ **No empty rows or columns:** Sorry, but you can't put an empty row or column in the middle of the worksheet list.

Product ID	Product Name	Production Cost	Packaging	Ship Cost	Sale per Unit	Profit	Warehouse	Supervisor
11100	Widget	1.19	0.14	0.45	4.11	2.33	Trenton	Munoz
11101	Gasket	2.24	0.29	0.89	4.14	0.72	Pickford	Salazaar
11102	Tappet	4.13	1.11	0.18	7.12	1.70	Trenton	Munoz
11103	Widget	8.19	3.40	0.45	14.80	2.76	LaRue	Smith
11104	Pludget	6.41	0.29	0.32	7.89	0.87	Massy	Yee
11105	Placker	7.39	0.98	1.11	12.14	2.66	Pickford	Salazaar
11106	Stacker	11.00	1.14	0.89	14.89	1.86	LaRue	Smith
11107	Knacker	14.31	3.14	0.45	20.98	3.08	Massy	Yee
11108	Tipplet	2.11	0.14	0.32	5.81	3.24	Trenton	Munoz
11109	Culet	4.18	0.17	0.32	6.01	1.36	Trenton	Munoz
11110	Ropper	13.44	2.89	0.79	21.43	4.31	LaRue	Smith
11111	Knocker	23.08	2.10	0.89	32.89	6.82	Trenton	Munoz
11112	Topper	1.14	0.09	0.11	4.02	2.68	Pickford	Salazaar
11113	Rammer	2.15	0.16	0.32	5.10	2.47	Massy	Yee
11114	Cricker	3.34	0.27	0.33	6.12	2.18	LaRue	Smity
11115	Knicker	8.78	1.01	0.89	10.79	0.11	Trenton	Munoz
11116	Stamler	2.14	0.53	0.20	6.78	3.91	LaRue	Smith
11117	Doublet	9.46	1.01	0.99	14.33	2.87	Pickford	Salazaar

Figure 5-1:
A work-
sheet as
a list.

✦ **No blank columns on the left:** Don't allow any empty columns to appear to the left of the list.

✦ **A single worksheet:** The list must occupy a single worksheet. You can't keep more than one list on the same worksheet.

If you know anything about databases, the rules for constructing a worksheet list no doubt sound familiar. These are the same rules that apply to constructing a database table. You might consider managing your list as a database if it's a long and complex one. Book VI explains how to use *Access,* the database program in Office 2007.

Sorting a list

Sorting means to rearrange the rows in a list on the basis of data in one or more columns. Sort a list on the Last Name column, for example, to arrange the list in alphabetical order by last name. Sort a list on the ZIP Code column to arrange the rows in numerical order by ZIP code. Sort a list on the Birthday column to arrange it chronologically from earliest born to latest born. Here are all the ways to sort a list:

✦ **Sorting on a single column:** Click any cell in the column you want to use as the basis for the sort, and then click the Sort Smallest to Largest or Sort Largest to Smallest button on the Data tab or the Home tab A. (On the Home tab, you can get to these buttons by clicking the Sort & Filter button first, depending on the size of your screen.) For example, to sort item numbers from smallest to largest, click in the Item Number column and then click the Sort Smallest to Largest button.

✦ **Sort on more than one column:** Click the Sort button (on the Data tab). You see the Sort dialog box, as shown in Figure 5-2. Choose which columns you want to sort with and the order in which you want to sort. To add a second or third column for sorting, click the Add Level button.

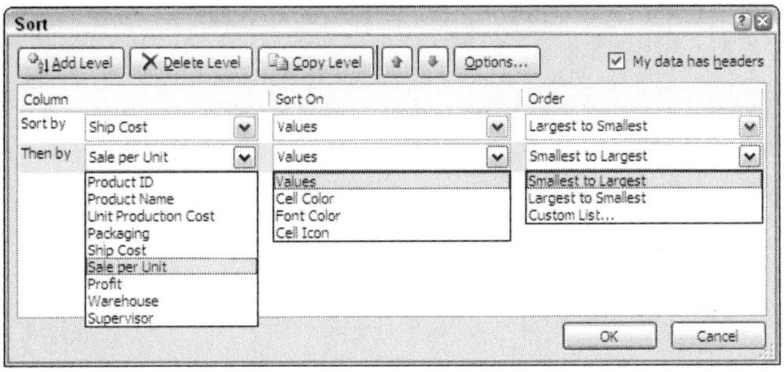

Figure 5-2:
Sort to
arrange the
list data in
different
ways.

Be careful about sorting rows with formula results. Sorting discombobulates the rows. If a formula refers to a cell that *isn't* in the same row and you give a sort command, you get a #VALUE! error because the formula won't compute using the correct cell address.

Filtering a list

Filtering means to scour a worksheet list for certain kinds of data. To filter, you tell Excel what kind of data you're looking for, and the program assembles rows with that data to the exclusion of rows that don't have the data. You end up with a shorter list with only the rows that match your filter criteria. Filtering is similar to using the Find command except that you get more than one row in the results of the filtering operation. For example, in a list of addresses, you can filter for only addresses in California. In a price list, you can filter for items that fall within a certain price range.

To filter a list, start by clicking the Filter button on the Data tab. As shown in Figure 5-3, a drop-down list appears beside each column header.

Your next task is to open a drop-down list in the column that holds the criteria you want to use to filter the list. For example, if you want to filter the list to items that cost more than $100, open the Cost column drop-down list; if you want to filter the list so that only the names of employees who make less than $30,000 annually appears, open the Salary drop-down list.

Click the Filter button.

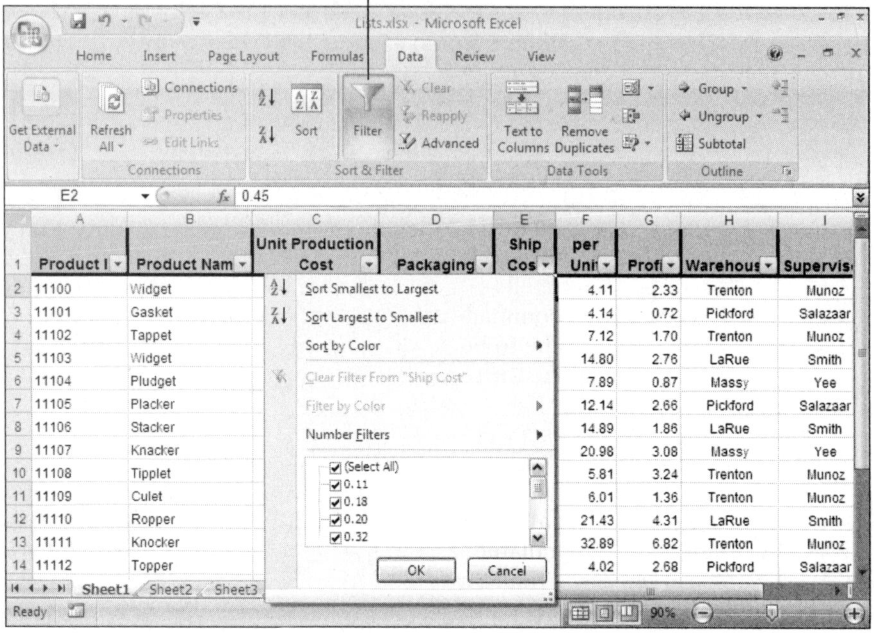

Figure 5-3:
Filter a
worksheet
to isolate
data.

After you open the correct column drop-down list, tell Excel how you want
to filter the list:

✦ **Filter by exclusion:** On the drop-down list, deselect the Select All check
box and then select the check box next to each item you *don't* want to
filter out. For example, to filter an Address list to addresses in Boston,
Chicago, and Miami, deselect the Select All check box and then select
the check boxes next to Boston, Chicago, and Miami on the drop-down
list. Your filter operation turns up only addresses in these three cities.

✦ **Filter with criteria:** On the drop-down list, choose Number Filters, and
then choose a filter operation on the submenu (or simply choose
Custom Filter). You see the Custom AutoFilter dialog box.

Choose an operator (equals, is greater than, or another) from the drop-
down list, and either enter or choose a target criterion from the list on
the right side of the dialog box. You can search by more than one criterion. Select the And option button if a row must meet both criteria to be
selected, or select the Or option button if a row can meet either criterion to be selected.

Click the OK button on the column's drop-down list or the Custom AutoFilter dialog box to filter your list.

To see all the data in the list again — to *unfilter* the list — click the Clear button on the Data tab.

Forecasting with the Goal Seek Command

In a conventional formula, you provide the raw data, and Excel produces the results. With the Goal Seek command, you declare what you want the results to be, and Excel tells you the raw data you need to produce those results. The Goal Seek command is especially useful in financial analyses when you want the outcome to be a certain way and you need to know which raw numbers will produce the outcome that you want.

Figure 5-4 shows a worksheet designed to find out the monthly payment on a mortgage. With the PMT function, the worksheet determines that the monthly payment on a $250,000 loan with an interest rate of 6.5 percent and to be paid over a 30-year period is $1,580.17. Suppose, however, that the person who calculated this monthly payment determined that he or she could pay more than $1,580.17 per month? Suppose the person could pay $1,750 or $2,000 per month. Instead of an outcome of $1,580.17, the person wants to know how much he or she could borrow if monthly payments — the outcome of the formula — were increased to $1,750 or $2,000.

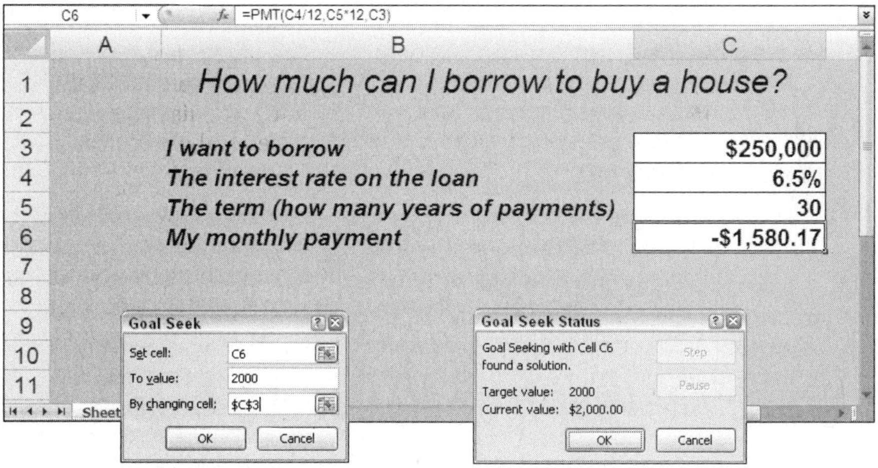

C6		ƒx =PMT(C4/12,C5*12,C3)	
	A	B	C
1		How much can I borrow to buy a house?	
2			
3		I want to borrow	$250,000
4		The interest rate on the loan	6.5%
5		The term (how many years of payments)	30
6		My monthly payment	-$1,580.17
7			
8			

Figure 5-4: Experimenting with the Goal Seek command.

Goal Seek
Set cell: C6
To value: 2000
By changing cell: $C$3
OK   Cancel

Goal Seek Status
Goal Seeking with Cell C6 found a solution.
Target value: 2000
Current value: $2,000.00
Step   Pause
OK   Cancel

To make determinations such as these, you can use the Goal Seek command. This command lets you experiment with the arguments in a formula to achieve the results you want. In the case of the worksheet in Figure 5-4, you can use the Goal Seek command to change the argument in cell C3, the total amount you can borrow, given the outcome you want in cell C6, $1,750 or $2,000, the monthly payment on the total amount.

Follow these steps to use the Goal Seek command to change the inputs in a formula to achieve the results you want:

1. **Select the cell with the formula whose arguments you want to experiment with.**

2. **On the Data tab, click the What-If Analysis button and choose Goal Seek on the drop-down list.**

   You see the Goal Seek dialog box, as shown in Figure 5-4. The address of the cell you selected in Step 1 appears in the Set Cell box.

3. **In the To Value text box, enter the target results you want from the formula.**

   In the example in Figure 5-4, you enter 1750 or 2000, the monthly payment you can afford for the 30-year mortgage.

4. **In the By Changing Cell text box, enter the address of the cell whose value is unknown.**

   To enter a cell address, select a cell on your worksheet. In Figure 5-4, you select the address of the cell that shows the total amount you want to borrow.

5. **Click OK.**

   The Goal Seek Status dialog box appears, as shown in Figure 5-4. It lists the target value that you entered in Step 3.

6. **Click OK.**

   On your worksheet, the cell with the argument you wanted to alter now shows the target you're seeking. In the case of the example worksheet in Figure 5-4, you can borrow $316,422, not $250,000, by raising your monthly mortgage payments from $1,580.17 to $2,000.

Performing What-If Analyses with Data Tables

For something a little more sophisticated than the Goal Seek command (which I describe in the preceding section), try performing what-if analyses with data tables. With this technique, you change the data in input cells and observe what effect changing the data has on the results of a formula. The difference between the Goal Seek command and a data table is that, with a data table, you can experiment simultaneously with many different input cells and in so doing experiment with many different scenarios.

Using a one-input table for analysis

In a *one-input table,* you find out what the different results of a formula would be if you change one *input cell* in the formula. In Figure 5-5, that input cell is the interest rate on a loan. The purpose of this data table is to find out how monthly payments on a $250,000, 30-year mortgage are different, given different interest rates. The interest rate in cell B4 is the input cell.

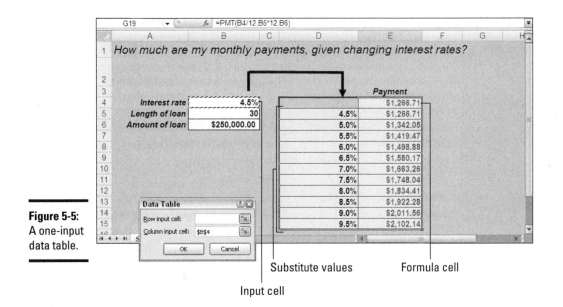

Figure 5-5:
A one-input
data table.

Substitute values   Formula cell

Input cell

Follow these steps to create a one-input table:

1. **On your worksheet, enter values that you want to substitute for the value in the input cell.**

   To make the input table work, you have to enter the substitute values in the right location:

   • *In a column:* Enter the values in the column starting one cell below and one cell to the left of the cell where the formula is located (refer to Figure 5-5).

   • *In a row:* Enter the values in the row starting one cell above and one cell to the right of the cell where the formula is.

2. **Select the block of cells with the formula and substitute values.**

   Select a rectangle of cells that encompasses the formula cell, the cell beside it, all the substitute values, and the empty cells where the new calculations will soon appear. In the case of a column, you select the formula cell, the cell to its left, as well as all the substitute-value cells and the cells below the formula cell. In the case of a row, select the formula cell, the cell above it, as well as the substitute values in the cells directly to the right and the now-empty cells where the new calculations will appear.

3. **On the Data tab, click the What-If Analysis button and choose Data Table on the drop-down list.**

   You see the Data Table dialog box.

4. **In the Row Input Cell or Column Input Cell text box, enter the address of the cell where the input value is located.**

   The input value is the value you're experimenting with in your analysis. In the case of Figure 5-5, the input value is located in cell B4, the cell that holds the interest rate.

   If the new calculations appear in rows, enter the address of the input cell in the Row Input Cell text box; if the calculations appear in columns (as shown in Figure 5-5), enter the input cell address in the Column Input Cell text box.

5. **Click OK.**

   Excel performs the calculations and fills in the table.

To generate the one-input table, Excel constructs an array formula with the TABLE function. If you change the cell references in the first row or plug in different values in the first column, Excel updates the one-input table automatically.

Using a two-input table for analysis

In a two-input table, you can experiment with two input cells rather than one. Getting back to the example of the loan payment in Figure 5-5, you can calculate not only how loan payments change as interest rates change, but how payments change if the life of the loan changes. Figure 5-6 shows a two-input table for examining monthly loan payments given different interest rates and two different terms for the loan, 15 years (180 months) and 30 years (360 months).

Column input cell   Row input cell

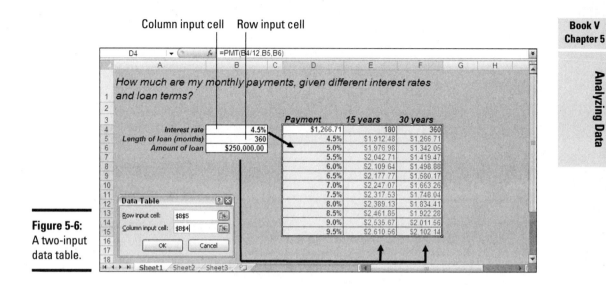

Figure 5-6:
A two-input
data table.

Follow these steps to create a two-input data table:

1. **Enter one set of substitute values below the formula in the same column as the formula.**

In Figure 5-6, different interest rates are entered from cell D5 to D15.

2. **Enter the second set of substitute values in the row to the right of the formula.**

In Figure 5-6, 180 and 360 are entered. These numbers represent the number of months of the life of the loan.

3. **Select the formula and all substitute values.**

Do this correctly and you select three columns, including the formula, the substitute values below it, and the two columns to the right of the formula. You select a big block of cells (the range D4:F15, in this example).

4. **On the Data tab, click the What-If Analysis button and choose Data Table on the drop-down list.**

The Data Table dialog box appears (see Figure 5-6).

5. **In the Row Input Cell text box, enter the address of the cell referred to in the original formula where substitute values to the right of the formula can be plugged in.**

   In Figure 5-6, for example, the rows to the right of the formula are for length of loan substitute values. Therefore, I select cell B5, the cell referred to in the original formula where the length of the loan is listed.

6. **In the Column Input Cell text box, enter the address of the cell referred to in the original formula where substitute values below the formula are.**

   In Figure 5-6, the substitute values below the formula cell are interest rates. Therefore, I select cell B4, the cell referred to in the original formula where the interest rate is entered.

7. **Click OK.**

   Excel performs the calculations and fills in the table.

Book VI

Access 2007

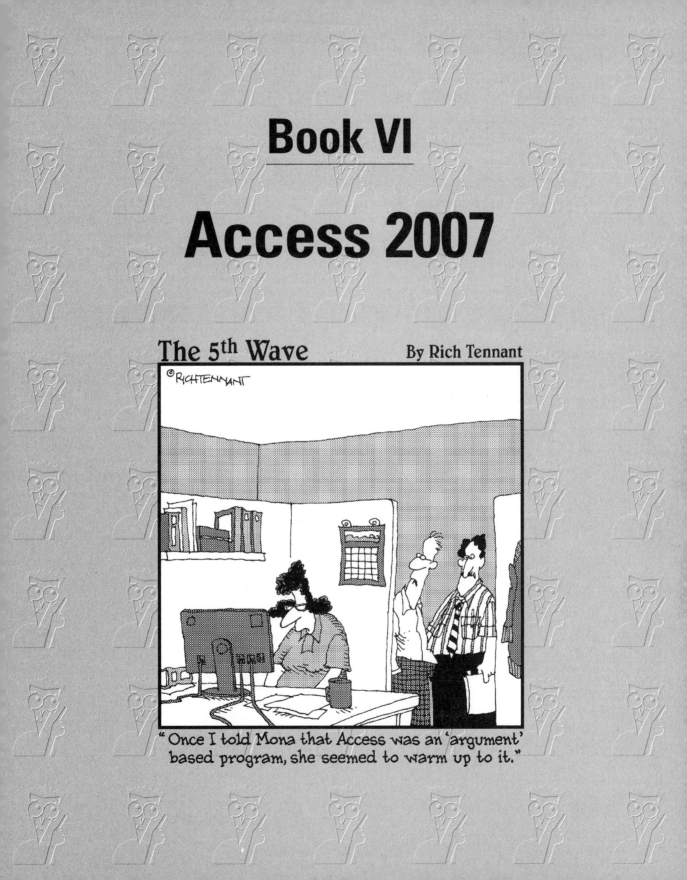

The 5th Wave   By Rich Tennant

"Once I told Mona that Access was an 'argument' based program, she seemed to warm up to it."

Contents at a Glance

Chapter 1: Introducing Access

In This Chapter

✔ **Understanding how databases work**

✔ **Looking at tables, queries, forms, and other database objects**

✔ **Creating a database**

✔ **Opening and closing tables**

✔ **Designing the tables, queries, forms, and the other parts of a database**

The word *database* is prone to making most people feel kind of queasy. Can you blame them? Database terminology — record, field, and filter — is the worst of the worst. It even puts other computer terminology to shame. Databases intimidate most people. Even brave souls with a considerable amount of experience in Word and Excel shy away from *Access,* the Office 2007 database program. However, Access can be invaluable for storing and organizing customer lists, inventories, addresses, payment histories, donor lists, and volunteer lists. What's more, Access is easy to use, after you get the hang of it. No kidding!

This chapter starts you down the road to the Land of Oz. In truth, it introduces databases and the concepts behind databases. It shows you how to create a database and database tables for storing information. The second half of this chapter explains how to design databases. Sorry, but you have to know about database design before you can start fooling with databases. You can't jump right in as you can with the other Office programs.

Access offers a practice database that you can experiment with as you get to know your way around databases. To open this database, start Access and then select Sample from the From Microsoft Office Online category on the left side of the Getting Started with Microsoft Office Access window. Choose Northwind 2007 from the sample templates, click Download at the right-side of the window to get the sample template from Microsoft Office Online (www.office.microsoft.com), and open it on your computer.

What Is a Database, Anyway?

Whether you know it or not, you're no stranger to databases. The address book on your computer is a database. The telephone directory in the desk drawer is, too. A recipe book is also a database in that recipes are categorized under different headings. If you ever arranged a CD collection in a certain way — in alphabetical order or by musical genre, for example — you created a database of CDs, one that makes finding a particular CD easier. Any place where information is stored in a systematic way can be considered a *database*. The only difference between a computerized database and a conventional database, such as a telephone directory, is that storing, finding, and manipulating data is much easier in a computerized database.

Imagine how long it would take to find all the New York addresses in an address list with 10,000 entries. In Access, you can query a 10,000-entry database and find all New York addresses in a matter of seconds. For that matter, you can query to find all the addresses in a certain ZIP code. You can put the list in alphabetical order by last name or in numerical order by ZIP code. Doing these chores without a computer requires many hours of dreary, monotonous labor.

Tables, Queries, Forms, and Other Objects

One problem with getting to know a database program — and the primary reason that people are intimidated by databases — is that you can't jump right in. You have to know how data is stored in a database and how it is extracted, to use programmer terminology. You have to know about *objects,* Access's bland word for database tables, queries, forms, and all else that makes a database a database. To help you get going, these pages offer a crash course in databases. They explain the different *objects* — tables, queries, forms, and reports — that make up a database. Fasten your seatbelt. If you complete the crash course without crashing, you're ready to create your first database.

Database tables for storing information

Information in databases is stored in *database tables* like the one in Figure 1-1. In a database table, you include one field for each category of information you want to keep on hand. *Fields* are the equivalent of columns in a table. Your first duty when you create a database table is to name the fields and tell Access what kind of information you propose to store in each field. The database table in Figure 1-1 is for storing employee information. It has six fields: ID, Company, First Name, Last Name, E-mail Address, and Job Title.

A database can comprise one database table or many different tables that are linked together. If you're dealing with a lot of information, storing data in more than one table is to your advantage. Later in this chapter, "Separating information into different database tables" explains why storing data across several database tables is advantageous.

A record   Cells

Figure 1-1:
A database
table.

A field

Forms for entering data

After you create the fields in the database table, you can start entering the
records. A *record* describes all the data concerning one person or thing. In
Figure 1-1, nine records are entered in the database table. Each record comprises a person's ID, company, first name, last name, e-mail address, and job
title. Records are the meat of the database. Information is stored in records.

Although you can enter records straight into a database table, the easiest
way to enter a record is with a form. Similar to a dialog box, a form has convenient text boxes and drop-down lists for entering information. Figure 1-2
shows the form for entering a record in the database table shown in Figure 1-1.
Notice that the form has one place for entering data in each field in the database table — First Name, Last Name, and so on. On a form, you can see
clearly what kind of information needs entering in each field.

Figure 1-2:
A form for
entering
data.

Fields

Access database terminology

Stumbling over database terminology is easy. To keep yourself from stumbling, fold back the corner of this page and return here if one of these database terms puzzles you:

✔ **Cell:** In a database table, a place for entering one piece of data. Cells appear in a database table where a field and record intersect.

✔ **Database:** A systematic way of organizing information so that it can be retrieved and manipulated easily.

✔ **Database table:** A collection of data records arranged into well-defined categories, or fields. Most databases have more than one table.

✔ **Dynaset:** The results of a search for data in a database. (This term is short for dynamic set.) A dynaset is not to be confused with a dinosaur.

✔ **Field:** One category of information in a database table. Fields are the equivalent of columns in a conventional table.

✔ **Filtering:** Finding the records in a database table that have the same or nearly the same field value. Filtering is a more convenient but not as sophisticated means of querying a database.

✔ **Foreign field:** In a relationship between two database tables, the field that is on the "many" side of a one-to-many relationship. The primary key field is on the "one" side.

✔ **Form:** Similar to a dialog box, a place with text boxes and drop-down lists for entering records in a database table.

✔ **Module:** A Visual Basic procedure whose job is to perform a certain task in Access.

✔ **Object:** The catch-all term for the tables, queries, forms, and reports that you create and open starting in the Navigation pane.

✔ **Primary key field:** The field in a database table where unique, one-of-a-kind data is stored. To query more than one database table at a time, the tables must have primary key fields.

✔ **Query:** A question asked of a database that yields information. Queries can be made of a single database table, several tables, or even other queries.

✔ **Record:** In a database table, all the data that's recorded about one person or thing. A record is the equivalent of a row in a conventional table.

✔ **Relational database:** A database program in which data is kept in more than one database table, relationships are established between tables, and queries can be conducted and reports made by assembling data from different tables. Access is a relational database. A database that permits only one table is a *flat-file database*.

✔ **Report:** Information gathered from a database and laid out in such a way that it's easy to read and understand. Reports are meant to be printed and distributed.

✔ **Sort:** To rearrange records in a database table so that the records appear in alphabetical, numerical, or date order in one field.

Queries for getting the data out

Figure 1-3 shows a simple query for finding out which employees in the database table shown in Figure 1-1 are Sales Representatives. A *query* is a question you ask of a database. The question here is, "Who is a Sales Representative?" Notice the criterion "Sales Representative" in the Job Title field on the Query grid.

**Book VI
Chapter 1**

Table being queried · Query Criteria

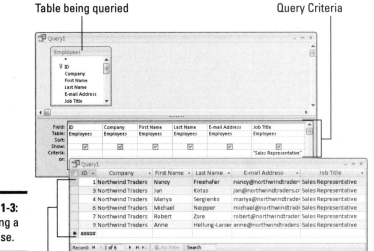

Figure 1-3:
Querying a
database.

Results of the query

In an address database, you can use a query to find all the people in a particular ZIP code or state. If information about contributions is stored in the database, you can find out who contributed more than $500 last year. Queries can get very complex. For example, you could find all the people in a particular city who contributed between $50 and $500 and volunteered more than eight hours in the past year. You can construct the query so that it produces each person's name and telephone number, or you can construct it so that all the information you have concerning each person appears in the query results.

When you get junk mail, it likely comes to your mailbox as the result of a database query. Companies routinely buy and sell customer databases. They query these databases to gather the names of people who they believe are well-disposed to purchasing the products they sell. Next time you get junk mail solicitation, study the letter and ask yourself, "How did I get in this database, and which database query produced my name?" The junk mailer is probably targeting extraordinarily beautiful, intelligent people.

After you create a query, you can save it and run it again. You can use it as the basis for constructing new queries. The information in database tables usually changes over time. Customers change addresses. New products come online, and others are discontinued. But no matter how much the data changes, you can find out exactly what you want to know from a database by running a well-crafted query.

Reports for presenting and examining data

Figure 1-4 shows a *report*. Reports can be made from database tables or from the results of queries. Reports are usually read by managers and others who don't get their hands dirty in databases. They're meant to be printed and distributed so that the information can be scrutinized and analyzed. Access offers many attractive reports. Don't worry — the program does most of the layout work for you, and exporting reports to a Word file is easy.

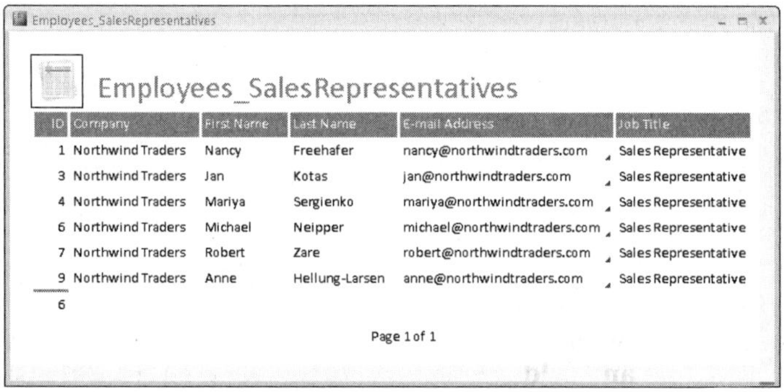

Figure 1-4: A report gathers data for scrutiny and analysis.

Employees_SalesRepresentatives

ID	Company	First Name	Last Name	E-mail Address	Job Title
1	Northwind Traders	Nancy	Freehafer	nancy@northwindtraders.com	Sales Representative
3	Northwind Traders	Jan	Kotas	jan@northwindtraders.com	Sales Representative
4	Northwind Traders	Mariya	Sergienko	mariya@northwindtraders.com	Sales Representative
6	Northwind Traders	Michael	Neipper	michael@northwindtraders.com	Sales Representative
7	Northwind Traders	Robert	Zare	robert@northwindtraders.com	Sales Representative
9	Northwind Traders	Anne	Hellung-Larsen	anne@northwindtraders.com	Sales Representative
6					

Page 1 of 1

Macros and modules

Macros and modules aren't covered in this mini-book, but they are also database objects. A *macro* is a series of commands. You can store macros for running queries and doing other Access tasks. (Book VIII, Chapter 7 explains macros.) A *module* is a collection of Visual Basic procedures and declarations for performing tasks in Access.

Creating a Database File

Creating a database is a lot of work, at least in the beginning. You have to design the database (a subject that I explain shortly). You have to enter the raw information into the table. You have to construct queries that allow yourself and others to read meaning into the data (see Chapter 4 of this mini-book). By contrast, creating a database file for storing the information is the easy part.

Access offers two ways to create a new database file. You can do it from scratch or get the help of a template. With a template, some of the work's done already for you. The template comes with prefabricated queries, forms, and reports. However, templates are for people who already know their way around Access databases. To make use of a template, you have to know how to modify a pre-existing database.

Before you create a database file, start by deciding where in your computer to store it. Unlike other Office programs, Access requires you to save and name a new file as soon as you create it.

Creating a blank database file

Follow these instructions to create a blank database file:

1. **Start Access (if you're not already running it), click the Office button, and choose New.**

   The Getting Started with Microsoft Office Access screen appears.

2. **Click the Blank Database link in the New Blank Database section in the middle pane.**

3. **In the Blank Database section on the right of the Access window, click the folder icon to open the File New Database dialog box and select the drive and folder where you want to keep the database file, enter a name in the File Name text box, and click OK to close the dialog box.**

4. **Click the Create button.**

   The Navigation pane and a blank table appear. Later in this chapter, "Finding Your Way around the Navigation Pane" explains what this pane is all about. I suggest you go there without delay or deferral.

Getting the help of a template

As I explain earlier, templates are wonderful if you have the wherewithal to modify them. Access offers prefabricated databases for tracking assets, keeping inventory, scheduling resources, and doing other things. Unfortunately, the only way to find out whether one of the templates is worthwhile is to go to the trouble to create a database from a template, open up the database file, and look around.

Follow these steps to create a database file from a template:

1. **Start Access or click the Office button and then choose New.**

The Getting Started with Microsoft Office Access screen appears.

2. **Click one of the Template Categories on the top left of the Access window or click a category under the From Microsoft Office Online.**

The available templates appear in the middle of the window. You can find databases for tracking tasks, sales, projects, assets, and other data.

3. **Select a template.**

The template name appears in the right section of the Access window, along with a rating and a filename.

4. **In the section on the right of the Access window (under the name of the chosen template), click the folder icon to open the File New Database dialog box and select the drive and folder where you want to keep the database file, enter a name in the File Name text box, and click OK to close the dialog box.**

5. **Click the Download button.**

Access downloads the template, creates a database file on your computer, and opens the file.

Finding Your Way around the Navigation Pane

The first thing you see when you open most database files is a Navigation pane like the one in Figure 1-5. This is the starting point for doing all your work in Access. From here, you can select an object — that horrible word again! — and begin working. You also add objects to the Navigation pane using the Create tab.

Here are shorthand instructions for doing this, that, and the other thing in the Navigation pane:

✦ **Choosing an object type:** Select a group (Tables, Queries, Forms, Reports, and so on) from the Object Type drop-down list at the top of the Navigation pane, or select All Access Objects to see all the groups, as shown in Figure 1-5.

✦ **Creating a new object:** Click the Create tab and then choose what type of object you want to create. When creating new forms and reports, click a table or query in the Navigation pane to base the new form or report on that table or query. You create different types of objects throughout this mini-book.

✦ **Opening an object:** To open a database table, query, form, or report, double-click it, select it and then press Enter, or right-click it and then choose Open from the shortcut menu.

✦ **Opening an object in Design view:** The task of formulating database tables, forms, and queries is done in Design view. If an object needs reformulating, right-click it and then choose Design View on the shortcut menu.

✦ **Finding objects:** Use the Search bar to display objects that contain the phrase in the name. Figure 1-5 shows the objects that contain the word *Customer*.

✦ **Manipulating the Navigation pane:** Click the Shutter Bar Open/Close button on the upper-right corner of the Navigation pane when you want to shrink it and get it out of the way. You can also resize this pane by clicking the far right edge and dragging it left or right.

No matter how cluttered the Access window gets with database tables, queries, and forms, you can quickly show the Navigation pane with these techniques:

✦ Click the Shutter Bar Open/Close button on the collapsed Navigation pane.

✦ Press F11.

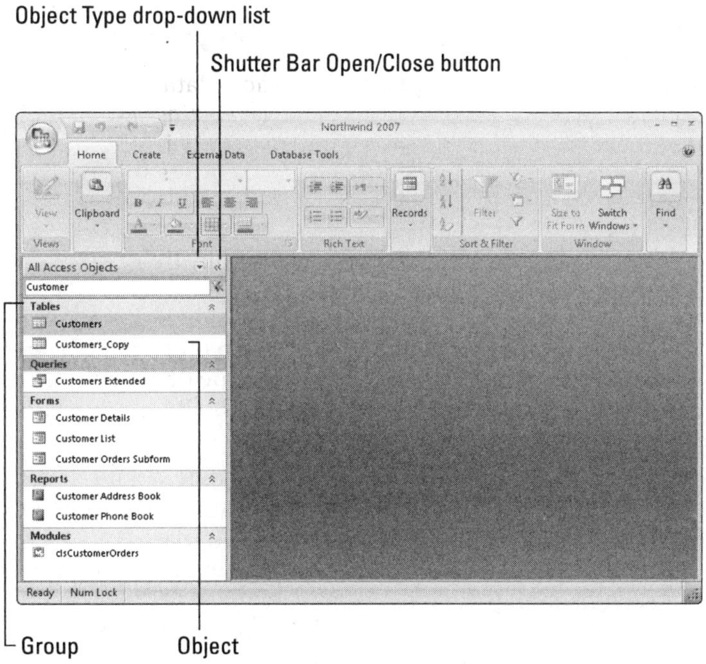

Object Type drop-down list

Shutter Bar Open/Close button

Figure 1-5:
The Access
Interface.

Group   Object

Access file formats

Not surprisingly, the default file format for database files you create with Access 2007 is Access 2007 and has an .accdb extension. If you work on your own or work with people who have the latest version of Access, you needn't worry about your Access files being compatible with older versions of the program.

Access 2007 also supports older file formats: Access 2000, Access 2002, and Access 2003, which have an .mdb extension. To use databases in these formats, simply open them in Access 2007. You can use some of the new features of Access 2007 while maintaining compatibility with your behind-the-times co-workers that still have the older version. You can even create new databases in the older format if these co-workers refuse to upgrade. Some people can be so stubborn!

Use one of the following methods to save your files in the latest version of Access:

✔ **Converting an older database version to Access 2007:** Open the older file in Access 2007, click the Office button, and choose Convert. The Convert Database Into dialog box appears. Select a folder and name for the database file and then click the Save button.

✔ **Converting an Access 2007 file to an older version:** Open the newer file in Access 2007, click the Office button, and choose Save As➪Access 2002-2003 or Access 2000 File Format. The Convert Database Into dialog box appears. Select a folder and name for the database file and then click the Save button.

✔ **Saving all files by default in a different version:** Click the Office button, choose Access Options, select Personalize on the left pane, and choose the Default file format from the drop-down list. Select from Access 2007, Access 2002-2003, or Access 2000.

Warning: After you use some features of an Access 2007 database, you can't convert it back into an older format. These features include attachments, multi-value lookup fields, and offline data.

Designing a Database

Being a database designer isn't nearly as glamorous as being a fashion designer, but it has its rewards. If you design your database carefully and correctly, it can be very useful to you and others. You can enter information accurately. When the time comes to draw information from the database, you get precisely the information you need. These pages explain everything you need to consider when designing a database. Pay close attention to "Separating information into different database tables" because the hardest part about designing a database is deciding how to distribute information across database tables and how many database tables to have.

Deciding what information you need

The first question to ask yourself is about the kind of information you want to get out of the database. Customer names and addresses? Sales information? Information for inventory tracking? Interview your co-workers to find out what information could be helpful to them. Give this matter some serious thought. Your goal is to set up the database so that every tidbit of information your organization needs can be recorded there.

A good way to find out what kind of information matters to an organization is to examine the paper forms that the organization uses to solicit or record information. These forms show precisely what the organization deems worthy of tracking in a database. Figure 1-6, for example, shows the paper form that players fill out to sign up for the little league whose database tables appear in Figure 1-7. Compare Figure 1-6 with Figure 1-7, and you can see that the Players, Teams, and Divisions database tables all have fields for entering information from this form.

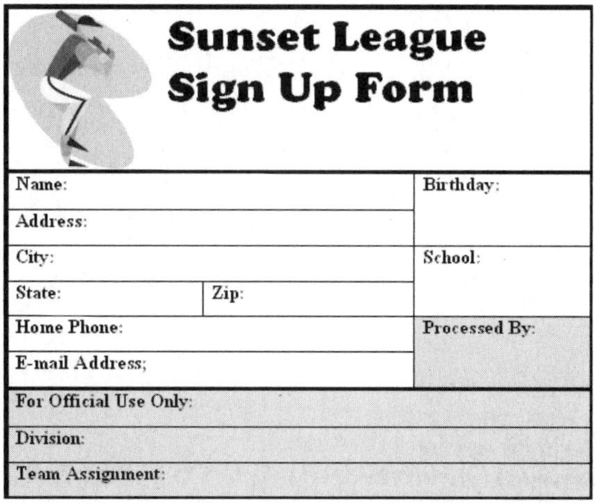

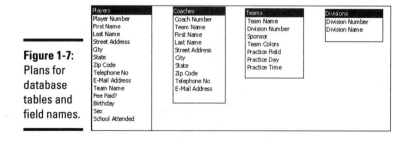

Figure 1-6: Paper forms also have fields.

Figure 1-7: Plans for database tables and field names.

Keeping object shortcuts in groups

In a database with many tables, queries, and reports, finding the one you want to work on can be a chore. To help you find objects, Access gives you the opportunity to create custom groups. After you create a group, its name appears in the Navigation pane, and the object you add to that group appears underneath the group's heading. Actually, only shortcuts to the objects appear in a custom group. Then, to open an object, all you have to do is double-click its shortcut.

To create custom groups, right-click the white space at the bottom of the Navigation pane and then choose Navigation Options from the drop-down list. The Navigation Options dialog box displays. Follow these instructions to set up your custom groups:

 ✔ **Creating a new category:** Click the Add Item button to create a new category. You see the new category appear, where you can type a name and press Enter. For example, you may want a category for Customers, Employees, or the Management team to keep them out of the important stuff. The Object Type category is the default and contains Tables, Queries, Forms, and so on.

 ✔ **Creating a new group:** Click the category to which you want to add the group and then

click the Add Group button. You see the new group appear, where you can type a name and press Enter. These groups appear in the Navigation pane after you select a Category from the Object Type drop-down list.

 ✔ **Putting a shortcut in a group:** At first, all the objects are in the Unassigned Objects group. To add them to your new group, close the Navigation Options dialog box, right-click the object, choose Add to Group, and choose the group's name in the submenu.

 ✔ **Opening a group:** Choose a category from the Object Type drop-down list and then expand the desired group name to display the objects you add to the group.

 ✔ **Removing a shortcut from a custom group:** Select the object, press the Delete button or right-click the object and then choose Remove from the drop-down list. The object returns to the Unassigned Objects group. If you're viewing actual objects — not shortcuts — you get a message asking if you want to permanently delete the object. Make sure you don't accidentally delete the real object instead of the shortcut.

Separating information into different database tables

After you know the information you want to record in the database, think about how to separate the information into database tables. Many are tempted to put all the information into a single database table, but Access is a *relational database,* you can query more than one table at a time, and in so doing, assemble information from different tables.

To see how it works, consider the simple database, as shown in Figure 1-7. The purpose of this little database and its four tables is to store information about the players, coaches, and teams in a little league. The Team Name field appears in three tables. It serves as the link between the tables and permits more than one to be queried. By querying individual tables or combinations of tables in this database, I can assemble team rosters, make a list of coaches and their contact information, list teams by division, put together a mailing list of all players, find out which players have paid their fee, and list players by age group, among other things. This database comprises four tables:

+ **Players:** Includes fields for tracking players' names, addresses, birthdays, which teams they're on, and whether they paid their fees

+ **Coaches:** Includes fields for tracking coaches' names, addresses, and the names of the teams they coach

+ **Teams:** Includes fields for tracking team names and which division each team is in

+ **Divisions:** Includes fields for tracking division numbers and names

Deciding how many database tables you need and how to separate data across the different tables is the hardest part of designing a database. To make the task a little easier, do it the old-fashioned way with a pencil and eraser. Here are the basic rules for separating data into different tables:

+ **Restrict a table to one subject only:** Each database table should hold information about one subject only — customers, employees, products, and so on. This way, you can maintain data in one table independently from data in another table. Consider what would happen in the little league database (refer to Figure 1-7) if coach and team data were kept in a single table, and one team's coach was replaced by someone new. You would have to delete the old coach's record, delete information about the team, enter information about the new coach, and re-enter information about the team that you just deleted. But by keeping team information separate from coach information, you can update coach information and still maintain the team information.

+ **Avoid duplicate information:** Try not to keep duplicate information in the same database table or duplicate information across different tables. By keeping the information in one place, you have to enter it only once, and if you have to update it, you can do so in one database table, not several.

Deciding how many tables to include in a database and how the tables relate to one another is probably the hardest task you undertake in Access. Entire books are written about database design, and this book can't do the subject justice. You can, however, store all your data in a single table if the data you want to store isn't very complex. The time you lose entering all the data in a single table is made up by the time you save not having to design a complex database with more than one table.

Choosing fields for database tables

As I explain earlier, *fields* are categories of information. Each database table needs at least one field. If the table itself is a subject, you could say that its fields are facts about the subject. An Address database table needs fields for recording street addresses, cities, states, and ZIP codes. A Products database table needs fields for product ID numbers, product names, and unit prices. Just the facts, ma'am. Within the confines of the subject, the database table needs one field for each piece of information that is useful to your organization.

When you're planning which fields to include in your database tables, follow these guidelines:

+ Break up the information into small elements. For example, instead of a Name field, create a First Name field and a Last Name field. This way, you can sort database tables by last name more easily.

+ Give descriptive names to fields so that you know what they are later. A more descriptive name, such as *Serial Number,* is clearer than *SN.*

+ Think ahead and include a field for each piece of information your organization needs. Adding a field to a database table late in the game is a chore. You have to return to each record, look up the information, and enter it.

+ Don't include information that can be derived from a calculation. As I explain in Chapter 4 of this mini-book, calculations can be performed as part of a query. For example, you can total the numbers in two fields in the same record or perform mathematical calculations on values in fields.

Deciding on a primary key field for each database table

Each database table must have a *primary key field.* This field, also known as the *primary key,* is the field in the database table where unique, one-of-a-kind data is stored. Data entered in this field — an employee ID number, a part number, a bid number — must be different in each record. If you try to enter the same data in the primary key field of two different records, a dialog box warns you not to do that. Primary key fields prevent you from entering duplicate records. They also make queries more efficient. In a query, you tell Access what to look for in database tables, Access searches through the tables, and the program assembles information that meets the criteria. Primary key fields help Access recognize records and not collect the same information more than once in a query.

Social security numbers make great primary key fields because no two people have the same social security number. Invoice numbers and serial numbers also make excellent primary key fields. Returning to the sample little league database (refer to Figure 1-7), which fields in the little league database tables are primary key fields? In the Teams table, Team Name can be the primary key field because no two teams have the same name. Division Number can also be a primary key field because divisions in the league are numbered and no two divisions have the same number.

The Players and Coaches database tables, however, present a problem when it comes to choosing a primary key field. Two players might have the same last name, which rules out Last Name as a primary key field. A brother and sister might have the same telephone number, which rules out a Telephone No. field. Because no field holds values that are certain to be different from record to record, I introduce fields called Player Number and Coach Number. For the purpose of this database, players and coaches are assigned numbers. (Chapter 2 in this mini-book explains how Access can assign sequential numbers for you in a database table.)

Mapping the relationships between tables

If your database includes more than one table, you have to map how the tables relate to one another. Usually, relationships are formed between the primary key field in one table and the corresponding field in another, called the *foreign key*. Figure 1-8 shows the relationships between the tables in the little league database. Because these tables are linked by common fields, I can gather information from more than one table in a query or report. Chapter 2 in this mini-book takes up the subject of linking tables in more detail. For now, when you design your database, consider how to connect the various tables with common fields.

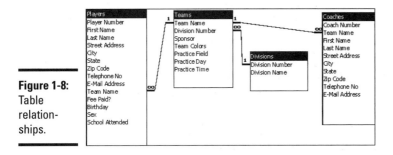

Figure 1-8:
Table
relation-
ships.

To get an idea how database tables can be linked, open the Northwind sample database and then look in the Relationships window. Click the Database Tools tab and then click Relationships in the Show/Hide group to open the Relationships window. The Relationships window shows you how the various tables are related to one another.

Chapter 2: Building Your Database Tables

In This Chapter

✔ **Creating database tables**

✔ **Creating fields for a database table**

✔ **Choosing a primary key field**

✔ **Using field properties to make data entries more accurate**

✔ **Indexing fields in a table**

✔ **Forming relationships between tables**

Database tables are the building blocks of a database. They hold the raw data. Relationships between the tables permit you to query and generate reports from several different tables. How well your database tables are put together and how accurately data is entered in the tables determine whether your database is a thing of beauty or a wilted flower.

This chapter explains how to create database tables and fields for the tables. It explains what primary key fields are and how primary key fields and indexed fields make it easier for Access to sort, search, and query a database. This chapter describes how to forge relationships between tables. Fasten your seatbelts. In this chapter, you can find numerous tips and tricks for making sure that data is entered accurately in your database tables.

Creating a Database Table

Raw data is stored in database tables (or in a single table if you decide to keep all the data in one place). The first and most important part of setting up a database is creating the tables and entering the data. After you enter the data, you can harass your database for information about the things and people your database keeps track of. If you haven't done so already, read the sections in Chapter 1 of this mini-book that pertain to storing information and designing a database before you create a database table. Chapter 1 of this mini-book explains what database tables are and how to fashion a splendid one.

The business of creating a database table starts on the Create tab, as shown in Figure 2-1.

Click the Create tab.

Figure 2-1:
Use the
Create tab
to create a
database
table.

Click Table, Table Templates,
or Table Design.

Select the Tables group in the Navigation pane to view the database's existing tables. As I explain in detail in the next pages, Access offers three ways to create a database table:

+ **Create the database table from scratch:** Enter and format the fields one at a time on your own.

+ **Get the help of a template:** Get prefabricated fields assembled in a table. This is the way to go if you know Access well, and you can modify database tables and table fields.

+ **Import the database table from another database:** This technique can be an enormous timesaver if you can recycle data that has already been entered in a database table in another Access database.

Creating a database table from scratch

Creating a table from scratch entails creating the table and then entering the fields one by one. Follow these steps to create a database table from scratch:

1. **Click the Create tab.**

2. **Click the Table Design button, located in the Tables group (see Figure 2-1).**

The Design window appears. From here, you enter fields for your database table. I hate to be like a City Hall bureaucrat who gives everybody the runaround, but I can't help myself. Turn to "Entering and Altering Table Fields" later in this chapter to find out how to enter fields in a database table.

3. **Click the Save button on the Quick Access toolbar.**

The Save As dialog box appears.

4. **Enter a descriptive name for your table and click OK.**

Return to the Navigation pane and you see the name of the table you created. If you don't believe me, click the Tables group to see the names of tables in your database.

Creating a database table from a template

If you know your way around Access and know how to modify database tables, you can do worse than create a database table with a template. Access offers a few different table templates to choose from. After you create a table with a template, you can remove any fields that you don't want. It's always easier to delete fields than to add new ones.

To create a table with a template, click the Table Templates button on the Create tab and then select a template from the list, as shown in Figure 2-2. Choose from Contacts, Tasks, Issues, Events, or Assets. Access creates the table.

Book VI Chapter 2

Building Your Database Tables

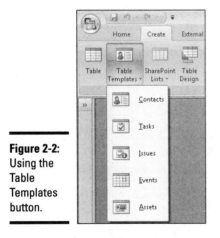

Figure 2-2: Using the Table Templates button.

A table appears on-screen, ready for you to enter data. First, you should explore the fields in your new table. If the table contains fields you don't want or you want to change the names of the fields, now is the time to do so. Turn to "Entering and Altering Table Fields" later in this chapter to find out how to change and delete fields in a database table.

Importing a table from another database

Few things are more tedious than entering records in a database table. If the records you need were already entered elsewhere, more power to you. Follow these steps to get a database table from another Access database:

1. **Click the External Data tab.**

2. **Click the Access button in the Import group.**

The Get External Data window opens.

3. **Enter a database name and path in the File Name text box or click the Browse button to find the Access database with the table you need.**

4. **Select the Import Tables, Queries, Forms, Reports, Macros, and Modules into the Current Database option button and click OK.**

You see the Import Objects dialog box, as shown in Figure 2-3.

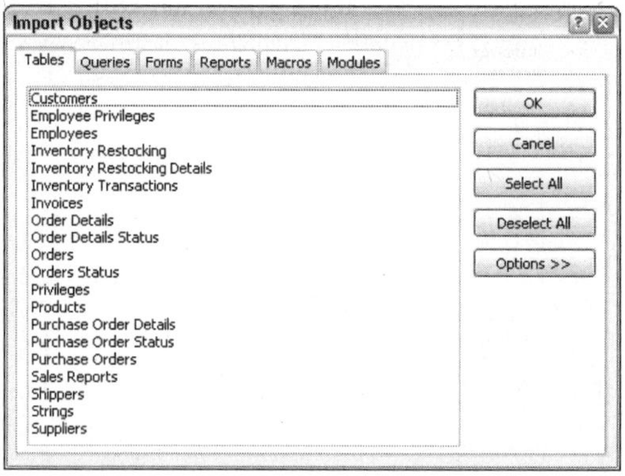

Figure 2-3:
Getting
data from
another
database.

Import Objects	? ✕
Tables | Queries | Forms | Reports | Macros | Modules	
Customers	OK
Employee Privileges	Cancel
Employees	
Inventory Restocking	Select All
Inventory Restocking Details	
Inventory Transactions	Deselect All
Invoices	
Order Details	Options >>
Order Details Status	
Orders	
Orders Status	
Privileges	
Products	
Purchase Order Details	
Purchase Order Status	
Purchase Orders	
Sales Reports	
Shippers	
Strings	
Suppliers	

5. **On the Tables tab, select the database table you want and click OK.**

You can import more than one database table by clicking multiple table names in the dialog box or clicking the Select All button.

If the table you want to import includes lookup fields, import the tables or queries that the lookup fields refer to as well as the table itself. Without those tables or queries, the lookup fields won't be able to obtain any values. Later in this chapter, "Creating a lookup data-entry list" explains what lookup fields are.

You can import a table structure — its field names and formats — without importing the data in the table. To do so, click the Options button in the Import Objects dialog box, and under Import Tables, select the Definition Only option button.

Opening and Viewing Tables

As with all the so-called objects in a database, you open tables by starting in the Navigation pane. Select the Tables group to view the database tables you created. How you open a table depends on whether you want to open it in Datasheet view or Design view. Figure 2-4 illustrates the difference between these views. Datasheet view is for entering and examining data in a table; Design view is for creating fields and describing their parameters.

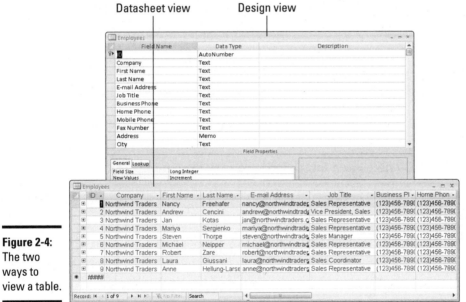

Figure 2-4: The two ways to view a table.

Select a table and follow these instructions to open it:

✦ **Opening in Design view:** Right-click the table and choose Design View on the shortcut menu.

✦ **Opening in Datasheet view:** Double-click the table or right-click and choose Open on the shortcut menu.

◆ **Switching views:** Click the View button on the far left of the Home tab. This button changes appearance, depending on whether you're in Design view or Datasheet view. You can also change views by right-clicking the table window's title bar and choosing Datasheet View or Design View on the shortcut menu.

Entering and Altering Table Fields

After you create a database table, the next task is to enter the fields, or if Access created the table for you, alter the fields to your liking. As Chapter 1 of this mini-book explains, fields represent categories of information in a database table. They are the equivalent of columns in a conventional table. Fields determine what kind of information is stored in a database table.

These pages explain how to create a field, choose the right data type, display data in fields, and designate the primary key field in a table. While I'm on the subject of fields, W.C. Fields said, "Horse sense is the thing a horse has which keeps it from betting on people."

Creating a field

Follow these steps to create a new field in a database table:

1. **Open the table and switch to Design view if you aren't already there.**

You can click the View command on the Home tab to change views.

2. **If necessary, insert a new row for the field.**

Insert Rows To do so, click in the field that is to go after the new field, and then click the Insert Rows command in the Tools group on the (Table Tools) Design tab. A blank row appears.

3. **Enter a name in the Field Name column.**

Names can't include periods or be longer than 64 letters, but you don't want to enter a long name anyway because it won't fit very well along the top of the table.

Some database programs don't permit spaces in field names. If you intend to export Access data to other database programs, don't include spaces in field names. Instead, run the words together or separate words with an underscore character, like this: underscore_character.

4. **Press the Tab key or click in the Data Type column, and choose a data type from the drop-down list, as shown in Figure 2-5.**

Data types classify what kind of information is kept in the field. The next section, "All about data types," in this chapter explains data types.

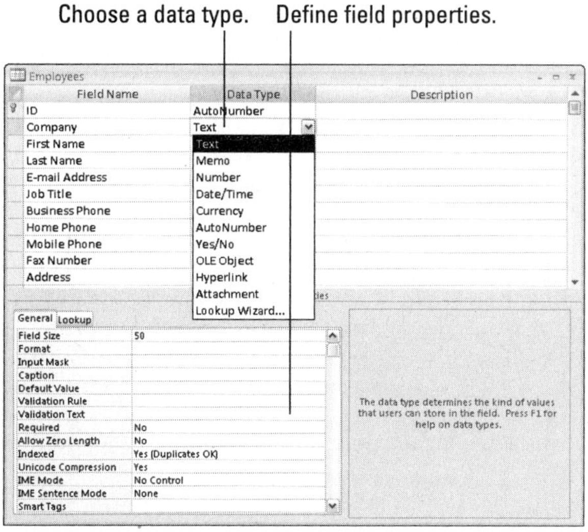

Choose a data type.   Define field properties.

Employees		
Field Name	**Data Type**	**Description**
ID	AutoNumber	
Company	Text	
First Name	Text	
Last Name	Memo	
E-mail Address	Number	
Job Title	Date/Time	
Business Phone	Currency	
Home Phone	AutoNumber	
Mobile Phone	Yes/No	
Fax Number	OLE Object	
Address	Hyperlink	
	Attachment	
	Lookup Wizard...	

General   Lookup

Field Size	50
Format	
Input Mask	
Caption	
Default Value	
Validation Rule	
Validation Text	
Required	No
Allow Zero Length	No
Indexed	Yes [Duplicates OK]
Unicode Compression	Yes
IME Mode	No Control
IME Sentence Mode	None
Smart Tags	

The data type determines the kind of values that users can store in the field. Press F1 for help on data types.

Figure 2-5:
Choosing a
data type.

Book VI
Chapter 2

Building Your
Database Tables

5. **(Optional) Enter a description in the Description column.**

These descriptions can be very helpful when you need to reacquaint yourself with a field and find out what it's meant to do.

In case the name you choose for your field isn't descriptive enough, you can give the field a second name. The name appears in Datasheet view, on forms, and on reports. To enter a second, descriptive field name, enter the name in the Caption field on the General tab of the Design view window.

Later in this chapter, "Field Properties for Making Sure That Data Entries Are Accurate" demonstrates how to define field properties in the Design view window to make it easier for data-entry clerks to enter the data.

Field templates

To get Access's help in creating a field, switch to Datasheet view and click the (Table Tools) Datasheet tab. Click the New Field button to display the Field Templates pane, which usually appears on the far right of the Access window (unless you move it). From this pane, select one or more fields to insert into your table. Just double-click or drag and drop a field from the list into the Datasheet view to add that field to the table. Do the sample tables and sample fields in this pane look familiar? These are the same fields you get when you create a database table from a template.

All about data types

To choose a data type for a field, open the Data Type drop-down list in the Design view window and choose a data type (see Figure 2-5). Data types are the first line of defense in making sure that data is entered correctly in a table. Try to enter text in a field assigned the Currency or Number data type, and Access tells you that your entry is invalid. You get the chance to fix your mistake as soon as you make it.

Table 2-1 explains the options on the Data Type drop-down list. Choose data types carefully because how you classify the data that is entered in a field determines how you can query the field for information. Querying for a number range is impossible, for example, if the field you're querying isn't classified as a Number or Currency field on the Data Type drop-down list.

Table 2-1	Data Types for Fields
Data Type	*What It's For*
Text	For storing text (city names, for example), combinations of text and numbers (street addresses, for example), and numbers that won't be calculated or used in expressions (telephone numbers and social security numbers, for example). By default, a Text field is 50 characters long but Text fields can be 255 characters if you need that many. If you need that many characters, however, you probably need the Memo data type, not the Text data type.
Memo	For storing long descriptions. Fields assigned this data type can hold 65,535 characters, not that anyone needs that many. If you fill this field programmatically, it can hold up to 2GB of data.
Number	For storing numbers to be used in calculations or sorting. (If you're dealing with monetary figures, choose the Currency data type.)
Date/Time	For storing dates and times and being able to sort data chronologically or use dates and times in calculations.
Currency	For storing monetary figures for use in calculations and sorting.
AutoNumber	For entering numbers in sequence that will be different from record to record. Use the AutoNumber data type for the primary key field if no other field stores unique, one-of-a-kind data. (See "Designating the primary key field," later in this chapter.)
Yes/No	For storing True/False, Yes/No, On/Off type data. Choose this data type to enter data with a check box in the field. When the box is selected, the data in the field is True, Yes, or On, for example.
OLE Object	For embedding an OLE link in your Access table to another object — an Excel worksheet or Word document.
Hyperlink	For storing hyperlinks to other locations on the Internet or on the company intranet.

Data Type	What It's For
Attachment	For storing images, spreadsheets, documents, charts, and other types of supported files to a record in your table. This is similar to attaching a file to an e-mail message. Attachments provide greater flexibility than OLE Object fields and are more efficient because they don't create a bitmap image of the original file.
Lookup Wizard	For creating a drop-down list with choices that a data-entry clerk can choose from when entering data. See "Creating a lookup data-entry list," later in this chapter.

Designating the primary key field

As I explain in Chapter 1 of this mini-book, no database table is complete without a primary key field. The *primary key field* identifies which field in the table is unique and contains data that differs from record to record. Duplicate values and null values can't be entered in the primary key field. (A *null value* indicates a missing or unknown value.) Choosing a primary key field is so important that Access doesn't let you close a table unless you choose one.

Deciding how the data in fields is displayed

To decide how numbers, times, dates, currency values, and Yes/No data are displayed in fields, open the Format drop-down list on the Field Properties part of the Design window and choose an option. These display options are useful indeed. Choose a number format with a dollar sign and comma ($3,456.79), for example, and you don't have to enter the dollar signs or commas when you enter data in the field. These marks are entered for you. You just enter the numbers.

✔ **@ (at symbol):** A character or space is required. For example, @@@@-@@ inserts a hyphen between the first set of numbers and the second. You don't have to enter the hyphen, only the text or numbers.

✔ **& (ampersand):** A character or space is optional. For example, @@@@@-&&&& in a ZIP Code field tells Access that either entry is correct, a five-character ZIP code or a five-character plus the four extra characters ZIP code.

✔ **> (right bracket):** Displays all characters in the field as uppercase. Merely by entering this symbol in the Format text box, you can display all entries in the field as uppercase without the data-entry clerk having to hold down the Shift or Caps Lock key.

✔ **< (left bracket):** Displays all characters in the field as lowercase.

If no field in your table holds one-of-a-kind data that is different from record to record, get around the problem with one of these techniques:

+ **The AutoNumber data type:** Create a new field, give it a name, choose AutoNumber from the Data Type drop-down list (refer to Figure 2-5), and make your new field the primary key field. This way, when you enter data, Access enters a unique number to identify each record in the field. (To generate random numbers instead of sequential numbers in an AutoNumber field, go the Field Properties tab of the Design view window and choose Random instead of Increment on the New Values drop-down list.)

+ **A multiple-field primary key:** Combine two or more fields and designate them as the primary key. For example, if you're absolutely certain that no two people whose names will be entered in your database table have the same name, you can make the First Name and Last Name fields the primary key. The problem with multiple-field primary keys, however, is that it takes Access longer to process them, and you run the risk of entering duplicate records.

Follow these steps to designate a field in a database table as the primary key field:

1. **In Design view, select the field or fields you want to be the primary key.**

   To select a field, click its *row selector,* the small box to its left; Ctrl+click row selectors to select more than one field.

Primary
Key

2. **Click the Primary Key button in the Tools group on the (Table Tools) Design tab.**

   A small key symbol appears on the row selector to let you know which field or fields is the primary key field.

To remove a primary key, click its row selector and then click the Primary Key button all over again.

Moving, renaming, and deleting fields

Suppose that you need to move, rename, or delete a field. To do so, switch to Design view and follow these instructions:

+ **Moving a field:** Select the field's row selector (the box to its left) and release the mouse button. Click again and drag the selector up or down to a new location.

+ **Renaming a field:** Click in the Field Name box where the name is, delete the name that's there, and type a new name.

✦ **Deleting a field:** Click in the Field Name box and click the Delete Rows button in the Tools group of the (Table Tools) Design tab. Alternatively, you can right-click the field and choose Delete Rows on the shortcut menu.

Field Properties for Making Sure That Data Entries Are Accurate

Unfortunately, entering the data in a database table is one of the most tedious activities known to humankind. And because the activity is so dull, people are prone to make mistakes when they enter data in a database table. One way to cut down on mistakes is to take advantage of the Field Properties settings on the General tab in the Design view window. Figure 2-6 shows the General tab.

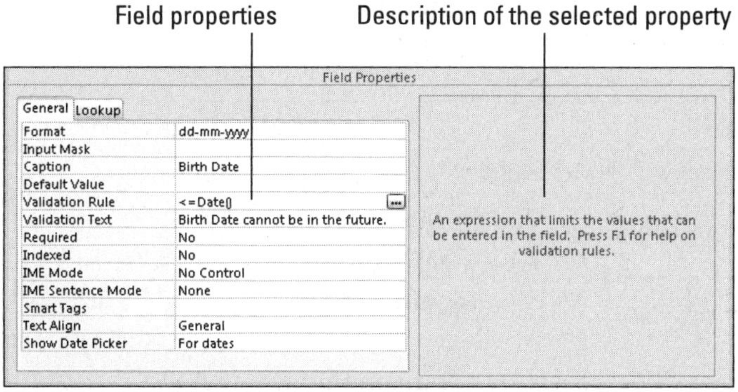

Book VI
Chapter 2

Building Your
Database Tables

Field properties   Description of the selected property

Field Properties

General	Lookup	
Format	dd-mm-yyyy	
Input Mask		
Caption	Birth Date	
Default Value		
Validation Rule	<=Date()	[...]
Validation Text	Birth Date cannot be in the future.	
Required	No	
Indexed	No	
IME Mode	No Control	
IME Sentence Mode	None	
Smart Tags		
Text Align	General	
Show Date Picker	For dates	

An expression that limits the values that can be entered in the field. Press F1 for help on validation rules.

Figure 2-6: Establishing field properties.

These properties determine what can and can't be entered in the different fields of a database table. Some of the settings are invaluable. The Field Size property, for example, determines how many characters can be entered in a field. In a State field where two-letter state abbreviations are to be entered, make the Field Size property 2 to be certain that no one enters more than two characters. If the majority of people you're tracking in an address database live in New York, enter NY in the Default Value property. That way, you spare data-entry clerks from having to enter NY the majority of the time. They won't have to enter it because NY is already there.

The Lookup tab in the Field Properties part of the Design view window is for creating a data-entry drop-down list. It, too, is invaluable. If you happen to know that only four items can be entered in a field, create a drop-down list with the four items. That way, data-entry clerks can choose from a list of four valid items instead of having to enter the data themselves and perhaps enter it incorrectly.

A look at the Field Properties settings

Especially if yours is a large database, you're encouraged to study the field properties carefully and make liberal use of them. The Field Properties settings safeguard data from being entered incorrectly. The following is a description of the different properties (listed here in the order in which they appear in the Design view window) and instructions for using them wisely. Which properties you can assign to a field depends on which data type the field was assigned.

Field Size

In the Field Size box for Text fields, enter the maximum number of characters that can be entered in the field. Suppose that the field you're dealing with is ZIP Code, and you want to enter five-number ZIP codes. By entering **5** in the Field Size text box, only five characters can be entered in the field. A sleepy data-entry clerk couldn't enter a six-character ZIP code by accident.

For Number fields, select a value for the field size from the drop-down list. Table 2-2 describes these field sizes.

Table 2-2	Numeric Field Sizes
Field Size	*Description*
Byte	A 1-byte integer that holds values from 0–255.
Integer	A 2-byte integer that holds values from 32,768–32,767.
Long Integer	A 4-byte integer that holds values from 2,147,483,648–2,147,483,647.
Single	A 4-byte floating point number that holds large values up to 7 significant digits.
Double	An 8-byte floating point number that holds large values up to 15 significant digits.
Replication ID	A 16-byte globally unique identifier (GUID) that's randomly generated.
Decimal	A 12-byte number with defined decimal precision. The default precision is 0, but you can set the scale up to 28.

The Single, Doubles, and Decimal field size options all hold different ranges of numbers. For now, if you need to store numbers after the decimal point, set the data type double so that you cover most situations. For more information on the ranges for all these field sizes, check the Access Help program by pressing F1 with your cursor in the Field Size box.

Format

Earlier in this chapter, "Deciding how the data in fields is displayed" explains the Format property. Click the drop-down list and choose the format in which text, numbers, and dates and times are displayed.

Decimal Places

For a field that holds numbers, open the Decimal Places drop-down list and choose how many numbers can appear to the right of the decimal point. This property affects how numbers and currency values are displayed, not their real value. Numbers are rounded to the nearest decimal point. The Auto option displays the number of decimal places that the format you choose on the Format drop-down list permits.

Input Mask

For Text and Date field types, this feature provides a template with punctuation marks to make entering the data easier. Telephone numbers, social security numbers, and other numbers that typically are entered along with dashes and parentheses are ideal candidates for an input mask (another ridiculous database term!). On the datasheet, blank spaces appear where the numbers go, and the punctuation marks stand at the ready to receive numbers, as shown in Figure 2-7.

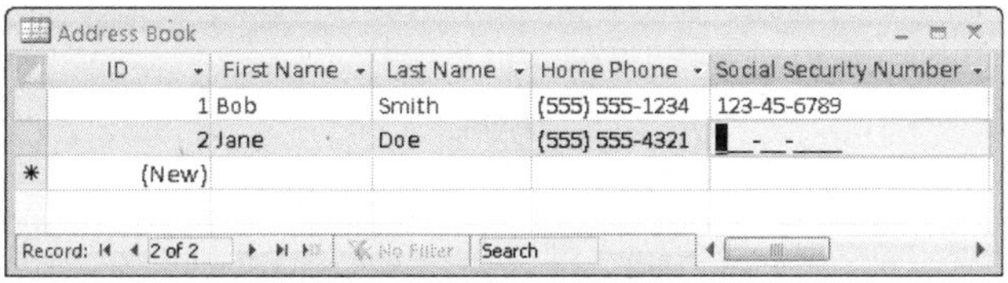

Figure 2-7:
Input masks.

ID	First Name	Last Name	Home Phone	Social Security Number
1 Bob		Smith	(555) 555-1234	123-45-6789
2 Jane		Doe	(555) 555-4321	- - _
(New)				

Record: 14 ◄ 2 of 2 ► ►I ►⊳ No Filter Search

In the Input Mask text box, enter a **0** where numbers go, and enter the punctuation marks where they go. For example, enter (000) 000-0000 or 000/000-0000 to enter an input mask for a telephone number like the one shown in Figure 2-7. You can also create input masks by clicking the three dots beside the Input Mask text box. Doing so opens the Input Mask Wizard dialog box, where you can fashion a very sophisticated input mask.

Caption

If the field you're working on has a cryptic or hard-to-understand name, enter a more descriptive name in the Caption text box. The value in the Caption property appears as the column heading in Datasheet view, as a label on forms, and on reports in place of the field name. People entering data understand what to enter after reading the descriptive caption.

Default Value

When you know that the majority of records require a certain value, number, or abbreviation, enter it in the Default Value text box. That way, you save yourself the trouble of entering the value, number, or abbreviation most of the time because the default value appears already in each record when you enter it. You can always override the default value by entering something different.

Validation Rule

As long as you know your way around operators and Boolean expressions, you can establish a rule for entering data in a field. For example, you can enter an expression that requires dates to be entered in a certain time frame. Or you can require currency figures to be above or below a certain value. To establish a validation rule, enter an expression in the Validation Rule text box. To use dates in an expression, the dates must be enclosed by number signs (#). Here are some examples of validation rules:

>1000	The value you enter must be over 1000.
<1000	The value you enter must be under 1000.
>=10	The value you enter must be greater than or equal to ten.
<>0	The value you enter cannot be zero.
>=#1/1/2007#	The date you enter must be January 1, 2007, or later.
>=#1/1/2007# And <#1/1/2008#	The date you enter must be in the year 2007.

To get help forming expressions, click the three dots beside the Validation Rule text box to open the Expression Builder, as shown in Figure 2-8, and build an expression there. Try clicking the Help button in the Expression Builder dialog box. Doing so opens the Access Help program, where you can get advice about building expressions.

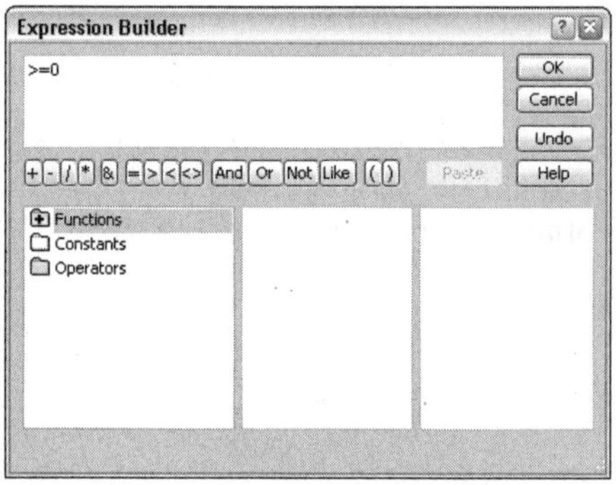

Figure 2-8:
Creating a validation rule.

Validation Text

If someone enters data that violates a validation rule that you enter in the Validation Rule text box, Access displays a standard error message. The message reads, "One or more values are prohibited by the validation rule set for [this field]. Enter a value that the expression for this field can accept." If this message is too cold and impersonal for you, you can create a message of your own for the error message dialog box. Enter your friendly message in the Validation Text text box.

Required

By default, no entry has to be made in a field, but if you choose Yes instead of No in the Required box and you fail to make an entry in the field, a message box tells you to be sure to make an entry.

Allow Zero Length

This property allows you to enter zero-length strings in a field. A *zero-length string* — two quotation marks with no text or spaces between them ("") — indicates that no value exists for a field. To see how zero-length strings work, suppose that your database table calls for entering e-mail addresses. If you didn't know whether one person has an e-mail address, you would leave the E-Mail Address field blank. If, however, you knew that the person didn't have an e-mail address, you could indicate as much by entering a zero-length string. Choose Yes on the drop-down list to permit zero-length strings to be entered in the field.

Indexed

Indicates that the field has been indexed. As "Indexing for Faster Sorts, Searches, and Queries" explains later in this chapter, indexes make sorting a field and searching through a field go faster. The word *No* appears in this text box if the field has not been indexed.

Unicode Expression

Choose Yes from the Unicode Expression drop-down list if you want to compress data that is now stored in Unicode format. Storing data this way saves on disk space, and you probably don't want to change this property.

Smart Tags

If you intend to enter Smart Tags in the field, indicate which kind you enter by clicking the three dots next to the Smart Tags box and choosing an option in the Smart Tags dialog box. Book VIII, Chapter 1 explains Smart Tags.

Text Align

This property determines how the text is aligned in a column or on a form or report. Select General to let Access determine the alignment, or select Left, Right, Center, or Distribute.

Text Format

Available on Memo fields, this drop-down list lets you choose to allow rich text in the field. With this property set to Rich Text, you can make different words bold, italic, underline, and change font sizes and colors. Set it to Plain Text for plain, boring text with no formatting. I wonder why that isn't the setting's name.

Append Only

Available on Memo fields, this lets you add data only to a Memo field to collect a history of comments.

Show Date Picker

Available on Date/Time field, setting this to For Dates shows a button next to the column that lets you use a calendar to select a date instead of typing numbers. Set this to Never if you don't want to use the date picker, but why would you do that?

Creating a lookup data-entry list

Perhaps the best way to make sure that data is entered correctly is to create a data-entry drop-down list. Whoever enters the data in your database table has to only choose an item from the list, as shown in Figure 2-9. This saves time and prevents invalid data from being entered. Access offers two ways to create the drop-down list:

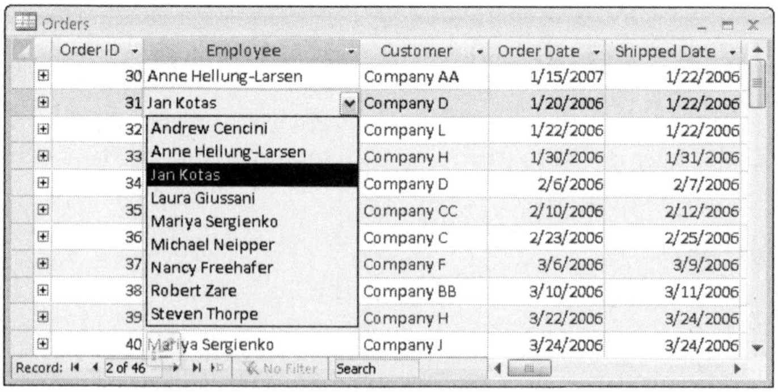

Figure 2-9:
A so-called
lookup list.

✦ **Create the list by entering the items yourself:** Go this route when you're dealing with a finite list of items that never change.

✦ **Get the items from another database table:** Go this route to get items from a column in another database table. This way, you can choose from an ever-expanding list of items. When the number of items in the other database table changes, so does the number of items in the drop-down list because the items come from the other database table. This is a great way to get items from a primary key field in another table.

Creating a drop-down list on your own

Follow these steps to create a drop-down, or *lookup,* list with entries you type:

1. **In Design view, click the field that needs a drop-down list.**

2. **Open the Data Type drop-down list and choose Lookup Wizard, the last option in the list.**

The Lookup Wizard dialog box appears.

3. **Select the second option, I Will Type in the Values That I Want, and click the Next button.**

4. **Under Col1 in the next dialog box, enter each item you want to appear in the drop-down list; then click the Next button.**

You can create a multicolumn list by entering a number in the Number of Columns text box and then entering items for the list.

5. **Enter a name for the field, if necessary, and click the Finish button.**

Switch to Datasheet view and open the drop-down list in the field to make sure that it displays properly.

**Book VI
Chapter 2**

**Building Your
Database Tables**

 To see what's on a drop-down list, start in Design view, select the field for which you created the list, and select the Lookup tab in the Field Properties pane. As shown in Figure 2-10, you can edit the list by editing or removing items in the Row Source text box. Be sure that a semi-colon (;) appears between each item. Even easier, click the three dots beside the Row Source text box to edit the list items. To remove a lookup list from a field, choose Text Box on the Display Control drop-down list.

Figure 2-10:
Editing a
lookup list.

General	Lookup	
Display Control	Combo Box	
Row Source Type	Value List	
Row Source	"Winter";"Spring";"Summer";"Fall"	...
Bound Column	1	
Column Count	1	
Column Heads	No	
Column Widths	1"	
List Rows	8	
List Width	1"	
Limit To List	No	
Allow Multiple Values	No	
Allow Value List Edits	Yes	
List Items Edit Form		

Getting list items from a database table

Before you can get list items from another database table, you might want to define a relationship between the tables; it's not required, but it's recommended. The next section of this chapter, "Indexing for Faster Sorts, Searches, and Queries," explains how to do that. Follow these steps to get items in a drop-down list from another database table:

1. **In Design view, click the field that needs a list, open the Data Type drop-down list, and choose Lookup Wizard.**

The Lookup Wizard dialog box appears.

2. **Select the first option, I Want the Lookup Column to Look Up the Values in a Table or Query, and click Next.**

You see a list of tables in your database.

3. **Select the table with the data you need and click the Next button.**

The dialog box shows you a list of available fields in the table.

4. **Select the field where the data for your list is stored.**

5. **Click the > button.**

The name of the list appears on the right side of the dialog box, under Selected Fields.

6. **Click the Next button.**

Normally, lists are displayed in ascending order, but you can select a field and click the Ascending button to reverse the order of the list. (Note that the button turns into the Descending button.)

7. **Click the Finish button.**

If you're so inclined, you can change the width of the list before clicking Finish, but you can always do that on the datasheet, as the section about changing the appearance of the datasheet explains in Chapter 3 of this mini-book.

Suppose that you obtain the items from the wrong field or wrong database table? To fix that problem, select the field for which you created the list, and in Design view, select the Lookup tab (refer to Figure 2-10). Choose Text Box instead of Combo Box on the Display Control drop-down list and start all over.

Indexing for Faster Sorts, Searches, and Queries

Indexing means to instruct Access to keep information about the data in a field or combination of fields. Because Access keeps this information on hand, it doesn't have to actually search through every record in a database table to sort data, search for data, or run a query. In a large database table, indexes make sorting, searching, and querying go considerably faster because Access looks through its own data rather than the data in tables. The performance difference between querying a database table that has and has not been indexed is astonishing. That's the good news. The bad news is that indexes inflate the size of Access files.

By default, the field you choose as the primary key field is indexed. I recommend choosing other fields for indexing if you often conduct queries and searches. When you choose a field to index, choose one with data that varies from record to record and is likely to be the subject of searches, sorts, and queries. That way, the index means something. However, a field with data that is mostly the same from record to record is a waste of a good index, not to mention disk space. By the way, Access automatically indexes fields whose names include the words *ID, Code, Num,* and *Key,* the idea being that these fields are likely to store essential information worthy of indexing.

Indexing a field

To index a field, switch to Design view, select the field you want to index, and on the General tab of the Field Properties part of the Design window, open the Indexed drop-down list and choose one of these options:

+ **Yes (Duplicates OK):** Indexes the field and allows duplicate values to be entered in the field.

+ **Yes (No Duplicates):** Indexes the field and disallows duplicate values. If you choose this option, the field works something like a primary key field in that Access does not permit you to enter the same value in two different records.

Indexing based on more than one field

Creating indexes on more than one field makes sorting, querying, and searching the database table go faster. It's especially valuable in sorting operations where records in one field are often the same but records in a companion field are different. If you plan on searching through or sorting on individual fields, create an index on each field you plan on using.

A *multifield index* is one index created on multiple fields. Use this type of index when you plan on searching more than one field at a time. For example, if you're going to search through a database for *Bob Smith,* it's faster if you create a multifield index on the First Name and Last Name fields than if you created individual indexes for both fields.

Follow these steps to generate a multifield index:

Indexes

1. Starting in Design view, click the Indexes button in the Show/Hide group of the (Table Tools) Design tab.

You see the Indexes dialog box, as shown in Figure 2-11. The dialog box lists the primary key field already because it's indexed by default. You also see any fields to which you set the Indexed property to Yes.

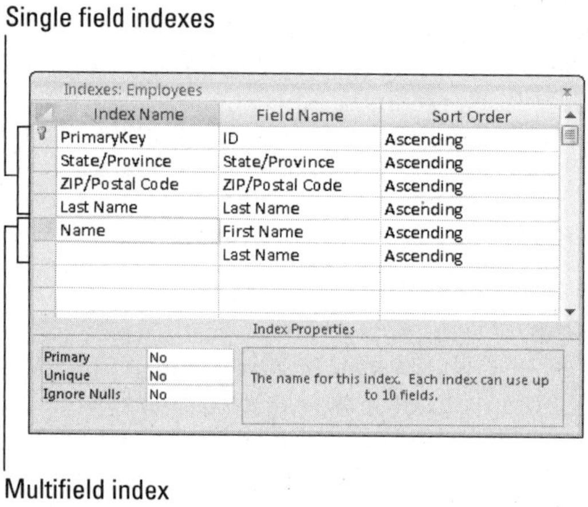

Single field indexes

Indexes: Employees			
Index Name	**Field Name**	**Sort Order**	
PrimaryKey	ID	Ascending	
State/Province	State/Province	Ascending	
ZIP/Postal Code	ZIP/Postal Code	Ascending	
Last Name	Last Name	Ascending	
Name	First Name	Ascending	
	Last Name	Ascending	

Index Properties

Primary	No	
Unique	No	The name for this index. Each index can use up
Ignore Nulls	No	to 10 fields.

Figure 2-11:
The Indexes
dialog box.

Multifield index

2. On a blank line in the dialog box, enter a name for the index in the Index Name column.

3. In the Field Name column, open the drop-down list and choose the first field you want for the multifield index.

Access sorts the records first on this field and then on the second field you choose.

4. In the next row, leave the Index Name blank and choose another field name from the drop-down list.

This field is the second field in the index. You can use as many as ten different fields in a multifield index. In Figure 2-11, two fields are in the index: First Name and Last Name.

5. Choose Descending in the Sort Order column if you want the field sorted in descending order.

Most of the time, you want leave the Sort Order set to Ascending because most people read from A to Z.

6. **Click the Close button.**

   Click the Indexes button in Design view if you need to return to the Indexes dialog box and change how fields are indexed.

Establishing Relationships between Database Tables

As the section about mapping the relationships between tables in Chapter 1 of this mini-book explains, you have to establish relationships between tables if you want to query or generate reports with data from more than one database table. Relationships define the field that two separate tables have in common. To understand why relationships between tables are necessary, consider the query shown in Figure 2-12. The purpose of this query is to list all companies that ordered items in 2006, list the companies by name, and list the city and country where each company is located. Figure 2-13 shows the results of the query.

Table relationship

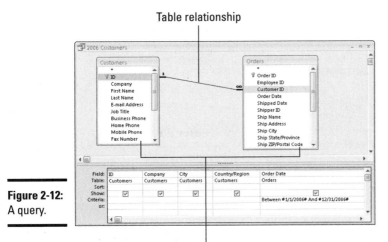

Tables being queried

Figure 2-12:
A query.

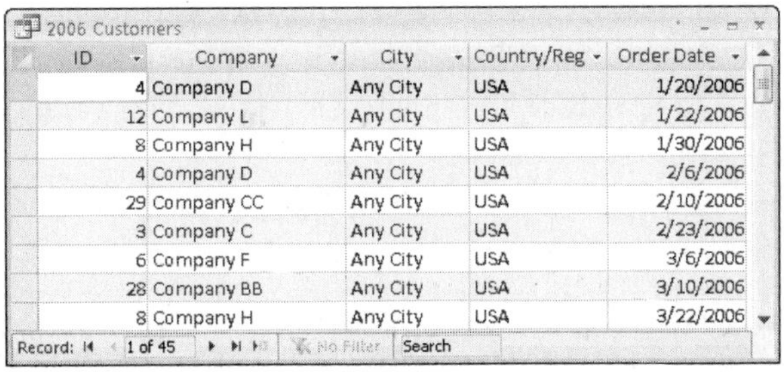

Figure 2-13:
Results of
the query in
Figure 2-12.

Consider what Access does to run this query:

✦ Access deals with two database tables, Customers and Orders.

✦ In the Orders table, Access looks in the Order Date field to isolate all records that describe orders made in the year 2006. The expression for finding these records is shown on the Criteria line in Figure 2-12: Between #1/1/2006# And #12/31/2006#.

✦ Because there is a relationship between the ID field in the Customers table and the Customer ID field in the Orders table — because the two fields hold the same type of information — Access can match the 2006 records it finds in the Orders table with corresponding records in the Customers table. Where the Customer ID of a 2006 record in the Orders table and an ID in the Customers table match, Access assembles a new record and places it in the query results. As Figure 2-13 demonstrates, the query records list customer IDs, company names, cities, countries, and order dates.

✦ Data for determining which records appear in the query results is found in the Order Date field in the Orders table. But the information compiled in the query results — customer IDs, company names, cities, and countries — comes from fields in the Customers table. Thanks to the relationship between the ID and Customer ID fields in these tables, Access can draw upon information from both tables.

Types of relationships

The vast majority of relationships between tables are *one-to-many relationships* between the primary key field in one database table and a field in another. Table relationships fall in these categories:

✦ **One-to-many relationship:** Each record in one table is linked to many records in another table. The relationship in Figure 2-12 is a one-to-many relationship. Each ID number appears only once in the ID field of the Customers table, but in the Orders table, the same Customer ID number can appear in many records because the same customer can order many different products. When you link tables, Access creates a one-to-many relationship when one of the fields being linked is either a primary key field or an indexed field assigned the No (No Duplicates) setting. (See "Indexing for Faster Sorts, Searches, and Queries" earlier in this chapter.)

✦ **One-to-one relationship:** Two fields are linked. This relationship is rare and is sometimes used for security purposes.

✦ **Many-to-many relationship:** This complex relationship actually describes crisscrossing relationships in which the linking field is not the primary key field in either table. To create a many-to-many relationship, an intermediary table called a *junction table* is needed. This relationship is rare.

Sometimes, fields in separate tables that hold the same data also have the same name, but that isn't necessary. For example, a field called ZIP Code in one table might be called Postal Code in another. What matters is that fields that are linked have the same data type and size. For example, you can't create a relationship between a text field and a number field.

Finding your way around the Relationships window

To display the tables in a database and link tables to one another or see how they're related to each other, click the Relationships button on the Database Tools tab. You see the Relationships window, as shown in Figure 2-14. Notice the field names in each table. The primary key field is shown with a picture of a key next to it. Lines in the window show how relationships have been established between tables.

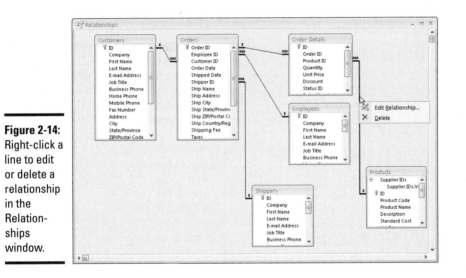

Figure 2-14:
Right-click a line to edit or delete a relationship in the Relationships window.

Apart from linking tables (a subject I explain shortly) in the Relationships window, here's all you need to know about this window:

✦ **Handling the tables:** Each table appears in its own window. Drag tables from place to place, drag a border to change a window's size, and scroll to see field names.

✦ **Removing a table from the window:** Right-click the table and choose Hide Table on the shortcut menu.

✦ **Removing all tables from the window:** Click the Clear Layout button on the (Relationship Tools) Design tab and select Yes in the confirmation box.

✦ **Placing tables back on the window:** To put selected tables back in the window, click the Show Table button, and in the Show Table dialog box, select the tables and click the Add button. To put all the tables with relationships back in the window, click the All Relationships button, also on the (Relationship Tools) Design tab.

✦ **Studying a table's relationships:** Click the Clear Layout button to remove all tables from the window; then place the table back in the window, select it, and click the Direct Relationships button on the (Relationship Tools) Design tab. All tables that are related to the selected table are added to the layout.

Placing tables in the Relationships window

The first time you open the Relationships window, you see the Show Table dialog box. The purpose of this dialog box is to find out which tables to put in the Relationships window. Ctrl+click to select tables and then click the Add button.

If you create a new database table and need to place it in the Relationships window, click the Relationships button to display the Relationships window; then click the Show Table button on the (Relationship Tools) Design tab. The Show Table dialog box appears. Select your new table and click the Add button.

Show Table   ? ✕

Tables   Queries   Both

Address Book
Customers
Customers_Copy
Employee Privileges
Employees
Inventory Restocking
Inventory Restocking Details
Inventory Transactions
Invoices
Order Details
Order Details Status
Orders
Orders Status
Privileges
Products

Add   Close

Forging relationships between tables

Make sure that both tables are on display in the Relationships window and then follow these steps to forge a relationship between them:

1. Click to select the field in one table; then hold down the mouse button, drag the pointer to the field in the other table where you want to forge the link, and release the mouse button.

You see the Edit Relationships dialog box, as shown in Figure 2-15. This dragging between table fields is probably the most awkward thing you undertake in Office 2007! If you do it right, a bar appears where the pointer is while you move it over the second table, and the names of the two fields appear in the Edit Relationships dialog box.

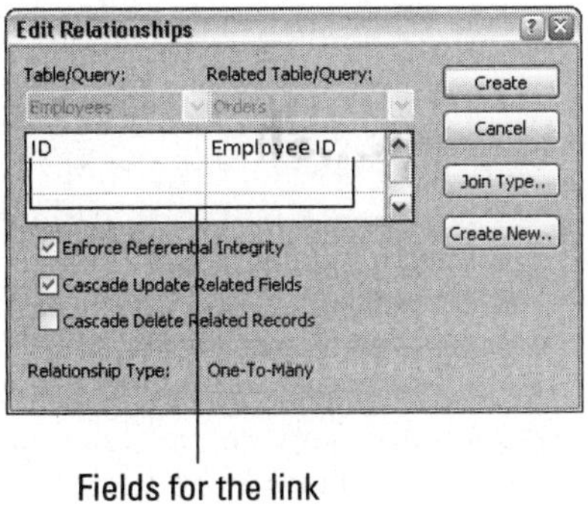

Figure 2-15:
Creating a
table
relationship.

Fields for the link

Notice the Relationship Type at the bottom of the dialog box. If you accidentally create a link to the wrong field, choose the correct field from the drop-down list in the dialog box.

2. Select the Enforce Referential Integrity check box.

If you don't select this box, the relationship between the tables is indeterminate, instead of being a one-to-many relationship. *Referential integrity* (another hideous database term!) has to do with whether values in the two different fields corroborate each other.

3. (Optional) Select Cascade options.

One of these options is excellent, and the other is dangerous:

* *Cascade Update Related Fields:* If you change a value on the "one" side of the relationship, a matching value on the "many" side changes as well to preserve referential integrity. For example, if

you create a multifield primary key of First Name and Last Name and then change the name of someone, the related fields in the other table change automatically to preserve referential integrity. This is a great way to make sure that information is up to date.

- *Cascade Delete Related Records:* If you delete a record in the "one" table, all records in the "many" table to which the deleted record is linked are also deleted. In Figure 2-15, for example, if I delete an employee from the "one" table, all records in the "many" table that include that employee are deleted! Access warns you before making the deletion, but still! This option is dangerous, and I don't recommend selecting it.

4. **Click the Create button to forge the relationship.**

   In the Relationships window (refer to Figure 2-14), a line is drawn between the table fields. The number 1 appears on the "one" side of the relationship and the infinity symbol (∞) appears on the "many" side.

If you mistakenly establish a relationship between the wrong fields, right-click the line between the fields, choose Delete on the shortcut menu (refer to Figure 2-14), and select Yes in the confirmation box. Choose Edit Relationship to open the Edit Relationship dialog box and rethink the link (hey, that rhymes!).

After you create a one-to-many relationship between tables with the Enforce Referential Integrity check box selected, you can't enter a value in the "many" table unless it's already in the "one" table. For example, suppose that the "one" table includes a primary key field called Employee Number, and this field is linked to a field in the "many" table that's also called Employee Number. If you enter an Employee Number in the "many" table that isn't in the "one" table, Access warns you that it can't be done without violating referential integrity. The best way to solve this problem is to create a lookup data-entry list in the "many" table with values from the primary key field in the "one" table. See "Creating a lookup data-entry list," earlier in this chapter.

To generate and print an Access report that shows how tables in your database are linked, open the Relationships window and click the Relationship Report button on the (Relationship Tools) Design tab. Then save the report and print it. I explain Access reports in Chapter 5 of this mini-book.

Subdatasheets

In Datasheet view, Access gives you the opportunity to view the "many" records that are linked to a field when a relationship is established between tables. The records appear on a *subdatasheet*. In the database shown in this illustration, the Orders and Order Details tables are linked on the Order ID field — the primary key of the Orders table and the "one" side of the relationship. In the Order Details table, I can click the plus sign (+) in a record to see the "many" records that are linked to Order ID, the primary key field. For this illustration, I clicked the plus sign to see the details for Order 31. The information on the subdatasheet comes from the Order Details table. Click the minus sign (–) to hide a subdatasheet.

Orders					
Order ID ▾	Employee ▾	Customer ▾	Order Date ▾	Shipped Date ▾	
⊞ 30	Anne Hellung-Larsen	Company AA	1/15/2007	1/22/2006	Shi
⊟ 31	Jan Kotas	Company D	1/20/2006	1/22/2006	Shi

	ID ▾	Product ▾	Quantity ▾	Unit Price ▾	Discount ▾	Sta
	29	Northwind Traders Dried Pears	10	$30.00	0.00%	Invoi
	30	Northwind Traders Dried Apples	10	$53.00	0.00%	Invoi
	31	Northwind Traders Dried Plums	10	$3.50	0.00%	Invoi
*	(New)		0	$0.00	0.00%	

Order ID	Employee	Customer	Order Date	Shipped Date	
⊞ 32	Mariya Sergienko	Company L	1/22/2006	1/22/2006	Shi
⊞ 33	Michael Neipper	Company H	1/30/2006	1/31/2006	Shi
⊞ 34	Anne Hellung-Larsen	Company D	2/6/2006	2/7/2006	Shi

Record: I◄ ◄ 1 of 3 ► ►I ►▣ 🔧 No Filter   Search

Chapter 3: Entering the Data

In This Chapter

✔ **Entering data on a datasheet**

✔ **Changing the look of a datasheet**

✔ **Creating a form for entering data**

✔ **Finding records in a field or database table**

✔ **Finding and replacing your data**

*A*t last — you can start entering the data. If you set up your database tables, named the fields, and established relationships between the tables, you're ready to go. This short chapter explains how to enter the data in a database table. It shows you how to enter data on a datasheet or enter data by way of a form. This chapter also describes how to find missing records in case one goes astray.

There's no getting around it. Entering data is truly a tedious activity. But if you set up the fields well and take advantage of input masks and other field properties, it isn't so bad. It's better than stepping on a shovel blade, anyway.

The Two Ways to Enter Data

When it comes to entering data in a database table, you can take your pick between Datasheet view and a form. Figure 3-1 compares and contrasts the two. Here are the advantages of entering data in Datasheet view:

✦ Many records appear at once.

✦ You can compare data easily between records.

✦ You can sort by column with the commands in the Sort and Filter group on the Home tab (as discussed in Chapter 4 of this mini-book).

✦ You can scroll up or down to locate records.

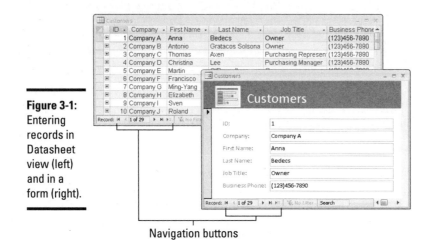

Figure 3-1:
Entering
records in
Datasheet
view (left)
and in a
form (right).

Navigation buttons

Here are the advantages of entering the data in a form:

✦ You don't have to scroll left or right to see all the fields.

✦ You can display data in a logical format instead of rows and columns.

✦ Fields are clearly labeled so that you always know what to enter.

Entering the Data in Datasheet View

Entering data in Datasheet view is like entering data in a conventional table. As with a table, a datasheet has columns and rows. Records are entered in rows, and each column represents a field. Fans of Datasheet view like being able to look at a dozen records simultaneously. They like being able to open subdatasheets. (Chapter 2 of this mini-book explains what those are.) For fans of Datasheet view, these pages explain how to enter data in a datasheet and change a datasheet's appearance.

Database tables open in Datasheet view when you double-click their names in the Navigation pane. But if you happen to be gazing at a table in Design view, click the View command on the far left of the Home tab.

Entering data

In Datasheet view, the bottom of the window tells you how many records were entered in the datasheet and which record the pointer is in. To enter a new record, move to a new, empty row and start entering the data. To create a new row, do one of the following:

+ Click the New command in the Records group on the Home tab.

+ Click the New Record button in the Navigation buttons that appear at the bottom of the Datasheet view window.

+ Scroll to the bottom of the Datasheet view window and begin typing in the row with an asterisk (*) next to it.

+ Press Ctrl++ (the plus key).

A pencil icon appears on the row selector to let you know which record you're dealing with. To get from field to field, click in a field, press the Tab key, or press Enter. Table 3-1 lists keyboard shortcuts for getting around in a datasheet.

Book VI
Chapter 3

Entering the Data

Table 3-1	Datasheet Shortcuts
Press. . .	*To Move. . .*
↑	To the previous record. You can also press the Previous button on the Navigation buttons.
↓	To the next record. You can also press the Next button.
Tab or Enter	To the next field in the record.
Shift+Tab	To the previous field in the record.
Home	To the first field in the record.
End	To the last field in the record.
Ctrl+Home	To the first field in the first record. You can also press the First button.
Ctrl+End	To the last field in the last record. You can also press the Last button.
Page Up	Up one screen.
Page Down	Down one screen.

To delete a record, click its row selector and then click the Delete command in the Records group on the Home tab, or press the Delete key. Access asks whether you really want to delete the record. Click Yes in the confirmation box.

Two tricks for entering data quicker

In a database table with many fields, it's sometimes hard to tell what data to enter. When the pointer is in the sixth or seventh field, for example, you can lose sight of the first field, the one on the left side of the datasheet that usually identifies the person or item whose record you're entering. To freeze a field so that it appears on-screen no matter how far you travel toward the right side of the datasheet, right-click the column's heading and choose Freeze Columns from the shortcut menu. To unfreeze the fields, right-click the column heading and choose Unfreeze All Columns from the shortcut menu. You can freeze more than one field by dragging across field names at the top of the datasheet before choosing to freeze the columns. Is it getting cold in here?

Another way to handle the problem of not being able to identify where data is supposed to be entered is to hide columns in the datasheet. To perform this trick, select the columns you want to hide by dragging the pointer across their names; then right-click the column heading and choose Hide Columns from the shortcut menu. To see the columns again, right-click any column heading and choose Unhide Columns from the shortcut menu. Any fields that are checked appear in the datasheet.

The fastest way to hide a column is to drag the border between it and the next column to the left until the column disappears.

Entering data in the Zoom box

To make putting a long entry in a field a little easier, Access offers the Zoom box. Instead of having to stay within the narrow confines of a datasheet field, you can press Shift+F2 to open the Zoom box and enter the data there. After you click OK, the data is entered in the field. The Zoom box is especially convenient for entering data in a Memo field. As Chapter 2 in this mini-book explains, Memo fields can hold a whopping 65,535 characters, including rich text. Move the cursor into a field and press Shift+F2 to open the Zoom box and read all the text in the field.

Zoom   x

This is Rich Text Field. It allows me to make things **BOLD** or *Italic* or ***BOTH.*** I can even make things RED or BLUE. The Zoom box allows me to edit text in this window instead of a small field on a datasheet.|

OK

Cancel

Font...

Changing the appearance of the datasheet

To make the datasheet a little less cluttered and unwieldy, try experimenting with its appearance. Access offers a few handy shortcuts for doing just that:

✦ **Rearranging columns:** To move a column to a different location, click its name at the top of the datasheet and drag it to the left or right.

✦ **Resizing columns:** Move the pointer between column names at the top of the datasheet, and when you see the double-headed arrow, click and start dragging. To make a column just large enough to fit its widest entry, move the pointer between column names and double-click when you see the double-headed arrow.

✦ **Changing fonts:** The default font for a datasheet is Calibri 11-point, but you can choose commands in the Font group on the Home tab to perhaps make entering data a little less mind-numbing.

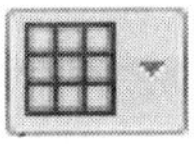

✦ **Changing the look of gridlines:** Open the drop-down list on the Gridlines button and choose options to change the number and thickness of gridlines.

✦ **Alternate row colors:** Open the drop-down list on the Alternate Fill/Back Color button and choose options to change the background colors of the datasheet or to add a background color to alternating rows.

To experiment all at one time with the many options for changing a datasheet's appearance, click the Font group button on the Home tab and play with options in the Datasheet Formatting dialog box, as shown in Figure 3-2. If you want a customized look for all the datasheets you work on, click the Office button and select Access Options. Then select Datasheet in the left pane of the Access Options dialog box and go to town.

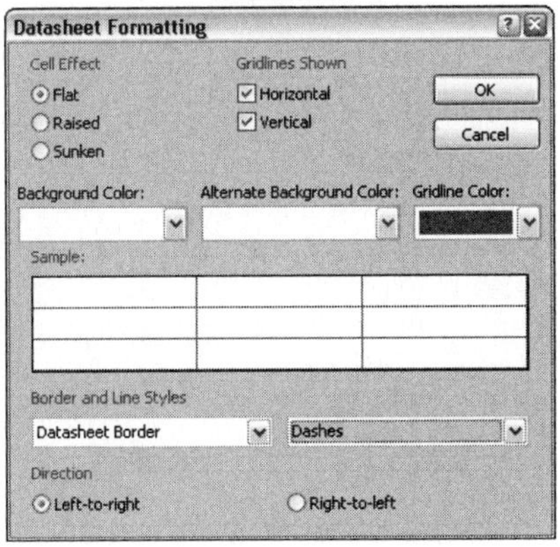

Figure 3-2:
The Datasheet Formatting dialog box.

Entering the Data in a Form

Forms like the one shown in Figure 3-3 are very convenient for entering data. The labels tell you exactly what to enter. Personally, I prefer entering data in a form to entering data on a datasheet. On a form, you take it one step — make that one record — at a time. Not looking at a dozen records makes the task of entering data a little easier. These pages explain how to create a form for entering information in a database table. You also get tried-and-true advice for moving around with the Navigation buttons.

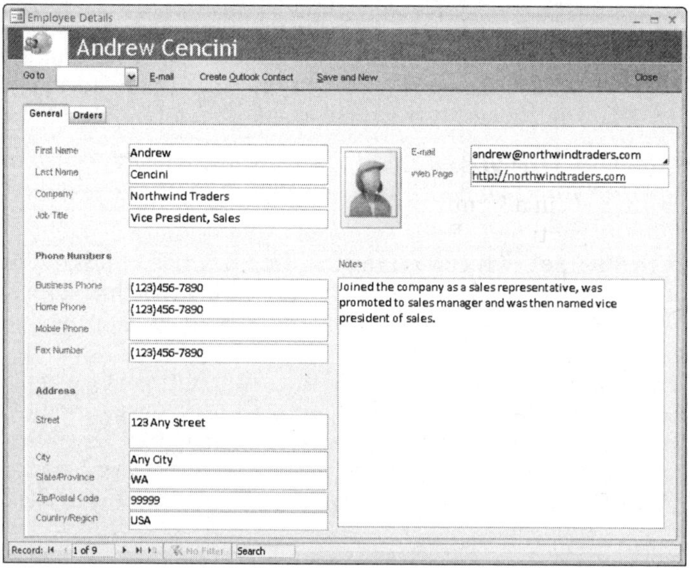

Figure 3-3:
A form.

Creating a form

Fortunately, the Form Wizard makes it very simple to create a form for entering information in a database table. All you have to do is start the wizard, choose the table, and make a couple of design decisions. To create a form, click the Create tab and choose Form Wizard from the More Forms drop-down list. You see the first of several Form Wizard dialog boxes. Answer these questions and keep clicking the Next button until the time comes to click Finish:

✦ **Tables/Queries:** From the drop-down list, choose the name of the database table you need to enter data in.

✦ **Selected Fields:** Click the >> button to enter all the field names in the Select Fields box.

+ **Layout:** Select the Columnar option button. The other layouts aren't much good for entering data in a table. If you choose Tabular or Datasheet, you may as well enter data straight into the datasheet rather than rely on a form.

+ **Style:** Choose a look for the form.

Click the Save button to save and name your form. (I suggest naming it after the database table you create it for.) When you want to enter data by way of the form you create, select the Forms group in the Navigation pane and double-click the form.

If you're in a hurry to create a form, select a table in the Navigation pane and click the Create tab. Select Form, Split Form, or Multiple Items from the Forms group. Just like magic, Access creates a new form for you.

Entering the data

To enter data in a form, click the New Record button on the Navigation buttons and start typing. Press the Tab key, press the Enter key, or click to move from field to field. You can move backwards through the fields by pressing Shift+Tab. If you enter half a record and want to start over, press the Esc key to empty the current field. Press Esc again to empty all the fields.

The Navigation buttons (refer to Figure 3-3) at the bottom of the form window tell you how many records are in the database table and which record you're looking at. Click the different Navigation buttons to do the following:

+ Go to the first record in the database table. You can also press Ctrl+Home.

+ Go to the previous record.

+ Go to the next record.

+ Go to the last record. You can also press Ctrl+End.

To delete a record from a form, click the Delete command's drop-down list in the Records group on the Home tab, and choose Delete Record. Access asks whether you really want to delete the record. Click Yes in the confirmation box.

Finding a Missing Record

Sometimes data goes astray. You scroll through a datasheet but simply can't find the item or record you need so bad. For times like those, Access offers the Find command. Use the command to scour a database for errant information.

Open the database table with the data that needs finding. If you know in which field the data is located, click in the field. You can save a little time that way. Then click the Find command on the far right of the Home tab or press Ctrl+F. You see the Find and Replace dialog box, as shown in Figure 3-4. Fill in the dialog box as follows:

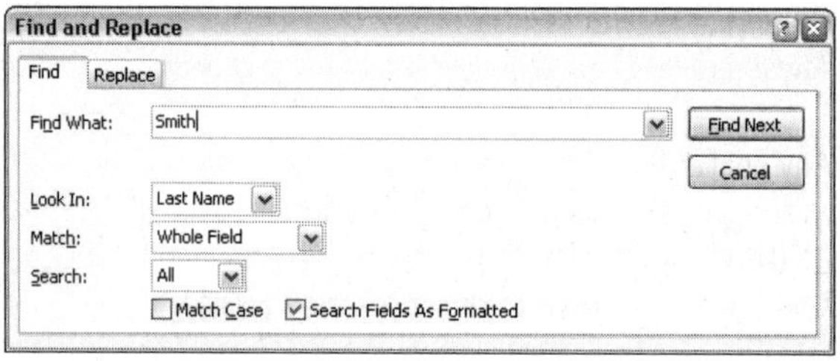

Figure 3-4:
Finding
data.

Find and Replace dialog box showing Find What: Smith, Look In: Last Name, Match: Whole Field, Search: All, Search Fields As Formatted checked, with Find Next and Cancel buttons.

+ **Find What:** Enter the item you're looking for. If you're looking for a null value, enter **null** in this text box. Enter **""** (two double-quotation marks) to find zero-length strings. Table 3-2 describes the wildcard characters you can use in searches.

+ **Look In:** If you click in a field before choosing the Find command, the field's name appears in this box. To search the entire database table, choose its name from the drop-down list.

+ **Match:** Choose the option that describes what you know about the item. Choosing the Any Part of Field option can make for a long search. For example, a search for the letters *chin* finds, among others, China, Ching, and itching — any word with the consecutive letters *chin*.

+ **Search:** Choose an option — All, Up, or Down — that describes which direction to start searching.

+ **Match Case:** If you know the combination of upper- and lowercase letters you're after and you enter the combination in the Find What text box, select this check box.

+ **Search Fields As Formatted:** If you're searching for a field that has been formatted a certain way, select this check box and make sure that the text or numbers you enter in the Find What text box are formatted correctly. For example, if you're searching for a record with the date July 31, 1958, and you choose the *mm/dd/yyyy* format, enter the date as 07/31/1958.

Click the Find Next button to conduct the search. The item might be found in more than one location. Keep clicking Find Next until you find the item or you die of thirst on the hot sands of the digital desert.

Table 3-2	Wildcard Characters for Searches	
Character	*Description*	*Example*
?	A single character	**b?t** finds *bat, bet, bit,* and *but.*
#	A single numeric digit	**9411#** finds *94111, 94112, 94113,* and so on.
*	Any group of consecutive characters	**t*o** finds *to, two,* and *tattoo.*
[xyz]	Any character in the brackets	**t[aio]pper** finds *tapper, tipper,* and *topper,* but not *tupper.*
[!xy]	Any character not in the brackets	**p[!io]t** finds *pat* and *pet,* but not *pit* and *pot.*
x–z	Any character in a range of characters	**[1–4]000** finds *1000, 2000, 3000,* and *4000,* but not *5000.* The range must be in ascending order.

To quickly find the first value of a search term, start typing in the Search box at the bottom of the form window (refer to Figure 3-3), and the pointer jumps to find the data while you type. Access finds only the first value, but you can press Ctrl+F and click Find Next to find the next match. This works in forms and in Datasheet view.

Finding and Replacing Data

Finding and replacing data is remarkably similar to finding data. The difference is that you enter data in the Replace With text box as well as the familiar Find What text box and other option boxes. Figure 3-5 shows the Replace tab of the Find and Replace dialog box. Does it look familiar? If it doesn't, read the preceding section in this chapter.

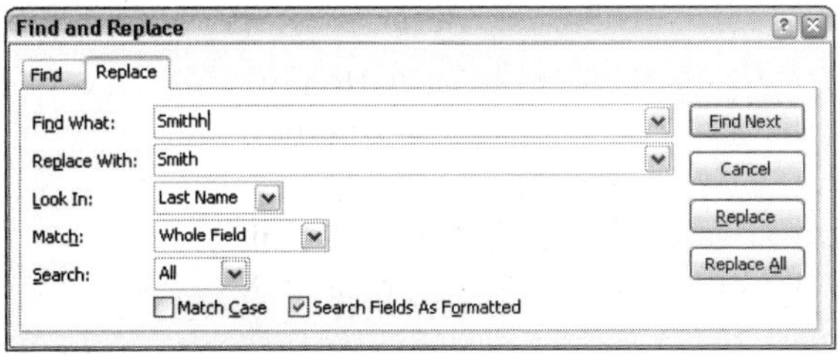

Figure 3-5: Replacing data.

Choose Replace from the Find group on the Home tab (or press Ctrl+H) to open the Replace tab of the Find and Replace dialog box. After you enter the replacement data in the Replace With text box, make sure that Whole Field is selected in the Match drop-down list. Conducting a find-and-replace operation with Any Part of Field or Start of Field selected in the Match drop-down list can have unintended consequences. For example, a search for *Brook* also finds *Brooklyn, Middlebrook,* and other words that include *brook.* Blindly replacing the *brook* text string with *stream* produces, for example, *Streamlyn* and *Middlestream.*

Unless you're as confident as a gambler with four aces, don't click the Replace All button to replace all instances of the text or numbers in the database table or field you're searching in. Instead, click the Replace button to find and replace text or numbers one instance at a time.

You can also find and replace data with an update query. See the section about update queries in Chapter 4 of this mini-book.

Chapter 4: Sorting, Querying, and Filtering for Data

In This Chapter

✔ Sorting, or rearranging, records in a database table

✔ Filtering records in a table to see only the records you need

✔ Querying to collect and examine information stored in a database

✔ Looking at different kinds of queries

*N*ow that you've laid the groundwork, you can put your database through its paces and make it do what databases are meant to do — provide information of one kind or another. This chapter explains how to pester a database for names, addresses, dates, statistical averages, and what not. It shows how to sort records and filter a database table to see records of a certain kind. You also find out how to query a database to get it to yield its dirty little secrets and invaluable information.

Sorting Records in a Database Table

Sorting rearranges records in a database table (or subdatasheet) so that the records appear in alphabetical, numerical, or date order in one field. By sorting the records in a database, you can locate records faster. What's more, being able to sort data means that you don't have to bother about the order in which you enter records because you can always sort them later to put them in a particular order.

Records can be sorted in ascending or descending order:

✦ **Ascending order:** Arranges records in alphabetical order from A to Z, numbers from smallest to largest, and dates chronologically from earliest to latest.

✦ **Descending order:** Arranges text from Z to A, numbers from largest to smallest, and dates chronologically from latest to earliest.

The database tables, as shown in Figure 4-1, present the same information. In the table on the left, records have been sorted in ascending order in the Order

ID field. In the table on the right, records have been sorted in descending order in the Order Date field. Notice the sort indicator in the column heading; ↑ indicates an ascending sort, and ↓ indicates a descending sort.

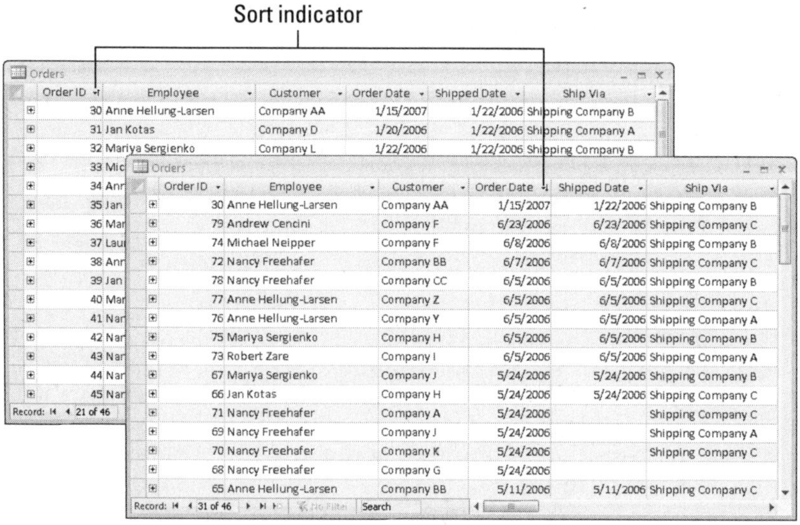

Sort indicator

Figure 4-1:
Sorting a
database
table.

Follow these steps to sort the records in a database table:

1. **In Datasheet view, click anywhere in the field by which you want to sort the records.**

2. **Click the Sort A to Z or Sort Z to A button in the Sort & Filter group on the Home tab.**

You can also right-click a field name at the top of a column and choose to sort from A to Z or Z to A on the shortcut menu. The menu choices change based on the type of data. For Number fields, you can sort smallest to largest and vice versa; for Date fields, choose to sort oldest to newest, or vice versa.

You can sort on more than one field by clicking a field and sorting ascending or descending and then clicking a second field and sorting ascending or descending. Just make sure you sort the fields in reverse order. For example, to sort the database by the Employee, Customer, and Order ID fields, click in Order ID and then sort it ascending; click in Customer and then sort it ascending; click in Employee and then sort it ascending. If you mess up and forget how the table is sorted, click the Clear All Sorts button — located underneath the Sort A to Z and Sort Z to A buttons on the Home tab.

Filtering to Find Information

Filtering isolates all the records in a database table that have the same field values or nearly the same field values. Instead of all the records in the table appearing on the datasheet, only records that meet the search criteria appear, as shown in Figure 4-2. The basic idea behind filtering is to choose a field value in the database table and use it as the standard for finding or excluding records. For example, you can find all the orders for a particular customer, all orders taken in the month of April, or all the orders that a particular customer placed in April. For that matter, you can filter by exclusion and see the records of all the orders in a database table *not* taken in April and *not* for a particular customer. Filtering is useful when you need to find records with specific information in a single database table.

Figure 4-2:
Results of
a filtering
operation.

Filter indicators

Different ways to filter a database table

Here are shorthand descriptions of the four ways to filter a database table. These techniques are described in detail in the upcoming pages.

✦ **Common Filters:** Select from several popular filters by clicking the icon in the column header. This type of filter is available for all field types except OLE Objects and calculated fields. This filtering method keeps you from spending time trying to get the filter criteria correct.

✦ **Filter by Selection:** Select all or part of a field in the database table and click the Selection button in the Sort & Filter group on the Home tab. Access isolates all records with the data you select. This method works best when you can't quite decide what you're looking for and permits you to look for data found in the whole field or in part of a field. It even lets you filter data that doesn't match the selection.

✦ **Filter by Form:** With the database table displayed, select Filter by Form from the drop-down list on the Advanced button. You see a form with one drop-down list for each field in your table. From the drop-down lists, make choices to describe the records you're looking for and then click the Toggle Filter button. This method is more flexible than filtering by selection because you can choose more than one field to filter with and you can search for different kinds of information in the same field. For example, you can isolate the records of people named Smith who also live in California, or the people who live in California or New York.

✦ **Advanced Filter/Sort:** Choose Advanced Filter/Sort from the drop-down list on the Advanced button, and in the Filter window, drag the name of the field you're filtering onto the grid. Then enter a search criterion, choose a Sort option, and click the Apply Filter button. This filtering technique has more in common with queries than filters. Truth be told, the Advanced Filter/Sort command is merely a way to query a single table.

You can tell when you're looking at a subset of filtered records rather than a database table because Filtered appears at the bottom of the window next to the Navigation buttons (refer to Figure 4-2). Also, the filter icon (a funnel) appears in the column heading, and the Toggle Filter command on the Ribbon appears highlighted. If you can't tell if a table has been filtered, a trip to the eye doctor is long overdue.

When you have finished filtering a database table and you want to see all the records in the table again, click the Toggle Filter button in the Sort & Filter group on the Home tab or click Filtered at the bottom of the window. To apply the same filter, click Toggle Filter or Unfiltered at the bottom of the window. After you define a filter, you can turn it on and off using these methods. To clear the filter so that you can start over, choose Clear All Filters from the drop-down list on the Advanced button. After you clear the filter, you can't use it again unless you rebuild it.

Common filters

A *common filter* is a powerful new tool that lets you get data that you want in a clear, easy-to-use interface. The list of filters that are available depends on the selected field's data type and values. Because a picture is worth a thousand words, take a look at Figure 4-3 to see the Filtering options for the Category field.

Clicking the down arrow in the column heading shows the available options for that field. From this menu, you can sort the field as ascending or descending, clear the filter for the field, apply patterns and ranges (text, number, and date) for the field, and select check boxes for actual data values. You don't have to remember all the data in a field. Let the database do the work for you.

Custom text filters for the Category field let you define patterns of data. For Text fields, you can select a filter that equals, begins with, contains, or ends with a value. You can also select a filter that doesn't match any of those specifications. Choose the option from the Text Filters submenu, and a Custom Filter dialog box appears, enabling you to enter the filter's criteria.

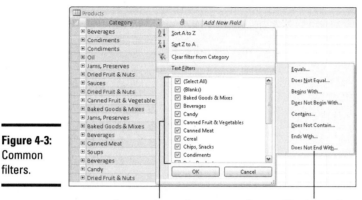

Figure 4-3:
Common
filters.

Current data values   Custom filtering options

Custom number filters include filtering for data that equals, does not equal, is greater than, is less than, or between two values. Date fields let you choose from these same options but add many more for today, tomorrow, this quarter, last quarter, and way too many more to mention here. This book is heavy enough!

The hands-down, best in show Filtering option is the list of data values at the bottom of the menu. From this list, select and deselect the data values you want to see and then click OK. If you just want to see Beverages and Cereal, for example, check those values in the list.

To filter one or two items in the list, deselect the Select All check box to clear all the check boxes and then select the values that you want to see in your filter. To see records that don't contain any values in the selected field, select the Blanks check box.

Filtering by selection

Filtering by selection is the fastest way to filter a database table. It's also the best way when you're not sure what you're looking for because you can search for partial words and phrases. Follow these steps to filter by selection:

1. **Display the database table that needs filtering in Datasheet view.**

2. **Tell Access how to filter the records.**

To find all records with the same value or text in a particular field, simply click in a field with the value or text. If you aren't quite sure what to look for, select part of a field. For example, to find all names that start with the letters *St,* select St in one of the name fields.

3. **Click the Selection button in the Sort & Filter group on the Home tab to display the Selection options.**

The options are similar to the custom filter options described in "Common filters," only these options are specific to the data in the current cell. For example, if you click a Last Name field that contains the name *Smith* and click the Selection command, you see options, such as Equals Smith and Does Not Contain Smith. Select an option, and the filter is applied immediately.

Filtering by form

Filtering by form permits you to search more than one field in a database table as well as search fields more than once. For example, you can tell Access to look in the Last Name field for people named *Martinez,* as well as look in the City field for *Martinezes* who live in Los Angeles *or* San Francisco. Searching twice in the same field is an *OR search.* To be included in the filtering results, a record has only to satisfy one *or* the other criterion. Follow these steps to filter by form:

1. **In Datasheet view, choose Filter by Form from the drop-down list on the Advanced button.**

Only field names appear on the datasheet, as shown in Figure 4-4.

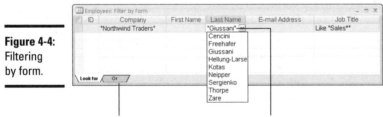

Figure 4-4:
Filtering
by form.

Click to search more than
once in the same field.

Select or enter a criterion.

2. **Click in a field, open its drop-down list, and choose the value or text you want to search for.**

To search in more than one field, open another drop-down list and choose a value or text entry from it. In Number and Currency fields, you can enter comparison operators to search for values. Table 4-1 explains the comparison operators.

3. **To perform an Or search on the data, click the Or tab and then choose a value or text from the drop-down list in any field.**

   When you click the Or tab, the search choices you made previously disappear from the screen. Don't worry — Access remembers them on the Look For tab. You can click the Or tab again if you want to enter more criteria for Or searching.

4. **Click the Toggle Filter button.**

   The results of the filtering operation appear in the datasheet.

Table 4-1	Comparison Operators for Filtering and Querying	
Operator	*Name*	*Example*
<	Less than	<10, any number smaller than ten
<=	Less than or equal to	<=10, ten as well as any number smaller than ten
>	Greater than	>10, any number larger than ten
>=	Greater than or equal to	>=10, ten as well as any number equal to or larger than ten
=	Equal to	=10, ten — not any other number
<>	Not equal to	<>10; all numbers except ten (instead of <>, you can enter the word not)
Between . . . And . . .	Between	Between 10 And 15, a number between 10 and 15 or equal to 10 or 15

If you click the Filter by Form button to try to filter by form a second time, the criteria you entered previously appear in the datasheet window. Choose Clear Grid — also in the drop-down list on the Advanced button — to empty the datasheet and start all over.

Some kinds of filtering operations can be saved and ran again, but to save them, you must save them as queries. With the desired filter in Filter by Form view, choose Save As Query from the drop-down list on the Advanced button; then enter a name in the Save As Query dialog box and click OK to save results of the filtering operation. Choose Load from Query to apply the saved filter. Later in this chapter, "Querying: The Basics" explains how to run queries.

Running an Advanced Filter/Sort

This command — choose Advanced Filter/Sort from the drop-down list on the Advanced button to activate — works exactly like a query except that it works on only one database table. If you're tempted to use this command, resist the temptation. Run a query instead.

The difference between a filter and a query

The biggest difference between filtering and querying is that you can save a query and call upon it more than once. Queries are kept at the ready in the Navigation pane. A filter, on the other hand, is as good as the first time you use it, although you can save and run it as a query. Filters apply to a single database table, whereas you can query to assemble information from more than one table. In the results of a query, you can include as many fields as you want, but the results of a filtering operation show all the fields in the database table, whether you want them or not.

When it comes to examining data, a query is more sophisticated than a filter. Although you can use standard comparison operators to find records by filtering, querying gives you the opportunity to use complex expressions as well as comparison operators. You can filter, for example, to find people whose income is greater than or less than a certain amount. However, because you can write expressions in queries, you can query to find people whose income falls within a certain range.

Querying: The Basics

Querying means to ask a question of a database and get an answer in the form of records that meet the query criteria. Query when you want to ask a detailed question of a database. "Who lives in Los Angeles and donated more than $500 last year?" is an example of a query. So is, "Which orders were purchased by people who live in California and therefore, have to pay sales tax, and how much sales tax was charged with these orders?" A query can search for information in more than one database table. For that matter, you can query other queries for information. A query can be as sophisticated or as simple as you need it to be. In the results of the query, you can show all the fields in a database table or only a few necessary fields.

Access offers several different ways to query a database. (The techniques are described later in this chapter in "Six Kinds of Queries.") Still, no matter which kind of query you're dealing with, the basics of setting up and running a query are the same. You start with the Create tab to build new queries. Or, you use the Queries group in the Navigation pane to open an existing query by double-clicking its name. The following pages introduce you to queries, how to create them, and how to modify them.

Creating a new query

To create a new query, start from the Create tab and click Query Design or Query Wizard (in the Other group).

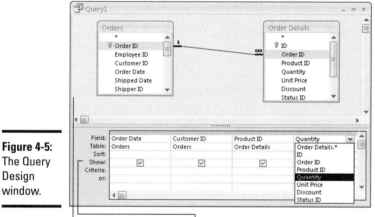

✦ **Create the query in Design view:** Click the Query Design button to see the Query Design window, as shown in Figure 4-5, as well as the Show Table dialog box for telling Access which database tables to query. Construct your query in the Query Design window (the following pages explain how).

Figure 4-5: The Query Design window.

Table pane   Design grid

✦ **Create the query with a wizard:** Click the Query Wizard button to display the New Query dialog box and then choose a wizard option (four possible Query Wizards are available) and answer the questions that the Query Wizard asks. You're asked which table or tables to query, which fields to include in the query, and which fields to include in the query results (the following pages explain these issues).

Finding your way around the Query Design window

The Query Design window (see Figure 4-5) is where you construct a query or retool a query you constructed already. You see this window straightaway after you click the Query Design button to construct a new query. Right-click a query in the Navigation pane and then choose Design View on the shortcut menu to open the Query Design window and fiddle with the query design to make it better.

The Query Design window is divided into halves:

✦ **Table pane:** Lists the database tables you're querying as well as the fields in each table. You can drag the tables to new locations or drag a table border to change its size and view more fields.

✦ **Design grid:** Lists which fields to query from the tables, how to sort the query results, which fields to show in the query results, and criteria for locating records in fields.

To run a query starting in the Query Design window, click the Run button in the Results group on the (Query Tools) Design tab.

Run

Choosing which database tables to query

To choose which database tables (and queries as well) to get information from, click the Show Table button in the Query Setup group on the (Query Tools) Design tab. You see the Show Table dialog box. The Tables tab lists all the database tables you create for your database. Ctrl+click to select the tables you want to query and then click the Add button. To query a query, go to the Queries tab and select the query.

Show Table

The tables and queries you choose appear in the Table pane of the Query Design window (refer to Figure 4-5). To remove a table from a query, right-click it in the Table pane and choose Remove Table on the shortcut menu.

In order to query more than one table, you need to establish relationships between tables. (See the section in Chapter 2 of this mini-book about establishing relationships between database tables.) So-called *join lines* in the Query Design window show how the tables are related to one another.

If you haven't defined relationships between the tables, you can still join them together by dragging a field from one table onto a field in another table. This is the same method used to create relationships between tables. Joining tables in a query doesn't create an actual relationship; it's just a temporary join for the sake of the query.

Choosing which fields to query

If you selected which tables to query, the next step is to choose which fields to query from the tables you selected. The field names in each table appear in the Table pane. The object is to list fields from the Table pane in the first row of the Design grid, as shown in Figure 4-6. As the figure shows, the fields whose names you enter in the Design grid are the fields that produce query results.

Field:	Order Date	Customer ID	Product ID	Quantity	Unit Price	
Table:	Orders	Orders	Order Details	Order Details	Order Details	
Sort:						
Show:	☑	☑	☑	☑	☑	
Criteria:						
or:						

Query1

Order Date	Customer	Product	Quantity	Unit Price
1/15/2007	Company AA	Northwind Traders Beer	100	$14.00
1/15/2007	Company AA	Northwind Traders Dried Plums	30	$3.50
1/20/2006	Company D	Northwind Traders Dried Pears	10	$30.00
1/20/2006	Company D	Northwind Traders Dried Apples	10	$53.00
1/20/2006	Company D	Northwind Traders Dried Plums	10	$3.50
1/22/2006	Company L	Northwind Traders Chai	15	$18.00
1/22/2006	Company L	Northwind Traders Coffee	20	$46.00
1/30/2006	Company H	Northwind Traders Chocolate Biscuits Mix	30	$9.20
2/6/2006	Company D	Northwind Traders Chocolate Biscuits Mix	20	$9.20
2/10/2006	Company CC	Northwind Traders Chocolate	10	$12.75
2/23/2006	Company C	Northwind Traders Clam Chowder	200	$9.65
3/6/2006	Company F	Northwind Traders Curry Sauce	17	$40.00

Record: 15 of 55   No Filter   Search

Figure 4-6:
How query fields translate into query results.

Access offers these techniques for listing field names in the first row of the Design grid:

✦ **Dragging a field name:** Drag a field name into a column on the Design grid. The field name appears on the grid, as does the name of the table that you drag the field name from.

✦ **Double-clicking a field name:** Double-click a field name to place it in the next available column in the Design grid.

✦ **Choosing a table and field name:** Click in the Table row and choose the name of a table from the drop-down list. Then, in the Field box directly above, choose a field name from the drop-down list.

✦ **Selecting all the fields in a table:** In the unlikely event that you want all the fields from a table to appear in the query results, either double-click the asterisk (*) at the top of the list of field names or drag the asterisk into the Design grid. Access places the name of the table followed by an asterisk in the Field text box. The asterisk signifies that all the fields from the table are included in the query.

To remove a field name from the Design grid, select it and press the Delete key, or click the field name and then click the Delete Columns button in the Query Setup group on the (Query Tools) Design tab.

Sorting the query results

At the start of this chapter, "Sorting Records in a Database Table" explains what sorting is. The Sort row of the Design grid — directly underneath the Table name — contains a drop-down list. To sort the query, click the drop-down list in a field and choose Ascending or Descending to sort the results of a query on a particular field. To sort the results on more than one field, make sure that the first field to be sorted appears to the left of the other fields. Access reads the sort order from left to right.

You can move fields in the query grid by clicking the tiny gray box above the field name and dragging the field to the left or right.

Choosing which fields appear in query results

Although you include a field in the Query grid, it isn't always necessary to display information from the field in the query results. Consider the Query grid, as shown in Figure 4-7. The object of this query is to show the orders shipped in 2006. Therefore, the Criteria cell of the Shipped Date field shows the expression Between #1/1/2006# And #12/31/2006#. However, when you generate the results, you might not want to see the Shipped Date field because you're just concerned with other information about the order.

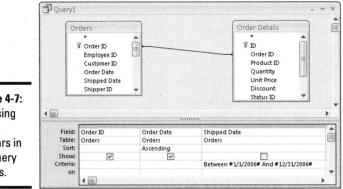

Figure 4-7: Choosing what appears in the query results.

Moving field columns on the Query grid

The order in which field names appear in the Query grid is also the order in which they appear in the query results (refer to Figure 4-6). Follow these steps to move field columns to the right order in the Query grid:

1. **Click a column's selector button to select a column.**

This button is the narrow gray box directly above the field name. The pointer turns into a down-pointing arrow when you move it over the selector button.

2. **After you select the column, click the selector button again and drag the column to the left or right.**

When a field's Show check box is selected, results from the field appear in Query results. If a field is necessary for producing records in a query but not necessary in the query results, deselect its Show check box. If you save and reopen the query, Access moves deselected fields to the right side of the Query grid (and you usually have to scroll to see them).

Entering criteria for a query

What separates a run-of-the-mill query from a supercharged query is a *criterion,* an expression or value you enter on the Criteria line under a field. Enter criteria on the Criteria line of the Query grid. By entering criteria, you can pinpoint records in the database with great accuracy. In Figure 4-8, the Query grid instructs Access to search orders taken in 2006 and shipped to New York or California where the unit price is more than $50. Notice the word *Or* between "NY" and "CA" in the criterion for the Ship State/Province field.

Book VI
Chapter 4

Sorting, Querying, and Filtering for Data

Figure 4-8:
Including criteria in a query.

Field:	Order ID	Order Date		Ship State/Province	Unit Price	
Table:	Orders	Orders		Orders	Order Details	
Sort:		Ascending				
Show:	☑	☑		☑	☑	
Criteria:		Between #1/1/2006# And #12/31/2006#		"NY" Or "CA"	>50	
or:						

Using Or between multiple values allows you to see rows containing one of those values. The query, as shown in Figure 4-8, retrieves rows for orders shipped to either New York or California. Using Or between values is similar to selecting multiple data values while filtering data, as I describe in "Common filters" earlier in this chapter.

As Figure 4-8 shows, Access places double quotation marks ("") around text criteria and number signs (#) around date criteria. When you enter text or date criteria, don't enter the double quotation marks or number signs. Access enters them for you.

When you need help writing an expression for a query, try clicking the Build button to construct your query in the Expression Builder dialog box.

Entering numeric criteria

Enter numeric criteria in Number and Currency fields when you want to isolate records with specific values. Earlier in this chapter, Table 4-1 describes comparison operators you can use for querying and filtering. These operators are invaluable when it comes to mining a database for information. Use the greater than (>) and less than (<) operators to find values higher or lower than a target value. Use the Between operator to find values between two numbers. For example, *Between 62 And 55* in a Currency field isolates records with all items that sell for between $62.00 and $55.00.

Do not include commas in numbers when you enter them as criteria. For example, enter 3200, not 3,200. Enter a comma and you get a "The expression you entered contains invalid syntax. . ." error message.

Entering text criteria

To enter a text criterion, type it in the Criteria text box. For example, to find students who attended Ohio State University, enter Ohio State in the Criteria text box of the University field. Access places double quotation marks ("") around the text you enter as soon when you move the pointer out of the Criteria text box.

Wildcards and the Not operator can come in very handy when entering text criteria:

 + **Wildcards:** Wildcards make it possible to query for data whose spelling you aren't quite sure of. (In Chapter 3 of this mini-book, Table 3-2 explains what the wildcard characters are and how to use them.) For example, entering Sm?th in the Criteria box of the Last Name field finds all Smiths and Smyths. Entering E* in the Company field finds all company names that begin with the letter *E*.

 + **Not operator:** Use the Not operator to exclude records from query results. For example, to exclude records with Belgium in the Shipped To field, enter Not Belgium in the Criteria text box. This is a great way to strip unneeded records from a query.

Entering date criteria

All the operators that work for numeric data (see Table 4-1 earlier in this chapter) also work for data entered in a Date field. For example, enter >7/31/1958 in a Birth Date field to find all people born after (greater than) July 31, 1958. Enter Between 1/1/1920 And 12/31/1929 to retrieve data about people born in the Roaring Twenties.

Access places number signs (#) around date criteria after you enter it. You can enter dates in these formats:

 + 11/22/07
 + 11/22/2007
 + 22-Nov-07
 + November 22, 2007

For the purpose of entering two-digit years in dates, the digits 30 through 99 belong to the 20th Century (1930–1999), but the digits 00 through 29 belong to the 21st Century (2000–2029). For example, *>4/1/24* refers to April 1, 2024, not April 1, 1924. To enter a date in 1929 or earlier, enter four digits instead of two to describe the year: *>4/1/1929*. To enter a date in 2030, or later, enter four digits instead of two: *>4/1/2038*. To avoid any confusion, enter four-digit years all the time. Make your application Y3K compliant now.

The Date() function can come in very handy when you want to retrieve data relative to today's date, whatever it happens to be. For example, to retrieve purchase orders made between January 1, 2007, and today's date, enter this expression: **Between 1/1/2007 And Date()**.

At last — saving and running a query

To save a query and inscribe its name forever in the Navigation pane, click the Save button on the Quick Access toolbar and enter a descriptive name in the Save As dialog box. The name you enter appears in the Queries group in the Navigation pane.

After you laboriously construct your query, take it for a test drive. To run a query:

Run

✦ **Starting from the Query Design window:** Click the Run button on the (Query Tools) Design tab.

✦ **Starting from the Navigation pane:** Double-click an existing query's name, or right-click its name and choose Open on the shortcut menu.

View

If the query doesn't work the way you want it to, click the Design View button, or right-click the Query window's title bar and choose Design View on the shortcut menu to return to the Query Design window and start tinkering.

Six Kinds of Queries

For your pleasure and entertainment, these pages describe six useful types of queries. Access offers a handful of other queries, but I won't go there. Those queries are pretty complicated. If you become adept at querying, however, you're invited to look into the Help system for advice about running the query types that aren't explained here.

Select query

A *select query* is the standard kind of query, which I explain earlier in this chapter. A select query gathers information from one or more database tables and displays the information in a datasheet. A select query is the most common query, the primal query, the starting point for most other queries.

Top-value query

A *top-value query* is an easy way to find out, in a Number or Currency field, the highest or lowest values. On the Query grid, enter the name of the Number or Currency field you want to know more about; then choose Ascending in the Sort drop-down list to rank values from lowest to highest or Descending in the Sort drop-down list to rank values from highest to lowest. Finally, in the Return drop-down list in the Query Setup group on the (Query Tools) Design tab, enter a value or choose a value from the drop-down list:

✦ **Highest or lowest by percentage:** Enter or choose a percentage to find, for example, the highest or lowest 25 percent of the values. To enter a percentage, type a percent sign (%) after your entry and press the Enter key.

✦ **Highest or lowest by ranking number:** Enter or choose a number to find, for example, the top-ten or lowest-ten values. Press the Enter key after you enter a number.

This may seem counterintuitive, but to see the top values, you have to sort the field you're ranking in descending order. For example, if you sort employees by number of sales in descending order, the employees with the top sales appear at the top. To see the bottom values, sort in ascending order.

Summary query

Similar to a top-value query, a *summary query* is a way of getting cumulative information about all the data in a field. In a field that stores data about sales in Kentucky, for example, you can find the average amount of each sale, the total amount of all the sales, the total number of all the sales, and other data.

Σ
Totals

To run a summary query, click the Totals button in the Show/Hide group on the (Query Tools) Design tab. A new row called Total appears on the Query grid. Open the Total drop-down list in the field whose contents you want to summarize and choose a function. Table 4-2 describes the functions.

Table 4-2	Summary Query Functions
Function	*Returns*
Sum	The total of all values in the field
Avg	The average of all values
Min	The lowest value
Max	The highest value
Count	The number of values
StDev	The standard deviation of the values

Function	Returns
Var	The variance of the values
First	The first value
Last	The last value

The Group By, Expression, and Where choices in the Totals drop-down list let you include fields you're not performing a function on:

✦ **Group By:** This option lets you pick which fields to show totals for.

✦ **Expression:** This option lets you create a calculated field.

✦ **Where:** This option lets you set criteria, but it doesn't include the field in the query.

Calculation query

A *calculation query* is one in which calculations are performed as part of the query. For example, you can calculate the sales tax on items sold or total the numbers in two fields in the same record. The beauty of a calculation query is that the data is recomputed each time you run the query. If the data used to make a calculation changes, so does the result of the calculation. If you were to include the calculation in a database table, you would have to recalculate the data yourself each time one of the values changed. With a calculation query, Access does the math for you.

To construct a calculation query, create a new field in the Query grid for storing the results of the calculation; then enter a name for the field and a formula for the calculation. Follow these steps to create a calculation query:

1. **Create a query as you normally would and be sure to include the fields you want to use for calculation purposes in the Query grid.**

2. **In the Field box of a blank field, enter a name for the Calculation field and follow it with a colon.**

   In Figure 4-9, I enter **SubTotal:**. The purpose of the new SubTotal field is to calculate the Unit Price × the Quantity.

3. **After the colon, in square brackets ([]), enter the name of a field whose data you use for the calculation.**

   In Figure 4-9, data from the Unit Price and Quantity fields are used in the calculation, so their names appear in square brackets: [Unit Price] and [Quantity]. Be sure to spell field names correctly so that Access can recognize them.

New field's name

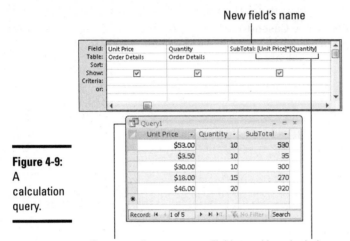

Figure 4-9:
A
calculation
query.

Query results   Fields used in calculation

4. **Complete the calculation.**

How you do this depends on what kind of calculation you're making. In Figure 4-9, I enter an asterisk (*) to multiply two fields together. The equation multiplies the values in the Unit Price and Quantity fields. You can add the data from two different fields — including calculated fields — by putting their names in brackets and joining them with a plus sign, like so: [SubTotal]+[Shipping Cost].

Sometimes the results of the query aren't formatted correctly on the datasheet. To assign a new format to a field you create for the purposes of making a calculation query, right-click the field on the Query grid and choose Properties. The Property Sheet appears. On the General tab, click the Format drop-down list and choose the correct format for your new, hand-crafted field.

Delete query

Be careful about running delete queries. A *delete query* deletes records and doesn't give you the opportunity to get the records back if you change your mind about deleting them. If used skillfully, however, a delete query is a great way to purge records from more than one database table at once. Back up your database file before running a delete query. Edith Piaf didn't regret her delete query, but you might regret yours.

To run a delete query, start a new query, and in Query Design view, click the Delete button in the Query Type group on the (Query Tools) Design tab. Then make as though you're running a select query but target the records you want to delete. Finally, click the Run button to run the query.

You can delete records from more than one table as long as the tables are related and you chose the Cascade Delete Related Records option in the Edit Relationships dialog box when you linked the tables. (See the section in Chapter 2 of this mini-book about forging relationships between tables.)

To preview the records that will be deleted before you run the delete query, click the Datasheet View button in the Results group on the (Query Tools) Design tab. The delete query will only delete records when you click the Run button. After clicking run, wave goodbye to that data.

Update query

An *update query* is a way to reach into a database and update records in several different tables all at one time. Update queries can be invaluable, but as with delete queries, they can have untoward consequences. Back up your database before you run an update query; then follow these steps to run it:

**Book VI
Chapter 4**

Sorting, Querying, and Filtering for Data

1. **Starting in Design view, click the Update command in the Query Type group on the (Query Tools) Design tab.**

A new line, Update To, appears on the Query grid.

2. **Set up the query as you normally would and then click the View button to see which records the query collects.**

The records appear in Datasheet view. Take this step to make sure that you're updating the records correctly.

3. **Click the View button again to return to Design view.**

4. **In the field with the data that needs updating, enter text or a value in the Update To line. You can even enter another field name in square brackets ([ ]).**

What you enter in the Update To line replaces what's in the field of the records you collect.

5. **Click the Run button.**

To update records in more than one table, you must have chosen the Cascade Update Related Fields option in the Edit Relationships dialog box when you linked the tables. (See the section in Chapter 2 of this mini-book about forging relationships between tables.)

Chapter 5: Presenting Data in a Report

In This Chapter

✔ **Creating a new report**

✔ **Opening a report**

✔ **Changing the look of a report**

*T*he prettiest way to present data in a database table or query is to present it in a report. Even people who are allergic to databases can put up with database material in a report. Reports are easy to read and understand. They succinctly present the data so that you and others can interpret it. This brief chapter explains how to create reports, open them, and edit them.

Creating a Report

Access comes with all kinds of complicated tools for fashioning your own report — for laying out the pages in different ways and making data fields show up in different parts of the page. If ever a task called for relying on a wizard, creating a report is it. You can save yourself a lot of trouble, and fashion sophisticated-looking reports as well, by dispensing with the fancy report-making tools and letting the wizard do the job.

What's more, the easiest and best way to make a report is to base your report on a query. As part of fashioning a report with a wizard, you can tell Access which database tables and which fields to get the data from — in other words, you can query your database from inside the Report Wizard. However, doing that requires turning somersaults and cartwheels. It's far easier to run a query to produce the results you want in your report, save your query, and then fashion a report from the query results. Chapter 4 in this mini-book explains how to create a query.

To create a report with the Report Wizard, start by clicking the Report Wizard command in the Reports group on the Create tab. You see the first of several Report Wizard dialog boxes. Negotiate the dialog boxes as follows, clicking the Next button as you go along:

✦ **Tables/Queries:** Open this drop-down list and choose the query where the information in the report will come from. A list of fields in the query appears in the Available Fields box.

✦ **Available Fields:** Select the fields whose data you want in the report by selecting the fields one at a time and clicking the > button. Doing so moves field names to the Selected Fields box. Add all the fields by clicking the >> button.

✦ **How Do You Want to View Your Data?:** Choose a field to define the grouping level. A *grouping level* is like a report subheading. For example, if you make Last Name the grouping level, information in the report is presented under people's last names.

✦ **Do You Want to Add Any Grouping Levels?:** Include subheadings in your report by selecting a field name and clicking the > button to make it a subheading. If you're building your report on a query that includes related tables, the Report Wizard automatically adds subheadings.

✦ **What Sort Order Do You Want?:** Select up to four fields to sort the data in your report. Even if you sort the fields in a query, the report handles sorting on its own. If you include grouping levels, the report already sorts on these fields.

✦ **How Would You Like to Lay Out Your Report?:** Experiment with the options, and watch the Preview box, to choose a layout for your report. If your report has a lot of fields, you may want to print it in Landscape view.

✦ **What Style Would You Like?:** Click the options to preview the different designs and choose the one that makes you happiest. As shown in Figure 5-1, this dialog box asks you to choose a design for your report. (Later in this chapter, "Tweaking a Report" explains how to change designs.)

✦ **What Title Do You Want for Your Report?:** Enter a descriptive title. The name you choose appears in the Reports group in the Navigation pane. From there, you double-click the name when you want to see the report.

✦ **Preview the Report:** Select this option button and click Finish. The report appears in the Preview window. How do you like it?

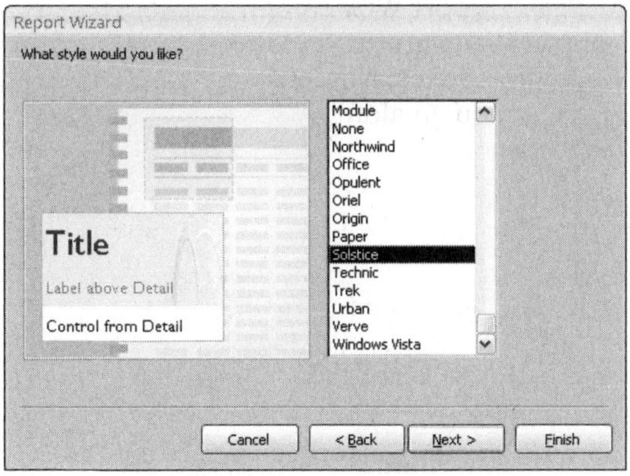

Figure 5-1:
Choosing a design for the report.

Opening and Viewing Reports

If you've spent any time whatsoever in Access, you know the drill for opening a so-called object. Follow these steps to open a report:

1. In the Navigation pane, click the Reports group.

You see the names of reports you created.

2. Double-click a report name or right-click a name and choose Open from the shortcut menu.

The report appears in Report view. From here, you can apply filters to the report in much the same way you do to a datasheet or a form. Reports in Access 2007 are interactive. (Chapter 4 in this mini-book explains how to apply a filter to a datasheet.)

3. Click the Office button and choose Print⇨Print Preview.

The report appears in the Preview window. Experiment with the report's settings by changing the layout between Portrait and Landscape, viewing one or more pages at a time, and creating a PDF (portable document format). Oh, I almost forgot, you can print the report, too; that's why you made it in the first place! Click the Close Print Preview command on the Ribbon after you're done playing around.

Tweaking a Report

As I mention at the start of this chapter, Access offers a bunch of complex tools for changing the layout and appearance of a report. If you're courageous and have lots of time on your hands, you're invited to take these tools in hand and go to it. In the Reports group of the Navigation pane, right-click a report and choose Design View from the shortcut menu. You see your report in the Report Design window, as shown in Figure 5-2. Have you ever seen anything scarier?

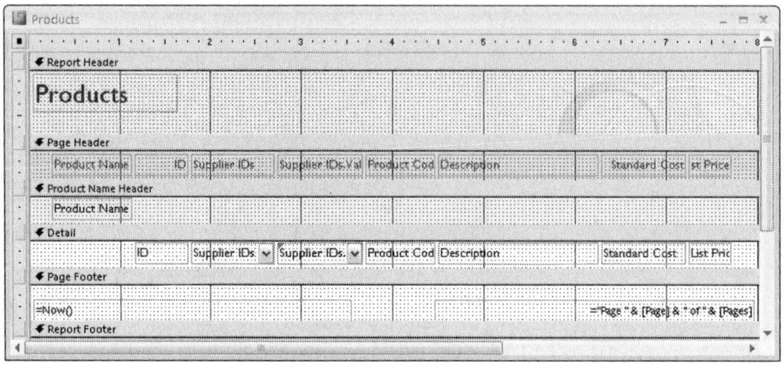

Figure 5-2:
The Report
Design
window.

I tell you how to create a report with the Report Wizard in order to avoid your having to visit this imposing window. However, you can change a report's appearance in the Report Design window without going to very much trouble if you follow these instructions:

+ **Choosing a new design:** If the design you choose in the Report Wizard isn't cutting it, click the AutoFormat command in the AutoFormat group on the (Report Design Tools) Arrange tab. You see a drop-down list containing the design formats that were also available in the Report Wizard. Click the desired format to change the report's design.

+ **Removing the header and footer:** Access places today's date and page numbers in the footer of reports. To remove these items, choose the Page Header/Footer command in the Show/Hide group on the (Report Design Tools) Arrange tab. Click Yes in the confirmation dialog box if you want to remove these sections and all of the controls in these sections.

+ **Including page numbers:** To include page numbers on the report, click the Page Numbers command in the Controls group on the (Report Design Tools) Design tab. You see the Page Numbers dialog box, as shown in Figure 5-3. Choose the Page N option button to display a page number only, or select the Page N of M option button to display a page number as well as the total number of pages in the report (as in "Page 2 of 4"). Choose Alignment and Position options to describe where on the page to put the page number. To remove a page number, scour the Report Design window to find an ="Page" code and then delete it.

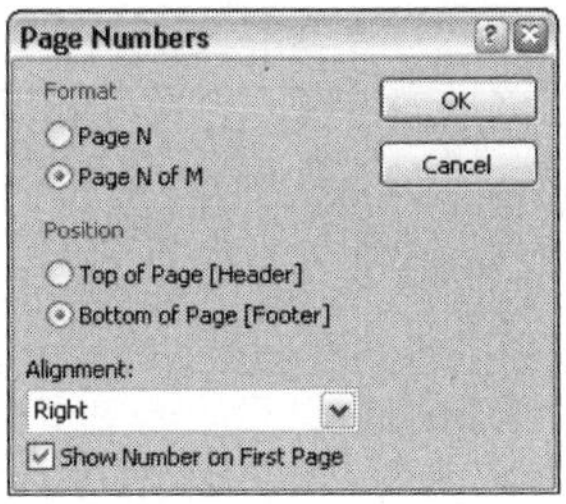

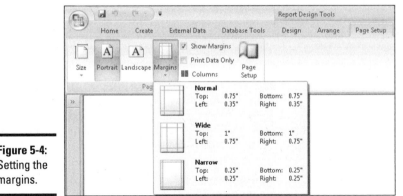

Figure 5-3:
Putting on
the page
numbers.

✦ **Changing the margins:** Choose Margins on the (Report Design Tools)
Page Setup tab and select the new margins. Choose from Normal, Wide,
or Narrow margins. The values of the Top, Left, Bottom, and Right
margin values are shown in Figure 5-4. The Margins command is also
available from the Print Preview view.

Figure 5-4:
Setting the
margins.

Access offers many more options for setting up a report. Click the Layout
View button to switch the report to Layout view. From this view, you can
resize the columns, change the column heading and the report's title, and
adjust fonts, colors, and sizes. You can also choose to add gridlines, adjust
the line thickness that appears, add additional fields, and adjust the spacing
between fields. The best part of Layout view is that you can do this while
viewing real live data.

An easier way to tweak a report — in Word

If you aren't comfortable in the Report Design window (who is?), try transferring your report to Microsoft Word and editing it there. Click the Word command in the Export group on the External Data tab. Choose a destination and filename, and then select the option to open the file after the export operation is complete. In a moment, your Access report appears in Word.

You can find the new Word file in the folder you chose when creating the file. The file is an RTF (rich text format file). To save it as a Word file, click the Office button and then choose Save As. In the Save As dialog box, name your file and choose Word Document on the Save As Type drop-down list. Books I and II describe how to work with files in Word.

Book VII

Publisher 2007

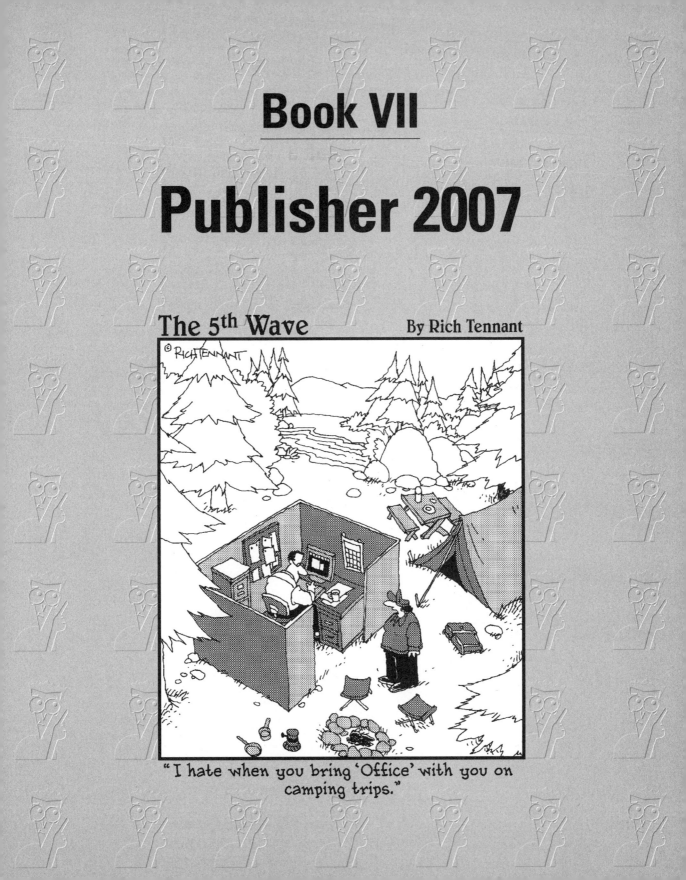

The 5th Wave   By Rich Tennant

"I hate when you bring 'Office' with you on camping trips."

Contents at a Glance

Chapter 1: Introducing Publisher

In This Chapter

- ✓ Understanding frames
- ✓ Creating a new publication
- ✓ Designing your publication
- ✓ Entering your business information
- ✓ Changing your view of the Publisher window
- ✓ Putting grid guides on pages
- ✓ Drawing a ruler guide

Welcome to Publisher. Not so long ago, creating professional publications like the kind you can create with Publisher required sophisticated printing equipment and a background in graphic design. However, even a novice can now create professional-looking publications with Publisher. As long as you rely on a publication design — a template that comes with Publisher — most of the layout work is done for you. All you have to do is enter the text and the other particulars.

"A Print Shop in a Can"

Publisher has been called "a print shop in a can" because the program is great for creating prefabricated brochures, business cards, calendars, newsletters, resumes, posters, and the like. To make these publications without going to a great deal of trouble, however, you have to stick to the publication designs. A *publication design* gives you the structure for creating a brochure, calendar, and so on. Chances are you can find a suitable publication design for whatever kind of publication you want to create. Figure 1-1 shows some examples of the publication designs for creating flyers. The designs include placeholders for graphics and text. To create a publication, you choose a publication type, choose a design, enter graphics and text in the publication design where the placeholders are, and tweak the publication to your liking.

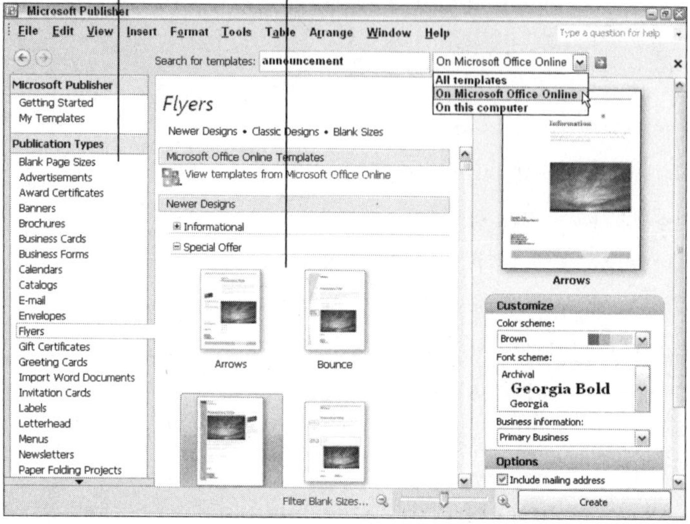

Choose a publication type.   Choose a design.

Figure 1-1:
Creating a
publication.

Striking out on your own and designing publications like those in Figure 1-1 can be done, but you need a thorough knowledge of Publisher and a full head of hair. You need the hair because much of it will have been pulled out in frustration by the time you finish your design. I venture to say that the people who invented Publisher expect everyone to work from ready-made publication designs. Designing publications from scratch is simply too difficult. Don't be discouraged, however, because you can almost always find a publication design for whatever you want to communicate.

Introducing Frames

The publications that you make with Publisher are composed of frames. A *frame* is a placeholder for text, a graphic, or a table. Complex publications have dozens of frames; simple publications have only a few. Frames keep text and graphics from overlapping. They make sure that everything stays on the page where it should be. As you create a publication, you enter your own text or graphics in frames.

The publication in Figure 1-2 is made up of several frames that are stitched together to form a poster. On the left side of the figure, I selected the frames, and you can see the frame boundaries; the right side of the figure shows what the poster looks like after it is printed. Frames make laying out publications easier. When you want to move text, a picture, a table, or an image, you simply drag its frame to a new location. After you select a frame, the commands you give apply to the text or graphic in the frame. Frames do not appear in the finished product — they are meant strictly to help with the laying out of text and graphics.

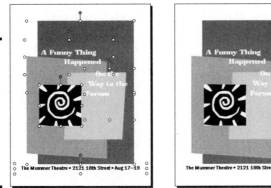

Figure 1-2:
A poster with frames showing (left); the poster as it looks when it is printed (right).

Creating a Publication

To create a new publication, choose File⇨New (or press Ctrl+N). You see the Welcome to Microsoft Office Publisher window (refer to Figure 1-1). Starting here, you can create a publication in any number of ways. When you search for a publication design, remember that you can click the Back and Forward buttons in the upper-left corner of the dialog box to retrace your search.

Use one of these techniques to create a publication:

**Book VII
Chapter 1**

Introducing
Publisher

✦ **Select a publication design:** Select a category under Publication Types, or click the icon representing a popular publication type. You see a dozen or more designs. Scroll through the list, select a design, and double-click it or click the Create button in the lower-right corner of the window.

✦ **Search for a publication design at Microsoft:** In the Search for Templates text box, enter the name of a publication type, choose On Microsoft Office Online on the drop-down list, and click the Search button (the green arrow). Then select a publication design and double-click it or click the Create button.

✦ **Use a template you created:** If you create your own design templates, you can use one to create a publication by clicking the My Templates button and then double-clicking a template name.

✦ **Start from another publication:** You can create a new publication by starting from one you've already designed. Select the publication's name in the Recent Publications list, or if the publication's name isn't listed, click the From File link (you can find it at the top of the Recent Publications list). In the Open Publication dialog box, locate the publication, select it, and click the Open button. Then get to work changing around your prototype publication to suit your purposes, but be sure to change its name if you want to preserve the original publication from which it was made.

After you select a design in the Welcome to Microsoft Office Publisher window (refer to Figure 1-1), you could choose a color scheme and font scheme for your publication. But I suggest waiting until you've created your publication before choosing colors and fonts. You can study your publication more closely after you create it. You can look through it and decide what you want it to look like. What's more, choosing new colors and fonts for a publication is as easy as pie, as I explain very shortly.

If you prefer *not* to see the Welcome to Microsoft Office Publisher window when you start Publisher, choose Tools⇨Options, select the General tab in the Options dialog box, and deselect the Show Publication Types When Starting Publisher check box. Click OK.

Redesigning a Publication

Make your design choices carefully. In theory, you can change publication designs, color schemes, and design options when you're well along in a project, but in practice, changing these designs can have unforeseen consequences. If you change the color of a headline, for example, and then choose a new color scheme, the headline might be swallowed or rendered invisible by a background color in the new scheme. If you enter a bunch of text, change the size of a few frames, and then choose a new publication design, you may turn your publication into corned-beef hash and have to start over.

To redesign a publication, choose Format⇨Format Publication. The Format Publication task pane appears, as shown in Figure 1-3. Starting at the Color Schemes, Font Schemes, Options, or Page Options category, you can choose colors, fonts, and even a different publication design. If your publication has more than one page, click page number buttons at the bottom of the window to visit different pages and see what they look like.

Choosing a different publication design

Not happy with the publication design you chose when you created your publication? To exchange it for a new one, select the Publication Options category in the Format Publication task pane (the category is named after the type of publication you're working on). Then click the Change Template button (see Figure 1-3). You return to see the Change Template window, where you can select a different publication design.

Figure 1-3: Changing designs, font schemes, color schemes, and page options in the Format Publication task pane.

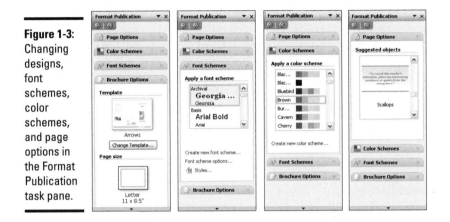

Book VII Chapter 1

Introducing Publisher

Choosing a font scheme

You'll be glad to know that most of the text formats that are available in Word are also available in Publisher on the Standard toolbar and Format menu. To boldface text, select it and click the Bold button. To change font sizes, choose an option on the Font Size drop-down list.

To avoid going to the trouble of formatting text, you can choose a *font scheme*, a pair of fonts for the headings and body text in a publication. Font schemes spare you the trouble of having to format the text on your own. The schemes were designed by people who know what they're doing. They look good.

To choose a font scheme, select the Font Schemes category in the Format Publication task pane (see Figure 1-3), and then select a scheme. If you really know what you're doing, you can click the Create New Font Scheme link and select fonts for heading text and body text in the dialog box that appears. And if you're a Publisher aficionado, you can click the Styles link and assign a font to different kinds of text — bulleted-list text, third- and fourth-level headings, and other text — in the Styles pane.

Choosing a color scheme

To choose a color scheme, select the Color Schemes category in the Format Publication task pane (refer to Figure 1-3) and then select a scheme. If you're daring, you can click the Create New Color Scheme link and fashion your own color scheme in the Create New Color Scheme dialog box.

Declaring the page size

Decide right away which page size to use for your publication. How large or small the page is determines how the headings, graphics, and text fit on the page. To declare the page size, select the Publication Options category in the Format Publication task pane (the category is named after the type of publication you're working on), scroll to the bottom of the task pane, and click the Change Page Size button. Then select a page size in the Page Sizes window. The bottom of the Publication Options category displays the page size you choose.

Choosing other design options

The last important step in designing a publication is to consider the other design options. These options vary depending on the kind of publication you're working on. When you're working on a brochure, for example, you can insert a sign-up form or space for a block quote. To examine the other design options, select the Page Options category in the Format Publication task pane. Select what Publisher calls an "object" to insert it on a page.

Getting Around in Publisher

The Publisher window can get kind of cluttered. In fact, the place has been known to cause claustrophobia. These pages are meant to help you conquer your fear of the Publisher window. They explain how to get from page to page and, more important, change views of the publication you're working on.

Zooming in and zooming out

As you create a publication, it's important to see the little details as well as the big picture; so Publisher offers special Zoom In and Zoom Out toolbar buttons as well as the Zoom menu. Click a Zoom button to quickly peer at or lean away from a document. You can also choose View⇨Zoom and select one of the intriguing options on the submenu. For example, select a frame and choose View⇨Zoom⇨Selected Objects when you want to focus on a single frame.

The View menu offers a command called View⇨Two-Page Spread for seeing facing pages in newsletters, brochures, and other publications with more than one page. Choose this command early and often. It permits you to see what readers of your publication will see when they view facing pages like the ones in Figure 1-4.

Entering business information

Brochures, newsletters, letterheads, envelopes, and a handful of other publication types include what Publisher calls "business information." Publisher plugs this information — an individual name, title, company name, address, phone number, motto, and even a logo — into the publication. The information comes from the Business Information dialog box. As long as the information in this dialog box is up to date, you needn't be concerned whether the information appears in the right places in a publication or whether it's accurate. And you don't have to enter the information directly into the publication you're working on.

To enter business information, choose Edit⇨ Business Information. You see the Create New Business Information dialog box. Enter information in this dialog box, choose a name for the information, and click the Save button. The information you enter will be plugged in to all publications you create in the future, as well as the publication you're working on (if you click the Update Information button).

If you need to edit the business information you entered or create secondary information about another business, choose Edit⇨Business Information, and in the Business Information dialog box, click the Edit button. You see the Edit Business Information Set dialog box, where you can enter information about another business and save it under a different name.

Notice the Select a Business Information Set drop-down list in the Business Information dialog box. Choose Edit⇨Business Information and select which business information set you need for the publication you're working on.

Publisher offers an unwieldy command for quickly entering business information one tidbit at a time: Select the frame where you want information to appear and choose Insert⇨ Business Information. You see the Business Information task pane. Select an information tidbit, open its drop-down list, and choose Insert This Field. Then adjust the frame in which the information appears (Chapter 2 of this mini-book explains how).

**Book VII
Chapter 1**

Introducing
Publisher

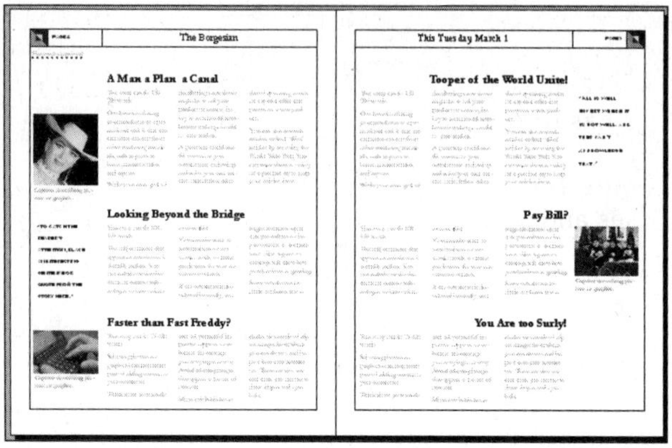

Figure 1-4:
A two-page spread.

Hiding and displaying toolbars

Toolbars can make the Publisher window look cluttered. Lucky for you, you can hide or display a toolbar in an instant with one of these techniques:

✦ Choose View➪Toolbars and select the name of a toolbar.

✦ Right-click any toolbar or the main menu and select a toolbar's name.

Going from page to page

Use these techniques to get from page to page in a publication:

✦ **Click a page navigation button:** In a publication with more than one page, click a page navigation button to go to a different page. The buttons are located on the status bar along the bottom of the window.

✦ **The Go to Page dialog box:** Choose Edit➪Go to Page (or press Ctrl+G) and enter a page number in the Go to Page dialog box.

To help you identify pages, you can name them. When you move the pointer over a page navigation button whose page has been given a name, the name appears in a pop-up box. To name a page, right-click its navigation button on the status bar and choose Rename on the shortcut menu. In the Rename Page dialog box, enter a descriptive name.

Understanding and Using the Layout Guides

Making frames, graphics, and lines of text line up squarely on the page is essential if your publication is to look smart and snappy. Readers tend to go cock-eyed when they see side-by-side columns with the text in one column slightly askew of the text in the column beside it. A graphic or text frame that spills onto the margin is a breach of etiquette punishable by death. A row of graphics has to be just that — a row, not a crooked line.

As shown in Figure 1-5, Publisher offers a bunch of different tools for making objects — frames and graphics — line up squarely. To wit, Publisher offers the following tools:

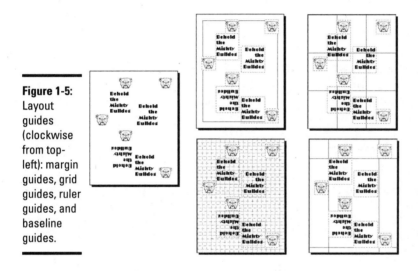

Figure 1-5:
Layout guides (clockwise from top-left): margin guides, grid guides, ruler guides, and baseline guides.

✦ **Margin guides:** Blue lines that clearly show where page margins begin and end. Use the margin guides to make sure objects don't stray too far into the margin.

✦ **Grid guides:** Blue lines that appear in grid form across the page. You can decide how tight or loose to make the grid. Frames and objects can be made to "snap to the grid." Because the objects snap, you're spared the trouble of aligning them because they line up on grid guides.

✦ **Ruler guides:** Green horizontal or vertical lines that you can place on the page for assistance in aligning frames and objects. Frames and objects can be made to "snap to" ruler guides, too. The ruler lines are easy to place on and remove from the screen.

✦ **Baseline guides:** Green horizontal and vertical lines that appear on the page to help with aligning frames and objects. You can decide how many baseline guides appear.

Use these techniques to hide or display the guides:

✦ **Margin guides, grid guides, and ruler guides:** Choose View➪ Boundaries and Guides (or press Ctrl+Shift+O).

✦ **Baseline guides:** Choose View➪Baseline Guides, and then choose Horizontal (or press Ctrl+F7) or Vertical (or press Ctrl+Shift+F7).

These commands make frames and objects "snap to" ruler guides or grid guides: Arrange➪Snap➪To Ruler Marks and Arrange➪Snap➪To Guides (press Ctrl+Shift+W). Snapping helps to make objects line up squarely.

Laying out the margin, grid, and baseline guides

Unless you create a new section (choose Insert➪Section), margin, grid, and baseline guides apply to every page in a publication. Follow these steps to tell Publisher how frequently to make guidelines appear on pages:

1. **Choose Arrange➪Layout Guides.**

You see the Layout Guides dialog box.

2. **On the Margin Guides tab, enter measurements to determine how wide to make the margins; on the Grid Guides tab, enter numbers to determine how many rows and columns form the grid; on the Baseline Guides tab, enter measurements to determine how tight or loose the guides are.**

The Preview box shows you precisely what your grid looks like and where the margins are. Think carefully about entering a number less than .2 in the Spacing boxes. If you enter 0, for example, object and frames touch each other when they "snap to the grid."

3. **Click OK.**

To remove grid guides, return to the Grid Guides tab of the Layout Guides dialog box and enter **1** in the Columns text box and **1** in the Rows text box.

Setting down ruler guides

Use a ruler guide to line up frames and other objects. Ruler guides can go anywhere on the page. You can draw ruler guides where you need them and remove the guides very easily when they get in the way. Whereas grid guides appear on every page in a publication, ruler guides appear on one page. You can, however, place the same ruler guide on every page by choosing View➪ Master Page and drawing the ruler guide on the master page.

Handling the Rulers

Rulers, when they aren't coming in very handy, get in the way. To hide or display rulers, choose View➪Rulers.

For precision work, you can drag a ruler into the middle of the window and use it as an aid for lining up frames and other objects. Hold down the Shift key, click a ruler, and drag it into the middle of the window. To move it back where it came from, Shift+drag all over again.

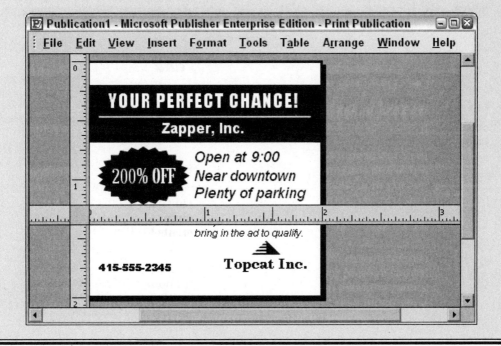

**Book VII
Chapter 1**

**Introducing
Publisher**

Publisher offers three ways to draw ruler guides:

✦ **Ruler Guides commands:** Choose Arrange➪Ruler Guides, and on the submenu, choose Add Horizontal Ruler Guide or Add Vertical Ruler Guide. A guide appears across the page. Drag it to a new location, if necessary.

✦ **Ruler Guides dialog box:** Choose Arrange➪Ruler Guides➪Format Ruler Guides. In the Ruler Guides dialog box, enter horizontal or vertical measurements for the guides and click OK.

Now you know all there is to know about ruler guides, except this stuff:

✦ **Moving a ruler guide:** Click and drag the guide to a new location.

✦ **Removing ruler guides:** Drag the guide off the page. To remove all guides, choose Arrange⇨Ruler Guides⇨Clear All Ruler Guides.

Chapter 2: Refining a Publication

In This Chapter

✔ **Entering and editing text**

✔ **Making text fit in frames**

✔ **"Flowing" text from frame to frame**

✔ **Wrapping text around frames and graphics**

✔ **Putting graphics in a publication**

✔ **Manipulating frames**

*T*his chapter picks up where the previous chapter left off. In Chapter 1 of this mini-book, you discover how to create a publication, find your way around the screen, and use the different guides. In this chapter, you explore how to make a publication your own. This chapter offers speed techniques for entering and editing text. It explains how to handle frames, make text "flow" from frame to frame, and put graphics and other kinds of art in a publication. *Bon voyage!*

Entering Text on the Pages

The placeholder text that appears in publication designs has to go, of course. One of your first tasks is to replace the generic text with your own words. In the case of a newsletter story, you have a lot of writing to do. (*Story* is the Publisher term for an article that reaches across several text frames.) If you're putting together a sign, you have only a handful of words to write.

To select all the text in a frame or story, click in the frame and press Ctrl+A (or choose Edit⇨Select All). Here's another trick that comes in handy when you're entering text: Click in the text and press F9 (or choose View⇨Zoom⇨Selected Objects) to zoom in and display text at its actual size.

Publisher offers these techniques for handling large blocks of text:

✦ **Writing the text in Microsoft Word:** Choose Edit⇨Edit Story in Microsoft Word. Microsoft Word opens, and you see the placeholder text in its entirety. Delete the text and enter your own text. You can call on all of the Word commands to edit the text. You can also copy text from elsewhere into the Word document. When you're finished writing, click the Office button and choose Close & Return to *Your Publication* on the drop-down list.

Notice that the placeholder text tells you roughly how many words fit into the story. As you compose the story in Word, glance at the status bar from time to time to see how many words are in the story and try to keep to the number of words you're allotted.

✦ **Inserting a text file:** Delete the placeholder text and choose Insert⇨Text File. In the Insert Text dialog box, select a file and click OK.

The problem with the techniques just described is that files you work on in Microsoft Word or import land in Publisher with their formats intact. If the text is bold and 26 points high, it is bold and 26 points high in your publication despite the publication design you've chosen. To fix the problem, choose Format⇨Font Schemes and select a font scheme in the task pane.

Making Text Fit in Text Frames

One of the biggest challenges in a publication is making text fit in text frames. What happens if the headline at the top of the story is too long to fit in the frame? Suppose that a story in a newsletter is too long to fit in the text frames allotted for the article by your publication design? These pages explain how to make text fit elegantly in frames.

Handling "overflow" text

The Text in Overflow icon appears at the bottom of a text frame when text doesn't fit in the frame and needs to go elsewhere, as shown in Figure 2-1. When you see this icon, it means that you must make decisions about how to fit the heading or story into your publication.

If you're dealing with a story that reaches across more than one frame, these are your options for handling overflow text:

✦ **"Flow" text from frame to frame on your own:** Direct the text from one frame to another. See "Making text jump from frame to frame," the next section in this chapter.

✦ **Use the "autoflow" mechanism:** Let Publisher suggest where to "flow" the text. After you insert a long story, you see the Autoflow dialog box. By clicking the Yes button in this dialog box, you can tell Publisher to pour the story into different frames in the publication. I don't recommend this technique. Publisher merely picks the next available text frame without regard to whether more than one story appears on the same page. Click No in the Autoflow dialog box to flow the text on your own.

Connect Text Boxes toolbar

Go to Previous Text Box icon

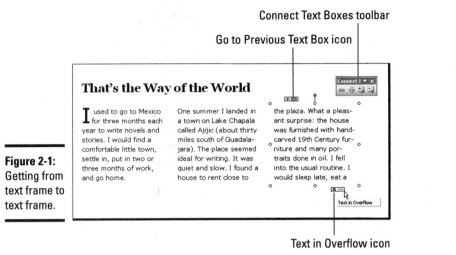

Figure 2-1:
Getting from
text frame to
text frame.

Text in Overflow icon

If you're dealing with a heading or paragraph that you want to fit in a single frame, try one of these techniques for making the heading or paragraph fit:

✦ **Shrink the text automatically:** Choose Format⇨AutoFit Text⇨Shrink Text on Overflow. This command shrinks the point size of text so that all text fits in the frame. Sometimes, however, shrinking the text this way makes the heading or paragraph hard to read.

✦ **Edit the text:** Snip out a word or sentence here and there to make the text fit. Have you ever wondered why magazine articles always fill the page and never end in the middle? That's because skillful editors and typesetters remove and add words here and there to make the story fit the page.

✦ **Make the text frame larger:** See "Changing the size and position of frames" later in this chapter.

✦ **Make the text frame margins smaller:** Like a page, text frames have internal margins to keep text from getting too close to the frame border. To shrink these margins and make more room for text, right-click the text frame and choose Format Text Box. Then, on the Text Box tab of the Format Text Box dialog box, enter smaller measurements for the text box margins.

One way to handle large blocks of text that don't fit text frames well is to try out a Tracking command. Select the text (press Ctrl+A) and choose Format⇨ Character Spacing. In the Character Spacing dialog box, choosing a Tracking option — Normal, Very Tight, Loose, and so on — to shrink or enlarge the text. The same tracking options are also available on the Measurement toolbar.

Making text jump from frame to frame

Follow these steps to direct text from frame to frame in a publication:

1. **Select the text frame with overflowing text.**

You can tell when text is overflowing because the Text in Overflow icon appears at the bottom of the text frame (refer to Figure 2-1).

2. **Click the Create Text Box Link button on the Connect Text Boxes toolbar.**

If you don't see this toolbar, right-click any toolbar and choose Connect Text Boxes. The pointer turns into an overflowing pitcher — or is that a beer stein? — after you click the button.

3. **Move the pointer over the box that you want the text to flow into.**

You may have to click a page navigation button to go to another page.

4. **Click in the target text box to make the text flow there.**

As I mention earlier, text frames linked this way are known as a story in Publisher-speak. Here are techniques for handling text frames that are linked in a story:

◆ **Going from text frame to text frame so that you can edit text:** When text travels from frame to frame, the Go to Previous Text Box and Go to Next Text Box icons appear above and below the frames (refer to Figure 2-1). Click an icon to go to the previous or next frame in the chain. You may also click the Previous Text Box or Next Text Box button on the Connect Text Boxes toolbar.

◆ **Selecting the text in all the text frames:** Press Ctrl+A or choose Edit⇨ Select All.

◆ **Breaking the link between frames:** Select the frame that you want to be the last one in the chain and click the Break Forward Link button on the Connect Text Boxes toolbar.

In a crowded publication, it's easy to overlook a text frame with overflowing text. To find these text frames, choose Tools⇨Design Checker. Then, in the Design Checker task pane, look for "Story with Text in Overflow Area."

Filling out a text frame

The opposite of an "overflow" problem is a text frame with too much blank space. Here are some techniques for handling vacant text frames:

◆ **Use an AutoFit Text option to fill the frame:** Choose Format⇨AutoFit Text⇨Best Fit. This command enlarges the text so that it fills the frame. Sometimes, however, the command makes text too big.

Continuation slugs

A *continuation slug* is a notice that tells the reader where to turn to continue reading an article or where an article is continued from. Publisher offers a nifty command for entering continuation slugs at the bottom or top of text frames:

1. **Right-click the text frame that needs a slug and choose Format Text Box.**

2. **On the Text Box tab of the Format Text Box dialog box, select the Include "Continued on Page" or Include "Continued from Page" check box and click OK.**

+ **Edit the text:** Add a word or sentence here or there. In the case of headings, write a subheading as well.

+ **Insert a graphic or Design Gallery object:** Placing a small graphic or Design Gallery object makes the page livelier and fills the dead space. See "Inserting a new frame" later in this chapter.

Making Text Wrap Around a Frame or Graphic

Wrap text around a frame, clip-art image, picture, or WordArt image and you get a very elegant layout. Figure 2-2 shows text that has been wrapped around a clip art image. Looks nice, doesn't it? Wrapping text may be the easiest way to impress innocent bystanders with your layout prowess. As Figure 2-2 shows, text wrapped tightly follows the contours of the picture, whereas text wrapped squarely runs flush with the picture's frame.

**Book VII
Chapter 2**

Refining a Publication

Figure 2-2: Text wrapped tightly (left) and squarely (right).

The ship is leaving soon. All aboard for the fun-filled adventure!

The ship is leaving soon. All aboard for the fun-filled adventure!

Here are shorthand instructions for wrapping text:

1. **Select the item that text is to wrap around.**

In Figure 2-2, you would select the clip-art image.

2. Display the Picture toolbar, click the Text Wrapping button on the toolbar, and choose a wrapping option on the drop-down list.

For Figure 2-2, I chose Tight for the picture on the left and Square for the picture on the right. As the figure shows, you can drag the Text Wrapping drop-down list away from the toolbar and make the Text Wrapping toolbar appear. Clicking the buttons on the toolbar makes it easier to experiment with wrapping options.

Replacing the Placeholder Graphics

As you might have noticed, publication designs are littered with generic clip-art images and graphics. Besides writing your own words where the generic ones are, replace the generic graphics with graphics of your own. Well, do it if you please. You're welcome to pass off the generic pictures as your own. I won't tell anybody.

Follow these steps to put a graphic where a placeholder graphic is now:

1. Right-click the picture and choose Change Picture.

2. On the submenu, choose what kind of picture you want to import.

What happens next depends on what kind of picture you're dealing with. Book VIII, Chapter 3 describes how to handle graphics in all Office programs. You'll be delighted to discover that graphics are handled the same way, no matter which program you're toiling in.

The next section in this chapter explains how to put a graphic on the page without the benefit of a placeholder graphic.

Inserting Frames on the Pages

Publications are made of frames — text frames, table frames, WordArt frames, picture frames, and Design Gallery frames. Nothing appears on the pages of a publication unless it appears within the confines of a frame. These pages explain everything you need to know about frames. You can find out how to insert a new frame, adjust the size of a frame, align frames, and place borders around frames. You can also see how to make frames and the words or images inside them overlap.

Inserting a new frame

To insert a new frame, click one of the six frame tool buttons — Text Box, Draw Vertical Text Box, Insert Table, Insert WordArt, Picture Frame, or

Design Gallery Object — on the Objects toolbar, click in your publication, and drag. As you drag, you form a rectangle. Release the mouse button when the frame is the right size. (The next section in this chapter explains how to adjust the size and position of a frame.) Do the following to create a text-box (or vertical-text-box), table, WordArt, picture, or clip-art frame:

✦ **Text frame for paragraphs, headings, and stories:** Click in the frame and start typing. Earlier in this chapter, "Entering Text on the Pages" offers speed techniques for entering text. By clicking the Draw Vertical Text Box button, you can enter text that reads sideways.

✦ **Table frame for tables:** You see the Create Table dialog box, as shown in Figure 2-3. Choose the number of rows and columns you want, and in the Table Format list, select a layout for your table.

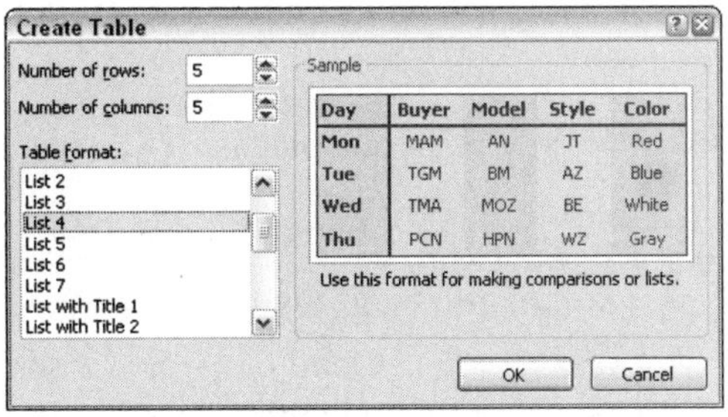

Figure 2-3:
Inserting
a table.

Day	Buyer	Model	Style	Color
Mon	MAM	AN	JT	Red
Tue	TGM	BM	AZ	Blue
Wed	TMA	MOZ	BE	White
Thu	PCN	HPN	WZ	Gray

Create Table. Number of rows: 5. Number of columns: 5. Table format: List 2, List 3, List 4, List 5, List 6, List 7, List with Title 1, List with Title 2. Use this format for making comparisons or lists. OK Cancel

✦ **WordArt frame for WordArt images:** The WordArt Gallery dialog box opens when you create a WordArt frame. Select an image and click OK.

✦ **Picture frame for clip art:** Click the Picture Frame button and choose Clip Art on the drop-down list. In the Clip Art task pane, find and select a clip-art image. Book VIII, Chapter 4 explains clip art.

✦ **Picture frame for art from a file:** Click the Picture Frame button and choose Picture from File on the drop-down list. The mouse pointer changes to a cross-hair. After you drag to form the picture frame, the Insert Picture dialog box appears so that you can choose a picture.

To delete a frame, all you have to do is select it and press the Delete key. You can tell when a frame is selected because round selection handles appear on the corners and sides.

Changing the size and position of frames

After you click a frame and see the selection handles, you're ready to change the size of the frame or adjust its position on the page. Use these standard techniques for resizing and moving frames:

✦ **Changing the size of a frame:** Move the pointer over a round selection handle and start dragging. If you're dealing with anything but a text frame, be careful about dragging a selection handle on the side of the frame. Dragging a side handle changes the frame's size as well as its proportions. Images can blur or become distorted when you change their proportions.

✦ **Changing the position of a frame:** Move the pointer onto the frame (or the perimeter of a frame if you're dealing with a text box), and click and drag when you see the four-headed arrow. To move more than one frame simultaneously, Ctrl+click the frames you want to move.

As I explain in Chapter 1 of this mini-book, frames snap to the grid as you move them, but you can hold down the Alt key as you drag to adjust frames with precision. You can also choose Arrange⇨Nudge and choose Up, Down, Left, or Right on the submenu to move a frame ever so slightly.

Making Frames Overlap

When frames overlap, you have to tell Publisher which frame goes in front of the other. And you are hereby invited to overlap frames because overlapping frames are artful and look good on the page. Figure 2-4 shows a portion of a newsletter. If you look closely, you can see where frames overlap in the figure. Overlapping frames like these make for a sophisticated layout.

Figure 2-4: Examples of overlapping frames.

Order toolbar

Making frames overlap like the ones in Figure 2-4 requires a delicate balancing act using these commands:

✦ **Text wrapping:** Wrapping must be turned off for frames to overlap. Select the frames, click the Text Wrapping button on the Picture toolbar, and choose None on the drop-down list.

✦ **Fill Color:** For frames and objects on the bottom of the stack to show through, the frames and objects above them cannot have a fill color that would obscure other objects. To remove the fill color, select the object, open the Fill Color drop-down list on the Formatting toolbar, and choose No Fill.

✦ **Object and frame order:** To tell Publisher which object goes where in the stack, right-click each object in turn, choose Order on the shortcut menu, and choose an option on the submenu. As Figure 2-4 shows, you can drag this submenu onto the screen and thereby have the Order toolbar at your command. Click buttons on the toolbar until objects are in the right order in the stack.

Inserting, Removing, and Moving Pages

Suppose that you have too many pages or you need to add a page or two. Follow these instructions to insert, remove, or move a page:

✦ **Inserting a new page:** Click a page navigation button to move to the page where you want to insert pages; then choose Insert⇨Page or press Ctrl+Shift+N. In the Insert Page dialog box, enter the number of pages you want to insert and click an option button to put the new pages before or after the page you're on. Then, under Options, choose an option to tell Publisher what to put on the new page or pages and click OK.

✦ **Removing a page:** Go to the page you want to remove and choose Edit⇨ Delete Page.

✦ **Moving a page:** Go to the page you want to move and choose Edit⇨ Move Page. Give instructions for moving the page in the Move Page dialog box and click OK.

**Book VII
Chapter 2**

**Refining a
Publication**

Chapter 3: Putting On the Finishing Touches

In This Chapter

✔ Using horizontal rules and drop caps

✔ Decorating frames with borders and color backgrounds

✔ Putting a background on a page

✔ Putting objects and frames on the master page

✔ Inserting a Design Gallery object

✔ Preparing publications so that they can be printed commercially

T his final chapter in Book VII is devoted to the Project to Beautify Publications, a joint effort of the Dummies Press and the author to try to make publications less bland and more original. The author has noticed, on the bulletin boards and lampposts in his neighborhood, that the rummage sale and lost pet notices look a little rough around the edges. The neighbors are using sophisticated software to produce their notices, but they're not using it well. They're relying solely on templates, which make the publications look alike. These pages explain a few simple tricks for making publications more sophisticated.

This chapter explores drop caps and horizontal rules, page backgrounds and borders, borders and backgrounds for frames, and how to place a logo in the same place on each page in a publication. It shows you Publisher's excellent Design Checker and Graphics Checker. Finally, this chapter offers advice for printing publications at a commercial print shop.

Decorating the Text

Herewith are a couple of tricks to amaze your friends and frighten your ene-mies. These pages explain how horizontal rules and drop caps can make a publication a little livelier. Don't worry — horizontal rules have nothing to do with which side of the bed to sleep on, and drop caps don't explode when you unroll them on the sidewalk and strike them with a hammer.

Drawing a horizontal rule

A *horizontal rule* is a horizontal line that divides one part of a page from another and directs the reader's eye on the page. There are four horizontal rules in Figure 3-1. By varying the width of the lines — the width is known as the *weight* — and placing lines in strategic places, you can make a publication look more elegant and graceful. How you draw a horizontal rule depends on whether you want to draw it above or below a frame, or above or below a text paragraph. The horizontal rules in Figure 3-1 appear above and below frames. Rules appear between paragraphs to mark an abrupt transition between paragraphs. In a mystery story, for example, the horizontal rule appears right after the murderer gets away.

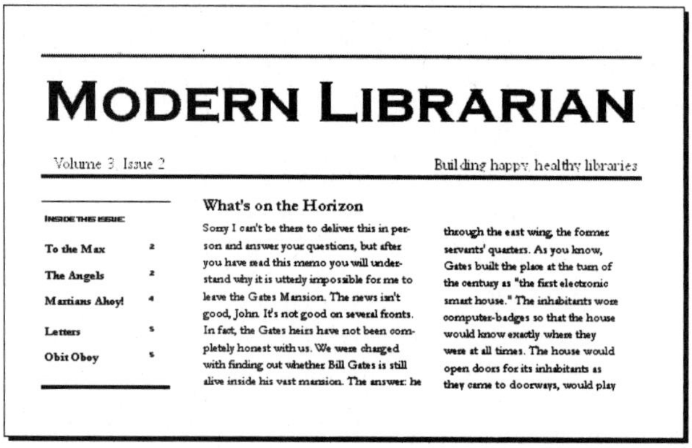

Figure 3-1: Examples of horizontal rules.

Usually where horizontal rules come in pairs, the bottommost rule is thicker than its twin. The thicker bottom line encourages the reader's eye to move down the page and find an article to read.

A horizontal rule on a frame

Follow these steps to draw a horizontal rule on a frame:

1. **Select the frame, right-click it, and choose Format.**

   The Format command has different names depending on what type of frame or object you are working with. You see the Format dialog box.

2. **Select the Color and Lines tab.**

3. **In the Preview box, click the top of the box to draw a rule above the frame or the bottom of the box to draw a rule below.**

By clicking part of the Preview box, you tell Publisher where you want to draw the rule.

4. **On the Color menu, choose a line color for the horizontal rule.**

5. **On the Style menu, choose the kind of line you want.**

   If you want a dashed line, choose it from the Dashed drop-down list. You can adjust the thickness of the line in the Weight text box, if necessary.

6. **To draw a second rule on the frame, click again in the Preview box and repeat Steps 4 and 5.**

7. **Click OK.**

To remove a horizontal rule on a frame, select the frame, open the Format dialog box, and choose No Line on the Color drop-down list.

A horizontal rule on a paragraph

Follow these instructions to draw a horizontal rule above or below a paragraph:

1. **Click in the paragraph and choose Format⇨Horizontal Rules.**

   You see the Horizontal Rules dialog box.

2. **Select the Rule before Paragraph or Rule after Paragraph check box, or both check boxes if you want to draw two horizontal rules.**

3. **Choose options to describe the thickness, color, and style of the line you want.**

   Lines extend from margin to margin or column to column, but you can shorten the lines by entering measurements in the From Left Margin and From Right Margin text boxes.

   To put more distance between the rule and paragraph text, enter a measurement in the Before Paragraph or After Paragraph text box.

4. **Click OK.**

   To remove horizontal rules from a paragraph, click the paragraph, choose Format⇨Horizontal Rules, and remove the check marks from the Rule before Paragraph and Rule after Paragraph check boxes.

Dropping in a drop cap

A *drop cap* is a large capital letter that "drops" into the text. Drop caps are usually found in the first paragraph of an article or chapter. Pound for pound, considering how little effort is required, a drop cap yields the most reward for the least amount of work. Follow these steps to place a drop cap in a publication:

1. **Click the paragraph that is to receive the drop cap and choose Format⇨ Drop Cap.**

You see the Drop Cap dialog box, as shown in Figure 3-2.

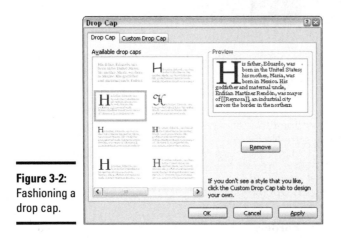

Figure 3-2: Fashioning a drop cap.

2. **Select one of the drop caps and click OK.**

If the drop caps on the Drop Cap tab don't do the trick, visit the Custom Drop Cap tab, where you can choose how far to drop the capital letter or select a font for the letter. To remove a drop cap, return to the Drop Cap dialog box and choose the first option.

Techniques for Decorating Pages

No one likes a dull publication. Following are some simple techniques to make pages a little bit livelier. Read on to find out how to put borders and color backgrounds on frames. You also find instructions for painting an entire page with a background color or gray shade.

Putting borders and color backgrounds on frames

As shown in Figure 3-3, putting borders and background colors on text frames makes the frames stand out. Everybody knows what a border is. A background color is a color or gray shade that fills a frame. Borders and background colors are ideal for calling readers' attention to important notices and items in publications. To really get readers' attention, for example, try using black for the background and white for the font color.

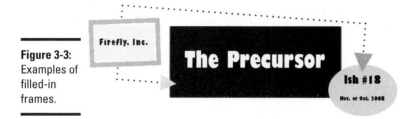

Figure 3-3:
Examples of
filled-in
frames.

Select a frame and follow these instructions to give it background color or a border:

✦ **Background color:** Open the drop-down list on the Fill Color button and choose a color. Choose No Fill to remove the background color or to create no background color so that frames below the frame you're dealing with can show through.

✦ **Color for the border:** Open the drop-down list on the Line Color button and choose a color.

✦ **Line or dashed-line border:** Click the Line/Border Style button and choose a line. Or choose More Lines to open the Format dialog box and choose from many different lines or to put a border on only one, two, or three sides of the frame. (Earlier in this chapter, "Drawing a horizontal rule" explains how to draw a border on different sides of a frame.)

Instead of clicking buttons on the Formatting toolbar, you can handle borders and backgrounds in the Format dialog box. Right-click a frame and choose Format on the shortcut menu to open this dialog box. The Colors and Lines tab offers all kinds of commands for borders and backgrounds.

Backgrounds for pages

Yet another nifty trick is to put a color or gray-shade background on the page. Be sure to choose a light color or gray shade that doesn't get in the way of your publication or render it impossible to read. Shrink the publication to 33 percent so that you can see what backgrounds really look like; then follow these steps to give your publication pages a background:

1. **Choose Format⇨Background.**

The Background task pane opens, as shown in Figure 3-4.

2. **Experiment with the Tint buttons and Color choices until you find a suitable background.**

To remove the background color, return to the Background task pane and select No Fill, the first Color choice.

Choose a tint.

Choose a background.

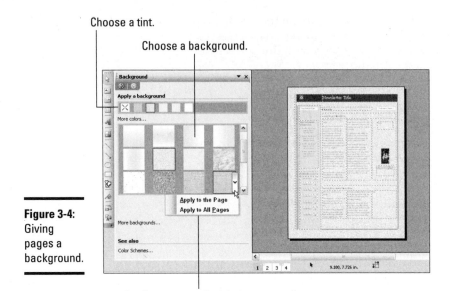

Figure 3-4:
Giving
pages a
background.

Apply to one or all of the pages.

The Master Page for Handling Page Backgrounds

In a publication with many pages, the same object sometimes goes on every page. A company logo on the corner of each page looks mighty elegant. Page numbers and copyright information are also found on all the pages of some publications. The good news is that you don't have to place the objects on each page individually. Instead, you can place the objects on the *master page*. Objects on the master page show up on every page.

To open the master page, choose View➪Master Page (or press Ctrl+M). You switch to Master view. Place objects and frames on the master page as if you were putting them on run-of-the-mill pages. You can tell when you're looking at a master page because the page navigation buttons show letters instead of numbers.

In a publication with facing pages, creating two master pages, one for the left-facing pages and another for the right-facing pages, is convenient. To create a second master page, choose Arrange➪Layout Guides, and in the Layout Guides dialog box, choose Two-Page Master. The original master becomes the master page for right-facing pages, the new master page becomes the one for left-facing pages, and Publisher copies everything on the original master page (right) to the second master page (left).

TIP

When background objects on the master page get in the way, choose View⇨ Ignore Master Page to prevent them from appearing on-screen. Click the Close Master View button on the Edit Master Pages toolbar when you're finished with master pages.

Taking Advantage of the Design Gallery

The Design Gallery is a collection of objects — logos, pull quotes, accent boxes, and thingamajigs — that you can throw into your publications. Figure 3-5 shows some examples of Design Gallery objects. They are great for filling blank spaces in a publication. After you've placed the object, you can change its size or shift its position by using the same techniques you use with other objects.

Figure 3-5:
Examples
of Design
Gallery
objects.

To insert a Design Gallery object, click the Design Gallery Object button on the Objects toolbar or choose Insert⇨Design Gallery Object. You see the Design Gallery dialog box. Select an object that tickles your fancy — there are about 250 objects in 22 categories — and click the Insert Object button.

Running the Design Checker

When at last your publication is ready for printing, be sure to run the Design Checker. This helpful tool can alert you to frames that fall on nonprinting parts of the page, stories that "overflow" without finding a text frame to go to, invisible objects, and a host of other problems.

Choose Tools⇨Design Checker to run the Design Checker. As shown in Figure 3-6, the Design Checker task pane opens and lists items that need your attention. Open an item's drop-down list and choose Go to This Item to locate it in your publication. Sometimes the drop-down lists offer quick fixes as well.

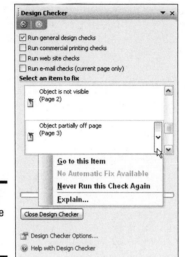

Figure 3-6:
Running the
Design
Checker.

To see which design flaws the Design Checker looks for, click the Design Checker Options hyperlink in the Design Checker task pane. Then, in the Design Checker Options dialog box, select the Checks tab and read the list.

Commercially Printing a Publication

You know the routine for printing a publication on your computer: Click the Print button; or choose File⇨Print, negotiate the Print dialog box, and click OK.

Sending a publication to a commercial printer is a different story. Commercial printers either print with process colors (also known as CMYK) or spot colors. To put it simply, process colors are made by mixing cyan, magenta, yellow, and black to make colors, whereas spot colors are premixed before printing begins. Before you hand over your publication to a commercial printer, find out which color system the printer prefers. It costs more to print with process colors than spot colors because process-color printing requires each color to be created on a different color plate. Process colors, however, produce color photographs much better than spot colors do.

Follow these steps to convert the colors in your publication to the color system that the commercial printer prefers:

1. **Choose Tools⇨Commercial Printing Tools⇨Color Printing.**

   You see the Color Printing dialog box.

2. **Under Define All Colors As, choose Spot Colors or Process Colors (CMYK).**

3. **Click OK.**

Publisher also offers the Pack and Go command for copying large files onto CDs and embedding fonts in the file. Whereas normally Publisher calls upon instructions from the computer to display fonts, embedding fonts make those instructions part of the file itself. These fonts display the same on all computers — including the computer your printer uses. Embedding fonts, however, makes files grow bigger.

To use the Pack and Go command, choose File⇨Pack and Go⇨Take to a Commercial Printing Service. The Pack and Go dialog box appears. Keep clicking Next and following the directions in the dialog box until your publication is "packed and gone."

Book VIII

Office 2007 — One Step Beyond

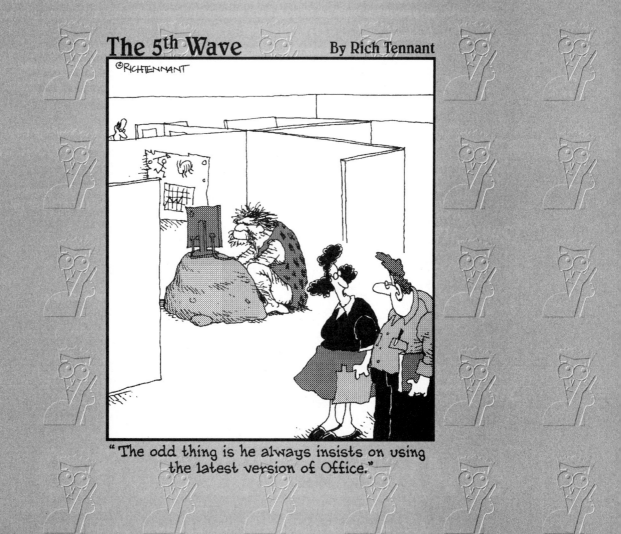

The 5th Wave   By Rich Tennant

"The odd thing is he always insists on using the latest version of Office."

Contents at a Glance

Chapter 1: Customizing an Office Program

In This Chapter

✔ **Changing around the Quick Access toolbar**

✔ **Choosing what appears on the status bar**

✔ **Choosing a new color scheme**

✔ **Changing the keyboard shortcuts in Word**

✔ **Deciding what to do about Smart Tags**

*T*his short chapter describes a handful of things you can do to customize Office 2007 programs. Don't be afraid to make like a software developer and change a program to your liking. Many people are wary of retooling Office programs, but you can always reverse the changes you make if you don't like them, as I explain throughout this chapter.

This chapter shows how to put your favorite button commands on the Quick Access toolbar. Instead of fishing around for your favorite commands, you can assemble them on the Quick Access toolbar and locate them right away. You also discover how to change around the status bar, dress up an Office program in a new set of clothes, designate your own keyboard short-cuts in Word, and handle Smart Tags, the data snippets that sometimes get mysteriously underlined in Office files.

Customizing the Quick Access Toolbar

No matter where you go in Word, Access, Excel, or PowerPoint, you see the Quick Access toolbar in the upper-left corner of the screen. This toolbar offers the Save, Undo, and Repeat buttons (and sometimes other buttons as well). However, which buttons appear on the Quick Access toolbar is entirely up to you. You can put your favorite buttons on the toolbar and keep them within reach. And if the Quick Access toolbar gets too big, you can move it below the Ribbon, as shown in Figure 1-1. Adding buttons to and removing buttons from the Quick Access toolbar is, I'm happy to report, a piece of cake. And moving the toolbar below the Ribbon is as easy as pie.

Figure 1-1:
Merely
by right-
clicking, you
can add a
button to the
Quick
Access
toolbar.

Right-click a button to add it to the toolbar.

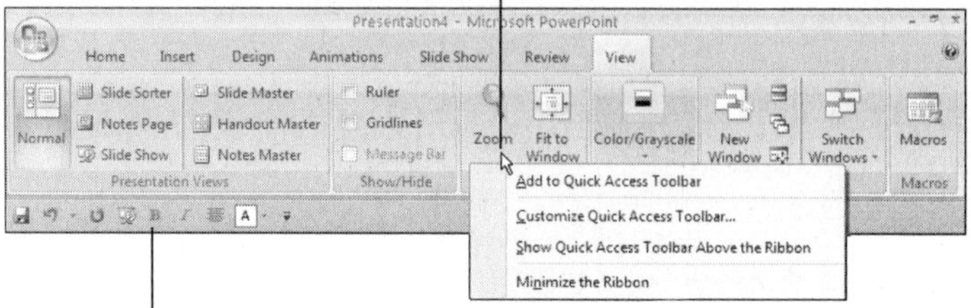

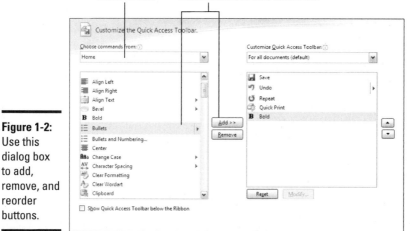

The Quick Access toolbar below the Ribbon.

Adding buttons to the Quick Access toolbar

Use one of these techniques to add buttons to the Quick Access toolbar:

✦ Right-click a button you want to see on the toolbar and choose Add to Quick Access Toolbar on the shortcut menu (see Figure 1-1).

✦ Click the Customize Quick Access Toolbar button and choose a button on the drop-down list. The list offers buttons deemed most likely to be placed on the Quick Access toolbar by the makers of Office.

✦ Click the Customize Quick Access Toolbar button and choose More Commands (or right-click any button or tab and choose Customize Quick Access Toolbar on the shortcut menu). You see the Customize category of the Options dialog box, as shown in Figure 1-2. On the Choose Commands From drop-down list, choose the name of the tab with the button you want to add to the Quick Access toolbar. Then select the button's name and click the Add button.

Select a tab.   Select a button and click Add.

Figure 1-2:
Use this
dialog box
to add,
remove, and
reorder
buttons.

To restore the Quick Access toolbar to its original buttons, click the Reset button in the Options dialog box (see Figure 1-2).

Unless you declare otherwise, changes you make to the Quick Access toolbar apply to all the files you work on. You can, however, construct a toolbar for one file only. To alter the Quick Access toolbar for one file, go to the Customize category of the Options dialog box (see Figure 1-2), open the Customize Quick Access Toolbar drop-down list, choose the name of your file, and then start altering the toolbar.

Changing the order of buttons on the Quick Access toolbar

Follow these steps to change the order of buttons on the Quick Access toolbar:

1. **Click the Customize Quick Access Toolbar button and choose More Commands on the drop-down list.**

   The Customize category of the Options dialog box appears (see Figure 1-2). You can also open this dialog box by right-clicking any button or tab and choosing Customize Quick Access Toolbar.

2. **Select the name of a button on the right side of the dialog box and click the Move Up or Move Down button.**

3. **Repeat Step 2 until the buttons are in the right order.**

4. **Click OK.**

Removing buttons from the Quick Access toolbar

Use one of these techniques to remove buttons from the Quick Access toolbar:

✦ Right-click a button and choose Remove from Quick Access Toolbar on the shortcut menu.

✦ Right-click any button or tab and choose Customize Quick Access Toolbar. You see the Customize category of the Options dialog box (refer to Figure 1-2). Select the button you want to remove on the right side of the dialog box and click the Remove button.

You can click the Reset button in the Options dialog box (refer to Figure 1-2) to remove all the buttons you placed on the Quick Access toolbar.

**Book VIII
Chapter 1**

Customizing an
Office Program

Placing the Quick Access toolbar above or below the Ribbon

The Ribbon is the stretch of ground along the top of the screen where the tabs and buttons are found. If your Quick Access toolbar contains many buttons, consider placing it below the Ribbon, not above it (refer to Figure 1-1). Follow these instructions to place the Quick Access toolbar above or below the Ribbon:

✦ **Quick Access toolbar below the Ribbon:** Right-click the toolbar, and on the shortcut menu, choose Show Quick Access Toolbar below the Ribbon.

✦ **Quick Access toolbar above the Ribbon:** Right-click the toolbar, and on the shortcut menu, choose Show Quick Access Toolbar above the Ribbon.

The Options dialog box offers a check box called Place Quick Access Toolbar below the Ribbon (refer to Figure 1-2). You can select this check box as well to move the toolbar above the Ribbon.

Customizing the Status Bar

The status bar along the bottom of the window gives you information about the file you're working on. The Word status bar, for example, tells you which page you're on, how many pages are in your document, and several other things. In PowerPoint, the status bar tells you which slide you're looking at and the theme you chose for your presentation. It also presents the view buttons and zoom controls.

To choose what appears on the status bar in Word, PowerPoint, Access, or Excel, right-click the status bar. You see a pop-up list similar to the one in Figure 1-3. By selecting and deselecting items in this list, you can decide what appears on the status bar.

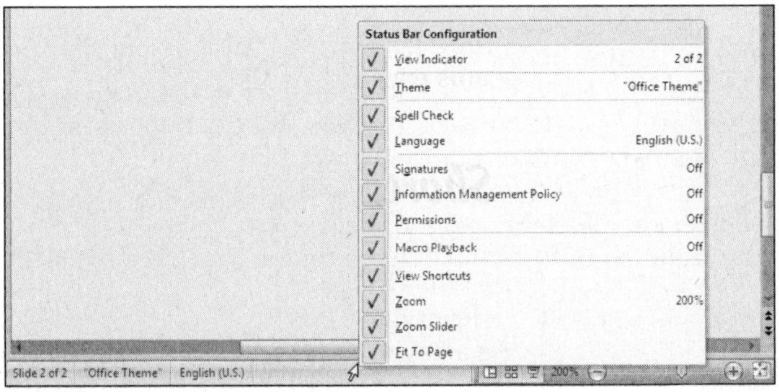

Figure 1-3: Right-click the status bar to customize it.

Changing Color Schemes

Figure 1-5 shows three color schemes with which you can dress up Excel, Outlook, Access, Word, and PowerPoint: Blue, Silver, and Black. Which do you prefer? Follow these steps to choose a color scheme for PowerPoint:

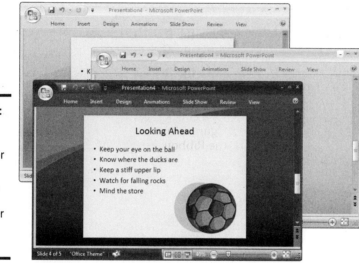

Figure 1-4:
Take your choice of these color schemes: Blue (top), Silver (middle), or Black (bottom).

1. **Click the Office button and choose Options.**

   You see the Options dialog box.

2. **Click the Popular category.**

3. **Open the Color Scheme drop-down list and choose Blue, Silver, or Black.**

4. **Click OK.**

   How do you like your new get-up? The color scheme you choose applies to all the Office programs except Publisher.

Customizing Keyboard Shortcuts in Word

In Microsoft Word, you can change the keyboard shortcuts. A *keyboard shortcut* is a combination of keys that you press to give a command. For example, pressing Ctrl+P opens the Print dialog box; pressing Ctrl+S gives the Save command. If you don't like a keyboard shortcut in Word, you can change it and invent a keyboard shortcut of your own. You can also assign keyboard shortcuts to symbols, macros, fonts, AutoText entries, and styles.

Follow these steps to choose keyboard shortcuts of your own in Microsoft Word:

1. **Click the Office button and choose Word Options.**

You see the Word Options dialog box.

2. **Select the Customize category.**

3. **Click the Customize button.**

You see the Customize Keyboard dialog box, as shown in Figure 1-5.

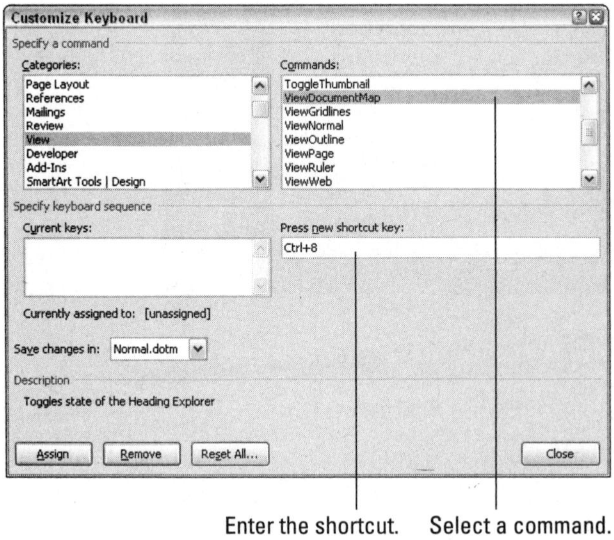

Customize Keyboard

Specify a command

Categories:

Page Layout
References
Mailings
Review
View
Developer
Add-Ins
SmartArt Tools | Design

Commands:

ToggleThumbnail
ViewDocumentMap
ViewGridlines
ViewNormal
ViewOutline
ViewPage
ViewRuler
ViewWeb

Specify keyboard sequence

Current keys:

Press new shortcut key:

Ctrl+8

Currently assigned to: [unassigned]

Save changes in: Normal.dotm

Description

Toggles state of the Heading Explorer

Assign   Remove   Reset All...   Close

Figure 1-5: Assigning keyboard shortcuts to commands.

Enter the shortcut.   Select a command.

4. **In the Categories list, choose the category with the command to which you want to assign the keyboard shortcut.**

At the bottom of the list are the Macros, Fonts, AutoText, Styles, and Common Symbols categories.

5. **Choose the command name, macro, font, AutoText entry, style, or symbol name in the Commands list.**

6. **In the Press New Shortcut Key box, type the keyboard shortcut.**

Press the actual keys. For example, if the shortcut is Ctrl+8, press the Ctrl key and the 8 key — don't type out C-t-r-l-+8.

If you try to assign a shortcut that's already assigned, the words "Currently assigned to" and a command name appear below the Current Keys box. You can override the preassigned keyboard assignment by entering a keyboard assignment of your own.

7. **If you want the keyboard shortcut changes you make to apply to the document you're working on, not to all documents created with the template you're working with, open the Save Changes In drop-down list and choose your document's name.**

8. **Click the Assign button.**

9. **When you're done, close the Customize Keyboard dialog box.**

To delete a keyboard shortcut, display it in the Current Keys box, select it, and click the Remove button.

You can always get the old keyboard shortcuts back by clicking the Reset All button in the Customize Keyboard dialog box.

Smart Tags, Smart Alecks

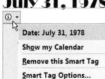

A *Smart Tag* is a snippet of data that Office programs recognize as a date, an address, a company ticker name, a place, a telephone number, or a person to whom you recently sent e-mail. If the program recognizes one of these entities, it places a purple dotted line underneath the data. Move the pointer over the purple dotted line and you see the Smart Tag icon. Click this icon and you see a shortcut menu with tasks, as shown in Figure 1-6.

July 31, 1978

ⓘ ▾
Date: July 31, 1978
Show my Calendar
Remove this Smart Tag
Smart Tag Options...

Figure 1-6: A Smart Tag in action.

Not everyone likes Smart Tags, however. Follow these steps to turn them off or otherwise tell Office which ones to recognize:

1. **Click the Office button.**

2. **Choose Options on the drop-down list.**

3. **Select the Proofing category of the Options dialog box, and click the AutoCorrect Options button.**

You see the AutoCorrect dialog box.

4. **Click the Smart Tags tab.**

5. **Deselect the Label Text with Smart Tags check box.**

   Rather than ditch Smart Tags altogether, you can select check boxes to tell Office which data types you want to "smart tag."

6. **Click OK.**

Chapter 2: Ways of Distributing Your Work

In This Chapter

✔ **Printing files**

✔ **Saving files so others can read them in Adobe Acrobat Reader**

✔ **Sending a file by e-mail**

✔ **Saving a file so it can be viewed in a Web browser**

✔ **Writing and keeping a blog from inside Word**

*T*his chapter explains how to distribute your work to co-workers and friends. You'll be glad to know that people who don't have Office 2007 can still read and review an Office 2007 file you created. You can print it for them, save it so it can be read in Adobe Acrobat Reader, or save it as a Web page. This chapter explains all that as well as how to send a file right away by e-mail and write and post blog entries from inside Word.

By the way, this book explains other ways to distribute your work. Book IV, Chapter 5 demonstrates how to provide audience handouts for PowerPoint presentations and ship presentations on CDs; Chapter 6 of this mini-book looks at how to trade files with SharePoint Services.

Printing — the Old Standby

In spite of predictions to the contrary, the paperless office is still a pipe dream. The day when Johnny at his computer is completely digitized and communicating with his colleagues without having to print anything on paper has yet to materialize. As for Jane, she can hardly go a day without printing reports, spreadsheets, and brochures. The office is still awash in paper, and all Jane and Johnny can do for consolation is try their best to recycle.

I describe the details of printing files elsewhere in this book, but here are the bare outlines of printing:

✦ **Printing right away:** Click the Office button and choose Print⇨Quick Print. The file you want to print goes straight to the printer.

✦ **Going first to the Print dialog box:** Press Ctrl+P or click the Office button and choose Print⇨Print to open the Print dialog box, as shown in Figure 2-1. From there, you can select a printer, choose how many copies to print, choose which parts of a file to print, and plump for other printing options.

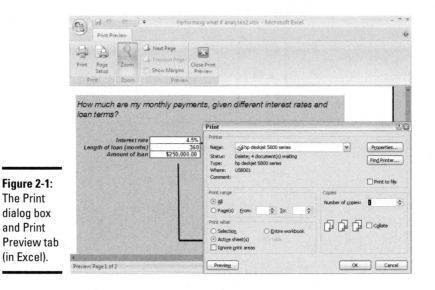

Figure 2-1:
The Print dialog box and Print Preview tab (in Excel).

✦ **Previewing before you print:** Click the Office button and choose Print⇨Print Preview. (Except in Word, you can also click the Preview button in the Print dialog box.) You see the Print Preview tab, as shown in Figure 2-1. The tab shows what your file looks like when you print it. You can tinker with your file before you print it on the Print Preview tab.

Distributing a File in PDF Format

As shown in Figure 2-2, you can save and distribute a file in the PDF (Portable Document File) format if the person to whom you want to give the file doesn't have the program with which it was created. For example, someone who doesn't have Excel can still view your Excel file in PDF format. Moreover, you can post PDF files on the Internet so others can view them there.

PDF files are designed to be viewed and printed in a program called Adobe Acrobat Reader. This program is very good at acquiring data from other programs and presenting it so it can be read and printed easily. Nearly every computer has Adobe Acrobat Reader. If someone to whom you sent a PDF file doesn't have the program, they can download it for free at this Web page:

www.adobe.com/acrobat

Figure 2-2:
A Word
document
as seen
through the
eyes of
Adobe
Acrobat
Reader.

To save an Office file as a PDF, you need a special add-in program from the Microsoft Web site. After you download and install the add-in, you can save files in the PDF format by clicking the Office button and choosing Save As⇨PDF.

To acquire the add@@hyin, go to the Microsoft Download Center at www.microsoft.com/downloads. Then, in the Search box, enter **Save as PDF** and click the Go button.

Sending Your File in an E-Mail Message

As long as you handle your e-mail with Outlook 2007, you can send the file you're working on to a friend or co-worker without having to open Outlook 2007. You simply choose a command and send the thing over the Internet. Follow these steps to send the file you're working on to a friend or co-worker:

1. **Click the Office button.**

2. **Choose Send⇨Email.**

An Outlook 2007 message window appears with the name of your file on the subject line and the file itself in the Attach box. Your presentation is ready to send along with the e-mail message.

3. **Enter the recipient's address in the To box and a message in the Message box.**

Book III, Chapter 3 explains how to address, compose, and send e-mail messages.

4. Click the Send button.

That was fast! It was faster than opening Outlook and attaching the file to the e-mail message on your own.

Saving an Office File as a Web Page

Figure 2-3 shows what an Excel file looks like after it is saved as a Web page and displayed in a Web browser. Looks like a normal Excel worksheet, doesn't it? Anyone with a Web browser can view a worksheet or other Office file after it's saved as a Web page. Save an Office file as a Web page and post it on the Internet or an intranet so that others who don't have Office can view it.

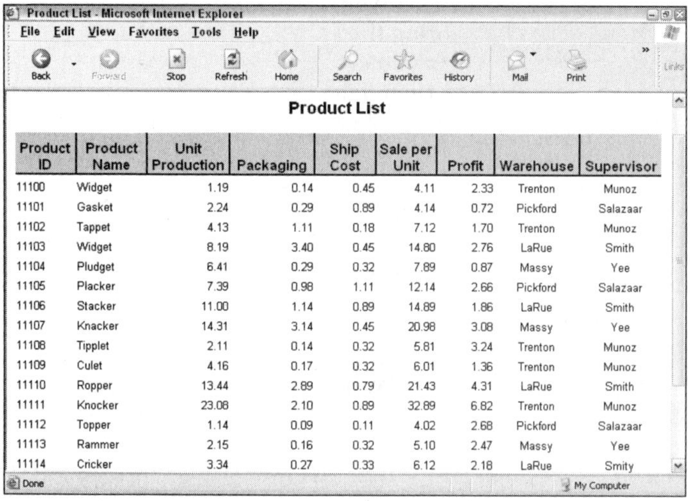

Product List

Product ID	Product Name	Unit Production	Packaging	Ship Cost	Sale per Unit	Profit	Warehouse	Supervisor
11100	Widget	1.19	0.14	0.45	4.11	2.33	Trenton	Munoz
11101	Gasket	2.24	0.29	0.89	4.14	0.72	Pickford	Salazaar
11102	Tappet	4.13	1.11	0.18	7.12	1.70	Trenton	Munoz
11103	Widget	8.19	3.40	0.45	14.80	2.76	LaRue	Smith
11104	Pludget	6.41	0.29	0.32	7.89	0.87	Massy	Yee
11105	Placker	7.39	0.98	1.11	12.14	2.66	Pickford	Salazaar
11106	Stacker	11.00	1.14	0.89	14.89	1.86	LaRue	Smith
11107	Knacker	14.31	3.14	0.45	20.98	3.08	Massy	Yee
11108	Tipplet	2.11	0.14	0.32	5.81	3.24	Trenton	Munoz
11109	Culet	4.16	0.17	0.32	6.01	1.36	Trenton	Munoz
11110	Ropper	13.44	2.89	0.79	21.43	4.31	LaRue	Smith
11111	Knocker	23.08	2.10	0.89	32.89	6.82	Trenton	Munoz
11112	Topper	1.14	0.09	0.11	4.02	2.68	Pickford	Salazaar
11113	Rammer	2.15	0.16	0.32	5.10	2.47	Massy	Yee
11114	Cricker	3.34	0.27	0.33	6.12	2.18	LaRue	Smity

Figure 2-3: Viewing an Excel worksheet in a Web browser.

These pages explain the different ways to save an Office file as a Web page, as well as how to save your Office file as a Web page and open a Web page you created in a Web browser.

Choosing how to save the component parts

When you save an Office file as a Web page, you have the choice of saving it as a Single File Web Page (`.mht`, `.mhtml`) or Web Page (`.htm`, `.html`).

- **Single File Web Page (`.mht`, `.mhtml`):** All component parts of the file — graphics, separate pages, and sounds, for example — are bundled into a single file. Keeping all the component parts in one file makes moving, copying, and sending the file easier. However, some browsers can't open or read .mht and .mhtml files. As of this writing, Internet Explorer can handle the files, but only the latest editions of Mozilla Firefox and Opera can handle them.

✦ **Web Page (.htm, .html):** All the component parts of the file are kept in separate files and are saved in the same folder. Keeping the component parts in separate files is the standard way to present pages on the Internet. Handling the half-dozen or more files that are needed to display the Web page can be troublesome, but you can be certain that the Web page displays properly in all browsers.

Turning a file into a Web page

Before you save your file as a Web page, create a folder on your computer or computer network for storing the page if you intend to save it in several files in the .htm format. Unless you create a folder for storing all the files, you'll have a hard time locating them later, and you must be able to locate them to transfer them to a Web server for display on the Internet or to send them to someone else.

Follow these steps to save an Office file as a Web page:

1. **Click the Office button and choose Save As on the drop-down list.**

The Save As dialog box appears.

2. **Open the Save As Type drop-down list and choose Single File Web Page (.mht; .mhtml) or Web Page (.htm; .html).**

Earlier in this chapter, "Choosing how to save the component parts" explains what these options are. New buttons — Change Title and Publish — appear in the Save As dialog box.

3. **Click the Change Title button, enter a descriptive title in the Set Page Title dialog box, and click OK.**

The title you enter will appear in the title bar along the top of the Web browser window (refer to Figure 2-3).

4. **Click the Publish button.**

The Publish As Web Page dialog box appears. This dialog box offers many options for deciding what the Web page looks like and how its files are organized.

5. **Click the Browse button, and in the Publish As dialog box, select the folder where you'll keep the Web page (and its support files); then click OK.**

You return to the Publish as Web Page dialog box.

6. Select the Open Published Web Page in Browser check box.

By selecting this box, you can see your presentation in a Web browser as soon as you save it as a Web page. The new Web page opens in your *default browser,* the one that opens automatically on your computer when your computer encounters a Web page.

7. Click the Publish button.

Office creates the Web page (and its support files if you chose Web Page [.htm; .html] in Step 2); it stores the file or files in the folder you selected in Step 5.

The Web page you created opens in your browser if you selected the Open Published Web Page in Browser check box.

Opening a Web page in your browser

To open a Web page you fashioned from an Office file, open the folder where you stored the Web page in My Computer or Windows Explorer and click the .htm or .hmtl file named after your file. For example, if your file is called Sales Projections, double-click the Sales Projections.htm or Sales Projections.html file to open the Web page.

While you're at it, you may consider bookmarking the Web page so you can open it in your browser. To bookmark a Web page in Internet Explorer, open the Web page you want to bookmark and choose Favorites⇨Add to Favorites.

Blogging from inside Word

The word *blog* is shorthand for *Web log.* A typical blog is a hodgepodge of commentary and links — to online news sources and often other blogs — where topics of concern to the blogger are discussed. Many blogs are online diaries. You get a daily picture of what the blogger is interested in — dating, technology, politics, and just about anything else under the sun.

To make it easier to keep a blog, Word offers special commands for writing blog entries and posting them immediately with a blogging service. Figure 2-4 shows the blogging feature in action. The title and the blog entry in the Word document are transported *in toto* to the blog without your having to enter a password or even visit a blogging service. To take advantage of Word's blogging feature, you must already have an account with a blogging service.

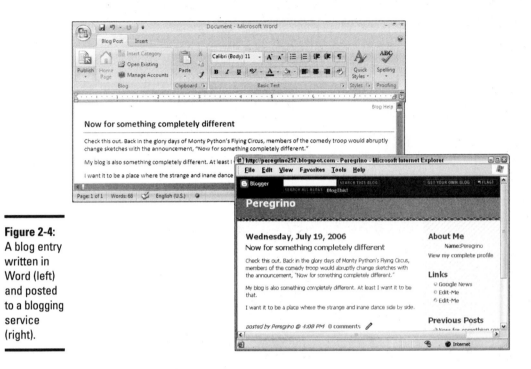

Figure 2-4:
A blog entry written in Word (left) and posted to a blogging service (right).

Describing a blog account to Word

Word can't post entries to a blog unless you tell it where the blog is located, what your password is, and some other juicy tidbits. As of this writing, Word is compatible with these blogging services: MSN Spaces, Blogger, Sharepoint, Community Server, TypePad, and WordPress. If you post blog entries at a different service, you need to know its blog post URL (the address to which you post entries) and its API protocol setting (either Atom or MetaWeblog).

Follow these steps to tell Word how and where to upload blog entries:

1. **Click the Office button and choose Publish⇨Blog.**

You go to the Blog Post tab (see Figure 2-4).

2. **Click the Manage Accounts button.**

The Blog Accounts dialog box appears. It lists places where you keep blogs.

3. **Click the New button.**

The New Blog Account dialog box appears.

4. **On the Blog Host drop-down list, choose where on the Internet your blog is stored and then click Next.**

Choose Other if your service isn't on the list.

5. **Enter your username, password, and other pertinent information.**

Which options you see next depends on which blogging service you use. You're asked for a username and password, and also perhaps an http or ftp address for publishing pictures on your blog.

When you're finished describing your blogging service, its name appears in the Blog Accounts dialog box. Return to this dialog box and click the Change button if you need to change your password or another particular.

Posting an entry to your blog

When you're ready to share your thoughts with the world, follow these steps to write and post an entry to your blog from inside Word:

1. **Write the title and the blog entry on the Blog Post tab.**

You can do that starting with a new document or a document you've already written.

- *New document:* Click the Office button, choose New, and in the New Document dialog box, double-click the New Blog Post icon. Then enter a title for the entry and the entry itself.

- *Already-written document:* Write the entry in a new document, click the Office button, and choose Publish⇨Blog. Word gives you a place to write the title ("Enter Post Title Here"). Enter the title.

Whichever method you choose, you land in the Blog Post tab (refer to Figure 2-4). It offers all the character styles and proofing tools that you find in Word. Go to the Insert tab to enter a hyperlink. (Book I, Chapter 2 explains hyperlinks.)

2. **Click the Publish button on the Blog Post tab.**

If all goes well, Word informs you that your post has been published on your blogging service, and it lists the time and date it was published. This information appears in the Word document itself.

Instead of publishing your blog entry right away, you can open the drop-down list on the Publish button and choose Publish as Draft. Doing so uploads the blog entry to your blogging service without posting it. The entry lands on the Editing page, where you can select it, click the Editing button, and edit it online before publishing it.

Chapter 3: Handling Graphics

In This Chapter

✔ Understanding the different graphic file formats

✔ Placing a graphic in a Word document, PowerPoint slide, or Excel worksheet

✔ Recoloring, cropping, and altering a graphic's brightness and contrast

✔ Compressing graphics

✔ Handling graphics with Office Picture Manager

A picture, so they say, is worth a thousand words. Whether it's worth a thousand words or merely 950 is debatable. What is certain is that visuals help people remember things. A carefully chosen image in a Power-Point presentation, Word document, or Excel worksheet helps others understand you better. The image reinforces the ideas or information that you're trying to put across.

This chapter explains how you can make pictures — photographs and graphics — part of your Word documents, PowerPoint presentations, and Excel worksheets. It looks into graphic file formats, copyrights, and other issues pertaining to graphics as well as how to touch up graphics in an auxiliary program called Office Picture Manager.

By the way, Chapter 4 in this mini-book looks at another way to decorate your work with images — by using clip art.

All about Picture File Formats

Graphics and photographs come in many different file formats, and as far as Office 2007 is concerned, some are better than others. These pages explain what you need to know about graphic files to use them wisely in Office files. Here, you find out what bitmap and vector graphics are, what resolution and color depth are, and how graphic files are compressed.

Bitmap and vector graphics

All graphic images fall into either the bitmap or vector category:

✦ A *bitmap graphic* is composed of thousands upon thousands of tiny dots called *pixels* that, taken together, form an image (the term pixel comes from "picture element").

✦ A *vector graphic* is drawn with the aid of computer instructions that describe the shape and dimension of each line, curve, circle, and so on.

The major difference between the two formats is that vector graphics do not distort when you enlarge or shrink them, whereas bitmap graphics lose resolution when their size is changed. Furthermore, vector images do not require nearly as much disk space as bitmap graphics. Drop a few bitmap graphics in a file and soon you're dealing with a file that is close to 750k in size and takes a long time to load.

Table 3-1 describes popular bitmap graphic formats; Table 3-2 lists popular vector graphic formats. The clip-art images that come with Office are Windows Metafile (WMF) files (Chapter 4 in this mini-book explains how to handle these clip-art images).

Table 3-1	Bitmap Graphic File Formats	
Extension	*File Type*	*Compression*
BMP, BMZ, DIB	Microsoft Windows Bitmap	None
FPX	FlashPix	Lossy
GFA, GIF	Graphics Interchange Format	Lossy
JPEG, JPG, JFIF, JPE	JPEG File Interchange Format	Lossy
PCD	Kodak Photo CD	Lossy
PICT	Macintosh PICT	None
PCX	PC Paintbrush	Lossless
PNG	Portable Network Graphics	Lossless
RLE	Bitmap File in RLE Compression Scheme	None
TIF, TIFF	Tagged Image File Format	Lossless

Table 3-2	Vector Graphic File Formats
Extension	*File Type*
CDR	CorelDRAW
CGM	Computer Graphics Metafile

Extension	File Type
DXF	AutoCAD Format 2-D
EMF	Enhanced Windows Metafile
EMZ	Windows Enhanced Metafile
EPS	Encapsulated PostScript
PCT	Macintosh PICT
WMF	Windows Metafile
WPG	WordPerfect Graphics

Resolution

Resolution refers to how many pixels comprise a bitmap image. The higher the resolution, the clearer the image is. Resolution is measured in *dots per inch* (dpi), sometimes called *pixels per inch* (ppi). Images with more dots — or pixels — per inch are clearer and display more fineness of detail. When you scan an image, your scanner permits you to choose a dots-per-inch setting.

High-resolution images look better but require more disk space than low-resolution images. Figure 3-1 illustrates the difference between a high- and low-resolution photograph.

Figure 3-1:
A high-resolution photo (left) and the same photo at low resolution (right).

Compression

Compression refers to a mathematical algorithm by which bitmap graphic files can be made smaller. In effect, compression enables your computer to store a bitmap graphic with less disk space. Some bitmap graphic types can't be compressed; the other bitmap graphic types are compressed using either lossless or lossy compression:

✦ **Lossless compression:** To maintain the picture's integrity, the same number of pixels is stored in the compressed file as in the original. Because the pixels remain intact, you can change the size of a file that has undergone lossless compression without losing picture quality.

✦ **Lossy compression:** Without regard for the picture's integrity, pixel data in the original picture is lost during compression. Therefore, if you try to enlarge a picture that has undergone lossy compression, the picture loses quality.

Choosing file formats for graphics

One of the challenges of using graphics and photographs in Office files is keeping file sizes to a minimum. A file that is loaded down with many photographs can take a long time to load and send over the Internet because graphics and photographs make files that much larger. The trick is to find a balance between high-quality, high-resolution graphics and the need to keep files sizes low. Here are some tips for choosing graphic file formats:

✦ Consider sticking with vector graphics if you're including graphics in your file strictly for decoration purposes. As Chapter 4 of this mini-book explains, Office provides vector clip-art images. These images are easy to come by, don't require very much disk space, and can be edited inside Word, PowerPoint, and Excel.

✦ For photographs, make JPEG your first choice for graphics. JPEG images have a fairly high resolution. If you intend to post your file on the Internet, you can't go wrong with JPEGs; they are the de facto photograph standard on the Internet.

✦ If you're dealing with black-and-white photos or resolution doesn't matter, use GIF files. These files eat up the least amount of disk space.

Inserting a Graphic in a File

After you weigh the merits of different kinds of graphics and decide which one is best for you, you can insert it. Inserting a graphic is as simple as choosing it in the Insert Picture dialog box. Follow these steps to insert a graphic on a PowerPoint slide, Word document, or Excel worksheet:

1. **Click the Insert tab.**

2. **Click the Picture button.**

You see the Insert Picture dialog box, as shown in Figure 3-2. In PowerPoint, you can also open this dialog box by clicking the picture icon in a content placeholder frame.

The all-important copyright issue

To save any image on the Internet to your computer, all you have to do is right-click it and choose Save Picture As. By starting from Google Image Search (www.images.google.com), you can scour the Internet for any image you need. Never before has it been easier to obtain images for your own use.

Still, obtaining images and using them legally are two different matters. Would it surprise you to know that the vast majority of graphics can't be used without the owner's permission? The copyright laws have a "fair use" provision for borrowing written words. You can quote others' words as long as you cite the author and work and you don't quote passages longer than 250 to a thousand words (the "fair use" provision is vague on this point). The copyright law regarding graphics is quite straightforward. Unless you have the owner's permission, you can't legally use a graphic.

Sometimes it's hard to tell who owns a graphic. The artist or photographer (or his or her estate) doesn't necessarily own the copyright because artists sometimes relinquish their copyrights when they create works for hire. The only way to get permission to use a graphic is to ask. Contact the owner of the Web site with the image you want, the publisher if the image is in a book, or the museum if the work is owned by a museum. You'll be asked to write a letter describing precisely how you intend to use the image, reproduce it, and distribute it. Your letter should also say how long you intend to use it and at what size you intend to reproduce it.

Select a picture file.   Switch to Thumbnails or Preview view.

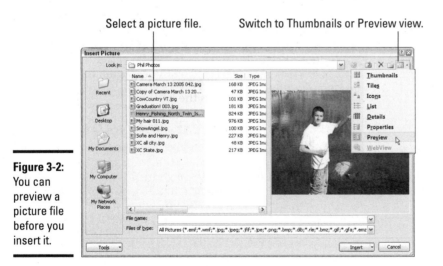

Figure 3-2:
You can preview a picture file before you insert it.

Book VIII
Chapter 3

Handling Graphics

3. **Select a file in the Insert Picture dialog box.**

As Figure 3-2 shows, you can open the drop-down list on the Views button and choose Preview to see what the graphic looks like before you import it. Thumbnails view can also be a help because it gives you a glimpse of several different files.

You can open the Files of Type drop-down list and choose a file type to locate files of a certain type in the dialog box.

4. **Click the Insert button.**

Select the (Picture Tools) Format tab to see all the different ways you can manipulate a graphic after you insert it. After a graphic lands on a file, it becomes an object. Book I, Chapter 8 explains how to manipulate objects — how to move them, change their size, and change their borders. The following pages look into various ways to change the appearance of graphics.

Touching Up a Graphic

Every graphic can be a *collaboration,* not the work of a single artist. In the (Picture Tools) Format tab, you can find commands for recoloring, changing the brightness, and changing the contrast of a graphic. You can collaborate with the original artist and create something new. You can also *crop* an image — that is, cut off part of it.

PowerPoint, Word, and Excel offer only a handful of tools for changing a graphic's appearance. If you have the time and the inclination, alter a graphic's appearance in a program designed especially for that purpose. You can find many more options for editing graphics in Photoshop, Paint Shop Pro, and Corel Photo-Paint, for example. Later in this chapter, "Using Microsoft Office Picture Manager" describes a nifty program that comes with Office for editing pictures.

Changing a graphic's brightness and contrast

Figure 3-3 shows a graphic that has been made over several times with the Brightness and Contrast commands. Select a graphic, go to the (Picture Tools) Format tab, and experiment with the Brightness and Contrast commands to alter a graphic's look. You'll find the Brightness and Contrast commands in the Adjust group.

Figure 3-3:
Experiments
with the
Brightness
and
Contrast
commands.

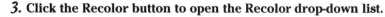

Brightness: Click the Brightness button and choose an option on the drop-down list. The positive percentage options make the picture brighter; the negative percentage options make it darker.

Contrast: Click the Contrast drop-down list and choose an option to enhance or mute the difference between light and dark colors or shades. The positive percentage options heighten the differences; the negative percentage options mute the differences.

You can also click the Picture Styles group button and then adjust the Brightness and Contrast settings in the Picture category of the Format Shape dialog box.

If you regret experimenting with the Recolor, Brightness, and Contrast commands and you want to start all over, click the Reset Picture button. Clicking this button restores a picture to its original condition.

Recoloring a graphic

Recolor a graphic when you want to bleach it a certain color. Recoloring gives a graphic a uniform color. Recolored graphics are useful for backgrounds because they allow the text to show through and be read, as shown in Figure 3-4. Follow these steps to recolor a graphic:

 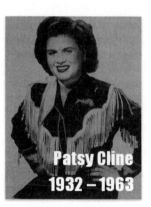

Figure 3-4: This graphic was recolored for use with a text.

1. **Select the graphic.**

2. **Click the (Picture Tools) Format tab.**

3. **Click the Recolor button to open the Recolor drop-down list.**

4. **Choose a Recolor option.**

Book VIII
Chapter 3

Handling Graphics

Live previewing really comes in handy when you're recoloring a graphic. Move the pointer over options on the Recolor drop-down list and watch your graphic to see what happens. Choose the More Variations option to open a submenu with many color options.

Cropping off part of a graphic

Cropping cuts off part of a graphic. I'm afraid you can't use the Office cropping tool — like a pair of scissors or an Xacto knife — to cut zigzag around the edges of a graphic or cut a hole in the middle. You can, however, cut strips from the side, top, or bottom. In Figure 3-5, the cropping tool was used to cut off all but the head of a figure to turn a portrait into a head shot.

Drag a handle to crop part of a graphic.

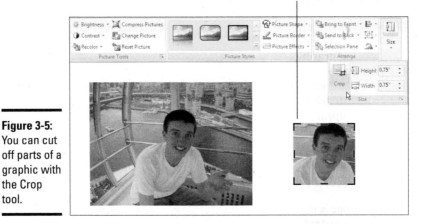

Figure 3-5:
You can cut off parts of a graphic with the Crop tool.

Follow these steps to crop off part of a graphic:

1. **Select the graphic.**

2. **Click the (Picture Tools) Format tab.**

3. **Click the Crop button.**

Depending on the size of your screen, you may have to click the Size button to get to the Crop button, as shown in Figure 3-5. You see the cropping pointer, and instead of selection handles, cropping handles appear around the graphic. You see eight cropping handles, one on each side and one on each corner.

4. **Drag a handle to crop start cropping.**

You may drag more than one handle to crop the image on more than one side.

5. **Release the mouse button when only the portion of the graphic that you want is inside the dashed lines.**

If you cropped too far, grab a cropping handle and drag away from the center of the image. What you cropped reappears.

6. **Click the Crop button again or press Esc after you finish cropping your graphic.**

When you crop a graphic, you don't cut off a part of it — not as far as your computer is concerned. All you do is tell Office not to display part of a graphic. The graphic is still whole. You can, however, compress a graphic after you crop it, and in so doing, truly shave off a part of the graphic and thereby decrease the size of the file you're working with, as "Compressing Graphics to Save Disk Space" explains later in this chapter.

Compressing Graphics to Save Disk Space

By compressing graphics, you reduce their file size and consequently the size of the file you're working on. Not all graphics can be compressed, as "Compression" explains earlier in this chapter, and some types of graphics lose their integrity when they're compressed. You can't resize lossy-compressed graphics without their looking odd.

Changing a picture's shape

Another way to crop a graphic is to change its shape. Changing from the standard rectangle to a diamond, for example, crops off the corners of the graphic. Follow these steps to change a picture's shape:

1. **Select the graphic.**

2. **Click the (Picture Tools) Format tab.**

3. **Click the Picture Shape button.**

A drop-down list of shapes appears.

4. **Choose a shape.**

If you don't like the shape you choose, either click the Undo button or reopen the Picture Shape drop-down list and choose a different shape. Choosing the Rectangle shape restores a picture to its original shape.

Book VIII
Chapter 3

Handling Graphics

Compress graphics to make files load faster and make e-mail messages with file attachments travel faster over the Internet. Compressing a graphic file reduces its pixels per inch (ppi) setting. Follow these steps to compress graphics:

1. **(Optional) Select the graphic or graphics you want to compress if you want to compress only one or two graphics.**

   The Compress Pictures command compresses all the graphics in a file unless you select graphics first.

2. **Click the (Picture Tools) Format tab.**

3. **Click the Compress Pictures button.**

   You see the Compress Pictures dialog box.

4. **Select the Apply to Selected Pictures Only check box if you selected graphics in Step 1 and you want to compress only a couple of graphics.**

5. **Click OK.**

By clicking the Options button in the Compress Pictures dialog box, you can open the Compression Settings dialog box and declare how you want to compress your graphics:

✦ **Automatically Perform Basic Compression on Save:** Select this check box to compress graphic files each time you save your file.

✦ **Delete Cropped Areas of Pictures:** As "Cropping off part of a graphic" explains earlier in this chapter, Office crops graphics in name only. Office retains the cropped part of the graphic in case you want it back, but you can remove the cropped part as well by selecting this check box.

✦ **Target Output options:** These options — Print (220 ppi), Screen (150 ppi), and E-mail (96 ppi) — tell Office which pixels per inch (ppi) setting to use when compressing graphics. Choosing a higher setting makes the graphics look sharper but also requires more disk space. In other words, the higher setting doesn't compress the graphic as much.

Using Microsoft Office Picture Manager

You may not know it, but you installed a program for managing and editing pictures when you installed Office. The program is called Microsoft Office Picture Manager, and you can use it to organize graphics and touch up graphics before inserting them in a PowerPoint, Word, Excel, or Publisher file. As shown in Figure 3-6, Picture Manager displays graphics so that you can see precisely what your editorial changes do to them. The program makes it easy to find and organize graphic files on your computer. In most Office programs, you can find commands for editing graphics, but you often have to dig in obscure dialog boxes to find them. Picture Manager puts the editing commands on the side of the screen where you can find them easily.

Select a folder where graphics are stored.   Zoom in or out.

Change views.   Edit a graphic.

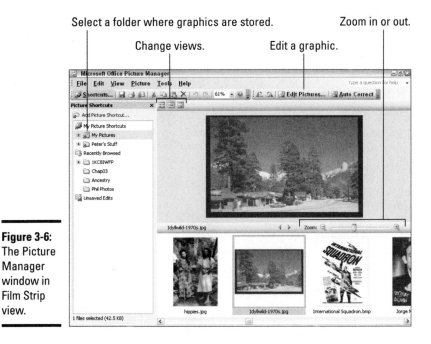

Figure 3-6:
The Picture Manager window in Film Strip view.

To open Picture Manager, click the Start button and choose All Programs⇨ Microsoft Office⇨Microsoft Office Tools⇨ Microsoft Office Picture Manager. You see the window, as shown in Figure 3-6. Starting there, you can display a graphic on your computer and change its appearance in several different ways.

Mapping the graphic files on your computer

The first step in using the Picture Manager is to tell the program what kind of graphic files you work with and point to the folders on your computer where these graphic files are located. After you tell Picture Manager which folders graphic files are kept in, shortcuts to the folders appear in the Picture Shortcuts pane on the left side of the window (see Figure 3-6). By clicking one of these shortcuts, you can open a folder, view its contents, and edit a graphic file.

Follow these instructions to get started in Picture Manager:

✦ **Telling the program which graphic file types you use:** Choose Tools⇨ File Types to open the File Types dialog box. Select the file types you want to manipulate with Picture Manager and click OK. Earlier in this chapter, Tables 3-1 and 3-2 explain what these files types are.

✦ **Telling the program which folders contain graphic files:** Choose File⇨ Add Picture Shortcut or click the Add Picture Shortcut link in the Picture Shortcuts pane (click the Shortcuts button to see this pane). The Add Picture Shortcut dialog box opens. Select a folder where you store graphics that you want to work with and click the Add button.

Instead of pointing to folders one at a time, you can choose File⇨Locate Pictures and have Picture Manager scour your computer or network for the graphic file types you select in the File Types dialog box. Shortcuts to folders with those file types appear in the Picture Shortcuts task pane. If you go this route, however, you'll likely discover many, many folders on your computer where graphic files are kept, and shortcuts to these folders will crowd the Picture Shortcuts task pane.

Click the Shortcuts button (or choose View⇨Shortcuts) to display the Picture Shortcuts task pane. To remove a shortcut from the task pane, right-click it and choose Remove Shortcut.

Displaying the graphic file you want to work with

After you've created shortcuts to the folders where you keep graphic files, you can display a graphic file by following these steps:

1. **Click the Shortcuts button, if necessary, to display the Picture Shortcuts task pane.**

2. **Click a shortcut to a folder.**

   Graphic files in the folder appear in the middle window (refer to Figure 3-6).

3. **Scroll to or choose a different view to pinpoint the file.**

   Picture Manager offers three views: Thumbnails, Filmstrip, and Single Picture. Click a View button to change views (refer to Figure 3-6).

Double-click a thumbnail image to see a graphic in Single Picture view. To zoom in and out, drag the Zoom slider.

Editing a picture

With the graphic you want to edit on display, you're ready to start editing. Your next task is to display the editing tools you need on the right side of the window, as shown in Figure 3-7. Picture Manager offers two ways to get the editing tools you need:

✦ Click the Edit Pictures button to display the Edit Pictures task pane. It lists the names of editing tools. Click the link that represents the kind of editing you want to do. For example, to crop a graphic, click the Crop link.

✦ Open the Picture menu and choose a task — Brightness and Contrast, Color, Crop, Rotate and Flip, Red Eye Removal, Resize, or Compress Pictures. For example, choose Picture⇨Crop to cut off part of a graphic.

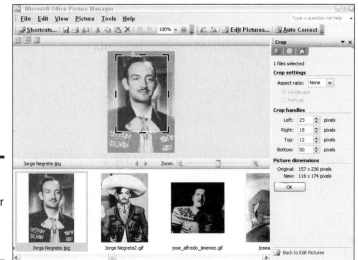

Figure 3-7: The editing tools appear on the right side of the window.

To let Picture Manager try its hand at improving your graphic, click the Auto-Correct button (or choose Picture⇨AutoCorrect).

If you regret making changes to a graphic, choose Edit⇨Discard Changes. All changes you made are reversed, and you get your original graphic back.

Click the Save button (or press Ctrl+S) to save your graphic after you've finish editing it. For that matter, choose File⇨Save As before you start editing and save the file under a new name so that you have the original in reserve.

If you edit one picture and go to another without saving the first one, Picture Manager takes notice. Copies of unsaved files are kept in the Unsaved Edits folder. To see the contents of this folder, click Unsaved Edits in the Picture Shortcuts task pane. Unsaved graphics appear on-screen so that you can select and save them, if you so choose.

Adjusting the brightness and contrast

Select a graphic and choose Picture⇨Brightness and Contrast or click the Brightness and Contrast hyperlink in the Edit Pictures task pane to adjust a graphic's tonal intensity. You see a Brightness, Contrast, and Midtone slider on the Brightness and Contrast task pane. Without going into too much detail, here is what these sliders do:

✦ **Brightness:** Adjusts the inherent brightness value in each pixel. Increasing the brightness makes the image lighter; decreasing it makes the image darker.

✦ **Contrast:** Increasing the contrast, in the words of a laundry detergent manufacturer, "makes your whites whiter and your darks darker," whereas decreasing the contrast making the tones more similar.

✦ **Midtone:** Redefines the *midtones,* or tonal values between light and shadow, of an image. Dragging the slider to the right brightens the image.

If dragging the sliders doesn't provide the results you want, say the heck with it and just click the Auto Brightness button to let Picture Manager adjust the brightness and contrast for you.

Balancing the colors

Select a graphic and choose Picture⇨Color or click the Color hyperlink in the Edit Pictures task pane to fine-tune a graphic's colors.

You can have Picture Manager do the fine-tuning for you. Click the Enhance Color button and then click a part of the graphic that is supposed to be white. If you don't like the results, try balancing the colors in the graphic yourself by dragging these three sliders:

✦ **Amount:** Increasing this value magnifies the hue and saturation settings; decreasing this value minimizes them.

✦ **Hue:** Increasing this value further distinguishes the colors from one another; decreasing this value makes the colors blend.

✦ **Saturation:** Increasing the value makes colors more luminous; decreasing this value makes colors grayer.

Cropping a graphic

Select a graphic and choose Picture⇨Crop or click the Crop hyperlink in the Edit Pictures task pane to cut off parts of a graphic. Picture Manager shows precisely how much of the graphic you will crop when you click the OK button (refer to Figure 3-7). The Crop task pane is especially useful if you want your graphic to be a certain size. Under Picture Dimensions, you can see exactly how many pixels high and wide your graphic is. By dragging the selected part of the graphic — the part that isn't grayed out — you can be very precise about what part of the graphic remains after you crop.

The Crop task pane offers two ways to crop a graphic:

✦ **Crop at will:** In the Aspect Ratio drop-down list, choose None and then drag a corner or side cropping handle.

✦ **Maintain symmetry when you crop:** Choose an option from the Aspect Ratio drop-down list and select the Landscape or Portrait option button before you drag a corner or side cropping handle. *Aspect ratio* proportionally describes the relationship between a graphic's width and height. For example, at the 4 x 6 aspect ratio, the graphic in Portrait mode is a third taller than it is wide (⅔); in Landscape mode, the graphic is a third wider than it is tall. Choose an aspect ratio setting when you want your graphic to have symmetry.

Cropping a graphic doesn't reduce its file size. To reduce a graphic's file size after you've cropped it, compress the graphic. See "Compressing a graphic" later in this chapter.

Rotating and flipping graphics

Select a graphic and choose Picture⇨Rotate and Flip, or click the Rotate and Flip hyperlink in the Edit Pictures task pane to rotate or flip graphics. The Rotate commands turn the graphic on its side; the Flip commands provide mirror images of the original graphic. You can rotate a graphic by degrees by entering a value in the By Degree text box. The Formatting toolbar also offers Rotate buttons for rotating graphics.

Removing "red eyes" from a graphic

Sometimes the subject of a photo appears to have *red eyes,* not because the subject didn't get enough sleep, but because the camera flash made the subject's irises turn red. Follow these steps to remove red eye from a digital flash photograph:

1. **Choose Picture⇨Red Eye Removal or click the Red Eye Removal hyperlink in the Edit Pictures task pane.**

2. **Drag the Zoom slider to the right so that you get a good look at the red eyes in the photo.**

3. **Click each red eye to select it.**

4. **Click the OK button.**

   You can click the Reset Selected Eyes button to start all over, if you need to do that.

Resizing a graphic

To change the size of a graphic, select it and choose Picture⇨Resize or click the Resize hyperlink in the Edit Pictures task pane. You land in the Resize task pane. It offers three ways to change the size of a graphic:

✦ **Predefined Width x Height:** Select this option button, and on the drop-down list, choose the setting that best describes the graphic's size. For example, if you intend to post the graphic on a Web page, choose Web - Large or Web - Small.

✦ **Custom Width x Height:** Select this option button and enter pixel measurements for the width and height of the graphic. Be careful with this option because the graphic doesn't maintain its original proportions unless you calculate the proportions yourself, and when a resized graphic loses its original proportions, it can be skewered or blurred.

✦ **Percentage of Original Width x Height**: Select this option button and enter the percentage by which you want to enlarge or shrink the graphic.

The bottom of the task pane tells you how many pixels wide and high your graphic was to start with and how wide and high it is after resizing.

Compressing a graphic

Near the beginning of this chapter, "Compression" explains what compressing a graphic entails. Compress a graphic to reduce its file size. Compressing a graphic file reduces its pixels per inch (ppi) setting. Some graphic types, however, can't be compressed.

To compress a graphic, select it and choose Picture⇨Compress Pictures or click the Compress Pictures hyperlink in the Edit Pictures task pane. You see the Compress Pictures task pane. The bottom of the task pane tells you how much the graphic shrinks in size after you compress it. Choose a Compress For option button and click OK.

Chapter 4: Decorating Files with Clip Art

In This Chapter

✔ **Understanding what clip art is**

✔ **Placing a clip-art image on a page, slide, or worksheet**

✔ **Changing the look of a clip-art image**

✔ **Using the Clip Organizer to store, organize, and insert clip art**

This chapter explains how you can use clip art to decorate Word documents, PowerPoint slides, and Excel worksheets. You also find a treatise on how to use the *Microsoft Clip Organizer,* an auxiliary program for storing clip art and other kinds of media files so that you can find the files in a hurry. If you often use media files in your work, you owe it to yourself to look into the Clip Organizer.

What Is Clip Art?

In the old days, long before the invention of computers, people would buy clip-art books. They would literally cut, or clip, images from these books and paste them into posters, letters, and advertisements. Today's clip art is the digital equivalent of old-fashioned clip art: You can paste clip art into computer programs such as Word, PowerPoint, Excel, and Publisher. You can resize clip-art images without the images losing their integrity. The clip art that comes with Office 2007 isn't encumbered by licensing restrictions; it's in the public domain, and you can use it as you please.

Figure 4-1 shows examples of some clip-art images that come with Office. Use images like these to decorate your files. Use them to help illustrate an idea or simply to add a little liveliness to your work. In my experience, the hardest task where clip art is concerned is finding the right image. You can choose from so many images that finding the right one is a chore.

Figure 4-1:
Examples
of clip-art
images.

Inserting a Clip-Art Image

To insert a clip-art image, you open the Clip Art task pane, search in the Clip Organizer for the image you want, and insert the image. The trick to finding the right image is knowing your way around the Clip Organizer. The majority of this chapter explains how to organize the art on your computer so that you can get it by way of the Clip Organizer. For now, you can follow these basic steps to insert a clip-art image in a page, slide, or worksheet:

1. **Click the Insert tab.**

2. **Click the Clip Art button.**

You see the Clip Art task pane, as shown in Figure 4-2. In PowerPoint, you can also click the Clip-Art icon to insert a clip-art image in a content placeholder frame.

Choose where to search.

Search by keyword.

Choose what to search for.

Figure 4-2:
Inserting a
clip-art
image by
way of the
Clip Art task
pane.

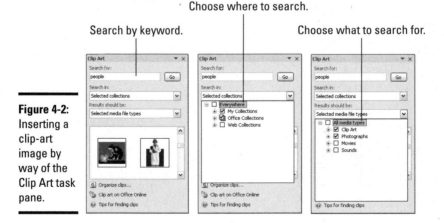

The Clip Art task pane is actually an entrée into the *Clip Organizer,* the Microsoft program for organizing and quickly inserting clip art. (The Clip Organizer is explained in more detail later in "Handling Media Files with the Clip Organizer.")

3. **In the Search For text box, enter a keyword that describes the clip-art image you need.**

   Later in this chapter, "Searching for a media file in the Search pane" explains how keywords work.

4. **In the Search In drop-down list, choose the collections you want to search in (see Figure 4-2).**

   Later in this chapter, "Searching for a media file in the Search pane" describes what these collections are.

5. **In the Results Should Be drop-down list, choose Clip Art (see Figure 4-2).**

6. **Click the Go button.**

   The bottom of the task pane shows the clip-art images found in your search. You may have to scroll through the task pane to see all the images.

7. **Double-click an image or open its drop-down list and choose Insert to place it in your Word document, PowerPoint slide, or Excel worksheet.**

   Your next task is to move the image into position and perhaps change its size. Book I, Chapter 8 explains how to manipulate clip-art images and other objects.

Tinkering with a Clip-Art Image's Appearance

Sometimes a clip-art image doesn't sit well with the rest of the page, slide, or worksheet. The image is too bright or too dark. It clashes with the colors in the rest of the file. When an image clashes, you don't have to abandon it in favor of another image. As Figure 4-3 shows, you can alter a clip-art image's appearance in different ways. Select your image, go to the (Picture Tools) Format tab, and change the image's appearance with these techniques:

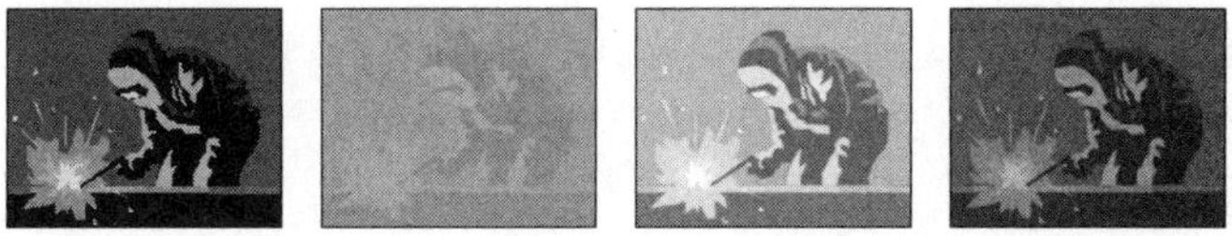

**Book VIII
Chapter 4**

**Decorating Files
with Clip Art**

Figure 4-3:
You can
change the
look of a
clip-art
image.

✦ **Recoloring:** Click the Recolor button and choose an option to remake the clip-art image in a different tint.

✦ **Changing the brightness:** Click the Brightness button and choose an option to make the image brighter or darker.

✦ **Changing the contrast:** Click the Contrast button and choose an option to enhance or mute the difference between light and dark colors or shades in the image.

Handling Media Files with the Clip Organizer

As computers get faster and better, media files — clip art, graphics, video clips, and sound files — will play a bigger role in computing. Dropping a clip-art image in a Word document or PowerPoint slide won't be a big deal. Playing video clips on PowerPoint slides will be commonplace.

Well aware that the future is closing in on us, Microsoft created the Clip Organizer to help you manage the media files on your computer. By using the Clip Organizer, you can place graphics, video clips, and sound files in Word documents, PowerPoint presentations, Excel worksheets, and Publisher publications. More important, the Clip Organizer is the place to organize media files in your computer so that you can find them and make good use of them. These pages explain how to manage the Clip Organizer.

Do either of the following to open the Clip Organizer:

✦ **Open the Clip Organizer from inside an Office program:** Open the Clip Art task pane (on the Insert tab, click the Clip Art button). Then click the Organize Clips link at the bottom of the task pane.

✦ **Open the Clip Organizer:** Click the Start button and choose All Programs➪Microsoft Office➪Microsoft Office Tools➪Microsoft Clip Organizer.

Knowing your way around the Clip Organizer

As shown in Figure 4-4, the Clip Organizer is divided in two parts, with a pane on the left and a window for displaying files on the right. The Clip Organizer offers two panes: Collection List and Search.

✦ **Collection List task pane:** Use the Collection List task pane to organize your media files and to quickly locate and insert a media file. To display the Collection List task pane, click the Collection List button or choose View➪Collection List.

Click to display a different task pane.   Search results

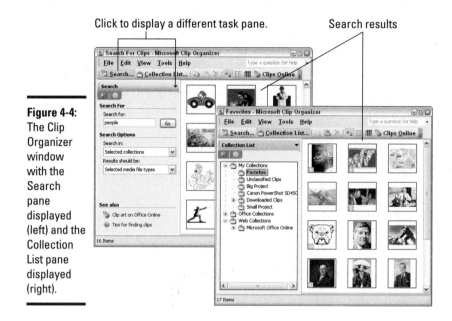

Figure 4-4:
The Clip
Organizer
window
with the
Search
pane
displayed
(left) and the
Collection
List pane
displayed
(right).

✦ **Search task pane:** Use the Search task pane to locate a media file on
your computer. Notice that this task pane is similar to the Clip Art task
pane in Office programs (refer to Figure 4-2). To display the Search task
pane, click the Search button or choose View⇨Search.

Locating the media file you need

The Clip Organizer presents two ways to find a media file you need. Starting
from the Search pane, you can conduct a keyword search; starting from the
Collection List pane, you can select folders and subfolders to display clip art
and other media files on the right side of the window.

Searching for a media file in the Search pane

By entering a keyword in the Search For text box, telling the Clip Organizer
where to look, and telling it what kind of files to look for, you can pinpoint
the clip-art image you need:

✦ **Search For text box:** Enter a keyword that describes what kind of clip-
art image you want. As Figure 4-5 shows, each clip-art image has been
assigned descriptive keywords. If the keyword you enter matches a
keyword assigned to a clip-art image, the image appears in the search
results. (To view an image's keywords, open its drop-down list and
choose Preview/Properties.)

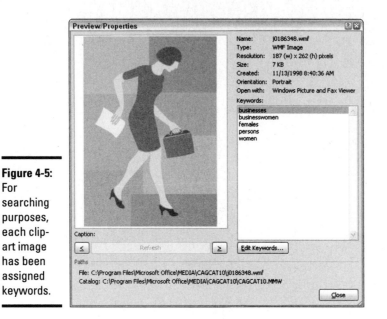

Figure 4-5: For searching purposes, each clip-art image has been assigned keywords.

+ **Search In drop-down list:** Select the Everywhere check box to look on your computer and at the Office clip-art Web site for clip-art images. You can narrow your search to My Collections, Office Collections, or Web Collections:

  - *My Collections:* Search among media files you've deemed favorites, files you placed in folders of your own making, and files you downloaded from Microsoft. Later in this chapter, "Storing your own files in the My Collections folders" explains how to place media files in the Favorites folder and create your own folders for organizing media files.

  - *Office Collections:* Search among the media files that you installed on your computer when you installed Office. These files are organized into categories. Select only a few categories to narrow your search.

  - *Web Collections:* You can search online at the Microsoft Web site that stores media files by selecting Web Collections. As are Office Collections, Web Collections are organized by category.

+ **Results Should Be:** Choose which type of media you're seeking — clip art, photographs, movies, or sounds. By clicking the plus sign (+) next to a media type, you can look for files of a certain kind. To look for JPEG photographs, for example, click the plus sign next to Photographs and select the check box beside JPEG File Interchange Format.

Click the Go button when you're ready to conduct the search. The results of the search appear on the right side of the window (refer to Figure 4-4).

Locating a media file in the Collection List

If you know that the media file you want is stored on your computer, you can find it by starting with the Collection List.

The folders in the Collection List pane work just the same as folders in Windows Explorer. Click a folder name to display its contents on the right side of the screen. Display or hide subfolders by clicking the plus sign (+) or minus sign (–) next to folder names.

When you select a folder (or subfolder) in the Collection List pane, its contents appear on the right side of the Clip Organizer window (refer to Figure 4-4). These are the top-level folders in the Collection List pane:

✦ **My Collections:** Includes the Favorites subfolder (where you can store media files you use most often), subfolders you create yourself for different projects, and the Downloaded Clips subfolder (where clip art you downloaded from Microsoft is stored). How to store a file in the Favorites folder or a folder you create yourself is explained later in this chapter in "Creating your own My Collections subfolder for the Clip Organizer."

✦ **Office Collections:** Includes many subfolders, each named for a clip-art category. Select a subfolder to view clip art in a category. You installed these clip-art images when you installed Office. The clip-art images are located on your computer.

✦ **Web Collections:** Includes many subfolders, each named for a clip-art category. To see these clip-art images, your computer must be connected to the Internet.

Inserting a media file

After you find the media file you want, either by searching in the Search pane or browsing among the folders in the Collection List pane, you can insert it in a Word document, PowerPoint slide, or Excel worksheet by following these instructions:

✦ **Clip Organizer:** Open the file's drop-down list and choose Copy. Then click in your file, go to the Home tab, and click the Paste button (or right-click and choose Paste).

✦ **Clip Art task pane in an Office program:** Either double-click the image or open its drop-down list and choose Insert.

Getting clip art from Microsoft

Microsoft permits users of Office to get their clip art, sound files, and video clips from a Microsoft Web site. To see what kind of media Microsoft offers online, connect your computer to the Internet and click the Clips Online button (you can find it on the right side of the Standard toolbar in the Microsoft Clip Organizer). You come to a Microsoft Web site where you can download collections of clip art and other media files to your computer.

When you find a file you like, select the check box below the image. To download the files to your computer, click the Download link in the Selection Basket (you can find this link on the left side of the window). Items you download from the Microsoft Web site land in the `My Documents\My Pictures\Microsoft Clip Organizer` folder on your computer. In the Clip Organizer, you can find the files in the `My Collections\Downloaded Clips` subfolder.

Storing your own files in the My Collections folders

The Collection List pane in the Clip Organizer is a convenient place to go when you need a media file. Wouldn't it be nice if you could go to the Clip Organizer when you want a file of a family photo, graphics that pertain to your work, or a video you're involved with?

It so happens that you can use the Clip Organizer for your own media files, not just the media files that come with Office. You can arrange it so that the media files you need are available to you simply by selecting the Favorites subfolder in the Collection List pane. For that matter, you can create a subfolder of your own in the Collection List and keep your media files there.

Adding your own media files to the Clip Organizer

If you're a fan of the Clip Organizer — if you think it's a convenient place to store and get media files — place your own files in the Clip Organizer. This way, you can open the Clip Organizer and get right to work making graphics or videos for a project you're working on.

Follow these steps to put your own media files in the Clip Organizer:

1. **Click the Collection List button, if necessary, to see the Collection List.**

2. **Choose File⇨Add Clips to Organizer⇨On My Own.**

The Add Clips to Organizer dialog box appears, as shown in Figure 4-6.

Select files.   Select a subfolder.

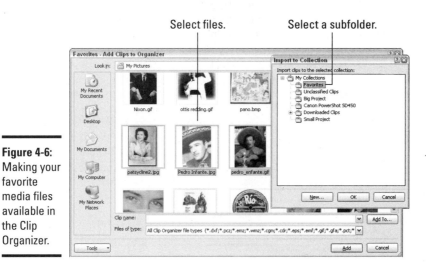

Figure 4-6: Making your favorite media files available in the Clip Organizer.

3. **Select the file or files whose names you want to store in the Clip Organizer.**

For example, open your My Pictures folder and select the graphic files that you often work with. You can select more than one file by Ctrl+ clicking.

4. **Click the Add To button.**

The Import to Collection dialog box appears, as shown in Figure 4-6. It lists subfolders of the My Collections folder.

5. **Select the subfolder where you want to store your file or files and click OK.**

6. **Click the Add button in the Add Clips to Organizer dialog box.**

**Book VIII
Chapter 4**

**Decorating Files
with Clip Art**

Automatically cataloging the media files on your computer

The first time you open the Clip Organizer, you see the Add Clips to Organizer dialog box, which asks whether you want to catalog the clip art, sound, and video files on your computer. Don't do it! If you click OK, you crowd the Clip Organizer with all kinds of extraneous files. You end up with sound files and graphics from every trivial program that's installed in your computer.

For now, click the Cancel button to postpone cataloging your media files. When you're ready to start cataloging, use one of these techniques:

✔ **Pick and choose which files to catalog:** Choose File⇨Add Clips to Organizer⇨On My Own and then select files in the Add Clips to Organizer dialog box. See "Adding your own media files to the Clip Organizer."

✔ **Catalog media files in folders:** Choose File⇨Add Clips to Organizer⇨Automatically to open the Add Clips to Organizer dialog box; then click the Options button. You see the Auto Import Settings dialog box. It lists every folder on your computer that holds media files. Go down the list, deselecting folders with meaningless media files and selecting folders with media files you may find useful. Then click the Catalog button to catalog the media files you really need.

Add Clips to Organizer

Add Media Clips

Clip Organizer can catalog picture, sound, and motion files found on your hard disk(s) or in folders you specify.

Click OK to catalog all media files. Click Cancel to quit this task. Click Options to specify folders.

| OK | Cancel | Options... |

When you add media files to the Clip Organizer, you don't move the files to a new location on your computer, although it may appear that way. Truth be told, the folders in the Clip Organizer don't really exist on your computer. The folders actually represent categories. Inside each category are shortcuts similar to the shortcuts on the Windows desktop that tell your computer where the files are located on your computer. When you place a file in the Clip Organizer, what you're really doing is placing a shortcut to a file located somewhere on your computer or network.

Organizing media files in the My Collections subfolders

The My Collections subfolders in the Collection List pane — Favorites and the others — are excellent places for storing the media files you use often. All you have to do to get them is select the Favorites subfolder or another subfolder in the Collection List. Follow these steps to copy or move a media file to the Favorites subfolder or another subfolder in the Clip Organizer (the next section in this chapter explains how to make subfolders of your own):

1. Find the media file or files you want to store in a subfolder.

Earlier in this chapter, "Locating the media file you need," explains how to locate a media file.

2. Select the file or files on the right side of the Clip Organizer window.

To select more than one file, Ctrl+click the files, or choose Edit⇨Select All to select them all.

3. Give the Copy to Collection or Move to Collection command.

You can give these commands two different ways:

- Open the file's drop-down list and choose Copy to Collection or Move to Collection.
- Open the Edit menu and choose Copy to Collection or Move to Collection.

You see the Copy to Collection or Move to Collection dialog box.

4. Select a folder in the dialog box.

If necessary, click a plus sign (+) beside a folder to display its subfolders.

5. Click OK.

To remove a file from a subfolder, select it and then press the Delete key, or open its drop-down list and then choose Delete from Clip Organizer. Deleting a file this way doesn't remove it from your computer; it just takes its name out of the Clip Organizer.

Creating your own My Collections subfolder for the Clip Organizer

If you work with a lot of media files, organize them into My Collections sub-folders. Put photographs in a Photographs subfolder. Put music files in a Music subfolder. That way, you can find media files simply by going to the subfolder where you place them. Follow these steps to create a new sub-folder in the Clip Organizer:

1. Choose File⇨New Collection.

The New Collection dialog box appears.

2. **Select the folder in which to place your new subfolder.**

   Selecting My Collections is probably the best choice, but place your new subfolder wherever you want.

3. **Enter a name for the subfolder in the Name box.**

4. **Click OK.**

If you need to rename a folder, select it in the Collection List, choose Edit⇨ Rename Collection, and enter a new name. To remove it, choose Edit⇨Delete from Clip Organizer.

Chapter 5: Note Taking with OneNote

In This Chapter

✓ Getting acquainted with OneNote

✓ Creating notebooks, sections, pages, and subpages for storing notes

✓ Writing and drawing notes

✓ Navigating in OneNote

✓ Organizing and finding stray notes

✓ Selecting, moving, and deleting notes, sections, and pages

✓ Using OneNote in conjunction with other Office programs

Microsoft OneNote is designed for taking notes — at meetings, at conferences, or when talking on the telephone. Rather than scribble notes indiscriminately in a Word document, you can enter them in OneNote and be able to retrieve them later. You can use your notes as building blocks for reports and white papers. You can copy them to Excel, PowerPoint, Word, or another Office 2007 program. OneNote comes with all sorts of amenities for finding and filing notes. OneNote can help you brainstorm and organize your ideas.

This chapter explains what OneNote is, how you can use it to write notes, and how to organize and find notes. Finally, it explains a couple of tricks for recycling notes into other Office programs.

Running OneNote

Do one of the following to run OneNote:

✦ Click the Start button and choose All Programs⇨Microsoft Office⇨ Microsoft Office OneNote 2007.

✦ Right-click the OneNote icon in the notification area (it's located in the lower-right corner of the screen next to the clock) and choose Open OneNote. If you don't see the icon in the notification area and you want to see it there, choose Tools⇨Options, select the Other category in the Options dialog box, and select the Place OneNote Icon in the Notification Area of the Taskbar check box.

OneNote opens to the notebook, section, and page or subpage that was open the last time you closed the program. What is a notebook, section, page, and subpage? Better keep reading.

Introducing OneNote

Figure 5-1 shows the OneNote window. The purpose of OneNote is to help you enter notes, keep track of notes, find notes when you need them, and organize your notes. From largest to smallest, the program offers these units for handling notes:

Notebooks (and Selections)

Notebook name   Sections in the open notebook

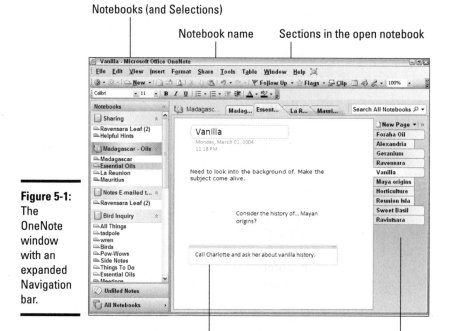

Figure 5-1:
The OneNote window with an expanded Navigation bar.

Notes   Pages and subpages in the open section

✦ **Notebook:** Create a notebook for each important project you're involved in. OneNote places one button on the Navigation bar for each notebook you create. The Navigation bar is located on the left side of the window (see Figure 5-1).

✦ **Sections:** Within each notebook, you can create different sections. A *section* is a subcategory of a notebook. In Figure 5-1, there are four sections — Madagascar, Essential Oils, La Reunion, and Mauritius — in the Madagascar notebook.

✦ **Pages and subpages:** Within each section, you can create pages and subpages for storing notes. Notes are stored on pages (see Figure 5-1).

OneNote is unusual among Office programs in that it doesn't have a Save button or Save command. Every 30 seconds, OneNote saves all the notes for you. You needn't concern yourself with whether notes are being saved.

Creating Storage Units for Notes

Before you write your first note, give a moment's thought to organizing notes in the notebook-section-pages hierarchy. Think of descriptive names for your notebook, sections, and pages. Then get to work creating the storage units you need for your notes. These pages explain how to do it.

Creating a notebook

Follow these steps to create a new notebook:

1. Open the drop-down list on the New button and choose Notebook.

You see the first of three New Notebook Wizard dialog boxes.

2. Enter a name and select a color for the notebook; then click Next.

Selecting a color can help you distinguish one notebook from another.

3. Click the option button that describes how many people will enter notes in the notebook; then click Next.

4. Select the folder where you will store notes.

To do so, click the Browse button and select a folder in the Select Folder dialog box. By default, notebooks are stored in the `C:\ Documents and Settings\`*Your Name*`\My Documents (or Documents)\ OneNote Notebooks` folder.

5. Click the Create button.

The new notebook opens on-screen. OneNote creates a section (called New Section 1) and a page (called Untitled Page) in your notebook, as shown in Figure 5-2.

Enter a new page name.　　Enter a new section name.

Figure 5-2:
A new
notebook
comes with
a generic
section and
page.

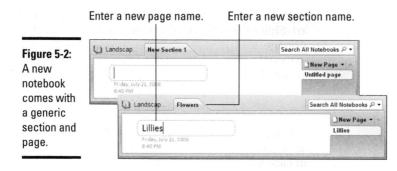

6. Change the name of the section and page.

Follow these instructions to change section and page names:

- *Changing the section name:* Right-click the section name, choose Rename on the shortcut menu, and enter a descriptive name. You can also double-click a name and enter a new one.

- *Changing the page name:* Enter a name in the text box at the top of the page provided for names (see Figure 5-2). After you enter the name, the new name appears as well on the page tab on the right side of the screen.

Creating sections, pages, and subpages for notes

Here are instructions for creating sections, pages, and subpages for your notes:

✦ **Creating a new section:** Click the New button and then type a name for the section on its section tab. (OneNote creates a new page — called Untitled Page — when you create a new section. To rename this page, enter a name in the text box at the top of the page, as shown in Figure 5-2.)

You can color-code sections to distinguish one section from the next. To change a section's color, right-click its tab, choose Section Color, and choose a color on the submenu. To rename a section, right-click its name, choose Rename, and enter a new name.

✦ **Creating a new page:** Each section comes with one page, but if you need more pages, press Ctrl+N, or open the drop-down list on the New button and choose Page. A new page appears, as does a Title text box for entering a descriptive title for the new page (refer to Figure 5-2). Enter a page title that identifies the notes you put on the page. You can also open the drop-down list on the New Page button and choose New Page to create a new page.

✦ **Creating a new subpage:** Display the page under which you create a subpage and press Ctrl+Shift+N or open the drop-down list on the New button and choose Subpage. In OneNote terminology, a page and all its subordinate pages are called a *group*. Enter a title for your subpage in the Title text box. You can also open the drop-down list on the New Page button and choose New Subpage to create a new page.

Each time you create a new section, you also create a new OneNote Sections (.one) file. These files are stored in the C:\Documents and Settings\ *Your Name*\My Documents (or Documents)\OneNote Notebooks\ *Notebook Name* folder, in case you're looking for them and want to back them up.

Writing Notes

Although the program is called OneNote, you can enter two kinds of notes — typed notes and drawings. Moreover, if you're using a Tablet PC to scribble your notes, OneNote can (at least in theory) recognize whether you're writing by hand or drawing. These pages explain how to write and draw notes.

Notes appear in what are called *containers,* as shown in Figure 5-3. Move the pointer over the top of a container and you see the four-headed arrow. At that point, you can click and drag a note elsewhere. Drag the right side of a note container to change its width.

Figure 5-3:
A typed note (left) and a drawn note (right).

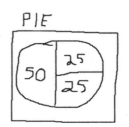

There is only one way to escape from bloodhounds who are chasing you: find water. By wading in the shallows of a creek or river you can make the dogs lose your scent.

Typing a note

To type a note, simply click and start typing. Press the Enter key to begin a new paragraph in a note. You can draw upon the commands on the Formatting toolbar — do you recognize them from Microsoft Word? — to format the text or change its color.

To get more room on a page for notes, try collapsing the Navigation bar and page tabs. To do so, press F11 or click the Full Page View/Normal View button.

**Book VIII
Chapter 5**

Note Taking with OneNote

Jotting down a side note

Suppose you're brainstorming and you come up with an idea that cries out to be preserved in a note. To quickly jot down your note, write a "side note" in the small but convenient Side Note window. This window works in cahoots with OneNote to help you record ideas before you forget them. When you enter a note in the window, it's entered as well in OneNote in the Unfiled Notes folder. Next time you open OneNote, you can go to the Unfiled Notes folder, locate your note, and copy or move it to another folder.

To open the Side Note window, click the OneNote icon in the notification area or press Windows key+N. Enter your note and then click the Close button in the Side Note window after you finish jotting down the note.

To find your note next time you open OneNote, click the Unfiled Notes button. You can find this button near the bottom of the Navigation bar. Your note is filed away on a page named after the note you entered. Later in this chapter, "Some House-keeping Chores" explains how to move notes.

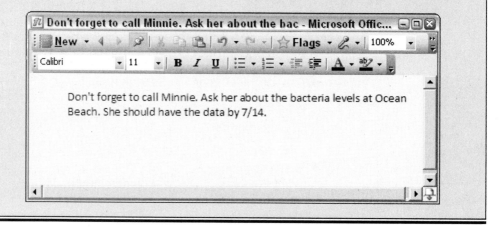

Don't forget to call Minnie. Ask her about the bacteria levels at Ocean Beach. She should have the data by 7/14.

Drawing with a pen or highlighter

Follow these steps to draw a note with a pen or highlighter:

1. **Display the My Pens toolbar.**

OneNote offers two ways to display this toolbar:

- Choose View⇨My Pens Toolbar.

- Right-click the menu or any toolbar and choose My Pens.

2. **Click a Pen or Highlighter button.**

OneNote offers 12 different options on the My Pens toolbar. The first four are thin pens, the next four are thick pens, and the next four are highlighters, not pens. As well as draw with them, you can use the highlighters to call attention to the text in notes.

3. **Press Esc when you're finished drawing or highlighting.**

Getting from Place to Place in OneNote

As you fill up notebooks with sections, pages, subpages, and notes, finding the place you need to be to enter or read a note gets more difficult. Here are ways to get from section to section or page to page in the OneNote window:

✦ **Going to a different notebook:** Click a notebook button on the Navigation bar. Use one of these techniques to find out where clicking a notebook button takes you:

  • Move the pointer over a button. You see a notebook's name and the folder where it is stored in a ScreenTip box.

✦ If the Navigation bar is collapsed, click the Expand Navigation Bar button. Now you can see the names of notebooks as well as the names of notebook sections on the Navigation bar (refer to Figure 5-1). The Expand Navigation Bar button is located at the top of the Navigation bar.

✦ **Going to a different section:** Click a section tab along the top of the window (refer to Figure 5-1). You can also expand the Navigation bar so you can see sections as well as notebook names and then click a section name.

✦ **Go to a different page:** Click a page or subpage tab on the right side of the window (refer to Figure 5-1). To make more room for page and subpage names, click the Expand Page Tabs button. You can find it to the right of the New Page button.

You can also click the Back and Forward buttons on the Standard toolbar to revisit pages.

Finding and Keeping Track of Notes

If you're an habitual note taker, you may find yourself drowning in notes. You won't be able to find the note you're looking for. The great idea you had may be lost forever. To keep notes from getting lost, these pages explain how to find stray notes and how to organize notes so that they don't get lost in the first place.

Flagging notes for follow up

The best way to keep notes from getting lost is to carefully place them in note-books, sections, and pages. Short of that, you can flag notes to make it easier to follow up on them. OneNote offers numerous ways to flag notes. After you flag a note, you can search for it by opening the Note Flags Summary task pane, arranging notes according to how they were flagged, and pinpointing the note you want, as shown in Figure 5-4.

Choose how to arrange notes in the task pane.

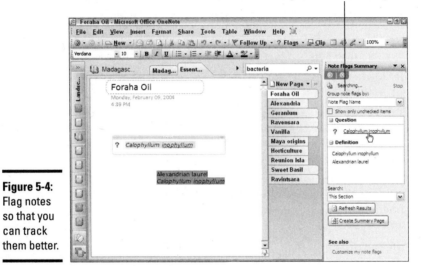

Figure 5-4:
Flag notes
so that you
can track
them better.

Flagging a note

Follow these steps to flag a note:

1. **Select the note, if necessary.**

2. **Open the drop-down list on the Flags button and choose a flag option.**

All options — except Remember for Later and Definitions — place an icon on the note. The aforementioned options highlight the note text, respectively, in yellow or green.

The fastest way to flag a note is to display the Note Flags toolbar and then click a button on the toolbar. To display the toolbar, right-click the menu or any toolbar and choose Note Flags.

Arranging flagged notes in the task pane

Follow these steps to arrange notes that you flagged in the Note Flags Summary task pane:

? Flags ▾

1. **Open the drop-down list on the Flags button and choose Show All Flagged Notes.**

   You see the Note Flags Summary task pane (refer to Figure 5-4). You can also open this task pane by choosing View⇨All Flagged Notes.

2. **Open the Group Notes By drop-down list and choose an option.**

   These options determine the order in which flagged notes appear in the task pane. Note Flag Name, for example, arranges notes according to which icon they're tagged with; Section arranges notes under section names; Note Text arranges notes in alphabetical order.

3. **Open the Search drop-down list and choose an option.**

   These options determine which notes appear in the task pane. This Section, for example, assembles only flagged notes from the section that appears on-screen; This Notebook gathers flagged notes from all sections in the notebook you're viewing.

   A list of notes appears in the task pane.

4. **Click the name of a note you want to visit.**

   OneNote opens the page with the note whose name you clicked and selects the note.

To remove flags from notes, select the notes and press Ctrl+0 (zero), or open the drop-down list on the Flags button and choose Remove Note Flags from Selection.

Finding a stray note

To find a lost note, you must be able to remember a word or two in the note. Follow these steps to chase down a lost note:

1. **Enter the word or phrase you're looking for in the Search box.**

   This box is located in the upper-right side of the OneNote window. If you don't see it, press Ctrl+F or choose Edit⇨Find.

2. **Click the Find button.**

   If the search text can be found, OneNote moves to the first instance of the search text. If the text is found in more than one note, click the Next Match (or Previous Match) button to go to the next or previous instance of the search text. You can also click the View List button to see a list of all notes with the search terms in the Page List task pane. Select a note in the task pane to view a note.

3. **Click the Close button beside the Search box when the search is complete.**

Some Housekeeping Chores

Unless you play loud soul music while you're doing it, housekeeping can be a tedious and irksome activity. Here are methods for handling a few house-keeping chores:

✦ **Selecting notes:** Click the bar along the top of a note to select it. Ctrl+ click to select several notes. If you have trouble selecting notes, click the Selection Tool button and drag across the notes.

✦ **Moving notes to another page:** Use the tried-and-true cut-and-paste method. Select the note, right-click, choose Cut, right-click the page where you want to move the note, and choose Paste. You can also use the keyboard shortcuts: Ctrl+X to cut, Ctrl+C to copy, and Ctrl+V to paste.

✦ **Moving a page to another section**: Right-click the page's tab and choose Move Page To⇨Another Section. You see the Move or Copy Pages dialog box. Select a section name and click the Move or Copy button.

✦ **Removing a notebook from the Navigation bar:** To remove a notebook's name from the Navigation bar and keep the bar from getting too crowded, right-click the notebook's button and choose Close This Notebook (or choose File⇨Close This Notebook). To reopen a notebook, choose File⇨ Open Notebook and then select the notebook's name in the Open Note-book dialog box.

✦ **Deleting notes:** Select the notes you want to delete and press the Delete key.

✦ **Deleting a section:** Right-click the section tab and choose Delete. Because each section is actually a file, you can recover a section you deleted accidentally by retrieving it from the Recycle Bin.

✦ **Deleting a page or subpage:** Right-click the page tab and choose Delete. You can't recover a page of notes that you delete this way.

OneNote and Other Office Programs

OneNote works hand in hand with its brothers and sisters in the Office suite. These pages describe how to copy notes into other programs, send notes by e-mail, and make a note into an Outlook task.

Copying a note into another Office program

To copy a note into another program, use the copy-and-paste command. Select the note, right-click, and choose Copy. Then go to the other program, right-click, and choose Paste. Typed notes land in the other program in the form of text. Drawn notes land as Portable Network Graphics (.png) files.

Sending notes by e-mail

As long as Outlook is installed on your computer, you can send the notes on a page by e-mail to someone else. The notes arrive as file attachments. As long as the recipient has OneNote, he or she can read the notes. Follow these steps to send notes by e-mail:

1. **Open the page with the notes you want to send.**

Unfortunately, you can't send a single note unless it's the only one on the page.

2. **Click the E-Mail button on the Standard toolbar or press Ctrl+Shift+E.**

You see a new message window open with the OneNote section within the message area.

3. **Address the message and enter some words to accompany the notes.**

4. **Click the Send button.**

The page of notes is sent by way of Outlook.

Transferring notes to a Word document

Follow these steps to transfer all the notes on a page or subpage to a Word document:

1. **Open the page with the notes that need transferring.**

2. **Choose File⇨Send To⇨Microsoft Office Word.**

Word opens (if it isn't already open) and creates a new document for your notes. Either save the document or copy the notes to a document you already created.

Turning a note into an Outlook task

As Book III, Chapter 5 explains, an Outlook task is a reminder to do something. You can make a note into an Outlook task and place the task in the Outlook Tasks window by following these steps:

1. **Select the note.**

2. **Open the drop-down list on the Follow Up button and choose the option that describes a due date for the task.**

   For example, choose Tomorrow if you want the note to be filed in the Outlook Tasks window under Due Date: Tomorrow.

Chapter 6: Collaborating with SharePoint Services

In This Chapter

✔ Getting ready to use SharePoint Services

✔ Logging on to a SharePoint Services Web site

✔ Navigating the Web site

✔ Uploading, download, viewing, and deleting files

✔ Exploring other ways to collaborate with SharePoint Services

SharePoint Services is a software product by which people who work in different locations can collaborate. Co-workers can share files, list tasks that need to be done, and discuss their work with one another. Think of SharePoint Services as a digital office. Instead of gathering in the conference room to share files and ideas, you share them online at a Web site. Co-workers in different states, countries, and continents — but not different planets — can work conveniently together.

If you're reading this in an office or cubicle, ask the person nearest you whether your company shares files with SharePoint Services, and if your co-worker answers "yes," keep reading. This chapter explains how to get equipped to share files, visit a SharePoint Services Web site, upload and download files, and do one or two other tasks that fall under the sharing information category.

Getting Equipped and Getting Started

To use SharePoint Services, you must have access to a SharePoint Services Web site similar to the one shown in Figure 6-1. These Web sites are maintained on a company intranet or on the Internet. Each Web site has an *administrator*, the person responsible for letting people into the Web site or barring the door, handing out passwords, and giving permission to do different tasks.

Click to go to different parts of the Web site.

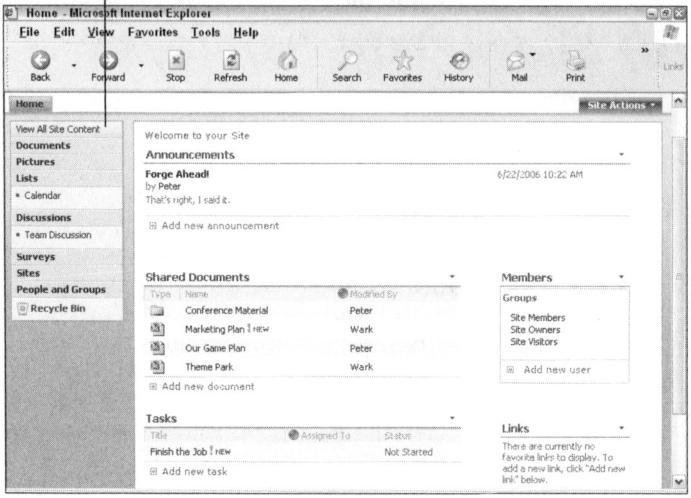

Figure 6-1:
The Home
page of a
SharePoint
Services
Web site.

To visit a SharePoint Services Web site and share files, you must first obtain the following from the administrator:

✦ **The address of the SharePoint Services site:** The URL of the SharePoint site. Typically, the address is `http://companyweb` if the site is located on a company intranet. If it's located on the Internet, the address typically ends with `.com`, `.net`, or `.org`.

✦ **A username:** A name that identifies you to the Web site.

✦ **A password:** A password for gaining admission.

Often you receive this information in the form of an e-mail message from the administrator. (SharePoint Services has a special command for issuing invitations to new members by e-mail.)

Visiting a SharePoint Services Web Site

If you received an e-mail invitation to join the SharePoint Services site, click the hyperlink in the e-mail to visit the site. Otherwise, follow these steps to gain entry to a SharePoint Services Web site:

1. **Open Internet Explorer or another Web browser.**

2. **Enter the address of the SharePoint Services site in the Address box and press Enter.**

The Connect To dialog box appears.

3. Enter your username and password, and then click OK.

Provided you entered the correct username and password, you land on the Web site's Home page (refer to Figure 6-1).

Getting from Place to Place in the Web Site

Use the View All Site Content bar on the left side of the window to get from place to place (refer to Figure 6-1). By clicking Documents, Pictures, Lists, Discussions, and so forth, you can get to a new page and undertake a new task. You can also use the Back and Forward buttons in your browser to get around. Click the Back button, for example, to return to the previous page you visited.

Click the Home button — it's shaped like a tab and located in the upper-left corner of the window — to return to the Home page.

Handling and Managing Files

Think of the SharePoint Services Web site as your computer home away from home. Starting at the Shared Documents folder (or one of its subfolders), you can upload files so others can work on them, download files to your computer, edit files, and delete files, as the following pages explain.

Going to the Shared Documents folder

No matter what you want to do with files — upload them, download them, or open them — start by going to the Shared Documents folder on the SharePoint Services Web site. Use one of these techniques to go to this all-important folder:

✦ Click the Documents link on the View All Site Content bar to open the Document Libraries window, and then click the Shared Documents folder.

✦ On the Home page, click the Shared Documents link. (You can find it in the middle of the window.)

Figure 6-2 shows the Shared Documents folder. This folder lists files that have been uploaded to the Web site, as well as subfolders that the administrator created to store additional files. (Click a folder name to see the files that are stored inside it.)

Upload a file.   Download a file.

Figure 6-2:
Files on the
SharePoint
Services
Web site
are stored in
the Shared
Documents
folder
and its
subfolders.

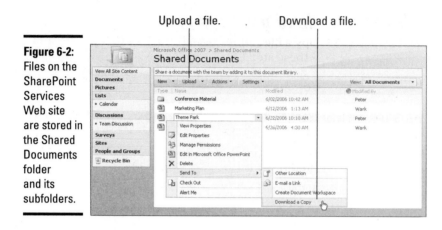

Uploading files

Uploading means to send a file across an intranet or the Internet to a Web
server so that others can view, open, and download it. Starting in the Shared
Documents folder (or one of its subfolders), use one of these techniques
to upload a file or files from your computer to a folder on the SharePoint
Services site:

✦ **Uploading one file:** Click the Upload button (see Figure 6-2), and in the
Upload Document window, click the Browse button. You see the Choose
File dialog box, which presents folders and files on your computer.
Locate the file you want to upload, select it, and click the Open button.
Click OK in the Upload Document window.

✦ **Uploading many files:** Open the drop-down list on the Upload button
and choose Upload Multiple Documents. You go to the Upload
Document window. Select a folder in your computer and click the check
box next to the names of files you want to upload. Then click OK.

The Upload Document window offers a check box called Overwrite Existing
Files. When this check box is selected, files you upload erase and take the
place of files in the folder with the same name. If the check box isn't
selected, a second copy of the file may be uploaded. Whether the second
copy is uploaded depends on whether the administrator permits different
versions of the same file to remain on the Web site.

You can also upload a file from inside an Office 2007 program. Click the
Office button and choose Publish➪Document Management Server. The Save
As dialog box appears. Enter the address of your SharePoint Services site in
the File Name text box and click the Save button. If the Office program asks
for them, enter your username and password. Then select Shared
Documents in the dialog box and click the Save button.

Downloading a file to your computer

Downloading means to copy a file from a place on the Internet or an intranet to your computer. Follow these steps to download a file from a SharePoint Services Web site to your computer so you can edit it in the security and safety of your own home or office:

1. **Locate the file you want to download in the Shared Documents folder or one of its subfolders.**

Earlier in this chapter, "Going to the Shared Documents folder" explains how to reach the Shared Documents folder.

2. **Open the drop-down list on the file and choose Send To⇨Download a Copy (refer to Figure 6-2).**

You see the File Download dialog box.

3. **Click the Save button.**

The Save As dialog box appears.

4. **Select the folder on your computer where you want to save the file and click the Save button.**

The file arrives on your computer so you can edit it at leisure. You find the file in the folder you selected.

Viewing and editing a file

As well as downloading a file to your computer, you can view and edit a file inside the SharePoint Services Web site by following these steps:

1. **Find and select the file that needs your attention in the Shared Documents folder or one of its subfolders.**

Earlier in this chapter, "Going to the Shared Documents folder" explains how to locate files.

2. **Double-click the file's name.**

You can also open its drop-down list and choose Edit in *Office Program*. The Office programs opens (if it's not already open), and the Connect To dialog box appears.

3. **Enter your username and password, and then click OK.**

If the file has been designated read-only or someone else is also editing it, you have to click the Edit button in order to start editing. You're asked to save a copy of the file to your computer and edit it there.

Next time you want to open a file online from the SharePoint Services Web site, try opening it by way of the Recent Documents menu. (Click the Office button to view this menu.) The names of presentations you opened online are placed on this menu alongside the names of other presentations you recently opened. You can tell which files are kept on the SharePoint Services Web site because the address of the Web site appears in a pop-up box when you move the pointer over these files' names.

Deleting a file

To delete a file, locate it in the Shared Documents folder (or one of its subfolders), select it, open its drop-down list, and choose Delete. Then click Yes in the message box that asks if you're sure you want to delete the file. Whether you can delete a file, however, depends on which permissions you've been given by the administrator.

Files that you delete land in the Recycle Bin folder. To undelete a file, go to the Recycle Bin folder, select the file's check box, and click the Restore Selection link. Click the Delete Selection link to permanently and irrevocably delete a file so that it can't be recovered in the Recycle Bin.

Other Ways to Collaborate at a SharePoint Services Web Site

Besides file sharing, SharePoint Services offers these amenities to people who live far apart but want to work closely together:

✦ **Pictures:** Use the Picture Libraries to share photographs with co-workers. Upload, download, and view photographs by using the same techniques that you use to share files.

✦ **Lists:** Use announcement, calendar, link, and task lists to manage your work and your deadlines better. The Links list is for listing Web sites that are of use to the people you work with.

✦ **Discussions:** Hold newsgroup-style discussions to iron out the problems that engage you at work. No gossiping is allowed.

✦ **Surveys:** Conduct a survey of co-workers to gauge people's opinions and establish goals and objectives.

✦ **Sites:** Use the Sites window to create more workspaces for sharing files and otherwise collaborating.

✦ **People and Groups:** Use this window to store and obtain your co-workers' contact information.

Chapter 7: Automating Tasks with Macros

This brief chapter explains how macros can make your work a little easier. I describe how to display the Developer tab on the Ribbon, record a macro, run a macro, and edit a macro. I also look into macro security issues and show you how to place a macro button on the Quick Access toolbar.

What Is a Macro?

A *macro* is a set of command instructions recorded under a name. When you activate a macro, the program you're working in carries out the instructions in the macro. Macros help automate repetitive and complex tasks. Instead of entering commands yourself, the macro does it for you — and it enters the commands faster and more efficiently. Instead of reaching into several dialog boxes to get a task done, you can run a macro and let it do the work.

Not that you necessarily need to know it, but playing a macro involves running command sequences in *Visual Basic for Applications* (VBA), a programming language built into all the major Office 2007 applications. Behind the scenes, the application you're working in executes VBA code when you run a macro.

Displaying the Developer Tab

Before you can run a macro or do anything in the wonderful world of macros, you must display the Developer tab. Figure 7-1 shows the Developer tab in PowerPoint. Follow these steps to display or remove this tab:

Figure 7-1:
The
Developer
tab (in
Power-
Point).

1. **Click the Office button and choose Options on the drop-down list.**

You see the Options dialog box.

2. **Click the Popular category.**

3. **Click the Show Developer Tab in the Ribbon check box.**

4. **Click OK.**

When you display the Developer tab in one Office program, it appears in the other programs as well. Likewise, when you undisplay it, it is removed from your other Office programs.

Managing the Macro Security Problem

A macro is a little (and sometimes not so little) computer program in its own right. As such, macros can contain computer viruses. When you run a macro in a PowerPoint presentation, Word document, Excel workbook, or any other file, you run the risk of infecting your computer with a virus.

To help protect you against macro viruses, Office gives you the opportunity to decide how you want to handle files that contain macros. You can disable all macros, disable some macros, or enable all macros. (If you're working in an office on a network, the network administrator may have decided for you whether you can run macro files on your computer. Network administrators can disable all files that contain macros.)

Follow these steps to tell Office how you want to handle macros:

1. **On the Developer tab, click the Macro Security button.**

You see the Macro Settings category of the Trust Center dialog box, as shown in Figure 7-2.

2. **Under Macro Settings, declare how you want to handle PowerPoint files that contain macros.**

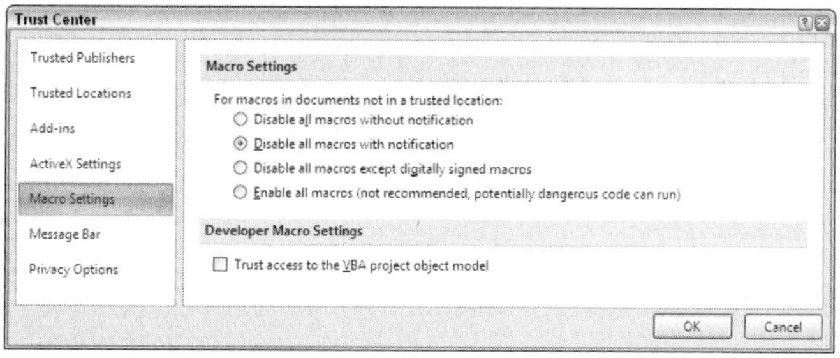

Figure 7-2:
Choosing how to handle macro security.

Your choices are as follows:

- *Disable All Macros without Notification:* You can't run macros, and moreover, you're not alerted to the fact that your file contains macros or given the opportunity to enable the macros.

- *Disable All Macros with Notification:* When you open a file with macros, you see the panel shown in Figure 7-3. It tells you that macros have been disabled, but gives you the opportunity to enable the macros by clicking the Enable Content button.

Figure 7-3:
Choose whether to run macros.

- *Disable All Macros Except Digitally Signed Macros:* You can run only macros that have been certified with a digital signature. Developers can apply for digital signatures that deem their macros safe to run. When you open a file with digitally signed macros, a dialog box tells you who developed the macros and gives you the opportunity to decide whether you want to allow them. However, you can't run macros that don't have a digital signature.

- *Enable All Macros:* You can run all macros, no matter where they came from and who made them. Choosing this option is a risky proposition. Choose it only if you get Office files from people or parties you know and trust.

3. Click OK.

Book VIII
Chapter 7

Automating Tasks
with Macros

Excel, PowerPoint, and Word files that contain macros have a file extension that ends in the letter *m* (the *m* stands for "macro"). Excel files have the extension .xlsm, PowerPoint files the extension .pptm, and Word files the extension .docm. Even if you disable macros, you can glance at a file's extension letters to tell whether it includes macros.

Recording a Macro

Recording a macro in an Office application is a matter of turning on the Macro Recorder and giving commands. The Macro Recorder is modeled after a tape recorder. You turn on the recorder, choose commands, and turn the thing off. Following are ground rules and instructions for recording macros.

Unless you want to construct them on your own using VBA code, you can't record your own macros in PowerPoint 2007 (although you can in Word, Excel, Publisher, Access, and Outlook). To make use of macros in PowerPoint, you have to obtain them from a developer or have them already in your PowerPoint presentation.

Ground rules for recording macros

Before you record a macro, observe these ground rules:

✦ Plan ahead. If the actions you intend to record in the macro are complex, write them down beforehand so that you can execute the commands without making any mistakes.

✦ Set up the program the way it will be when you play back the macro. Before creating a macro that manipulates information in a worksheet, for example, open a worksheet that is typical of the kind of worksheet on which you'll run the macro. Unless you prepare yourself this way, you may have to pause the Macro Recorder (you can do that in Word) as you record, or you may have to edit the macro in the Visual Basic Editor later.

✦ Toggle commands that you can switch on and off have no place in macros because when the macro starts running, the Macro Recorder can't tell whether the command is on or off.

✦ Close open files that might get in the way. For example, before creating a macro that copies information from one file to another, close any open files that might confuse the issue.

✦ If you intend to include a Find or a Find-and-Replace operation in a Word macro, open the Find dialog box in Word before you start recording the macro, click the More button, and then click Cancel. This way, you can get to all the find-and-replace options when you open the dialog box as part of recording the macro.

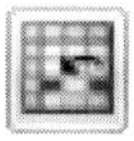

✦ In Excel, click the Use Relative References button on the Developer tab if you want to record cell references as relative, not absolute, references.

Recording a macro

Having read and followed the ground rules, follow these steps to record a macro in Word and Excel:

1. On the Developer tab, click the Record Macro button.

The Record Macro dialog box opens, as shown in Figure 7-4.

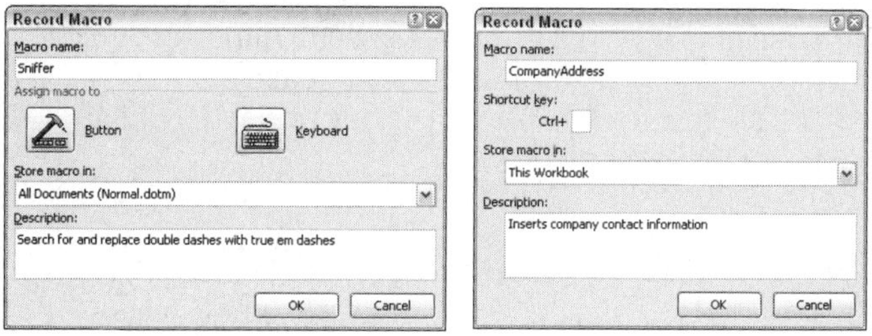

Figure 7-4:
The Macro Recorder dialog box in Word (left) and Excel (right).

If you can't find the Record Macro button, chances are an administrator removed it to prevent you from using or recording macros. Depending on which version of Windows you have, administrators can remove all macro and VBA functionality from Office by not installing the VBA component, or they can install the component but prevent individuals from accessing macros and VBA.

2. In the Macro Name text box, enter a name for your macro.

Macro names can be 80 characters long, must begin with a letter, and can include numbers and underscores. Blank spaces, symbols, and punctuation are not allowed in macro names.

3. If you so desire, assign a toolbar button or keyboard shortcut to the macro.

In Word, you can click the Button or the Keyboard icon and assign a button or keyboard shortcut for activating the macro. Later in this chapter, "Running a Macro from a Button on the Quick Access Toolbar" explains how to put a macro on the Quick Access toolbar. Chapter 1 of this mini-book explains how to assign a keyboard shortcut to a Word macro.

Book VIII
Chapter 7

Automating Tasks with Macros

In Excel, you can assign a Ctrl+key combination to a macro by entering a key in the Ctrl+ text box.

4. **In the Store Macro In drop-down list, decide where to store the macro you're about to record.**

   In Word, you can store macros in the document you're working on, the template the document is attached to, or the Normal template (the global template that's always loaded). Store a macro with a template if you'd like to be able to run the macro in all documents you create with your template.

   In Excel, you can store macros in the workbook you're working on (choose the This Workbook menu item), a new workbook, or the Personal.Macro Workbook. The Personal.Macro Workbook is designed expressly for storing macros. It is created automatically the first time you choose Personal.Macro Workbook. The workbook is called `Personal.xlsb`, and it's stored in this folder if your machine runs Windows XP:

   ```
   C:\Documents and Settings\Your Name\Application Data\Microsoft\Excel\
       XLSTART
   ```

   The `Personal.xlsb` workbook is stored in this folder if your machine runs Windows Vista:

   ```
   C:\Users\Your Name\AppData\Roaming\Microsoft\Excel\XLStart
   ```

5. **In the Description text box, enter a concise description of what the macro does.**

6. **Click OK.**

   The Record Macro dialog box closes.

7. **Perform the actions you want to record in the macro.**

   The Macro Recorder records every action you take, but it doesn't record actions in real time. Take your time when recording a macro. Concentrate on taking the actions in the right order so that you don't need to adjust the code afterward.

   Word offers the Pause Recording button. You can click it to suspend recording. Click it again to resume recording.

   In Excel, the Developer tab includes a Use Relative References button. Click it to switch between recording absolute cell references and relative cell references.

   Avoid using the mouse as you record a macro (although you can use it to open menus and select menu commands). The Macro Recorder interprets some mouse actions ambiguously. Select data by using key presses. (In Excel, you can select cells with the mouse because the Macro Recorder is able to recognize cell addresses.)

When you visit a dialog box as part of recording your macro, take into account all the dialog box settings. For example, if you visit the Font dialog box and choose 12 points on the Font Size drop-down list, the Macro Recorder duly records the 12-point font size, but it also records the Times Roman font in the macro if Times Roman happens to be the font that is chosen in the Font dialog box. The moral: Take account of all the settings in a dialog box when you visit it while recording a macro.

In dialog boxes with tabs, you can't click tabs to switch from tab to tab and choose commands. Instead, click OK to close the dialog box, reopen it, click a different tab, choose a command on the tab, and close the dialog box again.

8. **Click the Stop Recording button.**

That's all she wrote — your macro is recorded. I suggest you test it to see how well it runs.

To delete a macro, click the Macros button on the Developer or View tab, and in the Macros dialog box, select the macro you want to delete and then click the Delete button.

Running a Macro

Before you run a macro, take note of where the cursor is located. The macro may require the cursor to be in a certain place to run properly. Follow these steps to run a macro:

1. **On the Developer or View tab, click the Macros button (or press Alt+F8).**

The Macros dialog box appears, as shown in Figure 7-5.

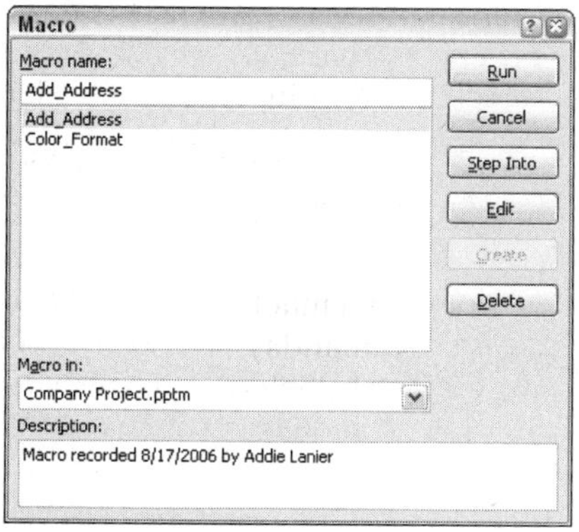

Figure 7-5:
The Macros dialog box.

2. **Select the macro that you want to run.**

Macros have cryptic names, but you can usually tell what they do by glancing at their descriptions.

If you don't see the macro you want, make a new selection in the Macro In drop-down list.

3. **Click the Run button.**

If your macro is a long one and you need to stop it from running, press Ctrl+Break. (On most keyboards, the Break key is located along with the Pause key on the right side of the keyboard, to the right of the F12 key.)

Editing a Macro

Editing a macro entails opening the Visual Basic Editor and editing Visual Basic codes, which is not for the faint of heart. If your macro is an uncomplicated one, you're better off re-recording it. This book isn't a developer's guide, so it can't go into the details of using the Visual Basic Editor. However, the following pages explain the basics of reading a macro in the Visual Basic Editor, deleting parts of a macro, and editing the text in a macro.

Follow these steps to view a macro in the Visual Basic Editor:

1. **On the Developer tab, click the Macros button (or press Alt+F8).**

You see the Macro dialog box (refer to Figure 7-5).

2. **Select the name of the macro that needs editing.**

3. **Click the Edit button.**

You see the Visual Basic window, as shown in Figure 7-6.

4. **Choose File⇨Save Normal (or press Ctrl+S) after you finish editing your macro.**

The name of the macro you selected appears in the Procedure box on the right side of the window. Those computer codes in the Code window are scary, aren't they? You can find one line of code for each command in your macro. Edit computer codes the same way that you edit text in a Word document. For example, click to the left of a line to select it and then press Delete to delete a line. Or type in the Code window to add commands or change the text that the macro enters in documents.

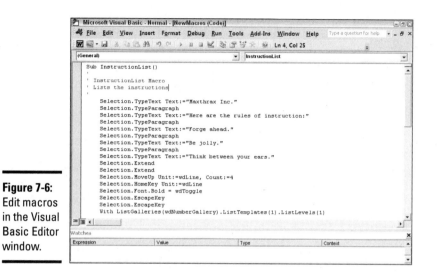

Figure 7-6:
Edit macros
in the Visual
Basic Editor
window.

Reading a macro in the Code window

Before you can do any editing in the Visual Basic Editor, you have to know how to read the codes in the Code window. Observe these attributes of the Code window:

✦ **Sub and End Sub line:** A macro begins with the Sub line and ends with the End Sub line.

✦ **Apostrophes (') at the beginning of lines:** Lines that begin with an apostrophe (') are descriptive comments and aren't part of the macro except insofar as they help you understand what it does. Notice, for example, that the descriptive line near the top of the macro appears after an apostrophe. Enter blank lines and lines of commentary to make macros easier to read and understand.

✦ **Text enclosed in double quotation marks ("):** Text that is typed in as part of the macro is enclosed in double quotation marks ("). If you need to edit the text in your macro, edit the text inside double quotation marks.

✦ **With and End With lines:** Codes that pertain to choices made in a dialog box begin with the With line and end with the End With line.

✦ **All dialog box options are recorded:** Even if you select only a single option in a dialog box, the macro records all the options in the dialog box. A visit to the Font dialog box, for example, adds more than 20 lines to a macro — one for every option in the dialog box. However, you can edit out lines that your macro does not require.

Editing the text that a macro enters

As I mention earlier, text that is typed during a macro procedure is enclosed in double quotation marks (") in the Code window. To edit the text in a macro, you can edit the text between double quotation marks in the Code window. Edit this text as though you were editing it in Word.

Deleting parts of a macro

Delete part of a macro when you want to remove a command or command sequence. For that matter, you may delete parts of a macro if they are unnecessary. Deleting unnecessary lines makes a macro easier to read and run faster. As I mention in the preceding section of this chapter, a visit to a dialog box, such as the Font dialog box, adds many lines to a macro, most of which are unnecessary. Your macro requires only the lines that pertain to changing settings.

To delete part of a macro, delete the lines as though they were text in a Word document: Click or click and drag in the left margin and then press the Delete key.

Running a Macro from a Button on the Quick Access Toolbar

Any macro that you run often is a candidate for the Quick Access toolbar. As Book VIII, Chapter 1 explains, you can place your own buttons on the Quick Access toolbar and move the toolbar below the Ribbon as well. Follow these steps to assign a macro to a button and place the button on the Quick Access toolbar:

1. **Right-click any button or tab and choose Customize Quick Access Toolbar on the shortcut menu.**

   You see the Customize category of the Options dialog box.

2. **In the Choose Commands From drop-down list, choose Macros (you can find it near the top of the list).**

   The cryptic names of macros in your file appear in the dialog box.

3. **Select the macro you want to assign to a button and click the Add button.**

   The macro's name appears in the right side of the dialog box alongside the names of buttons already on the Quick Access toolbar.

4. Make sure that your macro is still selected and click the Modify button.

The Modify Button dialog box appears. It offers symbols you can place on your macro button.

5. Select a symbol and click OK.

6. Click OK in the Options dialog box.

A button representing your macro appears on the Quick Access toolbar. You can click this button to run your macro. If you want to remove the button, right-click it and choose Remove from Quick Access Toolbar.

**Book VIII
Chapter 7**

**Automating Tasks
with Macros**

Chapter 8: Linking and Embedding in Compound Files

In This Chapter

✔ Understanding what object linking and embedding (OLE) is

✔ Embedding foreign data in a file

✔ Linking to foreign data in another file

A compound file is a computer file that brings together data created in different programs. A year-end report is a classic example of a compound file. Typically, a year-end report includes word-processed text, worksheet tables, and graphics. Thanks to object linking and embedding (OLE), you can create compound files. They can include data from different sources — Excel worksheets, Word text, or Paint graphic files. What's more, you can copy and continuously update material from other programs without leaving the Office 2007 program you're working in.

All this magic is accomplished with something called object linking and embedding (OLE). This chapter explains OLE, tells you how to embed data from another file in PowerPoint, and explains how to link data from another file so that your files are updated automatically.

By the way, OLE is pronounced the same as *olé* ("oh-lay"), which is the word that the bullfighting audience shouts when the bull passes under the matador's cape. *¿Loco, verdad?*

What Is OLE, Anyway?

Object linking and embedding (OLE) is a means of putting more than one program to work on the same file. You can think of OLE as a high-powered version of the standby Copy and Paste commands. As you probably know, the Copy and Paste commands are for copying material from one place or program to another. For example, with the Copy and Paste commands, you can copy text from an Excel worksheet into a Word document. You can copy columns and rows from a Word table and paste them straight into a PowerPoint table.

Linking and embedding

Object linking takes the copy-and-paste concept a step further. When you copy text from a Word document to a PowerPoint slide, you can *link* the Word file and PowerPoint slide so that changes made to the Word text are made as well to the same text on your PowerPoint slide. In effect, linking means you can run the Copy and Paste commands in the background without having to actually choose Copy or Paste. Linking establishes a connection between the two objects — in this case the text in the Word document and the text in the PowerPoint slide — so that the one automatically updates the other.

Similarly, *embedding* enables you to keep, or embed, foreign data from another program in the file you're working on. The program you're working in understands that the data is foreign. When you click the data, the program's tabs and buttons disappear to be replaced by tabs and buttons belonging to the program designed to handle the data. For example, when you click an Excel worksheet embedded in a Word document, you see Excel tabs and buttons for handling the worksheet data. In effect, you can open a second program inside the first program and use the second program to create data without having to copy the data from the second program. The object — the Word document or Excel worksheet — isn't connected to another file but is contained within the file.

Figure 8-1 shows an Excel worksheet embedded in a Word document. Notice the Excel tabs and buttons in the window. The tabs and buttons are at the ready. After you finish using them, you can click outside the embedded object — you can click outside the Excel worksheet — and go back to using the Word tabs and buttons. Although the table data was made in Excel, it looks like a Word table. Embedding an object spares you from having to open a different program, construct material there, and copy it into the file you're working on.

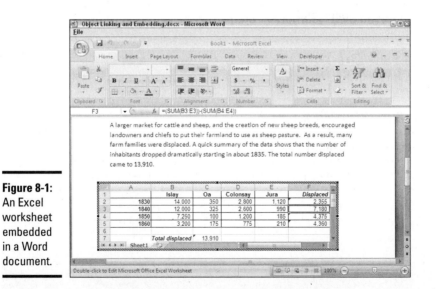

Figure 8-1: An Excel worksheet embedded in a Word document.

A *linked object* is a little bit different from an embedded object. When you double-click a linked object, the program you're currently using shouts out to the program where the material was created to find out whether the material has been edited or altered in any way. If the material has been updated, you can tell Office to gather the updated material and incorporate it into your current file. Linking is an opportunity for you to keep your files up-to-date. You can fold the work that you or a co-worker did to the original file into your file without having to go outside the program you're using, and then copying and pasting it.

Uses for linking

Linking was designed to let files dynamically share information. The object — the Excel worksheet or Word file, for example — remains connected to its source. As the source file is updated, the files to which it is linked can be updated, too.

Linking saves you the trouble of updating files that often change. Co-workers can maintain a library of source files and use them to update the files to which the source files are linked. Here are some examples of object linking coming in handy:

✦ Your PowerPoint presentation contains sales data, and you want the data to be up-to-date. You create a link to the Excel worksheet where the sales data is stored so that your PowerPoint slide remains up-to-date as sales data changes.

✦ A co-worker has created an Excel worksheet with demographic data that often changes. In your Word report, you create a link to your co-worker's worksheet so that demographic data appears in your report and is always up-to-date.

✦ Your company maintains a Word file with a list of branch office addresses and telephone numbers, and you want this list to be available to employees. You link your Word file to the company's Word file. Your address and telephone list document stays up-to-date as addresses and telephone numbers change.

Uses for embedding

Embedding enables you to work inside an Office program on data that the program isn't equipped to handle or display. Embed an Excel worksheet in a Word document if you want to have a table with complex mathematical formulas. Embed a Word document in an Excel worksheet if you want to write paragraphs of explanatory text and be able to call upon Word formatting commands. Consider embedding an object if you want to attempt something that you can't normally do in the program you're working in.

Pitfalls of linking and embedding

Linking and embedding aren't for everybody. Here are some OLE pitfalls:

✦ **File size:** Including embedded objects in a file makes the file grow in size — and I mean really grow. A large file can be unwieldy and hard to store. It takes longer to load on-screen. By linking, you solve the file-size problem because the item has to be stored only once — in its original location.

✦ **Carrying charges:** Links are broken if you move your file or you or someone else moves a file to which your file is linked. A file with links can't be sent over the Internet or copied to a laptop without the links being broken. Linking is out of the question in the case of files that travel to other computers. If you link to files over a network, establish a scheme for storing files with your co-workers so that files aren't moved inadvertently.

✦ **Formatting embedded and linked objects:** Unfortunately, linked and embedded objects are often hard to format. Selecting the same fonts and colors as the fonts and colors in your file can be difficult because you have to rely on the commands in the source file to do the formatting. The end result is that linked and embedded objects sometimes look out of place.

Before you undertake any activity regarding object linking and embedding, save the file you're working on. The program with which you're working needs to know precisely where OLE objects go in order to execute OLE commands. Therefore, your file must be completely up-to-date for OLE commands to work.

Linking to Data in another File

Link a slide, document, or worksheet to another file so that changes made to the other file are made automatically to your slide, document, or worksheet. Earlier in this chapter, "Uses for linking" explains the benefits of linking to another file. These pages explain how to establish the link between your files, how to update the link, how to break a link, and how to mend broken links.

Links are broken when files are renamed or moved to different folders. Linking files is more trouble than it's worth if you often move or rename files. Very carefully create or choose folders for storing linked files so that you don't have to move them.

Before you link one file to another, save the file you're working on. Your program needs to know precisely where OLE objects go in order to execute OLE commands. Therefore, your file must be completely up-to-date — and saved — for OLE commands to work.

Establishing the link

For the purposes of linking, the original file with the data you will link to is the *source*. Follow these steps to establish a link between your file and the source file so that your file can be updated whenever the source file is changed:

1. **Open the source file with the data that you'll link to your file.**

2. **Select the data you need and copy it to the Windows Clipboard.**

   You can do that by right-clicking and choosing Copy or pressing Ctrl+C.

3. **Click in the file where you want the linked data to appear.**

4. **Click the Save button.**

   As I explain earlier, all files must be saved and up-to-date for links to be successfully made.

5. **On the Home tab, open the drop-down list on the Paste button and choose Paste Special.**

   The Paste Special dialog box appears.

6. **Select the Paste Link option button, as shown in Figure 8-2.**

   In the As list, your program chooses an Object option for you, depending on which type of data you selected in Step 2.

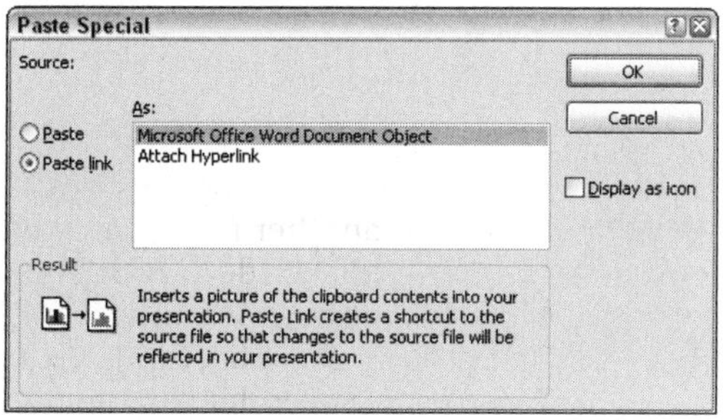

Figure 8-2: Creating a data link between two files.

Book VIII Chapter 8

Linking and Embedding in Compound Files

7. **Click OK.**

   Your file creates a pointer to data in the source file, and the data appears in your file.

8. **Save your file by clicking the Save button.**

   Congratulations. The link is established.

Opting for manual rather than automatic links

Some people prefer to update links manually rather than automatically. A manual link is updated when you tell a program to update it. These links don't tax your computer's memory as much as automatic links. Follow these steps to make links in your file manual rather than automatic:

1. **Click the Office button and choose Prepare➪ Edit Links to Files.**

   You see the Links (or Edit Links) dialog box.

2. **In the Links list, Ctrl+click to select the links that you want to update manually rather than automatically.**

3. **Select the Manual Update option button.**

4. **Click OK.**

To update a manual link, right-click the linked object that needs updating and choose Update Link on the shortcut menu.

To change the size of a linked object, move the pointer over a selection handle and drag. To move a linked object, move the pointer over the object and drag when you see a four-headed arrow.

Updating a link

Each time you open and save your file, the program you're working in checks the source file to find out whether its source data has been changed in any way. If the data has changed, new, up-to-the-minute data is inserted into your file.

Editing data that is linked with a source file

Suppose, while staring at the linked data in your file, you notice something wrong. The numbers in the table aren't accurate. There's a misspelling in the list. On those occasions, you can open the source file and edit the data with one of these techniques:

✦ **Editing the data inside your program:** Right-click the linked object and choose Object➪Edit Link. (The Object command is named for the kind of data you're editing.) If your program can manage it, tabs and buttons for editing the data appear. Edit the data and click Save.

✦ **Editing the data in the source file:** Double-click the linked object, or right-click it and choose Object➪Open Link on the shortcut menu. The program with which the source file was created and the source file itself both open. Edit the data and click the Save button.

Breaking and reestablishing links

As shown in Figure 8-3, the Links (or Edit Links) dialog box offers commands for breaking and reestablishing links. To open this dialog box, click the Office button and choose Prepare➪Edit Links to Files. Select a link in the Links (or Source) list and go to it:

✦ **Breaking links:** Break a link when you want your file to stay the same no matter what happens to the data in the source file. To break a link, click the Break Link button.

✦ **Reestablishing a link when the source file has changed locations:** Reestablish a link if you or someone else moves the source file to a different folder, rendering its link to your slide invalid. To reestablish a link, click the Change Source button, find and select the source file in the Change Source dialog box, and click the Open button.

✦ **Opening the source file:** Click the Open Source button to open the source file and perhaps edit the original data there. (You can also open the source file by right-clicking the linked object and choosing Object➪Open Link.)

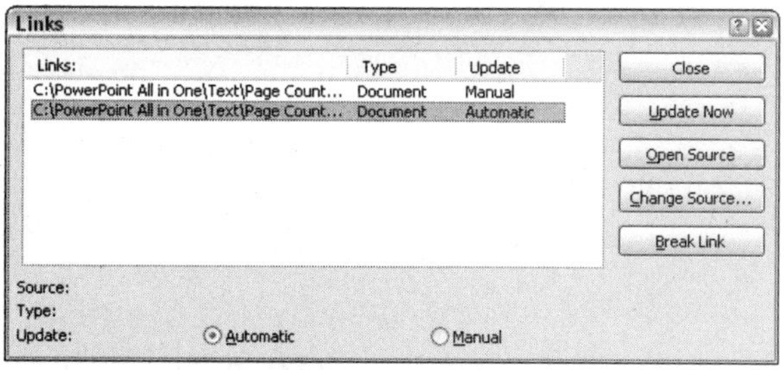

Figure 8-3:
Go to this dialog box to break and reestablish links.

Links:	Type	Update	
C:\PowerPoint All in One\Text\Page Count...	Document	Manual	Close
C:\PowerPoint All in One\Text\Page Count...	Document	Automatic	Update Now
			Open Source
			Change Source...
			Break Link

Source:
Type:
Update: ⦿ Automatic   ○ Manual

Embedding Data from Other Programs

By embedding data, you can enter and edit foreign data without leaving the program you're working in. An Excel worksheet, for example, can be embedded in a Word document (refer to Figure 8-1). When you double-click the embedded object, the computer program with which it was created opens so that you can start editing.

Embedding foreign data

How you embed data that is foreign to the program you're working in depends on whether the data has already been created. You can get a head start embedding data if you or someone else has already created it. Following are instructions for embedding an object so you can enter the data on your own and embedding data that has already been created.

**Book VIII
Chapter 8**

Linking and
Embedding in
Compound Files

Creating an embedded object from scratch

Create an embedded object from scratch if the data you need hasn't been created yet. Follow these steps:

1. **Click the Insert tab.**

   If your aim is to create an Excel table, click the Table button, choose Excel Spreadsheet, and be done with it.

2. **Click the Object button (and, in Word, choose Object on the drop-down list).**

   You see the Object (or Insert Object) dialog box, as shown on the left side of Figure 8-4.

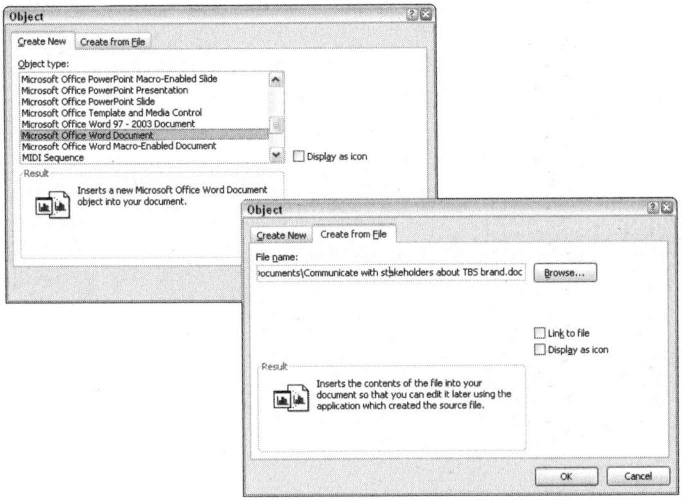

Figure 8-4: Creating space for embedding data (left) and embedding an entire file (right).

3. **Click the Create New option tab (or option button).**

4. **In the Object Type list, choose the name of the program that handles the kind of data you want to embed.**

   For example, to insert a space for Word text, choose Microsoft Office Word Document.

5. **Click OK.**

   Where your program's tabs and buttons used to be, you see different tabs and buttons. Use them to create and edit data.

Click outside the data when you're finished working on it.

Embedding data that has already been created

If the data you want to embed has been created already in another program, you can embed the data in your file by following these steps:

1. **Open the file with the data you want to embed.**

   Open the file in the program with which it was created.

2. **Copy the portion of the file you want to embed with the Copy command.**

   For example, right-click the portion of the file and choose Copy in the shortcut menu.

3. **Return to the program where you want to embed the data.**

4. **Click the Home tab.**

5. **Open the drop-down list on the Paste button and choose Paste Special.**

   You see the Paste Special dialog box, as shown in Figure 8-5.

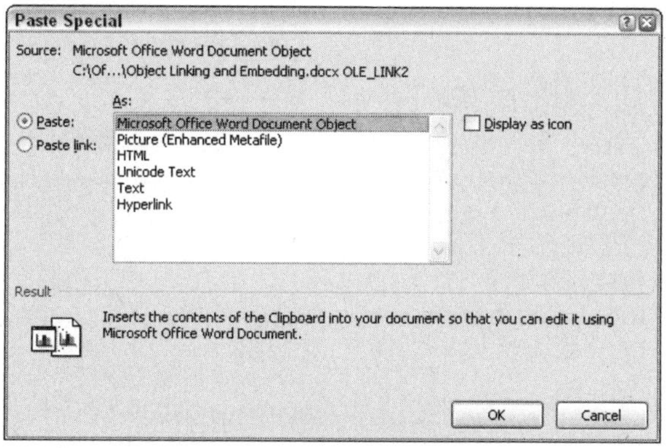

Figure 8-5:
Choose the program where the embedded data comes from.

Paste Special

Source: Microsoft Office Word Document Object
C:\Of...\Object Linking and Embedding.docx OLE_LINK2

As:

○ Paste: Microsoft Office Word Document Object
○ Paste link: Picture (Enhanced Metafile)
               HTML
               Unicode Text
               Text
               Hyperlink

☐ Display as icon

Result

Inserts the contents of the Clipboard into your document so that you can edit it using Microsoft Office Word Document.

OK   Cancel

6. **Select the Paste option button.**

7. **In the As list, choose an option with the word *Object* in its name.**

   Which options appear in the list depends on which type of object you're embedding. The options without Object in their names are for pasting the data in picture format.

8. **Click OK.**

   The data lands in your file.

Embedding an entire file

You can embed an entire file in the file you're working on by following these steps:

1. **On the Insert tab, click the Object button (and, in Word, choose Object on the drop-down list).**

   You see the Object (or Insert Object) dialog box (refer to Figure 8-4).

2. **Select the Create from File tab (or option button).**

   You see the version of the Object (or Insert Object) dialog box, as shown on the right side of Figure 8-4 (shown previously).

3. **Click the Browse button.**

   The Browse dialog box opens.

4. **Select the file you want to embed in your file and click OK (or Insert).**

5. **Click OK in the Object (or Insert Object) dialog box.**

   That's all there is to it.

Editing embedded data

To edit an embedded object, double-click it. Where your program's tabs and buttons used to be, you see a new set of tabs and buttons — ones belonging to the program normally used to edit the type of object you're editing. When you're finished editing the foreign data, click outside it.

To change the look of embedded data, right-click it and choose Format Object. Then choose formatting commands in the Format Object dialog box.

The techniques for changing the size and position of embedded objects are the same as the techniques for resizing and repositioning shapes, graphics, clip-art images, and other objects (Book I, Chapter 8 enumerates these techniques). To reposition an embedded object, move the pointer onto its perimeter and drag. To resize an embedded object, move the pointer over a selection handle and then drag.

Index

Symbols and Numerics

(pound signs) in an Excel cell, 463
& (ampersand), 561
@ (at symbol), 561
< (left bracket), 561
< (less than) operator, 597, 604
<= (less than or equal to) operator, 597
<> (not equal to) operator, 597
= (equals sign), entering a formula, 494, 505
= (equal to) operator, 597
> (greater than) operator, 597, 604
> (right bracket), 561
>= (greater than or equal to) operator, 597
( ) (parentheses) in formulas, 493
/ (slash), starting AutoCorrect entries, 68
3D
  chart, 127
  diagrams, 148
  reference, 499

A

.accdb extension, 31, 546
Access
  color scheme for, 657
  database addresses, 261
  description of, 10
  file formats, 546
  files in the latest version, 546
  Spelling button on the Home tab, 70
  status bar, 656
Account Settings dialog box, 299
Accounting Number Format, 470
accounts
  handling e-mail, 333
  sending messages, 326–327
action buttons in user-run presentations, 448–450

active cell
  describing, 459, 460, 461
  designating, 462
  scrolling to, 477
  selecting column or row of, 483
activities
  canceling, 355
  categorizing, 356
  rescheduling, 356
  scheduling, 353–355
Add Assistant command, 140
Add Bullet button, 144
Add Clips to Organizer dialog box, 693, 694
Add Contact Photo button, 307
Add Custom Dictionary dialog box, 74
Add New Category dialog box, 294
Add Shape commands, 136–137, 138, 139–140
address block, 263
address book, 290
Address Cards view, 310
address labels, printing, 259–260
addresses
  entering in the Contact form, 307
  importing into Outlook, 300
  mapping, 309
  printing on envelopes, 257–258
administrator for a Web site, 709
Adobe Acrobat Reader, 663
Advanced E-Mail Options dialog box, 332
Advanced Filter/Sort Command, 594, 597
Advanced Find dialog box in Outlook, 297
Align button, 167–168, 169
Align commands, 167–168, 417
aligning objects, 167–168
Alignment group button, 510
All Accounts group, 333
All Caps text, 44
All Day Event check box, 355

F

1

O

S

T

BUSINESS, CAREERS & PERSONAL FINANCE

0-7645-9847-3

0-7645-2431-3

Also available:
- Business Plans Kit For Dummies
  0-7645-9794-9
- Economics For Dummies
  0-7645-5726-2
- Grant Writing For Dummies
  0-7645-8416-2
- Home Buying For Dummies
  0-7645-5331-3
- Managing For Dummies
  0-7645-1771-6
- Marketing For Dummies
  0-7645-5600-2

- Personal Finance For Dummies
  0-7645-2590-5*
- Resumes For Dummies
  0-7645-5471-9
- Selling For Dummies
  0-7645-5363-1
- Six Sigma For Dummies
  0-7645-6798-5
- Small Business Kit For Dummies
  0-7645-5984-2
- Starting an eBay Business For Dummies
  0-7645-6924-4
- Your Dream Career For Dummies
  0-7645-9795-7

HOME & BUSINESS COMPUTER BASICS

0-470-05432-8

0-471-75421-8

Also available:
- Cleaning Windows Vista For Dummies
  0-471-78293-9
- Excel 2007 For Dummies
  0-470-03737-7
- Mac OS X Tiger For Dummies
  0-7645-7675-5
- MacBook For Dummies
  0-470-04859-X
- Macs For Dummies
  0-470-04849-2
- Office 2007 For Dummies
  0-470-00923-3

- Outlook 2007 For Dummies
  0-470-03830-6
- PCs For Dummies
  0-7645-8958-X
- Salesforce.com For Dummies
  0-470-04893-X
- Upgrading & Fixing Laptops For Dummies
  0-7645-8959-8
- Word 2007 For Dummies
  0-470-03658-3
- Quicken 2007 For Dummies
  0-470-04600-7

FOOD, HOME, GARDEN, HOBBIES, MUSIC & PETS

0-7645-8404-9

0-7645-9904-6

Also available:
- Candy Making For Dummies
  0-7645-9734-5
- Card Games For Dummies
  0-7645-9910-0
- Crocheting For Dummies
  0-7645-4151-X
- Dog Training For Dummies
  0-7645-8418-9
- Healthy Carb Cookbook For Dummies
  0-7645-8476-6
- Home Maintenance For Dummies
  0-7645-5215-5

- Horses For Dummies
  0-7645-9797-3
- Jewelry Making & Beading For Dummies
  0-7645-2571-9
- Orchids For Dummies
  0-7645-6759-4
- Puppies For Dummies
  0-7645-5255-4
- Rock Guitar For Dummies
  0-7645-5356-9
- Sewing For Dummies
  0-7645-6847-7
- Singing For Dummies
  0-7645-2475-5

INTERNET & DIGITAL MEDIA

0-470-04529-9

0-470-04894-8

Also available:
- Blogging For Dummies
  0-471-77084-1
- Digital Photography For Dummies
  0-7645-9802-3
- Digital Photography All-in-One Desk Reference For Dummies
  0-470-03743-1
- Digital SLR Cameras and Photography For Dummies
  0-7645-9803-1
- eBay Business All-in-One Desk Reference For Dummies
  0-7645-8438-3
- HDTV For Dummies
  0-470-09673-X

- Home Entertainment PCs For Dummies
  0-470-05523-5
- MySpace For Dummies
  0-470-09529-6
- Search Engine Optimization For Dummies
  0-471-97998-8
- Skype For Dummies
  0-470-04891-3
- The Internet For Dummies
  0-7645-8996-2
- Wiring Your Digital Home For Dummies
  0-471-91830-X

* Separate Canadian edition also available
† Separate U.K. edition also available

Available wherever books are sold. For more information or to order direct: U.S. customers visit www.dummies.com or call 1-877-762-2974.
U.K. customers visit www.wileyeurope.com or call 0800 243407. Canadian customers visit www.wiley.ca or call 1-800-567-4797.

SPORTS, FITNESS, PARENTING, RELIGION & SPIRITUALITY

0-471-76871-5   0-7645-7841-3

Also available:
- Catholicism For Dummies
  0-7645-5391-7
- Exercise Balls For Dummies
  0-7645-5623-1
- Fitness For Dummies
  0-7645-7851-0
- Football For Dummies
  0-7645-3936-1
- Judaism For Dummies
  0-7645-5299-6
- Potty Training For Dummies
  0-7645-5417-4
- Buddhism For Dummies
  0-7645-5359-3

- Pregnancy For Dummies
  0-7645-4483-7 †
- Ten Minute Tone-Ups For Dummies
  0-7645-7207-5
- NASCAR For Dummies
  0-7645-7681-X
- Religion For Dummies
  0-7645-5264-3
- Soccer For Dummies
  0-7645-5229-5
- Women in the Bible For Dummies
  0-7645-8475-8

TRAVEL

0-7645-7749-2   0-7645-6945-7

Also available:
- Alaska For Dummies
  0-7645-7746-8
- Cruise Vacations For Dummies
  0-7645-6941-4
- England For Dummies
  0-7645-4276-1
- Europe For Dummies
  0-7645-7529-5
- Germany For Dummies
  0-7645-7823-5
- Hawaii For Dummies
  0-7645-7402-7

- Italy For Dummies
  0-7645-7386-1
- Las Vegas For Dummies
  0-7645-7382-9
- London For Dummies
  0-7645-4277-X
- Paris For Dummies
  0-7645-7630-5
- RV Vacations For Dummies
  0-7645-4442-X
- Walt Disney World & Orlando
  For Dummies
  0-7645-9660-8

GRAPHICS, DESIGN & WEB DEVELOPMENT

0-7645-8815-X   0-7645-9571-7

Also available:
- 3D Game Animation For Dummies
  0-7645-8789-7
- AutoCAD 2006 For Dummies
  0-7645-8925-3
- Building a Web Site For Dummies
  0-7645-7144-3
- Creating Web Pages For Dummies
  0-470-08030-2
- Creating Web Pages All-in-One Desk
  Reference For Dummies
  0-7645-4345-8
- Dreamweaver 8 For Dummies
  0-7645-9649-7

- InDesign CS2 For Dummies
  0-7645-9572-5
- Macromedia Flash 8 For Dummies
  0-7645-9691-8
- Photoshop CS2 and Digital
  Photography For Dummies
  0-7645-9580-6
- Photoshop Elements 4 For Dummies
  0-471-77483-9
- Syndicating Web Sites with RSS Feeds
  For Dummies
  0-7645-8848-6
- Yahoo! SiteBuilder For Dummies
  0-7645-9800-7

NETWORKING, SECURITY, PROGRAMMING & DATABASES

0-7645-7728-X   0-471-74940-0

Also available:
- Access 2007 For Dummies
  0-470-04612-0
- ASP.NET 2 For Dummies
  0-7645-7907-X
- C# 2005 For Dummies
  0-7645-9704-3
- Hacking For Dummies
  0-470-05235-X
- Hacking Wireless Networks
  For Dummies
  0-7645-9730-2
- Java For Dummies
  0-470-08716-1

- Microsoft SQL Server 2005 For Dummies
  0-7645-7755-7
- Networking All-in-One Desk Reference
  For Dummies
  0-7645-9939-9
- Preventing Identity Theft For Dummies
  0-7645-7336-5
- Telecom For Dummies
  0-471-77085-X
- Visual Studio 2005 All-in-One Desk
  Reference For Dummies
  0-7645-9775-2
- XML For Dummies
  0-7645-8845-1

HEALTH & SELF-HELP

0-7645-8450-2

0-7645-4149-8

Also available:
- Bipolar Disorder For Dummies
  0-7645-8451-0
- Chemotherapy and Radiation
  For Dummies
  0-7645-7832-4
- Controlling Cholesterol For Dummies
  0-7645-5440-9
- Diabetes For Dummies
  0-7645-6820-5* †
- Divorce For Dummies
  0-7645-8417-0 †

- Fibromyalgia For Dummies
  0-7645-5441-7
- Low-Calorie Dieting For Dummies
  0-7645-9905-4
- Meditation For Dummies
  0-471-77774-9
- Osteoporosis For Dummies
  0-7645-7621-6
- Overcoming Anxiety For Dummies
  0-7645-5447-6
- Reiki For Dummies
  0-7645-9907-0
- Stress Management For Dummies
  0-7645-5144-2

EDUCATION, HISTORY, REFERENCE & TEST PREPARATION

0-7645-8381-6

0-7645-9554-7

Also available:
- The ACT For Dummies
  0-7645-9652-7
- Algebra For Dummies
  0-7645-5325-9
- Algebra Workbook For Dummies
  0-7645-8467-7
- Astronomy For Dummies
  0-7645-8465-0
- Calculus For Dummies
  0-7645-2498-4
- Chemistry For Dummies
  0-7645-5430-1
- Forensics For Dummies
  0-7645-5580-4

- Freemasons For Dummies
  0-7645-9796-5
- French For Dummies
  0-7645-5193-0
- Geometry For Dummies
  0-7645-5324-0
- Organic Chemistry I For Dummies
  0-7645-6902-3
- The SAT I For Dummies
  0-7645-7193-1
- Spanish For Dummies
  0-7645-5194-9
- Statistics For Dummies
  0-7645-5423-9

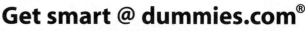

Get smart @ dummies.com®

- **Find a full list of Dummies titles**
- **Look into loads of FREE on-site articles**
- **Sign up for FREE eTips e-mailed to you weekly**
- **See what other products carry the Dummies name**
- **Shop directly from the Dummies bookstore**
- **Enter to win new prizes every month!**

* Separate Canadian edition also available

† Separate U.K. edition also available

Available wherever books are sold. For more information or to order direct: U.S. customers visit www.dummies.com or call 1-877-762-2974.
U.K. customers visit www.wileyeurope.com or call 0800 243407. Canadian customers visit www.wiley.ca or call 1-800-567-4797.

Do More with Dummies

Instructional DVDs • Music Compilations
Games & Novelties • Culinary Kits
Crafts & Sewing Patterns
Home Improvement/DIY Kits • and more!

Check out the Dummies Specialty Shop at www.dummies.com for more information!